The Humanities in the Western Tradition

The Humanities in the Western Tradition

IDEAS AND AESTHETICS

Marvin Perry
Baruch College, City University of New York

J. Wayne Baker
The University of Akron

Pamela Pfeiffer Hollinger
The University of Akron

George Bock
Editorial Associate

HOUGHTON MIFFLIN COMPANY
Boston   New York

Cover: Edouard Manet. *Claude Monet and His Wife in the Floating Studio.* Neue Pinakothek, Munich, Germany. *Source: Art Resource, NY.*

Senior Sponsoring Editor: Nancy Blaine
Development Editor: Julie Dunn
Senior Project Editor: Bob Greiner
Editorial Assistant: Wendy Thayer
Senior Production/Design Coordinator: Jodi O'Rourke
Manufacturing Manager: Florence Cadran
Senior Marketing Manager: Sandra McGuire

Printed in the U.S.A.

Library of Congress Catalog Number: 2002105244

ISBN: 0-395-84812-1

2 3 4 5 6 7 8 9-QUK-06 05 04 03

CONTENTS

The Humanities in the Western Tradition: Ideas and Aesthetics surveys Western thought, literature, and the arts from antiquity to the present. The text has two principal aims: (1) It explores those profound questions about the human experience elicited by a study of the ideas and aesthetics that have characterized Western thought, literature, art, and music—those cultural concerns that are called the Humanities. (2) It strives for synthesis, that is, it seeks to say something significant about the stages of Western history and the nature and meaning of the Western tradition. The text is written with the conviction that without a knowledge of Western history in general, and Western Humanities in particular, those who share in the Western tradition cannot fully know themselves. Without knowledge of our historic artistic, musical, and literary achievements, elicited from a study of the Humanities, our aesthetic tastes and moral awareness will be much the poorer. Without an understanding of the historical evolution of reason, freedom, and respect for human dignity, the dominant ideals of the Western tradition, commitment to these ideals will diminish. The authors hope to convey to students that the Western tradition is a living, vital tradition and that the study of thought, literature, and the arts—subjects that comprise the Humanities—will enrich their lives.

How this text came to be written sheds light on the authors' intent and objectives. Before his retirement, J. Wayne Baker was Course Director for the Humanities in the History Department, The University of Akron. A historian specializing in the Renaissance and Reformation, Baker, over the years of teaching the Humanities course, had also acquired an interest in art history. Pamela Hollinger, whose special interests are music history and British and American literature, had for many years worked closely with Baker in the Humanities program at The University of Akron, especially by creating a multimedia format for lecture presentations that integrated the various components of the Humanities. They had been thinking about producing a Humanities text that integrated more biographical information and human interest into discussions of music and art and provided deeper analyses of the great works of literature, a proposal they submitted to Houghton Mifflin Company.

Marvin Perry, whose special concerns are intellectual history and the evolution and nature of the Western tradition, has written several widely used texts for Houghton Mifflin, including *Western Civilization: Ideas, Politics, and Society* (senior author and general editor); *Sources of the Western Tradition* (senior editor); and *An Intellectual History of Modern Europe*. Coincidentally, he had proposed a Humanities text grounded in a solid historical framework and rich in ideas drawn from the West's philosophic, scientific, and religious traditions. It was clear that the two approaches complemented each other and the project was born.

The text took six years to complete, requiring endless hours of research, dialogue, and revision. We hope that instructors will find the finished work a helpful pedagogical instrument and that it will kindle in students an enduring appreciation for and interest in the Humanities.

APPROACH AND ORGANIZATION

To realize the project's overarching concerns, the authors devised an approach for each of the disciplines treated in a Humanities course. Realizing that many students enrolled in a Humanities program may never have studied European history, the authors provide a strong historical framework that facilitates comprehension of the Western cultural tradition. In our treatment of thought and the arts we have been careful to relate literary, art, and music productions to the historical eras in which they emerged. We also try to define the essential character of an age—classical Greece, the Middle Ages, the Enlightenment—by focusing on crucial questions: How did representative thinkers view nature, society, and the purpose of life? How did they assess the value of reason, faith, and clerical authority? What was their conception of political freedom? How did developments in literature and the arts show both an inheritance from the past and new points of departure?

Another feature of the text is the significant attention given to Western philosophy and religion in the shaping of those unique patterns of thought and systems of values that constitute the Western heritage. Thus the text contains discussions of the West's principal thinkers, often quoting passages from their works; it also devotes an entire chapter to the ancient Hebrews and another to Early Christianity, and in appropriate places throughout both volumes, important religious issues are treated. Because of the growing importance of Islam in today's world, we have included an extensive treatment of medieval Islamic civilization.

The literature sections are decidedly more than a list of books with brief summaries of plots; rather, we have tried to breathe life into literary discussions by incorporating appropriate biographical information about the authors, source extracts, and analyses of the important ideas the works convey.

The art sections reveal how people in each era interpreted their culture visually. Carefully chosen images of paintings, sculptures, and architectural works provide visual evidence of the essential values and beliefs that men and women held in a particular historical era. In some cases, images illustrate how artists were ahead of their time, cutting against the grain of contemporary thinking and introducing new artistic styles and approaches. In addressing the important issues that concern art historians, the authors have tried to make the text accessible to students with little prior knowledge of art history.

The music sections place composers in their cultural milieu; also, carefully selected details from their personal lives and careers give them a human face. Knowing that many students (and instructors) have little or no background in music theory, we have kept technical discussions to a bare minimum; however, where technical accomplishments were crucial to the development of Western music, we have made every effort to achieve clarity.

To convey to students the enduring importance of particular historical developments or the achievements in thought, literature, and the arts that they had just studied, each chapter contains an endpiece that searches for larger meaning. These endpieces are not chapter summaries, but interpretive and conceptual essays that compel students to ponder crucial questions about the Humanities and the nature and meaning of Western civilization. Examples of endpieces in Volume 1 are "The Greek Achievement: Reason, Freedom, Humanism" in Chapter 4; "Christianity and Classical Humanism: Alternative Worldviews" in Chapter 7; "Christianity and the Arts" in Chapter 11; and "The Middle Ages and the Modern World: Continuity and Discontinuity" in Chapter 12.

Endpieces in Volume 2 include "The Renaissance and the Rise of Modernity" in Chapter 13; "The Enlightenment and the Modern Mentality" in Chapter 17; "Enlightenment Values and the Arts" in Chapter 18; "The Enlightenment Tradition in Disarray" in Chapter 23; "The Modern Predicament" in Chapter 25; and "The Western Tradition in a Global Age" in Chapter 26.

The Humanities in the Western Tradition: Ideas and Aesthetics contains twenty-six chapters, twelve in Volume I and fourteen in Volume II. The chapters are grouped into five parts, two in Volume I and three in Volume II: (1) The Birth of the West: The Greco-Roman and Judeo-Christian Heritage; (2) The Middle Ages: The Christian Centuries; (3) The Early Modern West: From the Renaissance to the Enlightenment; (4) The Modern West: From Classicism to Modernism; and (5) Modernism and Beyond.

WORLD CULTURES

We now live in a global age in which Western ideals, institutions, and cultural styles have spread throughout the world. The globalization process also means that cultural elements—particularly religious beliefs, cuisines, and music—from Asian, African, and Middle Eastern lands have moved westward. That many non-Western students now attend American universities is another illustration of globalization. Although this text is concerned essentially with the Western humanities, we of course recognize the immense achievements of the other civilizations of the world. To facilitate an understanding and appreciation of all the world's civilizations, the text incorporates a special feature—"World Cultures" boxes that contain source material from the literary traditions of non-Western cultures. For example, Volume I contains excerpts from the *Rig Veda* and the *Bhagavad-Gita*, key ancient Hindu documents, and from the writings of Confucius, the Chinese sage, Han fei Tzu, the Chinese legalist philosopher, and Lu Yu, a prominent Chinese poet. Also included are selections from the journal of Sei Shonagon, an attendant to the empress of Japan in the late tenth century; a narrative by the fourteenth-century Islamic African, Ibn Battuta, about his travels; and *Popul Vuh*, the ancient sacred book of the Mayan people of Guatemala.

Volume II contains an Aztec account of the Spanish conquest of their land and Simon Bolivar's "Proclamation to the People of Venezuela" calling for liberation from Spanish rule. Two documents concern Africa: an excerpt from the memoirs of Olaudah Equiano, an educated former slave who took part in the antislavery movement in England, and a traditional African folktale. The excerpts from Japanese literature consist of a passage from a play by Chikamatsu Monzaemon, a late-seventeenth–early-eighteenth-century dramatist, who is called the "Japanese Shakespeare," and a sampling of modern Japanese lyric poetry. Emperor Ch'ien-lung's confidence in the superiority of Chinese civilization is revealed in his haughty reply to King George III's letter requesting the establishment of a British trading center at Peking (present-day Beijing). A representative illustration of twentieth-century Chinese poetry is also included. Excerpted too is Mohandas Gandhi's appeal for passive resistance, which had a profound influence on Martin Luther King, Jr.

SPECIAL FEATURES

The Humanities in the Western Tradition has been designed with a variety of features to help students master the material, including:

Comparative Timelines   Each of the book's five parts contains a two-page comparative timeline. These timelines allow students to visualize and compare events in four categories: Politics/Society; Art/Architecture; Literature/Music; and Philosophy/Science/Religion.

Key Terms   Every chapter of the book contains a list of important terms that students should know. These terms are highlighted within the narrative and listed at the end of the chapter for easy review.

Glossary   A glossary containing definitions of all the key terms appears at the end of each volume.

Annotated Bibliography   Organized by chapter, this bibliography appears at the end of the text. A searchable version also appears on the text's website.

TEACHING RESOURCES

We understand the challenges that instructors face when developing and teaching a Humanities course. The resources that exist are often difficult to locate, too general for the course, or too expensive to purchase. With these concerns in mind we developed the full package of ancillaries that accompany *The Humanities in the Western Tradition.*

Online Study Guide   A free study guide for students appears on the text-specific website and features chapter summaries and outlines; a glossary of key terms; web activities and links; and a self-testing quiz program. The site also features special art and music sections that trace major artistic movements, identify important terms, and allow students to explore additional works on the web.

ClassPrep CD-ROM   This CD-ROM includes all the resources that a professor needs to teach *The Humanities in the Western Tradition.* An Instructor's Manual features chapter summaries, lecture suggestions, bibliographic information, and classroom discussion questions and activities. A Testbank offers more than 700 multiple-choice, fill-in-the-blank, and essay questions. PowerPoint slides of all the maps and 100 of the art images from the text have been included to enable instructors to highlight visuals in the classroom.

Music CDs   Students may purchase a two-volume CD package to help supplement the music coverage in the text. Each CD features more than one hour of music and is designed to accompany specific discussions in the text (see CD icon in the margins).

Blackboard and WebCT   Course material is offered in both Blackboard and WebCT formats for those institutions that use these learning environments.

Computerized Testbank   A computerized version of the Testbank is available.

ACKNOWLEDGMENTS

The authors are grateful to the staff of Houghton Mifflin Company. Both Jean Woy (Editor-in-Chief) and Pat Coryell (now Editor-in-Chief for English, Education, ESL, and Student Success titles) recognized the merit of our proposals and brought the team together. Nancy Blaine, Senior Sponsoring Editor, and Julie Dunn, Development Editor, who continually impressed us with their commitment to the project, provided effective guidance. Bob Greiner, Senior Project Editor, conscientiously and skillfully supervised the manuscript through production. Karen Slaght, who edited the manuscript, provided helpful suggestions. Carole Frohlich researched and coordinated all of the art for the book; Jodi O'Rourke coordinated the production; and Janet Theurer provided us with a beautiful design in which to showcase the text.

Marvin Perry and Wayne Baker wish to thank their spouses, Phyllis Perry and Linda Kersker, for their encouragement, support, and patience. Marvin Perry is also grateful to his wife for her computer expertise, which saved him much time and frustration.

Pamela Pfeiffer Hollinger particularly appreciates the efforts of her friend and colleague, Robert DeMass, Jr., for his capable assistance in researching, selecting, and documenting the musical selections. Similarly, without the support and encouragement of her colleagues Marjorie Keil, Chris Kolaczewski-Ferris, and Joy LiCause, she is not certain if she could have kept her good humor during stressful times. To her capable student assistants, Joshua Davis and Scott Lockett, who helped to stimulate her thinking on some of the more contemporary art and music issues, "thank you." But most importantly, she is grateful for the love, patience, and understanding of her husband Greg and their daughters, Gretchen and Jenna.

Many instructors provided valuable suggestions on early drafts of the manuscript. The authors wish to thank the following people for their critical reading and insightful comments:

Phillip N. Bebb, *Ohio University*

Sherry Blum, *Austin Community College*

William J. Bogard, *Black Hills State University*

Edward T. Bonahue, *Santa Fe Community College*

Carolyn V. Copeland, *Bethune-Cookman College*

Tina M. Crocco, *Georgia Perimeter College*

Robert Eisner, *San Diego State University*

Kimberly Felos, *St. Petersburg College*

David H. Fenimore, *University of Nevada, Reno*

Matthew David Fisher, *Ball State University*

Ann M. Green, *Jackson Community College*

Jon D. Green, *Brigham Young University*

Thomas W. Hardy, *Northern Virginia Community College*

Siegfried E. Heit, *University of Central Oklahoma*

John Jay Hilfiger, *Saint Francis College*

Seth R. Katz, *Bradley University*

Kevin Kennedy, *Arapahoe Community College*

Richard D. Kortum, *East Tennessee State University*

Charlie McAllister, *Catawba College*

Bruce Naschak, *San Diego Mesa College*

Merry Ovnick, *California State University, Northridge*

Danney Ursery, *St. Edward's University*

Theresa A. Vaughan, *University of Central Oklahoma*

Richard A. Voeltz, *Cameron University*

LeeAnn E. Westman, *Ferris State University*

Sonia Yetter, *University of Northern Iowa*

Joel Zimbelman, *California State University, Chico*

M. P.

J. W. B.

P. P. H.

The Humanities in the
Western Tradition

PART III: The Early Modern West

A.D. 1300	A.D. 1400	A.D. 1500

Politics/Society

Beginning of the Italian Renaissance (c. 1350)

Gutenberg invents movable metal type (c. 1445)

Saint Bartholomew's Day Massacre (1572)

English fleet defeats the Spanish Armada (1588)

Art/Architecture

Brunelleschi constructs the dome (Il Duomo) for the Santa Maria del Fiore (1420–1436)

Masaccio paints *The Tribute Money* (1427)

Van Eyck brothers paint the *Ghent Altarpiece* (1432)

Donatello's sculpture of *David* (c. 1440)

Botticelli paints *Birth of Venus* (1486)

Da Vinci paints the *Mona Lisa* (1503)

Michelangelo paints the ceiling of the Sistine Chapel (1508–1512)

Raphael paints the *School of Athens* (1509–1510)

Titian paints the *Venus of Urbino* (c. 1538)

El Greco paints *Burial of Count Orgaz* (1586)

Literature/Music

Dufay's *Missa Se la face ay pale* (c. 1450)

Machiavelli, *The Prince* (1513)

More, *Utopia* (1516)

Castiglione, *The Book of the Courtier* (1528)

Rabelais writes *The Histories of Gargantua and Pantagruel* (1532–1546)

Byrd, first great composer of the English "Golden Age" (1543–1623)

Shakespeare, regarded as the West's finest playwright (1564–1616)

Montaigne writes his *Essays* (1571–1580)

Ballet Comique de la Royne, the first traditional ballet (1581)

Philosophy/Science/Religion

Luther writes his Ninety-five Theses; start of the Reformation (1517)

Pope Leo X excommunicates Martin Luther (1520)

Huldrych Zwingli leads the Reformation in Zurich (1523-1531)

John Calvin leads the Reformation in Geneva (1536–1564)

Publication of Copernicus' *On the Revolutions of the Heavenly Spheres* marks the beginning of modern astronomy (1543)

Council of Trent (1545–1563)

● Thirty Years' War (1618–1648)

● Reign of King Louis XIV in France (1643–1715)

● Revolution in England; end of Absolutism (1688–1689)

Declaration of Independence (1776) ●

Adam Smith's *The Wealth of Nations* begins concept of ●
laissez-faire economics (1776)

French Revolution begins (1789) and
Declaration of theRights of Man and of the Citizen (1789) ●

● Baroque artistic style (c. 1600–1750)

● Rembrandt paints *The Night Watch* (1642)

● Wren rebuilds Saint Paul's Cathedral in London
(1675–1710)

● Construction of the Gallery of Mirrors at Versailles
(1678–1684)

Work begins on the *Salon de la Princesse,*
example of French Rococo architecture (1732) ●

Boucher paints *Diana Leaving the Bath* (1742) ●

Hogarth paints series of paintings,
Marriage à la Mode (1742–1744) ●

● Cervantes writes *Don Quixote* (1603–1605)

● Development of modern French theater—Cornielle,
Molière, and Racine (1635–1691)

● Milton, *Paradise Lost* (1667)

● Bunyan's *Pilgrim's Progress* is published in two volumes
(1678–1684)

● Johann Sebastian Bach (1685–1750), preeminent organist-
composer of the Baroque age

Defoe publishes his first novel, *Robinson Crusoe* (1719) ●

Vivaldi publishes *The Four Seasons* in a collection of ●
concertos (c. 1725)

Publication of Swift's *Gulliver's Travels* (1726) ●

Richardson's *Pamela*, first epistolary novel (1740) ●

Handel composes the *Messiah* (1742) ●
Johnson publishes first English-language dictionary (1755) ●

● Bacon, *Advancement of Learning* (1605)

● Publication of Galileo's *The Starry Messenger,* asserting the
uniformity of nature (1610)

● The church condemns Galileo's teachings; he is placed under house arrest (1632)

● Newton, *Principia Mathematica* (1687)

● Locke, *Two Treatises of Government* (1690)

Voltaire, *Letters Concerning the English Nation* (1733) ●

Publication of the *Encylopedia* edited by ●
Diderot (1751–1765)

13

The Italian Renaissance: Transition to the Modern Age

D URING THE LATE FOURTEENTH AND FIFTEENTH CENTURIES, Italy witnessed a profound cultural transformation known as the **Renaissance,** or rebirth. It was characterized by a fresh respect for the humanistic and worldly culture of ancient Greece and Rome, the rise of a new type of scholarship known as humanism, an appreciation of the capabilities of the individual, and an innovative approach to the arts. For many historians, these developments mark the end of the Middle Ages and the dawn of the modern era. The Renaissance began in the northern Italian city–states, which had grown prosperous from the revival of trade during the Middle Ages. Wealthy Italian merchants and bankers patronized authors and artists and acquired libraries and works of art. Surrounded by reminders of their ancient past—amphitheaters, monuments, and sculpture—these prosperous patrons were drawn to classical culture and thought. Beginning in the late fifteenth century, Renaissance ideas spread to France, Spain, Germany, and England, primarily due to the invention of printing, which made editions of the ancient authors and the works of the Italian humanists available to a larger reading public.

THE BREAK WITH THE MIDDLE AGES

Although Renaissance individuals were by no means anti-Christian, they valued worldly activities and interests to a much greater degree than did people of the Middle Ages, whose outlook was dominated by Christian otherworldliness. Lewis W. Spitz, a student of the Renaissance, describes this shift in cultural orientation:

> In all areas of life, aesthetic, moral, social, political, and religious, there was a renewed and very intense interest in man's achievements. Nor was the age secular in the sense of being irreligious. . . . There was, however, a subtle shift toward interest in and anxiety about man in the here and now, as well as in the hereafter. . . . The change [in view] during this period may be described as a move away from official other-worldliness to an interest in man in this world— sometimes a very religious interest, in fact. There was a change of course in man's mental evolution from the medieval to the modern world, for life was no longer merely a period of probation for the life beyond.[1]

Renaissance individuals were fascinated by *this* world and by life's joys and possibilities; they aspired to live a rich and creative life on earth and to fulfill themselves through artistic and literary activity. The new secularism bestowed intrinsic worth on worldly pleasure and activity. Reviving the Greco-Roman

Leonardo da Vinci,
Mona Lisa, 1503–1506,
oil on panel, 30 1/4 x
21" (76.8 x 53.3 cm),
Musée du Louvre,
Paris, France.

The subject of the painting is Lisa Gherardini del Giocondo, the wife of a prominent Florentine businessman. Although the portrait is famous for Mona Lisa's enigmatic smile, the sfumato of the background cloaks an equally haunting setting of craggy rocks and roads, which seemingly lead to nowhere.

(Louvre/Erich Lessing/Art Resource, NY)

view that the complete individual is a political animal who participates actively in civic affairs, many Renaissance figures were critical of monastic withdrawal and asceticism and of the scholastics' purely contemplative life. In the centuries to come, a growing secular outlook would hold that the individual should be emancipated from domination by otherworldly concerns, theological dogma, and ecclesiastical authority and should focus on the full development of human talents and on improving the quality of earthly existence.

Individualism was another hallmark of the Renaissance. The urban elite sought to demonstrate their unique talents, to assert their own personalities, and to gain recognition for their accomplishments. Traditional medieval values of birth and place in a fixed hierarchy were superseded by a desire for individual achievement. In the tradition of the ancient Greeks, Renaissance figures expressed confidence in human nature and urged talented people to realize their capacities. They ascribed to human beings a special dignity: they had the intelligence and talent to accomplish wonders on earth and a special duty to fulfill their potential. The attainment of excellence—of greatness—depended on human intelligence and will, not on God's providence. Renaissance Italy produced a distinctive type of "universal man": a many-sided person, who demonstrated mastery of the ancient classics, an appreciation of talent for the visual arts, and a concern for the day-to-day affairs of the city. Such individuals sought to mold their lives into a work of art. Disdaining Christian humility, Renaissance individuals took pride in their talents and worldly accomplishments— "I can work miracles," said the great Leonardo da Vinci. Renaissance artists portrayed the individual character of human beings, captured the rich diversity of human personality, produced the first portraits since Roman times, and affixed their signatures to their works. Renaissance writers probed their own feelings, demonstrating a self-awareness that characterizes the modern outlook. This new outlook, however, applied almost exclusively to an elite—princes, courtiers, court ladies, wealthy urban families, and exceptionally talented artists and writers.

To be sure, the Renaissance was not a complete or abrupt break with the Middle Ages. Many medieval elements and attitudes, particularly scholastic learning, persisted into the Renaissance and beyond, and several components of Renaissance culture have medieval antecedents. For example, the revival of classical learning, which is the distinguishing feature of the Renaissance, dates back to the cultural awakening of the twelfth and thirteenth centuries.

Yet, there are three important differences between the Twelfth-Century Awakening, which was the high point of medieval civilization, and the Renaissance. First, many more ancient works were restored to circulation during the Renaissance than during the cultural revival of the Middle Ages. Whereas Roman authors were widely known in the Middle Ages, some Latin writers, such as Lucretius and Tacitus,* were rediscovered only during the Renaissance. Renaissance scholars had a much better knowledge of classical Latin and of Latin authors than their medieval forbears. For the most part, medieval thinkers did not know the Greek language and were unfamiliar with many important works of Greek literature, which had not been translated into Latin. Some Renaissance scholars mastered Greek and translated into Latin the whole corpus of ancient Greek literature, making many texts available to western Europeans for the first time; and they produced new and better translations of Roman works. Second, medieval scholastics had tried to fit the ideas of the ancients into a Christian framework; Renaissance scholars, on the other hand, valued ancient literature for its own sake. They admired its graceful style and believed that Greek and Roman authors could teach much about the art of living and the performance of civic duties. Third, Renaissance humanists approached ancient civilization with a critical attitude; they studied texts in a historical context and examined them for authenticity and accuracy. In contrast, medieval thinkers generally did not relate a text to its times but accepted it uncritically as an authoritative work of wisdom.

Renaissance figures were aware that they were living in a new and special time. They regarded the centuries immediately preceding them (unfairly, as we now know) as a dark age, in which antiquity's cultural splendor had been snuffed out; and they described their own age as a *rebirth* of the arts and learning—a *renaissance*, the name by which the period is known—after an interval of medieval darkness and sterility. It was Renaissance humanists (see following) who arranged history into three periods: ancient, medieval, and modern. The humanists also conceived the embryo of the modern idea of progress. In their exuberance and self-confidence, they dared to believe that they, "the moderns," could surpass the cultural brilliance of the ancient Greeks and Romans.

*Lucretius (c. 96–c. 55 B.C.) was the leading Roman Epicurean philosopher (see Chapter 6). **Tacitus** (A.D. 55–c. 118) was a Roman historian who denounced the Roman imperial system in his writings (see Chapter 6).

RENAISSANCE THOUGHT AND LITERATURE

During the Late Middle Ages, Italy was a patchwork quilt of city–states, along with one large monarchy. Florence, Venice, and Milan controlled most of northern Italy; the pope ruled Rome and the papal states in central Italy; and the king of Naples ruled the kingdom of Naples and Sicily in southern Italy. The intermittent warfare among them was brought to an end by the Peace of Lodi in 1454, which ushered in a forty-year period of relative peace. The illusion of Italian unity and security was shattered, however, when the French invaded Italy in 1494. For decades thereafter, Italy was the battleground for the wars between the French and the Spanish. A defining moment in this struggle was the sack of Rome, in 1527, by the army of Emperor Charles V, who was also king of Spain. Finally, in 1559, Spanish hegemony in Italy was established by the Treaty of Cateau-Cambrésis. Renaissance culture commenced, subsequently flourished, and ultimately faded within this historical context.

Humanism

The Renaissance revival of classical learning was fostered by the humanist movement, an educational and cultural program based on the study of ancient Greek and Latin literature. Humanists revived the worldly spirit and civic virtue of the ancient Greeks and Romans, which they believed had been lost during the Middle Ages, through their use of the *studia humanitatis* (the Humanities)—grammar, rhetoric, poetry, history, and moral philosophy. Humanists were fascinated by the writings of the ancients. They sought guidelines for living well in this world and looked for stylistic models for their own literary efforts in the works of Thucydides, Plato, Cicero, Seneca,* and other ancient authors. Their appreciation of Greek literature led them to introduce the study of Greek into the university curriculum.

Humanists believed that the study of Greek and Roman literature was the only fitting education for anyone engaged in public service. To the humanists, the ancients had written in an incomparable literary style, on friendship, citizenship, statesmanship, love, bravery, beauty, excellence, and every other topic devoted to the enrichment of human life. Humanists admired ancient authors for their insights into the human condition and viewed them as guides for moral self-development. Humanists strove to imitate the brilliant style of the ancients and to speak as eloquently and to write as gracefully as the Greeks and Romans. Toward these ends, they sought to read, print, and restore into circulation every scrap of ancient literature that they could find. They searched monastery libraries for these lost treasures. Humanists were neither anti-Christian nor irreligious, but in contrast to medieval thinkers, they did not subordinate secular studies to the requirements of Christian teachings, and they placed the human being and worldly activities at the center of their outlook.

Originally, humanism was not a philosophy or a movement, but an educational program, based on the study of the ancient authors. The first humanists were private individuals, lawyers, and public officials. As the new humanities curriculum circulated widely, the values of the humanists gained prominence. By the middle of the fifteenth century, many fields of learning, including philosophy and history, were imbued with the methodology, literary style, and central ideas of humanism.

The Origins of Humanism in Florence

In the early fifteenth century, Florence appeared to be a republic, but was, in reality, ruled by a patrician oligarchy led by the Albizzi family. The leader of the opposition party was Cosimo de' Medici (1389–1464), who in 1434 became the virtual ruler of Florence when his supporters gained a majority in the Signoria, the supposed ruling body of the republic. Although Cosimo carefully maintained the republican institutions of Florence, he also made sure that those elected to the Signoria were friendly to his regime. The Medici bank, which reached its height under Cosimo, was another important source of his power. By the time Cosimo died, the Florentines had accepted the Medici as hereditary leaders of Florence. Cosimo was succeeded by his son, Piero the Gouty (1414–1469); Piero's son, Lorenzo the Magnificent (1449–1492); and Lorenzo's son, Piero (1471–1503)—each of whom became head of the bank and ruler of the Florentine republic.

The Florentines that scholars view as the progenitors of humanism are Dante, Petrarch, and

---

***Thucydides** (c. 460–c.400 B.C.) was a Greek historian (see Chapter 4). **Plato** (c. 429–347 B.C.) was one of the greatest philosophers of ancient Greece (see Chapter 3). His thought was extremely influential during the Renaissance. **Cicero** (106–43 B.C.) was a Roman statesman and rhetorician whose Latin style was greatly admired during the Renaissance (see Chapter 6). **Seneca** (4 B.C.–A.D. 65) was an important advocate of Stoicism during early imperial times in Rome (see Chapter 6).

Boccaccio,* each of whom was deeply interested in classical literature. Humanism further blossomed under the leadership of two humanist chancellors of Florence—Coluccio Salutati (1331–1406) and Leonardo Bruni (1374–1444). Salutati and Bruni extolled the value of studying the humanities, and at the same time, stressed the importance of active involvement in public affairs—an outlook called *civic humanism*. Their ideal was Cicero, who used his wisdom and eloquence to serve the public good and the state at the end of the Roman Republic.

Both Salutati and Bruni glorified Dante, Petrarch, and Boccaccio as the forebears of humanism and declared that Florence was the center of the new learning. A fervid collector of manuscripts and an ardent student of the ancient authors, Salutati maintained that good literature had only recently been revived by Dante, Petrarch, and Boccaccio, "all of whose works, unless I am mistaken, posterity will honor."[2] In his *Life of Petrarch* (1436), Bruni lauded Dante, Petrarch, and Boccaccio as the three muses of Florence. He called Petrarch, who excelled in writing both prose and poetry, "the first who . . . restored to light the ancient elegance of style which was lost and dead." When Petrarch died, "the Florentine Muses, as if by hereditary succession, passed to Boccaccio, and in him dwelt the fame of the aforesaid studies. And this succession was also temporal, for when Dante died, Petrarca was seventeen years old, and when Petrarca died, Boccaccio was nine years younger than he, and thus by succession went the Muses."[3]

Bruni was one of the first humanists to define the *studia humanitatis*. About 1404, he wrote a letter to Baptista di Montefeltro, the daughter of the Duke of Urbino. Baptista was one of a significant number of patrician women who were educated in the *studia humanitatis* in the same manner as their brothers. In the letter, Bruni offers advice for her course of study and laments that "true learning has almost died away amongst us." This leads him "to press home this truth . . . that the foundations of all true learning must be laid in the sound and thorough knowledge of Latin: which implies study marked by a broad spirit, accurate scholarship, and careful attention to details." He states that Baptista can gain this knowledge first by reading Christian authors, such as Augustine,

and then by turning to classical authors, especially Cicero, who is "unapproachable in wealth of ideas and of language, in force of style, indeed, in all that can attract in a writer!"[4] As she reads these authors, she must pay close attention to grammar, which is necessary for good writing. Religion and moral philosophy, he says, should "hold the first place in the education of a Christian lady." As guides, she should read Augustine, Epicurus, and Aristotle.[†] History is also valuable and "must not on any account be neglected by one who aspires to true cultivation. . . . For the careful study of the past enlarges our foresight in contemporary affairs and affords to citizens and to monarchs lessons of incitement or warning in the ordering of public policy."[5] Finally, poetry is "a subject with which every educated lady must shew herself thoroughly familiar. For we cannot point to any great mind of the past for whom the Poets had not a powerful attraction."[6]

Nonetheless, Bruni also asserted that "there are certain subjects"—arithmetic, geometry, astrology—in which women should have only "a modest proficiency." Moreover, he viewed rhetoric as "positively unbecoming" for a woman, because "rhetoric in all its forms—public discussion, forensic argument, logical [defense], and the like—lies absolutely outside the province of [a] woman."[7]

Philosophy

Knowledge of the Greek language was almost nonexistent in the West during the Late Middle Ages and the Early Renaissance. Neither Dante nor Boccaccio knew Greek, and Petrarch was unsuccessful when he tried to learn the language. But when Salutati invited the Byzantine scholar Manuel Chrysoloras to come to Florence in 1397, the humanists began to master Greek. Bruni himself was one of Chrysoloras' best students, and he translated parts of Plato's and Aristotle's works into Latin. In his memoirs, *Commentary on Things Done in His Own Time*, Bruni recalls his inner conflict between continuing with the study of law or learning Greek. After much soul-searching, he decides that there are plenty of lawyers, but that he has only one chance to study Greek: "Overcome at length by these reasons, I gave myself to Chrysoloras, with such zeal to learn, that

---

*Dante (1265–1321) was a poet who greatly influenced **Petrarch** (1304–1374), who is often called the father of humanism. **Boccaccio** (1313–1375), a gifted poet and storyteller, wrote among other things a biography of Dante (see Chapter 12).
†**Augustine** (354–430) was one of the most influential church fathers whose thought influenced theologians during the

Middle Ages and in modern times (see Chapter 7). **Epicurus** (342–270 B.C.) was a Greek philosopher who denied the power of the gods over humans and advocated a moderate lifestyle that would free the individual from pain and worry (see Chapter 5). **Aristotle** (384–322 B.C.) was a leading Greek philosopher who had an enormous influence among medieval and Renaissance scholars (see Chapter 3).

what through the wakeful day I gathered, I followed after in the night, even when asleep."[8] Additional momentum was given to Greek studies when a large number of Byzantine scholars and philosophers attended the Council of Ferrara-Florence from 1438 to 1439. During the council, the Byzantine Platonist Gemistos Pletho gave a speech on Plato, which convinced Cosimo de' Medici about the truth of the Platonic philosophy.

Subsequently, in 1462, Cosimo founded the Florentine Academy under the leadership of Marsilio Ficino (1433–1499), his physician's young son, for whom Cosimo provided a villa near Florence, a library of Greek manuscripts, and a lifetime income. For the remainder of his life, Ficino devoted himself to the study of the works of Plato and the Neo-Platonists.* The villa soon became known as the "Platonic Academy," because members of the leading families and the humanists of Florence gathered there for discussions about Platonic philosophy. Over time, Ficino's reputation alone attracted scholars from the rest of Italy and northern Europe.

To make the Platonic tradition available to other scholars, Ficino published his Latin translation of all the works of Plato, Plotinus, and other Neo-Platonists. Immersed in the Platonic doctrines, Ficino stressed the dignity and the abilities of the human being. In 1474, he published *The Platonic Theology Concerning the Immortality of Souls*. Combining Platonic ideas and Christian theology, Ficino argues that truth has been transmitted through a variety of philosophers through the centuries—from Plato, to the Stoics and the Neo-Platonists of the early Christian period, until his own day. Although he accepts the Bible as God's truth, he does not make a strict distinction between the *revealed* truth of Scripture and the *inspired* truth of the ancient philosophers. He contends that through reason Plato and later Platonists had discovered God.

Ficino viewed the universe as the Great Chain of Being, descending from the purest spirit, God, down to the lowest form of physical matter on earth. In this great chain of being, the human being occupies the central place—humans are linked to the material realm through their bodies, and to the spiritual realm through their souls. Because of their immortal souls, humans possess a unique dignity that no other creature can claim. Therefore, through inspired contemplation favored by Neo-Platonists, the human soul can ascend to the spiritual realm and find union with God. This inner striving toward God is made possible by

Jesus, who frees human souls from physical matter. Consequently, the role of the church is to keep humans in contact with the spiritual world so that after death, the soul will rise to the realm of the spirit. Ficino's Christianization of Neo-Platonism made it both a pious philosophy and a learned religion.

Ficino also developed a doctrine of spiritual love for which he coined the term **"platonic love."** In opposition to carnal love, platonic love is the spiritual intimacy and fervent companionship of two people in a mutual love of God. This spiritual love of the lover and the beloved imitates the manner in which God, through Jesus, loves humanity. The idea of platonic love became increasingly popular in later Renaissance literature.

One of Ficino's pupils at the Florentine Academy, Giovanni Pico della Mirandola (1463–1494), surpassed him in his praise of human potential. Pico, in his attempt to reconcile Christianity with Platonic philosophy, made use of Aristotle, some Arabic and Hebrew philosophy, Pythagoreanism, and Zoroastrianism.[†] His eclectic approach was based on his conviction that there is unity of truth in all philosophies and all religions—each of which, including Christianity, reveals a sacred theology and truth.

Pico, believing that Ficino's conception of the potential of humans was inadequate, offered his own view of human nature in his *Oration on the Dignity of Man*. In it, God addresses Adam at the moment of his creation:

> You, who are confined by no limits, shall determine for yourself your own nature, in accordance with your own free will, in whose hand I have placed you. I have set you at the centre of the world, so that from there you may more easily survey whatever is in the world. We have made you neither heavenly nor earthly, neither mortal nor immortal, so that, more freely and more honourably the moulder and maker of yourself, you may fashion yourself in whatever form you shall prefer. You shall be able to descend among the lower forms of being, which are brute beasts; you shall be able to be reborn out of the judgment of your own soul into the higher beings, which are divine.[9]

Humans, therefore, unlike the animals, are not constrained by their nature. Rather human beings are masters of their own nature and can become whatever they choose. This is the basis for human dignity, for when God created humans, he endowed them

---

*Neo-Platonism (see Chapter 6) was a mystical, semireligious restatement of Plato's thought by Plotinus (c. A.D. 205–270).

†Pythagoras (c. 580–507 B.C.) was a Greek philosopher whose work influenced both Socrates and Plato (see Chapter 3). Zoroastrianism is a monotheistic religion that began in Persia about 500 B.C. (see Chapter 1).

with all kinds of seeds and with the germs of every way of life. Whatever seeds each man cultivates will grow and bear fruit in him. If these seeds are vegetative, he will be like a plant; if they are sensitive, he will become like the beasts; if they are rational, he will become like a heavenly creature; if intellectual, he will be an angel and a son of God. And if, content with the lot of no created being, he withdraws into the centre of his own oneness, his spirit, made one with God in the solitary darkness of the Father, which is above all things, will surpass all things. Who then will not wonder at this chameleon of ours?[10]

Although Pico warns that humans can degrade themselves to the level of plants and animals, he exhorts people to attain the Neo-Platonic union with God through philosophical contemplation, the highest of all achievements. Pico thus sums up the Renaissance view that people have the power to shape their own lives, to rise as high as they aspire, a mind-set that was to become a key element in the emergence of the modern outlook.

The thoughts of both Ficino and Pico were based on the Platonic concept of the immortality of the soul, an idea that had a great impact on sixteenth-century theology and philosophy. But in 1516, an Aristotelian philosopher, Pietro Pomponazzi, published a work that was the antithesis of both the philosophy of the Florentine Academy and the teaching of the church—*On the Immortality of the Soul.* Following Aristotle, Pomponazzi argued that although the soul can rise above bodily functions to grasp abstract truths, it is, nonetheless, absolutely mortal. The soul cannot function without the body—it is born with the body, and it dies with the body. As a Christian, Pomponazzi accepts immortality as a *matter of faith, on the authority of the church,* but, as a philosopher, he will not teach it. Furthermore, in opposition to the teaching of the church that virtue and vice will be rewarded and punished in an afterlife, he contends:

The essential reward of virtue is virtue itself, which makes man happy." Since virtuous behavior leads to a happier and more secure life, human beings do not need the promise of heaven to act virtuously. Nor is hell the only proper punishment for the wicked, for, continues Pomponazzi, vice produces its own earthly punishment—misery and unhappiness. [Aristotle shows] that the life of the vicious man . . . is to be shunned, for the vicious man all things are discordant. Faithful to no one, not even to himself, neither awake nor asleep is he at peace; he is beset by horrible tortures of body and soul: a most unhappy man. . . . Hence no vicious man is left unpunished, since vice itself is the punishment of the vicious man.[11]

Pomponazzi thus developed a purely naturalistic, secular ethic, independent of Christianity.

History

Renaissance humanists valued historical thinking and history was one of the subjects of the *studia humanitatis;* consequently, the humanists studied the ancient historians—such as Livy and Julius Caesar*—for both moral guidance and the lessons about life they could teach. The humanists also imitated the ancient historians by writing histories of their own time.

BRUNI   Leonardo Bruni, one of the first humanists to write history, set the standard for both the style and the organization in the writing of history during the Renaissance. Inspired by Livy's *History of Rome,* he wrote his Latin *History of the Florentine People* in 1415. Bruni asserts that history is important because citizens and political leaders can learn from the ethical, moral, and political behavior of the past. Holding that imperial despotism caused the decline of Roman civilization, he concluded that political freedom is a necessary condition for healthy civic life. Bruni viewed the period between antiquity and his own time as a middle period of barbarism. Consequently, he presented the history of Florence in his own day as the resurgence of the civic freedom and republicanism that had distinguished Athens and Rome in their best days. Bruni's history became the model that other humanist historians followed.

VALLA   Bruni's student, Lorenzo Valla (1407–1457), had a sure sense of the impact of the new history and of how historical criticism could be used effectively. By viewing ancient works as historical phenomena—products of a particular people at a particular time—Valla helped create a more critical historical awareness. Valla was also a pioneer in the science of textual criticism, which seeks to establish the most accurate version of an antique text and the date that it was written. In his *Annotations on the New Testament,* he demonstrated a critical approach by treating the sacred text like any other writing and stating that "none of the words of Christ have come down to us, for Christ spoke in Hebrew and never wrote down anything."[12]

In 1440, while he was employed as secretary and historian to Alfonso of Aragon (1416–1458),

---

*Livy (59 B.C.–A.D. 17) wrote histories that glorified the Roman character and accomplishments. **Julius Caesar** (c. 100–44 B.C.) was a renowned Roman military commander and statesman who also wrote historical treatises (see Chapter 6).

King of Naples, Valla wrote his *Declamation Concerning the False Donation of Constantine,* which exemplified the new critical spirit of the age. The Donation of Constantine, used by popes to support their claim to temporal authority throughout the Middle Ages, stated that the fourth-century Roman emperor Constantine* gave the papacy dominion over the Western empire. Valla, by showing that some of the words in the document were unknown in Constantine's time and therefore could not have been used by the emperor, proved that the document was forged by church officials several hundred years after Constantine's death.

MACHIAVELLI AND GUICCIARDINI   During the sixteenth century, the writing of history progressed through the works of Nicolò Machiavelli (1469–1527) and Francesco Guicciardini (1483–1540). Although Machiavelli was born into an established middle-class Florentine family, his branch of the family had only modest wealth and could not hope to measure up to the wealth and influence of the family of his younger contemporary, Guicciardini. Throughout the fifteenth century, the Guicciardini family played a leading role in Florentine politics, as part of the small group of prominent families that supported the Medici oligarchy. Guicciardini studied civil law at the universities at Florence, Ferrara, Padua, and Pisa, whereas Machiavelli's education was less formal and focused more on the ancient authors. In contrast to the earlier humanists, who wrote in Latin, both Machiavelli and Guicciardini wrote in the vernacular Italian.

Machiavelli's *History of Florence,* written in the 1520s and published in 1532, covers Florentine affairs from the origins of the city until the death of Lorenzo de' Medici in 1492. Machiavelli was more a political theorist (see later discussion) than a historian, and consequently, his history of Florence is more an illustration of his rules for political conduct than an interpretation of the city's past. In contrast, Guicciardini was more a historian than political theorist. In attempting to recreate the past, he made an unprecedented use of original source materials—official government notes, correspondence, and other documents. His *History of Florence* and *The History of Italy* deal with the crucial events of the late fifteenth and early sixteenth centuries, including the invasion of Italy in 1494 by the king of France, Charles VIII, who intended to validate his dynastic claim to the

Kingdom of Naples. Guicciardini recounts that as Charles' army of 30,000 soldiers marched down the peninsula and took Naples almost without opposition, it was like "everything was turned upside down as if by a sudden storm; the unity of Italy was broken and shattered, and so was the consideration and care which all used to give to their common affairs."[13]

Fra Girolamo Savonarola: A Reaction Against Florentine Secularism and Humanism

During the time just prior to the French invasion, the zealous Dominican monk Fra Girolamo Savonarola (1452–1498)—who came to Florence in 1489, at the invitation of Lorenzo de' Medici—rose to a position of authority as a prophet. Savonarola regarded the rule of the Medici as a vaguely disguised tyranny that had brought about the moral dissolution of the Florentines. He criticized Lorenzo for his patronage of the arts, for his affinity for worldly pleasures, and for surrounding himself with preachers who did nothing to stem the tide of moral decay. Savonarola's prophesies about the future from the book of Revelation attracted a large number of Florentines, who came to see him as a prophet and holy man.

In 1494, as the French army, led by Charles VIII, neared Florence on its march south, Piero de' Medici met with Charles and agreed to his every demand. Consequently, Piero and his family fled the city the very next day, and the terrified Florentines, fearing that Charles would sack the city, turned to Savonarola. Invoking his keen diplomatic skills as well as a call to Christian compassion, Savonarola met with Charles and was able to prevent the sack of Florence. Exhilarated by this accomplishment, Savonarola decided that he could now fulfill his mission to build a New Jerusalem, an equitable and God-fearing society in which citizens would enjoy "holy liberty." His vision also encompassed an attack on the new secular and humanist spirit. Savonarola whipped the Florentines into a frenzy of moral zeal, which Guicciardini described:

> There was no public gambling. . . . The taverns . . . were closed. Sodomy was suppressed and punished severely. Women . . . gave up indecent and lascivious dress. Boys were almost all reformed from many wicked ways and led to a decent and God-fearing life. They were gathered together in companies, . . . attended church, wore their hair short, and pursued with stones and insults wicked

---

*Contantine, who was the first Christian emperor, ruled Rome from 306 to 337 and divided the Empire into eastern and western portions (see Chapter 6).

men and gamblers and immodestly dressed women. At carnival time they went about collecting dice, cards, cosmetics, indecent pictures and books, which they burned publicly.[14]

On February 7, 1497 (the day before the beginning of Lent), Savonarola organized a purifying "Bonfire of the Vanities." Thrown into the bonfire were "paintings and sculpture, many of them the work of great masters," as recorded by the Florentine art historian Giorgio Vasari (see later in the chapter).[15] Savonarola was opposed by some Florentines, who regarded him as a tyrant, and by Pope Alexander VI (1492–1503), whom Savonarola constantly criticized. Many Florentines were disappointed by his failure to perform a miracle, and public opinion suddenly welled up against him. After a riot ensued between the followers of Savonarola and a Franciscan friar, who had denounced him, during which hundreds were injured and killed, Savonarola was imprisoned and severely tortured; he reputedly confessed that his prophesies were lies. Alexander VI then sent a papal commission, which on May 22, 1503, judged Savonarola to be guilty of heresy. The next day, he and two of his companions were hanged, then burned, and their ashes dumped into the Arno River. The religious zeal generated by Savonarola during his four years of power demonstrated that many Florentines were distressed with the secular spirit of the Renaissance.

Machiavelli: The Politics of Reality

Less than a month after Savonarola's execution, Machiavelli acquired a relatively minor post in the government of the republic, which had survived Savonarola. Machiavelli was a confidant of Piero Soderini, the leader of the government. Machiavelli's duties included both domestic and foreign affairs, and he was sent on several diplomatic missions—to the king of France, to the court of the Emperor Maximilian, and to other Italian states, including Rome. The republic continued to exist until 1512, when Cardinal Giovanni de' Medici, soon to be elected Pope Leo X (1513–1521), entered Florence with a victorious army to restore the Medici family to power. Because of his close ties to Soderini, Machiavelli was dismissed from his government position and forced into exile when the Medici family was restored to power in 1512. The following year, a conspiracy against the Medici failed, and the conspirators were executed. Suspected of involvement in the conspiracy (probably mistakenly), Machiavelli was arrested and tortured but confessed to nothing.

After his release, the exiled Machiavelli retired to his farm in the country. There, having observed firsthand major rulers and political figures and deeply affected by the political events of his day, he wrote two treatises on politics that had a profound influence on the further development of modern political theory—*The Prince* and *The Discourses on the First Ten Books of Livy*. In a famed letter to a friend, dated 10 December 1513, he described his love for ancient authors:

> I read about their amorous passions and about their loves, I remember my own, and I revel for a moment in this thought. . . . When evening comes, I return to my home, and I go into my study; and on the threshhold, I take off my everyday clothes, which are covered with mud and mire, and I put on regal and curial robes; and dressed in a more appropriate manner I enter into the ancient courts of ancient men and am welcomed by them kindly. . . . I become completely part of them. . . . I composed a little work, *De principatibus* [The Prince], where I delve as deeply as I can into . . . discussing what a principality is, what kinds there are, how they are acquired, how they are maintained, why they are lost.[16]

The Prince is a handbook advising individual rulers how to gain and maintain power. *The Discourses*, which Machiavelli wrote between 1513 and 1517, focuses on the broader issues of preserving social and political stability within the state, and it reveals Machiavelli's republican sympathies. It is written in the form of a commentary on Livy's *History of Rome*, but Machiavelli uses it as a platform for the further development of his own theories about government.

Machiavelli believed that both ancient and medieval theorists, who sought to define the best form of constitution, the just regime, the ideal state, were irrelevant. Classical political thought maintained that ethics and politics are interrelated, that it is the state's purpose to promote the virtuous life. Greek philosophers wanted the human community to accord with natural law—rules of conduct whose principles are ascertainable by reason. Christian thinkers wanted to fashion the earthly city according to the divine commandments revealed in Scripture and interpreted by the church.

Machiavelli had no patience with an approach that sought to shape political life in accordance with ideal standards. Such visionary expectations, he held, bring the state to ruin, for we do not live in the world of the "ought," the fanciful utopia, but in the world of the "is," the real world of real human beings. Machiavelli aimed to discover how states functioned in the real world and how rulers must behave if they are to protect their states against the threats posed by domestic and foreign enemies and the unruly passions of their subjects. In *The Prince*, Machiavelli makes it clear that he is aware that his approach to the study of politics in the cold light of reason, free of illusions about human nature, and devoid of idle speculation about higher worlds and imaginary and unattainable commonwealths, represents a new departure.

> [It] seemed more suitable to me to search after the effectual truth of the matter rather than its imagined one. And many writers have imagined for themselves republics and principalities that have never been seen nor known to exist in reality; for there is such a gap between how one lives and how one ought to live that anyone who abandons what is done for what ought to be done earns his ruin rather than his preservation.[17]

Machiavelli's rigorous investigation of politics led him to examine human nature from the standpoint of its limitations and imperfections; a bleak and pessimistic view of human nature, the antithesis of the optimistic view of Ficino and Pico, pervades his works. The astute prince, said Machiavelli, looks at men as they are and not as he would like them to be. He recognizes that human beings are by nature selfish, corrupt, cowardly, faithless, base, dishonest, and prone to violence and that deception and coercion are necessary to hold in check a flawed human nature that threatens civil order. In his *Discourses*, Machiavelli stresses that "it must needs be taken for granted that all men are wicked and that they will always give vent to the malignity that is in their minds when opportunity offers. . . . [M]en never do good unless necessity drives them to it."[18] For Machiavelli, politics is not the pursuit of moral virtue but the pursuit of the state's security and well-being. When conditions require it, the wise prince sets aside conventional morality and does what is necessary, even if these actions are generally considered morally wrong.

Although Machiavelli did not advocate wickedness, he does say that actions are permissible in politics that would be condemned in personal behavior. The successful prince separates political morality from private morality; no private conscience constrains his public acts. As Machiavelli sums it up in *The Prince*:

> [F]or a man who wishes to make a vocation of being good at all times will come to ruin among so many who are not good. Hence it is necessary for a prince who wishes to maintain his position to learn how not to be good, and to use this knowledge or not to use it according to necessity.[19]

Machiavelli maintains that the state is purely a human creation and that the actions of princes should be governed solely by necessity. The successful prince, concerned only with preserving and strengthening the state's power, dismisses issues of morality and immorality as irrelevant. The course of action that he chooses is determined by the needs of a particular situation and not by any moral purpose or by any system of justice given to man by God or rooted in the natural order of things. As he writes in *The Discourses*, all means are permitted the prince if the state's survival is at stake.

> For when the safety of one's country wholly depends on the decision to be taken, no attention should be paid either to justice or injustice, to kindness or cruelty, or to its being praiseworthy or ignominious. On the contrary, every other consideration being set aside, that alternative should be wholeheartedly adopted which will save the life and preserve the freedom of one's country.[20]

Successful princes, Machiavelli concludes, have always been indifferent to moral and religious considerations—a lesson of history that rulers ignore at their own peril.

> How praiseworthy it is for a prince to keep his word and to live by integrity and not by deceit every one knows; nevertheless, one sees from the experience of our times that the princes who have accomplished great deeds are those who have cared little for keeping their promises and who have known how to manipulate the minds of men by shrewdness; and in the end they have surpassed those who have laid their foundations upon honesty.
>
> You must, therefore, know that there are two means of fighting: one according to the laws, the other with force; the first way is proper to man, the second to beasts; but because the first, in many cases, is not sufficient, it becomes necessary to have recourse to the second. Therefore, a prince must know how to use wisely the natures of the beast and the man. . . .
>
> A wise ruler, therefore, cannot and should not keep his word when such an observance of faith would be to his disadvantage and when the reasons which made him promise are removed. And if men were all good, this rule would not be good; but since men are a sorry lot and will not keep their promises to you, you likewise need not keep yours to them.[21]

A wise prince gives the appearance of being virtuous, for such a pretense will assist him in governing his subjects. But when the security of the state requires it, the prince is prepared to abandon all virtue. In the world of politics, blunders—not crimes—are unpardonable. Machiavelli says that it is good for a prince to seem merciful, faithful, humane, forthright, religious, and to be so; but his mind should be disposed in such a way that should it be necessary not to be so, he will be able and know how to change to the contrary. And it is essential to understood this: that a prince, and especially a new prince, cannot observe all those things by which men are considered good, for in order to maintain the state he is often obliged to act against his promise, against charity, against humanity, and against religion.[22]

If the prince's policy proves successful, his ruthlessness will be forgiven and forgotten: "[I]n the actions of all men, and especially of princes, . . . one must consider the final result.* Let a prince therefore act to seize and to maintain the state; his methods will always be judged honorable and will be praised by all; for ordinary people are always deceived by appearances."[23] In justifying unscrupulous behavior, Machiavelli did not condone needless acts of cruelty and violence: the prince resorts to repression and terror for reasons of state, never for private passion, pride, whim, or petty revenge, and he employs violence judiciously and deftly.

Machiavelli's interpretation of history and politics is devoid of the religious concerns that occupied a central place for Christian moralists. Only the world of the here and now concerned him. Machiavelli favored the virtues of classical civilization and regarded the Christian ideals of compassion, meekness, humility, turning the other cheek, yearning for salvation, and contempt for the worldly life as detrimental to the state's well-being. Whereas the ruler who tries to govern on the basis of Christian teachings condemns himself to political impotence, the morality of Pericles' Athens and Scipio's† Rome, which valued personal achievement, courage, strength, pride, glory, civic responsibility and patriotism, fosters the development of a strong and vigorous republic. As Machiavelli wrote in *The Discourses:*

> [T]he old religion did not beatify men unless they were replete with worldly glory: army commanders, for instance, and rulers of republics. Our religion has glorified humble and contemplative men, rather than men of action. It has assigned as man's highest good humility, abnegation, and contempt for mundane things, whereas the other identified it with magnanimity, bodily strength,

and everything else that conduces to make men very bold. And, if our religion demands that in you there be strength, what it asks for is strength to suffer rather than strength to do bold things.[24]

For Machiavelli, religion has value, not because of its revelation, but because it is socially useful; a wise ruler should utilize religion to unite his subjects and to promote civic obedience, public-spiritedness, and patriotism. As he writes in *The Discourses:*

> It will also be seen by those who pay attention to Roman history, how much religion helped in control of the armies, in encouraging the plebs, in producing good men, and in shaming the bad. . . . Nor in fact was there ever a legislator who, in introducing extraordinary laws to a people, did not have recourse to God, for otherwise they would not have been accepted, since many benefits of which a prudent man is aware, are not so evident to reason that he can convince others of them. . . . The rulers of a republic or of a kingdom, therefore, should . . . keep their commonwealths religious, and, in consequence, good and united.[25]

Such an outlook requires that churches always remain subordinate to the interests of the state—a complete reversal of the essential character of medieval political thought.

Completely rejecting the otherworldly orientation of medieval political thought, Machiavelli ascribed no divine origin or purpose to the state. He viewed the state as an autonomous entity that recognized no higher religious-ethical power. For good or for ill, he removed political thought from a religious frame of reference and viewed the state and political behavior from a purely secular perspective. Machiavelli thus initiated trends in political thought that we now recognize as distinctively modern. Nonetheless, in the sixteenth century, both the northern humanists and the Protestant reformers (see Chapter 14) continued to cling to the ideal of a state that promoted morality and religion. Not until the seventeenth century did political philosophy become largely independent of a Christian orientation through the work of Thomas Hobbes and John Locke (see Chapter 17), Machiavelli's true successors.

Castiglione: The Ideal Courtier

Baldassare Castiglione (1478–1529) was born into an illustrious Lombard family near Mantua. He received a humanist education in Latin and Greek and had a distinguished career serving in the courts of Italian dukes and Charles V in Spain.

By the early sixteenth century, the era of the republics was at an end in Italy, and the princely

---

* The Italian original—*si guarda al fine*—has often been mistranslated as "the ends justify the means."
† **Pericles** (c. 495–429 B.C.) was the democratic leader of Athens during its Golden Age (see Chapter 3). **Scipio** (d. 211 B.C.) was a political and military leader of Rome during the Republic.

courts had become the new social and political ideal. At the same time that Machiavelli was defining the new *political* ideal—the consummate prince and the politics of reality—in his *Prince,* Castiglione was describing the new *social* ideal— the Renaissance courtier who served princes—in his *The Book of the Courtier.* Castiglione chose the court of Urbino as the setting for his *Courtier*—written in the form of a conversation among the courtiers and ladies of the court. Federico da Montefeltro had made the court of Urbino a center of humanist culture and courtly manners, a tradition that was carried on by his son, Guidobaldo, who was well versed in Latin and Greek literature and a sponsor of chivalric games and musical performances.

In the first two books of *The Courtier,* Castiglione describes the ideal courtier as a complete person with breadth of interest and versatility of accomplishment. The perfect courtier ought to be "born of a noble and genteel family. . . . For noble birth is like a bright lamp that makes manifest and visible deeds both good and bad, kindling and spurring on to virtue as much for fear of dishonor as for hope of praise."[26] As a matter of bodily skill and grace, "his first duty [is] to know how to handle every kind of weapon, both on foot and on horse, and know the advantages of each kind; and be especially acquainted with those arms that are ordinarily used among gentlemen."[27] He should, in all endeavors, "practice . . . a certain *sprezzatura* [nonchalance], so as to conceal all art and make whatever is done or said appear to be without effort and . . . [a]lmost without any thought about it."[28] Regarding his education, he should be "more than passably learned in letters, at least in those studies which we call the humanities. Let him be conversant not only with the Latin language, but with Greek as well. . . . Let him be versed in the poets, as well as in the orators and historians, and let him be practiced also in writing verse and prose."[29] He should also be a musician who "besides understanding and being able to read music, . . . can play various instruments."[30] The ideal courtier should also display "a knowledge of how to draw and an acquaintance with the art of painting itself." In his demeanor he should "be cautious in his every action and see to it that prudence attends whatever he says or does . . . [and] he should avoid affectation above all else."[31] In his daily conversation he should strive for "a gentle and pleasant manner."[32] In his dress, the courtier ought "to be neat and dainty in his attire, and observe a certain modest elegance, yet not in a feminine or vain fashion."[33] The ideal courtier should "devote all his thought and strength of

spirit to loving and almost adoring the prince he serves,"[34] but should only obey the prince as long as he does good, for "[i]n dishonorable things we are not bound to obey anyone."[35]

In the third book, Castiglione portrays the ideal court lady:

> For I hold that many virtues of the mind are as necessary to a woman as to a man; also, gentle birth; to avoid affectation, to be naturally graceful in all her actions, to be mannerly, clever, prudent, not arrogant, not envious, not slanderous, not vain, not contentious, not inept, to know how to gain and hold the favor of her mistress and of all others, to perform well and gracefully the exercises that are suitable for women. And I do think that beauty is more necessary to her than to the Courtier. . . . Also she must be more circumspect, and more careful not to give occasion for evil being said of her.[36]

Moreover, she should be prudent, magnanimous, kind, discreet, be able "to manage her husband's property and houses and children . . . and [display] all qualities that are requisite in a good mother."[37] However, one member of the circle, Signor Gasparo, makes some disparaging remarks about women:

> [W]omen are imperfect creatures, and consequently have less dignity than men. . . . [V]ery learned men have written that, since nature always intends and plans to make things most perfect, she would constantly bring forth men if she could; and that when a woman is born, it is a defect or mistake of nature. . . . Thus, a woman can be said to be a creature produced by chance and accident.[38]

But Gasparo is soundly reproved by everyone.

In the fourth book, Castiglione deals with the relationship between the courtier and his prince:

> [T]he Courtier will in every instance be able adroitly to show the prince how much honor and profit will come to him and to his [court] from justice, liberality, magnanimity, gentleness, and the other virtues that befit a good prince; and on the other hand, how much infamy and harm result from the vices opposed to these virtues. . . . [T]here is no good more universally beneficial than a good prince, nor any evil more universally pernicious than a bad prince: likewise, there is no punishment atrocious and cruel enough for those wicked courtiers who . . . seek their prince's favor in order to corrupt him, turn him from the path of virtue, and bring him to vice.[39]

The fourth book concludes with Castiglione's discussion of beauty and love. His description of the yearning of the human soul for beauty is reminiscent of Dante's account of his love for Beatrice in

The New Life and Petrarch's sonnets for his beloved Laura. In each instance, the personification of beauty is the Lady, and the love of beauty transforms her Lover. Once the Lover has beheld the beauty that is comprehended through the eyes of the mind, he ultimately achieves the love of the intellect—the highest form of love—but only if he perseveres:

> And thus, burning with this most happy flame, it rises to its noblest part, which is the intellect; and there, no longer darkened by the obscure night of earthly things, it beholds divine beauty; . . . love gives the soul a greater happiness; for, just as from the particular beauty of one body it guides the soul to the universal beauty of all bodies, so in the highest stage of perfection beauty guides it from the particular intellect to the universal intellect. Hence, the soul, aflame with the most holy fires of true divine love, flies to unite itself with the angelic nature; . . . transformed into an angel, it understands all things intelligible, and without any veil or cloud views the wide sea of pure divine beauty, and receives it into itself, enjoying the supreme happiness of which the senses are incapable.[40]

Castiglione's handbook became one of the most influential books of the day, providing instruction to aristocrats and nonaristocrats alike about how to be the perfect courtier or court lady. It was subsequently translated into every major European language by the end of the sixteenth century, thus making Castiglione the arbiter of aristocratic manners throughout the century. Attesting to the depth of its appeal is the fact that Emperor Charles V reputedly kept three books at his bedside—the Bible, Machiavelli's *The Prince*, and Castiglione's *The Book of the Courtier*.

ITALIAN RENAISSANCE ART

Like the humanist movement, Renaissance art also marked a break with medieval culture. The art of the Middle Ages had served a religious function: its purpose was to lift the mind to God. Medieval art perfectly expressed the Christian view of the universe and the individual. The Gothic cathedral, with its flying buttresses, soared toward heaven, rising in ascending tiers; it reflected the medieval conception of a hierarchical universe with God at its apex. Painting also expressed gradations of spiritual values—dark colors expressed evil, light colors good. Spatial proportion was relative to spirituality—the less spiritually valuable a thing was, the less form it had (or the more deformed it was). Renaissance artists continued to utilize religious themes, but they shattered the dominance of religion over art by shifting attention from heaven to the natural world

and to the human being. Renaissance artists depicted the human qualities of men and women and celebrated the beauty and grace of the human form. Renaissance artists also developed a new conception of visual space, which resulted in a naturalistic, three-dimensional rendering of the real world. It was a quantitative space in which the artist, employing reason and mathematics, portrayed the essential form of the object in perspective, as it would appear to the human eye.

Pivotal Treatises on Art

Between the 1390s and 1550, two treatises, written by men who were both artists and writers, helped to define the development of a new style of art and architecture distinct from the medieval style and placed Renaissance art into a historical and humanistic perspective—Alberti's *On Painting*, and Giorgio Vasari's (1511–1574) *Lives of the Painters, Sculptors, and Architects*. Like the humanists, the works of these men advanced the very idea of the Renaissance as a dynamic cultural movement, and as a uniquely "modern" phenomenon, separate from and superior to the Middle Ages.

ALBERTI   In his work *On Painting*, Leon Battista Alberti (1404–1472)—the first modern art theoretician—formulated the mathematical theory of artistic perspective that became commonly used by the artists. His work enabled artists to depict objects as if they were seen through a glass window by creating the illusion of three dimensions on a two-dimensional surface. To achieve this illusion, Renaissance artists had to establish a precise mathematical relationship between the object and the observer.

Alberti thus linked the art of painting with the pursuit of truth. To render an object in three-dimensional, realistic visual space, the painter must place it in perspective and painstakingly adapt the size, shape, and color of the painted object to show how it would appear to the eye at any given distance from the observer. The painter, said Alberti, situates the object

> at a definite distance with definite lights and a definite position of centre in space and in a definite place in respect to the observer. Each painter, endowed with his natural instinct, demonstrates this when [while painting] he places himself at a distance as if searching [for] the point and angle of the pyramid from which point he understands the thing painted is best seen.[41]

He admonishes painters to remember "that a painted thing can never appear truthful where there is not a definite distance for seeing it."[42]

In aspiring to show nature as it appeared to the eye, Renaissance artists were inspired by the representational art of classical antiquity, and like their classical predecessors, they emphasized the immeasurable importance of the viewer. Moreover, Renaissance art creatively restated and expressed the ideals of classical humanism, which celebrated the dignity, worth, and creative capacity of the individual human being and the beauty of the human form.

VASARI   Although art historians have come to recognize that Giorgio Vasari (1511–1574) sometimes manipulated facts for his own purposes, his *Lives* remains a vivid and informative history of the art of the period. Vasari offers his own platonic interpretation of art as an organic evolution—bloom, decay, and rebirth. He contends that art bloomed with Greek culture, and the decline began during the time of the Emperor Constantine. The sculpted figures on Constantine's triumphal arch exemplified the degeneration of art.

> Very rude also are some scenes of small figures in marble below the reliefs and the pediment, representing victories, while between the side arches there are some rivers, also very crude, and so poor that they leave one firmly under the impression that the art of sculpture had begun to decline even before the coming of the Goths and other barbarous and foreign nations who combined to destroy all the superior arts as well as Italy.[43]

The decay continued into the Middle Ages, said Vasari, and he coined the term *Gothic* to describe barbaric northern European culture as opposed to civilized Greek culture: "[N]ew architects arose who created that style of building, for their barbarous nations, which we call Gothic, and produced some works which are ridiculous to our modern eyes, but appeared admirable to theirs."[44]

Vasari divides the history of the development of art during the Renaissance into three periods. During the "first and earliest period [the fourteenth century] the three arts are seen to be very far from perfection, and though they possess some amount of excellence, yet this is accompanied by such imperfections that they certainly do not merit extravagant praise."[45] Vasari believed that the two most important artists of this period were Cimabue and Giotto (see Chapter 12).

The second period, which has come to be known as the Early Renaissance, began with Donatello (c.1386–1466), Brunelleschi (1377–1446), and Masaccio (1401–1428) and covered most artists of the fifteenth century; and the third period, usually designated as the High Renaissance, began with Leonardo da Vinci (1452–1519) and reached its climax with Michelangelo (1475–1564). Comparing the two latter periods, Vasari doubts that another group of artists will ever surpass the greatness of those of the High Renaissance.

Early Renaissance (1400–1495)

The Florentine Renaissance, which helped to usher in the modern world, has often been compared to the cultural flowering in ancient Athens, which marked the foundation of the Western humanist and intellectual tradition. Vasari suggests that, like the humanists, the artists of the Early Renaissance looked back to antiquity for inspiration. Early Renaissance sculptors owed the most to antiquity in their depiction of the human form.

SCULPTURE   The sculpture of the thirteenth and fourteenth centuries was essentially subordinate to the Christian worldview and the requirements of Gothic religious architecture, constricting it within cramped wall reliefs and cornices. Early Renaissance sculptors disengaged the human figure from the architectural setting and were preoccupied with creating a natural, freestanding human figure in the round. The sculpted figures in the reliefs of Donatello occupy a shallow physical space and appear to emerge naturally from the background of infinitely receding pictorial space. Even though they still convey religious motifs, the freestanding figures of Donatello also mark a sudden break with tradition, for they occupy an entirely new space, crafted with stark realism and compassion, which penetrates the human essence of the figure.

Sculpture in Florence thus took a new turn with the work of Donatello. He surpassed his predecessors by sculpting the first freestanding nude figures since antiquity. Writing of Donatello, Vasari states: "[J]ust as in the days of the ancient Greeks and Romans, many combined to attain perfection, so he, single-handed, brought perfection and delight back to our age by the multitude of his works."[46]

In the early 1430s, Donatello spent an extended time in Rome admiring the monuments of the ancient world. In about 1440, he cast his bronze *David* (Figure 13.1). Rendered quite unheroically, the statue derives its exceptional quality more from the modeling of the subject's body and his contrapposto stance—a pose between walking and resting, in which the weight of the body rests on one foot—than from the prowess of his physique. Not only does the brilliant surface of the bronze contrast with the rough styling of his hair, but similarly, the serene expression on David's face is the antithesis of the contorted face of his adversary,

Figure 13.1   Donatello, *David,* **c. 1425–1430, bronze, height 62 1/4" (158 cm), Museo Nazionale del Bargello, Florence, Italy.** This statue is the first freestanding nude since antiquity. During both the Middle Ages and the Renaissance, David's triumph over Goliath was a symbol of Christ's victory over sin, death, and the law; and David's nudity symbolized the soul being exposed before God. *(Museo Nazionale del Bargello, Florence/Alinari/Art Resource, NY)*

Goliath. During both the Middle Ages and the Renaissance, David's triumph over Goliath was a symbol of Christ's victory over sin and death; and David's nudity symbolized the soul being exposed before God. David's laurel-encircled hat stands in opposition to the warrior helmet of Goliath, but the meaning of his open-toed leather boots is a matter of speculation. Nonetheless, the link to contemporary politics is also unmistakable: Goliath represents the enemies of Florence whereas David symbolizes the vulnerable, but undaunted, republic of Florence.

As a sculptor, Donatello was trained by Lorenzo Ghiberti (1378–1455), and beginning in 1403, he worked with Ghiberti on the bronze doors for the

north side of the Baptistery of San Giovanni. The doors, with their twenty-eight panels drawing on scenes from the New Testament, were finally installed in 1424. Four years later, Ghiberti was given another commission, this time to cast a pair of doors, with scenes drawn from the Old Testament, for the east side of the Baptistery, thereafter known as *The Gates of Paradise* (Figure 13.2), so named by Michelangelo. In describing the ten thirty-one-inch-square panels, Ghiberti discerns that his sense of perspective is one of the hallmarks of his accomplishment:

> Truly I worked with the greatest diligence and love. There were ten stories altogether and all the architectural settings introduced were in perspective, and so true to life that they looked like sculpture in the round seen from the right distance. They are carried out in very low relief and the figures visible on the nearer planes are bigger than those on the distant ones, just as they appear in real life.[47]

The stories depicted on the panels, from left to right and top to bottom, begin with the story of "the creation of Man and Woman, and how they disobey the Creator of all Things," and their expulsion from Paradise. The second panel portrays Cain and Abel making sacrifices to God, "Cain killing Abel out of jealousy" for the superiority of his sacrifice, and God's questioning of Cain. The third panel shows Noah and his family "emerging from the Ark, . . . offering sacrifices, . . . planting . . . the vine, Noah's subsequent drunkenness, . . . and the covering of his nakedness." The fourth panel contains the story of Abraham's sacrifice of his son, Isaac, and how "the Angel, who, pointing at the ram, stays the hand that holds the knife." The fifth panel shows Jacob deceiving his father, Isaac, and thus obtaining his blessing in place of his twin brother, Esau (Genesis 27).

The sixth panel is especially noteworthy because of the deep perspective provided by its architectural setting. It tells the long, complicated story of Jacob's son, Joseph. The story begins in the upper right-hand corner of the panel, as Joseph is sold into bondage by his brothers (Genesis 37:28) and brought before the Egyptian pharaoh to interpret his dreams. The scene in the lower left corner portrays "How he interprets Pharaoh's dream as a prophecy of great famine," how Joseph becomes ruler of Egypt, and the time when his brothers come to Egypt to buy grain (Genesis 40–42). The center of this scene depicts the discovery of Joseph's silver cup, which he had placed in his youngest brother's bag of grain (Genesis 44:2). Finally, in the upper left, Joseph reveals his true identity to his brothers (Genesis 45).

The seventh panel depicts Moses' reception of "the Tablets of the Law upon the mountain top, whilst Joshua remains halfway up, and the multitude is terrified by the raging of lightning, thunder, and earthquake." The eighth panel renders Joshua's arrival in Jordan, "How he surrounds the city, gives orders for trumpets to be blown, and how after seven days, the walls totter and the city is captured." In the ninth panel, "David kills Goliath and the people of Israel defeat the Philistines." The tenth panel concludes the cycle as "the Queen of Sheba and a great retinue [arrives] to visit Solomon."[48]

Ghiberti demonstrated a mastery of skill and perspective that none of the other contestants could match. Moreover, setting Old Testament stories in Classical architectural settings illustrates a regard for the Classical antiquity that was more important than historical accuracy. The panels also depict individualized faces and body language

for each person—an attention to human uniqueness that epitomizes the Renaissance.

ARCHITECTURE Gothic architecture—with the vertically upward motion of its lines and the ambiguity of its loosely defined boundaries and interior spaces—was perfectly consonant with the otherworldliness and mystery of the Christian worldview. In comparison, Renaissance architecture—ever conditioned by an awareness of antiquity even in its ecclesiastical structures—boldly reflected the orientation of the Greeks and Romans. Renaissance architectural style, typified by its stress on horizontal and measurable lines and its explicitly defined boundaries, produced an architectural space not unlike the visual, mathematically defined, perspectival space of the Renaissance painter.

Unlike Gothic architecture, Renaissance architects designed their buildings to relate to and to

Figure 13.2   Lorenzo Ghiberti, *Gates of Paradise,* **the east door of the Baptistery of San Giovanni, Florence, Italy, c. 1435, gilt bronze, height 15' (4.57 m).**   The ten thirty-one-inch-square panels, nicknamed "The Gates of Paradise" by Michelangelo, portray scenes drawn from the Old Testament with a definite sense of linear perspective. *(Baptistery of San Giovanni, Florence/Scala/Art Resource, NY)*

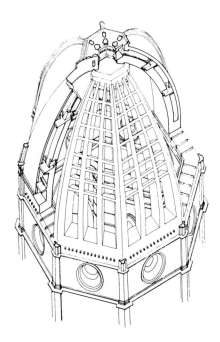

Figure 13.3   *Il Duomo:* **Dome for the** *Florentine Cathedral.*   Between 1420 and 1436, Filippo Brunelleschi utilized the Gothic principles of rib construction for the dome spanning the 138-foot-diameter octagonal crossing of the *Florentine Cathedral.* This exterior shot of the red tile roof clearly shows the eight massive ribs that divide the octagonal space. *(Scala/Art Resource, NY)*

Figure 13.4   **Filippo Brunelleschi: Diagram for the dome of the** *Florentine Cathedral. (From Peter Murray,* Renaissance Architecture © *1971 Electa International Publications. Drawing by Pepi Merisio)*

reflect everything in proportion to the human figure. Moreover, they utilized the notion (following such ancient authors as Vitruvius) that the parts of a building should be interrelated in much the same manner as the parts of the human body. The human being, awed and overwhelmed by the scale and otherworldliness of Gothic structures, was at ease and comfortable in buildings constructed by Renaissance architects. Renaissance architecture also departed from the medieval Gothic style by a corresponding shift from religious to secular architecture. Although they continued to build ecclesiastical structures, Renaissance architects also produced a profusion of civic buildings and palaces.

Brunelleschi, the foremost architect of the Early Renaissance, was trained as a goldsmith and a sculptor. After losing the competition for the commission for the north door of the Baptistery to Ghiberti, he reputedly went to Rome with Donatello to study and to measure the architectural monuments of antiquity. In 1417, at the age of forty, he engaged in another competition with Ghiberti, for the commission to build a dome to complete the Gothic Florentine Cathedral.

Brunelleschi's plan was daring and innovative; he won the commission. Although Brunelleschi was awed by the hemispherical, solid concrete dome of the Roman Pantheon, he knew that he could not build such a dome to span the existing 138-foot-diameter octagonal crossing of the Florentine Cathedral. Instead, between 1420 and 1436, he built a drum—a vertical supporting wall—on the octagonal crossing. He then assembled the dome on the drum utilizing the Gothic principles of rib construction. The octagonal space is divided by eight massive ribs, which are clearly visible from the exterior against the red tile roof (Figure 13.3). These eight primary ribs, plus the sixteen secondary ribs (two within each section), form pointed arches. The twenty-four ribs are tied together with eight horizontal ties. Thus, the dome (Figure 13.4), the largest since the Pantheon, is essentially an eight-sided Gothic vault. Brunelleschi did not live to witness the completion of the lantern, but he left a model showing how it should be constructed. The lantern, crowning the dome and tying the ribs together, was constructed according to his plans. Overshadowing the city of Florence, the Cathedral was consecrated on March 25, 1436—the Marian Feast Day of the Annuciation—as *Santa Maria del Fiore,* but ever since has been known as *Il Duomo.*

Contrasting sharply with the complex design of the Gothic dome is Brunelleschi's *Pazzi Chapel* (Figure 13.5) in Florence, a work of his later years, which evidences his true genius. The chapel, with its simple harmonious combination of the circle and the square, established a new direction for Early Renaissance architecture. The chapel is named for the Pazzi family, who gave it to the church of Santa Croce; it was used for their family masses as well as for meetings of the monks.

Although Brunelleschi was not a painter, he was a pioneer in **linear perspective**. From his study of Roman architectural examples, he devised a new way of representing space that was eagerly adopted by painters of the age. He formulated the principles of single-point (linear) perspective when he made drawings of ancient buildings while he was in Rome. Linear perspective makes it possible to represent three-dimensional space on a flat surface. The central feature of single-point perspective is a vanishing point toward which parallel lines converge. This innovation made it possible to replicate landscapes, people, or buildings as seen through the human eye.

Figure 13.5 *Pazzi Chapel,* **Florence.** Filippo Brunelleschi employed a classical design for the *Pazzi Chapel,* in Florence, which was named for the Pazzi family who used it for their family masses. They then gave it to the church of Santa Croce, whose monks used it for their meetings. *(Santa Croce, Florence/Nicolas Sapieha/Art Resource, NY)*

PAINTING   Like sculpture, medieval painting—adorning the walls of churches, as mural decorations, mosaics, and frescoes—was subordinated to a religious and architectural function and was dedicated to representing the truths of the Christian faith. Like the Renaissance sculptors, Renaissance painters freed painting from its architectural function—paintings were no longer confined to church walls; they were done on wood panels or canvases. These portable works could be transported to the homes of the elite, where they became objects of pleasure and pride.

Renaissance painters transformed medieval painting by depicting human beings and the world about them in more secular terms. Although religious motifs continued to prevail, Renaissance painters subordinated the supernatural to the natural and produced works that were perspectival, naturalistic, realistic, and humanistic. Thus they reflected the contemporary enthusiasm for inquiry and the growing curiosity about human beings and their world. This growing preoccupation with individual tastes, and with the natural world and human beings—a search for reality and truth in art—induced Renaissance artists to produce new artistic genres. The fifteenth and sixteenth centuries saw the progressive development of portraiture, and in the sixteenth century, artists showed a growing feeling for nature by painting landscapes and still life.

Masaccio, the third artistic giant of the Early Renaissance in Florence, was the chief beneficiary of Brunelleschi's and Donatello's stylistic innovations. According to Vasari, Masaccio originated the style that became the hallmark of Early Renaissance painting.

> For the good style of painting we are chiefly indebted to Masaccio. Desiring to acquire renown, he reflected that as painting is nothing more than an imitation of all natural living things, with similar design and colouring, so he who should follow Nature most closely would come nearest to perfection. . . . Masaccio introduced movement, vigour and life into the attitudes, giving the figures a certain appropriate and natural relief that no painter had ever succeeded in obtaining before. . . . His works possess harmony and sweetness, the flesh-colour of the heads and of his nudes blending with the tints of the draperies, which he delighted to make in a few easy folds, with perfect nature and grace.[49]

As an example of this, Vasari details how Masaccio executed *The Holy Trinity* (Figure 13.6) for the church Santa Maria Novella in Florence:

> [H]e painted a Trinity . . . between Our Lady and St. John the Evangelist, who are contemplating the

crucified Christ. . . . But the most beautiful thing there beside the figures is a barrel vault represented in perspective, and divided into squares . . . which gradually diminish so realistically that the building seems hollowed in the wall.[50]

The crucified Christ is within the arch; God the Father is behind and above him; and the Holy Spirit is represented by the descending white dove, just above the head of Christ. The two figures outside the arch are the two donors. Below the scene is a painted skeleton, above which are the words, "I was once that which you are, and that which I am you also will be." The painting is notable because it incorporates Masaccio's version of Brunelleschi's perspective and the painter's modeling of Donatello's human figures.

These characteristics are further enhanced in Masaccio's *The Tribute Money* (Figure 13.7), which was commissioned in 1427 by the Brancacci family to ornament their chapel in the church of Santa Maria del Carmine in Florence. This theme was especially important, for in that year the Florentines considered imposing a tax, based on one's ability to pay, for the defense of the city against Milanese aggression. Vasari describes this fresco as "the most notable of all" of Masaccio's works. The fresco reflects the story of Peter's confrontation with the tax collector and Jesus telling Peter to catch a fish, in which he will find a coin to pay the tribute (Matthew 17:24–27). The group in the center portrays Jesus and his apostles being approached by the tax collector; on the left, Peter catches the fish and discovers the coin; on the right, Peter pays the tax collector.

Although this fresco concerns a biblical theme, Masaccio portrays the story in a naturalized setting, containing real people—solid in form, with detailed bones and muscles, whose expressions exude energy. Unlike Giotto, who simply modeled a mass, Masaccio separated the human forms from the fabric of their garments. The sculptural modeling of the human form is accomplished through the use of light and shadow. Whereas Giotto's light came from a source within the fresco (most notably haloes), Masaccio's light appears to come from a natural source outside the painting, which reflects on it and operates independently of the figures. The light creates shadows on and around the figures, thereby rounding them and giving them volume. The light and atmosphere reveal some figures and completely obscure others, creating a sense of realistic space imbued with light casting shadows. Other Renaissance painters emulated Masaccio's creative use of light.

Equally important for future advancements in painting was Masaccio's use of both linear and aerial perspective in *The Tribute Money*. The purpose of both types of perspective is to create an illusion of real space by representing three-dimensional forms in a manner that gives the same perception of relative size and distance as the human eye perceives them. Linear perspective (Figure 13.8) uses a series of parallel lines receding from the viewer's vantage point that meet at a vanishing point on the horizon—in this case, just above Christ's head. Masaccio achieved aerial perspective by altering the color and hue of the

Figure 13.6   Masaccio, *The Holy Trinity*, 1425, Santa Maria Novella, Florence, Italy.   The crucified Christ is within the arch, God the Father is behind and above him, and the Holy Spirit is represented by the descending white dove, just above the head of Christ. *(Santa Maria Novella, Florence/Scala/ Art Resource, NY)*

Figure 13.7   Masaccio, _The Tribute Money_   This fresco was commissioned in 1427 by the Brancacci family to ornament their chapel in the church of Santa Maria del Carmine in Florence. The fresco reflects the story of the apostle Peter's confrontation with the tax collector and Jesus telling Peter to catch a fish, in which he will find a coin to pay the tribute (Matthew 17:24–27). _(Brancacci Chapel, Santa Maria del Carmine, Florence/ Scala/Art Resource, NY)_

landscape in the distance thus making objects in the distance muted and less distinct.

When Masaccio died at the early age of twenty-seven, he left no talented students to carry on his new style. His torch subsequently passed to the gifted monk, Fra (meaning brother) Filippo Lippi (c.1406–1469), who, according to Vasari, decided to become a painter after watching Masaccio paint in the Brancacci Chapel. Later, Vasari declares that Filippo made such progress in his painting "that many declared that the spirit of Masaccio had entered into the body of Fra Filippo,"[51] and he attracted the attention of Cosimo de' Medici, who became his patron. But in his later years, Filippo developed a more intimate and sensual approach, evidenced in his _Madonna and Child with Two Angels_ (Figure 13.9). A shimmering light highlights the foreground, and the distinctly outlined figures are fully rounded by the use of this light and the shadows it creates. Filippo's Madonna is neither fragile nor spiritual, but a beautiful young woman; the Child and the angel radiate both youth and beauty. The entire scene of soft colors exudes a worldliness and humanity, and the landscape, visible through the window, was an innovation that was widely copied by later painters.

Sandro Botticelli (1444–1510) was a student of Filippo Lippi. Vasari recounts how he "followed and imitated his master so well that Filippo became very fond of him and taught him so carefully that he soon attained to an excellence that no one would have thought possible."[52] Botticelli is best known for two allegorical paintings, both of which Vasari describes in a single sentence: "One is a Birth of Venus wafted to land by the breezes, with cupids; the other is also a Venus in company with the Graces and flowers, denoting Spring, expressed by him with much grace."[53] These

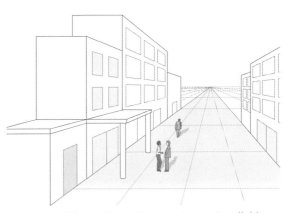

Figure 13.8   Linear Perspective.   Parallel lines recede into the painting and meet at a vanishing point in the distance. Therefore, figures in the foreground are larger than the figure walking up the street toward the vanishing point.

Figure 13.9   Fra Filippo Lippi, *Madonna and Child with Two Angels*, c. 1465, 24 3/8" x 37 3/8" (95 x 62 cm), Galleria degli Uffizi, Florence.   This Madonna is neither fragile nor spiritual, but a beautiful young woman, and the Child and the angel radiate both youth and beauty. A shimmering light highlights the foreground, and the distinctly outlined figures are fully rounded by the use of this light and the shadows it creates. *(Uffizi Gallery, Florence/Scala/Art Resource, NY)*

paintings were commissioned by Lorenzo di Pierfrancesco de' Medici, a cousin of Lorenzo the Magnificent and an enthusiastic adherent of Ficino's Neo-Platonic philosophy, which also inspired Botticelli as he painted them.

In about 1478, Botticelli painted his panel *Primavera* or *Allegory of Spring* (Figure 13.10), depicting Venus, the Roman goddess of love, at the center of a luxurious garden laden with fruit and flowers. The textual foundation for *Primavera* comes from several ancient authors—Hesiod, Lucretius, Horace, Ovid, and Seneca—all of whom described the primeval deities of spring. The descriptive narrative must be interpreted from right to left: Zephyr, the wind god, chases Chloris, who is then transformed into Flora, the goddess of flowers; the Three Graces (Chastity, Beauty, and Voluptuousness), daughters of Zeus and constant attendants of Venus, dance in their diaphanous

drapery; and Mercury, a god of spring, restrains the elements, while the blindfolded, winged Cupid shoots his arrows of love from above. Beyond the literal narrative, the painting reflects the Neo-Platonic teaching that human beings communicate with the Divine through Love. Venus mediates and ameliorates physical love, represented by the capricious Cupid discharging his blazing arrows and Zephyr enveloping Chloris in his captivating breath; her transformation into Flora represents the first blossoming goodness of the early spring. Thus, Flora is both the symbol for the idea of love as it first grows in the human mind and the goddess who anticipates and ushers in Divine Love (symbolized by Venus), the full vitality and beauty of the season.

A further expression of Divine Love can be found in Botticelli's *Birth of Venus* (Figure 13.11, p. 26), painted on canvas in 1486. This is the Venus of classical mythology, born from the sea and enriched by the dismembered genitalia of the Titan god, Saturn (Greek, Kronos, see Chapter 4). However, the painting must be interpreted within the light of Ficino's philosophy, for it is an allegory that concerns the birth of the idea of Beauty in the human mind, which is fertilized by the Divine. The sensuous, yet modest Venus, who attempts to cover her nude body with her golden wisps of hair, stands on a pink shell that appears to float gently on the pale green sea. The figures on the right represent amorous winds, whereas the figure of Hora (one of the Hours, or Seasons, present at the birth of classical figures) drifts in with an airy lightness to cover further the naked Venus with a floral robe. Reminiscent of the fashioning of the Three Graces in *Primavera*, the simple and solemn Venus is delicately modeled. Such purity of line and the cadence of linear rhythms evoke the method of relief sculpture. However, Botticelli did not paint his figures in real space; rather he introduced anti-naturalistic elements into his paintings, including V-shapes for waves and the unnatural rendering of Venus' long neck and the curvature of the joints of her left arm.

Soon after Botticelli painted these two masterpieces, Savonarola came to Florence, and Vasari claims that Botticelli came under the spell "of Fra Girolamo Savonarola . . . and this led him to abandon painting."[54] It is true that Botticelli became a follower of Savonarola, but he did continue to paint, although his style gradually changed in the last two decades of his life. The graceful, idealized figures of his earlier paintings are replaced with intense and passionate figures that resonate with religious meaning. This new style is especially evident in his *Mystical Crucifixion* (c.1500), which shows the salvation of a repentant Florence. In this

Figure 13.10   Sandro Botticelli, *Primavera* or *Allegory of Spring,* c. 1478, tempera on panel, 6′8″ x 10′4″ (2.03 x 3.15 m), Galleria degli Uffizi, Florence, Italy.   The descriptive narrative uncharacteristically reads from right to left. Zephyr, the wind god, chases Chloris, who is then transformed into Flora, the goddess of flowers, as the Three Graces dance. As Mercury, a god of spring, restrains the elements, the blindfolded Cupid shoots his arrows of love from above. *(Uffizi Gallery, Florence/Scala/Art Resource, NY)*

later period, Botticelli also painted several portraits, including one of Dante. By this time, portrait painting had become a popular art form in keeping with the humanists' belief in the inherent dignity of human beings.

Although Domenico Ghirlandaio's (1449–1494) style of painting reflects the techniques of Masaccio and the style of Filippo Lippi, he was the only Florentine painter inclined toward Flemish realism (see Chapter 14). About him, Vasari declares:

> [F]or the excellence, size and multitude of his works [he] deserves to be considered one of the best masters of his age. . . . Endowed by Nature with great ability, admirable taste and good judgment in painting, he always studied design . . . making extraordinary likenesses, a story which is largely borne out by the number of excellent portraits which he produced.[55]

Among his most heartwarming portraits is *An Old Man and His Grandson* (Figure 13.12, p. 27), which tenderly portrays the love and trust between a grandfather and his grandson. Ghirlandaio's fig-

ures are represented realistically ("warts and all"), and the landscape, which gives the painting spatial depth, is reminiscent of Filippo Lippi.

Ghirlandaio's most famous achievement, depicting scenes from the lives of Mary and John the Baptist, is a fresco cycle for the church of Santa Maria Novella. Ghirlandaio's most famous apprentice, Michelangelo, probably worked on the frescoes with him, and a quarter of a century later, he was destined to surpass his master when he executed the frescoes for the ceiling of the Sistine Chapel.

High Renaissance (1495–1520)

The High Renaissance as a period of art began with the paintings of Leonardo da Vinci (1452–1519) and lasted until the death of Raphael Sanzio (1483–1520). The High Renaissance ushered in a new style characterized by classical values—balance, simplicity, and harmony—reinforced by authentically proportioned human bodies with natural poses, painted with complementary colors in real space employing

Figure 13.11   Sandro Botticelli, *The Birth of Venus*, c. 1486, tempera on canvas, 5'8 7/8" x 9' 1 7/8" (1.8 x 2.8 m), Gallera degli Uffizi, Florence, Italy.   The sensuous, yet modest Venus attempts to cover her nude body with her golden wisps of hair as she stands on a pink shell that floats on the pale green sea. The figures on the left represent amorous winds, whereas the figure of Hora drifts in with an airy lightness to cover Venus with a floral robe. *(Uffizi Gallery, Florence/Scala/Art Resource, NY)*

realistic perspective. In 1503, when Julius II was elected pope, he dreamed of rekindling the greatness of ancient Rome and embarked on an ambitious project to rebuild Saint Peter's in a towering classical style. Although the new style was grounded in the Florentine tradition, Rome suddenly became the heart of Italian art during the High Renaissance. After 1520, Venice began to rival both Florence and Rome, becoming the center of the Italian art world.

LEONARDO DA VINCI The works of Leonardo da Vinci—his drawings, paintings, sculpture, innumerable inventions, and copious writings—exemplify the Renaissance spirit. They announced a new way of looking at nature and the individual. Leonardo examined objects in all their diversity and represented them realistically. For Leonardo, visual art was a means of arriving at nature's truths. Truth was attained when the artist brought human reason and creative capacity to bear on the direct experiences of the senses. Leonardo visually delineated the natural world with unprecedented scientific precision and simul-

taneously asserted his spiritual and intellectual freedom to do so. Through his art Leonardo helped pave the way for modern science.

In his notebooks, Leonardo sketched an infinite variety of objects—inorganic, organic, human— and recorded fragmentary thoughts about them. Everywhere, he demonstrated a concern for the concrete specificity of things, which he depicted in minute detail. He is revealed in his notebooks, not only as a gifted artist, but as an architect, engineer, inventor, musician, physicist, botanist, astronomer, geologist, and geographer.

He is, however, best known as the founder of a new style of painting. Leonardo developed two important design techniques that became standard features of High Renaissance painting: circular motion and the pyramidal grouping of figures. **Circular motion** is achieved by placing figures in a group in such a way that each seems to be leaning toward, looking at, or pointing to another figure; **pyramidal design** establishes a three-dimensional effect by positioning one figure as if at the apex of an imaginary pyramid and then allowing the other figures to fix the corners of the pyramid.

According to Vasari, the High Renaissance began with the works of Leonardo who initiated what "I will call the modern [style], notable for boldness of design, the subtlest imitation of Nature in trifling details, good rule, better order, correct proportion, perfect design and divine grace, . . . diving to the depths of art, endowing his figures with motion and breath."[56] Leonardo was born in Vinci near Florence, but he lived and worked in Florence until 1481, when he moved to Milan. There he executed many of his important early works for his patron, Lodovico Sforza, who ruled the duchy of Milan from 1481 until 1499.

Leonardo's most famous work in Milan is a mural, *The Last Supper* (Figure 13.13), executed for the monastic church of Santa Maria delle Grazie between 1495 and 1498. Unfortunately, the medium Leonardo used for it—an emulsion of oil and tempera paint—began to peel almost as soon as it was completed. Most scholars acknowledge that this mural is the first definitive assertion of the standards of the High Renaissance. The perspec-

Figure 13.12   Domenico Ghirlandaio, *An Old Man and His Grandson*, c. 1480, tempera and oil on wood panel, 24 1/8" x 18" (61.2 x 45.5 cm), Musée du Louvre, Paris, France. This tender portrait depicts the love and trust between a grandfather and his grandson. Although Ghirlandaio painted his figures realistically ("warts and all"), the landscape gives the painting spatial depth. *(Louvre/Erich Lessing/Art Resource, NY)*

tive is straightforward, with the vanishing point located immediately behind Jesus' head. This is reinforced with the open doorway behind him, which creates a halo effect. The grouping of the disciples in four groups of three is equally unique. The entire scene reflects the wide range of emotions experienced by the disciples as Jesus serenely states: "One of you will betray me" (Matthew 26:21, Mark 14:18, and Luke 22:21). On Jesus' right, John's expression is one of calm integrity in contrast to Philip, who places his hands on his chest in disbelief; whereas on Jesus' left, James's face reveals revulsion. Breaking with tradition, Leonardo places Judas on the same side of the table as the other disciples (rather than alone on the opposite side), virtually hidden in the shadows as he clutches the bag of silver, his payment for betraying Christ. Vasari notes the psychological introspection portrayed in the mural as well as Leonardo's eye for detail:

> All their faces are expressive of love, fear, wrath or grief at not being able to grasp the meaning of Christ, in contrast to the obstinacy, hatred and treason of Judas, while the whole work, down to the smallest details, displays incredible diligence, even the texture of the tablecloth being clearly visible.[57]

When Milan fell to the French in 1499, Leonardo returned to Florence. In 1503, he began his most famous work—*Mona Lisa* (see chapter opening). The subject of the painting is Lisa Gherardini del Giocondo, the wife of a prominent Florentine businessman. She is posed half-length in the seated position, her posture is relaxed, and her gaze is direct. The softening of the edges of the background—effecting a fine haze (called *sfumato*)—creates a sense of intimacy and psychological drama. The sfumato for *Mona Lisa* cloaks a haunting setting of craggy rocks and roads, which seemingly lead to nowhere. Vasari was overwhelmed by the portrait:

> This head is an extraordinary example of how art can imitate Nature, because here we have all the details painted with great subtlety. The eyes possess the moist lustre which is constantly seen in life, and about them are those livid reds and hair which cannot be rendered without the utmost delicacy. The lids could not be more natural, for the way in which the hairs issue from the skin. . . . The nose possesses the fine delicate reddish apertures seen in life. The opening of the mouth, with its red ends, and the scarlet cheeks seem not colour but living flesh. To look closely at her throat you might imagine that the pulse was beating.[58]

During Leonardo's later restless years, he traveled between Florence, Milan, and Rome. He

Figure 13.13   Leonardo da Vinci, *The Last Supper*, Santa Maria delle Grazie, c. 1495–1498, 15′2″ x 28′10″ (4.6 x 8.8 m), Milan, Italy. This scene reflects the wide range of emotions experienced by the disciples as Jesus serenely states: "One of you will betray me." On Jesus' right, John's expression is one of calm integrity in contrast to Philip, who places his hands on his chest in disbelief; on Jesus' left, James's face reveals revulsion. Virtually hidden in the shadows is Judas, clutching the bag of silver he received for betraying Christ. *(Santa Maria delle Grazie, Milan/Scala/Art Resource, NY)*

painted fewer paintings, but broadened his interests in a variety of fields. He reputedly sculpted a number of works (although none of them is extant), and he did theoretical architectural designs, structures, and elevations. In 1513, he journeyed to Rome, where he dedicated himself to scientific experimentation. He gained an unprecedented understanding of human anatomy by performing numerous dissections on human cadavers, even though they were forbidden by the church. From 1516 until his death in 1519 at the age of 67, he was an esteemed guest of King Francis I of France.

MICHELANGELO BUONARROTTI In evaluating the lives and works of the Renaissance artists, Vasari saved his highest praise for Michelangelo Buonarrotti (1475–1564). Vasari saw Michelangelo as the high point of all the visual arts—painting, sculpture, and architecture—during the Renaissance in Italy:

The great Ruler of Heaven looked down and . . . resolved . . . to send to earth a genius universal in each art, to show single-handedly the perfection of line and shadow, and who should give relief to his paintings, show a sound judgment in sculpture, and in architecture should render habitations convenient, safe, healthy, pleasant, well-proportioned, and enriched with various ornaments. He further endowed him with true moral philosophy and a sweet poetic spirit, so that the world should marvel at the singular eminence of his life and works and all his actions, seeming rather divine than earthly.[59]

After creating some statues in Florence that proved "Michelangelo's superiority to all the moderns in statuary," he went to Rome where "he made such progress in art that his conceptions were marvellous and he executed difficulties with the utmost ease, frightening those who were not accustomed to see such things."[60]

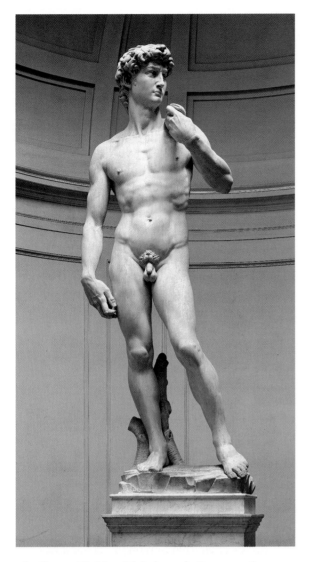

Figure 13.14 Michelangelo Buonarroti, *David*, 1501–1504, marble, 13'5" (4.09 m), Galleria dell' Accademia, Florence, Italy. In this statue, Michelangelo deftly blends the classical model of a victorious athlete crowned with a laurel wreath with the biblical hero as a defender of the faith. David is a mature young man of consummate beauty, and his bare skin contrasts with the rough leather strap of the slingshot, as he leans against a realistic tree trunk. *(Galleria dell'Accademia, Florence/Scala/Art Resource, NY)*

In 1501, Michelangelo's friends in Florence informed him that a block of marble, originally cut for Donatello's design for a statue of David, was about to be commissioned. Subsequently, Michelangelo returned to Florence and attempted to obtain the now badly damaged marble from wardens of the cathedral. Vasari relates Michelangelo's efforts:

They gave it to him as worthless, thinking that anything he might do would be better than its present useless condition. Accordingly Michelangolo

[Michelangelo]* made a wax model of a youthful David holding the sling to show that the city should be boldly defended and righteously governed, following David's example. . . . [He] finished it without anyone having seen him at work.[61]

Of the unveiling of *David* (Figure 13.14) in 1504, Vasari recalls:

When the statue was finished and set up Michelangelo uncovered it. . . . The legs are finely turned, the slender flanks divine, and the graceful pose unequalled, while such feet, hands and head have never been excelled. After seeing this no one need wish to look at any other sculpture of the work of any other artist.[62]

The 13'5" tall statue marks the further development of Renaissance sculptural style. Michelangelo fashioned the marble in a new, more natural manner—David's bare skin contrasts with the rough leather strap of the slingshot, and his right leg leans against a realistic tree trunk. Whereas Donatello, following the biblical story, depicted his bronze *David* as a youth, Michelangelo's *David* is a mature young man of consummate beauty. Although most portrayals of David show him resting his foot on the slain Goliath's head, Michelangelo chooses the moment before David launches the stone (held in the hollow of his right hand). Michelangelo's statue deftly blends the classical model of a victorious athlete crowned with a laurel wreath with the biblical hero as a defender of the faith. Michelangelo's *David* was placed in a location of secular significance, in the plaza in front of the Palazzo Vecchio (the seat of government), where it became the symbol of Florentine civic virtue.

In 1505, Michelangelo was summoned to Rome to design the tomb for Pope Julius II. The project, abandoned in 1506 until after Julius' death in 1513, brought the artist much anguish and is often referred to as "the tragedy of the tomb." By far the most impressive of the three pieces of sculpture that survive is the formidable Moses (Figure 13.15), finished between 1513 and 1515 (the other two statues are the *Rebellious Slave* and the *Dying Slave).* The work may have been inspired by the Hellenistic sculpture of the *Laocoön Group,* which Michelangelo had carefully studied after supervising its excavation. The 7' 8 1/2" *Moses* was to be placed on the second level of the monument and thus to be seen from below. Vasari

---

*Vasari consistently refers to Michelangelo as Michelangolo, but, henceforth, the authors will use the better recognized spelling of the name.

Figure 13.15 Michelangelo Buonarroti, *Moses*, c. 1515, marble, 7′ 8 1/2″ (2.35 m), San Pietro in Vincoli, Rome, Italy. Pope Julius II summoned Michelangelo to Rome to design his tomb. The project brought the artist much anguish and is often referred to as "the tragedy of the tomb." Michelangelo believed that instead of creating figures, he simply released their forms from the stone that imprisoned them. *(San Pietro in Vincoli, Rome/Alinari/Art Resource, NY)*

considered *Moses* "unequalled by any modern or ancient work":

> Seated in a serious attitude, he rests with one arm on the tables [the Ten Commandments], and with the other holds his long glossy beard, the hairs, so difficult to render in sculpture, being so soft and downy that it seems as if the iron chisel must have become a brush. The beautiful face, like that of a saint and mighty prince, . . . so splendid and shining does it appear, and so well has the artist presented in the marble the divinity with which God had endowed that holy countenance. The draperies fall in graceful folds, the muscles of the arms and bones of the hands are of such beauty and perfection, as are the legs and knees, the feet being adorned with excellent shoes, that Moses may now be called the friend of God more than ever, since God has permitted his body to be pre-

pared for the resurrection before the others by the hand of Michelangelo. The Jews still go every Saturday in troops to visit and adore it as a divine, not a human thing.[63]

Michelangelo steadfastly maintained that, rather than creating his figures, he released their imprisoned forms from the stone:

> The best artist has no concept which some single marble does not enclose within its mass, but only the hand which obeys the intelligence can accomplish that. . . . Taking away . . . brings out a living figure in . . . hard stone, which . . . grows the more as the stone is chipped away.[64]

This evidences Michelangelo's Neo-Platonic bent of mind—the human soul, imprisoned in the body, struggles toward the divine. Moreover, unlike Leonardo, he considered sculpture to be the superior art form.

Vasari relates that because Bramante and Raphael (see later discussion) were envious of Julius II's preference for Michelangelo's sculpture, they persuaded the pope to commission Michelangelo to paint the vaulted ceiling of the Sistine Chapel, an incredibly difficult enterprise, which they hoped Michelangelo would not be able to accomplish. Vasari further recounts how Michelangelo profusely protested, but "seeing that the Pope was resolute, Michelangelo decided to do it . . . resolving to prove himself superior to those who had worked there before, and to show modern artists the true way to design and paint. The circumstances spurred him on in his quest of fame and his desire for the good of art."[65]

During the 1480s, several artists (including Ghirlandaio and Botticelli) had executed the frescoes for the upper walls of the Sistine Chapel. But the vaults of the 130-foot-long ceiling were simply adorned with stars on a blue background. Michelangelo's commission was the most challenging enterprise of the Renaissance. Between 1508 and 1512, he completed the entire ceiling by himself (his fourteen assistants were employed only to move the scaffolding about). Vasari describes his ordeal: "The work was executed in great discomfort, as Michelangelo had to stand with his head thrown back, and he so injured his eyesight that for several months he could only read and look at designs in that posture."[66]

Working much like a sculptor, Michelangelo's monumental figures on the *Sistine Ceiling* (Figure 13.16) are highly expressive. They communicate his belief that physical beauty manifests the spiritual beauty of the soul, and he presents the human body—whether nude or draped—in its most elemental form. Moving away from the altar, the nine central panels portray the world described in Genesis from Creation to the Drunkenness of Noah—God dividing the Light from the Darkness, Creation of the Sun and the Moon, God Separating the Waters from the Land, The Creation of Man, The Creation of Woman, The Original Sin and Banishment from the Garden, The Sacrifice of Noah, The Flood, and the Drunkenness of Noah. In the sections above the windows and in the lunettes around the windows, Michelangelo portrayed the forty generations of ancestors prior to Christ, and in the large corners of the chapel he depicts important scenes drawn from the Old Testament.

Michelangelo adapted his figures to fit the contours of the ceiling. Among the most renowned panels of the ceiling is the *Creation of Adam* (Figure 13.17), which modifies the biblical story of how God created man "from the ground, and breathed into his nostrils the breath of life" (Genesis 2:7). In an unprecedented image of one of the most profound human mysteries, a divine spark passes from God's outstretched hand to enliven Adam. Vasari not only describes "God being borne by a group of little angels, who seem to be supporting the whole weight of the world," but also the character of God at the moment of Adam's creation: "The venerable majesty of God with the motion as He surrounds some of [the] cherubs with one arm and stretches the other to an Adam of marvellous beauty of attitude and out-

line, seem a new creation of the Maker rather than one of the brush and design of such a man."[67]

Desiring to excel in all art forms, Michelangelo also wrote poetry. His most productive period began in 1536, when he met Vittoria Colonna (1490–1547), who inspired some of his best poetry and gave renewed meaning to his life. Born into the noble Colonna family, Vittoria received a humanist education. She married the Marchese di Pescara, Ferdinando Francesco d'Avalos, at the age of seventeen. Throughout much of their eighteen-year marriage, her husband was preoccupied with wars. After his death in 1525, she wrote fine poetry in his memory. Because her family had a long-running feud with the papacy over its political ambitions, Vittoria composed poems criticizing the worldliness of the clergy and the corruption of the church. Nonetheless, despite her work as a poet, Vittoria is best known for the relationships she kept—she was respected by Italian humanists such as Baldassare Castiglione, and she became the soul mate of Michelangelo, on whom she had an extraordinary influence. No other woman is known to have influenced him in such a way; when he did mention other women, they were either his female servants or relatives.

Whether Michelangelo wrote to Vittoria or to his young men (he was homosexual), he expressed the timeless beauty and spirituality that had been revealed to his mortal eyes. The relationship between Vittoria and Michelangelo was pure,

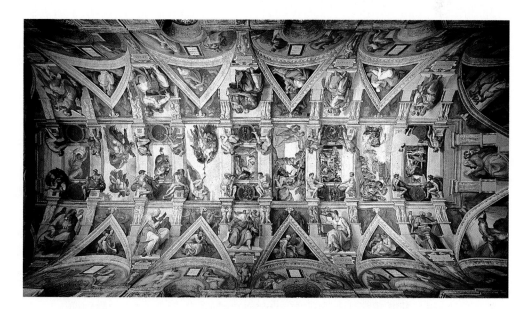

Figure 13.16 Michelangelo Buonarroti, *The Sistine Chapel Ceiling*, 1508–1512, Vatican, Rome, Italy. Michelangelo's commission to adorn the vaults of the 130-foot-long ceiling, which were originally bedecked only with stars on a blue background, was the most challenging enterprise of the Renaissance. Although he adapted his monumental figures to fit the contours of the ceiling, they are highly expressive and communicate Michelangelo's belief that physical beauty manifests the spiritual beauty of the soul. *(Vatican Museums)*

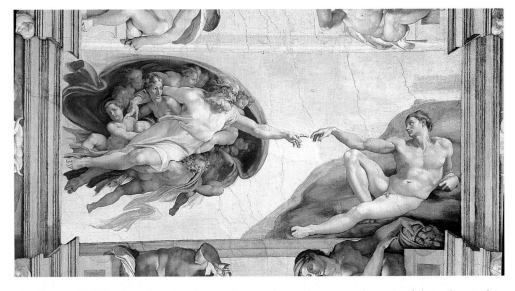

Figure 13.17 Creation of Adam Among the most renowned panels of the ceiling is the *Creation of Adam*. In an unprecedented image of one of the most profound human mysteries (creation), a divine spark passes from God's outstretched hand to enliven Adam. *(Vatican Museums)*

based on a platonic love that enabled her to be his intellectual equal. In one of his most famous sonnets about her, Michelangelo refers to Vittoria as *un uomo in una donna* (a man within a woman) and tells how she drew him out of his brooding and reclusive behavior:

A man within a woman, nay, a god,
Speaks through her spoken word:
I therefore, who have heard,
Must suffer change, and shall be mine no more.
She lured me from the paths I whilom [willingly]
   trod.
Borne from my former state by her away,
I stand aloof, and mine own self deplore.

About all vain desire
The beauty of her face doth lift my clay;
All lesser loveliness seems carnal mire.
O lady, who through fire
And water leadest souls to joys eterne [eternal],
Let me no more unto myself return.[68]

While Vittoria and Michelangelo were friends, he received a commission from Pope Paul III to paint a fresco on the enormous altar wall of the Sistine Chapel, painted between 1536 and 1541. The awe-inspiring design of the *Last Judgment* was inspired by a passage from the New Testament concerning the Second Coming of Christ: "And they will see the Son of man coming on the clouds of heaven with

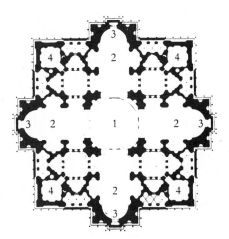

Figure 13.18 Donato Bramante, *Plan for Saint Peter's Rome.*

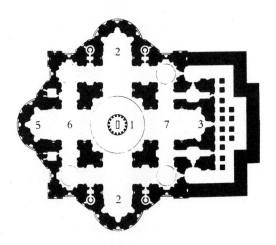

Figure 13.19 Michelangelo Buonarroti, *Plan for Saint Peter's Rome.*

power and great glory; and he will send out his angels with a loud trumpet call and they will gather his elect from the four winds, from one end of heaven to the other" (Matthew 24: 30–31).

Soon after completing the *Last Judgment,* the "tragedy of the tomb" finally found closure. By mutual agreement, Michelangelo and the pope's heirs agreed to a small structure at San Pietro in Vincoli, in Rome. The only sculpture chiseled by Michelangelo's hand to be included was his *Moses.* Tragedy subsequently struck on February 25, 1547, when Vittoria Colonna died with Michelangelo at her side. Michelangelo wrote a sonnet acknowledging the significance of his personal loss and her importance to his creative endeavors:

> The sculptor's hammer according to his will
> Gives to the rugged stone a human form.
> The hammer of itself knows not the norm
> And must be guided by the sculptor's skill.
> The hammer forged remains a hammer still.
> There is a power that rides above the storm,
> Beauty alone creates, invests with form,
> Able to recreate and also kill.
> The hammer, if the hand be lifted high,
> Descends with greater force upon the stone.
> Mine upraised was snatched with her away.
> Untouched about me now my carvings lie.

> I know not what to do. I am alone,
> Unless the great Artificer will show the way.[69]

Following her death, Michelangelo worked on only two more sculptures, both Pietàs, the second of which he intended for his own tomb.

In 1546, the seventy-one-year-old Michelangelo found an outlet for his creative energies in architecture, when he accepted the challenge of completing the construction of Saint Peter's. Pope Julius II had originally awarded the commission for Saint Peter's to Donato Bramante (1444–1514), known as an architect devoted to the revival of the architectural models of antiquity. Bramante's original centralized design (Figure 13.18) consisted of a Greek cross (four arms of equal length), with an apse on the end of each arm.

Julius II's death in 1513 and Bramante's in 1514 caused a suspension in the construction of Saint Peter's. When Michelangelo took over the project in 1546, Bramante's four grand arches were overgrown by trees, and Michelangelo decided to simplify Bramante's original plan (Figure 13.19). He thickened the four central piers, discarded the corner porches and towers, compressed the four Greek crosses into one cross and square, and added a porch of freestanding columns. In his treatment of the exterior (Figure 13.20), he

Figure 13.20   *Saint Peter's,* Rome.   In designing the dome for *Saint Peter's in Rome,* Michelangelo borrowed the vertical Gothic profile and ribs of Brunelleschi's dome for the Florentine Cathedral, and he fashioned a colonnade of paired Corinthian columns between each window at the base of the dome's drum. *(Scala/Art Resource, NY)*

virtually abandoned Bramante's design. In designing the dome, Michelangelo borrowed the vertical Gothic profile and ribs of Brunelleschi's dome for the Florentine Cathedral and fashioned a colonnade of paired Corinthian columns between each window at the base of the dome's drum. Due to these vertical elements, the overall effect looks like a single piece of monumental sculpture.

Michelangelo died before Saint Peter's was completed. Although he was buried with great pomp in Rome, his nephew, Leonardo, knowing of his uncle's desire to be buried in Florence, later brought his body back to that city, where another funeral ceremony was performed. In attendance were all the dignitaries and artists of Florence, and Michelangelo was buried in a crypt, designed by Vasari, in the church of Santa Croce. Eulogizing his friend, Vasari wrote, "He was sent into this world to help artists to learn from his life, his character and his works what a true artist should be."[70]

RAPHAEL Vasari begins his account of the life of Raphael by comparing him with Michelangelo:

"Nature created Michelangelo Buonarroti to excel and conquer in art, but Raphael to excel in art and in manners also."[71] A native of Urbino, Raphael was first taught to paint by his father. In 1504, at the age of twenty-one, he went to Florence where he studied the works of Masaccio, Leonardo, and Michelangelo. Subsequently, he began a series of Madonnas, known for their grace, charm, and gentility, which brought him widespread attention as an artist. Although he imitated the pyramidal design of his teacher, Leonardo, his Madonnas do not replicate the technicality and artifice of his mentor. Instead, Raphael painted balanced and harmonious compositions, with untroubled figures arranged in compact clusters, in gentle repose and within serenely peaceful landscapes.

In 1508, Bramante persuaded Julius II to summon Raphael to Rome. There, according to Vasari, he "acquired great renown" and developed "a graceful style [which] commanded the admiration of all."[72] Raphael's principles of compositional harmony, so evident in the most majestic of his Madonnas—the *Sistine Madonna* (Figure 13.21)—became the standard of High Renais-

Figure 13.21 Raphael Sanzio, *Sistine Madonna*, 1512, oil on canvas, 8' 8 1/2" x 6'5" (2.65 x 1.955 m), Gemäldegalerie, Dresden, Germany. The balanced, pyramidal composition is accomplished through the use of various pairings: the two angels, the two figures on either side of the Virgin, the Virgin and Child between the pair of draperies. *(Staatliche Kunstsammlungen - Alte Meister, Dresden/Erich Lessing/Art Resource, NY)*

Figure 13.22 Raphael Sanzio, *School of Athens*, 1510–1511, fresco, Stanza della Segnatura, Vatican Palace, Rome. The arches of the painting draw the eye into the depths of the scene, creating a straightforward perspective, which culminates between the figures of Plato and Aristotle. Other great thinkers of antiquity are grouped around them. *(Stanza della Segnatura, Vatican Palace, Rome/Scala/Art Resource, NY)*

sance painting. The balanced, pyramidal composition (beginning at the bottom and ascending to the top) is accomplished through the use of various pairings: the two angels, the two figures on either side of the Virgin, and the Virgin and Child between the pair of draperies. Barely distinguishable in the background are many additional faces of angels, painted using the softest sfumato. The idealized Virgin appears to be standing on the clouds, and no real space is depicted. Painters of the eighteenth and nineteenth centuries, instead of looking back to Michelangelo, were inspired by Raphael.

In contrast to the setting of the *Sistine Madonna,* Raphael's designs for the Vatican frescoes in the four stanzas (papal apartments) are created with real pictorial space. Julius II requested that the stanzas embody the Neo-Platonic ideals of Goodness, Truth, and Beauty. The most remarkable of the "Raphael Stanzas" is the composition representing natural Truth—known as the *School*

of Athens (Figure 13.22). It was executed for the so-called "Stanza of the Signature," because the chief papal documents were signed and sealed there. As one views the fresco, the first arch is actually part of the vaulting of the room, whereas the arches of the painting draw the eye into the depths of the scene, creating a straightforward perspective that culminates between the figures of Plato (with the features of Leonardo da Vinci) and Aristotle. Holding his *Timaeus,* Plato points toward the heavens, the world of Being, as Aristotle, grasping his *Ethics,* gestures toward the earth. Other figures from antiquity are grouped around them. On the left are Epicurus, crowned with grape leaves; the turbaned Averroës,* leaning over

*Averroës (1126–1198) was a Spanish Muslim philosopher whose work influenced Christian European philosophers in the twelfth and thirteenth centuries (see Chapter 10). **Socrates** (c. 469–399 B.C.), one of the most important Greek philosophers, was the teacher of Plato (see Chapter 3).

the shoulder of the bearded Pythagoras; and, above them, the olive-mantled Socrates arguing about wisdom. The group on the right, in the foreground, includes Euclid (a portrait of Bramante), bending over with a compass in hand; next to him in the gold mantle, Ptolemy, holding the earth; face to face with him, Zoroaster, holding the heavens; and to his right, a portrait of Raphael himself. Sprawled on the steps is the philosopher of cynicism, Diogenes. Scholars assume that the brooding figure in the center foreground is a portrait of Michelangelo as Heraclitus,* which Raphael added in 1511, after he had viewed the ceiling of the Sistine Chapel.

Raphael is also famous for his extensive production of portraits. Although his Florentine portraiture was generally homogenous in both pose and mood, he developed the talent to depict the unique personality of each individual he painted in Rome. Raphael painted a portrait of his patron, Pope Julius II, as well as his successor, Leo X, who gave him a position in the papal court, which enabled Raphael to further his interests in architecture, painting, and archaeology. In assessing Raphael's importance, Vasari interpreted Raphael's sudden death, at the age of thirty-seven, as a public tragedy:

> With the death of this admirable artist painting might well have died also, for when he closed his eyes she was left all but blind. We who remain can imitate the good and perfect examples left by him, and keep his memory green for his genius and the debt which we owe to him. It is, indeed, due to him that the arts, colouring and invention have all been brought to such perfection that further progress can hardly be expected, and it is unlikely that anyone will ever surpass him.[73]

TITIAN The Florentine style of painting also affected the development of painting in northern Italy, most notably in Venice. The new style was introduced into northern Italy by Giovanni Bellini (c. 1430–1516), the first teacher of Tiziano Vecellio (c. 1490–1576), known as Titian. Although the Venetian school of painting appropriated the Florentine concern for logical and controlled space and proportion, it revolutionized the concept of coloring. This new coloring was made possible by

the use of oil paints on canvas, borrowed from the Netherlands (see Chapter 14), by which painters could make it appear that there was a source of light within the painting itself.

By 1517, Titian was the unchallenged master painter in Venice, and he struck out in new directions that affected the future of painting both in Italy and throughout northern Europe. Like Raphael, Titian worked to please his patrons, but in his portraiture he created an assortment of poses that were imitated by his successors for centuries to come—most notably by van Dyck, Rubens, and Rembrandt (see Chapter 16). Moreover, Titian modeled his figures using color and tone, creating uniquely individualized portraits, instead of following the Florentine tradition of sculptural massing and line.

Although he also painted many religious and mythological scenes, Titian is best known for his female nudes. Commissioned by the Duke of Urbino on the occasion of his wedding (c. 1538), *Venus of Urbino* (Figure 13.23) is Titian's most famous female nude. The scene depicts a beautiful, sensuous young woman who is aware of her own beauty and who welcomes an assessment of it by appreciative eyes. Reclining on a pillowed couch, the draperies behind her further augment her sensuality. Nonetheless, there are images that represent marital fidelity—the small dog symbolizes faithfulness, and the chest in the background being opened by her attendants is most likely her trousseau. Titian's coloring is indicative of the Venetian style—the gold tones of her flesh vividly contrast with the reds of her pillows and the ivory color of her linens. His image of the reclining female nude was to become a theme for both painters and sculptors for generations to come.

According to Vasari, Michelangelo liked Titian's "colouring and style," but criticized him for not studying design better and commented on his potential as an artist: "If this man . . . were aided by art and design as he is by Nature, especially in copying from life, he would not be surpassed, for he has ability and a charming and vivacious style."[74] In Vasari's own assessment of Titian's significant contribution to the development of painting in Italy, he states: "[Titian] deserves the honour of artists, and [is] to be imitated in many things, for his works will endure as long as the memory of famous men."[75]

TINTORETTO The foremost painter in Venice during the second half of the sixteenth century was Jacopo Robusti (1518–1594), known as Tintoretto, which means "the little dyer," so named after the profession of his father. He reputedly advertised outside his studio that he combined

---

*Euclid (c. 300 B.C.) wrote *Elements*, an original synthesis of mathematical knowledge in his day (see Chapter 5). **Ptolemy** (c. A.D. 90–168) summed up antiquity's knowledge about astronomy and was the authority during the Middle Ages and Renaissance. **Diogenes** (c. 412–323) B.C. was the most famous Greek Cynic philosopher (see Chapter 5). **Heraclitus** (c. 535–475 B.C.) was an early Greek philosopher who maintained that strife and change are natural conditions of the universe.

Figure 13.23 Titian, *Venus of Urbino*, c. 1538, oil on canvas, 47″ x 65″ (1.19 x 1.65 m), Galleria degli Uffizi, Florence, Italy.   Titian's image of the reclining female nude was to become a theme for both painters and sculptors for generations to come. *Venus of Urbino*, commissioned by the Duke of Urbino on the occasion of his wedding, depicts a beautiful, sensuous young woman who is aware of her own beauty and who welcomes the assessment of appreciative eyes. *(Uffizi Gallery, Florence/Scala/Art Resource, NY)*

"the drawing of Michelangelo with the coloring of Titian," and he contended with Titian for prominence in Venice until Titian died in 1576. Tintoretto's style, disposition, and technique, however, differ acutely from Titian's. For example, his portraits lack the personal qualities of Titian's and favor a sort of abstract, Byzantine iconography. Tintoretto's later works were profoundly influenced by the Catholic Reformation (see Chapter 14), evidenced in his *Last Supper* (Figure 13.24), painted between 1592 and 1594. Breaking with the tradition begun by Leonardo of straightforward perspective, Tintoretto employs a diagonal perspective, which draws the eye toward the focus of the painting—the figure of Christ. He further departs from Leonardo's interpretation by relegating Judas to an insignificant position on the left end of the table. The painting's hallmark is the luminescent light that seems to emerge from within the painting itself—the figures are set aglow by the rays that emanate from the head of Christ and from the lamp. Although the illumination and the ghostly angels in the upper right corner suggest a holy scene, the servants attend to mundane tasks such as removing uneaten food and cleaning up. This unearthly, almost mystical, scene marks a definitive break from the style of the High Renaissance.

Mannerism

Vasari considered himself to be a Mannerist painter, and he was the first person to use the Italian word *maniera* to mean "style." Hence, the term **mannerism** is generally given to the period of Italian art from the death of Raphael until about 1600. The inspiration for the new style may be found in three political and religious events of the early sixteenth century: (1) the loss of republican liberty in Florence to the Medici family in 1512; (2) the fracturing of Christendom by the Protestant Reformation, beginning in 1517; and (3) the sack of Rome by the troops of Emperor Charles V, in 1527. Mannerism was a sudden, deliberate departure from the classical values esteemed during the High Renaissance—balance, simplicity, and harmony. These values were superseded by an emphasis on instability and discord—the proportions of human bodies are distorted, often with unnatural poses; the principles of space and perspective are similarly violated; and the naturalistic colors are replaced by subjective coloring. Michelangelo was one of the forebears of the Mannerist style, both as painter and as sculptor. His *Last Judgment*, with its contorted figures, has Mannerist elements, and even his *David*, with its disproportionate hands and head, has been viewed as anticipating Mannerist tendencies.

Figure 13.24 Jacopo Tintoretto, The Last Supper, (1592–1594), oil on canvas, 12′ x 18′8″ (3.7 x 5.6 m), San Giorgio Maggiore, Venice, Italy. Tintoretto employs a diagonal perspective that draws the eye toward the focus of the painting—the figure of Christ. The hallmark of the painting is the luminescent light that seems to emerge from within the painting itself. *(S. Giorgio Maggiore, Venice/Scala/Art Resource, NY)*

PARMIGIANINO Francesco Mazzuoli (1503–1540) of Parma, known as Parmigianino, was a progenitor of the Mannerist style. He was schooled in painting by his two uncles, who raised him. Recognizing his talent in 1524, they granted his wish to go to Rome to study the works of the artists he hoped to emulate—Michelangelo and Raphael. After the sack of Rome in 1527, Parmigianino went to Bologna, where his style of painting underwent transformation—his graceful figures became infused with an aura of mystical spirituality. In 1531, he returned to Parma and became so fascinated with alchemy that his work as a painter virtually ceased.

During this period, in 1534, Parmigianino received a commission for his *Madonna with the Long Neck* (Figure 13.25), which was still incomplete when he died in 1540. His delight in distortion is obvious not only in the long neck of the Virgin, but also in her elongated figure and that of the Child, whose pose resembles Christ's in a Pietà composition. The smooth, porcelainized skin is complemented by the velvet draperies and lustrous satin. The figure of the scrawny man (in the lower right corner) holding a scroll seems decidedly misplaced. Although his proportions suggest that he should be more than a hundred yards away, his

actual presence is immediately behind the Madonna. Parmigianino's drawing for the painting shows that he intended to paint a Corinthian portico in the background, but completed only the one huge column, without a capital. The base contains a baffling row of columns. The relationship of the figures to each other and to the setting has invoked much argument and speculation, but in the end the true meaning of Parmigianino's work remains impenetrable.

EL GRECO Born in Crete, Domenikos Theotokopoulos (1541–1614), known as El Greco ("The Greek"), moved to Venice in the 1560s and learned the techniques of the Venetian masters, especially Titian and Tintoretto. El Greco brought to his art a deeply religious intensity and often imbued religious themes with an ecstatic, emotional, and mystical quality. Sometime in the 1570s, he sojourned to Rome to study the work of Michelangelo and Raphael, and around 1577 he went to Toledo, Spain, where he spent the remainder of his life. El Greco's *Burial of Count Orgaz* (Figure 13.26, p. 40), painted in 1586, reflects the influence of his travels as well as the impact of the Catholic Reformation (see Chapter 14). Painted for the church of Santo Tomé, the scene conveys the traditional message that good works will merit the intercession of the saints in the matter of salvation and attaining heaven.

The actual funeral of the pious Count Orgaz took place in 1323, when, according to the legend, Saint Augustine and Saint Stephen miraculously appeared to bury him. El Greco, however, portrays the burial as an event that has just occurred and even depicts contemporary nobles as mourners. The action in the painting operates on three levels—death, the funeral, and the arrival of the Count's soul in heaven. Below the painting on the wall is a plaque, the front of which was meant to be the face of the coffin. Above the plaque, within the painting, Saint Stephen and Saint Augustine

lower the Count's body into his grave. Immediately above the row of mourners, the Count's soul is carried into the presence of Christ.

El Greco meticulously differentiates the earthly sphere from the heavenly realm. In the terrestrial domain the figures are painted with the rich detailing of the Venetian school—including the armor of the Count, the brocaded robes of the two saints, and the somber, yet resplendent Spanish noblemen. The heavenly sphere captures El Greco's mystical, Mannerist tendencies. Elongated, flame-like forms appear to float into the presence of Mary and John the Baptist and then on toward Christ himself. The distortions and undefined space of the heavenly sphere further reveal the nature of the immaterial world, which is imbued with a tranquil, celestial light.

SOFONISBA ANGUISSOLA   There were female artists in ancient Greece and Rome, but none of their work is extant. Similarly, during the Middle Ages, women worked as anonymous illuminators of manuscripts. However, by the middle of the sixteenth century, a few women became conspicuous as artists. The first Italian woman to be widely recognized as an artist during her own lifetime was Sofonisba Anguissola (c. 1535–1625). The eldest of six daughters, she was born into a wealthy family in Cremona, near Parma, in northern Italy. Because women were not permitted to study anatomy, Sofonisba specialized in portrait paintings, which are infused with psychological truth about human emotions. In her early thirties she became friends with Michelangelo (then in his eighties), and some scholars speculate that it was she who inspired some of his poetry, called "September Songs," in which he laments the passing of the passion of his youth. Moreover, Michelangelo wrote her a letter praising her artistic works.

In 1555, Sofonisba painted *Portrait of the Artist's Three Sisters with Their Governess* (Figure 13.27, p. 41), described by Vasari: "I have this year seen a picture in her father's house at Cremona, most carefully finished, representing her three sisters playing at chess, in the company of an old lady of the house, making them appear alive and lacking speech only."[76] The scene is a suspended moment in time: as the governess looks on, the oldest sister is poised to make her next move, while the youngest sister smiles mischievously as she anticipates her other sister's countermove.

By 1559, Sofonisba was such a distinguished portrait painter that Elizabeth of Valois, queen of Spain and the third wife of Philip II, summoned her to be her court painter. Sofonisba remained in the Spanish court at Madrid for more than ten years, before returning to Italy to be married.

Figure 13.25 Parmigianino, *The Madonna with the Long Neck,* c. 1535, oil on panel 7'1" x 4'4" (2.2 x 1.3 m), Galleria degli Uffizi, Florence, Italy.   Painting in the Mannerist style, which often features distortion, Parmigianino deliberately not only distorted the lengthened neck of the Virgin, but he also elongated her body and that of the Child, whose pose resembles Christ's in a Pietà composition. *(Uffizi Gallery, Florence/Scala/Art Resource, NY)*

Figure 13.26 El Greco, *The Burial of Count Orgaz*, 1586, oil on canvas, 16′ x 11′10″ (4.9 x 3.6 m), Santo Tomé, Toledo, Spain   The scene conveys the traditional message that good works will merit the intercession of the saints in the matter of salvation and attaining heaven. The action operates on three levels: death, the funeral, and the arrival of the Count's soul in heaven. *(Museo del Prado, Madrid/Institut Amatller d'Art Hispanic, Barcelona)*

Sofonisba became quite a celebrity, and her self-portraits were in great demand. In the year before her death, the celebrated Flemish portrait painter Anthony Van Dyck (see Chapter 16) painted her portrait. Sofonisba's achievements as an artist encouraged other women to become artists.

GIORGIO VASARI   Giorgio Vasari was not only one of the first art historians but was also a painter of some ability. His major murals can still be seen in Florence and in Rome, and he distinguished himself as an architect, designing a number of palaces and churches in Pisa and in his hometown of Arezzo. His masterpiece is the *Palazzo degli Uffizi,* which was built to house the governmental offices of Florence. In 1582, the third floor was converted into a gallery for the exhibition of the Medici art collection. Through the years, other works of art belonging to the Medici family, gathered from throughout Italy, were exhibited within its walls. Anna Maria Ludovica, the last of the Medici and Electress of the Holy Roman Empire, gathered many additional works of art belonging

to the Medici and, in 1743, willed the entire collection to the people of Florence, provided that all the works remain in Tuscany. Today, many of the works of art discussed in this chapter can be viewed in the renowned Uffizi Museum in Florence.

The Italian Renaissance lasted from Petrarch's age until about the time when Michelangelo painted the *Last Judgment.* By the middle of the sixteenth century, there was an awareness that a period of great creativity had reached its consummation. Vasari undoubtedly realized this when he sat down to write his *Lives* in 1544, where he relates that he had witnessed "the renaissance of the arts."[77]

MUSIC

Most music historians argue that there never was a real musical Renaissance in Italy during the fifteenth century. As evidence of this, they point out that there were no significant new inventions or techniques in music nor did any innovative styles

Figure 13.27   Sofonisba Anguissola, *Portrait of the Artist's Three Sisters with Their Governess*, 1555, oil on canvas, 27 9/16" x 37" (70 x 94 cm), Narodowe Museum, Poznan, Poland.   The scene is a suspended moment in time: as the governess looks on, the oldest sister is poised to make her next move, while the youngest sister smiles mischievously as she anticipates her other sister's countermove. *(Narodowe Museum, Poznan, Poland/The Bridgeman Art Library International)*

emerge during the period. Instead, the music of the period was simply a continuation of medieval music. Music for the mass continued to be predominant in church music; and secular music did not change significantly. In both sacred and secular music, polyphony continued to be emphasized. Musical innovation in the fifteenth century did take place, but in northern Europe (see Chapter 14). Nonetheless, in the late sixteenth century, a new musical expression began to emerge in Italy, which ultimately led to the development of opera (see Chapter 15).

In 1589, the grand wedding of Ferdinand de Medici (grand duke of Tuscany from 1587 until 1609) to Christine of Lorraine took place in Florence. Their wedding, one of the most spectacular and talked-about social events in the history of Florence, was a celebration that included banquets, elegant receptions, parades, and plays. The highlight of the entertainment was intended to be the performance of the five-act play, *La Pellegrina* (The Pilgrim), by Girolamo Bargagli. It was designed to include ***intermezzi*** ("in the middle")—musical interludes before the play, between acts, and at the end of the play. Unfortunately for Bargali, the magnificence of the *intermezzi* totally overshadowed the play itself. Ferdinand was so

enamored of them that he not only had the *intermezzi* replayed numerous times in the days following, but he also had the music and the texts published. Consequently, we know that the music included flamboyant solos, large-scale choral works, and dances.

These *intermezzi* are seen as the forebears of opera because the musicians and thinkers involved in creating them were engaged in the same sort of dialogue that ultimately resulted in opera. Such artistic intellectuals were members of the Accademia degli Alterati, which was founded in Florence in 1579 with the avowed purpose "to alter" or advance its associates "through the cultivation of elegant speech, good conduct, and a knowledge of the arts and sciences."[78] As part of the arts, they sought to rediscover Greek drama, which they believed ought to be sung. By 1592, this association was called the *camerata* (taken from the word *camera*, meaning private chamber)—in reference to the fact that the groups met in a member's private quarters.

Aware that polyphonic music detracted from the text, the members of the camerata wanted to create music that would facilitate a straightforward recitation of the text, but without losing the emotion attached to the words. The solution to their

another theme of German humanists—a type of romantic cultural nationalism. Referring to the "ancestral virtue and invincible strength" of Germans, he beseeched his audience, "O men of Germany, assume those ancient passions by which you were so often a dread and terror to the Romans."[2]

French Humanism

Lefèvre d'Étaples (1455–1536) was the foremost Christian humanist in France. During a visit to Italy in 1491 and 1492, he was inspired to learn Greek. Although he was drawn to the Neoplatonism of Ficino and the cabalistic learning of Pico, he was also captivated by Aristotle, and for over thirty years he edited and commented on most of Aristotle's writings. In 1512, he published one of his most important works, *Commentary on the Epistles of St. Paul,* in which his own Latin translation from the Greek appeared alongside the Latin Vulgate text. Subsequently, in 1530, he published his French translation of the Bible. Because of his emphasis on faith and grace in the matter of salvation, many of Lefèvre's contemporaries saw him as an evangelical predecessor to Martin Luther and as sympathetic toward Protestantism. Later French humanists—François Rabelais, Marguerite of Navarre, and Michel Montaigne—are discussed in Chapter 15.

Spanish Humanism

In Spain, the most important humanist was Cardinal Francisco Ximénez de Cisneros (1436–1517). A man of great conviction, Ximénez lived an austere and ascetic life. In 1492, he was appointed confessor to Queen Isabella, and three years later, as the Archbishop of Toledo, he became the most powerful churchman in the land. Soon after Isabella's death in 1504, Ximénez was drawn into the political arena when he became viceroy of Castile, a position he held until 1516 when Charles became king of a united Spain. In 1507, he was named Grand Inquisitor of Castile, an office he used to reform the church and to ensure by torture and fire, if necessary, that converted Moors and Jews were actually sincere Christians. In 1509, Ximénez himself led an army that conquered the Muslim city of Oran in North Africa; he released Christian captives and turned the mosques into churches. Ximénez was also a great patron of learning. In 1504, he founded the University of Alcalá, one college of which was devoted to the study of Latin, Greek, and Hebrew. At Alcalá, between 1510 and 1517, Ximénez produced the *Complutensian Polyglot Bible* (*Complutum* is Latin for Alcalá), which he dedicated to Pope Leo X. It was one of the first Bibles to be printed in the original Hebrew and Greek, with both languages appearing in parallel columns, along with the Latin text of the Vulgate.

The high point of Spanish Renaissance literature came with Miguel de Cervantes Saavedra, who wrote *Don Quixote* early in the seventeenth century (see Chapter 15).

English Humanism

John Colet (1467–1519) was one of the first important humanists in England. In the 1490s, he left Oxford to spend four years in Italy, where he was greatly influenced by Ficino and Pico. Following his return to England, he was appointed Dean of Saint Paul's in London in 1505. Using most of the fortune he had inherited from his father's estate, he established Saint Paul's School for the education of boys, patterning it after the humanist schools in Italy. Although he never learned Greek and published very little, he was, nonetheless, the leader of the Christian humanist circle in England that included Thomas More (1478–1535), who was the most distinguished of the early English humanists.

Thomas More is probably best known for his principled refusal to approve of Henry VIII's (Figure 14.1) divorce (see following) or to swear an oath accepting Henry's supremacy over the Church of England, actions for which he lost his life in 1535. By profession a lawyer, he learned Greek as a young man; later he became close friends with Erasmus (see following) and published widely as a humanist. In about 1510, More translated some of Pico's works and a *Life of Pico* (written by Pico's nephew) into English. He also defended the new humanist learning against conservative theologians who felt threatened by the reformist spirit of the Christian humanists. More had already established a reputation on the European continent when, in 1516, he published his masterpiece, *Utopia,* which comes from two Greek words—*ou,* "no," and *topos,* "place."

Influenced by Plato's *Republic,* More's *Utopia* was the first modern description of a perfect state—a society in which there are no social or economic injustices. Raphael, the narrator, claims to have sailed to the new world with Amerigo Vespucci, a Florentine merchant and explorer after whom the Americas are named. Raphael recounts for More the perfect society he reputedly witnessed on the island of Utopia. He describes Utopia as a communal society in which there is no poverty—there is no money economy, no private property, and the Utopians share all things. Scholars, however, disagree about More's intentions when he wrote *Utopia*. Is it a monastic order imposed on the entire society, or is it a precursor of

Figure 14.1 Hans Holbein the Younger, *Henry VIII,* **c. 1540, oil on panel, 32 1/2" x 29" (82.6 x 74.5 cm), Galleria Nazionale d'Arte, Antica, Rome.** This portrait of Henry VIII, painted by Holbein in 1540, is the best known of all of Henry's portraits. Although the king is painted half-length, Holbein has successfully captured Henry's regal bearing, finely detailed dress, the impact of his 6'2″ frame, and Henry's imperturbable, aloof expression. *(Galleria Nazionale d'Arte Antica, Rome/Scala/Art Resource, NY)*

modern socialism? The clearest statement of what may have been More's purpose is found near the end of *Utopia,* where Raphael declares:

> Elsewhere, people are always talking about the public interest, but all they really care about is private property. In Utopia, where there's no private property, people take their duty to the public seriously. . . . [I]n Utopia, where everything's under public ownership, no one has any fear of going short. . . . Everyone gets a fair share, so there are never any poor men or beggars. . . . Now will anyone venture to compare these fair arrangements in Utopia with the so-called justice of other countries? . . . In fact, when I consider any social system that prevails in the modern world, I can't . . . see it as anything but a conspiracy of the rich to advance their own interests under the pretext of organizing society. . . . [The Utopians] have eliminated the root-causes of ambition, political conflict, and everything like that.[3]

More, however, has the final word: "I cannot agree with everything that he [Raphael] said, for all his undoubted learning and experience. But I freely admit that there are many features of the Utopian Republic which I should like—though I hardly expect—to see adopted in Europe."[4]

The high point of English Renaissance literature in the sixteenth and early seventeenth centuries came with the writings of Edmund Spenser, Christopher Marlowe, and William Shakespeare (see Chapter 15).

Erasmus: The Prince of Christian Humanists

The greatest scholar and most popular humanist author of the early sixteenth century was the Dutch humanist Desiderius Erasmus (c. 1469–1536; see chapter opening), who shared More's commitment to reform and his relatively optimistic view of human nature. His satiric masterpiece, *The Praise of Folly,* is an indictment of poets, rhetoricians, philosophers, the clergy, the papacy, and especially self-absorbed theologians, who think they are better than the rest of humanity:

> Then there are the theologians, a remarkably supercilious and touchy lot. I might perhaps do better to pass over them in silence . . . lest they marshal their forces for an attack with innumerable conclusions

and force me to eat my words. If I refuse they'll denounce me as a heretic on the spot. . . . In addition, they interpret hidden mysteries to suit themselves. . . . Is it a possible proposition that God the Father could hate his Son; could God have taken on the form of a woman, a devil, a donkey, a gourd, or a flintstone? . . . Shall we be permitted to eat and drink after the resurrection? We're taking due precaution against hunger and thirst while there's time. . . . Such is the erudition and complexity they all display that I fancy the apostles themselves would need the help of another Holy Spirit if they were obliged to join issue on these topics with our new breed of theologian.[5]

Although Erasmus claimed that writing *The Praise of Folly* was merely a way of amusing himself while recuperating from an illness, it became his most famous work. First published in 1511, during his lifetime it went through thirty-six Latin editions and was translated into Czech, French, and German. In many ways, it was also his most controversial work, for twice before his death, it was officially condemned—in 1527, by the theologians of Paris, and in 1533, by the Franciscans—and several more times after his death.

One of Erasmus's greatest ambitions was to revive the writings of *Christian* antiquity in much the same spirit that the Italian humanists had revived *classical* antiquity. He hoped that the spiritual purity of the early Christians would inspire Christians of his own day. In this endeavor, his most important contribution was the publication of his Greek New Testament in 1516. Erasmus was encouraged and instructed by Valla's *Annotations on the New Testament*, which he edited and published in 1505. Hoping to clarify the meaning of the Greek text, Erasmus also included, in a parallel column, his own Latin translation. In the preface of his New Testament—the "Paraclesis" (the Greek word for "exhortation")—Erasmus admonishes the reader to follow "the philosophy of Christ" (the teachings of Jesus) contained in the New Testament, which, he believed, all Christians ought to be able to read in vernacular languages:

I disagree very much with those who are unwilling that Holy Scripture, translated into the vulgar tongue, be read by the uneducated, as if Christ taught such intricate doctrines that they could scarcely be understood by very few theologians, or as if the strength of the Christian religion consisted in men's ignorance of it. . . . Christ wishes his mysteries published as openly as possible. . . . To me he is truly a theologian who teaches . . . by his very life that riches should be disdained, that the Christian should not put his trust in the supports of this world but must rely entirely on

heaven, that a wrong should not be avenged, that a good should be wished for those wishing ill, . . . that all good men should be loved and cherished equally as members of the same body, . . . and that death should even be desired by the devout, since it is nothing other than a passage to immortality. . . . But if anyone objects that these notions are somewhat stupid and vulgar, I should respond to him only that Christ particularly taught these rude doctrines. . . . He is not a Platonist who has not read the works of Plato; and is he a theologian, let alone a Christian, who has not read the literature of Christ? . . . Only a very few can be learned, but all can be Christian, all can be devout, and—I shall boldly add—all can be theologians.[6]

The "Paraclesis" was thus a short summary of what Erasmus believed true Christianity to be. He clearly hoped for a reform of faith and morality, and he was convinced that the values of the Christian humanists could effect such a reform.

In 1516, the same year that More published his *Utopia*, Erasmus published a more formal treatise on politics, *The Education of a Christian Prince*, for the sixteen-year-old Prince Charles—the future Emperor Charles V. In contrast to Machiavelli's pragmatic prince, Erasmus exhorts his prince to be a true Christian—one who pursues righteousness and justice, as well as peace, and who places a special emphasis on education:

A prince who is about to assume control of the state must be advised at once that the main hope of a state lies in the proper education of its youth. . . . Pliable youth is amenable to any system of training. Therefore the greatest care should be exercised over public and private schools and over the education of the girls, so that the children may be placed under the best and most trustworthy instructors and may learn the teachings of Christ and that good literature which is beneficial to the state. As a result of this scheme of things, there will be no need for many laws or punishments, for the people will of their own free will follow the course of right.[7]

This treatise reflects Erasmus's mitigated optimism about the possibilities of reform, which he shared with More and other Christian humanists.

Erasmus, as the prince of the humanists, had a large following of younger admirers. When Martin Luther (1483–1546) appeared on the scene in 1517, many people regarded him as one of these younger humanists. Because both men criticized current theology, condemned abuses in the church, and proclaimed the need for reform, they even were seen as collaborators. Erasmus, however, sensed that he and Luther were of a different mind. Although many labeled Erasmus a Lutheran, and others thought that Luther was an Erasmian, they were mistaken, for Luther's message marked a break with Catholicism to which Erasmus remained committed.

THE PROTESTANT REFORMATION

The Protestant* Reformation ushered in a spiritual revolution that had a great impact on the Western world. The reformation of the Western Christian church in the sixteenth century was precipitated and largely defined by the Augustinian monk Martin Luther. Luther had no intention of founding a new church or overthrowing the political and ecclesiastical order of his native Germany. Rather, it was a search to resolve his own spiritual crisis that led to the permanent schism within the church and had a profound effect on European life.

The Lutheran Reformation

By the middle of the fifteenth century, many Christians were angered by the luxurious lifestyle of the upper clergy and the behavior of Renaissance popes, who enhanced their political power at the expense of other rulers and who seemed more concerned with land and wealth than with Christ's message. Concerned Christians yearned to revive the intense spirituality displayed by the first followers of Christ. This quest for a deeper commitment to the essential Christian mission took several forms: a growing interest in mysticism as a way of communicating directly with the divine; the study of the Bible to arrive at a greater understanding of Christ's life and teachings; the development of communal ways for laypeople to live and to work following the apostles' example; a heightened search for ways within secular society to imitate more perfectly the life of Christ; and a revival of pious practices, such as veneration of the saints, acquisition of relics, and popular support for the cult of Mary. In addition, the reformist spirit was buttressed by the humanists' dedication to religious education and their interest in biblical study; nearly all the religious reformers of the sixteenth century were influenced by the methods and ideals of the Christian humanist movement.

In German lands, a spirit of discontent with social and economic conditions coincided with the demand for reform of the church and religious life. For several decades before Luther's break from the Catholic church, the economic conditions of the

knights, the peasants, and the lower-class urban workers had deteriorated. The knights' grievances included loss of their political power to the centralizing governments of the German princes and increasing restrictions on their customary feudal privileges. Peasants protested that lords had steadily withdrawn certain of their customary rights and had added burdens in order to increase the lords' income and control over their estates. The knights and peasants were squeezed into an ever-worsening social and economic niche. In the cities, the lower-class artisans and laborers were similarly oppressed. Those individuals in the urban upper classes, who controlled town governments, enhanced their own economic privilege at the expense of lower-class citizens. To the economically weak, the church, which was a major landowner and active in commercial enterprises in towns, could be seen as an oppressor. All these grievances formed the explosive background to Luther's challenge to the authority of the church and the imperial government.

Martin was one of eight children born to Margarethe and Hans Luther. Martin's father was relatively prosperous, progressing from working simply as a laborer in the mines to owning shares in several mines. He was thus able to support a large family and to finance Martin's education through his master's degree in the liberal arts at the University of Erfurt in 1505. Obedient to his father's wishes, Martin entered law school but, because of a deep-seated spiritual despondency, soon dropped out. Like many of his contemporaries, Luther sought to save his soul from the temptations of the flesh, the devil, and the world. "Why would a righteous God choose a sinner like me to be saved?" This was the question that tormented him. Consequently, he contemplated entering a monastery, because he believed that only the perfection of a monastic life could calm his tormented soul. His resolve was stiffened further when, during a thunderstorm, he was knocked to the ground by a bolt of lightning that struck nearby; terrified, he reputedly made a vow: "Help me, Saint Anne [mother of the Virgin Mary], and I will become a monk." Despite his father's anger at his decision, Luther soon entered the Augustinian monastery at Erfurt. Although he was a fastidiously conscientious monk, he did not find the spiritual solace he was seeking in the monastery. Nevertheless, he persevered as a monk, was ordained into the priesthood in 1507, and studied theology at Erfurt. In 1512, Luther received the doctoral degree and became professor of theology at the University of Wittenberg; two years later, he was appointed preacher at the Castle Church at Wittenberg.

---

* When Emperor Charles V rescinded the freedom previously given to cities and territories to exist as Lutheran entities at the Diet of Speyer in 1529, the Lutheran territories and cities "protested"—hence the name "Protestants."

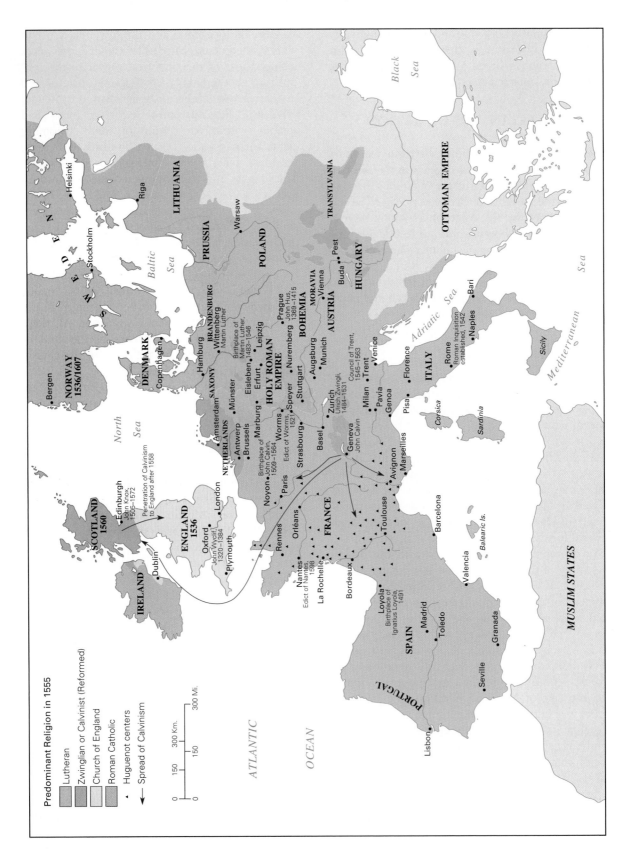

Predominant Religion in 1555

Lutheran

Zwinglian or Calvinist (Reformed)

Church of England

Roman Catholic

▲ Huguenot centers

→ Spread of Calvinism

While lecturing at the university on the apostle Paul's Epistle to the Romans, Luther discovered the answer to his anxieties about sin and the assurance of his salvation. He came to understand that God freely forgave sins through the righteousness of Christ:

> Though I lived as a monk without reproach, I felt that I was a sinner before God with an extremely disturbed conscience. . . . I did not love, yes, I hated the righteous God who punishes sinners, and secretly, . . . I was angry with God. . . . Thus I raged with a fierce and troubled conscience. . . . At last, by the mercy of God, meditating day and night, I gave heed to the context of the words, namely, "In it the righteousness of God is revealed, as it is written, 'He who through faith is righteous shall live'" [Romans 1:17]. There I began to understand that the righteousness of God is that by which the righteous lives by a gift of God, namely by faith. . . . Here I felt that I was altogether born again and had entered Paradise itself through open gates. . . . And I extolled my sweetest word with a love as great as the hatred with which I had before hated the words "righteousness of God."[8]

Luther's understanding of the "righteousness of God" was the basis for his distinctive teaching of *justification by faith alone, through God's grace alone.* **Justification,** a theological term, is derived from two Latin words—*iustus* (righteous) and *facere* (to make)—and means "to make a person righteous." For Luther, however, justification was a *passive righteousness,* attained through God's gift of faith, and not through any human efforts. Justification by faith alone, through God's grace alone, became the core of Luther's new evangelical theology, which was the foundation of the theology of all Protestant reformers.

Luther's theology deviated from the official doctrines of the Roman Catholic Church in several ways. The church maintained that *both* faith, a sincere belief in God, and good works—church attendance, acts of charity, fasting, and pilgrimages—were necessary to achieve salvation. For Luther, however, faith alone was the avenue to heaven; good works did not bring a person closer to salvation. A person of faith, he said, does good

Map 14.1 Catholics and Protestants in 1555 At the time of the Peace of Augsburg, Christendom in western Europe was divided into three major groups. Lutheran influence was largely confined to parts of Germany and Scandinavia, while Reformed influence was strong in Switzerland, Scotland, the Low Countries, and parts of France. Ultimately northern Europe became predominantly Protestant and southern Europe remained Catholic.

works—for example, demonstrating active love toward one's neighbor—in thanksgiving to God, but such actions are not rewarded with eternal life. The church taught that the clergy were intermediaries between human beings and God, that a person reached God by going through the clergy, as, for example, when confessing to a priest. Luther, however, asserted that the clergy were no different from and possessed no more power than the laity. In effect, all believers are priests. This means that the Christian's path to God is direct; no clerical intermediary is required. Luther believed that the only authority for the Christian is Holy Scripture, God's word to men and women. Luther also dismissed the authority of canon law, ecclesiastical courts, and the exclusive power of the clergy to interpret the Scriptures. Furthermore, he retained only two of the seven sacraments—baptism and the Eucharist (see following). Luther viewed Christianity as a personal relationship between the individual and God. His idea that the individual reaches God and attains salvation without clerical intermediaries diminished the importance of the institutional church and its clergy.

It was Luther's rejection of the sacrament of penance that opened the floodgates of the Protestant Reformation. The dispute over the sacrament of penance began innocently—as an argument about the efficacy of indulgences. In the sacrament of penance, the priest absolved the truly contrite sinner from the guilt of sin but gave the sinner a penalty or penance to fulfill. If the penance was either insufficient or not completed before one's death, the remainder would be fulfilled in purgatory—the place where sinners made recompense for their sins before being allowed into heaven. In theory, an **indulgence** allowed a sinner to draw on the treasury of merit accrued by Christ, the Virgin Mary, and the saints to remit the temporal punishment for sins.

In 1507, Pope Julius II proclaimed an indulgence to finance the construction of the new Saint Peter's basilica in Rome, which was renewed by Leo X in 1513. The indulgence promised Christians, living or dead, the remission of ecclesiastical penalties for sin and thus the possibility of avoiding purgatory. By April 1517, John Tetzel, a Dominican monk, was preaching the indulgence near Wittenberg, but he preached that the indulgence was itself a means to salvation, which could easily be purchased. Tetzel, playing on the emotions of those who had lost loved ones, reputedly said:

> As soon as the coin in the box rings,
> the soul from purgatory to heaven springs.[9]

To sincere Christians, it seemed as if the church was espousing an abhorrent idea—that people could buy their way into heaven. In 1517, Luther denounced the abuses connected with the preaching of the indulgence in his *Ninety-Five Theses Concerning the Efficacy of Indulgences,* written in Latin, which he posted on the north door of the Castle Church on All Saints' Eve (October 31) 1517. This quarrel led quickly to other and more profound theological issues. Luther refused to recant his views at the Diet of Augsburg in 1518, and two years later, he burned the papal bull excommunicating him, both of which gained him popular notoriety. In his *Address to the Christian Nobility of the German Nation Concerning the Reform of the Christian Estate* (August 1520), written in German, Luther attacked the whole system of papal governance. Arguing that the papacy was blocking any reform of the church, Luther appealed to the nobility and the leaders of the imperial cities in Germany to intervene by summoning a "free council" to reform the church.

In April 1521, Luther was summoned to appear at the meeting of the **Imperial Diet at Worms,** where he was shown a pile of his books, asked to admit that he was the author of them, and to recant of his errors contained in them. Luther, before the emperor and all the dignitaries of both the Empire and the church, readily admitted that he had authored the books but refused to admit that they contained any error.

> Unless I am convinced by the testimony of the Scriptures or by clear reason (for I do not trust either in the pope or in councils alone, since it is well known that they have often erred and contradicted themselves), I am bound by the Scriptures I have quoted and my conscience is captive to the Word of God. I cannot and I will not retract anything, since it is neither safe nor right to go against conscience. I cannot do other wise, here I stand, may God help me, Amen.[10]

When Luther began his spiritual journey, he had no intention of breaking with Rome, but a rupture had developed between the papacy and Luther and his followers—one that never healed. Luther's dictum at Worms—that he was "bound by the Scriptures" and "captive to the Word of God"—reflected his rejection of the authority of the papacy and of the Roman clergy.

At Worms, Luther was condemned as a heretic and declared an outlaw by an imperial edict. Cognizant of the fate of Jan Hus, the fourteenth-century heretic who was burned at the stake by the Council of Constance in 1415, Luther was abducted, for his own safety, by agents of Elector Frederick the Wise of Saxony to the Wartburg, a medieval castle in Eisenach. There, Luther began his translation of the Bible into German, which was instrumental in standardizing the German language. Meanwhile, Luther's evangelical theology gained a large following in Wittenberg, including some fanatical evangelicals who broke into monasteries and destroyed images. Therefore, shortly before Christmas of 1521, Luther, disguised as a knight, returned to Wittenberg to aid in restoring order.

On June 27, 1525, Luther married Katharina von Bora (1499–1552), a former nun, and their friend, Lucas Cranach the Elder (1472–1553), painted their wedding portraits (Figure 14.2). The couple then moved into an old monastery, where they often hosted as many as thirty people for dinner and conversation. To supplement their income, Katharina ran a brewery in the basement of their home, bred cattle, and leased plots of land for gardening. Luther, on the other hand, was so preoccupied with returning the church to its apostolic origins that he was nearly oblivious to the politicization of the Reformation in Germany. In 1525, the German peasants, using portions of Luther's writings about the "freedom of a Christian," revolted against their lords. Luther, however, denounced the Peasants' Revolt because he believed that it was a rebellion against "the powers that be" (Romans 13:1), and that it was inspired by the devil. The revolt was cruelly crushed by the lords.

In 1531, the Lutherans formed the Schmalkaldic League—a defensive military alliance against the Catholic Emperor Charles V. In 1547, the year after Luther died, the cataclysmic war, which he dreaded for so long, finally began. The wars continued until the signing of the Peace of Augsburg in 1555, which divided the German lands into Lutheran and Catholic territories on the basis of the religion of their rulers.

The Reformed Tradition

HULDRYCH ZWINGLI   In addition to Luther's *Evangelical* Protestantism, there emerged the *Reformed* tradition. Since the time of the Reformation, the term Reformed has been used to identify the Protestant churches of Switzerland—Zurich and Geneva—to distinguish them from the Lutheran church. This Reformed tradition was founded by Huldrych Zwingli (1484–1531), the biblical humanist and disciple of Erasmus, who became known as the "Reformer of Zurich." Like Luther, Zwingli rejected the authority of the clergy, including the pope, and insisted that Scripture was the highest authority for Christians. Zwingli also agreed with Luther that there were only two sacraments—baptism and the Eucharist—but he disagreed with Luther's interpretation of Scripture about the meaning of the Eucharist.

Figure 14.2   Lucas Cranach the Elder, *Martin Luther and Katharina von Bora*, c. 1526, Wartburg Collection, Eisenach, Germany.   The dinners hosted by Luther and his wife, "My Katie," resulted in ardent and consequential discussions about the Protestant cause; notes on them were subsequently collected and published as Luther's *Table Talk*. *(Uffizi Gallery/Scala/Art Resource, NY)*

Luther totally rejected the Catholic view that in the ceremony of the Eucharist the "substance" or the "essence" of the bread and the wine actually changed into the body and the blood of Christ *(transubstantiation)*. Instead, he believed that, although there is no change in the substance of the bread and wine, Christ is, nonetheless, really present in them "as fire is to red hot coals" *(consubstantiation)*. Zwingli, however, based on his reading of Scripture, agreed with neither the Catholics nor Luther. Rather than Christ being really present in the bread and the wine, Zwingli asserted that he is spiritually present—the bread and the wine are symbols of Christ's presence. The Christian thus partakes of the Eucharist in remembrance of the death and resurrection of Christ, not as a "good work" that could help assure salvation.

The issue became so destabilizing that Philip, ruler of Hesse, convened a meeting at his castle at Marburg in 1529 that included Luther and Zwingli. During the three-day meeting, Luther and Zwingli vehemently disagreed on the Eucharist, with Luther carving the Latin words from Matthew 26:26, "Hoc est corpus meum" (This is my body) on a tabletop while Zwingli insisted that the "is" in the sentence must be understood metaphorically and not literally. Their failure to agree meant that the Lutheran and the Reformed churches would not present a united Protestant front against the Catholics in the German-speaking lands.

During the final two years of his life, Zwingli played the roles of both reformer and politician—a position that involved Zurich in the first of the religious wars. The Catholic states of the Swiss Confederation declared war on Zurich on October 9, 1531, and soundly defeated the meager Protestant forces two days later at the battle of Kappel, where 500 Zurichers, including Zwingli, lost their lives in battle. Zwingli's body was quartered and burned and mixed with dung, which showed the intensity of the contempt that the Catholics held for the arch-heretic from Zurich.

JOHN CALVIN   The Reformed tradition, begun by Zwingli, was further advanced by another reformer, John Calvin (1509–1564). After studying the liberal arts at the University of Paris and law at the University of Orléans, Calvin (Figure 14.3) returned to Paris in 1531, where he joined a group of humanists led by Lefèvre d'Étaples (see previous discussion). Although the circumstances surround-

Figure 14.3 John Calvin
This portrait of John Calvin is attributed to the German artist Hans Holbein the Younger (see Chapter 15). It was painted around 1538, when the reformer was 29 years old, at the beginning of his career at Geneva. *(H. Henry Meeter Center for Calvin Studies, Calvin College and Calvin Theological Seminary)*

ing Calvin's conversion to Protestantism are unclear, it probably occurred between 1532 and 1534. When the French government stepped up its persecution of Protestants in 1534, Calvin fled to the Swiss city of Basel. There he composed a summary of his understanding of the new Protestant theology, *The Institutes of the Christian Religion*, which was revised four times before his death. Written in the elegant Latin style favored by the humanists, the work was translated into French and became the principal theological text for French, Scottish, Dutch, and English Protestant reformers. He lived in Basel until 1536, when he traveled to Italy to visit fellow Protestants in Ferrara, where he met his future wife, Idelette de Bure. In 1536, Calvin was persuaded to stay in Geneva to participate in the reform of the city. Except for a brief time, he remained there for the rest of his life.

Calvin's theology was in most respects similar to Luther's. Both reformers gave primary importance to the authority of the Bible. Similarly, they both believed that human beings are totally corrupt and in bondage to sin and that the only path to salvation is justification by God's grace and the gift of faith. Consequently, both also believed in **predestination**— that even before their birth God determined that some human beings would be saved and others con-

demned—but Calvin's statement was the most emphatic of all of the Protestant Reformers:

> We call predestination God's eternal decree, by which he compacted with himself what he willed to become of each man. For all are not created in equal condition; rather, eternal life is foreordained for some [the elect], eternal damnation for others [the reprobates]. Therefore, as any man has been created to one or the other of these ends, we speak of him as predestined to [eternal] life or to [eternal] death.[11]

Although Luther adhered to predestination, it was not central to his theology. Nor, like Calvin, did he dwell on the damned, preferring instead to emphasize God's love for human beings, his mercy, and his redemptive grace. Luther's followers did the same, and over generations predestination became increasingly less significant for Lutherans. Calvin's followers, however, made the teaching a core principle of their theology, and their daily life was profoundly affected by it.

By the seventeenth century, many Calvinists believed that they had a special covenant with God, that God had predestined them for salvation; they considered themselves to be God's elect and held that Jesus had died only for the elect. They regarded themselves as God's instruments chosen to carry out his will on earth, and it was their divine mission to make society conform to God's law as revealed in Scripture. Such an outlook produced, even among ordinary people, determined and disciplined individuals, supremely confident that their aims and actions accorded with God's will. Buoyed by this conviction, such people believed that they could move mountains. The Puritans, the English followers of Calvin, demonstrated just such strength when they settled in America, which they viewed as a new promised land.

Calvin made the *zeal for public morality* a vital part of the Reformed Protestant tradition. Thus, the church in Geneva established the **consistory**— a morals court made up of lay elders and pastors— which enforced Christian discipline. The consistory warned people who were violating God's law as contained in the Scriptures. They targeted such sins as adultery, drunkenness, profanity, failure to attend church services, and usury. If people refused to amend their ways, the consistory excommunicated them. Moreover, the consistory could refer charges to the civil court for additional punishment. Calvin struggled with the city council for years to establish the authority of the consistory. By the final decade of his life, the consistory's authority was virtually unchallenged.

The Spread of Calvinism and the Development of Resistance Theory

During the second half of the sixteenth century, Calvin's theological teachings spread from Geneva to France, the Netherlands, England, and Scotland, as well as parts of Germany and eastern Europe. Catholics viewed this rapid expansion with alarm and often used force to suppress the Calvinists.

FRANCE Despite severe persecution of suspected Protestants by the French royal authorities, Calvinism won a sizable minority of followers among all social ranks. When Henry II (1547–1559) died, there were more than 2,000 French Calvinist or Huguenot* churches with nearly three million members. Soon France was engulfed in a vicious religious war between Huguenots and Catholics that lasted some thirty years. When Henry III (1574–1589) died, Henry of Navarre, a Huguenot, became King Henry IV (1589–1610). The wars continued for another five years, until Henry, seeking to secure his authority over all of France, converted to Catholicism, reputedly declaring, "Paris is worth a Mass." In 1598, Henry assuaged the apprehensions of the

Huguenots by issuing a decree of partial toleration—the Edict of Nantes.

A pivotal event during the religious wars, instigated by Catherine de' Medici, the Queen Mother, and Charles IX, was the **Saint Bartholomew's Day Massacre** (August 24, 1572), when thousands of Huguenots were brutally murdered in France, particularly in Paris, the center of the atrocity, and throughout France. This event inspired a number of Huguenot political writers to go much farther than any of the earlier reformers in making a case for rebellion against a ruler who was perceived to be a tyrant. Calvin, who had a horror of disobedience to the civil authorities, believed that all authority comes from God and that bad kings or tyrants were to be accepted as an expression of God's wrath and as just punishment for the people's sins. Nonetheless, by 1561, Calvin was forced by circumstances in France and the Netherlands to moderate his position and to justify disobedience to rulers who defied God's law. This teaching laid the groundwork for resistance by Calvinists not only in France, but also in the Netherlands and Scotland.

The most influential of these treatises, *Defense of Liberty Against Tyrants*, was published anonymously at Basel in 1579. It was actually written by a Huguenot noble and councilor to Henry of Navarre—Philippe du Plessis-Mornay (1549–1623). Mornay held that there is a religious covenant between God, on the one hand, and the ruler and the people on the other. The ruler and the people promise that they will be God's people, and they swear to obey his law. Should the ruler fail to fulfill the stipulations of the covenant, the people have the right "of enforcing its performance." Consequently, "the people as a whole, or the officers of the kingdom . . . very gravely sin against the Covenant with God" if they do not forcibly resist "a king who corrupts God's Law . . . to confine him to his proper bounds."[12] Mornay, taking the religious idea of the covenant and applying it to the political realm, then asks the crucial question: "May a prince who oppresses or devastates a commonwealth be resisted?" Kings, he states, "are created by the people . . . [and] that the people as a whole is greater than the king."[13] The instrument that creates the king is the covenant made "between the king and the people."

Hence, if a ruler becomes a tyrant by persistently violating the political covenant, he must be forcibly removed, because "tyranny is like a raging fever. At the beginning it is easy to cure but difficult to detect; afterwards, it is easy to recognize but very difficult to cure."[14] Mornay's argument advocating active resistance to tyranny permanently affected the development of political thought, and his concept of the political covenant

---

* Although the origin of the term *Huguenot* is not known with certainty, it may have come from the Swiss German word *Eidgenossen*—confederates.

caused him to label those whom he perceived to be his enemies as the "Antichrist Incarnate." He applied the label not only to Jews, but to Catholics and Turkish Muslims as well. Luther firmly believed that Jews, who obstinately refused to recognize Jesus as the Messiah and rejected the Christian faith, impeded the Second Coming; conversely, their conversion to the Christian faith would hasten it. For this reason, Luther was particularly irritated and dismayed by what he thought was Jewish intransigence, and his later writings about the Jews became increasingly polemical and intolerant.

In August 1536, John Frederick (1532–1546), the Elector of Saxony, ordered the expulsion of Jews. Because of Luther's earlier statements about the Jews, Josel of Rosheim, a scholarly German Jew, appealed to him for assistance. Luther, however, refused to help Josel, because in his eyes the protection of the Jews was the responsibility of the civil authorities. In 1543, convinced that the end of the world was rapidly approaching, Luther admonished the civil authorities to place further limits on the Jews, because their window of opportunity to convert before the Last Judgment was swiftly closing. In his most acrimonious treatise—*On the Jews and Their Lies*—Luther describes the Jew as a "devil incarnate" and advises civil and clerical authorities to treat the Jews harshly in order to be rid "of the unbearable devilish burden of the Jews."

> First, to set fire to their synagogues or schools and to bury and cover with dirt whatever will not burn, so that no man will ever again see a stone or cinder of them. . . . Second, I advise that their houses also be razed and destroyed. For they pursue in them the same aims as in their synagogues. Third, I advise that all their prayer books and Talmudic writings, in which such idolatry, lies, cursing, and blasphemy are taught, be taken from them. Fourth, I advise that their rabbis be forbidden to teach henceforth on pain of loss of life and limb. . . . Fifth, I advise that safe-conduct on the highways be abolished completely for the Jews. . . . Sixth, I advise that usury be prohibited to them, and that all cash and treasure of silver and gold be taken from them and put aside for safekeeping.[16]

Luther then admonishes the princes and lords to do as he directs and concludes his treatise with a prayer that Christ will yet convert the Jews: "May Christ, our dear Lord, convert them mercifully and preserve us steadfastly and immovably in the knowledge of him, which is eternal life. Amen."[17] Although some anti-Jewish measures were introduced, the authorities did not heed Luther's proposals to raze synagogues and homes. For several centuries, Lutheran theologians paid little mind to Luther's statements against the Jews. But in the late nineteenth and twentieth centuries, German nationalists revived Luther's treatise and the Nazis gleefully circulated his words as an authoritative endorsement of their anti-Semitic ideology. In 1994, the Church Council of the Evangelical Lutheran Church in America acknowledged "with pain . . . Luther's anti-Judaic diatribes and violent recommendations . . . against Jews. . . . [W]e reject this violent invective and yet more do we express our deep and abiding sorrow over its tragic effect on subsequent generations. In concert with the Lutheran World Federation, we particularly deplore the appropriation of Luther's words by modern anti-Semites for the teaching of hatred toward Judaism or toward Jewish people in our day."

Even though other reformers, most notably Martin Bucer in Strasbourg and Huldrych Zwingli in Zurich, chastised Luther for his vehement outbursts against the Jews, they shared his fundamental belief that unbaptized Jews threatened the very fiber of the Christian community. Later, as Protestants themselves became the victims of persecution, they began to see themselves as sharing in the same covenant that God made with the Hebrew patriarchs, Abraham, Isaac, and Jacob. This attitude toward the Jews is evident in some of Calvin's late sermons in which he stresses the dispersion and homelessness of both Jews and persecuted Christians. Later, this new sense of Jewish–Christian community advanced from France and the Netherlands to England and Scotland, and finally, to North America.

The Catholic Reformation

The criticisms of Catholic beliefs and practices by Luther, Calvin, and other Protestant reformers generated a host of theological defenses of traditional Catholicism. However, there was also a general admission that grave abuses in Catholic clerical morals and discipline had been allowed to go uncorrected. Almost everyone agreed that a new general council of the church was necessary to clarify and affirm Catholic doctrine and to institute reforms in clerical discipline and practices.

In the middle of the sixteenth century, Pope Paul III (1534–1549) convened a council that he hoped would be instrumental in healing the schism within Western Christendom. The council assembled at Trent, located in the Alps of northeastern Italy near the Austrian border. Between 1545 and 1563, the Council of Trent met in three sessions to reaffirm Catholic dogma, to condemn Protestant teachings on justification and the sacraments, and to initiate internal reform within the church itself. The papacy was firmly in control, and no Protestant theologians participated in the conciliar sessions. Therefore, rather than healing the schism, as Paul III wished, Trent made accord between Catholics and Protestants improbable. But it did provide the basis for the rejuvenation of Catholicism.

Even before the Council of Trent had been called, the Basque nobleman Ignatius Loyola (1491–1556) founded a new religious order, the **Society of Jesus,** popularly called the Jesuits. A former soldier, Ignatius underwent a spiritual conversion in 1521 to 1522 and, after seeking guidance about his vocation, decided to become a priest. Later, while studying at the University of Paris, Ignatius and several companions founded a new order, which received papal recognition in 1540.

The new Jesuit order was characterized by three distinctive features. First, the members took a special oath of obedience to the pope, which bound them to support the papacy and its programs with special devotion. Second, they rejected the traditional monastic ideal of a life of contemplation and instead espoused a life of active service in the world. Third, they were especially committed to the Christian education of youth and to missionary work among pagans and heretics.

Although other new orders were established to work among the poor, sick, and orphans, the Jesuits were particularly important, for they soon became the vanguard of the Roman Catholic Church's effort to resist what it believed to be Protestant errors. Not only did they labor for the restoration of Catholicism in those lands where it no longer was the dominant religion, but they also worked to fortify the Council of Trent's dicta regarding the authenticity of transubstantiation, the intercession of priests, and the efficacy of good works pertaining to salvation. Ignatius himself thought it vital for his followers, and for the Catholic laity as well, to "think with the mind of the Church." To help Catholics achieve a higher spiritual life, Ignatius composed a book between 1521 and 1535, *The Spiritual Exercises,* which became a guide for Jesuit confessors or counselors in leading penitents to a greater spiritual maturity. It was a summary of practical ways to order one's life through the imitation of Christ.

In the last section of *The Spiritual Exercises,* Ignatius gave final instructions to his followers. These guidelines reflect the response of reformed Catholicism to the great theological issues raised by the Protestants. One particularly poignant reflection affirms the authority of the Roman Catholic hierarchy—"If we wish to be sure that we are right in all things, we should always be ready to accept this principle: I will believe that the white that I see is black, if the hierarchical Church so defines it."[18]

The **Index of Forbidden Books**—a list of dangerous works that no Catholic could read under threat of excommunication—was also used to counteract Protestantism. The first Index was published in 1559 under Pope Paul IV, partially revised by the Council of Trent, and then promulgated as the Tridentine Index in 1564. The list included the works of all Protestant authors as well as some classics by the humanists, including Boccaccio's *Decameron,* Machiavelli's *The Prince,* and the works of Erasmus, who, ironically, had once been offered a cardinal's hat. The *Index,* which over the centuries included works by many prominent thinkers, was not abolished until 1966.

The Reformation and the Modern World

Like the Renaissance, the Reformation helped to usher in the modern world. By dividing Christendom into Catholic and Protestant, the Reformation destroyed the religious unity of Europe, the distinguishing feature of the Middle Ages, and weakened the church, the chief institution of medieval society. By strengthening monarchs at the expense of church bodies, the Reformation furthered the growth of the modern secular and centralized state. Protestant rulers repudiated all papal claims to temporal authority and extended their power over the newly established Protestant churches in their lands. In Catholic lands, the weakened church was reluctant to challenge monarchs, whose support it now needed more than ever. This subordination of clerical authority to the throne permitted kings to build strong centralized states, which characterize the political life of the modern West.

Although absolute monarchy was the immediate beneficiary of the Reformation, Protestantism indirectly contributed to the growth of political liberty—another feature of the modern West. To be sure, neither Luther nor Calvin championed political freedom. Luther believed that a good Christian was an obedient subject, and he explicitly stated that subjects should obey their rulers' commands: "It is no wise proper for anyone who would be a Christian to set himself up against his government, whether it act justly or unjustly."[19] He also declared: "Those who sit in the office of magistrate sit in the place of God, and their judgment is as if God judged from heaven. . . . If the emperor calls me, God calls me."[20] When the longsuffering German peasants rose up against the lords, Luther, regarding the uprising as a threat to the social order, approved its suppression by the lords. Calvinists created a Christian government in Geneva that closely regulated citizens' private lives, and Calvin strongly condemned resistance to political authority as wicked. He held that God selects rulers, and punishment of bad rulers belongs only to God and not to the rulers' subjects.

Nevertheless, the Reformation also provided a basis for challenging monarchical authority. Protestant theorists, such as Mornay, supported resistance to political authorities whose edicts appeared to contravene God's law as expressed in the Bible. This religious justification for revolution against tyrannical authority helped to fuel the resistance of English Calvinists, or Puritans, to the English monarchy in the seventeenth century. Like their English counterparts, American Puritans believed that the Bible contained a law higher than the law of the state. They also challenged political and religious authorities who, in their view, went against God's law. Thus, American Puritans acquired two habits that were crucial to the development of political liberty: dissent and resistance. When transferred to the realm of politics, these Puritan tendencies led Americans to resist authority that they considered unjust. Both the English Civil War and the American Revolution were instrumental in creating the modern constitutional state, which limits the powers of government.

The Reformation advanced the idea of equality. Equality is rooted in the Judeo-Christian belief that all people are the creatures of a single God. In two important ways, however, medieval society contravened the principle of equality. First, feudalism stressed hereditary distinctions between nobles and commoners. Medieval society was a hierarchy of legal orders, or estates—ascending from commoners to nobles and then to clergy. Second, the medieval church taught that only the clergy could administer the sacraments, which provided people with the means of attaining salvation; for this reason, the clergy were above the laity. Because Luther believed that there was no spiritual distinction between laypeople and clergy, this meant that there was a spiritual equality of all believers: all men and women were equal before God; all were equally priests. The entire hierarchical concept of society was challenged.

The Reformation fostered a religious individualism that was the counterpart of the intellectual individualism of the Renaissance. In their rebellion against clerical authority and accepted orthodoxy, Protestant reformers asserted the primacy of private judgment and individual conscience. When Luther was ordered by the authorities to recant at the Diet of Worms, he refused to go against his conscience as informed by "the Word of God."

Because for Protestants there was no official interpreter of Scripture as there was for Catholics, each person had the responsibility of interpreting the Bible according to the commands of his or her own conscience. Everyone had to decide individually which path to take toward God. Thus, Protestants confronted the prospect of salvation or damnation entirely on their own. No church provided them with security or certainty, and no priesthood interceded between them and God. The Protestant church was a community of equal believers guided by their own consciences, not a hierarchy of offices with special powers and prerogatives. Piety was not determined by the church but by the autonomous individual, whose conscience, illuminated by God, was the source of judgment and authority.

For the Protestant, faith was personal and inward. This new arrangement called for a personal relationship between each person and God and called attention to the individual's inner religious capacities. Certain that God had chosen them for salvation, many Protestants developed the inner self-assurance and assertiveness that characterized the modern westerner. Thus, the Protestant emphasis on private judgment in religious matters—on an inner personal conviction—helped to mold new and distinctively modern Europeans, who had confidence in their own judgment and who were unafraid to resist authority.

Whether or not the Protestant Reformation, particularly Calvinism, had a profound influence on the emergence and growth of modern capitalism was hotly contested by scholars during the first half of the twentieth century. This was primarily due to the publication of *The Protestant Ethic and the Spirit of Capitalism* (1904) by the German sociologist Max Weber. Weber acknowledged that capitalism existed in Europe before the Reformation; for example, merchant bankers in medieval Italian and German towns engaged in capitalistic activities. But, he argued, Protestantism gave to capitalism a special dynamism. Protestant businessmen believed that they had a religious obligation to succeed, and their faith gave them the self-discipline to do so. Weber argued that Calvinists, convinced that prosperity was God's blessing and poverty his curse, had a spiritual inducement to labor industriously and to avoid sloth. Calvin taught that God had already determined in advance who would be saved; consequently, salvation could not be attained through any worldly actions and there was no definite way of determining who had received God's grace. By the seventeenth century, however, some Calvinists distorted Calvin's teachings to mean that certain activities were signs of their election by God— hard work, diligence, dutifulness, efficiency, frugality, and a disdain for hedonism (all virtues that contributed to rational and orderly business procedures and to business success). Thus, argued Weber, Protestantism, unlike Catholicism, gave religious approval to moneymaking and the businessman's way of life.

Critics of Weber's thesis have argued that both Luther and Calvin personally opposed unbridled capitalism. Both reformers railed against usury and exploitation of labor by those who sought to become wealthy, and Calvin never taught that material prosperity is a sign of God's election. However, while recognizing the limitations of Weber's thesis, scholars generally agree that Protestantism did produce a highly individualistic religiosity that valued inner strength, self-discipline, and methodical and sober behavior—necessary traits for a middle class seeking business success in a highly competitive world.

Did the Protestant emphasis on individual conscience and individual interpretation of Scripture promote liberty of conscience, that is, toleration of differing religious views, which is another fundamental characteristic of the modern world? There is no easy answer to this question. Luther himself opposed propagation of beliefs that in his view misinterpreted Scripture, and Lutheran princes slaughtered Anabaptists. Calvin condoned the burning to death in 1553 of Michael Servetus, who held unorthodox views on the Trinity, as a heretic. But revulsion against torturing and killing people for their religious views also produced spokepersons for toleration. Thus, the execution of Servetus prompted Sebastian Castellio (1515–1563) to proclaim the principle of toleration in his *Concerning Heretics, Whether They Are to Be Persecuted and How They Are to Be Treated*—a book of lasting influence that went through more than 100 editions. Toleration became one of the chief concerns of secular-minded thinkers of the eighteenth-century Enlightenment, who were disgusted by the brutal history of religious persecution.

The Reformation released a torrent of religious intolerance, culminating in persecution and the "wars of religion" between Protestants and Catholics, which devastated Europe until 1648, the end of the Thirty Years' War. Nor did Europe rid itself of this fanaticism. In a broad view of Western history, it could be argued that the fanaticism of the wars of religion was channeled in the nineteenth and twentieth centuries into the even more destructive wars of nationality.

Key Terms

New Devotion
justification
indulgence
Imperial Diet at Worms
predestination
consistory

Saint Bartholomew's
  Day Massacre
Anabaptists
Society of Jesus
Index of Forbidden
  Books

Notes

1. Quoted in Lewis W. Spitz, *The Religious Renaissance of the German Humanists* (Cambridge: Harvard University Press, 1963) p. 22.
2. Excerpted in Lewis W. Spitz, ed., *The Northern Renaissance* (Englewood Cliffs, NJ: Prentice Hall, 1972), pp. 17, 19, 25–26.
3. Thomas More, *Utopia*, trans. Paul Turner (Baltimore: Penguin Books, 1965), pp. 128–131.
4. Ibid., p. 132.
5. Desiderius Erasmus, *Praise of Folly*, trans. Betty Radice, in *Collected Works of Erasmus*, ed. A. H. T. Levi (Toronto: University of Toronto Press, 1986), vol. 27, pp. 126–127.
6. John C. Olin, ed., *Desiderius Erasmus: Christian Humanism and The Reformation. Selected Writings* (New York: Harper and Row, 1965), pp. 96–100.
7. Desiderius Erasmus, *The Education of a Christian Prince*, trans. Lester K. Born (New York: W. W. Norton & Company, 1968), pp. 212–213.
8. Lewis W. Spitz, ed., *Luther's Works: Volume 34, Career of the Reformer IV* (Philadelphia: Muhlenberg Press, 1960), pp. 336–337.
9. Quoted in Carter Lindberg, *The European Reformations* (Cambridge, MA: Blackwell Publishers, 1996), p. 75.
10. George W. Forell, ed., *Luther's Works: Volume 32, Career of the Reformer II* (Philadelphia: Fortress Press, 1958), pp. 112–113.
11. John T. McNeill, ed., *Calvin: Institutes of the Christian Religion*, The Library of Christian Classics, 21 (Philadelphia: The Westminster Press, 1960), p. 926.
12. Julian H. Franklin, ed. and trans., *Constitutionalism and Resistance in the sixteenth Century: Three Treatises by Hotman, Beza, & Mornay* (New York: Pegasus, 1969), p. 157.
13. Ibid., p. 161.
14. Ibid., p. 190.
15. Walther I. Brandt, *Luther's Works: Volume 45, The Christian in Society II*, (Philadelphia: Fortress Press, 1962), p. 229.
16. Franklin Sherman, ed., *Luther's Works: Volume 47, The Christian in Society IV* (Philadelphia: Fortress Press, 1971), pp. 268–272.
17. Ibid., p. 306.
18. Ignatius, of Loyola, Saint, *The Spiritual Exercises of St. Ignatius*, trans. Anthony Mottola (Garden City, NY: Doubleday & Company, 1964), pp. 140–141.
19. Quoted in George H. Sabine, *A History of Political Thought* (New York: Holt, Rinehart and Winston, 1961), p. 361.
20. Quoted in Roland H. Bainton, *Here I Stand* (New York: Abingdon, 1950), p. 238.

Later Humanism, Art, and Music

T HE SECTARIAN VIOLENCE UNLEASHED by the Reformation is a principal backdrop for the literature of later humanism. The years from 1562 until 1609 encompassed the religious wars in France (1562–1594), the Dutch revolt against Spain (1570–1609), and the attack of the Spanish Armada on England (1588). The antagonisms between Catholics and Protestants played an important role in all of these developments. During these violent and precarious times, later humanist writers discovered a tragic discontinuity between life as it is and how it ought to be, and they often expressed disillusionment with the human condition. At the same time they continued to perpetuate the secular spirit of the earlier humanists, to study the Greek and Roman classics, and to dedicate themselves to an eloquent rhetorical and grammatical style.

During the sixteenth century, lands north of the Alps adopted many of the artistic innovations, including a careful rendering of the human form initiated earlier by the masters of the Italian Renaissance. Northern artists also gave expression to the deep religiosity that prevailed in these lands and helped to produce the Protestant Reformation. Among the important developments in music during the sixteenth century were the growing importance of instrumental arrangements, which the church had traditionally opposed, and the emergence of counterpoint; by blending together different voices, counterpoint opened up new avenues of musical expression.

LITERATURE

France

The religious conflict between Huguenots and Catholics that culminated in the devastating wars of religion affected not only the participants themselves but the cultural life of France as well. The three important writers during this period, Marguerite of Navarre, François Rabelais, and Montaigne, were Catholics who demonstrated tolerance and refused to involve themselves in the sectarian violence. Their frank examination of human behavior, including the frailty of the clergy, often led them into doubt and disillusionment.

MARGUERITE OF NAVARRE   One of the foremost prose writers in France to embrace this reflective mood was Marguerite of Navarre (1492–1549), whose second husband was Henry II, King of Navarre. At times, her circle of friends included humanists, as well as the Protestant theologian John Calvin. Marguerite presumably remained a Catholic throughout her life.

Jan van Eyck, *Portrait of Giovanni Arnolfini and his Wife*, c. 1434, oil on panel, 33″ x 22 1/2″ (83.7 x 57 cm), The National Gallery of London, England.

In 1434, Jan reputedly attended the marriage of Giovanni Arnolfini and Giovanna Cenami and decided to portray the event. In this painting, as Giovanni holds his betrothed's right hand in his left, he raises his right hand in a solemn oath of fidelity to her.

(National Gallery, London/The Bridgeman Art Library International)

Although women were less prominent in northern courts than they were in Italy, Marguerite was an exception to the rule. She read Latin and learned Italian from her mother, Louise of Savoy, which enabled her to read the sonnets of Dante and Petrarch, as well as Castiglione's *Book of the Courtier* (see Chapter 13). However, she patterned the structure of her most famous work, *Heptaméron,* after Boccaccio's *Decameron.* She intended to write 100 tales *(nouvellas)* like Boccaccio, but she only completed 72 of them, and the work was not published until nine years after her death. The larger story involves a group of travelers (reputedly fashioned after her own circle of friends) who are delayed by a flood from returning home from a spa in the Pyrenees Mountains. To pass the time, they tell tales about virtue and vice (often satirically and pointedly aimed at lascivious clergy and deceitful monks), which illustrate their disillusionment with life.

In the tale that closes book one of her nouvellas, Marguerite recounts the tragic fate of "a gentleman whose devotion to St. Francis was such that he imagined all those who wore that saint's habit were . . . as holy as the sainted founder of their order."[1] However, the gentleman's wife (who has recently delivered him a newborn son) is duped into having sex with a monk living in their home "who gratif[ies] the criminal passion which had long poisoned his heart."[2] Horrified by the violation of her honor, the woman decides to kill herself by "strangling herself with her own hands." The tragedy of the situation is compounded when "the unfortunate woman pressed her foot upon her infant's face, and its innocence could not secure it from a death as piteous as its mother's."[3] The woman's brother, jumping to the conclusion that her husband is responsible for both deaths, kills the gentleman and seeks "satisfaction of justice" by going to the court of King Francis I to "solicit his pardon."[4] Following the conclusion of the tale, one of the travelers cynically remarks: "It is they [the clergy] who unite us with our wives in the bonds of wedlock, and they have the wickedness to try to disunite us, and make us break the oath they have imposed upon us."[5]

FRANÇOIS RABELAIS   Around 1511, at the age of eighteen, François Rabelais (c. 1494–1553) became a Franciscan friar. In the monastery, he spent his leisure time studying the Greek and Roman classics. Nonetheless, in 1525, hoping to be able to pursue his humanistic studies more freely, he transferred to the Benedictine order. In

1536, he became a secular priest, which gave him even more freedom to study and to write.

In 1532, Rabelais began to write his most famous book—*The Histories of Gargantua and Pantagruel.* The "history" is divided into five books, which were published at various times during Rabelais' life—*Pantagruel* (1532), *Gargantua* (1534), *Third Book* (1546), *Fourth Book* (1552), and an incomplete *Fifth Book,* the authenticity of which is still in dispute. Because Rabelais' contemporaries delighted in scholarly puns and inside jokes, the work is filled with seemingly disparate material that often dumbfounds the modern reader. The narrator of the tales is Alcofribas Nasier, who many scholars contend is the alter ego of Rabelais himself, and the names of his two giants—Gargantua and his son, Pantagruel—were borrowed from already extant minor literary works. In Chapters 52–58 of the first book, concerning the life of Gargantua, we learn how he founded the Abbey of Thélème when he was a young man.

The abbey is designed to be the ideal place for learning to occur, free of any restraints. Consequently, certain "undesirable" types are excluded, including "vile hypocrites and bigots," "beggars in blankets," "stirrers up of troubles," "lawyers insatiable," "lawyers' clerks, devourers of the people, holders of office, scribes, and pharisees, ancient judges who tie up good citizens like stray dogs with cord on their necks." Similarly banned are "miserly usurers, gluttons, and lechers, . . . tricksters and swindlers."[6] In contrast, those who "shall be most welcome" are "noble gentlemen," "you who preach with vigor Christ's Holy Gospel, never mind who scoffs," and "ladies of high lineage." Breaking with the asceticism of traditional medieval monasteries, the rules of the imaginary monastery of Rabelais celebrated the worldly life.

All their life was regulated not by laws, statutes, or rules, but according to their free will and pleasure. They rose from bed when they pleased, and drank, ate, worked, and slept when the fancy seized them. Nobody woke them; nobody compelled them either to eat or to drink, or to do anything else whatever. So it was that Gargantua had established it. In their rules there was only one clause:

DO WHAT YOU WILL

. . . So nobly were they instructed that there was not a man or woman among them who could not read, write, sing, play musical instruments, speak five or six languages, and compose in them both verse and prose. Never were seen such worthy knights, so valiant, so nimble both on foot and horse; knights more vigorous, more agile, handier with all weapons than they were. Never were seen ladies so good-looking, so dainty, less tiresome, more skilled with the fingers and the needle, and in every free and honest womanly pursuit than they were.[7]

Later, Gargantua writes to his son Pantagruel, studying in Paris. In the letter, he describes a truly liberal education, one befitting a Renaissance humanist.

It is my earnest wish that you shall become a perfect master of languages. First of Greek, . . . secondly, of Latin; and then of Hebrew, on account of the Holy Scriptures; also of Chaldean and Arabic, for the same reason; and I would have you model your Greek style on Plato and your Latin on that of Cicero. Keep your memory well stocked with every tale from history. . . . Of the liberal arts, geometry, arithmetic, and music, I gave you some smattering when you were still small, at the age of five or six. Go on and learn the rest, also the rules of astronomy. . . . Of civil law I would have you learn the best texts by heart, and relate them to the art of philosophy. And as for the knowledge of Nature's works, I should like you to give careful attention to that too, so that there may be no sea, river, or spring of which you do not know the fish. All the birds of the air, all the trees, shrubs, and bushes of the forest, all the herbs of the field, all the metals deep in the bowels of the earth, the precious stones of the whole East and the South—let none of them be unknown to you.

Then scrupulously peruse the books of the Greek, Arabian, and Latin doctors once more, not omitting the Talmudists and Cabalists,* and by frequent dissections gain a perfect knowledge of that other world which is man. At some hours of the day also, begin to examine the Holy Scriptures. First the New Testament and the Epistles of the Apostles in Greek; and then the Old Testament in Hebrew. In short, let me find you a veritable abyss of knowledge.[8]

Through his stories, characters, and digressions, Rabelais lampoons, parodies, chastises, satirizes, and ridicules the intellectual pretensions not only of the church, but also of polite French humanist society. Due to the coarseness of his language and his penchant for scatological metaphors and analogies, Rabelais' writings have often been

banned. The essence of his message appears to be that human beings must come to grips with their situation in life and approach their difficulties with humor, for as he noted in his "Advice to Readers":

When I see grief consume and rot
You, mirth's my theme and tears are not,
For laughter is man's proper lot.[9]

MICHEL EYQUEM†␣DE MONTAIGNE The greatest French literary figure of the sixteenth century was Michel de Montaigne (1533–1592). During his lifetime, religious upheaval dominated not only the affairs of France, but Montaigne's private life as well. His father, Pierre, remained a staunch Catholic until the day he died. On the other hand, his mother, Antoinette de Loupes, born into a Spanish family of converted Jews, became a Calvinist, along with his sister, Jeanne, and his brother, Thomas.

Montaigne was well schooled. He learned Latin as a child, because "it was an unbreakable rule that neither my father nor mother, manservant nor maid, should speak anything in my presence but . . . Latin." By the age of six, "I had . . . learned to speak as pure a Latin as my teacher himself."[10] He subsequently studied at the Collège de Guyenne for seven years before taking up dialectics, logic, and law at Bordeaux. He entered public life as a magistrate, but in 1570, two years after his father's death, he sold his post to retire (at the age of thirty-eight) to the country estate he inherited—the Château de Montaigne. There, between 1571 and 1580, Montaigne wrote his *Essays,* which are considered by many scholars to be the finest example of the genre ever written. The first two books of his *Essays* appeared in 1580, and the third in 1588, just four years before his death.

In the *Essays,* Montaigne reflects on the human condition—often in paradoxical ways—exploring humanity's strength and fragility, compassion and hostility, joy and sorrow, morality and degeneracy, faithfulness and infidelity, piety and irreverence. In addition, the *Essays* demonstrate Montaigne's concern for humanity, his wit, and his wisdom. Nonetheless, Montaigne was not a naive believer in human goodness and rationality. He believed that human beings were vain, stupid, and wicked, and that human reason could not ascertain absolute truth or prove God's existence.

*Talmudists are students of the collection of writings on Jewish civil and religious laws, and Cabalists refers to students of a medieval Jewish occult tradition based on a mystical interpretation of the Hebrew Scriptures.

†Montaigne was fourth-generation nobility in the Bordeaux region of France, and the first person to drop the surname "Eyquem," preferring instead to refer to himself by the name of his father's estate—Montaigne.

Montaigne also doubted the humanists' belief in the essential dignity and goodness of the individual:

> The most vulnerable and frail of all creatures is man, and at the same time the most arrogant. He feels and sees himself lodged here, amid the mire and dung of the world, nailed and riveted to the worst, the deadest, and most stagnant part of the universe, on the lowest story of the house and the farthest from the vault of heaven, . . . and in his imagination he goes planting himself above the circle of the moon, and bringing the sky down beneath his feet. It is by the vanity of this same imagination that he equals himself to God, attributes to himself divine characteristics, picks himself out and separates himself from the horde of other creatures, carves out their shares to his fellows and companions the animals, and distributes among them such portions of faculties and powers as he sees fit.[11]

Montaigne was a skeptic who believed that humans were incapable of achieving certain truth, including knowledge of God's existence, by rational means. Nonetheless, even though knowledge of God is beyond human reason or understanding, Montaigne concluded that God exists: "But what is, then, that which really exists? . . . God alone exists, not according to any measure of time, but according to an unchangeable and immovable eternity."[12] He thus revealed himself to be a *fideist*—one who simply believes in God without objective, rational proof of God's existence.

Spain: Miguel de Cervantes

Although humanism flourished in Spain under Cardinal Francisco Ximénez de Cisneros (see Chapter 14), soon after the publication of his Polyglot Bible, the Spanish Inquisition began to persecute individuals suspected of being Protestant. This had a chilling effect on most literary efforts in Spain. For example, the renowned Spanish humanist Juan Luis Vives (1492–1540) spent most of his adult life in France, England, and the Netherlands, and Juan de Valdes (1500–1541) left Spain in 1530 because of the Inquisition.

Nonetheless, the sixteenth and seventeenth centuries are known as Spain's "Golden Age" of literature. Both the climax and decline of the Golden Age is spanned by the life of Spain's most illustrious author—Miguel de Cervantes (1547–1616). At the age of twenty-three, Cervantes became a mercenary soldier in Italy and embarked on expeditions to Naples, Sardinia, and Sicily. Cervantes was wounded at the Battle of Lepanto, where he lost the use of his left hand, accepting his disability as a badge of honor. When he decided to return to

Spain in 1575, Moorish pirates boarded his ship, Cervantes was taken captive, and for the next five years, despite his repeated attempts to escape, he was a galley slave in Algiers. Finally, in 1580, Cervantes was ransomed and returned to Valencia, Spain. At the age of thirty-seven, he married a nineteen-year-old girl and began to write plays, but for the next fifteen years, he was actually a frustrated businessman who was sued and jailed several times.

Cervantes' raucous and unconventional life all came to bear when, between 1603 and 1605, he wrote his masterpiece—*The Most Ingenious Knight, Don Quixote of La Mancha. Don Quixote* consists of two books, the first written when Cervantes was in his later fifties and the second just before his death. An immediate best-seller, it brought the near-penniless author great fame but little financial reward. The book was subsequently translated into French, German, Italian, and English and is considered to be the first modern novel.

Its original purpose was to ridicule the popular romances glorifying medieval chivalry. But Cervantes portrays his characters so well and his insights are so great that the book rises far above satire. Swinging from rollicking humor to lofty idealism, from realism to fantasy, *Don Quixote* has a worldwide appeal and a quality of timelessness achieved by few other books. Cervantes creates an absurd world, which his protagonist, Don Quixote, interprets as the real world.

The style and structure of the novel draw not only on the *picaresque* narrative form, which developed in Spain during the sixteenth century, but are also reminiscent of Chaucer's *Canterbury Tales*. In the first instance, a *picaro*—a knave or rogue—gallivants from one escapade to another and, along the way, meets people drawn from all walks of life. In the second instance, just as Chaucer's pilgrims traveled to the shrine of Thomas à Becket at Canterbury Cathedral, so too did pilgrims in Spain journey to the shrine of Saint James the Greater at Santiago de Compostela.

The *picaresque* novel also is characterized by a narrator who, on the surface, appears to be relating his own autobiography. Such is the case of Cervantes' hero, Don Quixote, who imagines himself as a gallant knight who devotes all his time to reading books about knighthood.

> [A]nd in the end, through his little sleep and much reading, he dried up his brains in such sort as he lost wholly his judgment. His fantasy was filled with those things that he read, of enchantments, quarrels, battles, challenges, wounds, wooings, loves, tempests, and other impossible follies. And these toys did so firmly possess his imagination

with an infallible opinion that all that *machina* [machinery] of dreamed inventions which he read was true. . . . Finally, his wit being wholly extinguished, he fell into one of the strangest conceits that ever a madman stumbled on in this world; to wit, it seemed unto him very requisite and behooveful, as well for the augmentation of his honour as also for the benefit of the commonwealth, that he himself should become a knight-errant, and go throughout the world, with his horse and armour, to seek adventures, and practise in person all that he had read was used by knights of yore; revenging of all kinds of injuries, and offering himself to occasions and dangers, which, being once happily achieved, might gain him eternal renown. The poor soul did already figure himself crowned, through the valour of his arm, at least Emperor or Trapisonda; and led thus by these soothing thoughts, and borne away with the exceeding delight he found in them, he hastened all that he might, to effect his urging desires.[13]

Subsequently, Don Quixote chooses a simple peasant boy, Sancho Panza, "an honest man, . . . but one of a very shallow wit,"[14] to be his knightly squire—promising him great glory. Furthermore, Don Quixote selects Dulcinea as his ladylove—who does not know that he loves her—imitating the relationships of Dante with Beatrice and Petrarch with Laura.

One of the most famous incidents in the story of Don Quixote is his battle with "thirty or forty monstrous giants." In reality, the supposed giants are only windmills, a fact that Sancho calls to his attention, but to no avail: "What giants? . . . I pray you understand . . . that those which appear there are no giants, but windmills; and that which seems in them to be arms, are their sails, that swung about by the wind, do also make the mill go."[15] This incident, among others, was immortalized in the Broadway musical *Man of La Mancha* by Mitch Leigh and Joe Darion, which gave rise to the ever-popular song—"The Impossible Dream."

In 1615, Cervantes published a sequel that ever since has been included as part of the original novel, but stylistically, it is generally regarded as inferior to the first book. By April of 1616, Cervantes was quite ill and decided to prepare for the end of his earthly life. Consequently, he took his final vows as a Franciscan on April 18, and the next day, he received the sacrament of last rites. Cervantes died on April 23, the same day as William Shakespeare (see following) and was buried the following day—adorned in his Franciscan habit.

England

During the early years of her reign, Elizabeth I deftly balanced the opposing forces that hoped to further their own agendas. The papal bull of 1570, which excommunicated Elizabeth, was a turning point because it galvanized support for her among her subjects. Despite her differences with the House of Commons, she was able to appeal to the emotional bonds that linked her to the English people, and she freely employed the powers of the crown, which had been expanded under the rule of the Tudor monarchs during the sixteenth century. In 1601, she gave her last address to Parliament, the "Golden Speech," in which she proclaimed:

> There will never be a Queen sit in my seat with more zeal to my country, care for my subjects, and that will sooner with willingness venture her life for your good and safety, than myself. For it is my desire to live nor reign no longer than my life and reign shall be for your good. And though you have had and may have many princes more mighty and wise sitting in this seat, yet you never had, nor shall have, any that will be more careful and loving.[16]

During the last years of her reign, Elizabeth managed to avoid direct conflict over two important issues—the relationship between the crown and Parliament and the challenge of the Puritans, who wished to establish a more Calvinistic form of Protestantism. These issues, however, did afflict the Stuart monarchs, who succeeded Elizabeth.

EDMUND SPENSER *The Faerie Queen,* by Edmund Spenser (1552/53–1599), illustrates the great literary creativity that marked the forty-five-year reign of Elizabeth I. The first three books were published in 1590 and the second three books in 1596. The nine-line stanzas that Spenser employed in *The Faerie Queen* became known as the "Spenserian Stanzas." When Spenser died and was buried near his cherished Chaucer in the so-called "Poets' Corner" of Westminster Abbey, the work was still incomplete. Nonetheless, we can learn much about Spenser's intentions from a letter he wrote to Sir Walter Raleigh, his friend and a courtier of the queen, which accompanied the first edition.

> The general end therefore of all the book is to fashion a gentlemen or noble person in virtuous and gentle discipline. In which I have followed all the antique poets historical. First Homer, who in the persons of Agamemnon and Ulysses hath ensampled a good governor and a virtuous man. . . . Then Virgil, whose like intention was to do in the person of Aeneas. After him Ariosto

comprised them both [the man of private virtue and the politically involved one] in his Orlando. And lately Tasso* . . . in his Rinaldo . . . [and] his Godfredo.[17]

As his example of a virtuous noble, Spenser tells Raleigh that he has chosen "Arthur [legendary king of Europe], before he was king, the image of a brave knight perfected in the twelve private moral virtues as Aristotle hath devised [in his *Nicomachean Ethics*]." Moreover, in the fashion of Virgil's "prophecy" concerning the Roman emperor, Augustus' greatness, Spenser describes how his epic will trace Arthur's genealogy down to the time of Elizabeth. In doing so, Arthur will envision England as "Faeryland," and Arthur will catch a glimpse of "the Faery Queen," and "in a dream or vision" he will come to realize she is none other than Oriana (Elizabeth) herself— "In that Faery Queen I mean glory is my general intention, but in my particular I conceive the most excellent and glorious person of our sovereign the Queen, and her kingdom in Faeryland."[18]

A committed Puritan, Spenser sought to fuse Christian revelation with Greek and Roman sources. Furthermore, Spenser's epic, incorporating the pervasive Elizabethan interpretation of the Book of Revelation, viewed the blood spilled by Protestant martyrs as the victory of Protestantism over the corrupt clergy and the Roman church.

Spenser begins the first book of *The Faerie Queen* with the adventures of the Red Cross Knight—a type of *everyman* who wanders in error, but who emerges as a Christlike figure. Spenser's heroic knight encounters not only the allegorical representation of the seven deadly sins but also "true religion" in the guise of the beloved Una—Spenser's symbol for Protestantism, which is reminiscent of Unitas in the medieval allegory *Piers Plowman*. In another adventure, reminiscent of Dante's *Divine Comedy*, the Red Cross Knight does battle with Error, employing human reason (symbolized by the Dwarf); but it is Una who tells him that he must add Faith to his arsenal, especially when he engages the monster Duessa— Spenser's symbol for false religion.

In the final analysis, Spenser connects Britain with Augustine's "City of Man" and the "City of God" with the New Jerusalem described in the Book of Revelation. Faeryland, however, remains outside of the Augustinian mold, which stressed an irreconcilable conflict between the heavenly and earthly cities and emerges as a philosophical and spiritual ideal that unites the two cities.

CHRISTOPHER MARLOWE   In contrast to the adventures of Spenser's Red Cross Knight, the heroes of Christopher Marlowe (1564–1593), reminiscent of Machiavelli's prince, throw themselves into the fray in an attempt to gain unbridled power. Marlowe thus stands in stunning contrast to his contemporaries—including William Shakespeare—who were more deeply influenced by the mood of later humanism, which valued talent and learning more than power. *Tamburlaine the Great,* his first major play and the first tragedy written in English, premiered in 1587. It tells the story of the famous Mongol chieftain who hungers for ruling power. This play, along with *Edward the Second, The Jew of Malta,* and *Doctor Faustus,* established Marlowe as a major dramatist. Even though the play is set in the Middle Ages, Marlowe's *Doctor Faustus,* instead of focusing on eternal salvation as the sole purpose of earthly life, becomes a humanist with an obsessive craving for knowledge—a contrast to Tamburlaine's lust for ruling power.

Marlowe was killed on May 30, 1593, when he was only twenty-nine years old, reputedly stabbed to death at the inn of the Widow Bull in a tavern brawl over who was going to pay the bill. Numerous scholars now suspect, however, that his death was part of a deliberate plot to assassinate him, perhaps for engaging in undercover work for the crown. Marlowe died just as Shakespeare was launching his career as a playwright, and in many ways it was Marlowe who laid the foundation for the popular English theater on which Shakespeare built.

WILLIAM SHAKESPEARE   By dealing with classical themes and figures, setting his plays in Renaissance Italy and ancient Greece, and probing the full range of people's motives, actions, and feelings, William Shakespeare (1564–1616), widely regarded as the West's finest playwright, gave expression to the Renaissance spirit. On April 26, 1564, Mary Arden and John Shakespeare christened their first son in the town of Stratford-on-Avon. Although little reliable information exists concerning Shakespeare's early life, it is certain that at the age of eighteen he married Anne Hathaway who was eight years his senior. Less than a year later, in 1583, she bore him a daughter, Susanna; two years later, the Shakespeares had twins, Judith and Hamnet, but Hamnet died when he was but eleven years old. When and why Shakespeare left Stratford has led to much speculation by scholars, but they do agree that by 1592, he was already an established actor and playwright in London.

---

*Toquato Tasso (1544–1595) was an Italian contemporary of Spenser who wrote *Rinaldo and Jerusalem Delivered.* Lodovico Ariosto (1474–1533) was another Italian poet, who authored the *Orlando Furioso,* after whose work Spenser patterned his epic.

Shakespeare wrote ten historical plays about the reigns of seven kings of England—*King John* (1199–1216), *Richard II* (1377–1399), *1 and 2, Henry IV* (1399–1413), *Henry V* (1413–1422), *1, 2, and 3, Henry VI* (1422–1471), *Richard III* (1483–1485), and *Henry VIII* (1509–1547). This genre, often referred to as the "chronicle" play, was entirely English and came into existence during the Elizabethan period. The dramas deal with, among other topics, the unrest and strife of the Hundred Years' War (1337–1453) between England and France and the Wars of the Roses (1460–1485), the series of civil wars that resulted in the establishment of the house of Tudor on the throne of England, beginning with Henry VII (1485–1509). In his chronicle plays, Shakespeare evidences his unbridled affection for England, glorifying the kings of England despite their human failings, helping to authenticate the tenuous claim of the Tudors to the throne, and bolstering the feeling of patriotism in England after the invasion of the Spanish Armada in 1588.

Shakespeare found his material in contemporary histories, but he did not hesitate to modify characters and events to intensify the dramatic effect—creating his own personalized version of English history. Shakespeare brought to the stage tormented individuals, who were often faced with life-altering dilemmas. Shakespeare's characters reveal themselves in both word and deed, but he allows the reader (or spectator) to judge the characters' failings and frailties in light of historical events. For example, in his play about Henry VIII, Shakespeare fashioned a speech for Cardinal Wolsey, the chief minister of Henry VIII from 1515 to 1529, who has just fallen from power because he could not get the pope to grant Henry a divorce from Catherine (see Chapter 14). The speech reflects on the dark side of life:

Farewell! a long farewell, to all my greatness!
This is the state of man: to-day he puts forth
The tender leaves of hopes; to-morrow blossoms,
And bears his blushing honours thick upon him;
The third day come a frost, a killing frost,
And, when he thinks, good easy man, full surely
His greatness is a-ripening, nips his root,
And then he falls, as I do. I have ventur'd,
Like little wanton boys that swim on bladders,
This many summers in a sea of glory,
But far beyond my depth. By high-blown pride
At length broke under me, and now has left me,
Weary and old with service, to the mercy
Of a rude stream that must for ever hide me.
Vain pomp and glory of this world, I hate ye!
I feel my heart new open'd. O how wretched
Is that poor man that hangs on princes' favours!
There is, betwixt that smile we would aspire to,

That sweet aspect of princes, and their ruin,
More pangs and fears than wars or women have;
And when he falls, he falls like Lucifer,
Never to hope again.[19]
Henry the Eighth, Act III, Scene ii, lines 351–372

Even while writing his historical plays, Shakespeare also authored a number of comedies. Because of his sympathy for and understanding of the human condition, Shakespeare did not write pure comedy, compelling spectators to laugh *at* his characters; instead, he depicts the foibles and follies of ordinary human beings *with* whom anyone can identify. The moods of Shakespeare's comedies vary widely. Plays such as *The Taming of the Shrew* and *The Comedy of Errors* are boisterous farces, whereas *The Merchant of Venice, Much Ado About Nothing,* and *As You Like It* reveal Shakespeare's clever wit. Moreover, *Love's Labour's Lost* and *A Midsummer Night's Dream* indicate that Shakespeare was authoring his comedies for a courtly audience. Finally, Shakespeare wrote a number of more serious comedies that are darker, almost tragic, in some cases. *The Tempest, The Winter's Tale, Troilus and Cressida,* and *All's Well That Ends Well* fall into this category. Nonetheless, in all of these types, the way of steadfast love (rarely the subject of tragedy) is a universal theme. Whether the impediment to true love be parents, amorous rivals, comedic love triangles, or deceitful friends, Shakespeare acknowledges that "the course of true love never runs smooth."

Ay me! for aught that I could ever read,
Could ever hear by tale or history,
The course of true love never did run smooth; . . .
Or, if there were a sympathy in choice,
War, death, or sickness did lay siege to it,
Making it momentary as a sound,
Swift as a shadow, short as any dream,
That, in a spleen, unfolds both heaven and earth,
And ere a man hath power to say 'Behold!'
The jaws of darkness do devour it up:
So quick bright things come to confusion.[20]
A Midsummer-Night's Dream, Act I, Scene i, lines 132–149

Moreover, Shakespeare recognizes the debilitating effect love can have on rational thought:

Lovers and madmen have such seething brains,
Such shaping fantasies, that apprehend
More than cool reason ever comprehend.
The lunatic, the lover, and the poet,
Are of imagination all compact.
One sees more devils than vast hell can hold;
That is, the madman. The lover, all as frantic,
See Helen's beauty in a brow of Egypt.[21]
A Midsummer-Night's Dream, Act V, Scene i, lines 1–11

Coincident with his historical plays and comedies, Shakespeare also proved his skill as a poet—composing sonnets and two remarkable narrative poems: *Venus and Adonis* and *The Rape of Lucrece*. Today Shakespeare's reputation rests on his accomplishments as a dramatist, but in his own day, his literary reputation was founded on these two poems, both of which were "retellings" of classical tales.

Although Shakespeare proved himself as a playwright in his histories and comedies, his tragedies are his crowning achievement. Prior to 1600, he had written only three tragedies—*Titus Andronicus* (c. 1593), *Romeo and Juliet* (1595), and *Julius Caesar* (1599). But for the next nine years following the turn of the century, Shakespeare immersed himself in the writing of seven enduring tragedies—*Hamlet, Othello, King Lear, Macbeth, Timon of Athens, Antony and Cleopatra,* and *Coriolanus*.

In the first tragedy of the period, *Hamlet*, Shakespeare drew on a number of stories and themes we have already encountered—the murder of a father and the incestuous marriage of a mother (as in Sophocles' *Oedipus the King*), the vengeance of the son (as in Aeschylus' *Oresteia*), madness versus insanity (as in Cervantes' *Don Quixote*), and the idealistic, yet conflicted, humanist who seeks to balance reason and emotion (as in Petrarch's *Secretum*). The intrigue of the play centers on the death of Hamlet's father—the king of Denmark and the victim of a conspiracy between Hamlet's mother, the adulterous Queen Gertrude, and Hamlet's uncle, Claudius, now the new king. Vowing to avenge his father's death, Hamlet feigns madness to discover the truth. In such a precarious state, Shakespeare permits Hamlet to reflect on the place of human beings in the Great Chain of Being and also to assert and to question the optimistic outlook of the Renaissance humanists:

> What a piece of work is man! How noble in reason! How infinite in faculty, in form and moving! How express and admirable in action! How like an angel in apprehension! How like a god! The beauty of the world! The paragon of animals! And yet, to me, what is this quintessence of dust? Man delights not me,—no, nor woman neither.[22] *The The Tragedy of Hamlet, Prince of Denmark,* Act II, Scene ii, lines 315–322

The timelessness of Shakespeare's masterpiece is due mostly to his ability to portray the struggle waged within Hamlet's soul—his dream of revenge and the forces that deprive him of it. One of Shakespeare's most famous soliloquies comes when Hamlet contemplates revenge against his mother and Claudius and reflects on the possible consequences of his actions:

> To be, or not to be: that is the question.
> Whether 'tis nobler in the mind to suffer
> The slings and arrows of outrageous fortune,
> Or to take arms against a sea of trouble,
> And by opposing end them. . . .
>   To die; to sleep; —
> To sleep? Perchance to dream! Ay, there's the rub;
> For in that sleep of death what dreams may
>   come,
> When we have shuffl'd off this mortal coil,
> Must give us pause.[23]
> *The Tragedy of Hamlet, Prince of Denmark,*
>   Act III, Scene i, lines 56–68

Hamlet's soliloquies allow us to see his inner torment and to reflect on our own struggle to exist in a world that often seems to conspire against us. Moreover, Hamlet's "tragic flaw"—his fiery passion, which results in his death and the death of a number of those whom he loved—reminds each of us of our frailty as human beings and our ever-present need to quell the inner forces that well up inside us seeking to overcome and to destroy us. Finally, we are made aware of that nobility of soul that endures "the slings and arrows of outrageous fortune" before acquiescing to the ultimate defeat—death.

In other tragedies, Shakespeare explores additional powerful themes related to the human condition: how all people, both good and bad, cannot violate natural law with impunity *(Romeo and Juliet)*; how a tragic hero's physical deterioration can foster moral purification *(King Lear* and *Othello)*; and how the pursuit of worldly power and fortune can result in moral dissolution *(Macbeth)*.

In all of his tragic masterpieces, Shakespeare plumbs the depths of the human condition with the beauty of his poetic language, the carefulness of his characterizations, and the spontaneity of his creative imagination. In the process, he offers insights worthy of a profound philosopher, as in the famous passage from *Macbeth*:

> To-morrow, and to-morrow, and to-morrow
> Creeps in this petty pace from day to day
> To the last syllable of recorded time;
> And all our yesterdays have lighted fools
> The way to dusty death. Out, out, brief candle!
> Life's but a walking shadow, a poor player
> That struts and frets his hour upon the stage
> And then is heard no more. It is a tale
> Told by an idiot, full of sound and fury,
> Signifying nothing.[24]
> *The Tragedy of Macbeth,* Act V, Scene v,
>   lines 19–28

Beginning in 1599, Shakespeare became a shareholder in the *Globe Theater,* where most of his greatest plays were performed. The original structure was built in approximately thirty weeks. Because the stage was not modified for individual scenes, it was the structure itself, not the scenery, that framed the action of each play. One side of the platform, measuring 25′ x 45′, was attached to the stage wall, and the other side extended into the middle of the surrounding yard. Therefore, a significant part of Shakespeare's audience stood or sat very near to the actors. Halfway between the front edge of the stage and the stage wall were two pillars used to support some kind of cover, or curtain, for the stage. The stage wall contained two doors for entry and exit of the actors, and there probably was a third door on some sort of upper level acting area. In the floor, there was a trapdoor so that actors could "disappear" from the stage rather than simply walking off. Because the stage area was so open, very few properties (props) were used in the plays. To introduce props, Shakespeare generally wrote them into his plays, by having them carried onto the stage by one of his characters or by being discovered by one of them. Whether or not huge props (including scaffolds, enclosures, and tents) were consistently used remains in dispute. But all scholars agree that due to the formal limitations of the stage itself, the success of Shakespeare's plays depended heavily on the actors' movements coming on and moving off the stage and that an actor's gestures had to be turned toward the audience to maximize their effectiveness. Because the only area in which the entire audience could view all actors was in front of the pillars, at the very center of the stage, all the significant events advancing the action of the play occurred in this area. Thus, the number of actors on stage at any given time was generally limited to less than five. In 1613, during a performance of Shakespeare's play *Henry VIII,* the Globe burned down.

Three years later, Shakespeare himself died (on the same day as Cervantes). At the time of his death in 1616, no collected edition of Shakespeare's plays was in circulation. Therefore, in 1623, two members of his acting company published a collection of what they considered to be his authentic plays—the *First Folio.* When it appeared, Shakespeare's great rival, critic, and friend, Ben Jonson (1573–1637), affirmed Shakespeare's superiority to all other playwrights—either past or present:

> Triumph, my Britain, thou hast one to show
> To whom all scenes of Europe homage own.
> He was not of an age, but for all time![25]

BEN JONSON Ben Jonson is regarded as the last of the great Elizabethan writers both for his masterful epigrams—in the style of Martial*—and for his superb lyric poetry—rendered in the man-

ner of Horace.† One of his lyric poems contains the famous line: "Drink to me only with thine eyes." After a stint in the army, he began his career as an actor and playwright in 1595. The star of his first play, *Every Man in His Humour,* was none other than his friend, William Shakespeare. The play was the first in a series of "comedies of humour"—plays that satirize the passions and eccentricities of the characters. Two of the most outstanding plays of this genre are *Volpone* (The Fox, 1606), an attack on human greediness, and *The Alchemist* (1610), a study of human naïveté. Although Jonson was put in prison for insulting the Scots shortly after James I became king of England, he was active in James's court from 1616 onward. The failure of a number of his later plays and Jonson's acerbic criticism of others made him an easy target for satirists.

JOHN DONNE Jonson's circle of friends included not only Shakespeare but also the preeminent poet John Donne (1571–1631). Donne was born into a Roman Catholic family when anti-Catholic sentiment was running high in England, but during his twenties, he quietly abandoned Catholicism. Donne, ingenuous, witty, and with a voracious appetite for learning and living, became a man of the world—traveling, partying, dancing, and enjoying the ladies. He even participated in two raiding expeditions to Spain with Sir Walter Raleigh. In 1598, he was appointed the private secretary to Sir Thomas Egerton, but in 1601, attempting to advance his station in life, he made a fatal mistake—he clandestinely married Egerton's sixteen-year-old niece, Anne More. Her father had Donne arrested, stripped of his post, and imprisoned for a brief period. For the next ten years, Donne, fighting health problems, could barely eke out an existence for himself, his wife, and his ever-increasing family. During this time, he composed a number of anti-Catholic polemics, epigrams reminiscent of Martial, and love elegies in the style of the Roman poet Ovid.

Because King James declared that Donne would never receive preferential treatment at the court unless he became an Anglican priest, much of Donne's poetry from this period is introspective. In it, he both doubts his religious commitment and seeks assurance of his salvation. Finally, in 1615, Donne did take priestly orders. He was subsequently appointed royal chaplain, and became one of the great preachers of the age.

---

*Martial (c. A.D. 38/41 to c. 104) was a Roman poet of the Silver Age who was well-known for his witty *Epigrams* (see Chapter 6).
†Horace (65–8 B.C.) was a major poet of the Augustan Age who was famous for his *Epodes* and *Odes* (see Chapter 6).

In August 1617, Donne's wife died giving birth to their twelfth child. Consequently, Donne entered a long period of grief during which his religious devotion increased. In 1621, he was made dean of Saint Paul's Cathedral, London (see Chapter 16), where he preached until his death. In 1623, while Donne was quite ill, he wrote his *Private Devotions,* one of which—*Meditation VII*—gave rise to the title of a famous novel by Ernest Hemingway, *For Whom the Bell Tolls* (see Chapter 24), and inspired the title of a tune popular in the 1960s by Simon and Garfunkel, "I Am a Rock, I Am an Island."

> No man is an island, entire of itself; every man is a piece of the continent, a part of the main. If a clod be washed away by the sea, Europe is the less. . . . Any man's death diminishes me because I am involved in mankind, and therefore never send to know for whom the bell tolls; it tolls for thee.[26]

One of Donne's most famous **conceits** (a fixed image that evokes a form of dramatic contrast that is comprehended with intense intellectual effort) is the image of the compass, whose fixed feet he uses to express the love he and his wife shared. He employed the image in his poem, "A Valediction: Forbidding Mourning," which he wrote while he was on the Continent, and his pregnant wife was home alone where she subsequently gave birth to a stillborn child. Therefore, it would appear that Donne had a premonition of the tragedy that was about to befall them.

> If they be two, they are two so
>   As stiff twin compasses are two;
> Thy soul, the fixed foot, makes no show
>   To move, but doth, if th' other do.
>
> And though it in the center sit,
>   Yet when the other far doth roam,
> It leans and hearkens after it,
>   And grows erect, as it comes home.
>
> Such wilt thou be to me, who must
>   Like th' other foot, obliquely run;
> Thy firmness makes my circle just,
>   And makes me end where I begun.[27]

Following his death, Donne's poetry went through several editions, and his influence spread to America. But during the eighteenth and nineteenth centuries, his "conceited" poetry fell into disfavor, only to be revived in the twentieth century.

ART OF NORTHERN EUROPE

Italian Renaissance art was characterized by an identification with the secular spirit of antiquity, the use of mathematical perspective, a rendering of the human form that revealed both an appreciation of the body's inherent beauty and a sophisticated comprehension of anatomy, and a fondness for the classical style in architecture. These artistic achievements were slow to spread to other lands, particularly north of the Alps, where a strong Gothic tradition persisted. With the exception of southern France, these lands, unlike Italy, contained few architectural and artistic remains from Roman days to emulate. However, in the early sixteenth century, northerners—several of whom had studied in Italy–enthusiastically embraced the stylistic innovations initiated by the Italian masters.

Artists of the Northern European Renaissance are sometimes called *Romanists,* because they had knowledge of Italian style, either firsthand, through personal contact, or indirectly through one of their teachers. Nonetheless, northern artists exhibited personal styles derived from their national traditions. Because many northern artists were individualists, they do not easily fit into Italian Renaissance categories.

As the market for secular objects and small paintings expanded, some northern artists actually specialized in particular types of art—still life, landscape, or portraiture—which became popular for people to display in their homes. With the aid of assistants, these artists essentially mass-produced their work with only slight variations on a theme.

Hubert and Jan van Eyck

The founders of the northern school of Flemish* painting were the two van Eyck brothers—Hubert (1366/1370–1426) and Jan (c. 1390–1441)—whose work marks a definitive break from the Middle Ages. Eschewing the mathematical perspective of their Italian contemporaries, they nevertheless paid painstaking attention to minute details, seeking to replicate the visible, natural world. This level of detail is indicative of the brothers' training as miniaturists. Their technical artistry is particularly evident in the depiction of textures—including metal, flowers, rocks, jewels, and fabrics—which set the standard for all subsequent northern artists. Moreover, they perfected the technique of oil painting, which enabled painters to apply their paints in transparent layers. This resulted in paintings that have a vibrant intensity, that seem to sparkle with highlights and half-tones.

Flemish refers to the province of Flanders, which today would include parts of the Netherlands, Belgium, and northeastern France.

Figure 15.1 Hubert and Jan van Eyck, *Ghent Altarpiece*–**open, 1432, oil on panel, 11′5 3/4″ x 15′1 1/2″ (3.5 x 4.61m), Saint Bavon Cathedral, Ghent, Belgium.** The van Eycks created the altarpiece in the customary triptych—a central panel with two hinged side arms. In the upper portion of the central panel are Jesus, Mary, and John the Baptist; on either side of them are angel musicians. On the far left and right, respectively, are Adam and Eve, and above them is a depiction of the sacrifice of Cain and Abel. The five lower panels embody the entire drama of salvation, culminating in the central panel portraying *The Adoration of the Lamb,* which blends the beauty of the natural world with the glories of the other world. *(St. Savo Cathedral, Ghent/Giraudon/The Bridgeman Art Library International)*

One of the most renowned works in the history of Flemish art is the *Ghent Altarpiece* (Figure 15.1), which Hubert and Jan executed for Saint Bavon Cathedral in Ghent. The post-dated inscription (1432) reads: "The painter Hubert van Eyck, than whom none was greater, began this work, which his brother Jan, who was second to him in art, completed at the behest of Jodoc Vijdt, and which he invites you by this verse to contemplate on 6 May [1432]," and it has caused much debate among art historians about how much each brother contributed to it. However, the controversy does not diminish the impact of the work. It was conceived in the format typical of altarpieces—the *triptych*—a central panel with two hinged side arms. Each of the three units contained four panels, which were painted on both sides. In the upper portion of the central panel are the monumental figures of Jesus

between Mary and John the Baptist. Next to them, on either side, are angel musicians—paintings presumably intended for the shutters of an organ. Adam (on the far left) and Eve (on the far right) mark the termination of the upper part of the triptych. The nude figures of the shame-faced Adam and Eve are the earliest known nudes in northern panel painting, and the dignity of their natural forms is in direct contrast to the scenes of evil immediately above them—the sacrifice of Cain and Abel (above Adam) and Cain killing Abel (above Eve). By establishing a direct relationship between the subject and the viewer (whose position is just beneath the figures), the van Eycks connected real space to pictorial space. This type of perspective is a forceful reminder of the sort employed by Masaccio in his *Holy Trinity* (see Chapter 13), a painting Jan van Eyck may well have seen when he visited Florence.

The five lower panels embody the entire drama of salvation and culminate in the central panel portraying *The Adoration of the Lamb,* which blends the beauty of this world—in a picturesque meadow—with the glories of the other world. The Lamb is perched on an altar as blood pours from his breast into a chalice—symbolizing both Christ's redemption of sinful humanity and the sacrament of the Eucharist. Beside the Lamb are angels who hold the column on which Christ was flogged and the cross on which he was crucified. In front of the Lamb is the Fountain of Life—a reference to Revelation 22:1, "the river of the water of life, bright as crystal, flowing from the throne of God and of the Lamb." Immediately above the Lamb, but below the throne of God, is the dove symbolizing the Holy Spirit. In the foreground (to the left of the Fountain of Life) are twelve prophets; behind them, the Old Testament patriarchs; on the right are the New Testament apostles; behind them, Christian martyrs, who are joined, at a short distance, by other saints. In the distant landscape are pinnacles, spires, and a Gothic dome—depicting the glory of the New Jerusalem. In the paired panels to the left of the Lamb are righteous judges and Christian knights who advance toward the Lamb on docile horses; in the pair of panels on the right, Saint Christopher (patron saint of travelers) leads both pilgrims and hermits into the presence of the Lamb.

Jan van Eyck's most famous painting, *Giovanni Arnolfini and his Wife* (see chapter opener), is also filled with symbolism. In 1434, Jan reputedly attended the marriage of Giovanni Arnolfini and Giovanna Cenami and decided to portray the event. In this painting, as Giovanni holds his betrothed's right hand in his left, he raises his right hand in a solemn oath of fidelity to her. The luminescent light of the interior augments the lustrous textures of the groom's purple velvet frock, the bride's opulent green gown, and the red spread on the bed. The room of the bride's house in which the marriage takes place is filled with objects alluding to Netherlandish marriage customs—the carved chair post is topped by a statuette of Saint Margaret, guardian of childbirth; the brass chandelier bears the customary nuptial candle, the last light to be extinguished on the wedding night; on a chest and the window sill are ripening peaches, symbolizing fertility; in the foreground are clogs, pushed aside, to represent the holy ground of matrimony; and the little dog, symbolizing fidelity, completes the allegorical scene.

Perhaps the most fascinating portion of the painting is the convex mirror and the inscription on the back wall, which reads "Johannes de Eyck fuit hic 1434" (Jan van Eyck was here 1434). The mirror not only reflects the room and the bridal couple from behind, but also two other figures—believed to be Jan and the bride's father. The mirror is surrounded by ten painted roundels depicting scenes of Christ's Passion.

Hieronymus Bosch

Except for a few references to Hieronymus Bosch (c. 1450–1516) in public documents, nothing is known about his life and training—not even the date of a single painting. Even though Bosch painted many traditional Christian subjects—the Seven Deadly Sins, The Nativity, and scenes of Christ's Passion—he is arguably the most enigmatic and original painter of the northern Renaissance. So-named for s'Hertogenbosch, the small Dutch town on the German border where he lived, Bosch broke from the jewel-like luster of the Flemish tradition established by the van Eycks, not only with his derisive humor about human folly but also through the unconventional images he incorporated into his paintings.

Bosch's triptych, *Garden of Earthly Delights* (Figure 15.2), is one of the most daring and disconcerting paintings in the history of art. In contrast to the customary practice of commissioning triptychs for altarpieces, this one was commissioned by an aristocrat from Brussels for his home. The left panel, a perverse rendering of the Garden of Eden, illustrates the marriage of Adam and Eve performed by God. In the pool beneath them and in the fountain behind them, Bosch places a myriad of animals, some of which are easily identifiable—the cat with a mouse in its mouth in the foreground, and a unicorn, an elephant, and a giraffe in the background—others, however, are a fantastical union of hybrid forms.

In the central panel, Bosch appears to condemn, yet is captivated by, all carnal activity. Although no erotic activity is explicit, as the figures caress one another as couples, or in groups of three or four, they are surrounded by animals known for their appetites—pigs, goats, and horses—and they partake of fruits that have decidedly sexual connotations: strawberries, pomegranates, grapes, and cherries. Furthermore, the central pool contains a comparatively new theme—sensuous women bathing who charm and enslave the male onlookers with their beauty. The rocky landscape is littered with nude women and men who cavort amid gigantic birds, fishlike forms, and thorny outcroppings of stone and metal. Nevertheless, in his depiction of Hell in the right panel, Bosch, always the harsh moralist, suggests that all lustful pleasure is as fleeting as the taste of a sensuous fruit.

Figure 15.2   Hieronymus Bosch, *Garden of Earthly Delights* (c. 1504), oil on panel, center—7'2 1/2" x 6'4 3/4" (2.2 x 1.95 m), each wing—86 1/2" x 38" (219.7 x 97cm), Museo del Prado, Madrid, Spain.   Bosch's bizarre portrayal of earthly existence, his dire depiction of Hell, and his failure to include any hope of heavenly redemption was commissioned by an aristocrat from Brussels for his home. *(Museo del Prado, Madrid/The Bridgeman Art Library International)*

Bosch's Hell is a scene of darkness illumined only by the light of fires. The "king" of this realm is a forlorn looking fiend whose head is crowned with a disk and bagpipe and whose face turns toward the viewer with a look of melancholy as tiny people crawl through his body—a broken egg with tree trunks for legs, which poke through the bottom of boats. Above and to the left of him is a war engine—a huge pair of ears pierced by an enormous knife and an arrow. At the very top are the Styx River and a city ablaze with fire. At the bottom of the painting, Bosch impales some of his sinners on the strings of musical instruments; others are eaten, then excreted in bubble form, by a ghoulish hawk-faced monster, while still others are eaten by phantasmagorical animals.

In spite of Bosch's bizarre portrayal of earthly existence, his dire depiction of Hell, and his failure to include any hope of heavenly redemption, the painting was copied for tapestries commissioned by a cardinal and Francis I of France in 1566; and following the Netherlands' revolt, the original triptych ended up in the possession of the ardently religious Philip II of Spain. Furthermore, Bosch's private world of dream imagery presages the twentieth century's search for self by means of psychoanalysis, as well as the artistic movement known as Surrealism (see Chapter 24).

Albrecht Dürer

In contrast to the life of Bosch, much is known about the character, career, and thought of Albrecht Dürer (1471–1528)—the most important artist of the northern Renaissance. Dürer was as temperamental and obsessive as Michelangelo and yet as discerning, discriminate, and detailed as Leonardo. Dürer was born in Nuremberg and trained as a goldsmith in his father's workshop. Later, he not only learned painting but also copper and wood engraving, and in 1494, his father arranged his marriage to Agnes Frey, whose substantial dowry increased Dürer's social standing. Following his marriage, Dürer traveled alone to Venice to learn about Renaissance philosophy and the Renaissance style of painting from his humanist friend, Willibald Pirckheimer. While in Venice, Dürer began his lifelong study of human proportions and did many drawings of animals, exotic figures, and nature. On the trip back to Nuremberg, Dürer documented his trip to Italy by painting a series of landscapes using watercolors. Upon his return to Nuremberg, Dürer established himself in his own workshop, where he did both wood and copper engravings. By 1497, he was so successful that he adopted his distinctive "AD" monogram to prevent others from copying his work.

16

The Age of the Baroque in Literature, Art, and Music

THE AGE OF THE BAROQUE ENCOMPASSES THE PERIOD roughly from the last decades of the sixteenth century to the opening decades of the eighteenth century. To art historians, the ***Baroque Age*** was primarily defined during the seventeenth century when popes, kings, and aristocrats, eager to demonstrate their wealth and power, appropriated an artistic style characterized by majesty, opulence, sensuality, tension, and drama. The preeminent expression of the Baroque style in France is Louis XIV's extravagant palace complex at Versailles. Because Louis recognized the relevance of the arts in furthering his concept of royal glory, his Versailles fuses architecture, sculpture, painting, and gardens to create an awe-inspiring whole. Such a magnificent combination of art forms was what the Germans called *Gesamtkunstwerk* (total work of art). Like contemporary artists, Baroque composers and writers often expressed extreme emotions, including exuberance, grief, wrath, anguish, melancholia, and morbidity.

LITERATURE

Writers of the Baroque Age gave expression to a variety of themes, including the catastrophic consequences of the Thirty Years' War (1618–1648), the foibles of the clergy, natural disasters, and the lives of ordinary people. These efforts resulted in an explosion of fresh literary forms, including grand epic poems using the innovation of "blank verse," and new forms of drama and satire. The period also occasioned the "greatest allegory ever written," John Milton's *Paradise Lost,* and an outburst of popular literature, which was read by an increasingly literate populace.

French Theater

France emerged from the religious wars in a precarious state, but in the early seventeenth century, the authority of the French monarchy was rejuvenated. During the reign of Louis XIV (1643–1715), French royal absolutism became the envy of every ruler in Europe. The foundations for such a strong monarchy were first laid by Henry IV (1589–1610), but when he was assassinated by a demented monk in 1610 as his carriage was traversing a narrow street in Paris, France entered a period of crisis. Louis XIII (1610–1643), only nine years old when he became king, was first dominated by his mother, Marie de' Medici (1573–1642). In 1624, he appointed Cardinal Richelieu (1585–1642) as his chief minister. Over the next eighteen years, Richelieu curbed the power of the nobility and extended the tentacles of royal power into all the provinces of France. When Louis XIII died a few months after his chief minister, he left the throne to his five-year-old son, Louis XIV. Because Louis was too young to rule, Cardinal Mazarin (1602–1661) directed the government until his death in 1661, at which time the eighteen-year-old Louis began his personal rule, which was to last for fifty-four years.

One of Louis' first decisions was to move the royal court from Paris to a royal chateau at Versailles, twelve miles to the west, where he later built a magnificent new palace (see the later discussion). Louis subsequently compelled all of the chief nobility of France to live at his Versailles' court as effete courtiers, and rather than employ aristocrats in his government, he recruited his ministers, counselors, and local officials from the upper bourgeoisie. Thus, the so-called "Sun King" effectively muzzled the aristocracy, which enabled him to impose his own authority over all of France; as Louis exulted, *"L'état, c'est moi"*—"I am the state!" The French Revolution, which began in 1789 (see Chapter 19) would challenge successfully the absolute power of the "divine right" Bourbon monarchs.

During the seventeenth century, French theater came into its own in Europe. French playwrights contributed three key concepts that influenced generations of playwrights who followed in their footsteps. First, there was to be unity of time—all action of the play should take place within one day; secondly, unity of place—all of the action must occur in only one location; and finally, unity of action—the play ought to have one plot line and avoid any subplots. These three unities gave rise to what came to be called *"classical" French drama,* which was first compellingly expressed by Pierre Corneille (1606–1684).

CORNEILLE   Corneille received a good education from the Jesuits in his hometown of Rouen, in northern France. He became a lawyer and subsequently served as the king's counsel in the department of forests and waterways from 1628 until 1650. Despite his legal training, he was fascinated by drama and wrote his first play when he was only twenty years old. He then wrote four comedies and attracted the attention of Cardinal Richelieu, who included him in a circle of writers known as "the society of the five authors." Richelieu provided outlines for the plays the writers were to compose, but in 1635, when Corneille departed from Richelieu's outline in Act III of his comedy *La Comédie des Tuileries (The Comedy of the Tuileries)*, he fell into disfavor for a time. Also in 1635, Corneille experimented with the three

unities in his tragedy *Médée* (Medea). He then began to write his masterpiece, *Le Cid* (The Cid), which was first performed in 1637. However, Richelieu instigated a "pamphlet war" among Corneille's rivals, who called the tragicomedy morally deficient and dramatically improbable and who were quick to point out that the play did not employ the three unities. Moreover, the newly formed Académie Française published a report, *The Opinion of the French Academy About the Tragi-comedy of The Cid,* that enabled Richelieu to prevent public performances of the play.

For the next three years, Corneille wrote nothing, but beginning in 1640, his fortune began to change. He published two widely successful Roman tragedies—*Horace* (1640) and *Cinna* (1641). In 1643, Corneille wrote *Polyeucte*, which many critics consider to be his finest play. Collectively, these four plays comprise Corneille's "classical tetralogy."

Corneille's rendering of *Le Cid* does not emphasize the violence of the Spanish soldier's adventures, which have been romanticized in a number of literary works. The Cid fought against the Moors, but was banished in 1081 by Alfonso VI, who did not trust him. Subsequently, he fought against both Moors and Christians in the service of the Muslim ruler of Zaragoza. In 1094, he conquered Valencia and ruled there until his death in 1099. Corneille's version emphasizes The Cid's passionate devotion to his family, his honor, and his loyalty. His *Horace* is based on a story by the Roman historian Livy recounting the death-duel between two Romans. The plot of *Cinna* revolves around a commanding Emperor Augustus who, being informed of a conspiracy against him, chooses not to kill his adversaries, but rather, to grant them a political pardon, boasting that he possesses the power to be compassionate. Finally, Corneille presents the Christian martyr Polyeucte as a hero who spurns his family in favor of the road to *la glorie* (the glory) of the heavenly world.

MOLIÈRE   Although Jean-Baptiste Poquelin (1622–1673), better known by his stage name Molière, acknowledged Corneille as his master, he was dissatisfied with his "classical" themes. For inspiration, Molière turned instead to the pensive introspection of Montaigne's *Essays*. Like Montaigne, Molière was fascinated by the complexity and the folly of human nature—themes that he incorporated into his prodigious output of comedic plays, but to a point where they fell just short of being tragic.

Educated at the prestigious Jesuit College of Claremont, where he excelled in both Latin and Greek studies, he received his degree in law in

1642, but the very next year changed his name to Molière and joined the Dufrense Company acting troupe. For twelve years he honed his skills as an actor, director, and playwright. In 1658, the repertory company returned to Paris and performed before Louis XIV. Subsequently, the king's brother became Molière's patron, and ultimately, he and his associates were given their own theater at the Palais Royal and placed in charge of the king's entertainment.

In 1659, Molière's production of *The Affected Young Ladies* established him as the most popular comedic playwright of the time. But he soon aroused the ire of religious authorities, who viewed his plays as scandalous attacks on religion. For example, in *Don Juan* (which the church banned for the duration of Molière's life), the lead character, Don Juan, in his quest to be the perfect aristocrat, renounces all forms of commitment—to doctors, to parents, and even to God—but he assumes they will still honor their obligations to him.

The church also waged war against Molière's *Tartuffe*—which attacked religious hypocrisy—but only managed to prevent performances until 1669. The main character of the play is Orgon, a wealthy middle-aged man of the bourgeoisie, who has fallen on bad times. To compensate for his diminished power and authority, he adopts an extreme form of religious piety, but only for self-aggrandizing reasons. To instruct his conscience, Orgon solicits the "holy" layman, Tartuffe, who proves to be a calculating opportunist. Once he has become entrenched in Orgon's moral life, Tartuffe plays his patron for a fool and conspires to swindle Orgon out of everything he has. Consequently, Orgon's brother-in-law, Cléante, launches an indictment against such religious hypocrisy:

> So there is nothing that I find more base
> Than specious piety's dishonest face—
> Than these bold mountebanks [charlatans], these
>   histrios [actors]
> Whose impious... [absurd] and hollow shows
> Exploit our love of Heaven, and make a jest
> Of all that men think holiest and best;
> These calculating souls who offer prayers
> Not to their Maker, but as public wares,
> And seek to buy respect and reputation
> With lifted eyes and sighs of exaltation;
> These charlatans, I say, whose pilgrim souls
> Proceed, by way of Heaven, toward earthly
>   goals,
> Who weep and pray and swindle and extort,
> Who preach the monkish life, but haunt the
>   court,
> Who make their zeal the partner of their vice—
> Such men are vengeful, sly, and cold as ice,

> And when there is an enemy to defame
> They cloak their spite in fair religion's name,
> Their private spleen and malice being made
> To seem a high and virtuous crusade,
> Until, to mankind's reverent applause,
> They crucify their foe in Heaven's cause.[1]

Such satiric portrayals of church figures and religious zealots offended the church authorities, who denounced Molière as "a demon in the human flesh."[2]

In spite of ill health, Molière continued to write and to produce plays exposing what he perceived as the hypocrisy of the clergy and the aristocracy. During his own performance in *The Imaginary Invalid* on February 17, 1673, Molière collapsed on stage and died at home the same evening. Four days later, he was buried at Saint Joseph's Cemetery, but church officials refused to give him a formal interment. Seven years later, Louis XIV combined Molière's company with a rival company to form the Comédie Française, which continued to perform his plays in the fashion he intended.

RACINE Molière was a friend of Jean Racine (1639–1699) and, in 1664, staged Racine's first play, *The Thebaid*. But a feud broke out between the two playwrights during the staging of the second one, *Alexander the Great*, in 1665. After a two-week run of the play, Racine grew dissatisfied with Molière's production and transferred its performance rights to a rival repertory company—in the process, stealing Molière's star actress Mademoiselle du Parc. Many stories arose in Paris concerning Racine's illicit love affairs, including one that imputed that Racine poisoned one of his mistresses. Nonetheless, between 1667 and 1677, Racine entered his greatest period as a writer of "pure" tragedy. He based three of his plays—*Andromache* (1667), *Iphigenia* (1672), and *Phaedra* (1677)—on plots drawn from Euripides the ancient Greek dramatist. These dramas illustrate the full range of human emotions, including jealousy, passion, love, and hate. Other plays from this period deal with themes about madness, death, and the consequences of criminal behavior. In 1677, Racine was appointed royal historiographer and underwent some type of religious conversion experience. Consequently, his last two plays—*Esther* (1689) and *Athalie* (1691)—consider themes relating to God's anger, justice, and providence. Racine's legacy as a playwright was his ability to combine classical formulations—as in his reinterpretations of the tragic figures of Andromache, Iphigenia, and

Phaedra*—with psychological insights into the characters' motivations, prompting audiences to think in fresh ways about the human condition.

Germany: Grimmelshausen

By the terms of the Peace of Augsburg in 1555, dividing Germany into Lutheran and Catholic territories on the basis of the religion of the ruler, religious warfare in Germany was temporarily halted. The next year, an exhausted Emperor Charles V abdicated all of his titles and gave up his vast lands. His son, Philip, inherited Spain and its colonies, as well as the Netherlands; his brother, Ferdinand, acquired the Austrian territories and was elected emperor of the German lands. Thus, two branches of the family were formed—the Austrian Hapsburgs and the Spanish Hapsburgs. Throughout the sixteenth century, the Austrian Hapsburgs barely managed to control the sprawling and deeply divided German territories. The Austrian Hapsburg emperors, however, never missed an opportunity to further the cause of Catholicism or to strike at the power of the German nobility.

The Jesuit-trained Ferdinand, king of Bohemia, became Emperor Ferdinand II in 1619. When the fervent Ferdinand attempted to impose Catholicism on Bohemia in 1618, the Protestant nobles revolted against him and put a Calvinist king on their throne. Spain and Austria responded by sending troops into Bohemia; this was the beginning of the *Thirty Years' War* (1618–1648). Bohemia was virtually decimated during the war—almost 75 percent of its villages and cities were pillaged and set ablaze, and the aristocracy was almost eliminated.

The Hapsburgs also used the occasion of the war to buttress their authority in Europe. The Hapsburg plan of domination was thwarted by Protestant Sweden, which, under the leadership of Gustavus Adolphus and with the encouragement of France, intervened. The French, fearing encirclement by the Spanish and Austrian Hapsburgs, entered the war themselves in 1635. The Treaty of Westphalia of 1648 ended the war and effectively neutralized Hapsburg power. The Austrian Hapsburgs were able to keep Austria as a dynastic state and to retain control of the German imperial office. Nonetheless, the balance of power in Germany shifted to the territorial princes, who were intent on preserving their own interests. Thus, the Hapsburg dreams of uniting Germany under their rule and of dominating Europe were dashed.

The Thirty Years' War was the backdrop for the German masterpiece of seventeenth-century prose—*Simplicius Simplicissimus*—written by the German novelist Johann Jacob Christoph von Grimmelshausen (1621–1676). When his small hometown of Gelnhausen, in Hesse, was sacked, Grimmelshausen's family fled, and he was compelled to join the Hessian army as a musketeer. In 1637, Grimmelshausen reappeared as a member of the emperor's forces, and when the war was over, he became regimental secretary to the imperial field commander and converted to Catholicism. Grimmelshausen later married, served as a steward for several wealthy families, and in 1667 became the mayor of the small town of Renchen, near Strassburg.

Like Cervantes, Grimmelshausen based the structure of his novel on the Spanish picaresque novel, but his narrative style also includes satire, allegory, and autobiographical material. Reminiscent of Dante's journey from hell to paradise in *The Divine Comedy* and Christian's journey to the Celestial City in *The Pilgrim's Progress* (see later discussion), Simplicius' wanderings enable him to be a guide to other Christians. Simplicius tells the reader about his boyhood ignorance of God, how he happened to become a Christian, and how he fell away from God's grace and became worldly-wise. Moreover, Simplicius relates his feeble attempts at repentance, the despair he felt when he realized that his life was empty, and how he became a distraught hermit. Finally, he details his return to the world and the contentment he now finds in the contemplative world of the spirit.

Not only was the source material of Grimmelshausen's novel drawn from his personal experience in the Thirty Years' War, but he also researched published accounts of the war. He provides the reader with vivid descriptions of one of the most destructive wars in European history:

In the battle itself each man tried to prevent his own death by killing the man approaching him. An awful music was performed by the cruel shots, the clashing of armor plates, the splintering of pikestaffs, the screams of the attackers as well as the wounded, by the blare of trumpets, the roll of drums, and the shrill sound of fifes. Heavy dust and dense smoke covered the scene, as if to hide the ghastly sight of the wounded and dead. From the darkness one heard the pitiful moaning of the dying and the joyful shouting of those still full of

---

*Andromache** was the dedicated wife of Hector who warned him about the dangers of participating in the Trojan War. **Iphigenia** was the daughter of Agamemnon and Clytemnestra who, because her father killed one of the stags of the goddess Artemis, was to be sacrificed as propitiation for the offense. However, when Agamemnon raised his hand to slay her, a beautiful stag appeared in her place. **Phaedra**, enamored of her stepson Hippolytus, sought to make him love her. However, his rejection of her overtures led her to hang herself, but she left a note incriminating Hippolytus for attacking her.

courage. . . . The earth that is accustomed to covering the dead was, herself, now covered by corpses. In one place lay heads that had lost their masters, and elsewhere lay bodies without heads. Out of some bodies entrails hung in a cruel and ghastly manner. The heads of others had been crushed and the brains spattered all over. Here one saw lifeless bodies robbed of their blood; there, some still alive and gory with the blood of others. Here lay severed arms with the fingers still twitching as if they itched to get back into the melee.[3]

However, the novel is not only a historical narrative, for woven into the story are folktales, anecdotes, allusions to Greco-Roman mythology, biblical references, and a majestic description of the Black Forest, for which the work is famous:

I lived on a high mountain range called the Moss, a part of the Black Forest that is covered by a somber stand of firs. I had a beautiful view east into the Oppenau valley and its branches, and south into the valley of the Kinzig and Geroltseck County, where the lofty castle rises among the neighboring heights like a kingpin in a game of ninepins. To the west I could see upper and lower Alsace, and to the north in the direction of lower Baden, down the Rhine, where the city of Strasbourg, with its high cathedral tower, stands out like the heart enclosed by its body.[4]

Due to the popularity of the first five books of the novel, Grimmelshausen wrote a "Continuation" only a year after they appeared, which was later incorporated into the novel as Book Six. Buoyed by his success, Grimmelshausen subsequently wrote several sequels, including one about a wandering woman named Courage, which became the basis of the acclaimed twentieth-century play—*Mother Courage and Her Children*—by the German playwright, director, and poet, Bertolt Brecht (see Chapter 25).

England

James I (reigned 1603–1625), who had already been king of Scotland for forty-one years, became the first Stuart king of England on the death of Elizabeth I in 1603. As a foreigner, he did not understand the constitutional balance between the monarch and Parliament that had evolved under the Tudors. Claiming that the king alone was the true legislator, James considered himself an absolute monarch. In a speech to Parliament in 1610, he asserted: "The state of monarchy is the supremest thing upon earth: for kings are not only God's lieutenants upon earth and sit upon God's throne, but even by God himself they are called gods."[5] James's successor, his son, Charles I (reigned 1625–1649), even more inflexible in his

relations with Parliament, ruled without Parliament from 1629 to 1640.

Those who belonged to the Church of England and who favored a church governed by bishops—episcopal form of government—were called Anglicans, and James was a devout Anglican who had developed an immense mistrust of Presbyterianism while he was king of Scotland. Therefore, as king of England, he refused to negotiate with the Puritans.* The single most-important achievement in religion during the reign of James was a translation of the Bible that greatly enriched English literature—the *King James Version.* Under Charles, religious tension was further exacerbated when he encouraged the Archbishop of Canterbury to strictly enforce Anglican worship and church organization and to suppress the Puritan movement. Influential people were also angered when Charles married Henrietta Maria, the Catholic sister of Louis XIII of France. The turning point was Charles' attempt to bring the established Presbyterian church in Scotland into a closer accord with the Church of England by ordering it to use the Anglican prayer book and to accept the authority of the bishops. This sparked a rebellion among the Scots. In 1640, Charles called Parliament into session to raise money to deal with the revolt.

Parliament, however, immediately seized the opportunity to try to limit the king's power. The situation finally came to a head in 1642, when the king marched on Parliament with several hundred troops to arrest five parliamentary leaders. When the five escaped, Charles left London to travel to Oxford to meet with those members of Parliament who supported him. The lines of battle were drawn—Charles and his royalist supporters (the Cavaliers) remained outside London, and his opponents (the **Roundheads,** many of whom were Puritans) remained in London. Both began to enlist soldiers, and the English Civil War—often called the Puritan Revolution—broke out during the summer. In 1643, the Roundhead cause was bolstered when it formed an alliance with the Scots. The commander of the Roundheads was the Puritan Oliver Cromwell (1599–1658), whose troops defeated the Cavalier army and took Charles prisoner. In January of 1649, after a Parliamentary court found Charles I guilty of "high treason," he was executed. Soon thereafter, the monarchy and the House of Lords were abolished.

*The term Puritan is used here to identify those who refused to accept the authority of the Church of England and who wanted either a Congregational or Presbyterian form of church government. Under the Presbyterian system the church was under the rule of several church courts, composed of lay elders and clergy, ascending from the congregational level to the national level, while the Congregationalists gave a significant degree of independence to each local church.

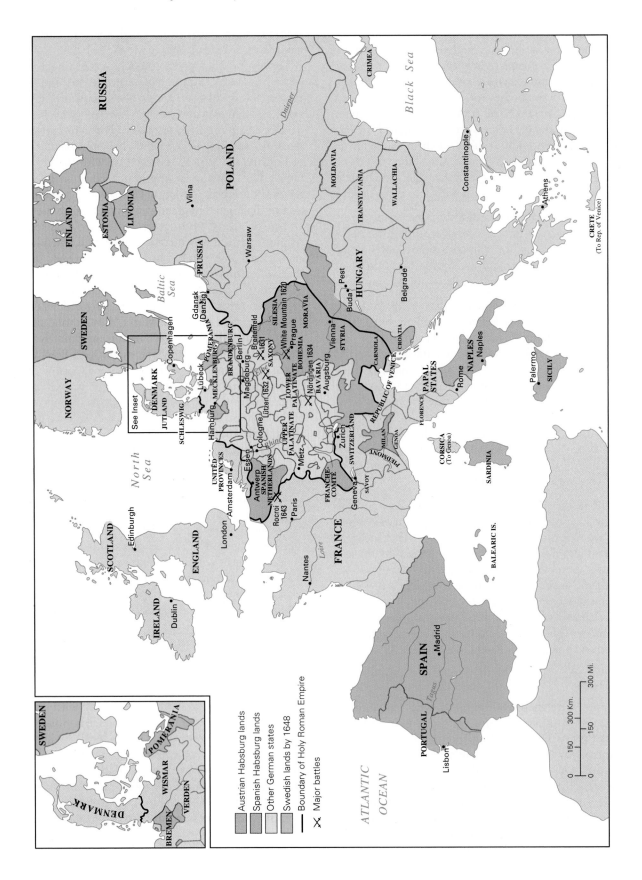

This led to the establishment of a new government—first the Commonwealth, which ended in 1653, then the Puritan Protectorate, which lasted until Cromwell's death in 1658.

The *Period of the Restoration* began in 1660, when Charles I's oldest son became King Charles II (1660–1685). During his early reign, Charles II not only reestablished the Church of England but restricted the activities of all those he viewed as Dissenters. Catholics, Presbyterians, Baptists, and Congregationalists were collectively labeled Dissenters and persecuted for their beliefs. Through a series of *Acts of Uniformity* (in 1549, 1552, 1559, and 1662), Parliament sought to create religious conformity to the Church of England. However, having learned the lesson of civil war and remembering his father's execution, Charles did not try to impose royal absolutism. Upon Charles' death in 1685, his Catholic brother acceded to the throne as James II (1685–1688). Eschewing the moderation of his brother, James sought to rule absolutely. In 1688, the situation intensified when James' Catholic wife gave birth to a son, which seemed to ensure that England would be ruled by a Catholic dynasty. This caused the two major political factions in Parliament to unite—the Tories (the royalist Anglicans) and the Whigs (who affirmed the supremacy of Parliament). Together, they drove James from the throne and offered it to his Protestant son-in-law, William of Orange, from the Dutch Republic, who agreed to reign as a limited monarch. In November 1688, William invaded southwestern England, and James fled to France, but without abdicating the throne. Parliament, however, proclaimed the English throne vacant. The crown was bestowed on William, who became King William III (1689–1702), and his wife, Mary, the Protestant daughter of James II. They ruled together until Mary's death from smallpox in 1694.

To ensure that only Protestants would accede to the throne, Parliament also passed the Act of Settlement in 1701. It stipulated that on the death of Queen Anne (1702–1714), the last of James II's Protestant daughters, the crown would pass to his Protestant granddaughter Sophia, the Electress of Hanover in Germany and, subsequently, to her heirs. Thus, the Hanoverian line of kings began with George I (1714–1727), and there was political stability in England throughout the eighteenth century.

The Bloodless or **Glorious Revolution** of 1688–1689 was a crucial event in English history

Map 16.1 Europe During the Thirty Years' War, 1618–1648 The Thirty Years' War was fought largely within the borders of the Holy Roman Empire. It was the result of conflicts within the empire as well as the meddling of neighbors for their own strategic advantages.

and the history of liberty. It ensured that parliamentary government and the rule of law, not the tyrannical power of a monarch, would prevail in England. That this was England's last revolution attests to the revolution's success and the effectiveness of the English parliamentary system. In the years to come, other lands came to view the British parliamentary system as a model to be emulated.

These religious, political, and constitutional events had an impact on, and are reflected in, the literature of the period. Of all the literary forms, drama was England's greatest accomplishment. Like the French dramatists, the English often attempted to blend classical forms with national content. However, when English repertory companies performed publicly, they encountered opposition from the Puritans, who thought that such public displays not only caused people to stay away from work, but also contributed to fires, accidents, and the spread of the plague. Similarly, because men played female roles, and scripts included oaths and blasphemies, the Puritans thought that the plays contributed to a general environment of irreverence and ungodliness. Nevertheless, the monarchy had to be entertained—especially on occasions of state and when foreign dignitaries visited the realm. It was within this context that English dramatists began to employ the devices and language of poetry. This buoyed the hopes of a number of poets that they, too, could become courtiers.

MILTON The course of contemporary English history—as well as the ideals of the Renaissance and Reformation—found their fullest expression in the works of the writer John Milton (1608–1674). Sometime after 1615, Milton matriculated at Saint Paul's School in London, where he demonstrated his facility for Hebrew, Greek, and Latin. He subsequently enrolled in Christ's College, Cambridge, where he was enamored of Latin verse and immersed himself in classical tragedies and comedies. There Milton had an ongoing dispute with a number of faculty and friends over the blatantly scholastic curriculum, based on medieval philosophy-religion. He preferred, instead, the humanistic studies of Renaissance scholars. He did, however, receive his baccalaureate degree in 1629 and his master's degree three years later. His earliest poems from this period—"On the Morning of Christ's Nativity," "Il Penseroso" (The Pensive One), and "L'Allegro" (The Lively One)—show him to be a master of poetic image, grace, and style. His scholarly gifts led teachers, family, and friends to assume that he would become a minister. Instead, Milton retired to his family's homes at

Hammersmith (until 1635) and Horton (until 1638) to cultivate the sort of humanist education he had not received at Cambridge.

While at Horton, Milton wrote the poem "At a Solemn Music," which hints at the grandiose theme of good versus evil that was to culminate in his monumental poem, *Paradise Lost,* the heroic epic for which he would forever be remembered (see later discussion).

> Hymns devout and holy psalms
> Singing everlastingly:
> That we on Earth, with undiscording voice,
> May rightly answer that melodious noise;
> As once we did, till disproportioned Sin
> Jarred against Nature's chimes, and with harsh din
> Broke the fair music that all creatures made . . .
> O, may we soon again renew that song,
> And keep in tune with Heaven, till God ere long
> To his celestial consort us unite,
> To live with Him, and sing in endless morn of
>   light![6]

In 1642, Milton married Mary Powell, a woman half his age, who left him one month later to return to her family. Mary's departure prompted Milton to write his pamphlet, *Doctrine and Discipline of Divorce,* in which he argued that divorce should be granted not only for adultery, but also in cases of incompatibility or a loveless marriage. Almost immediately, both Puritans and Catholics condemned Milton, but he wrote three more treatises on the same subject.

During the same period (1643–1644), Milton published two of his most famous pamphlets—*On Education,* a discourse on the value of a humanistic education, and *Aeropagitica,* a plea for freedom of the press and an indictment of royal censorship. Following the public execution of Charles I, Milton (an event that he reportedly attended) published his first political treatise, *The Tenure of Kings and Magistrates.* Echoing Mornay's *Defense of Liberty Against Tyrants* (see Chapter 14), which was published in English translation in 1642 and 1648, Milton asserted the right of the people to execute a tyrannical king. One month later, Milton was asked to become part of Cromwell's Council of State as secretary of foreign languages. However, Milton's excitement at the fall of the Stuarts was tempered by the loss of his eyesight (probably from glaucoma), which left him totally blind by the age of forty-three.

When the monarchy was restored in 1660, Milton wrote his last political tract, *The Readie and Easie Way to Establish a Free Commonwealth,* an indictment of the English people who chose to become slaves of the monarchy. Subsequently, royalists in Parliament issued a warrant for Milton's arrest. Imprisoned briefly, he was forced to pay an exorbitant fine.

Although the prodigious output of prose during these twenty years of Milton's life is four times greater than his entire poetic production, it is for his poetry that he is remembered. During his later life, Milton began to dictate *Paradise Lost,* the first of three monumental heroic epic poems. While he worked, Milton closely identified with the situation of the ancient poet Homer, who was reputedly blind when he composed the *Iliad* and the *Odyssey.* The subject of *Paradise Lost* is humanity's fall from God's grace, and with a note of irony attached, Milton chose Satan as an atypical protagonist (anti-hero) "[to] assert Eternal Providence, and justify the ways of God to men."[7]

The epic reminds the reader of a Greek tragedy written in five acts. The setting is Paradise; the period covers the time from just before The Fall until Adam and Eve are expelled from Paradise. The plot, however, is secondary to the ruminations and reflections of Milton's characters, including Gabriel, Adam, Eve, and most importantly, Satan. In Book IX, Satan's soliloquy reveals his bitterness about being expelled from heaven for leading a rebellion of angels and his desire to reap vengeance on God by destroying his creation of six nights and days, particularly Adam, whom God formed from the dust of the earth:

> For only in destroying I find ease
> To my relentless thought; . . .
> To mee shall be the glory sole among
> The infernal Powers, in one day to have marr'd
> What he *Almighty* styl'd, six Nights and Days
> Continu'd making, and who knows how long
> Before had been contriving. . . .
> But what will not Ambition and Revenge
> Descend to? . . .
> Revenge, at first though sweet,
> Bitter erelong back on itself recoils;
> Let it; I reck [care] not, so it light well aim'd,
> Since higher I fall short, on him who next
> Provokes my envy, this new Favorite
> Of Heav'n, the Man of Clay, Son of despite,
> Whom us the more to spite his Maker rais'd
> From dust: spite then with spite is best repaid.[8]

Milton's overwhelming sense of human guilt and sinfulness is drawn directly from the Protestant reformers, who viewed human nature as corrupt, but the abundance of classical allusions demonstrates his affinity for the Renaissance.

Milton composed the epic in **blank verse,** which rarely appeared outside drama. Blank verse is unrhymed **iambic pentameter,** which is the most natural form of English verse. An iambic foot is an unstressed syllable followed by a stressed one.

CHIKAMATSU: THE JAPANESE SHAKESPEARE

JAPAN'S GREATEST DRAMATIST, CHIKAMATSU MONZAEMON (1653–1725), is often called the Japanese Shakespeare. He wrote more than one hundred plays, mostly for the puppet theater, including *The Love Suicides at Sonezaki,* which was inspired by an actual double suicide one month before its first performance on June 20, 1703. It is the story of Tokubei, a clerk in a shop, who falls in love with the prostitute, Ohatsu, and refuses to marry the girl his uncle has chosen for him. Tokubei must persuade his stepmother to return the dowry money, but after receiving it, he lends the money to his friend, Kuheiji, for a few days. When Kuheiji refuses to return the money, Tokubei and Ohatsu, in despair, commit suicide. The following selection from the play, which is performed with large, almost life-sized puppets, is from the dramatic, violent conclusion.

Tokubei: My parents died when I was a boy, and I grew up thanks to the efforts of my uncle. . . . It disgraces me to die without repaying his kindness. Instead I shall cause him trouble which will last even after my death.

Soon I shall see my parents in the other world. Father, Mother, welcome me there!

Narrator: He weeps. Ohatsu also joins her hands.

Ohatsu: I envy you. You say you will meet your parents in the world of the dead. My father and mother are in this world and in good health. . . . Tomorrow, when word reaches the village of our suicides, how unhappy they will be! Now I must bid farewell for this life to my parents, my brothers and sisters. . . . please appear before me, if only in dreams. Dear Mother, beloved Father!

Narrator: She sobs and wails aloud. Her husband also cries out and sheds incessant tears in all too understandable emotion.

Ohatsu: We could talk forever, but it serves no purpose. Kill me, kill me quickly!

Narrator: She hastens the moment of death.

Tokubei: I'm ready.

Narrator: He swiftly draws his dagger. . . . But when he tries to bring the blade against the skin of the woman he's loved, and held and slept with so many months and years, his eyes cloud over, his hands shake. He tries to steady his weakening resolve, but sill he trembles, and when he thrusts, the point misses. Twice or thrice the flashing blade deflects this way and that until a cry tells it has struck her throat.

Narrator: He twists the blade deeper and deeper, but the strength has left his arm. When he sees her weaken, he stretches forth his hands. The last agonies of death are indescribable.

Tokubei: Must I lag behind you? Let's draw our last breaths together.

Narrator: He thrusts and twists the razor in his throat, until it seems the handle or the blade must snap. His eyes grow dim and his last painful breath is drawn away at its appointed hour. No one is there to tell the tale, but. . . they have become models of true love.

Source: *Donald Keene, trans.,* Major Plays of Chikamatsu *(New York: Columbia University Press, 1990), pp. 55–56.*

Therefore, pentameter means that there are five iambic feet per line. Milton explained to the reader why he chose to use this form for his epic:

> The measure is English heroic verse without rime [rhyme], as that of Homer in Greek, and of Virgil in Latin—rime being no necessary adjunct or true ornament of poem or good verse . . . but the invention of a barbarous age, to set off wretched matter and lame metre.[9]

Thus, the famous line, quoted above, is accented as follows: "|and jús|ti-fý|the wáys|of Gód|to mén.|"
1   2   3   4   5

Included in the front matter was the poem "On Paradise Lost," written by Andrew Marvell (1621–1678), Milton's poetic contemporary and one of his governmental assistants. Although he was initially suspicious of Milton's intentions, Marvell came to realize how *Paradise Lost* was composed, to understand its major plots and themes, and subsequently to predict that Milton's epic would be counted among the great works of English literature.

> When I beheld the Poet blind, yet bold,
> In slender Book his vast Design unfold,
> *Messiah* Crown'd, God's Reconcil'd Decree,
> Rebelling Angels, the Forbidden Tree,
> Heav'n, Hell, Earth, Chaos, All; the Argument
> Held me a while misdoubting his Intent,
> That he would ruin . . .
> The sacred Truths to Fable and old Song . . .
> The World o'rewhelming to revenge his sight.
>
> . . . .
>
> But I am now convinc'd, and none will dare
> Within the labours to pretend a share.
> Thou hast not miss'd one thought that could be
>   fit,
> And all that was improper dost omit:
> So that no room is here for Writers left,
> But to detect their Ignorance or Theft.
> That Majesty which through thy Work doth
>   Reign
> Draws the devout, deterring the Profane.
>
> . . . .
>
> Thy Verse created like thy Theme sublime,
> In Number, Weight, and Measure, needs not
>   Rhime.[10]

Milton followed *Paradise Lost* with another epic poem, *Paradise Regained*—the story of how Christ, as the second Adam, overcame Satan's temptations and redeemed fallen humanity.

> I who erewhile the happy Garden [Paradise] sung,
> By one man's [Adam's] disobedience lost, now
>   sing Recovered Paradise to all mankind,
> By one man's [Christ's] firm obedience fully tried

> Through all temptations, and the Tempter [Satan]
>   foiled
> In all his wiles, defeated and repulsed,
> And Eden raised in the waste Wilderness.[11]

Included with *Paradise Regained* was *Samson Agonistes*—a dramatic poem patterned after ancient Greek tragedy. Paralleling his own blindness, Milton chose a blind man as his hero—the biblical strongman, Samson, after he had been taken captive and blinded by the Philistines (Judges 16).

All three of these epic poems demonstrate how Milton overcame despair and found meaning in suffering. Moreover, he designed them to reflect the Protestant faith's emphasis on salvation through God's grace, and the humanist belief in the capacity of the human soul to prevail against adversity. On November 8, 1674, Milton died from complications of his painful gout.

BUNYAN Whereas Milton united classical humanistic thought with his deep-seated Protestant beliefs, John Bunyan (1628–1688) combined everyday speech with the eloquent verse of the King James Version of the Bible into a vivid narrative style. Like Luther and Milton, Bunyan understood human nature to be corrupt, and throughout his life, he sought assurance of his salvation from sin. Bunyan's father was a Bedfordshire tinker (a person who makes and mends metal pots), and Bunyan had little formal education before deciding to assume his father's trade. From 1644 until 1647, Bunyan participated in the English Civil War but saw little actual fighting. He suffered lifelong guilt over the death of the young man who came to replace him. After his discharge from the army, Bunyan married a fervently pious woman and entered into a long period of spiritual crises, which lasted about five years. During this time, he often felt that he was assailed by devils, physically abused, and threatened with damnation. He recounted these painful encounters in his spiritual autobiography, *Grace Abounding to the Chief of Sinners.*

> I thought I was as with a tempest driven away from God, for always when I cried to God for mercy, this would come—It is too late, I am lost, God hath let me fall, not to my correction, but condemnation; my sin is unpardonable. . . . Then was I struck into a very great trembling, insomuch that at some times I could for whole days together feel my very body, as well as my mind, to shake and totter under the sense of the dreadful judgment of God. . . . Thus did I wind and twine and shrink under the burden that was upon me; which burden also did so oppress me, that I could neither stand, nor go, nor lie, either at rest or quiet.[12]

Bunyan eventually recovered from his dark night of despair and became an electrifying preacher. However, his activities as a preacher drew the attention of the authorities, and he was charged with not following the liturgy of the Church of England. When he refused to conform, Bunyan was sent to prison, where he remained for the greater part of twelve years. During his imprisonment, Bunyan preached to his fellow prisoners, studied, and supported his family by making and selling shoelaces. But most importantly, he wrote *Grace Abounding* and began *The Pilgrim's Progress*—a book that was destined to become the most successful allegory ever written in English.

Part I of *The Pilgrim's Progress* is told in the guise of a dream as it details the spiritual journey of Christian (the leading character) to the Celestial City. On his journey, Christian must overcome despair, fear, corruption, the burden of sin, "Vanity Fair," and the "Valley of the Shadow of Death" before he finds Faith, who leads him into the knowledge of God's grace. Soon thereafter, Christian finds Hopeful, and he masters Temptation, defeats Ignorance, and is delivered from the Fear of Death. At the end of Part I, Bunyan admonishes the reader to interpret the metaphors of his dream correctly:

> Now, reader, I have told my dream to thee,
> See if thou canst interpret it to me,
> Or to thyself or neighbor; but take heed
> Of misinterpreting; for that, instead
> Of doing good, will but thyself abuse:
> By misinterpreting, evil ensues.
>
> . . . .
>
> Put by the curtains, look within my veil,
> Turn up my metaphors and do not fail,
> There, if thou seekest them, such things to find
> As will be helpful to an honest mind.[13]

It was not until 1684 that Bunyan published Part II of *The Pilgrim's Progress*—detailing the journey of Christiana, Christian's wife, and their children. Written in a lighter tone than Part I, Christiana and her children meet Mr. Sagacity and the characters of Mercy and Prudence. After they pass through the Valley of Humiliation, they encounter "a sweet grace," Humility.[14] Bunyan injects scenes of humor, including the confrontation between Mr. Great-Heart and Mr. Honest concerning "reasons why good men are so in the dark."[15] The pilgrims also encounter Mr. Feeble-mind who "came from the town of Stupidity which lies four degrees northward of the City of Destruction."[16] Later, they are greeted by the shepherds—Knowledge, Experience, Watchful, and Sincere—and join with Great-Heart to kill the giant, Despair, and to demolish Doubting Castle. Just before they get to Enchanted Ground, Mr. Valiant-for-Truth recites poetic lines, which afterward became the text for a famous church hymn—"He Who Would Valiant Be."

> Who would true valor see,
> Let him come hither;
> One here will constant be,
> Come wind, come water;
> There's no discouragement
> Shall make him once relent
> His first avowed intent
> To be a pilgrim.
>
> Whoso beset him round
> With dismal stories
> Do but themselves confound—
> His strength the more is.
> No lion can him fright;
> He'll with a giant fight,
> But he will have a right
> To be a pilgrim.[17]

The pilgrims finally cross the River of Death and are welcomed into the Celestial City "with horses and chariots, with trumpeters and pipers, with singers and players on stringed instruments."[18] For centuries, Bunyan's images and characters inspired other writers, and his symbols became part of ordinary speech.

DRYDEN   The last great English literary figure of the seventeenth century was John Dryden (1631–1700), who, unlike Milton and Bunyan, was an enthusiastic supporter of the restored Stuart monarchy. Also unlike his literary predecessors, who looked inwardly and developed a persona based on their own private experiences, Dryden was a cosmopolitan commentator on the philosophical, political, artistic, and religious trends of his day. In 1654, Dryden received his baccalaureate degree from Trinity College, Cambridge, and shortly thereafter, he published his first two important poems—one on the occasion of Cromwell's death in 1658 and the other on the restoration of the Stuart monarchy. Most of Dryden's poems from these early years are "occasion" poems—celebrating such things as political events, coronations, or military triumphs. From 1664 to 1681, Dryden was a serious playwright. In 1668, he published his *Essay of Dramatic Poesy*, which not only distilled the importance of the Greco-Roman dramatists for his own age, but also synthesized contemporary English and French theater. In the same year, his successes as a poet and dramatist drew the attention of the king, who had Dryden appointed to royal poet laureate and historiographer.

It was at the age of 50, however, that Dryden discovered that his true talent was writing satire. Nonetheless, he did not cease to write plays. In

1677, he published *The State of Innocence,* which reduced Milton's *Paradise Lost,* a blank verse epic with no definite rhythm or rhyme, to rhymed dramatic verse. For this, Dryden was soundly criticized. The next year, he published his political satire, *Absalom and Achitophel,* which ridiculed the Earl of Shaftesbury, who was seeking to have legislation enacted that would have excluded James II from the throne. This was followed with two more attacks on opponents of the Stuarts—*The Medal* and *MacFlecknoe.* Dryden's plays also titillated his audiences with thinly veiled references to the sexual escapades of leading public figures.

Soon thereafter, political and religious tensions compelled Dryden to deal with more serious issues. In 1682, he defended the Church of England against the influx of deism, which eliminated God's involvement in the universe after its creation (see Chapter 17).

Soon after James II assumed the throne, Dryden and his two sons converted to Catholicism. The circumstances of their conversion led to much criticism of Dryden by his detractors, who questioned both his political and religious sincerity. Nonetheless, his religious affinity is evident in the poem, "The Hind and the Panther" (1688)—an allegory that characterizes the Roman Catholic church as the pure-white hind (deer) and the Church of England as a spotted panther. In his later life, Dryden produced five more plays, but when William and Mary acceded to the throne, he lost his position as poet laureate. Two months before his death, he published his *Fables Ancient and Modern*—excellent verse translations drawn predominately from the poetry of Ovid, Boccaccio, and Chaucer. Following his death on May 1, 1700, he was buried near Chaucer and Spenser in the Poets' Corner of Westminster Abbey.

The American Colonies

The colonists who founded the first English settlements in New England—Plymouth (1620), Salem (1628), and Massachusetts Bay (1630)—produced a body of literature detailing how they built their homes, tamed the wilderness, interacted with the Indians, and formed a civil society. *The Mayflower Compact* of November 11, 1620—signed by William Bradford (1590–1657) the leader of the landing party of persecuted English Dissenters (known as Pilgrims)—was the first American document to institute civil government by means of popular consent. Founded on the Protestant idea of covenant (see Chapter 14), the *Compact* states:

> We whose names are underwritten, the loyal subjects of our dread Sovereign Lord King James . . . Having undertaken, for the Glory of God and advancement of the Christian Faith . . . a Voyage to plant the First Colony in the Northern Parts of Virginia, do by these presents solemnly and mutually in the presence of God and one of another, Covenant and Combine ourselves together into a Civil Body Politic, for our better ordering and preservation . . . and by virtue hereof do enact, constitute and frame such just and equal Laws, Ordinances, Acts, Constitutions and Offices, . . . as shall be thought most meet and convenient for the general good of the Colony, unto which we promise all due submission and obedience.[19]

BRADSTREET The first work of true literary value produced in New England was the poetry of Anne Bradstreet (1612–1672). She was born in England to devout Puritans, Dorothy Yorke and Thomas Dudley, steward to the Earl of Lincolnshire. Due to her father's position, Anne received good tutoring and read widely, but was primarily drawn to Puritan writings emphasizing plainness, grace, and divine mission. In 1628, when Anne was sixteen, she married a Cambridge-schooled Puritan named Simon Bradstreet, and two years later, Anne and her father, along with the Bradstreet family, sailed to the New World to be part of the Puritan settlement at Massachusetts Bay. Anne's father served as the colony's governor for four terms and her husband was governor for ten years. Simon also represented the interests of the colony at the court of Charles II. Shortly after her arrival and continuing until at least 1643, Anne wrote poetry about her home, her faith, and her family. By all accounts, Anne and Simon Bradstreet (the parents of eight children) loved one another and were happily married—as evidenced by Anne's poem "To My Dear and Loving Husband."

> If ever two were one, then surely we.
> If ever man were loved by wife, then thee;
> If ever wife was happy in a man,
> Compare with me ye women if you can.
> I prize thy love more than whole mines of gold,
> Or all the riches that the East doth hold.
> My love is such that rivers cannot quench,
> Nor ought but love from thee give recompense.
> Thy love is such I can no way repay;
> The heavens reward thee manifold, I pray.
> Then while we live, in love let's so persever,
> That when we live no more we may live ever.[20]

In 1647, John Woodbridge, Anne's brother-in-law and pastor of the church in Andover, took the manuscript of her poetry with him to England without her consent. There, in 1650, her poetry appeared in print under the title *The Tenth Muse Lately Sprung up in America, by a Gentlewoman* of Those Parts.* Six years after her death, a second volume of her poetry surfaced—Several Poems—advertised as "Corrected by the Author, and enlarged by an Addition of several other Poems found amongst her Papers after her Death." However, it remains uncertain whether or not the "corrections" had really been made by Anne.

TAYLOR The leading poet of colonial America was Edward Taylor (c. 1645–1729), whose prolific body of work was not made public until the twentieth century. Taylor was born near Coventry, England, into a family of Dissenters. Because of Charles II's crackdown on Dissenters, Taylor was shunned by English universities. Consequently, he became a schoolteacher but felt stifled by the restrictive environment. Desiring an education and freedom of religion, he emigrated to New England. Taylor arrived in Boston in 1668 and was accepted into Harvard College. Upon his graduation from Harvard in 1671, Taylor became a minister in the village of Westfield, Massachusetts, where he remained for the rest of his life. He married twice and fathered thirteen children, but outlived most of them.

Around 1680, Taylor completed his first thirty-five poems, classified as *God's Determinations*. The poems reflect his struggles in the frontier village, his fear of Indian attacks, and his continual war to protect his soul from Satan. The predominance of Satan in Taylor's thought is always balanced by the omnipotence and majesty of God, the redeeming power of Christ (including images of Christ as the bridegroom and the church his bride), and the community of the elect. Beginning in 1682 and continuing for the next 44 years, Taylor wrote 200 poems, which he called his *Preparatory Meditations Before My Approach to the Lord's Supper*. Collectively, these poems serve as Taylor's spiritual autobiography—he renounces the vanities of this world, describes his ongoing battle with Satan, his spiritual union with Christ, his desire to be a poet like the biblical psalmist, David, and finally, his development as a preacher.

In his meditative poem, "Huswifery," Taylor makes use of an extended metaphor linked to the spinning of thread from raw wool or flax, then weaving it into cloth, and finally, using the cloth to make a garment.

> Make me, O Lord, thy Spin[n]ing Wheele
>   compleate.
> Thy Holy Worde my Distaff make for mee.
> Make mine Affections thy Swift Flyers neate
> And make my Soule thy holy Spoole to bee.
> My Conversation make to be thy Reele
> And Reele the yarn thereon spun of thy Wheele.

> Make me thy Loome then, knit therein this
>   Twine:
> And make thy Holy Spirit, Lord, winde quills
>   [spools]:
> Then weave the Web thyselfe. The yarn is fine.
> Thine Ordinances make my Fulling Mills
>   [cleaning with soap].
> Then dy[e] the same in Heavenly Colours Choice,
> All pinkt [ornamented] with varnisht Flowers of
>   Paradise.
> Then cloath [clothe] therewith mine
>   Understanding, Will,
> Affections, Judgment, Conscience, Memory,
> My Words, and Actions, that their shine may fill
> My Wayes with glory and thee glorify.
> Then mine apparell shall display before yee
> That I am Cloathd in Holy robes for glory.[21]

When Taylor died, his grandson, Ezra Stiles, inherited his manuscripts, but before his death, Taylor had made it clear that he did not want his poems published. When Stiles became the president of Yale College, the manuscripts were stored at Yale, and in 1883, a relative bequeathed them to the college, where they were rediscovered in 1939.

ART

Although most Baroque artists emphasized majesty and grandeur, they all rebelled against the clarity and harmony of Renaissance art, stressing instead the ambiguity and turbulence of line and color; they depicted the shadowy, the formless, and the mysterious in the visual image. As the Baroque style spread outward from Italy, it was modified to fit the differing tastes of indigenous traditions. Whereas it became more extravagant and flamboyant in Spain and Latin America, in predominantly Protestant countries, such as the Dutch Republic and England, it was tempered to accommodate more conservative preferences. Today, the Baroque artistic style refers to the major style of European art between Mannerism and Rococo, from 1600 to 1750.

Italy: Bernini

Italian Baroque styling was dominated by the boundless energy and spiritual conviction of Gianlorenzo Bernini (1598–1680). Bernini's father, Pietro, was an accomplished Florentine sculptor who moved his family to Rome when Bernini was about five years old. Initially trained by his father,

*According to classical mythology, the muses were the nine daughters of Zeus who presided over the arts; by making Bradstreet "the tenth muse," she is honored as a poet.

Figure 16.1   Gianlorenzo Bernini, *baldacchino*, 1624–1633, gilded bronze, approx. 100' (30.48 cm), Saint Peter's Basilica, Vatican, Rome.   This canopy, of gilded bronze, was fashioned over the site where Saint Peter is said to be buried. It reputedly was inspired by the serpentine columns of Solomon's Temple. Golden bees cling to the vines and leaves of the columns, gigantic angels top its four corners, and the structure is crowned by an orb and a cross. *(St. Peter's Basilica, Vatican City, Rome/Scala/Art Resource, NY)*

Bernini proved to be a sculptural prodigy. He studied the works of Raphael and Michelangelo (see Chapter 13) and enjoyed the patronage of Pope Paul V (1605–1621) and later, Urban VIII (1623–1644), who commissioned Bernini to be the architect for Saint Peter's in 1629.

One of Bernini's most important monumental works was the *baldacchino*—canopy (Figure 16.1)—which he fashioned for the site where Saint Peter is said to be buried within Saint Peter's basilica. Constructed between 1624 and 1633, the baldacchino of gilded bronze stands almost 100 feet tall and was reputedly inspired by the serpentine columns of Solomon's Temple. Golden bees—the Pope's family emblem—cling to the vines and leaves of the columns and gigantic angels top its four corners. The crown of the baldacchino consists of an orb and a cross that draw the eye upward into Michelangelo's dome.

When Urban VIII died, he was succeeded by Innocent X (1644–1655), who viewed Urban's

artistic tastes as extravagant. Consequently, for a time, Bernini fell into disfavor with the Vatican. During this time, he did commissions for a number of private patrons—including the decoration for the Cornaro Chapel of the Church of Santa Maria della Vittoria, dedicated to Theresa of Ávila (1515–1582), the patron saint of Spain. As a mystic, she restored a deep asceticism and spirituality to her Carmelite convent in particular and the Roman Catholic Church in general. Her spiritual writings are considered to be the equivalent of those of Ignatius of Loyola. In 1970, Pope Paul VI (1963–1978) declared Theresa of Ávila to be a "Doctor of the Church"—making her the first woman to be accorded such an honor.

One of Theresa's mystical experiences inspired Bernini's most famous sculptural work, *Ecstasy of Saint Theresa* (Figure 16.2). The dramatic scene shows an angel, representing Divine Love, piercing Theresa's heart with an arrow. The anguished Theresa falls into an ecstatic swoon, evident in the

Figure 16.2   Gianlorenzo Bernini, *The Ecstasy of Saint Theresa*, 1645–1652, bronze and marble, life size, Cornaro Chapel, Santa Maria della Vittoria, Rome.   The scene depicts an angel, representing Divine Love, piercing Theresa's heart with an arrow, causing her to fall into an ecstatic swoon. As marble figures float on marble clouds, the bronze rays of heaven's light shine down on them. *(Cornaro Chapel, Santa Maria della Vittoria, Rome/ Erich Lessing/Art Resource, NY)*

expression on her face. As the marble figures float on marble clouds, the bronze rays of heaven's light shine down on them. The entire scene is framed by the columns of the oval niche of the altar, which stands under a vaulted ceiling painted in the illusionistic style of Carracci. Bernini's true virtuosity is evident in his handling of textures. For example, the angel's gauzelike garment contrasts with the rough drapery of Theresa's robe, but the smooth flesh of her sensuous form is still visible. Bernini's theatrical blending of architecture, painting, and sculpture was emulated throughout Europe.

In 1665, Louis XIV called Bernini to France to work on a design for the Louvre, a design that was ultimately rejected. This rejection signaled the emerging disparity between Italian and French expectations for the Baroque.

Spain: Velázquez

The greatest of all Spanish Baroque painters was Diego Rodríguez de Silva y Velázquez (1599–1660). Born in Seville, he studied with the Mannerist painter Francisco Pacheco. In 1623, he traveled to Madrid to assume the post of court painter for King Philip IV (1621–1665), a position Velázquez held for thirty years. Between 1629 and 1631, Velázquez made the first of two trips to Italy, where he expressed his appreciation for Titian and Tintoretto but disdained the work of Raphael (see Chapter 13). For his paintings, Velázquez adopted Italian Renaissance design principles (particularly the pyramid) and incorporated Venetian color.

Late in the year 1648, Velázquez made a second trip to Italy to obtain statues and paintings for the royal palace. When he returned in 1651, he painted a magnificent portrait of Philip's new bride, Mariana of Austria, and one of the king himself. It was followed shortly by one of his great masterpieces, a group portrait popularly known as *Las Meninas* (*The Maids of Honor*, Figure 16.3). In the center of the painting is the five-year-old Infanta (Princess) Margarita, whose ladies-in-waiting (María Augustina Sarmiento and Isabella de Velasco) appear on either side of her. In the right corner of the painting are a dog and two dwarfs—Maria Bárbola and Nicolás de Bertusato. Although it was customary for dwarfs to be employed as playmates in the Spanish court, Velázquez is careful to paint them with compassion and understanding. The mirror on the rear wall reflects the images of the king and queen, who have entered the room. Next to them, in the doorway, stands the chamberlain, José Nieto, and in front of him are Doa Marcela de Ulloa and a chamber groom. To the far left is Velázquez himself, painting a huge canvas, and due to the posi-

Figure 16.3 Diego Rodríguez de Silva y Velázquez, *Las Meninas*, 1656, oil on canvas, 10′5″ x 9′1/2″ (3.18 x 2.76 m), Museo del Prado, Madrid. In the center of the painting is the five-year-old Princess Margarita, whose ladies-in-waiting are positioned on either side of her. The mirror on the rear wall reflects the images of the king and queen who have entered the room, and on the far left is Velázquez himself painting a huge canvas. (*Museo del Prado, Madrid/Art Resource, NY*)

tioning of the rulers' reflected image, a number of art historians believe Velázquez is actually painting their portrait. In 1658, Philip IV awarded Velázquez the distinguished Order of Santiago, and following his death in 1660, the king ordered that it be painted around Velázquez's neck within this painting. When the painting was cleaned in 1984, it was revealed that one of the paintings hanging on the rear wall of *Las Meninas* is *Minerva and Arachne* by Rubens (see following discussion).

France

The influence of the Italian Baroque, especially that of Caravaggio and Bernini, was strongly felt in France. However, French artists discarded what they viewed as the excessive exuberance of their Italian counterparts. They emphasized instead elegance and grace, and their body of work bears a conspicuous resemblance to Renaissance classicism.

POUSSIN The painter who best illustrates French classicism during the Baroque period was Nicolas Poussin (c. 1593–1665), who, although born in

France, lived most of his life in Rome. Traveling to Paris as a teenager from his native Normandy, Poussin became enamored of the paintings of Raphael and Titian (see Chapter 13). In 1624, Poussin left Paris to live in Rome, where he furthered his interest in classical antiquity, including Stoic philosophy. About 1630, while recovering from a serious illness, Poussin formulated his theory of art, which bears the mark of the sort of classicism that dominated French painting during the second half of the seventeenth century. Poussin's letters and notebooks detail what he calls *la maniera magnifico* (**the grand manner**)—the subject must be conceived without superfluous details, it must be painted naturally and without affectation, and the style of the painting must flow innately from the artist. Moreover, Poussin postulated "modes of painting," which he equated with the ancient Greek modes of music. For example, his painting, *The Rape of the Sabine Women* (Figure 16.4), illustrates the application of the Phrygian mode (intense and emotional), which, according to Poussin, Plato and Aristotle "held in high esteem" as a "vehement, furious, and highly severe Mode, that astonishes the spectator."[22] Painted between 1636 and 1637, the dynamically modeled figures are reminiscent of the sculpture of both the Hellenistic world and the Italian Renaissance in its realistic, individualized rendering of the human form. The action occurs within a limited space with clearly drawn perspective. Although the Sabine women are being abducted by the Roman men to ensure the perpetuation of the Roman people, the emotion of the scene is more like that of Raphael than the high drama and emotion more typical of the Baroque styling. Moreover, the action is placed under Poussin's orderly, rational control, further demonstrating his adherence to the artistic style of classical antiquity.

In 1640, Poussin traveled to Paris to meet with Louis XIII, who wanted him to decorate the ceiling of the Long Gallery of the Louvre. Poussin, however, rebuffed the king, telling him that placing people on the ceiling was unnatural, for human beings do not fly through the air.

RIGAUD   The best-known portrait of *Louis XIV* (see chapter opening) was painted by Hyacinthe Rigaud (1659–1743) in 1701. Louis, adorned in his coronation garment lined with ermine, stares directly at the viewer as he flaunts his legs (of which he was quite proud) bedecked with high-heeled shoes (which he reputedly invented to augment his small stature). Rigaud's ceremonial portrait succeeded in capturing the essence of the divine right absolutism of the king who had proclaimed, "L'etat, c'est moi" (I am the state).

VERSAILLES   The most spectacular manifestation of Louis XIV's absolute monarchy is his complex of palaces and gardens at Versailles, located twelve miles southwest of Paris. In 1669, Louis commissioned the architect Louis Le Vau (1612–1670) to transform an existing royal hunting lodge into an elaborate and extensive palace, the *Palais de Versailles* (Figure 16.5). Heavily influenced by the Italian Baroque, Le Vau enclosed the château on three sides but designed the garden side of stone and decorated it with Ionic pilasters and arcades. To the north were the king's quarters and to the south the queen's. Beginning in 1678, Jules Hardouin-

Figure 16.4   Nicolas Poussin, *The Rape of the Sabine Women*, 1636–1637, oil on canvas, 60 7/8 x 82 5/8" (154.4 x 209.8 cm), The Metropolitan Museum of Art, New York. The Sabine women are being abducted by the Roman men to ensure the perpetuation of the Roman people. But the violence of this scene is placed under Poussin's orderly, rational control, which demonstrates his adherence to the artistic style of classical antiquity. *(The Metropolitan Museum of Art, Harris Brisband Dick Fund, 1946 (46.160)   Photograph © 1992 The Metropolitan Museum of Art)*

Figure 16.5 Louis Le Vau and Jules Hardouin-Mansart, *Palais de Versailles*, 1668–1685, Versailles, France. In 1669, Louis commissioned Le Vau to transform an existing royal hunting lodge into an elaborate and extensive palace. To the north were the king's quarters and to the south the queen's. Beginning in 1678, Mansart took over the project and added new wings on the north and the south. *(Altitude)*

Mansart (1646–1708) took over the project and added new wings on the north and the south. Between 1678 and 1684, he supervised the construction of the *Hall of Mirrors*, Figure 16.6 and, beginning in 1689, the chapel. The hall is more than 200 feet long and is framed by seventeen windows and seventeen arched mirrors. In the evening, crystal chandeliers light the interior of the gallery. The ceiling is lined with six cameos, twelve medallions, and nine monumental paint-ings executed by Charles Le Brun (1619–1690), illustrating the life of Louis XIV. Le Brun's ceiling paintings not only demonstrate the influence of Carracci, but they also bear the mark of Poussin.

The styling of the grounds and the architectural decoration became the standard of the old regime. When the French Revolution began in 1789 (see Chapter 19), the interior design was modified to embrace the Rococo styling (see Chapter 18) and the silver furniture that had

Figure 16.6 Jules Hardouin-Mansart and Charles Le Brun, *Hall of Mirrors, Palais de Versailles*, begun 1678, Versailles, France. The hall is more than 200 feet long and is framed by seventeen windows and seventeen arched mirrors. In the evening, crystal chandeliers light the interior of the gallery. *(The Bridgeman Art Library International)*

graced the gallery was melted down, because the opulent furnishings offended the revolutionaries.

Flanders and the Dutch Republic

Under the leadership of Prince Frederick Henry (1625–1647), the Protestant Dutch Republic exerted itself as an artistic leader in Europe. In contrast to their French contemporaries, Dutch painters delighted in depictions of their own townspeople, landscapes, and still lifes. As such, their artistic production marks the further development of the Netherlandish style, which began with the van Eyck brothers (see Chapter 15). Dutch artists found fervent and willing patrons among the middle-class citizens of Utrecht, Haarlem, Amsterdam, Leiden, and Delft.

Beginning in 1598, the area known as Flanders enjoyed relative independence from the Hapsburgs, but in 1621, the Spanish Hapsburgs reasserted their authority over the predominantly Catholic region. The power and authority of both the Roman Catholic Church and the Hapsburg monarchy are reflected in the work of Peter Paul Rubens.

RUBENS Although Rubens (1577–1640) was born a Protestant in Germany, the family became Catholic when they moved to Antwerp after his father's death in 1587. For a number of years, Rubens studied painting with several Antwerp masters, and in 1598 he was employed as a master painter by the Antwerp Guild. A year later, he traveled to Italy to study the paintings of the Italian Renaissance masters as well as his Italian contemporaries. From Michelangelo, Rubens appropriated monumental figures; from Titian and Tintoretto, Venetian coloring; from Carracci, natural rendering of space; and from Caravaggio, the interpretation of light and shadow.

Between 1609 and 1610, Rubens painted one of his most important works, a triptych, *The Raising of the Cross* (Figure 16.7), executed for the altar of the Church of Saint Walpurga in Antwerp. Breaking with the traditional triptych form in which the wings bear little relation to the central panel, Rubens chose to continue the action in the side wings. The vivid drama of the central panel reveals the gruesome agony of Jesus as his persecutors struggle to raise the cumbersome cross into place. In the right wing are the soldiers who stand guard during his crucifixion; in the left wing are those who mourn his impending death. Thus, the Baroque propensity for unity of theme is carried out in grand fashion.

Because Rubens, quite a courtly gentleman, was also well schooled in the classics of antiquity and the literature of the Renaissance, he soon found himself with commissions from Philip IV of Spain,

Charles I of England, and Marie de' Medici, Queen Regent of France. In 1621, Marie de' Medici commissioned Rubens to paint a story of her life, which he did in a series of twenty-four paintings. The series not only allegorically depicts episodes from Marie's life, such as the founding of the Bourbon dynasty and its political triumphs, but Marie and her deceased husband, Henry IV, are portrayed as Roman deities overseeing the course of affairs in France. In 1630, Charles I made Rubens a knight and asked him to adorn the ceiling of the Banqueting House at Whitehall Palace in London. The same year, Rubens married for a second time, his first wife having died in 1626; his new wife, Hélène Fourment, was the seventeen-year-old daughter of an Antwerp silk merchant. Hélène came to inspire some of Rubens' most sensual and pleasantest paintings. Rubens' rendering of the luster and warmth of the nude female form is one of the things for which he is best remembered.

In 1635, Rubens began work on the decoration of his own country estate, Château de Steen, for which he executed some of his most memorable landscape paintings. One of Rubens' assistants for the project, Anthony van Dyck, later became famous in his own right.

VAN DYCK Born in Antwerp, Anthony van Dyck (1599–1641), the originator of the Baroque court portrait, already had his own studio with assistants by the age of sixteen. Nonetheless, in 1618 he chose to become Rubens' principal assistant, a position he held for three years. In 1621, he traveled to Italy to study Titian's style of painting. While in Italy, van Dyck modified the robust style he had learned from Rubens into something more refined and graceful. From 1630 until 1632, van Dyck served as court painter to the Archduchess Isabella Clara Eugenia in Antwerp. During this time, his portraits became more monumental and austere. In 1632, van Dyck journeyed to London to become the chief painter for the court of Charles I, whose portrait he painted many times. In 1633, van Dyck painted an equestrian portrait of Charles that was inspired by Titian's portrait of Emperor Charles V. Two years later, he painted *Charles I at the Hunt* (Figure 16.8), depicting the king standing on a precipice looking out over the landscape. Although the stature of the king is diminutive, he appears larger than both his horse and his page. The monarch's casual attire and appearance are capped off by his debonair cavalier's hat. Van Dyck subsequently painted Charles in his full royal regalia, and his triple portrait of Charles' face is said to have influenced Bernini. Van Dyck's attention to detail, graceful composition, luminescent surfaces, and carefully drawn landscapes revolutionized English painting and influenced generations of painters to come.

LEYSTER   One of the most important Dutch portrait painters was Judith Leyster (c. 1609–1660), about whose early years little is known. Her portraits capture both the individuality and spontaneity of her subjects, but so closely did they resemble the style of her contemporary, Frans Hals (c. 1580–1666), that a number of them were mistakenly attributed to him. Moreover, because she signed as a witness at the baptism of one of Hals' children, many art historians previously supposed that she was one of his students. However, she competed directly with Hals and is known to have upbraided him for stealing one of her apprentices away from her studio. Leyster was well known for her delicate brushwork and sensitive (often moralistic) portrayal of her subjects. Leyster painted her *Self-Portrait* (Figure 16.9) in 1635, representing herself as a successful artist, in a fashionable dress and sitting in an elegant chair. The subject of the

"painting within the painting" is a man playing a violin, but Leyster varied her technique to illustrate the difference between her own self-portrait and the painting she is supposedly painting. Moreover, the viewer cannot help but note the similarity between the way an artist holds a brush and palette and the manner in which the man holds the bow over his violin. In her handling of light and shadow, Leyster not only demonstrated her indebtedness to Caravaggio, but she also anticipated the work of the great Rembrandt van Rijn.

REMBRANDT   During his early years, Rembrandt (1606–1669) painted in his hometown of Leiden, where his work demonstrated the influence of Caravaggio's tenebrism. However, in the early 1630s, Rembrandt moved to Amsterdam and soon made a name for himself as a portrait painter, rivaling Hals and Leyster. The high point of his portrait-painting career in Amsterdam came in 1642 when he painted the group portrait *The Company of Captain Frans Banning Cocq*, also

Figure 16.7   Peter Paul Rubens, *The Raising of the Cross*, 1609–1610, oil on panel, 15'1" x 11'9 5/8" (4.6 x 3.6 m), Antwerp Cathedral.   The vivid drama of the central panel of this triptych reveals the gruesome agony of Jesus as his persecutors struggle to raise the cumbersome cross into place. In the right wing are the soldiers who stand guard during his crucifixion; in the left wing are those who mourn his imminent death. *(Onze Lieve Vroukerk, Antwerp Cathedral, Belgium/Peter Willi/The Bridgeman Art Library International)*

Figure 16.8 Anthony van Dyck, *Charles I at the Hunt*, 1635, oil on canvas, 8'11" x 6'11" (2.75 x 2.14 m), Musée du Louvre, Paris. The king is standing on a precipice looking out over the landscape. Although his stature is diminutive, he appears larger than both his horse and his page. Charles I's casual attire and appearance are capped off by his debonair cavalier's hat *(Louvre/Réunion des Musées Nationaux/Art Resource, NY)*

known as *The Night Watch* (Figure 16.10). Due to the excessive layer of grit and varnish that accumulated on the painting during the years, the scene was generally thought to have occurred at night—hence its title *The Night Watch*. However, a post–World War II restoration revealed that Rembrandt used a full palette of rich, golden colors. Moreover, during the eighteenth century, the painting was sized to fit into a space for Amsterdam's Town Hall; as a consequence, it is no longer evident that the company is about to cross a bridge.

The painting was commissioned by those who are depicted in it, including Captain Cocq (swathed in a sash of vibrant red) and his lieutenant, Willem van Ruyteburch (attired in lemon yellow). Even though all the officers portrayed would have contributed equally to the commission, Rembrandt eschewed Hals's policy of painting all subjects in a group portrait on equal footing. Instead, Rembrandt paints some men in shadows, including one to the far right whose eyes are the only visible part of his body. The inclusion of mischievous children—a young girl to the right of the captain, who emerges into a spotlight, and the young boy in

front of her, who appears to be firing a rifle at the lieutenant's plumed hat—has engendered much controversy as to their meaning. However, art historians have arrived at no consensus, and it could be that Rembrandt's eye for detail caused him to include them simply because they were part of the street life he was so fond of sketching.

Following the death of his wife, Saskia van Uylenburgh, in 1642, Rembrandt immersed himself in an intensely personal study of the Bible. During this time, he may also have been a member of the pacifist Mennonites, who believed in silent prayer and the Bible as the sole authority for the Christian faith. In 1648, Rembrandt painted one of his most important paintings of this period—*Supper at Emmaus* (Figure 16.11)—a rendering of Christ revealing himself to his disciples, over a meal, following his resurrection (Luke 24:30). Rather than paint the emotional event with the dramatic intensity of most Baroque painters, Rembrandt's version of the episode is quiet and restrained, a deeply spiritual and personal vision of what he believed the disciples experienced. Although the servant is oblivious to what is happening, the disciple to the right of Christ pulls

Figure 16.9 Judith Leyster, *Self-Portrait*, 1635, oil on canvas, 29 3/8" x 25 5/8" (74.9 x 65.4 cm), National Gallery of Art, Washington, D.C. Leyster represents herself as a successful artist, in a fashionable dress and sitting in an elegant chair. The subject of the "painting within the painting" is a man playing a violin. *(National Gallery of Art, Washington. Gift of Mr. And Mrs. Robert Woods Bliss, Photograph © 2002 Board of Trustees)*

Figure 16.10 Rembrandt, *The Company of Captain Frans Banning Cocq (The Night Watch)*, 1642, oil on canvas, 12′2″ x 14′7″ (3.8 x 4.4 m), Rijksmuseum, Amsterdam. All of the officers portrayed in the painting would have contributed equally to the commission, including Captain Cocq (swathed in a sash of vibrant red) and his lieutenant, Willem van Ruyteburch (attired in lemon yellow). *(Rijksmuseum)*

back in amazement as he realizes that the man with whom he is eating is Christ, risen from the dead. As Christ's head is bathed with a luminescent light, the niche behind him becomes an apse, and the table in front of him acts as an altar for the breaking of the bread.

During the 1630s and 1640s, Rembrandt was also a prolific printmaker. His etchings—pictures created on metal plates with acid—rival the engravings of Albrecht Dürer (see Chapter 15). Despite his successes as an artist, Rembrandt was prone to living beyond his means, and he incurred such severe financial losses in 1655 that he was forced to auction off his house and furnishings and to move to a poorer district of Amsterdam.

VERMEER Second only to Rembrandt among the Dutch virtuoso painters is Jan Vermeer (1632–1675). However, because his artistic production was less than forty canvases, Vermeer's contemporaries did not count him among the prominent artists of his day. Compared to the mysterious, haunting light of Rembrandt, Vermeer's depiction of natural light exudes a translucence that imbues his simple subjects (generally a sole woman immersed in an ordinary task) with an ethereal quality, which transcends ordinary time and space. Moreover, Vermeer's scrupulous sense of design with interlocking shapes, as well as his purity of color, set him apart from his contemporaries.

Little is known about Vermeer's training, and for most of his life he was an ineffectual art dealer in Delft, who, when he died, left his wife, Catherina Bolnes, and their eleven children in debt. In

1662, he was chosen to be a member of the Board of Saint Luke's Guild of Delft (a trade association of artists) and began to work on one of his most famous paintings—*The Artist's Studio* (Figure 16.12)—which Catherina called "the art of paint-

Figure 16.11 Rembrandt, *Supper at Emmaus*, 1648, oil on wood, 26 3/4″ x 25 5/8″ (68 x 65 cm). Musée du Louvre, Paris. Rembrandt's version of the emotional event—Christ revealing himself to his disciples, over a meal, following his resurrection—is quiet and restrained, a deeply spiritual and personal vision of what the disciples experienced. *(Louvre/Réunion des Musées Nationaux/Art Resource, NY)*

they experienced no change. Because the quintessential heavens differed totally from earth, the paths of planets could not follow the same laws that governed the motion of earthly objects. This two-world orientation blended well with the Christian outlook.

Like Aristotle, Ptolemy held that planets moved around the earth in perfect circular orbits and at uniform speeds. However, in reality the path of planets is not a circle but an ellipse, and planets do not move at uniform speed, but accelerate as they approach the sun. Therefore, problems arose that required Ptolemy to incorporate into his system certain ingenious devices that earlier Greek astronomers had employed. For example, to save the appearance of circular orbits, Ptolemy made use of epicycles, small circles attached to the rims of larger circles. A planet revolved uniformly around the small circle, the epicycle, which in turn revolved about the earth in a larger circle. If one ascribed a sufficient number of epicycles to a planet, the planet could seem to move in a perfectly circular orbit.

The Aristotelian–Ptolemaic model of the cosmos did appear to accord with common sense and raw perception: The earth does indeed seem and feel to be at rest. And the validity of this view seemed to be confirmed by evidence, for the model enabled thinkers to predict with considerable accuracy the movement and location of celestial bodies and the passage of time. This geocentric model and the division of the universe into higher and lower worlds also accorded with passages in Scripture. Scholastic philosophers harmonized Aristotelian and Ptolemaic science with Christian theology, producing an intellectually and emotionally satisfying picture of the universe in which everything was arranged according to a divine plan.

The Scientific Revolution shattered the medieval worldview, in which the earth occupied the central position, heaven lay just beyond the fixed stars, and every object had its place in a hierarchical and qualitative order.

A NEW VIEW OF NATURE

The Renaissance contributed to the Scientific Revolution. The revival of interest in antiquity during the Renaissance led to the rediscovery of some ancient scientific texts—including the works of Archimedes (287–212 B.C.), which fostered new ideas in mechanics—and to the improved translations of the medical works of Galen,* a contem-

* **Galen** (c. A.D. 130–201) summed up the medical knowledge of the Ancient World in a treatise that dominated medicine up to modern times.

porary of Ptolemy, which stimulated the study of anatomy. Renaissance art, too, was a factor in the rise of modern science, for it linked an exact representation of the human body to mathematical proportions and demanded accurate observation of natural phenomena. By defining visual space and the relationship between the object and the observer in mathematical terms and by delineating the natural world with a newfound appreciation for precision, Renaissance art helped promote a new view of nature, which later found expression in the astronomy of Copernicus and Kepler and the physics of Galileo.

The Renaissance revival of ancient Pythagorean and Platonic ideas, which stressed mathematics as the key to comprehending reality, also contributed to the Scientific Revolution. Extending the mathematical harmony found in music to the universe at large, Pythagoras (c. 580–507 B.C.) and his followers believed that all things have form, which can be expressed numerically, and that reality consists fundamentally of number relations, which the mind can grasp. Plato maintained that beyond the world of everyday objects made known to us through the senses lies a higher reality, the world of Forms, which contains an inherent mathematical order apprehended only by thought. The great thinkers of the Scientific Revolution were influenced by these ancient ideas of nature as a harmonious mathematical system knowable to the mind.

Nicolaus Copernicus: The Dethronement of the Earth

Modern astronomy begins with Nicolaus Copernicus (1473–1543), a Polish astronomer, mathematician, and church canon. He proclaimed that earth is a planet that orbits a centrally located sun together with the other planets. This *heliocentric theory* served as the kernel of a new world picture, which eventually supplanted the medieval view of the universe. Copernicus did not base his heliocentric theory on new observations and new data. What led him to remove the earth from the center of the universe was the complexity and cumbersomeness of the Ptolemaic system, which offended his sense of mathematical order. To Copernicus, the numerous epicycles (the number had been increased since Ptolemy, making the model even more cumbersome) violated the Platonic vision of the mathematical symmetry of the universe.

Concerned that his theories would spark a controversy, Copernicus long refused to publish his work, but persuaded by his friends, he finally relented. His masterpiece, *On the Revolutions of the Heavenly Spheres,* appeared in 1543. As Copernicus had feared, his views did stir up controversy, but the new astronomy did not become a passionate issue until the early seventeenth century, more than fifty years after the publication of *On the Revolutions*. The Copernican theory frightened clerical authorities, who controlled the universities as well as the pulpits, for it seemed to conflict with Scripture. For example, Psalm 93 says: "Yea, the world is established, that it cannot be moved." And Psalm 103 says that God "fixed the earth upon its foundation not to be moved forever." When Martin Luther became aware of the new Copernican cosmology, he rejected it as contrary to Scripture:

> There was mention of a certain new astrologer who wanted to prove the earth moves and not the sky, the sun, and the moon. . . . Whoever wants to be clever must agree with nothing that others esteem. He must do something of his own. This is what that fellow does who wishes to turn the whole of astronomy upside down. Even in these things that are thrown into disorder I believe the Holy Scriptures, for Joshua commanded the sun to stand still and not the earth (Joshua 10:12).[1]

Moreover, in 1616, the Catholic church placed *On the Revolutions* and all other works that ascribed motion to the earth on the *Index of Forbidden Books*.

Galileo: Uniformity of Nature and Experimental Physics

The seventeenth century has often been called "the century of genius," one of the principal reasons being the work of Galileo Galilei (1564–1642). A Pisan by birth, Galileo was a talented musician and artist and a cultivated humanist; he knew and loved the Latin classics and Italian poetry. He was also an astronomer and physicist, who helped shatter the medieval conception of the cosmos and shape the modern scientific outlook. Galileo was indebted to the Platonic tradition, which tried to grasp the mathematical harmony of the universe, and to Archimedes, the Hellenistic mathematician–engineer who had sought a geometric understanding of space and motion.

Galileo rejected the medieval division of the universe into higher and lower realms and proclaimed the modern idea of nature's uniformity. Learning that a telescope had been invented in Holland, Galileo built one for himself and used it to investigate the heavens—the first person to do so. From his observations of the moon, Galileo concluded

> that the surface of the moon is not smooth, uniform, and precisely spherical as a great number of philosophers believe it (and the other heavenly

bodies) to be, but is uneven, rough, and full of cavities and prominences, being not unlike the face of the earth, relieved by chains of mountains and deep valleys.[2]

This discovery of the moon's craters and mountains and spots on the supposedly unblemished sun led Galileo to break with the Aristotelian notion that celestial bodies were pure, perfect, and unchangeable. For Galileo, there was no difference in quality between celestial and terrestrial bodies. Nature was not a hierarchical order, in which physical entities were ranked according to their possession of or lack of quality; rather, it was a homogeneous system, the same throughout.

With his telescope, Galileo discovered the four moons that orbit Jupiter, an observation that overcame a principal objection to the Copernican system. Galileo showed that a celestial body could indeed move around a center other than the earth; that the earth was not the common center for all celestial bodies; and that a celestial body (the earth's moon or Jupiter's moons) could orbit a planet at the same time that the planet revolved around another body (the sun).

Galileo pioneered in experimental physics and advanced the modern idea that knowledge of motion should be derived from direct observation and from mathematics. In dealing with problems of motion, he insisted on applying mathematics to the study of moving bodies and did, in fact, study acceleration by performing experiments, which required careful mathematical measurement. For Aristotelian scholastics, a rock fell because it was striving to reach its proper place in the universe, thereby fulfilling its nature; it was acting in accordance with the purpose God had assigned it. Galileo completely rejected the view that motion is due to a quality inherent in an object. Rather, he said, motion is the relationship of bodies to time and distance. By holding that bodies fall according to uniform and quantifiable laws, Galileo posited an entirely different conceptual system. This system requires that we study angles and distances and search for mathematical ratios but avoid inquiring into an object's quality and purpose—the role God assigned it in a hierarchical universe.

For Galileo, the universe was a "grand book which . . . is written in the language of mathematics and its characters are triangles, circles, and other geometric figures without which it is humanly impossible to understand a single word of it."[3] In the tradition of Plato, Galileo sought to grasp the mathematical principles governing reality—only his reality was nature itself, not Plato's higher realm of which nature was only a poor copy—and ascribed to mathematics absolute authority. Like Copernicus and Kepler (see the following discussion), he believed that mathematics expresses the harmony and beauty of God's creation.

Attack on Authority

Insisting that physical truth is arrived at through observation, experimentation, and reason, Galileo strongly denounced reliance on authority. Scholastic thinkers regarded Aristotle as the supreme authority on questions concerning nature, and university education was based on his works. These doctrinaire Aristotelians angered Galileo, who protested that they sought truth not by opening their eyes to nature and new knowledge, but by slavishly relying on ancient texts. In *Dialogue Concerning the Two Chief World Systems—Ptolemaic and Copernican* (1632), Galileo upheld the Copernican view and attacked the unquestioning acceptance of Aristotle's teachings. Galileo also criticized Roman Catholic authorities for attempting to suppress the Copernican theory. He argued that passages from the Bible had no authority in questions involving nature.

A sincere Christian, Galileo never intended to use the new science to undermine faith. What he desired was to separate science from faith so that reason and experience alone would be the deciding factors on questions involving nature. He could not believe that "God who has endowed us with senses, reason and intellect,"[4] did not wish us to use these faculties in order to acquire knowledge. He was certain that science was compatible with Scripture rightly understood, that is, allowing for its metaphorical language and its disinterest in conveying scientific knowledge. For Galileo, the aim of Scripture was to teach people the truths necessary for salvation, not to instruct them in the operations of nature, which is the task of science.

Galileo's support of Copernicus aroused the ire of both scholastic philosophers and the clergy, who feared that the brash scientist threatened a world picture that had the support of venerable ancient authorities, Holy Writ, and scholastic tradition. Already traumatized by the Protestant threat, Catholic officials cringed at ideas that might further undermine traditional belief and authority.

In 1616, the ***Congregation of the Index,*** the church's censorship organ, condemned the teaching of Copernicanism. In 1633, the aging and infirm Galileo was summoned to Rome. Tried and condemned by the Inquisition, he was ordered to abjure the Copernican theory. Not wishing to bring harm to himself and certain that the truth would eventually prevail, Galileo bowed to the Inquisition. He was sentenced to life imprisonment—mostly house arrest at his own villa near Florence—the *Dialogue* was banned, and he was forbidden to write on Copernicanism. Not until 1820 did the church lift the ban on Copernicanism.

Johannes Kepler: Laws of Planetary Motion

Johannes Kepler (1571–1630), a German mathematician and astronomer, combined the Pythagorean–Platonic quest to comprehend the mathematical harmony within nature with a deep commitment to Lutheran Christianity. He contended that God gave human beings the ability to understand the laws of harmony and proportion.

As a true Pythagorean, Kepler yearned to discover the geometric harmony of the planets, which he too called the "music of the spheres." Such knowledge, he believed, would provide supreme insight into God's mind. No doubt, this mystical quality sparked the creative potential of the imagination, but to be harnessed for science, it had to be disciplined by the rational faculties.

Kepler discovered the three basic laws of planetary motion, which rendered Ptolemaic cosmology obsolete. In doing so, he utilized the data collected by Tycho Brahe, a Danish astronomer, who for twenty years systematically observed the planets and stars and recorded their positions with far greater accuracy than had ever been done. Kepler sought to fit Tycho's observations into Copernicus' heliocentric model.

Kepler's first law demonstrated that planets move in elliptical orbits—not circular ones, as Aristotle and Ptolemy (and Copernicus) had believed—and that the sun is one focus of the ellipse. This discovery that a planet's path was one simple oval eliminated all the epicycles that had been used to preserve the appearance of circular motion. Kepler's second law showed that planets do not move at uniform speed, as had been believed, but accelerate as they near the sun, and he provided the rule for deciphering a planet's speed at each point in its orbit. His third law drew a mathematical relationship between the time it takes a planet to complete its orbit of the sun and its average distance from the sun. On the basis of these laws, one could calculate accurately a planet's position and velocity at a particular time—another indication that the planets were linked together in a unified mathematical system.

Derived from carefully observed facts, Kepler's laws of planetary motion buttressed Copernicanism, for they made sense only in a heliocentric universe. But why did the planets move in elliptical orbits? Why did they not fly off into space or crash into the sun? To these questions Kepler had no satisfactory answers. It was Isaac Newton

MEMOIRS OF OLAUDAH EQUIANO, A FORMER SLAVE

OLAUDAH EQUIANO (1745–1797), born in what is now Nigeria, wrote about his kidnapping and enslavement in Africa, his subsequent sale to an English slave merchant, and his voyage to and first impressions of the West Indian port of Bridgetown, Barbados. Equiano's subsequent life diverged from the pattern of most slaves. He educated himself, purchased his freedom, traveled widely, and took part in the antislavery movement in England. In the following excerpts from his memoirs, he records his reaction at the age of eleven when he was placed aboard an English slave ship for the voyage to the West Indies.

> The first object which saluted my eyes when I arrived on the coast was the sea and a slaveship, which was then riding at anchor, and waiting for its cargo. These filled me with astonishment, which was soon converted into terror. . . . When I was carried on board I was immediately handled and tossed up, to see if I were sound, by some of the crew; and I was now persuaded that I had got into a world of bad spirits, and that they were going to kill me. . . . When I looked round the ship too, and saw a large furnace or copper [pot] boiling and a multitude of black people of every description chained together, every one of their countenances expressing dejection and sorrow, I no longer doubted of my fate; and, quite overpowered with horror and anguish, I fell motionless on the deck and fainted. When I recovered a little, I found some black people about me. . . . I asked them if we were not to be eaten by those white men with horrible looks, red faces and long hair. They told me I was not. . . . Soon after this, the blacks who brought me on board went off, and left me abandoned to despair. I now saw myself deprived of all chance of returning to my native country. . . .
>
> . . . At last, when the ship we were in had got in all her cargo . . . we were all put under deck. . . . The closeness of the place, and the heat of the climate, added to the number in the ship, which was so crowded that each had scarcely room to turn himself, almost suffocated us. . . . Happily perhaps for myself I was soon reduced so low here that it was thought necessary to keep me almost always on deck. . . .

The voyage from Africa to the West Indies took more than two months. Equiano's ship finally reaches Bridgetown, Barbados, where the slaves are to be sold.

> We were conducted immediately to the merchant's yard, where we were all pent up together like so many sheep in a fold, without regard to sex or age. . . . We were not many days in the merchant's custody, before we were sold after their usual manner, which is this: on a signal given (as the beat of a drum), the buyers rush at once into the yard where the slaves are confined, and make choice of that parcel they like best. . . . In this manner, without scruple, are relations and friends separated, most of them never to see each other again. I remember . . . several brothers who . . . were sold in different lots; and it was very moving . . . to see and hear their cries at parting. O, ye nominal Christians! might not an African ask you, learned you this from your God? who says unto you, Do unto all men as you would men should do unto you. Is it not enough that we are torn from our country and friends to toil for your luxury and lust of gain? Must every tender feeling be likewise sacrificed to your avarice? . . . Surely this is a new refinement in cruelty, which, while it has no advantage to atone for it, thus aggravates distress, and adds fresh horrors even to the wretchedness of slavery.

Source: *Philip D. Curtin*, Africa Remembered *(Madison: University of Wisconsin Press, 1967)*, *pp. 92–93, 95, 97–98.*

(1642–1727), the great British mathematician–scientist, who arrived at a celestial mechanics that linked the astronomy of Copernicus and Kepler with the physics of Galileo and accounted for the behavior of planets.

The Newtonian Synthesis

The publication in 1687 of Isaac Newton's *Mathematical Principles of Natural Philosophy* marks the climax of the Scientific Revolution. Newton postulated three laws of motion that joined all celestial and terrestrial objects into a vast mechanical system, whose parts worked in perfect harmony and whose connections could be expressed in mathematical terms, and he invented the calculus that facilitated the expression of physical laws in mathematical equations. Because Copernican astronomy was essential to his all-encompassing theory of the universe, Newton had provided mathematical proof for the heliocentric system and opposition to it dissipated.

Newton's first law is the *principle of inertia:* that a body at rest remains at rest unless acted on by a force and that a body in rectilinear motion continues to move in a straight line at the same velocity unless a force acts on it. A moving body does not require a force to keep it in motion, as ancient and medieval thinkers had believed. Once started, bodies continue to move; motion is as natural a condition as rest. Newton's second law states that a given force produces a measurable change in a body's velocity; a body's change of velocity is proportional to the force acting on it. Newton's third law holds that for every action or force there is an equal and opposite reaction or force. The sun pulls the earth with the same force that the earth exercises on the sun. An apple falling to the ground is being pulled by the earth, but the apple is also pulling the earth toward it. (However, because the mass of the apple is so small in comparison with that of the earth, the force that the apple exercises on the earth causes no visible change in the earth's motion.)

Newton asserted that the same laws of motion and gravitation that operate in the celestial world also govern the movement of earthly bodies. Ordinary mechanical laws explain both why apples fall to the ground and why planets orbit the sun. Both the planet and the apple are subject to the same force, and the very same mathematical formulas describe the sun's action on a planet and the earth's pull on an apple. Newtonian physics ended the medieval division of the cosmos into higher and lower worlds with different laws operating in each realm. The universe is an integrated, harmonious mechanical system held together by the force

of gravity. By demonstrating that the universe contains an inherent mathematical order, Newton realized the Pythagorean and Platonic visions. To his contemporaries, it seemed that Newton had unraveled all of nature's mysteries: The universe was fully explicable. It was as if Newton had penetrated God's mind.

Deeply committed to the Church of England, Newton retained a central place for God in his world system. God, for him, was the grand architect whose wisdom and skill accounted for nature's magnificent clockwork design. Newton also believed that God periodically intervened in his creation to restore energy to the cosmic system and that there was no conflict between divine miracles and a mechanical universe. However, in future generations, thinkers called deists (see the following discussion) came to regard miracles as incompatible with a universe governed by impersonal mechanical principles.

With his discovery of the composition of light, Newton also laid the foundation of the science of optics. He was a cautious experimentalist who valued experimental procedures, including drawing appropriate conclusions from accumulated data. Both Newton's mechanical universe and his championing of the experimental method were foundation blocks of the Age of Enlightenment.

Prophets of Modern Science

The accomplishments of the Scientific Revolution extended beyond the creation of a new model of the universe. They also included the formulation of a new method of inquiry into nature and the recognition that science could serve humanity. Two thinkers instrumental in articulating the implications of the Scientific Revolution were Francis Bacon and René Descartes. Both repudiated the authority of Aristotle and other ancients in scientific matters and urged the adoption of new methods for seeking and evaluating truth.

FRANCIS BACON: THE INDUCTIVE METHOD Sir Francis Bacon (1561–1626), an English statesman and philosopher, vigorously supported the advancement of science and the scientific method. Although he himself had no laboratory and made no discoveries, his advocacy of the scientific method has earned him renown as a prophet of modern science. Bacon attributed the limited progress of science over the ages to the interference of scholastic philosophers, who sought to bend theories of nature to the requirements of Scripture. Bacon also denounced scholastic thinkers for their slavish attachment to Aristotelian doctrines, which prevented independent thinking and the acquisition of new information about nature. To acquire new knowledge and improve the quality of human life, said Bacon, we should not depend on ancient texts; old authorities must be discarded. Knowledge must be pursued and organized in a new way.

The method that Bacon advocated as the way to truth and useful knowledge was the ***inductive approach:*** careful observation of nature and the systematic accumulation of data; drawing general laws from the knowledge of particulars; and testing these laws through constant experimentation. People committed to such a method would never subscribe to inherited fables and myths about nature or invent new ones. Rather, they would investigate nature directly and base their conclusions on observable facts. In his discovery of the circulation of blood, Bacon's contemporary, British physician William Harvey (1578–1657), successfully employed the inductive method championed by Bacon. Grasping the essential approach of modern natural science, Bacon attacked practitioners of astrology, magic, and alchemy for their errors, secretiveness, and enigmatic writings and urged, instead, the pursuit of cooperative and methodical scientific research that could be publicly criticized.

Bacon was among the first to appreciate the value of the new science for human life. Knowledge, he said, should help us utilize nature for human advantage; it should improve the quality of human life by advancing commerce, industry, and agriculture. Holding that knowledge is power, Bacon urged the state to found scientific institutions and praised progress in technology and the mechanical arts. In Bacon's transvaluation of values, the artisan, mechanic, and engineer advanced knowledge more and contributed more to human betterment than did philosopher–theologians who constructed castles in the air.

RENÉ DESCARTES: THE DEDUCTIVE METHOD   The scientific method encompasses two approaches to knowledge that usually complement each other: the empirical (inductive) and the rational (deductive). In the inductive approach, which is employed in such descriptive sciences as biology, anatomy, and geology, general principles are derived from analyzing data collected through observation and experimentation. The essential features of the inductive method, as we have seen, were championed by Bacon, who regarded sense data as the foundation of knowledge. In the ***deductive approach,*** which is employed in mathematics and theoretical physics, truths are derived in successive steps from first principles, indubitable axioms. In the seventeenth century, the

Figure 17.1   Franz Hals, *Portrait of Descartes*, c. 1649 , oil on canvas, 30 3/4" x 26 3/4" (76 x 66 cm), Musée du Louvre, Paris, France. Descartes rejected as false anything about which he could have the least doubt, and he searched for an incontrovertible truth that could serve as the first principle of knowledge and be the foundation for an all-encompassing philosophical system. *(Louvre/Réunion des Musées Nationaux/Art Resource, NY)*

deductive method was formulated by René Descartes (1596–1650), a French mathematician and philosopher, who is also regarded as the founder of modern philosophy (Figure 17.1).

In the *Discourse on Method* (1637), Descartes expressed his disenchantment with the learning of his day. In particular, he was responding to the seventeenth-century French skeptics, who, like Montaigne, doubted the possibility of discovering absolute truth. Descartes rejected as false anything about which he could have the least doubt, and he searched for an incontrovertible truth that could serve as the first principle of knowledge and be the foundation for an all-encompassing philosophical system.

[A]s I wanted to concentrate solely on the search for truth, I thought that I ought to . . . reject as being absolutely false everything in which I could suppose the slightest reason for doubt, in order to see if there did not remain after that anything in my belief which was entirely indubitable. So . . . I rejected as being false all the reasonings I had hitherto accepted as proofs. And finally, considering that all the same thoughts that we have when we are awake can also come to us when we are asleep, without any one of them then being true, I resolved to pretend that nothing which had ever entered my mind was any more true than the illusions of my dreams. But immediately afterwards I became aware that, while I decided thus to think that everything was false, it followed necessarily that I who thought thus must be something; and observing that this truth: *I think, therefore I am,* was so certain and so evident that all the most extravagant suppositions of the sceptics were not capable of shaking it, I judged that I could accept it without scruple as the first principle of the philosophy I was seeking.[5]

Descartes found one truth to be certain and unshakable: that it was he who was doing the doubting and thinking. With his dictum "I think, therefore I am," Descartes discovered his starting point for knowledge. Because he called for the individual to question and, if necessary, to overthrow all traditional beliefs, Descartes is viewed as the founder of modern philosophy. By proclaiming the mind's autonomy and importance, he asserted people's ability to understand truth and their capacity to comprehend the world through their own mental powers.

Descartes saw the method used in mathematics as the most reliable avenue to certain knowledge. By applying mathematical reasoning to philosophical problems, we can achieve the same certainty and clarity evidenced in geometry. Mathematics is the key to understanding both the truths of nature and the moral order underlying human existence. The mathematical, or deductive, approach favored by Descartes consists of finding a self-evident principle, an irrefutable premise, such as a geometric axiom, and then deducing other truths from it through a chain of logical reasoning. The Cartesian deductive method, with its mathematical emphasis, perfectly complements Bacon's inductive approach, which stresses observation and experimentation. The scientific achievements in modern times have stemmed from the skillful synchronization of both induction and deduction.

The Meaning of the Scientific Revolution

The radical transformation of our conception of the physical universe that was produced by the Scientific Revolution ultimately transformed our understanding of the individual, society, and the purpose of life. It replaced the medieval view with the modern conception of a homogeneous universe of unbounded space and an infinite number of celestial bodies. Gone were the barriers that separated the heavens and the earth. The glory of the heavens was diminished by the new view that

celestial objects were composed of the same stuff and subject to the same laws as all other natural objects. Gone also was the medieval notion that God had assigned an ultimate purpose to all natural objects and to all plant and animal life, that in God's plan everything had an assigned role: We have eyes because God wants us to see and rain because God wants crops to grow. Eschewing ultimate purposes, modern science examines physical nature for mathematical relationships and chemical composition.

Although the implications of the new cosmology caused great anguish in later centuries, only a few people at the time were aware of its full significance. For example, the devout Catholic Blaise Pascal (1623–1662), a French scientist and mathematician, was frightened by what he called "the eternal silence of these infinite spaces" and realized that the new science could feed doubt, uncertainty, and anxiety, which threatened belief. In succeeding centuries, this radical cosmological transformation proved as traumatic for the modern mind as did Adam's and Eve's expulsion from the Garden of Eden for the medieval mind. Today, we know that the earth is one of billions and billions of celestial bodies, a tiny speck in an endless cosmic ocean, and that the universe is some twelve billion years old. Could such a universe have been created just for human beings? Could it contain a heaven that assures eternal life for the faithful and a hell with eternal fires and torments for sinners?

The creators of modern science saw no essential conflict between traditional Christianity and the new view of the physical universe and made no war on the churches. Indeed, they believed that they were unveiling the laws of nature instituted by God at the Creation—that at last the human mind could comprehend God's magnificent handiwork. But the new cosmology and new scientific outlook ultimately weakened traditional Christianity, for it dispensed with miracles and the necessity of God's sustaining presence in the universe.

The new critical spirit led the thinkers of the Enlightenment to doubt the literal truth of the Bible and to dismiss miracles as incompatible with what science teaches about the regularity of nature. So brilliantly had God crafted the universe, they said, so exquisite a mechanism was nature, that its operations did not require God's intervention. In the generations after the Scientific Revolution, theology, long considered the highest form of contemplation, was denounced as a barrier to understanding or even dismissed as irrelevant, and the clergy rapidly lost their position as the arbiters of knowledge. To many intellectuals, theology seemed sterile and profitless in comparison with the new science. Whereas science promised the certitude of mathematics, theologians seemed to quibble endlessly over unfathomable and, even worse, inconsequential issues. In scientific academies, in salons, and in coffeehouses, educated men and some women met to discuss the new ideas, and journals published the new knowledge for eager readers. European culture was undergoing a great transformation, marked by the triumph of a scientific and secular spirit among the intellectual elite. Consequently, a wide breach opened between the intellectual elite and the masses, who remained steeped in popular superstitions and committed to traditional Christian dogma.

The Scientific Revolution repudiated reliance on Aristotle, Ptolemy, and other ancient authorities in matters concerning nature and substituted in their place knowledge derived from observation, experimentation, and mathematical thinking. Citing an ancient authority was no longer sufficient to prove a point or to win an argument. The new standard of knowledge derived from experience with the world, not from ancient texts or inherited views. This new outlook had far-reaching implications for the Age of Enlightenment. If the authority of ancient thinkers regarding the universe could be challenged, could not inherited political beliefs be challenged as well—for example, the divine right of kings to rule? Impressed with the achievements of science, many intellectuals started to urge the application of the scientific method to all fields of knowledge.

The new outlook generated by the Scientific Revolution served as the foundation of the Enlightenment. The Scientific Revolution gave thinkers great confidence in the power of the mind, which had discovered nature's laws, reinforcing the confidence in human abilities expressed by Renaissance humanists. In time, it was believed, the scientific method would unlock all nature's secrets, and humanity, gaining evergreater knowledge and control of nature, would progress rapidly.

THE AGE OF ENLIGHTENMENT: AFFIRMATION OF REASON AND FREEDOM

The Enlightenment of the eighteenth century was the culmination of the movement toward modernity initiated by the Renaissance. Aspiring to create a more rational and humane society, the thinkers of the eighteenth century, known as *philosophes*, attacked medieval otherworldliness, rejected theology as an avenue to truth, denounced the Christian idea of people's inherent depravity, and sought to understand nature and society

through reason alone, unaided by revelation or priestly authority. Adopting Descartes' method of systematic doubt, they questioned all inherited opinions and traditions. "We think that the greatest service to be done to men," said Denis Diderot (1713–1784), "is to teach them to use their reason, only to hold for truth what they have verified and proved."[6] The philosophes believed that they were inaugurating an enlightened age. Through the power of reason, humanity was at last liberating itself from the fetters of ignorance, superstition, and despotism with which tyrants and priests had bound it in past ages. Paris was the center of the Enlightenment, but there were philosophes and adherents of their views in virtually every leading city in western Europe and North America.

Drawing on many of the advancements of the Scientific Revolution and relying on Newton's methodology, which had established certain knowledge of the physical universe, the philosophes hoped to arrive at the irrefutable laws that operated in the realm of human society. They aspired to shape religion, government, law, morality, and economics in accordance with these natural laws. They believed that all things should be reevaluated to see if they accorded with nature, that is, if they promoted human well-being.

In championing the methodology of science, the philosophes affirmed respect for the mind's capacities and for human autonomy. Rejecting appeals to tradition or to clerical or princely authority, the self-sufficient mind relies on its own ability to think and trusts the evidence of its own experience. Thus, the philosophes wanted people to have the courage to break with beliefs and institutions that did not meet the test of reason and common sense and to seek new guideposts derived from experience and reason unhindered by passion, superstition, dogma, and authority. The numerous examples of injustice, inhumanity, and superstition in society outraged the philosophes. Behind their devotion to reason and worldly knowledge lay an impassioned moral indignation against institutions and beliefs that degraded human beings.

English Antecedents in Political Theory and Epistemology

Just as Newton's new view of the physical universe was a cornerstone of the Age of Enlightenment, the political thought, the epistemology, and the psychology of the age were profoundly affected by the ideas of Thomas Hobbes (1588–1679) and John Locke (1632–1704). Hobbes witnessed the agonies of the English Civil War, including the execution of Charles I in 1649. These developments fortified his conviction that absolutism was the most desirable and logical form of government. Only the unlimited power of a sovereign, Hobbes wrote in his major work, *Leviathan* (1651), could contain human passions that disrupt the social order and threaten civilized life; only absolute rule could provide an environment secure enough for people to pursue their individual interests.

Hobbes had a pessimistic view of human nature. Believing that people are innately selfish and grasping, he maintained that competition and dissension, rather than cooperation, characterize human relations. Without a stringent authority to make and enforce law, life would be miserable, a war of every man against every man, he said. Therefore, he prescribed a state with unlimited power because only in this way could people be protected from each other and civilized life preserved.

Influenced by the new scientific thought that saw mathematical knowledge as the avenue to truth, Hobbes aimed at constructing political philosophy on a scientific foundation and rejected the authority of tradition and religion as inconsistent with a science of politics. Thus, although Hobbes supported absolutism, he dismissed the idea advanced by other theorists of absolutism that the monarch's power derived from God. Instead, it derived from the will of the people. Hobbes stated that government is achieved by a "mutual pact," which he described as

> a covenant of every man with every man, . . . as if every man should say to every man, "I authorise and give up my right of governing myself, to this man, or to this assembly of men, on this condition, that thou give up thy right to him, and authorize all his actions in like manner."[7]

This political covenant created the absolute ruler that Hobbes called the "great LEVIATHAN, or rather, . . . that *mortal god.*"[8] Hobbes modeled his political covenant after the idea of the biblical covenant between human beings and God—a popular theological concept in seventeenth-century England—but he rejected the idea that the state should not be obeyed when it violated God's law. Like Machiavelli, Hobbes made no attempt to fashion the earthly city in accordance with Christian teachings.

Although the thinkers of the Enlightenment, called *philosophes,* generally rejected Hobbes' gloomy view of human nature, they embraced his secular approach to politics, particularly his denunciation of the theory of the divine right of kings. Hobbes' concern with protecting the social order from human antisocial tendencies is still a central consideration of modern political life.

In contrast to Hobbes, John Locke saw people as essentially good and humane and developed a conception of the state fundamentally different from Hobbes'. In the *Two Treatises of Government* (1690), Locke maintained that human beings are born with **natural rights** to life, liberty, and property, and they establish the state to protect these rights. Consequently, neither executive nor legislature—neither king nor assembly—has the authority to deprive individuals of their natural rights. Whereas Hobbes justified absolute monarchy, Locke explicitly endorsed constitutional government, in which the power to govern derives from the consent of the governed, and the state's authority is limited by agreement. Rulers hold their authority under the law; when they act outside the law, they forfeit their right to govern.

> [W]henever the *Legislators endeavour to take away, and destroy the Property of the People,* or to reduce them to Slavery under Arbitrary Power, they put themselves into a state of War with the People, who are thereupon absolved from any further Obedience. . . .Whensoever therefore the *Legislative* shall transgress this fundamental Rule of Society; and either by Ambition, Fear, Folly or Corruption, *endeavor to grasp* themselves, *or put into the hands of any other an Absolute Power* over the Lives, Liberties, and estates of the People; By this breach of Trust they *forfeit the Power,* the People had put into their hands, for quite contrary ends, and it devolves to the People, who have a right to resume their original Liberty, and, by the establishment of a new Legislative . . . provide for their own Safety and Security, which is the end for which they are in Society.[9]

Thus, if government fails to fulfill the end for which it was established—the preservation of the individual's right to life, liberty, and property—the people have a right to dissolve that government.

Both Hobbes and Locke agreed that the state exists in order to ensure the tranquillity, security, and well-being of its citizens. But they proposed radically different ways for attaining this end. Unlike Hobbes, Locke believed that social well-being encompassed personal freedom. Rejecting Hobbes' view that absolute power can remedy the defects of the state of nature, Locke stated the case for limited government, the rule of law, the protection of fundamental human rights, and the right of resistance to arbitrary power. Underlying Locke's conception of the state is the conviction that people have the capacity for reason and freedom: "We are born Free as we are born Rational."[10]

The value that Locke gave to reason and freedom and his theories of natural rights, the rule of law, and the right to resist despotic authority had a profound effect on the Enlightenment and the liberal revolutions of the late eighteenth and early nineteenth centuries. Thus, in *The Declaration of Independence,* Thomas Jefferson restated Locke's principles to justify the American Revolution. Locke's tenets that property is a natural right and that state interference with personal property leads to the destruction of liberty also became core principles of modern liberalism.

Locke's more optimistic view of human nature is evident in his *Essay Concerning Human Understanding* (1690), a work of immense significance in the history of philosophy, in which he articulated his epistemology, or theory of knowledge. Contrary to Descartes, Locke argued that human beings are not born with divinely implanted innate ideas, such as the idea of God, principles of good and evil, and rules of logic. Rather, said Locke, the human mind is a *tabula rasa* (a blank slate) on which are imprinted sensations derived from contact with the phenomenal world. For Locke, knowledge is derived from experience, which he defines as a process of gathering information through our senses and then reflecting on our sensory perceptions.

> Let us then suppose the Mind to be, as we say, white Paper, void of all Characters, without any *Ideas;* How comes it to be furnished? . . . Whence has it all the materials of reason and Knowledge? To this I answer, in one word, From *Experience:* In that, all our Knowledge is founded; and from that it ultimately derives it self. Our Observation employ'd either about external, *sensible Objects; or about the internal Operations of our Minds, perceived and reflected on by our selves, is that, which supplies our Understandings with all the materials of thinking.* These two are the Fountains of Knowledge, from whence all the Ideas we have, or can naturally have, do spring.[11]

Locke's theory of knowledge had profound implications. Embracing Locke's optimistic view of human nature, the philosophes thought that he had discovered the fundamental principles governing the human mind, an achievement comparable to Newton's discovery of the laws governing physical bodies. If there are no innate ideas, said the philosophes, then human beings, contrary to Christian doctrine, are not born with original sin, are not depraved by nature. All that individuals are derives from their particular experiences. If people are provided with a proper environment and education, they will behave morally; they will become intelligent and productive citizens. By the proper use of their reason, people could bring their beliefs, their conduct, and their institutions into harmony with natural law. This was how the reform-minded philosophes interpreted Locke. They preferred to believe that evil stemmed from faulty institutions and poor education, both of which could be remedied, rather than from a defective human nature.

Christianity Assailed: The Search for a Natural Religion

The philosophes waged an unremitting assault on traditional Christianity, denouncing it for harboring superstition, promulgating unreason, and fostering fanaticism and persecution. Relying on the facts of experience, as Bacon had taught, the philosophes dismissed miracles, angels, and devils as violations of nature's laws and figments of the imagination, which could not be substantiated by the norms of evidence. Applying the Cartesian spirit of careful reasoning to the Bible, they pointed out flagrant discrepancies between various biblical passages and rejected as preposterous the theologians' attempts to resolve these contradictions. With science as an ally, the philosophes challenged Christianity's claim that it possessed infallible truths, and they ridiculed theologians for wrangling over pointless issues and for compelling obedience to doctrines that defied reason.

Moreover, the philosophes assailed Christianity for viewing human nature as evil and human beings as helpless without God's assistance, for focusing on heaven at the expense of human happiness on earth, and for impeding the acquisition of useful knowledge by proclaiming the higher authority of dogma and revelation. The philosophes argued that people, frightened and confused by religion, were being held in subjugation by the clergy. Therefore, to establish an enlightened society, clerical power must be broken, Christian dogmas repudiated, and the fanaticism that produced the horrors of the Crusades, the Inquisition, and the religious wars purged from the European soul.

Many Christian dogmas are incomprehensible, yet Christians have slaughtered one another to enforce obedience to these doctrines, said the recognized leader of the French Enlightenment, François Marie Arouet (1694–1778), known to the world as Voltaire (see chapter opening). Few of the philosophes had a better mind and none had a sharper wit. Living in exile in Britain in the late 1720s, Voltaire acquired a great admiration for English liberty, commerce, science, and religious toleration. Voltaire's angriest words were directed against established Christianity, to which he attributed many of the ills of French society. He regarded Christianity as "the Christ-worshiping superstition," which someday would be destroyed "by the weapons of reason."[12]

Although some philosophes were atheists, most were deists, including Voltaire and Thomas Paine (1737–1809), the English–American radical. *Deists* sought to fashion a natural religion in accordance with reason and science, and they tried to adapt the Christian tradition to the requirements of the new science. They denied that the Bible was God's revelation, rejected clerical authority, and dismissed Christian mysteries, prophecies, and miracles—including the virgin birth, Jesus walking on water, and the Resurrection—as violations of a lawful natural order. They did consider it reasonable that this magnificently structured universe, operating with clockwork precision, was designed and created by an all-wise Creator. However, once God had set the universe in motion, he refrained from interfering with its operations. Thus, deists were at odds with Newton, who allowed for divine intervention in the world.

For deists, the essence of religion was morality—a commitment to justice and humanity—and not adherence to rituals, doctrines, or clerical authority. In *The Age of Reason* (1794–1795), Paine declared: "I believe in the equality of man; and I believe that religious duties consist in doing justice, loving mercy, and endeavoring to make our fellow-creatures happy."[13] Deists deemed it reasonable that after death, those who had fulfilled God's moral law would be rewarded, whereas those who had not would be punished.

Freedom of Conscience and Thought

The philosophes regarded religious persecution—whose long and bloodstained history included the burning of heretics in the Middle Ages, the slaughter of Jews and Muslims during the First Crusade, and the massacres of the religious wars—as humanity's most depraved offense against reason. Although the worst excesses of religious fanaticism had dissipated by the eighteenth century, examples of religious persecution still abounded, particularly in Catholic lands. In his pleas for tolerance, Voltaire spoke for all the philosophes:

> I shall never cease . . . to preach tolerance from the housetops . . . until persecution is no more. The progress of reason is slow, the roots of prejudice lie deep. Doubtless, I shall never see the fruits of my efforts, but they are seeds which may one day germinate.[14]

An issue closely related to religious intolerance was censorship, a serious and ever-present problem for the philosophes. After the publication of Voltaire's *English Letters,* his printer was arrested and the book confiscated and publicly burned as irreligious. On another occasion, when the author-

ities harassed Voltaire, he commented, "It is easier for me to write books than to get them published."[15] *On the Mind* (1758), by Claude-Adrien Helvetius (1715–1771), was burned by the public executioner because ecclesiastical and ministerial authorities thought it was a threat to religion and constituted authority.

In 1784, the German philosopher Immanuel Kant (1724–1804) published an essay entitled *What Is Enlightenment?* in which he contended that the Enlightenment marked a new way of thinking and eloquently affirmed the Enlightenment's confidence in and commitment to reason. In the introductory paragraph, he wrote:

> Enlightenment is man's leaving his self-caused immaturity. Immaturity is the incapacity to use one's intelligence without the guidance of another. Such immaturity is self-caused if it is not caused by lack of intelligence, but by lack of determination and courage to use one's intelligence without being guided by another. *Sapere Aude!* [Dare to be wise!]* Have the courage to use your own intelligence! is therefore the motto of the enlightenment.[16]

Kant went on to argue that "all that is required for this enlightenment is . . . the freedom for man to make *public* use of his reason in all matters,"[17] whether it be in the realm of scholarship, education, or politics, but especially in religion.

Denis Diderot (1713–1784) was the principal editor of the thirty-eight-volume *Encyclopedia,* begun during the 1740s, which attempted to bring together all human knowledge and to propagate Enlightenment ideas. More than 150 leading Enlightenment thinkers contributed numerous articles on science and technology, but only a limited number of articles concerned theological questions—attesting to the new interests of eighteenth-century intellectuals. At times, the French authorities suspended publication, and following the appearance of the first two volumes, they condemned the work for containing "maxims that would tend to destroy royal authority, foment a spirit of independence and revolt . . . and lay the foundations for the corruption of morals and religion."[18] In 1759, Pope Clement XIII condemned the *Encyclopedia* for having "scandalous doctrines [and] inducing scorn for religion."[19] It required careful diplomacy and clever ruses to finish the project and still incorporate ideas considered dangerous by religious and governmental authorities. With the project's completion in 1772, Diderot

---

* "Dare to be wise!" was the motto of the Society of the Friends of Truth, a group of German scholars during the Enlightenment.

and Enlightenment opinion triumphed over clerical, royal, and aristocratic censors.

An article in the *Encyclopedia*, "The Press," conveys the philosophes' yearning for freedom of thought and expression. For them, the term *press* designated more than newspapers and journals; it encompassed everything in print, particularly books.

> People ask if freedom of the press is advantageous or prejudicial to a state. The answer is not difficult. It is of the greatest importance to conserve this practice in all states founded on liberty. I would even say that the disadvantages of this liberty are so inconsiderable compared to the advantages that this ought to be the common right of the universe, and it is certainly advisable to authorize its practices in all governments.[20]

Political Thought of the French Philosophes

Besides established religion, the philosophes identified another source of the evil that beset humanity: despotism. If human beings are to achieve happiness, they must extirpate revealed religion and check the power of their rulers. "Every age has its dominant idea," wrote Diderot; "that of our age seems to be Liberty."[21] Central to the political outlook of the philosophes was the conviction that political solutions could be found for the ills that afflicted society. Affirming John Locke's theory that government had an obligation to protect the natural rights of its citizens, the philosophes generally favored constitutional government that protected citizens from the abuse of power. With the notable exception of Rousseau, the philosophes' concern for liberty did not lead them to embrace democracy, for they put little trust in the masses. Several philosophes, notably Voltaire, placed their confidence in reforming despots, such as Frederick II (the Great) of Prussia, who were sympathetic to enlightened ideas. However, the philosophes were less concerned with the form of government— monarchy or republic—than with preventing the authorities from abusing their power.

MONTESQUIEU The contribution of Charles Louis de Secondat, baron de la Brède et de Montesquieu (1689–1755), to political theory rests essentially on his *The Spirit of the Laws* (1748). Asserting that the study of political and social behavior should be based on empirical studies, Montesquieu concluded that different climactic and geographic conditions and different national customs, habits, religions, and institutions give each nation a particular character; each society requires constitutional forms and laws that pay heed to the character of its people. Montesquieu's

effort to explain social and political behavior empirically—to found a science of society based on the model of natural science—makes him a forerunner of modern sociology.

Montesquieu regarded despotism as a pernicious form of government, corrupt by its very nature, for the despot, ruling as he wishes and unchecked by law, knows nothing of moderation and institutionalizes cruelty and violence. To safeguard liberty from despotism, Montesquieu advocated the principle of separation of powers. In every government, said Montesquieu, there are three sorts of powers: legislative, executive, and judiciary. When one person or one body exercises all three powers—if the same body both prosecutes and judges, for example—liberty cannot be preserved. Where one person or body monopolizes sovereignty, power is abused and political liberty is denied. In a good government, one power balances and checks another power, an argument that impressed the framers of the U.S. Constitution.

Several of Montesquieu's ideals were absorbed into the liberal tradition—constitutional government and the rule of law, separation of powers, freedom of thought, religious toleration, and protection of individual liberty. The conservative tradition drew on Montesquieu's respect for traditional ways of life and his opposition to sudden reforms that ignored a people's history and culture.

VOLTAIRE Like Montesquieu, Voltaire sought to introduce several reforms into France, including freedom of the press, religious toleration, a fair system of criminal justice, proportional taxation, and curtailment of the privileges of the clergy and nobility. Voltaire, however, was not a systematic political theorist, but rather a propagandist and polemicist, who hurled pointed barbs at all the abuses of French society. Nevertheless, Voltaire's writings do contain ideas that form a coherent political theory, which in many ways expresses the outlook of the Enlightenment.

Voltaire disdained arbitrary power because it is based on human whim rather than on established law. He described a prince who imprisons or executes his subjects unjustly and without due process as "nothing but a highway robber who is called 'Your Majesty.'" For Voltaire, freedom consists of being governed by an established and standard code of law that applies equally to all. Without the rule of law, wrote Voltaire, there is no liberty of person, no freedom of thought or of religion, no protection of personal property, no impartial judiciary, and no protection from arbitrary arrest. Although Voltaire did not advocate revolution to achieve his goals, he did favor reforming society

Figure 17.2   *Panthéon.* Jacques-Germain Soufflot began his work in 1757, but died before it could be completed in 1789. He designed it in the shape of a Greek cross, which is capped by a magnificent dome. The structure is 427 feet long, 269 feet wide, and 272 feet high (130 x 82 x 83 m). The Panthéon's Neoclassical styling is evident in the peristyle of Corinthian columns. *(Foto Marburg/Art Resource, NY)*

through the advancement of reason and the promotion of science and technology. Nonetheless, he was no democrat. Voltaire had little confidence in the capacities of the common people, whom he saw as prone to superstition and fanaticism.

As a testament to Voltaire's greatness as a thinker, when the French *Panthéon* (Figure 17.2) became the repository for the mortal remains of great French national heroes, his coffin was moved there amid great pomp and ceremony, including a cortege of people adorned in garments reminiscent of Roman antiquity, and a chest full of Voltaire's writings.

ROUSSEAU In stark contrast to Voltaire, the Geneva-born French thinker Jean Jacques Rousseau (1712–1778) was an advocate of direct democracy. In 1762, he began *The Social Contract* with the stirring words: "Man is born free and everywhere he is in chains."[22] Rousseau considered the modern state to be unjust and corrupt, because it was dominated by the rich and the powerful, who used it to further their own interests

and to oppress the weak, who knew only misery. In Rousseau's view, the state deprived human beings of their natural freedom and fostered a selfish individualism, which undermined feelings of mutuality and concern for the common good.

Rousseau wanted the state to be a genuine democracy, a moral association that bound people together in freedom, equality, and civic devotion. For Rousseau, human character was ennobled when people cooperated with each other and cared for one another, fulfilling their moral potential not in isolation, but as committed members of the community. In *The Social Contract*, he sought to re-create the community spirit and the political freedom that characterized the ancient Greek city–state, the polis.

Rousseau proposed that each person unconditionally surrender all his rights to the community as a whole and submit to its authority. To prevent the assertion of private interests over the common good, Rousseau wanted the state to be governed in accordance with ***the general will***—an underlying principle that expressed what was best for the community. He did not conceive of the general will as a majority or even a unanimous vote, both of which could be wrong. Rather, it was a plainly visible truth, easily discerned through common sense and reason and by listening to one's heart. Therefore, just and enlightened citizens, imbued with public spirit, will have the good sense and moral awareness to legislate in accordance with the general will.

The state Rousseau envisioned was a direct democracy, like that of ancient Athens, in which the citizens themselves, not their representatives, constituted the lawmaking body. Consequently, the governed and the government were one and the same. Rousseau condemned arbitrary and despotic monarchy, the divine-right theory of kings, and the traditional view that people should be governed by their betters, lords and clergy, who were entitled to special privileges. He granted sovereignty to the people as a whole and affirmed the principle of equality.

Rousseau remains a leading theorist of democratic thought. His critics assert that his political thought, whose goal is a body of citizens who think alike, buttresses a dangerous collectivism and even totalitarianism. These critics argue that Rousseau did not place constitutional limitations on sovereignty or erect safeguards to protect individual and minority rights from a potentially tyrannical majority. They note, too, that Rousseau rejected entirely the Lockean principle that citizens possess rights independently of the state, as well as the right to act against the state.

Enlightened Economics

In *The Wealth of Nations* (1776), Adam Smith (1732–1790), professor of moral philosophy in Scotland, attacked the theory of mercantilism, which held that a state's wealth was determined by the amount of gold and silver it possessed. According to this theory, to build up its reserves of precious metals, the state should promote domestic industries, encourage exports, and discourage imports. Mercantilist theory called for government regulation of the economy so that the state could compete successfully with other nations for a share of the world's scarce resources. Smith argued that the real basis of a country's wealth was measured by the quantity and quality of its goods and services and not by its storehouse of precious metals. Government intervention, he said, retards economic progress; it reduces the real value of the annual produce of the nation's land and labor. On the other hand, when people pursue their own interests—when they seek to better their condition—they fos-

ter economic expansion, which benefits the whole society. However, this is not a result of the intention of the individual, but rather, it is a consequence of the "invisible hand" of the marketplace.

> By preferring the support of domestic to that of foreign industry, he intends only his own security; and by directing that industry in such a manner as its produce may be of the greatest value, he intends only his own gain, and he is in this, as in many other cases, led by an invisible hand to promote an end which was no part of his intention . . . . By pursuing his own interest he frequently promotes that of the society more effectually than when he really intends to promote it.[23]

Smith limited the state's authority to maintaining law and order, administering justice, and defending the nation. The concept of *laissez faire*—that government should not interfere with the market—became a core principle of nineteenth-century liberal thought.

Psychology, Education, and Social Reform

The philosophes rejected the Christian belief that human beings are endowed with a sinful nature, a consequence of Adam and Eve's disobedience of God. Influenced by the epistemology of John Locke, the philosophes generally believed in individuals' essential goodness and in their capacity for moral improvement. "Nature has not made us evil," wrote Diderot, "it is bad education, bad models, bad legislation that corrupt us."[24] And Voltaire declared that a person is "born neither good nor wicked; education, example, the government into which he is thrown—in short, occasion of every kind—determines him to virtue or vice."[25] But because they knew from experience that human beings behave wickedly and seem hopelessly attached to nonrational modes of thinking, they retained a certain pessimism about human nature.

The most important work of Enlightenment educational thought was Rousseau's *Émile* (1762), in which he suggested educational reforms that would instill in children self-confidence, self-reliance, and emotional security—necessary qualities if they were to become productive adults and responsible citizens. If the young are taught to think for themselves, said Rousseau, they will learn to cherish personal freedom. A strong faith in the essential goodness of human nature underlay Rousseau's educational philosophy. He also assumed that youngsters have an equal capacity to learn and that differences in intelligence are due largely to environmental factors.

Rousseau understood that children should not be treated like little adults, for children have their own ways of thinking and feeling. He railed against those who robbed children of the joys and innocence of childhood by chaining them to desks, ordering them about, and filling their heads with rote learning. Instead, he urged that children experience direct contact with the world to develop their body and senses and their curiosity, ingenuity, resourcefulness, and imagination. It is the whole child that concerned Rousseau.

Dedication to one's family, as defined by Rousseau, is evident in the famous painting, *Cornelia Pointing to Her Children as Her Treasures* (Figure 17.3), which was executed by the Swiss-born artist Angelica Kauffmann (1741–1807), a child prodigy in both music and painting, who produced her first commissioned work at the age of thirteen and who, in 1768, helped to found the British Royal Academy of Arts. Kauffmann portrays Cornelia, the Roman mother of Tiberius and Gaius, as a wealthy, aristocratic woman showing off her "treasures"—her children. A humanitarian spirit, which no doubt owed something to Christian compassion, pervaded the outlook of the philosophes. Convinced that human nature was essentially virtuous and that human beings were capable of benevolent feelings toward each other, the philosophes proposed a number of social reforms. They attacked torture, commonly used to obtain confessions in many European lands, cruel punishments for criminals, slavery, and war.

In *On Crimes and Punishments* (1764), Cesare Beccaria (1738–1794), an Italian economist and criminologist inspired in part by Montesquieu, condemned torture as inhuman, "a criterion fit for a cannibal."[26] He saw it as an irrational way of determining guilt or innocence, for an innocent person, unable to withstand the agonies of torture, will confess to anything, and a criminal with a high threshold for pain will be exonerated. Influenced by Beccaria's work, reform-minded jurists, legislators, and ministers called for the elimination of torture from codes of criminal justice, and several European lands abolished torture in the eighteenth century.

Though not pacifists, the philosophes denounced war as barbaric and an affront to reason. They deemed it to be a scourge promoted by power-hungry monarchs and supported by fanatical clergy, wicked army leaders, and ignorant commoners. Voltaire condemned the idea that God might ordain the outcome of a war, and he ridiculed the rituals of war. In addition, the article "Peace," in Diderot's *Encyclopedia*, described war in harsh terms, as

the fruit of man's depravity; it is a convulsive and violent sickness of the body politic. . . . [It] depop-

ulates the nation, causes the reign of disorder. . . makes the freedom and property of citizens uncertain . . . disturbs and causes the neglect of commerce; land becomes uncultivated and abandoned. . . . If reason governed men and had the influence over the heads of nations that it deserves, we would never see them inconsiderately surrender themselves to the fury of war; they would not show that ferocity that characterizes wild beasts.[27]

Montesquieu, Voltaire, Adam Smith, Benjamin Franklin, Thomas Paine, and other philosophes condemned slavery and the slave trade. For example, in Book 15 of *The Spirit of the Laws*, Montesquieu scornfully refuted all justifications for slavery. Ultimately, he said, slavery, which violates the fundamental principle of justice underlying the universe, derived from base human desires to dominate and exploit other human beings. In 1780, Paine helped draft the act abolishing slavery in Pennsylvania. An article in the *Encyclopedia*, "The Slave Trade," denounced slavery as a violation of the individual's natural rights:

If commerce of this kind can be justified by a moral principle, there is no crime, however atrocious it may be, that cannot be made legitimate. . . . Men and their liberty are not objects of commerce; they can be neither sold nor bought. . . . There is not, therefore, a single one of these unfortunate people regarded only as slaves who does not have the right to be declared free.[28]

In spite of their humanitarianism, the philosophes continued to view women as intellectually and morally inferior to men, even though they often enjoyed the company of intelligent and sophisticated women in the famous salons. Although some philosophes did argue for female emancipation, they were the exception. Most concurred with David Hume (1711–1776), a Scottish skeptic, who held that "nature has subjected" women to men and that their "inferiority and infirmities are absolutely incurable."[29] Rousseau, who also believed that nature had granted men power over women, regarded traditional domesticity as a woman's proper role.

I would a thousand times rather have a homely girl, simply brought up, than a learned lady and a wit who would make a literary circle of my house and install herself as its president. A female wit is a scourge to her husband, her children, her friends, her servants, to everybody. From the lofty height of her genius, she scorns every womanly duty, and she is always trying to make a man of herself.[30]

Figure 17.3   Angelica Kauffmann, *Cornelia Pointing to Her Children as Her Treasures*, 1785, oil on canvas, 40 x 50" (101.6 x 127 cm), Virginia Museum of Fine Arts, Richmond.   Kauffmann portrays Cornelia, the Roman mother of Tiberius and Gaius, as a wealthy, aristocratic woman showing off her "treasures"—her children. Not only are the names of her subjects classical, but so too are their dress and the background of the painting. *(Angelica Kauffmann, Cornelia Pointing to her Children as her Treasures, ca. 1785.   Oil on canvas, 40"H x 50"W.   Virginia Museum of Fine Arts, Richmond.   The Adolph D. And Wilkins C. Williams Fund.   Photo: Katherine Wetzel   © Virginia Museum of Fine Arts)*

Nevertheless, by clearly articulating the ideals of liberty and equality, the philosophes made a women's movement possible. The growing popularity of these ideals could not escape women, who measured their own position by them. Moreover, by their very nature, these ideals were expansive. Denying them to women would ultimately be seen as an indefensible contradiction.

Thus, Mary Wollstonecraft's *Vindication of the Rights of Woman,* written under the influence of the French Revolution, protested against the prevailing subordination and submissiveness of women and the limited opportunities afforded them to cultivate their minds. If women were also endowed with reason, why should men alone determine the standards and ground rules, she asked pointedly. She reminded enlightened thinkers that the same arbitrary power that they objected to when wielded by monarchs and slave owners they condoned when exercised by husbands in domestic life. She considered this power to be an act of tyranny, allowing women "to be excluded from a participation of the natural rights of mankind."[31]

The Idea of Progress

The philosophes were generally optimistic about humanity's future progress. Two main assumptions contributed to this optimism. First, accepting Locke's theory of knowledge, the philosophes attributed evil to a flawed but remediable environment, not to an inherently wicked human nature. Hopeful that a reformed environment would bring out the best in people, they looked forward to a day when reason would prevail over superstition, prejudice, intolerance, and tyranny. Second, the philosophes' veneration of science led them to believe that the progressive advancement of knowledge would promote material and moral progress.

A work written near the end of the century epitomized the philosophes' vision of the future: *Sketch for a Historical Picture of the Progress of the Human Mind* (1794) by Marie Jean Antoine Nicolas Caritat, Marquis de Condorcet (1743–1794). A mathematician and historian of science and a contributor to the *Encyclopedia,* Condorcet campaigned for religious toleration, the abolition of slavery, and the emancipation of women in his

Plea for the Citizenship of Women (1791). In *Sketch,* Condorcet lauded recent advances in knowledge that enabled reason to "lift her chains (and) shake herself free"[32] from superstition and tyranny. Passionately affirming the Enlightenment's confidence in reason and science, Condorcet expounded a theory of continuous and indefinite human improvement. He pointed toward a future golden age, characterized by the triumph of reason and freedom.

> Our hopes for the future condition of the human race can be subsumed under three important heads: the abolition of inequality between nations, the progress of equality within each nation, and the true perfection of mankind. . . . The time will therefore come when the sun will shine only on free men who know no other master but their reason; when tyrants and slaves, priests and their stupid or hypocritical instruments will exist only in works of history and on the stage; and we shall think of them only to pity their victims and their dupes; to maintain ourselves in a state of vigilance by thinking on their excesses; and to learn how to recognize and so to destroy, by force of reason, the first seeds of tyranny and superstition, should they ever dare to reappear amongst us.[33]

But the philosophes were not starry-eyed dreamers. They knew that progress was painful, slow, and reversible. "Let us weep and wail over the lot of philosophy," wrote Diderot. "We preach wisdom to the deaf and we are still far indeed from the age of reason."[34] Similarly, Voltaire's *Candide* (discussed in Chapter 18) was a protest against a naive optimism that ignored the granite might of human meanness, ignorance, and irrationality.

The Enlightenment and the Modern Mentality

The philosophes articulated core principles of the modern outlook. Asserting that human beings are capable of thinking independently of authority, they insisted on a thoroughgoing rational and secular interpretation of nature and society. They critically scrutinized authority and tradition and valued science and technology as a means for promoting human betterment. Above all, they sought to emancipate the mind from the bonds of ignorance and superstition and to rescue people from intolerance, cruelty, and oppression. Because of their efforts, torture (which states and Christian churches had endorsed and practiced) was eventually abolished in Western lands, and religious toleration and freedom of speech and of the press

became the accepted norms. Those who fought against the slave trade and called for emancipation utilized the arguments that the philosophes marshaled against slavery. Enlightenment economic thought, particularly Adam Smith's *Wealth of Nations,* gave theoretical support to a market economy based on supply and demand—an outlook that fostered commercial and industrial expansion. The separation of church and state, a basic principle of modern political life, owes much to the philosophes, who frequently cited the dangers of politics inflamed by religious passions. The philosophes' denunciation of despotism and championing of natural rights, equality under the law, and constitutional government are the chief foundations of modern liberal government, including the new United States.

The philosophes broke with the traditional Christian view of human nature and the purpose of life. In that view, men and women were born in sin; suffering and misery were divinely ordained, and relief could come only from God; social inequality was instituted by God; and for many, eternal damnation was a deserved final consequence. In contrast, the philosophes saw injustice and suffering as man-made problems that could be solved through reason; they expressed confidence in people's ability to attain happiness by improving the conditions of their earthly existence and articulated a theory of human progress that did not require divine assistance.

To be sure, the promise of the Enlightenment has not been achieved. More education for more people and the spread of constitutional government have not eliminated fanaticism and superstition, violence and war, or evil and injustice. In the light of twenty-first-century events, it is difficult to subscribe to Condorcet's belief in linear progress. As American historian Peter Gay observes:

> The world has not turned out the way the philosophes wished and half expected that it would. Old fanaticisms have been more intractable, irrational forces more inventive than the philosophes were ready to conjecture in their darkest moments. Problems of race, of class, of nationalism, of boredom and despair in the midst of plenty have emerged almost in defiance of the philosophes' philosophy. We have known horrors, and may know horrors, that the men of the Enlightenment did not see in their nightmares.[35]

Nevertheless, the philosophes' achievement should not be diminished. Their ideals became an intrinsic part of the liberal-democratic tradition and inspired nineteenth- to twenty-first-century reformers. The spirit of the Enlightenment will always remain indispensable to all those who cherish the traditions of reason and freedom.

Key Terms

heliocentric theory	natural rights
Congregation of the Index	*tabula rasa*
principle of inertia	deists
inductive approach	the general will
deductive approach	*laissez-faire*

Notes

1. *Luther's Works: Volume 54, Table Talk*, Theodore G. Tappert, (Philadelphia: Fortress Press, 1967), pp. 192–193.
2. Galileo Galilei, *The Starry Messenger*, in *Discoveries and Opinions of Galileo*, trans. and ed. Stillman Drake (Garden City, N.Y.: Doubleday Anchor Books, 1957), p. 31.
3. Galileo Galilei, *The Assayer*, in *Discoveries and Opinions*, pp. 237–238.
4. Galileo Galilei, "Letter to the Grand Duchess Christina," in *Discoveries and Opinions*, p. 183.
5. Descartes, *Discourse on Method and the Meditations*, trans. F. E. Sutcliffe (London: Penguin Books, 1968), pp. 53–54.
6. Quoted in Frank E. Manuel, *Age of Reason* (Ithaca, N.Y.: Cornell University Press, 1951), p. 28.
7. *The English Works of Thomas Hobbes*, ed. William Molesworth. Vol. III. Second Reprint (Darmstadt, Germany: Scientia Verlag Aalen, 1966), p. 587.
8. Ibid., p. 158.
9. John Locke, *Two Treatises of Government*, ed. Peter Laslett (Cambridge: University Press, 1963), chap. 19, sec. 222, pp. 430–431.
10. Ibid., chap. 6, sec. 61, p. 326.
11. John Locke, *An Essay Concerning Human Understanding*, ed. Peter H. Nidditch (Oxford: Clarendon Press, 1975), Book II, chap. I, p. 104.
12. Quoted in Ben Ray Redman, ed., *The Portable Voltaire* (New York: Viking Press, 1949), p. 26.
13. Thomas Paine, *The Age of Reason* (New York: Eckler, 1892), p. 5.
14. Voltaire, "Letter to M. Bertrand," in *Candide and Other Writings*, ed. Haskell M. Block (New York: Modern Library, 1956), p. 525.
15. Quoted in Peter Gay, *Voltaire's Politics* (New York: Random House, Vintage Books, 1965), p. 71.
16. *The Philosophy of Kant: Immanuel Kant's Moral and Political Writing*, ed. Carl J. Friedrich (New York: Random House, 1949), p. 132.
17. Ibid., p. 134.
18. Quoted in Stephen J. Gendzier, ed. and trans., *Denis Diderot's The Encyclopedia Selections* (New York: Harper Torchbooks, 1967), p. xxv.
19. Ibid., p. xxvi.
20. Excerpted in Ibid., p. 199.
21. Quoted in Paul Hazard, *European Thought in the Eighteenth Century* (New Haven: Yale University Press, 1954), p. 174.
22. Jean Jacques Rousseau, The Social Contract, in *The Social Contract and Discourses*, ed. and trans. G. D. H. Cole (New York: Dutton, 1950), bk. 1, chap. 1, p. 3.
23. Adam Smith, *An Inquiry into the Nature and Causes of the Wealth of Nations*, The Harvard Classics, ed. Charles W. Eliot (Danbury, Conn.: Grolier Enterprises Corp., 1984), p. 335.
24. Quoted in Peter Gay, *The Enlightenment: An Interpretation*, vol. 2, *The Science of Freedom* (New York: Vintage Books, 1966), p. 170.
25. Quoted in Steven Seidman, *Liberalism and the Origins of European Social Theory* (Berkeley: University of California Press, 1983), p. 30.
26. Cesare Beccaria, *On Crimes and Punishments*, trans. Henry Paolucci (Indianapolis: Library of Liberal Arts, 1963), p. 32.
27. Excerpted in Gendzier, *Diderot's Encyclopedia Selections*, pp. 183–184.
28. Excerpted in Ibid., pp. 229–230.
29. Quoted in Bonnie S. Anderson and Judith P. Zinsser, *A History of Their Own* (New York: Harper & Row, 1988), 2:113.
30. Jean Jacques Rousseau, *Emile*, trans. Barbara Foxley (London: Dent, Everyman's Library, 1974), p. 370.
31. Mary Wollstonecraft, *Vindication of the Rights of Woman* (London: Dent, 1929), pp. 11–12.
32. Antoine Nicolas de Condorcet, *Sketch for a Historical Picture of the Progress of the Human Mind*, trans. June Barraclough (London: Weidenfeld & Nicholas, 1955), p. 124.
33. Ibid., pp. 173–179.
34. Quoted in Gay, *The Enlightenment*, 1:20.
35. Gay, *The Enlightenment*, 2:567.

18

The Arts in the Age of Enlightenment

THE PHILOSOPHES OF THE ENLIGHTENMENT rebelled against dogmatic religious belief, metaphysical speculation, and the repression of human freedom. Enlightenment thought was secular, empirical, skeptical, pragmatic, and humane. These trends also found expression in the arts of the age. Indeed, several of the French philosophes were involved in the arts. Voltaire, Montesquieu, Diderot, Rousseau, and others wrote important literary works, and Diderot was an insightful art critic. Literary figures, particularly the French philosophes, produced works that attacked the intolerance, follies, and superstitions of their day. But the most popular literature was a type of prose that emphasized balance, refinement, coherence, and decorum.

Eighteenth-century artists and musicians generally abandoned the passion, mysticism, and somberness, as well as the grandeur, monumentality, and heavily modeled figures of the Baroque style. Instead, they favored a new style called the Rococo, characterized by elegance, refinement, grace, and fancifulness. Rococo music, the musical complement to Rococo art, was generally free of technical complexities and devoid of sweeping themes or pretentious passions so characteristic of Baroque styling.

Rococo and Neoclassicism were the principal artistic movements of the eighteenth century. The Romantic Movement, which dominated European cultural life in the early nineteenth century, also had roots in the eighteenth century. These movements were not entirely consecutive, but rather were overlapping developments. In this chapter, we discuss primarily the Rococo, which began with the reign of Louis XV (1715–1774) and lasted throughout the century. However, following excavations of Roman ruins in the late 1730s and 1740s, the public began to shun the fanciful ornamentation of the Rococo and to embrace both the virtues and the rational principles of classical antiquity, which stressed the primacy of intelligible form. In many ways *Neoclassicism* was the counterpart of the philosophes' stress on reason. This chapter treats the antecedents of Neoclassicism; the revolutionary Neoclassical style, which is directly associated with the French Revolution, is discussed in Chapter 19. Romanticism, which valued human emotions and drew inspiration from nature's wonders, was a reaction against the philosophes' emphasis on analytical reason. This crucial period in European cultural life will be discussed in Chapter 20.

The aristocracy set the standard in the arts, and the middle class copied aristocratic costumes, manners, and affectations. But by the end of the century, the aristocracy was imitating the middle class. As patronage waned, the modern public audience began to emerge as a powerful influence on the arts. This was a direct result of the burgeoning middle class, which initiated the popularization of the arts—a trend that continues to the present day. The artistic

Jean-Baptiste-Siméon Chardin, House of Cards, c. 1735, oil on canvas, 32-3/8 x 26 (82.2 x 66cm). National Gallery of Art, Washington, D.C.

The seriousness and concentration of this young child reflect the values of the middle class, as he arranges his cards like a row of dominoes on a table. Chardin's sensitive portrayal suggests that the slightest disturbance will cause the cards to fall.

(National Gallery of Art, Washington, Andrew W. Mellon Collection, Photograph @ 2002 Board of Trustees)

I don't know what to say about this man. Degradation of taste, color, composition, character, expression, and drawing have kept pace with moral depravity. What can we expect this artist to throw onto the canvas? What he has in his imagination. And what can be in the imagination of a man who spends his life with prostitutes of the basest kind? . . . I'd say this man has no conception of true grace; I'd say he's never encountered truth; I'd say the ideas of delicacy, forthrightness, innocence, and simplicity have become almost foreign to him.[28]

FRAGONARD   Although Boucher was his true mentor, Jean-Honoré Fragonard (1732–1806) first studied during 1751, somewhat briefly and unhappily, with Jean-Baptiste-Siméon Chardin (see following). In 1756, Fragonard traveled to Rome to further his education, where he admired the works of Raphael (see Chapter 13) and his Italian contemporary Giovanni Battista Tiepolo (see later discussion). By 1765, when Fragonard painted his version of the *Bathers* (Figure 18.3)— with its luxuriant vegetation, spiraling clouds, and voluptuous, Rubenesque nudes—he had developed his own unique style of painting. Fragonard's

brushwork displays an exuberance lacking in Boucher's smooth surfaces; his figures are reminiscent of Rubens' sculpturesque modeling of the human form; and the landscapes of his backgrounds anticipate those of nineteenth-century Romantic artists (see Chapter 20). During the 1770s, Fragonard replaced Boucher as the painter of decorative interiors. His most famous works in this medium were the fourteen canvases executed for Madame du Barry (1743–1793), Louis XV's favorite mistress, who was executed during the French Revolution. Madame du Barry, however, rejected the paintings and commissioned another series of paintings to be done in the new, Neoclassical style (see Chapter 19) that ascended as Fragonard's fortunes waned.

CHARDIN   The forced sentimentality and gaiety of the Rococo provoked a reaction that gave rise to paintings emphasizing humble, everyday life, infused with a sense of moral purpose. The leading moral genre painter in France was Jean-Baptiste-Siméon Chardin (1699–1779), the early mentor of Fragonard. During his early years, Chardin's artistic output was limited almost exclusively to still lifes—including arrangements of vegetables,

Figure 18.2   François Boucher, *Diana Leaving the Bath*, 1742, oil on canvas, 22 x 28 1/2" (56 x 73 cm), Musée du Louvre, Paris.   Madame de Pompadour was Boucher's devoted patron, and he painted her portrait several times, but he is best remembered for his fanciful depictions of mythological subjects, such as this one, which illustrates Boucher's graceful handling of overt sensuality. *(Louvre/Réunion des Musées Nationaux/Art Resource, NY)*

Figure 18.3   Jean-Honoré Fragonard, *Bathers*, c. 1765, oil on canvas, 25 1/2″ x 31 1/2″ (64.8 x 80 cm), Musée du Louvre, Paris.   Fragonard developed his own unique style of painting with paintings such as this one, replete with luxuriant vegetation, spiraling clouds, and voluptuous Rubenesque nudes. *(Louvre/ Erich Lessing/Art Resource, NY)*

fruits, pots, pans, and musical instruments. These unpretentious objects were associated with middle-class households, and Chardin portrayed them with a serenity and appreciation that stood in direct contrast to the glitz and glamour of princely courts. During the 1730s, as an extension of this type of painting, Chardin began to depict middle-class people engaged in ordinary, everyday tasks—young mothers reading to their children, kitchen maids preparing the evening meal, and governesses educating their young charges. Chardin's renderings are executed in powdery colors of blue, pink, grey, and brown. Moreover, he is careful to regulate the play of light as it casts shadows on his subjects. One of Chardin's most famous moral genre paintings is his *House of Cards* (see chapter opening), done in 1741, which shows a young, middle-class boy arranging his cards like a row of dominoes on a table. Chardin's sensitive portrayal of the scene suggests that the slightest disturbance will cause the cards to fall. Furthermore, the child's seriousness and concentration reflect the values of the middle class. Despite the simplicity of these middle-class, domestic scenes, such paintings did appeal to the French aristocrats. However, by the 1750s, Chardin's star was eclipsed by the work of the more sentimental genre paintings of Jean-Baptiste Greuze (1725–1805). As a consequence, during the 1770s, Chardin focused on pastel portraits.

HOGARTH   The first of the moral genre painters in England was William Hogarth (1697–1764), who combined his satirical wit and his highly developed moral sense with his extraordinary skills as a painter and engraver. His first successes were two series of moralistic paintings, called "progresses"—*The Harlot's Progress* (1732) and *The Rake's Progress* (1735)—which were later duplicated as engravings. Referring to himself as a comic writer of "burlesque," Henry Fielding called his friend Hogarth a "comic history painter," by which he meant one who paints satirically. In the preface to his novel, *Joseph Andrews*, Fielding likens Hogarth's progresses to what the Italians called *caricatura*—the aim of which is "to exhibit monsters, not men; and all distortions and exaggerations whatever are within its proper province." Furthermore, Fielding notes the correlation between himself and Hogarth:

Now, what Caricatura is in painting, Burlesque is in writing; and in the same manner the comic writer and painter correlate to each other. . . . [I]n

Figure 18.4   William Hogarth, first in series—*Marriage à la Mode*, 1743–1745, oil on canvas, 28" x 36" (71.7 x 92.3 cm), The National Gallery, London.   In this series, Hogarth advanced the idea that marriage should be based on love instead of parental arrangement. *(National Gallery, London/The Bridgeman Art Library International)*

the former the painter seems to have the advantage; so it is in the latter infinitely on the side of the writer; for the Monstrous is much easier to paint than describe, and the Ridiculous to describe than to paint. . . . He who should call the ingenious Hogarth a burlesque painter, would, in my opinion, do him very little honour; for sure it is much easier, much less the subject of admiration, to paint a man with a nose, or any other feature of a preposterous size, . . . than to express the affections of men on canvas. It hath been thought a vast commendation of a painter to say his figures seem to breathe; but surely it is a much greater and nobler applause, that they appear to think.[29]

Between 1742 and 1744, Hogarth produced his most popular series—*Marriage à la Mode*—advancing the idea that marriage should be based on love instead of parental arrangement. In April of 1746, Jean-André Rouquet wrote a commentary on *Marriage à la Mode* for his own brother and a friend, which was published in *Gentlemen's Magazine*. Hogarth later paid his former neighbor to transform them into the popular epistolary format of the day. In his commentary—the only contemporary description of Hogarth's own intentions for *Marriage à*

la Mode—Roquet captures the essence of the first of the six scenes (Figure 18.4):

The great find themselves insufficiently rich; the rich believe they are insufficiently great. The latter is the case with the alderman [magistrate] of London, and is also the motive which makes him covet for his daughter the alliance with a great lord, who for his part consents to the alliance only so as to enrich his son. This is what the artist calls a *marriage à la mode.* . . .The figures of the alderman and the earl are in every respect so well characterized in this picture that they explain themselves. The alderman counts his money with a well-to-do air . . . and the earl, full of his title and noble lineage, . . . has an attitude which suggests prideful egotism. . . . Everything about him bears marks of distinction; even his crutches, the humiliating consequence of his infirmities, are decorated with an earl's coronet. . . . For their part, the engaged couple are by no means attentive to one another. He looks in the mirror, takes snuff, and thinks of nothing; she plays nonchalantly with a ring and seems to listen indifferently to what she is being told by a kind of lawyer, who is present in order to execute the marriage articles. Another lawyer cries out in admiration of the building which appears in the distance, and on which the earl has spent his entire fortune, by no means enough to complete it. A troop of idle servants, who are in the courtyard of this building, complete the characterization of the ruinous display which surrounds the earl.[30]

REYNOLDS AND GAINSBOROUGH   Although Hogarth is considered the father of English painting, it was Joshua Reynolds (1723–1792) who established English painting within the European Continental tradition. In 1768, Reynolds was elected as the first president of the Royal Academy of the Arts, and over the next thirty years, he delivered fifteen *Discourses* to the Academy. In these *Discourses*, he developed a theory of art—based on his study of the masterworks of antiquity and the High Renaissance during his stay in Rome between 1749 and 1752—that served as an antecedent for Neoclassicism, discussed in the next chapter. In his inaugural Discourse for the opening of the Royal Academy on January 2, 1769, he recommended:

> [A]n implicit obedience to the *rules of art*, as established by the practice of the great Masters, should be exacted from the young Students. That those models, which have passed through the approbation of ages, should be considered by them as perfect and infallible Guides; as subjects for their imitation, not their criticism.[31]

Reynolds believed that these classical principles could best be expressed by "history" painting—in an epic, or grand, style. Consequently, he incorporated classical poses and mythological subject matter into his portraits of English aristocrats, and his lustrous colors reflect Italian influence.

Figure 18.5   Joshua Reynolds, *Lady Sarah Bunbury Sacrificing to the Graces*, 1765, oil on canvas, 7'10" x 5' (2.42 x 1.53 m), The Art Institute of Chicago, Chicago, Ill.   Adorned in the classical garb of a Roman priestess, Bunbury makes a sacrifice to the Three Graces, who are viewed as the personification of feminine beauty. *(Mr. and Mrs. W. W. Kimball Collection, 1922.4468 (E13314) © Art Institute of Chicago. All Rights Reserved)*

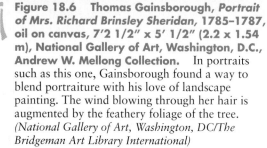

Figure 18.6   Thomas Gainsborough, *Portrait of Mrs. Richard Brinsley Sheridan*, 1785–1787, oil on canvas, 7'2 1/2" x 5' 1/2" (2.2 x 1.54 m), National Gallery of Art, Washington, D.C., Andrew W. Mellong Collection.   In portraits such as this one, Gainsborough found a way to blend portraiture with his love of landscape painting. The wind blowing through her hair is augmented by the feathery foliage of the tree. *(National Gallery of Art, Washington, DC/The Bridgeman Art Library International)*

Figure 18.7 Germain Boffrand, *Salon de la Princesse*, 1732, Hôtel de Soubise, Paris. Rejecting the Baroque styling, Boffrand designed the oval Salon with sculpted stuccoes, carved wood frames, and pastel panels framed with precious metal, all of which is reflected in mirrors. *(Scala/Art Resource, NY)*

Figure 18.8 Johann Balthasar Neumann, *Pilgrimage Church of the Vierzehnheiligen*, 1743–1772, Staffelstein, Germany. Neumann's plan called for seven interlinked ovals, which are so lavishly decorated with arabesques, stucco ornamentations, and wreaths that flat surfaces seem not to exist. *(Scala/Art Resource, NY)*

One of Reynolds's most famous portraits illustrating this style is *Lady Sarah Bunbury Sacrificing to the Graces* (Figure 18.5), painted in 1765. Adorned in the classical garb of a Roman priestess, Bunbury makes a sacrifice to the Three Graces—the personification of feminine beauty. The classicism of the scene is further amplified by the monumental, classical architecture of the background as a reflection of the former glory and grandeur of Rome. Reynolds thus conferred on the English aristocracy noble qualities borrowed from antiquity.

Thomas Gainsborough (1727–1788), like most of the artists of his day, supported his family by painting portraits, but his true passion throughout his lifetime was landscape painting. Gainsborough was a founding member of the Royal Academy, but both the Academy and Reynolds viewed landscape painting as inferior to the depiction of historical events and personages. Nonetheless, after 1759, Gainsborough found a way to blend portraiture with his love of landscape painting, as is evident in his *Portrait of Mrs. Richard Brinsley Sheridan* (Figure 18.6). Her informal pose, framed by a tree, is reminiscent of the portraits by van Dyck (see Chapter 16), but instead of the landscape being of secondary importance, the woman is assimilated by the landscape. Moreover, the feathery foliage of the tree is duplicated by the manner in which Gainsborough paints the wind blowing through the woman's hair. Although the overall effect is achieved by using both the softer colors and the brushwork of the earlier Rococo style, Gainsborough's rhapsodic appreciation of nature foreshadows the work of the great English landscape artists of the nineteenth century—John Constable and Joseph M. W. Turner (see Chapter 20).

KAUFFMANN One of the most important painters to paint in the style of Reynolds was Angelica Kauffmann (1741–1807)(see p. 143). Born in Switzerland, she was a child prodigy in both music and painting, producing her first commissioned work at the age of thirteen. In 1766, Lady Wentworth, the wife of an English ambassador, invited Kauffmann to London, where she became a close friend of Reynolds. During her English period (1766–1781), Kauffmann painted a number of self-portraits, commissioned portraits, and narrative history paintings portraying the virtues of the Roman Republic—a genre typically reserved for her male counterparts. As a result of her perseverance, she was one of the founding members of the British Royal Academy of Arts, established in 1768. Throughout the 1770s, Kauffmann produced large-scale works for the interiors of the homes of many prestigious English aristocrats. Following her marriage in 1781, Kauffmann moved to Rome, where she remained for the rest of her life with her husband, Antonio Zucchi, a Venetian painter.

Architecture

In architecture, the term *Rococo* refers mainly to the styling and decoration of interiors, not to a structural style, and it reached its height in France and Germany. At the same time, in England, the new Palladian school of architecture—named for the Late Renaissance architect Andrea Palladio (1508–1580)—was developing. During the second half of the eighteenth century, the **British Palladian style** served as a precursor to the revival of Neoclassical architecture. Moreover, the advent of Neoclassicism was hastened by the archaeological investigations into the ancient Roman ruins at Herculaneum in 1738 and Pompeii in 1748 and drawings that were made of Paestum in 1750. Collectively, these discoveries ignited the imagination of Europe, and once again, the classical world was in vogue.

BOFFRAND In 1745, Germain Boffrand (1667–1754) published an important book on architecture that aids in our understanding of the movement from the Baroque to the Neoclassical style. Nonetheless, his reputation rests on his *Salon de la Princesse* (Figure 18.7), begun in 1732 and located within the Hôtel de Soubise in Paris, which typified the French Rococo architecture of the day. Boffrand, a pupil of Mansart, was the architect for the Duke of Lorraine. He patterned many of his

monumental buildings after those of his teacher, but favored the delicacy of the Rococo for the styling of the *Salon*, thus rejecting the Baroque styling of both Mansart and Le Vau (see Chapter 16). The oval room—encompassing windows, doorways, and mirrors—is a visual confusion of gold, wood, plaster, and glass. The entire scene of sculpted stuccoes, carved wood frames, and pastel panels framed with precious metal is reflected in mirrors. The chaos of light is further heightened by the light of the candles reflecting off the jewel-like pendants of the chandelier. Some of the greatest painters of the day, including Boucher, decorated the panels above the doors and windows with mythological scenes. For example, the eight corner panels, painted by Charles Joseph Natoire (1700–1777), illustrate the mythical love story of Cupid and Psyche.

NEUMANN The spirit of the German Rococo style is epitomized by the *Pilgrimage Church of the Vierzehnheiligen* (Fourteen Auxiliary Saints), designed by Johann Balthasar Neumann (1687–1753). Built between 1743 and 1772, the church stands on the site where, during the fifteenth century, a shepherd had a vision of the infant Jesus surrounded by fourteen saints known as "the holy helpers" because they aided people in distress. Although the Baroque exterior of the church is somewhat restrained, the interior (Figure 18.8) is exuberantly Rococo. Neumann's plan called for seven interlinked ovals, which are so lavishly decorated with arabesques, stucco ornamentations, and wreaths that flat surfaces seem not to exist. Moreover, the columns have capitals embellished with fanciful gold foliage, as they are paired with the pilasters framing the openings into the side aisles. Finally, the entire scene of undulating motion is illumined by the light streaming in from the gold and white windows of the clerestory.

MUSIC

New Trends in Musical Theory

During the latter part of the eighteenth century, a decisive change took place in the development of musical thought. From the time of Pythagoras, Plato, and Aristotle, throughout the Renaissance, and even during the age of the Baroque, music served as a vehicle for other pursuits. Thus the Greeks could refer to the heavens as the "music of the spheres" because they believed that the mathematical ratios found in music also governed heavenly objects, and they held that musical modes, because of their "curative power," could affect human temperament. Moving away from this position, the music of the eighteenth century exhibited a trend that is decidedly modern: Music should be evaluated for its own intrinsic worth, that is, for its ability to express human emotions and to convey sound that has an aesthetic appeal.

This is seen in the work of Charles Burney (1726–1814), the organist-composer and friend of Samuel Johnson, who, in his monumental work, *A General History of Music from the Earliest Ages to the Present Period* (1789), defined music as "an innocent luxury, unnecessary, indeed, to our existence, but a great improvement and gratification of the sense of hearing."[32] Instead of trying to express grandiose themes—the crucifixion, for example—by using technically complex musical patterns, a practice typical of Baroque composers, Burney wanted music to be appreciated on its own terms and for its own aesthetic qualities. He was particularly critical of J. S. Bach's organ compositions, because of their technical complexity and their dense musical symbolism, including references to the crucifixion, such as the wrapping of Christ's death shroud and the Lutheran catechism. Burney praised the music of his day because of its ability to stir the emotions as never before. He said that this accomplishment was made possible by eliminating opaque symbolism and de-emphasizing the role of the human voice, whose words and connotations often distracted audiences away from beautiful instrumental passages.

The leading French composer and theorist of the eighteenth century, Jean-Philippe Rameau (1683–1764), was virtually unknown as a musician until the age of forty. In 1715, Rameau acceded to the position of organist at the cathedral in Clermont. There he began to investigate, and ultimately to overturn, traditional music theory founded on the ancients' interpretation of melody. In 1722, his pivotal treatise *Traité de l'harmonie (Traits of Harmony)*, brought Rameau immediate fame. His interpretation of music, starting with *harmony* instead of *melody*, has remained the standard for composition up to the present day. Operas and oratorios placed value on the human voice and the words and melodies it sang; now instrumental music was appreciated for the harmony of its own "voices" to express human emotion in conjunction with, or even apart from, the human voice.

Rameau is best known for his harpsichord pieces, but he also composed more than thirty operas and ballets. Between 1748 and 1754, Rameau reached the summit of his career when, in only eight days, he not only composed his masterpiece, *Pygmalion*, but he also wrote music celebrating the birth of the grandson of Louis XV, who would become Louis XVI (1774–1792). Although Rameau was respected by the circle of friends cen-

tered around Diderot, his celebrity waned as the new music, called "Classical," took hold.

Enlightenment Values and the Arts

Any particular historical period has a distinguishing characteristic or style that expresses itself, both in thought and in the arts. For example, early Greek thinkers, rejecting mythical explanations for natural occurrences, attempted a rational analysis of the physical world. The importance given to reason by these early philosophers gradually found expression in all other areas of cultural life—politics, political thought, historiography, drama, music, and art. Thus, the Greek temple is an organized unity obeying mathematical principles of equilibrium and harmony, classical sculpture captures the basic laws that govern life in motion, and vase painting reveals Greek realism and naturalism, a fascination with representing the vivid details of the visible world.

The Christian religion, which was at the center of medieval civilization, was the principal concern not only of philosopher–theologians, but also of artists, writers, and musicians. Scholastic philosophy, which sought to prove through reason the teaching of the church; Dante's *Divine Comedy*, which, in magnificent poetry, captures Christian feeling about heaven and hell; and the Gothic cathedral, which soared to the heavens; all reflect the importance of the religious impulse during the Middle Ages.

The distinguishing feature of the Age of Enlightenment was the confidence placed in human reason and its ability to understand nature and to improve the social world in accordance with rational principles. In treatises, essays, and historical works, the philosophes tirelessly attacked the traditions and institutions of their day for being contrary to reason. Several of the philosophes also produced imaginative works of literature, which continued the assault on bigotry, intolerance, tyranny, and religious dogmatism.

The value given to reason by Enlightenment thinkers and their humanitarian concerns also found expression in art and music. The spontaneity, merriment, and frivolity of the Rococo were assailed by many philosophes as representative of the superficiality and callousness of the aristocracy. Therefore, they welcomed artistic forms that celebrated the virtues and moral values of the middle class. This is evident in the many portraits of ordinary people, the themes of moral genre paintings, and the works of the Neoclassicists. In 1755, the great German archaeologist and art historian

Johann Joachim Winckelmann (1717–1768) published an essay, "Reflections on the Painting and Sculpture of the Greeks," that, echoing the philosophes, expressed admiration for the rational tradition of ancient Greece. In 1764, Winckelmann published his *History of the Art of Antiquity*, which is credited as being largely responsible for initiating the Neoclassical movement in the arts. Almost immediately Neoclassicism was adopted in France, where it harmonized with the outlook of the philosophes, including their affinity for science and reason.

Although Classical music evidences no direct link to ancient Greco-Roman models, music historians have, nonetheless, borrowed the term *classical* from art historians. Because the masters of the Classical period could not actually duplicate Greek music (because only two dozen compositions still exist, and the directions about how to decipher the musical manuscripts did not survive), they were content with the inspiration they derived from the ideas of the ancient Greeks. Consequently, Classical composers founded their music on discipline, clarity of form, intellectual coherence, and restraint, and we shall see in the following chapter that they sought to free their compositions from superfluous technical difficulties and to make them instantly pleasing to any sensitive listener's ears. The sentiments expressed in their music were intended to be natural, entertaining, universal in application, and expressed within the confines of good taste.

Key Terms

epistolary novel
the cult of the individual
Rococo
moral genre
British Palladian style

Notes

1. Donald F. Bond, ed., *The Spectator* (Oxford: The Clarendon Press, 1965), I: 44.
2. Ibid., I: 5.
3. Ibid., 1: 293–294.
4. Ibid., 1: 439.
5. Daniel Defoe, *The Life and Strange Surprising Adventures of Robinson Crusoe of York, Mariner*, ed. George A. Aitken (London: J. M. Dent & Co. 1895), pp. 228–229.
6. September 29, 1725. As quoted in W. B. Carnochan, *Lemuel Gulliver's Mirror for Man* (Berkeley: University of California Press, 1968), p. 87. See also Harold Williams, ed., *The Correspondence of Jonathan Swift* (Oxford, 1963–1965) 3: 103.
7. Alexander Pope, *The Best of Pope*, ed. George Sherburn (New York: The Ronald Press Company, 1940), pp.124–125.
8. Samuel Richardson, *Pamela or Virtue Rewarded* (New York: W. W. Norton & Company, Inc., 1958), p. 531.
9. Samuel Richardson, *Clarissa or The History of a Young Lady* (New York: Henry Holt and Co., n.d.), p. 458.
10. Excerpted in M. H. Abrams, ed., *The Norton Anthology of English Literature* (New York: W. W. Norton & Company, 1968), vol. 1, p. 1803.
11. Pope, *The Best of Pope*, p. 125.
12. Voltaire, *Candide or Optimism*, ed. Norman L. Torrey (New York: Appleton-Century-Crofts, 1946), p. 2
13. Ibid., p. 55.
14. Ibid., pp. 62–63.
15. Ibid., p. 107.
16. Ibid., p. 115.
17. Ibid., pp. 114–115.
18. Excerpted in, Christopher Thacker, *Voltaire. Profiles in Literature* (London: Routledge & Kegan Paul, 1971), p. 47.
19. Jean-Jacques Rousseau, *Julie, or the New Heloise. Letters of Two Lovers Who Live in a Small Town at the Foot of the Alps*, trans. Philip Stewart and Jean Vach. *The Collected Writings of Rousseau*, (Hanover and London: Dartmouth College, University Press of New England, 1997), Vol. 6, p. 342.
20. Ibid., IV. xvii, p. 428.
21. Ibid., VI. xii, p. 610.
22. Montesquieu, *The Persian Letters*, trans. George R. Healy (Indianapolis: Library of Liberal Arts, 1964), chap. 29, p. 53.
23. Ibid., chap. 60, pp. 101–102.
24. Ibid., pp. 47–48, 94.
25. Denis Diderot, *Rameau's Nephew and Other Works*, trans. Jacques Barzun and Ralph H. Bowen (Garden City, New York: Doubleday Anchor Books, 1956), pp. 196–197.
26. Ibid., pp. 198–199.
27. Ibid., pp. 206–207.
28. *Diderot on Art. Volume I: The Salon of 1765 and Notes on Painting*, ed. and trans. John Goodman (New Haven and London: Yale University Press, 1995), pp. 22–23.
29. Henry Fielding, *The History of the Adventures of Joseph Andrews and of his friend Mr. Abraham Adams, written in Imitation of the Manner of Cervantes, Author of Don Quixote* (New York: Holt, Rinehart and Winston, 1948), p. xx.
30. Excerpted in *Hogarth on High Life*, ed. and trans. Arthur S. Wensinger with W. B. Coley (Middletown, Conn.: Wesleyan University Press, 1970), pp. 126–127.
31. Quoted in H. W. Janson, *History of Art* (New York: Harry N. Abrams, Inc., 1995), p. 631.
32. Charles Burney, *A General History of Music from the Earliest Ages to the Present Period (1789)*, ed. Frank Mercer (New York: Harcourt, Brace and Company, 1935), p. 21.

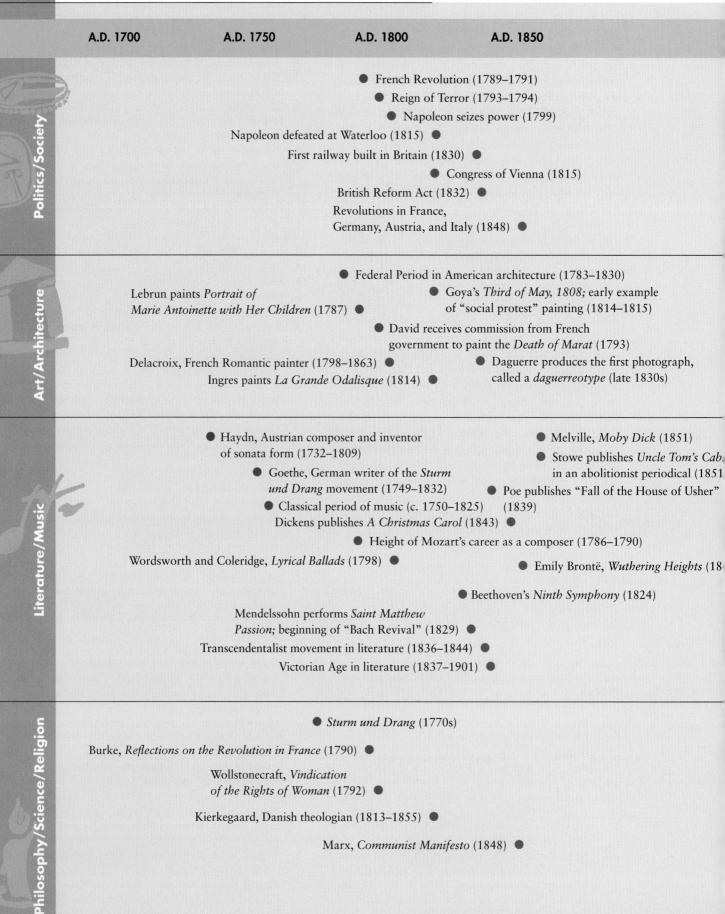

	A.D. 1700	A.D. 1750	A.D. 1800	A.D. 1850

Politics/Society

● French Revolution (1789–1791)

● Reign of Terror (1793–1794)

● Napoleon seizes power (1799)

Napoleon defeated at Waterloo (1815) ●

First railway built in Britain (1830) ●

● Congress of Vienna (1815)

British Reform Act (1832) ●

Revolutions in France,
Germany, Austria, and Italy (1848) ●

Art/Architecture

● Federal Period in American architecture (1783–1830)

Lebrun paints *Portrait of
Marie Antoinette with Her Children* (1787) ●

● Goya's *Third of May, 1808;* early example
of "social protest" painting (1814–1815)

● David receives commission from French
government to paint the *Death of Marat* (1793)

Delacroix, French Romantic painter (1798–1863) ●

Ingres paints *La Grande Odalisque* (1814) ●

● Daguerre produces the first photograph,
called a *daguerreotype* (late 1830s)

Literature/Music

● Haydn, Austrian composer and inventor
of sonata form (1732–1809)

● Melville, *Moby Dick* (1851)

● Goethe, German writer of the *Sturm
und Drang* movement (1749–1832)

● Stowe publishes *Uncle Tom's Cab
in an abolitionist periodical (1851

● Classical period of music (c. 1750–1825)

● Poe publishes "Fall of the House of Usher"
(1839)

Dickens publishes *A Christmas Carol* (1843) ●

● Height of Mozart's career as a composer (1786–1790)

Wordsworth and Coleridge, *Lyrical Ballads* (1798) ●

● Emily Brontë, *Wuthering Heights* (18

● Beethoven's *Ninth Symphony* (1824)

Mendelssohn performs *Saint Matthew
Passion;* beginning of "Bach Revival" (1829) ●

Transcendentalist movement in literature (1836–1844) ●

Victorian Age in literature (1837–1901) ●

Philosophy/Science/Religion

● *Sturm und Drang* (1770s)

Burke, *Reflections on the Revolution in France* (1790) ●

Wollstonecraft, *Vindication
of the Rights of Woman* (1792) ●

Kierkegaard, Danish theologian (1813–1855) ●

Marx, *Communist Manifesto* (1848) ●

- Unification of Italy (1859–1870)
  - Civil War in the United States (1861–1865)
    - Unification of Germany (1866–1871)
      - Franco-Prussian War (1870–1871)
        - Dreyfus Affair in France (1894–1899)

- Wagner composes the *Ring* cycle of operas (1857–1874)
  - Construction of the *Paris Opéra* under Charles Garnier (1861–1875)
    - Napoleon III orders the creation of the *Salon de Refusés* (1863)
      - Monet's *Impression—Sunrise* is exhibited at the First Impressionist Exhibition (1874)
        - Rodin's sculpture *The Kiss* (1888–1898)

- Flaubert's *Madame Bovary,* example of Realist novel (1856)
  - Tolstoy, *War and Peace* (1863–1869)
    - Eliot, *Middlemarch* (1872)
      - Tchaikovsky, "1812 Overture" premiers (1882)
        - Twain writes *The Adventures of Huckleberry Finn;* it is later banned in Boston (1884)

- Darwin writes *Origin of the Species* and introduces theory of evolution (1859)
- Mill, *On Liberty* (1859)

19

The Arts in the Era of the French Revolution

BETWEEN 1775 AND 1815, THE WEST WITNESSED two major upheavals—the American and the French Revolutions, both of which helped shape the Western liberal–democratic tradition. Equal in importance to these political revolutions was the Industrial Revolution—a social and economic phenomenon that transformed both society and the way people did their work—which began in Britain at approximately the same time (see Chapter 21). Although one might expect that the arts would also reflect such a "revolutionary" spirit, in reality, the converse was true. For the most part, a traditional Neoclassical style prevailed in the arts both in Europe and in the United States. In the tradition of ancient Greece and Rome and the Renaissance, Neoclassicism emphasized intelligible form, proper proportion, and balance. But in the early nineteenth century, artists, musicians, and poets began to look beyond the venerable Classical past for new frames of reference and searched for new forms of expression. Great painters such as Goya and musicians such as Beethoven aspired to integrate the Classical style with a growing concern for human feelings that the tumultuous times had underscored. Thus the era of revolution straddled two worlds: one drawn to a past Classical tradition; the other exploring new possibilities that pointed to a cultural change of direction that historians call Romanticism.

THE FRENCH REVOLUTION AND NAPOLEON

The outbreak of the French Revolution in 1789 stirred the imagination of Europeans. Both participants and observers sensed that they were living in a pivotal age. On the ruins of the Old Order, founded on privilege and despotism, a new era was emerging that promised to realize the ideals of the Enlightenment. These ideals included the emancipation of the human person from superstition and tradition, the triumph of liberty over tyranny, the refashioning of institutions in accordance with reason and justice, and the tearing down of barriers to equality. It seemed that the natural rights of the individual, hitherto a distant ideal, would now reign on earth, ending centuries of oppression and misery. Never before had people shown such confidence in the power of human intelligence to shape the conditions of existence. Never before had the future seemed so full of hope.

The Roles of the Enlightenment and the American Revolution

Revolutions are born in the realm of the spirit. Revolutionary movements, says George Rudé, a historian of the French Revolution, require "some unifying

Declaration of the Rights of Man and of the Citizen, whose spirit permeated the reforms of the Revolution, upheld the dignity of the individual, demanded respect for the individual, attributed to each person natural rights, and barred the state from denying these rights. It insisted that society and the state have no higher duty than to promote the freedom and autonomy of the individual. "It is not enough to have overturned the throne," said Robespierre; "our concern is to erect upon its remains holy Equality and the sacred Rights of Man."[5] The tragedy of the Western experience is that this humanist vision, brilliantly expressed by the Enlightenment and given recognition in the reforms of the French Revolution, would be undermined in later generations. And, ironically, by its fanatical commitment to a seductive ideology that promised worldly salvation—the creation of a republic of virtue and truth—the French Revolution itself contributed to the shattering of this vision. It had spawned total war, nationalism, terror as government policy, and a revolutionary mentality that sought to change the world through coercion and violence.

ART

Neoclassicism was a reaction to the excesses and extravagance of both the Baroque and the Rococo. Although initially a purely aesthetic movement, Neoclassicism took on a political tone during the American and French Revolutions. In the United States, it became known as the Federal style, and in France, Neoclassicism became the official style not only of the revolutionaries but also of Napoleon himself. In all the visual arts—painting, sculpture, and architecture—the classical republican virtues of duty, honor, patriotism, and loyalty were both appreciated and lauded. These themes are evident in the portraits of revolutionary leaders as well as important aristocrats. Moreover, a number of painters and sculptors appropriated Classical principles from High Renaissance artists (see Chapter 13) and created works that are simultaneously natural, realistic, and highly detailed. Particularly in the area of sculpture, the figures reflect the idealization of the human form that was evident in Classical Greek statues. Collectively, these characteristics reflect the Neoclassicists' rejection of the sensational and emotional works of the emerging Romantic artists, discussed in the next chapter.

Vigée-Lebrun

Among the most masterful portraitists of the eighteenth century was Marie-Louise-Élisabeth Vigée-

Figure 19.1 Marie-Louise-Élisabeth Vigée-Lebrun, *Portrait of Marie Antoinette with Her Children,* 1787, 9' 1/4" x 7' 5/8" (2.75 x 2.15 m), oil on canvas, Musée National du Château de Versailles. Vigée-Lebrun portrays the queen as a benevolent, stabilizing influence for her children. She cradles her youngest child in her lap, the young princess inclines her head tenderly against her mother's arm, and the young dauphin points to the empty cradle, indicating the loss of the queen's fourth child. *(Réunion des Musées Nationaux/Art Resource, NY)*

Lebrun (1755–1842). The daughter of the painter Louis Vigée, she began to paint at a young age and when her father died when she was only fifteen, she was able to earn enough money as a portraitist to support her mother and younger brother. In 1776, she married the renowned art dealer Jean-Baptiste-Pierre Lebrun. The following year, she was summoned to Versailles to paint the portrait of Queen Marie Antoinette and two years later became court painter to the queen. In 1783, due to the influence of Marie Antoinette, Vigée-Lebrun was selected to fill one of the four seats open to women at the *Royal Academy of Painting and Sculpture.* Following her admission to the Academy, she opened her own salon in Paris, where she exhibited many of her paintings. In contrast to the studied composition of the statuesque figures of her Neoclassical contemporaries, Vigée-Lebrun's subjects possess a guileless charm.

In 1787, she painted her famous *Portrait of Marie Antoinette with Her Children* (Figure 19.1). Holding to Rousseau's theme that women are naturally suited to educate their children, Vigée-Lebrun portrayed the queen as a benevolent, stabilizing influence for her children—an image in sharp contrast to the public perception of the queen as self-centered, lascivious, and indulgent. While the queen cradles her youngest child in her lap, the young princess inclines her head tenderly against her mother's arm and the young dauphin (who would never accede to his father's throne) points to the empty cradle, poignantly indicating the recent loss of the queen's fourth child. The coloring of the scene is reminiscent of Rubens, the group portrait style a reminder of Hals, and the singular figure of the queen an appropriation of the royal portraits of van Dyck. But the compassionate portrayal of her human subjects counters the dispassionate sensibilities of any of her predecessors.

When the French Revolution broke out, Vigée-Lebrun's connections with the monarchy caused her to be exiled from France. She returned to Paris in 1805 and she was elected to prestigious academies of fine arts in Italy, Russia, and Switzerland. During and after the Napoleonic era, Vigée-Lebrun continued to paint and to exhibit her works in salons in Paris, including her own, which was frequented by some of the greatest writers, artists, and composers of the age—among them Goethe and Byron (discussed in Chapter 20).

David

The leading French Neoclassical painter, Jacques-Louis David (1748–1825), was also the most celebrated artist of both the French Revolution and the Napoleonic era. Between 1775 and 1781, David studied in Rome, developing his Neoclassical style. After his return to Paris, David painted several austere paintings that reflect the classical ideals of clarity of composition and rational order and embody his reaction against the superficiality of the Rococo. These heroic paintings, with their cool colors and simple composition, championed the new virtues of civic devotion, duty, and honesty. *The Oath of the Horatii* (Figure 19.2), painted in 1784, is based on a Roman legend about a war between Rome and Alba in the seventh century B.C., which was the subject of Pierre Corneille's (see Chapter 16) seventeenth-century French tragedy, *Horace*. According to the legend, the conflict was to be settled by combat between two groups of triplet brothers. David's stark scene—with its background of Roman architecture—depicts the Horatii receiving their swords from

Figure 19.2   Jacques-Louis David, *Oath of the Horatii*, 1784, 10'8 1/4" x 14' (3.26 x 4.27 m), oil on canvas, Musée du Louvre, Paris.   This painting is based on a Roman legend about a war between Rome and Alba in the seventh century B.C. David depicts the Horatii receiving their swords from their father, Horace, as they pledge a sacred oath of obedience to Rome, before entering combat against the Alban brothers. *(Louvre/Erich Lessing/Art Resource, NY)*

Figure 19.3 Jacques-Louis David, *Death of Socrates*, 1787, 51" x 77 1/4" (129.5 x 196.2 cm), oil on canvas, Metropolitan Museum of Art, New York. Condemned to death by the Athenians, Socrates is portrayed as serene and at peace with himself. This classically balanced composition reminds the viewer that following the rule of law for the greater good of the state is one of the hallmarks of republican citizenship. *(The Metropolitan Museum of Art, Catharine Lorillard Wolfe Collection, Wolfe Fund, 1931 (31.45) Photograph © 1995 The Metropolitan Museum of Art)*

their father, Horace, as they pledge a sacred oath of obedience to Rome, just prior to engaging in combat with the Alban brothers. These precisely drawn, statuesque figures evoked memories of the virtues of citizenship in the Roman Republic—duty, honor, patriotism. Consequently, during the Reign of Terror this painting came to epitomize republican citizenship in revolutionary France.

Three years later, David painted another classically balanced composition, the *Death of Socrates* (Figure 19.3), which reminds the viewer of a second aspect of republican citizenship—following the rule of law for the greater good of the state. Condemned to death by the Athenians, Socrates, drinking the hemlock brew that will bring him a sure, but peaceful death, is portrayed as serene and at peace with himself. Surrounded by his friends, students, and family, he is discussing virtue and, perhaps, the immortality of the soul. Such close attention to realistic detail is a hallmark of Neoclassical painting, but the tenebrism, in which the figures emerge from the darker background illuminated by a light source that lies outside the painting, is reminiscent of Caravaggio (see Chapter 16).

David was an active participant in the French Revolution. As a deputy to the National Convention, he voted for the execution of King Louis XVI and supported the Reign of Terror. In 1793, he received a commission from the government to paint the *Death of Marat* (see chapter opening).

This martyr portrait of Jean-Paul Marat, a revolutionary leader during the Reign of Terror, raised portraiture to the level of cosmic tragedy. Marat was a radical political writer and a physician who had a painful skin disease that often forced him to sit in a medicinal bath while working. A young counterrevolutionary, Charlotte Corday d'Amont, gained entry to his workplace to present a petition for his signature, stabbed him to death in his bath, dropped the knife, and escaped. David, who was summoned immediately to make a sketch, reproduced the scene. He portrays Marat somewhat like a close-up photograph, because the subject appears to be nearly in the viewer's space. The lack of a background also enhances Marat's proximity. David again used tenebrism to depict Marat in this dramatic pietà-like pose, in the still of death, as a hero–saint of the Revolution.

When Robespierre was executed in 1794, David was imprisoned, but his estranged wife gained his release. When Napoleon came to power, David, an avid supporter of Napoleon, produced a series of paintings (1802–1807) that glorified the emperor's great deeds. Then, when Napoleon fell from power, David went into exile in Brussels. Although he continued to paint, his later works did not receive the critical acclaim of his revolutionary and Napoleonic paintings. He did, however, have a continuing influence on the development of French painting through the work of his students.

Ingres

David's greatest pupil, Jean-Auguste-Dominique Ingres (1780–1867), became the leader of a group of conservative painters who wished to preserve the Neoclassical tradition against the new burgeoning Romantic style (see Chapter 20). The more than twenty years that Ingres spent in Italy led him to appreciate not only the art and architecture of Classical antiquity but also the works of Renaissance artists, such as Michelangelo, Raphael, and Parmigianino (see Chapter 13).

Ingres thought of himself as a history painter, and it is in his history paintings—such as his *Apotheosis of Homer* and *School of Athens*—that his nonpolitical Neoclassicism is most apparent. He was, however, compelled by economic necessity to paint portraiture, which he claimed to disdain, believing it was beneath him. His portraits, with their nearly photographic accuracy, testify to his dictum that drawing is superior to painting. Ironically, today his portraits are viewed as his greatest works.

Nevertheless, Ingres is equally famous for his highly personal *La Grande Odalisque* (Figure 19.4), painted in Rome in 1814, which reflects a new interest in Near Eastern or oriental themes. Here he portrays an exotic and erotic *odalisque*— a female slave or concubine in a sultan's harem— whose soft iridescent flesh is accentuated by the rich colors of the drapery and the bed. The elongation of the odalisque's body is reminiscent of Mannerism, particularly Parmigianino's *Madonna with the Long Neck* (see Chapter 13), but the odalisque

also demonstrates that Ingres was not totally able to resist a romantic theme. Nonetheless, in the years following the fall of Napoleon, he resolutely fought against the emotionalism and sensationalism of French Romantic painting, especially the work of Eugene Delacroix (see Chapter 20).

Goya

The art of Francisco Goya y Lucientes (1746–1828) gave expression to the rationalism and objective realism of the Enlightenment. His artistic response to the atrocities committed during the Spanish uprising against Napoleon also revealed a commitment to the humanitarian spirit of the philosophes. However, in several ways, Goya's art went beyond the Enlightenment. In his depiction of the inner life of the individual, its uniqueness, and his concern with the dark and macabre side of human nature and human experience—terror, madness, cruelty, irrationality—Goya anticipated Romanticism and much of modern art.

Goya's first work was a series of elegant Rococo scenes that were used on tapestries, but then, rather than moving on to the contemporary style of Neoclassicism, he turned to a highly personalized style of portraiture. In 1786, under Charles III (1759–1788), he was appointed a court painter and in 1799, painter to King Charles IV (1788–1808). In 1800, he painted his *Family of Charles IV* (Figure 19.5), which was partially inspired by Velázquez's *Las Meninas* (see Chapter 16). Like Velázquez, Goya painted an image of

Figure 19.4   Jean-Auguste-Dominique Ingres, *La Grande Odalisque*, 1814, 35" x 64" (88.9 x 162.5 cm), oil on canvas, Musée du Louvre, Paris. An odalisque is a female slave or concubine in a sultan's harem. Here, Ingres portrays her as both exotic and erotic; her soft iridescent flesh is accentuated by the rich colors of the drapery and the bed. *(Louvre/Réunion des Musées Nationaux/Art Resource, NY)*

Figure 19.5 Francisco Goya y Lucientes, *Family of Charles IV*, 1800, 9'2" x 11' (2.79 x 3.36 m), oil on canvas, Museo del Prado, Madrid. Because of its stark realism, this painting is often viewed as an intense satire of the commonness, pomposity, and insolence of the royal family. But it is unlikely that Goya would have made a mockery of the king, his most important patron. *(Museo del Prado, Madrid/Institut Amatller d'Art Hispanic, Barcelona)*

himself, in the left background behind the easel, and the light comes from the side, as in *Las Meninas*. Because of its stark realism—the red-faced king and rather ugly, frowning queen—the painting is often viewed as an intense satire of the commonness, pomposity, and insolence of the royal family. It is unlikely, however, that Goya would have made a mockery of his most important patron, the king.

Goya was a member of a group of Spaniards who, captivated by the ideals of the French philosophes, encouraged Charles III to institute several liberal reforms, including the curtailment of the power of the Catholic Church in Spain. However, following the excesses of the Reign of Terror in France, Charles IV reversed the French-inspired reforms and reestablished the notorious Inquisition. During the same period, in 1793, Goya suffered a severe illness that left him deaf. Thereafter, his works reflect both his personal despair and his social disillusionment, which is clearly seen in his *Los Caprichos (The Caprices)*, a series of etchings using aquatint that were executed between 1796 and 1798. Goya was the first major artist to employ *aquatint*—a process using acid to create

tonal areas on a plate that had already been etched. The most famous of the series is the frontispiece of the second section—*The Sleep of Reason Produces Monsters* (Figure 19.6). Goya personifies Reason,

Figure 19.6 Francisco Goya y Lucientes, *The Sleep of Reason Produces Monsters*, 1796–1798, published 1799, 8 1/2" x 6" (21.6 x 15.2 cm), etching and aquatint, The Hispanic Society of America, New York. Goya personifies Reason, asleep on the table, as dark monsters of the night arise from his mind. *(Corbis)*

asleep on the table, as dark monsters of the night arise from the mind of the sleeping Reason. Goya's warning is clear: Spain must return to the rational policies of Charles III.

In 1808, Napoleon conquered Spain and put his brother, Joseph, on the throne. Goya was one of a group of Spaniards who welcomed Joseph and hoped for liberal reforms and a liberal constitution. Spanish nobles and clergy, hostile to the liberal and secular spirit of the French Revolution, rallied the intensely Catholic peasantry to resist the French. After only a day of fighting, French troops gathered together hundreds of Spaniards and executed them, thus ushering in six years of guerrilla warfare. Following the defeat of Joseph and the expulsion of the French, Goya painted *Third of May, 1808* (Figure 19.7). Produced between 1814 and 1815, this indictment of human evil—in which Goya depicts a French firing squad executing defenseless Spanish prisoners—is an early example of what came to be known as "social protest" paintings. The singular light emitted by the paper lantern in the foreground illuminates the bloody corpses of those already dead (on the left), the terror of those about to die (in the center), and the anguish of those awaiting their turn (on the right). The dominant figure is the man in the white shirt, in a pose reminiscent of the crucified Christ, who will be a martyr for liberty rather than for religion.

Although Goya probably never heard the term "Romanticism," his passion and his flair for the dramatic, as well as his fascination with the exotic and the macabre in his later works, justifiably place him within the sphere of the Romantic painters of the first half of the nineteenth century. For example, between 1813 and 1819, Goya executed a much darker series of engravings—*Los Disparates (The Follies)*. Similarly, between 1820 and 1822, Goya painted a series of gruesome frescoes—depicting irrationality, dread, and terror—for the walls of his own house.

Houdon

The greatest portrait sculptor of his day, Jean-Antoine Houdon (1741–1828) was born in Versailles. He studied in Rome between 1764 and 1768, where he was influenced by the works of ancient sculptors and those of Renaissance masters, especially Michelangelo. Specializing in natural, realistic portraiture, he often made plaster casts of live subjects and made precise measurements. Although his figures have a certain heroic aura, he captured the individual personalities of his subjects and gave the marble the appearance of living flesh.

In 1771, the year he became a member of the Royal Academy, Houdon exhibited the first of his sculpture portraits of eminent men, his bust of the philosophe Denis Diderot, which he followed with a prodigious number of portraits of famous men, including several busts of Voltaire and a death mask of Rousseau. In 1781, Houdon completed a statue of *Voltaire* (see Chapter 17 opening), which was commissioned by Catherine II of Russia. Voltaire posed for the sculpture as a frail old man, which is evident in the deep wrinkles of his face

Figure 19.7 Francisco Goya y Lucientes, *Third of May, 1808*, 1814–1815, 8′9″ x 13′4″ (2.67 x 4.06 m), oil on canvas, Museo del Prado, Madrid. Following the defeat of Joseph and the expulsion of the French, Goya painted this indictment of human evil by depicting a French firing squad executing defenseless Spanish prisoners. It is an early example of what came to be known as "social protest" paintings. *(Museo del Prado, Madrid/Institut Amatller Hispanic, Barcelona)*

Figure 19.8 Jean-Antoine Houdon, *George Washington*, 1788–1792, 6'2" (1.88 m), marble, State Capitol, Richmond, Virginia. Although Houdon adhered to a realistic portrayal of Washington's features, the classical contrapposto pose reflects the growing identification of classicism with republicanism. *(Robert Llewellyn)*

and the dry, papery skin of both his face and hands. Nonetheless, Houdon captures Voltaire's intellect and wit in his incisive gaze.

In 1778, Houdon modeled a bust of Benjamin Franklin based only on his memories of Franklin, whom he met at a few social events in Paris. Consequently, Houdon was invited to travel to America to sculpt a statue of George Washington. In 1785, he crossed the Atlantic and stayed for several weeks at Washington's home at Mount Vernon, observing Washington and making a cast of his features. Subsequently, Houdon returned to Paris and executed his monumental marble, *George Washington* (Figure 19.8), between 1788 and 1792. Although Houdon adhered to a realistic portrayal of Washington's features, the classical **contrapposto** pose reflects the growing identification of classicism with republicanism. Dressed in his general's uniform, Washington's left hand rests on a fasces (a bundle of rods carried before Roman magistrates as a symbol of authority). The thirteen rods also refer to the states of the new United States, of which Washington was now president. Attached to the fasces are a sword and a plowshare, alluding to Washington's preeminence in both war and peace. The marble statue was set up in the state capitol of Virginia, at Richmond, in 1796. Houdon's style of portraiture, with its elegant realism and individualized personalities, continued to exert a strong influence over Western sculptors for generations to come.

Figure 19.9 Antonio Canova, *Pauline Bonaparte as Venus Victorious*, 1805–1807, 62 7/8" x 78 3/4" (1.6 x 2 m), marble, Galleria Borghese, Rome. Canova's idealized classical figure is at once serenely sensuous and coolly aloof. She holds the apple that was given to Venus when she was declared by the shepherd Paris to be the most beautiful goddess. *(Galleria Borghese, Rome/Scala/Art Resource, NY)*

Figure 19.10 Thomas Jefferson, *Monticello*, 1770–1784, 1796–1806, Charlottesville, Virginia. While in Europe, as U.S. minister to France, Jefferson studied architecture. Upon his return, he redesigned Monticello to reflect French influences. *(Robert Llewellyn)*

Canova

The leading proponent of Neoclassicism in sculpture was Antonio Canova (1757–1822). Born near Venice, he moved to Rome in 1781 where, immersed in the revival of interest in ancient Greek and Roman styles, he soon established himself as a Neoclassical sculptor. However, in contrast to Houdon's painstakingly realistic portraits, Canova's Neoclassical sculptures are idealized figures like the statues of Classical Greece. Canova received some commissions from Napoleon, including a rendering of his sister Pauline, whom he sculpted between 1805 and 1807. The famous *Pauline Bonaparte as Venus Victorious* (Figure 19.9) depicts a reclining princess, partially nude, holding the apple that was given to the mythical Venus when the shepherd Paris declared her to be the most beautiful goddess. Canova's idealized classical figure is at once serenely sensuous and coolly aloof.

Jefferson

During the 1770s both French Neoclassicism and British Palladianism spread to America. From 1783 to 1830—the ***Federal period***—American architecture was dominated by the Neoclassical style. The preeminent American architect of this period was Thomas Jefferson (1743–1826), who, in 1801, became the third president of the United States.

In 1771, Jefferson began to build his home in Virginia—*Monticello* (from the Italian "little mountain," Figure 19.10)—based on a design he appropriated from Andrea Palladio's *Four Books on Architecture*. While Jefferson was the American minister to France, beginning in 1785, he traveled in France, Italy, and England studying architecture and landscape gardening. After his return to the United States, Jefferson completely redesigned Monticello. He not only adopted French doors and long narrow windows but also used a cornice to unify the structure. Consequently, he created a home that gives the illusion of being a single-story structure. While he was president, from 1801 to 1809, Jefferson was instrumental in planning the *United States Capitol* (Figure 19.11). The original design for the Capitol, with its large dome over a temple facade flanked by two large wings, came from William Thornton. But in 1803, Jefferson hired the British architect Benjamin Henry Latrobe (1764–1820) to construct the building. When the Capitol was partially destroyed in the War of 1812, Latrobe repaired the wings and designed a new dome. The present dome, which resembles Wren's dome for Saint Paul's Cathedral in London (see Chapter 16), was designed and constructed on a gigantic web of cast iron by Thomas Ustick Walter (1804–1887).

By 1812, the identification of Neoclassical architecture with republicanism was complete. In a letter to Latrobe, Jefferson made a clear connection between Neoclassicism and republicanism—and between the new United States and ancient Athens—by describing the Capitol as "the first temple dedicated to the sovereignty of

Figure 19.11   Benjamin Henry Latrobe, *United States Capitol,* c. 1808, Washington, D.C.   The original design for the Capitol was a large dome over a temple facade flanked by two large wings. But in 1803, Jefferson hired Latrobe to construct the building, and when the Capitol was partially destroyed during the War of 1812, Latrobe repaired the wings and designed a new dome. *(I.N. Stokes Phelps Collection, Miriam and Ira D. Wallach Division of Art, Prints and Photographs, New York Public Library, Astor, Lenox and Tilden Foundations)*

the people, embellishing with Athenian taste the course of a nation looking far beyond the range of Athenian destinies."[6]

CLASSICAL MUSIC

The Classical period in music lasted from approximately 1750 to 1825. Classical composers aspired to a musical style that was distinguished by its harmony, symmetry, simplicity, and clarity, one they believed expressed the aesthetics of Classical Greek art. Instrumental music gained in stature as courtly entertainment often included lighthearted dance music, such as the *minuet.* Moreover, further developments to the piano made sudden, dramatic shifts in musical dynamics possible, and the piano eventually replaced the harpsichord as the central keyboard instrument of the mature Classical style.

The musical works of the Classical period are often said to be composed in the "Viennese style," because Vienna, Austria, was the musical heart of Europe. This is due to the fact that the "three greats" of the period—Franz Josef Haydn, Wolfgang Amadeus Mozart, and Ludwig van Beethoven— were inextricably linked to Vienna. Composers from all over Europe came to study in and around Vienna, where they eventually established and formalized the musical forms of the *symphony,* the *sonata,* the *con-*

certo, and the *string quartet,* which became standard during the modern period.

The most important innovation of the Classical period was the *sonata form* (usually consisting of three movements), which became the basis for the Classical symphony, the Classical concerto, and the Classical string quartet. Sonata form dictates the structure of a single movement— *exposition, development,* and *recapitulation.* The exposition states the themes; the development enlarges the themes by varying such things as harmony, rhythm, and dynamics; and the recapitulation restates the themes and brings resolution to the dramatic tension created by the development section of each single movement.

Haydn

The man most responsible for the invention and cultivation of sonata form was the Austrian composer Franz Josef Haydn (1732–1809). During his tenure as musical director for the rich and powerful Esterházy family, Haydn not only transformed the sonata form, but he also helped to establish the practice of modern orchestral playing. Consequently, titles such as "father of the orchestra," "father of the symphony," and "father of the string quartet" have been conferred on him. Haydn had at his disposal approximately twenty-five gifted orchestra players and a dozen accomplished vocalists, all of whom were recruited from the finest music schools in Europe, including Vienna. In 1790, Haydn accepted an invitation to travel to London to compose and conduct two series of six symphonies. Haydn's twelve "London Symphonies" (1791–1792 and 1794–1795) are considered to be the summit of his musical career, for they contain all the elements of Haydn's nearly forty years of musical experience. Haydn was immediately thrust into the spotlight of the highly sophisticated, cosmopolitan culture of London. Although the aristocracy welcomed him warmly, Haydn's personal appearances at crowded public concerts earned him the appreciation of the middle class and the adulation of people such as Charles Burney (see Chapter 18), who wrote a poem lauding both Haydn's musical genius and the superiority of German instrumental music.

> Haydn! Great Sovereign of the tuneful art!
> Thy works alone supply an ample chart
> Of all the mountains, seas, and fertile plains,
> Within the compass of its wide domains,—
> Is there an Artist of the present day
> Untaught by thee to think, as well as play? . . .
> Thy style has gain'd disciples, converts, friends,
> As far as Music's thrilling power extends. . . .
> And though to Italy of right belong
> The undisputed sovereignty of *Song:*
> Yet ev'ry nation of the earth must now
> To Germany pre-eminence allow
> For *instrumental* powers, unknown before
> Thy happy flights had taught her sons to soar.[7]

Similarly, one of the London newspapers, commenting on Haydn's first concert on March 11, 1791, placed him in the same category as Shakespeare:

> It is not wonderful that to souls capable of being touched by music, HAYDN should be an object of homage, and even of idolatry; for like our own SHAKESPEARE, he moves and governs the passions at will.[8]

The symphony performed at Haydn's first London concert was "No. 92" of his more than 100 symphonies. Because Haydn was awarded an honorary doctorate from Oxford University the following year, the symphony has henceforward been known as the "Oxford Symphony." Another significant event in Haydn's career also occurred in 1791, when he attended a performance of Handel's *Messiah* (see Chapter 16) in Westminster Abbey. Reputedly, as the chorus concluded the second part of the oratorio with the singing of the "Hallelujah Chorus," Haydn burst into tears and proclaimed: "Handel is the master of us all."[9]

Haydn's *Symphony No. 94* was first performed on March 23, 1792. Because of the sudden *fortissimo* (a loud, orchestral crash) during the *andante* (slow) movement, the symphony is now simply known as Haydn's "Surprise Symphony." A contemporary London newspaper reviewer likened the so-called surprise to "a beautiful Shepherdess who, lulled to slumber by the murmur of a distant Waterfall, starts alarmed by the unexpected firing of a fowling-piece [gun]."[10]

In addition to his symphonies, Haydn composed more than 83 string quartets, 52 piano sonatas, 23 operas, and four oratorios, as well as 400 folk songs and seven Masses. Haydn composed his first Mass in 1782, before an imperial edict (in effect from 1783 until 1792) curtailed the use of instrumental accompaniment in the church. Haydn's final six Masses (composed between 1796 and 1802) reflect his predilection for the symphony. Perhaps the best known of these late Masses is the *Lord Nelson Mass* (1798), commissioned to commemorate the English victory of Vice Admiral Sir Horatio Nelson over the troops led by Napoleon Bonaparte at the Battle of the Nile, in August 1798, for control of Egypt. Of comparable stature are Haydn's *Missa in tempore belli (Mass in Time of War)*, composed in 1797, and *Harmoniemesse (Wind-band Mass)*, arranged in 1802.

Haydn's indebtedness to Handel's choral technique is not only evident in his Masses but also in his two best-known oratorios—*The Creation* (1798) and *The Seasons* (1801). Although both oratorios are primarily religious, they also are imbued with the love of Nature and the simple, natural life so highly prized during the Romantic Period, discussed in Chapter 20. *The Creation* is based on Milton's *Paradise Lost* (see Chapter 16) and the biblical book of Genesis. Parts I and II of *The Creation* cover the first six days of creation. The oratorio begins with "Representation of Chaos" as the orchestra paints a harmonic picture that foreshadows the propensities of the quintessential German Romantic composer, Richard Wagner (see Chapter 22). The transition from darkness into the light of the first day is accomplished in the next recitative and climactic chorus, which announces: "And God said, 'Let there be Light': and there was Light!" Part III of *The Creation* is idyllic and lyrical, and it is the one part that bears no resemblance to either Genesis or Milton. In it, the audience senses a childlike gladness, optimism, and a glorifying of the individual so characteristic of the thought and mood of the Enlightenment. Adam and Eve sing not about their expulsion from the Garden of Eden in despair, but rather, they sing about "this world so great, so wonderful." Similarly, the oratorio concludes with the chorus singing about God, the great Artisan of Creation:

> Sing the Lord, ye voices all,
> Magnify His name thro' all creation,
> Celebrate His power and glory,
> Let His name resound on high.
> Praise the Lord. Utter thanks.
> Jehovah's praise forever shall endure. Amen.

On the occasion of his seventy-sixth birthday on March 27, 1808, Haydn was honored with a performance of his oratorio in Vienna. Although in failing health, Haydn listened attentively as poems (in both German and Italian) were read in his honor, trumpets played, drums rolled, and applause shook the hall as those in attendance shouted: "Long live Haydn!" As he was about to depart the theater, Beethoven (see following) knelt down and kissed the hands and forehead of his former teacher. Moved to the verge of tears by all he had witnessed, Haydn, before he was carried out of the theater, raised his hand in the manner of a blessing, which he silently pronounced on the audience. As fate would have it, this was Haydn's last public appearance.

Following the dictation of his recollections and the preparation of a catalog of his works, Haydn died on May 21,1809. Subsequently, artists and musicians throughout Europe mourned the loss of one of the greatest musical giants. On June 15, Mozart's *Requiem* was performed in Haydn's honor; many high-ranking French officers from Napoleon's invasionary force attended.

Mozart

One of the most versatile composers of the age, Wolfgang Amadeus Mozart (1756–1791), was not only one of Haydn's pupils but also one of his closest friends. Unlike his teacher, who was most comfortable with symphonic music, Mozart was equally at home with both vocal and instrumental music. He composed masterpieces in many musical forms, including concertos, operas, symphonies, songs, and even a Requiem, which he never completed due to his untimely death at the age of thirty-five.

Soon after Mozart's birth in Salzburg, Austria, his father, Leopold, himself a composer and author of a renowned treatise on violin playing, recognized that his son was a musical genius. Consequently, Leopold abandoned his own musical career to commit himself to that of his talented son. By the age of five, Mozart was an accomplished organist, violinist, and clavier player. Therefore, his father decided to take him on a

grand tour of the European musical capitals in England, France, Germany, Holland, Italy, and Austria; between the ages of six and fifteen, Mozart performed for some of the most celebrated monarchs in Europe, including King George III of England, King Louis XV of France, and Empress Maria Theresa of Austria.

As a child prodigy, Mozart was acclaimed for his improvisational skills as well as his numerous compositions, which consisted of minuets (before he even reached his sixth birthday), a symphony (at age nine), an oratorio (by age eleven), and an opera (by the age of twelve). Throughout his entire life, Mozart worked as if possessed of some sort of "inner vision" that inspired him.

Mozart succeeded in combining the German and Italian traditions like no one since J. S. Bach (see Chapter 16). When comparing the German and Italian musical traditions, we discover that traditional German music is expressive and serious, that the primary medium is instrumental (especially symphonies), and that the textural quality is polyphonic. The Italian tradition emphasized the light, entertaining nature of music, the medium of the voice (particularly the cantata and opera), and the textural quality is homophonic. The general goals of the two traditions are also at odds with one another. Whereas Italian music seeks to please and appeals to people "with taste," German music values the science of counterpoint and intellectual acumen. Conceivably, Mozart's greatest musical contribution was his ability to fuse both the German and Italian styles, not only in opera, but also in every other musical form.

Mozart found it difficult to deal with his expenses, especially following his marriage to Constanze Weber on August 4, 1782. In ill health, and with few pupils or commissions, he finally landed an appointment as Chamber Music Composer for Emperor Joseph II (1765–1790). Unfortunately, Mozart was only paid half the salary of his predecessor. During these final ten years of his life, Mozart achieved his synthesis of the German and Italian traditions. Moreover, he immersed himself in the compositions of his friend Haydn and discovered the masterworks of J. S. Bach. The man most responsible for Mozart's interests in both areas was none other than Baron van Swieten, who had composed the librettos for Haydn's last two oratorios. As the Imperial Court Librarian, van Swieten was fascinated by the northern German composers. Relaxing in van Swietan's home, Mozart familiarized himself with *Bach's Well-Tempered Clavier,* as well as his *Art of Fugue,* arranged a number of Bach's fugues for string quartet, and composed an ambitious fugue for two pianos. Bach's abiding influence, particularly his pensive mood and contrapuntal textures, are most evident in two of Mozart's last works: his *Requiem* and the opera *Die Zauberflöte (The Magic Flute)*.

Mozart dedicated six string quartets to Haydn, his friend and former teacher. In addition to his "Haydn Quartets," Mozart mastered the form of the string *quintet*—in contrast to both Haydn and Beethoven. He composed two of these master-pieces (both in C-Major) during the spring of 1787. During the summer of 1788, over a period of only six weeks, Mozart composed three of his most famous symphonies: the symphonies in E-flat, G-minor, and C-Major (nicknamed the "Jupiter Symphony"). In addition, he composed seventeen concertos for piano and orchestra. On the surface, Mozart's piano concertos are reminiscent of Vivaldi's (see Chapter 16) in that the movements are ordered in a fast-slow-fast sequence. However, the relationship between the piano and the orchestra was unprecedented and unrivaled. Rather than competing with each other, the piano and the orchestra are placed on equal footing, thus creating a type of "symphonic" concerto.

During these same years, Mozart composed three of his best-known Italian operas: *Le nozze di Figaro (The Marriage of Figaro)* in 1786, *Don Giovanni (Don Juan)* in 1787, and *Cosi fan tutte (Thus Do They All)* in 1790. One of the most interesting commissions of Mozart's final years was for his opera *La clemenza di Tito (The Mercy of Titus)*, composed for the coronation of King Leopold II of Bohemia at Prague in 1791. He followed this with the German opera *Die Zauberflöte (The Magic Flute)* in which Mozart foreshadowed a significant line of German opera that came to fruition with the works of the German Romantic composer Richard Wagner.

Whereas, Mozart's Italian operas were hailed as the climax of the form, *The Magic Flute* is considered to be the first and, perhaps, one of the greatest modern German operas. Traditionally, the German opera was a *Singspiel* (literally, "a play with music") in which the recitatives were replaced with spoken dialogue and characters were often included simply for popular entertainment. However, the mood of *The Magic Flute* is somber. In it, Mozart synthesizes a number of Germanic traditions, including the folk humor of the Singspiel, the vocal resources of the Italian operatic tradition, solemn choral scenes worthy of any oratorio, and even con-trapuntal, Baroque chorale preludes. The result is both synthesis and an eclectic mix of the musical ideas of the late eighteenth century.

Early in December, Mozart struggled to com-plete his *Requiem* with the assistance of one of his pupils. However, suffering from partial paralysis due to rheumatic fever and an infection, he died on December 5, 1791. Mozart was buried a day later in an unmarked, common grave at Saint Marx cemetery, five miles outside Vienna. Haydn was in London when his friend died. In a letter dated December 20, 1791, Haydn declares his desire to go home to Vienna and comments on the impor-tance of Mozart's short, yet abundantly produc-tive life:

> I look forward tremendously to going home and to embracing all my good friends. I only regret that the great Mozart will not be among them. . . . Posterity will not see such a talent again in 100 years![11]

Beethoven

Although the Viennese aristocracy allowed Mozart to be buried in a pauper's grave, when Ludwig van Beethoven (1770–1827) arrived in Vienna at the age of 22 to study with Haydn, they bestowed many gifts on him. Like his prolific pre-decessors, Beethoven's musical output is prodi-gious, but he is best known for his thirty-two piano sonatas, two masses, one opera, and above all, his nine symphonies. Beethoven's music, par-ticularly his symphonies, not only revolutionized modern music, but it is also viewed as the bridge between the Classical and Romantic movements.

Beethoven was baptized in Bonn, Germany, on December 17, 1770. By the age of eleven, he was a substitute organist for the court organist of the Elector of Cologne at Bonn, and by the age of twelve he had published his first music. In the spring of 1787, at the age of sixteen, Beethoven had the good fortune to travel to Vienna, where he played for Mozart, who, at the time, was deeply immersed in his opera *Don Giovanni*. A witness to the encounter remembered it like this:

> Beethoven . . . was taken to Mozart and at that musician's request played something for him which he . . . praised in a rather cool manner. Beethoven observing this, begged Mozart to give him a theme for improvisation. . . . [H]e played in such a style that Mozart, whose attention and interest grew more and more, finally went silently to some friends who were sitting in an adjoining room, and said, vivaciously, "Keep your eyes on him; some day he will give the world something to talk about."[12]

Due to news of his mother's impending death, Beethoven was forced to abandon his studies with Mozart after only a few lessons in musical theory, and by the time Beethoven was able to return to Vienna, Mozart too was dead.

Unlike Mozart, whose work can be categorized into no less than thirty-five different periods, Beethoven's musical output is generally regarded as falling into three distinct periods: the early years (until about 1802), when the influence of Haydn's and Mozart's classicism is most evident; the middle years (from about 1803 until 1814), when his works became elongated and more daring; and the final years (approximately 1815 until 1827), when Beethoven composed profound music reflecting his personal tribulations—including his failed marital hopes and his complete deafness.

During the first period, Beethoven's most notable works are his first ten piano sonatas, the six string quartets, and the *Symphony No. 1 in C,* which premiered on April 2, 1800, at the Royal Imperial Court Theater, in Vienna. In these works, Beethoven revealed himself not only to be a master at evoking emotion through music but also as an innovator at using the sounds of the instruments of the orchestra as a whole. However, for such innovations as allowing the wind instruments to be virtual soloists, rather than following the Classical form of an integrated, harmonic whole, Beethoven was soundly criticized by the prestigious musical journal, *Allgemeine Musikalische Zeitung (General or Universal Musical Newspaper),* which is best known by its acronym AMZ.

The music of Beethoven's second period was less imitative of Classical forms than was his first, and it is characterized by musical forms that are unprecedented in length, originality, and exuberance. Moreover, it was during this period that Beethoven confronted his most disabling challenge—deafness. Although Beethoven began to have difficulties with his hearing as early as 1796, by the summer of 1802, while he was composing his effervescent *Symphony No. 2 in D,* he was forced to face the possibility that he was going to become completely deaf. Consequently, in the autumn of 1802, Beethoven wrote a long letter to his brothers Karl and Johann (the so-called *Heiligenstädter Testament*) in which he directly confronts his impending deafness, acknowledges the degree to which it has affected his personality, and confesses how only his music has saved him from total despair.

> Oh you men who think or say that I am malevolent, stubborn or misanthropic, how greatly do you wrong me. You do not know the secret cause which makes me seem that way to you. . . . [F]or 6 years now I have been hopelessly afflicted. . . . Though born with a fiery, active temperament, even susceptible to the diversions of society, I was soon compelled to withdraw myself, to live life alone. . . . [T]herefore forgive me when you see me draw back when I would have gladly mingled with you. My misfortune is doubly painful to me because I am bound to be misunderstood; . . . I must live almost alone like one who has been banished, I can mix with society only as much as true necessity demands. . . . But what a humiliation for me when someone standing next to me heard a flute in the distance and *I heard nothing,* or someone heard a *shepherd singing* and again I heard nothing. Such incidents drove me almost to despair, a little more of that and I would have ended my life—it was only my *art* that held me back. Ah, it seemed to me impossible to leave the world until I had brought forth all that I felt was within me. So I endured this wretched existence.[13]

Despite his affliction, Beethoven composed several overtures, a number of piano concertos and string quartets, the violin concerto, various piano sonatas, his opera, *Fidelio,* and five more symphonies.

Throughout 1803 and 1804, Beethoven worked on his *Symphony No. 3 in E-flat (Eroica—*"heroic"). The symphony was originally entitled *Bonaparte,* but after Napoleon made himself emperor in 1804, Beethoven reputedly changed the title page to read "on the memory of a great man." Nonetheless, the symphony stands as a tribute to heroic grandeur, with Beethoven himself conducting the first performance on April 7, 1805. Despite Beethoven's ability to arrange an extensive amount of divergent material into a compact, musical whole, the work was generally not well received. A reviewer divided the audience reaction into three distinct types:

> Some, Beethoven's particular friends, assert that it is just this symphony which is his masterpiece, that this is the true style for high-class music, and that if it does not please now, it is because the public is not cultured enough, artistically, to grasp all these lofty beauties; after a few thousand years have passed it will not fail of its effect. Another faction denies that the work has any artistic value and professes to see it as an untamed striving for singularity which had failed, however, to achieve in any of its parts beauty or true sublimity and power. . . . The third party, a very small one, stands midway between the others—it admits that the symphony contains many beauties, but concedes that the connection is often disrupted entirely and the inordinate length of this longest, and perhaps most difficult of all symphonies . . . is unendurable to the mere music-lover. . . . [I]f Beethoven continues on his present path both he and the public will be the sufferers.[14]

Soon thereafter, at the same theater, he premiered his only opera. The original title was *Lenore,* named for the heroine of the drama, who is an idealized, self-effacing woman of immense courage. The entire opera champions the humanitarian ideals of the French Revolution—liberty, equality, and fraternity—as well as idealized womanhood. The opera, however, was declared a failure. While revising it, Beethoven also composed his *Symphony No. 4 in B-flat*—the so-called "Romantic" symphony, because it is brighter and mellower than some of his other symphonies—which premiered on November 15, 1807, in Vienna.

In 1814, Beethoven finally resubmitted his opera under its new title—*Fidelio*—for its premier at the Kärnthnerthor Theater. Beethoven wrote no fewer than four different overtures for the opera. Today, the fourth "Lenore Overture" generally precedes the opera, and the third "Lenore Overture" is usually played between the scenes of Act II. In addition, the *Lenore Overtures* collectively often appear as a musical unit on the programs of many symphonic orchestras. Eager for the opera to succeed, especially for financial reasons, Beethoven listened to his friends and critics and cut a number of musical pieces and shortened the opera from three acts to two. But following the success of *Fidelio*, Beethoven never wrote another opera.

Beethoven worked on both his fourth and fifth symphonies simultaneously. In fact, the first two movements of the fifth were completed before he finished the fourth symphony. However, the two symphonies are "polar opposites" in terms of their mood. In contrast to the jocund *Symphony No. 4.* is his *Symphony No. 5 in C-minor.* Beethoven is said to have "grappled with Fate" as it knocked at his door in the opening four-note motive: short-short-short-long. What is truly revolutionary in this symphony is the manner in which Beethoven majestically moves from the key of C-minor to the triumphal key of C-Major in the final movement. Also revolutionary was Beethoven's use, for the first time, of trombones to announce the exultant major key.

At a joyous concert on December 22, 1808, Beethoven premiered both the *Fifth* and *Sixth* symphonies at the Theater an der Wein. Although his sketchbooks indicate that themes were formulating in Beethoven's mind as early as 1802, *his Symphony No. 6 in F* ("Pastoral") was reputedly inspired by a walk that he and his friend, Anton Schindler, took in the countryside of Heiligenstadt, outside Vienna. The titles of each of the five movements give a clear indication of Beethoven's intentions: I—"Awakening of Cheerful Feelings on Arriving in the Country," II—"Scene by the Brook," III—"Merry Gathering of the Country Folk," IV—"Thunderstorm," and V—"Shepherd's Song—Happy, Thankful Feelings After the Storm."

As Napoleon's troops besieged Vienna, Beethoven took refuge in his cellar, covering his head with pillows. Despite the siege, Beethoven completed his *Fifth Piano Concerto in E-flat*—nicknamed the "Emperor Concerto." It was not, however, dedicated to Napoleon, but rather to Beethoven's accomplished pupil and ardent supporter, Archduke Rudolph of Vienna, who had fled the city with his family. Beethoven later lamented their departure in the first movement of a piano sonata (Opus 81a).

In 1811, Beethoven began to work on his *Symphony No. 7 in A*, which he finished in 1812 and debuted on December 8, 1813, at the University of Vienna. While still at work on his symphony, between July 6 and 11 in 1812, Beethoven wrote a three-part letter to a woman identified only as his "Immortal Beloved." The letter, discovered among Beethoven's personal belongings following his death, has resulted in a voluminous amount of scholarly research and speculation (as well as a full-length motion picture of the same title) as to the identity of the woman whose identity is still shrouded in mystery. However, a number of scholars believe her to have been Antonie von Birkenstock-Brentano (1780–1869), the Viennese wife of a Frankfurt businessman. In the third part of the letter, Beethoven pours out his heart most intensely:

> Though still in bed, my thoughts go out to you, my Immortal Beloved, now and then joyfully, then sadly, waiting to learn whether or not fate will hear us—I can live only wholly with you or not at all. . . . No one else can ever possess my heart—never—never—Oh God, why must one be parted from one whom one so loves. And yet my life in V[ienna] is now a wretched life—Your love makes me at once the happiest and the unhappiest of men. . . . Oh continue to love me—never misjudge the most faithful heart of your beloved.[15]

By 1814, Beethoven had completed his revisions of *Fidelio* and was preparing to debut his *Symphony No. 8 in F;* unfortunately, only the opera was considered a success. Beethoven, however, continued to live in relative peace and prosperity—that is until he was appointed guardian of his ten-year-old nephew, Karl. Although it was he who sought joint guardianship with the boy's mother (whom he viewed as unfit), Beethoven's temperament was not well suited to being a parent. Similarly, Karl treated his uncle poorly, neglected his schoolwork, and even attempted suicide in 1826. Moreover, Beethoven's health began to spiral downward. Nonetheless, during his final years, Beethoven's musical will triumphed over his personal adversity. Between 1816 and 1821, he completed his last five piano sonatas, the *Mass in D (Missa Solemnis),* and his *Symphony No. 9 in D* ("Choral"). In all of these works, Beethoven displayed a reflective, meditative mood that belied his fiery personality.

Like J. S. Bach's *Mass in B minor* (see Chapter 16), Beethoven's Mass is intensely personal and is, at times, a private profession of faith. The Mass requires a full orchestra and a massive chorus. Due to these requirements and its inordinate length, Beethoven's *Missa Solemnis,* like Bach's *Mass in B minor,* is rarely performed as part of a typical liturgical church service. Like his symphonies, Beethoven's *Missa Solemnis* was conceived as a unified whole—five movements corresponding to the five principal divisions in the Roman Catholic mass.

On May 7, 1824, Beethoven performed three movements of the Mass—*Kyrie, Credo, and Agnus Dei*—and inaugurated his *Ninth Symphony* at the Kärnthnerthor Theater in Vienna. The symphony is based on a poem, "Ode to Joy," by the dramatist and poet Friedrich Schiller (1759–1805). In this, the largest and most complex of all of his symphonies, Beethoven proved that he was still an innovator. For the very first time, he used the voices of four soloists and the chorus like instruments of the orchestra. True to the democratic sentiments of both Schiller and Beethoven, the following excerpt from the choral text aptly describes the "voice" of Beethoven's symphony:

> Joy is drunk by all God's creatures
> Straight from earth's abundant breast,
> Good and bad, all things are Nature's,
> As with blameless joy are blessed.
> Joy gives love and wine; her gladness
> Makes the universe her zone,
> From the worm that feels spring's madness
> To the angels near God's throne. . . .
>
> Joy, thou source of light immortal,
> Daughter of Elysium,*
> Touched with fire, to the portal
> Of thy radiant shrine we come.
> Thy Pure magic frees all others
> Held in custom's rigid rings.
> Men throughout the world are brothers
> In the haven of thy wings.
>
> Millions, myriads, rise and gather!
> Share this universal kiss!
> Brothers, in a heaven of bliss
> Smiles the world's all-loving Father.
> Do the millions, his creation,
> Know him and his works of love?
> Seek him! In the height above
> Is his starry habitation![16]

---

*In ancient Greek mythology, Elysium was the place where happy souls went after death.

A London reviewer in attendance at the concert raved about the final movement and Beethoven's use of the soloists and chorus:

> [I]n the finale . . . the genius of this great master shines forth most conspicuously. We are here in an ingenious manner presented with a return of all the subjects in short and brilliant passages, and which, as in a mirror, reflect the whole. . . .The passages from Schiller's "Song of Joy" are made admirably expressive of the sentiments which the poet intended to convey and are in perfect keeping with the tone and character of the whole of this wonderful composition. Critics have remarked of the finale that it requires to be heard frequently in order to be duly appreciated.[17]

At the conclusion of the concert there was thunderous applause, but Beethoven had to be turned around to *see* it, because he simply could not *hear* it.

Today, Beethoven's melody for Schiller's text appears in many church hymnals as the song "Joyful, Joyful, We Adore Thee." On November 10, 1989, as the Berlin Wall (see Chapter 26) was being dismantled, an exuberant crowd substituted the word *freedom* for the word *joy* as they disassembled the hated symbol of oppression while singing Beethoven's hymn.

Beethoven intended a tenth symphony and a Bach overture, but he died on March 26, 1827. His funeral, attended by an estimated crowd of 10,000 people, took place two days later, and on April 3, Mozart's *Requiem* was performed in Beethoven's honor. The eulogy read at his funeral gives full meaning to Beethoven's historical importance:

> Standing by the grave of him who has passed away we are in a manner the representatives of an entire nation, of the whole German people, mourning the loss of . . . the last master of tuneful song, the organ of soulful concord, the heir and amplifier of Handel and Bach's, of Haydn and Mozart's immortal fame is now no more. . . . He was an artist—and who shall arise to stand beside him?[18]

Neoclassicism and the End of an Era

The term "Classical Style" refers to a work of art, literature, or music that embodies principles of order, proportion, balance, and rationality that underlay the aesthetics of ancient Greece and Rome and that were revived during the Renaissance. Classicism rests on the premise that inherent standards of beauty do exist and that the human mind can know them. Therefore, writers, artists, and composers alike should aspire to shape their phrases, melodies, or images in accordance with these defined standards. In literature, there were conventional forms for writing poems, dramas, and satires, and any violation was viewed with contempt, not only by critics but by the reading public as well.

The terms "Classicism" and "Neoclassicism" designate the predominant artistic style and temperament during the era of the Enlightenment and the French Revolution, a period that extolled reason, stressed the primacy of the intelligible form, and rebelled against types of thinking or behavior founded in irrationality, ignorance, or superstition. These concerns applied not only to thought and the social world but also to the arts. Artists, writers, and composers equally believed that there were time-honored, formal rules of composition that must be followed. To do otherwise was a violation of the natural order of things.

In the visual arts, the style called Neoclassicism derived its inspiration from the art of antiquity and the Renaissance, but it also found a model in the mechanically and mathematically harmonious universe fashioned during the Scientific Revolution. As a restated version of the art of Roman antiquity and the Renaissance, Neoclassicism depicted heroic motifs of moral virtue such as duty, family, patriotism, and honor. In addition, Neoclassical painters, sculptors, and architects sought to emulate the repose, serenity, balance, and form of these models. However, they seldom achieved the living vitality of the earlier originals.

The pervasive musical style of the late Enlightenment and the era of the French Revolution is called Classical by historians, but not because of any direct inheritance from antiquity. In the field of music, the term Classical is simply a convenient borrowing of the term from art history. Like Neoclassical artists, Classical composers emphasized formal rules of composition for the string quartet, sonata, concerto, or symphony. They believed that their clean, orderly style of music echoed the outlook of Classical Greek art. Classical composers viewed the music of their Baroque predecessors as too dense, too complicated, and too emotionally draining. Restraining passion and rejecting ultra complex harmonies, that is by balancing emotion and intellect, Classical composers created a style that exuded clarity and proportion.

Neoclassicism marked the end of an era, because in the late eighteenth century, the Romantic Movement took hold throughout Europe. Eschewing the simplicity, proportion, and restraint of Classical artists and composers, Romanticists valued feeling, intuition, passion, imagination,

and spontaneity. During the first half of the nineteenth century, Romanticism became the dominant cultural movement throughout Europe, particularly among musicians.

Key Terms

Estates	Federal period
Bastille	minuet
Reign of Terror	symphony
Concordat of 1801	concerto
Code Napoléon	string quartet
odalisque	string quintet
aquatint	sonata form
contrapposto	*Singspiel*

Notes

1. George Rudé, *Revolutionary Europe, 1783–1815* (New York: Harper Torchbooks, 1966), p. 74.
2. Henri Peyre, "The Influence of Eighteenth-Century Ideas on the French Revolution," *Journal of the History of Ideas*, 10 (1949):73.
3. Quoted in Carlton J. H. Hayes, *The Historical Evolution of Modern Nationalism* (New York: Richard R. Smith, 1931), p. 55.
4. Quoted in Hans Kohn, *Making of the Modern French Mind* (New York: D. Van Nostrand, 1955), p. 17.
5. Quoted in Christopher Dawson, *The Gods of Revolution* (New York: New York University Press, 1972), p. 83.
6. Quoted in David Watkin, *A History of Western Architecture*, 2nd ed. (London: Laurence King Publishing, 1996), p. 375.
7. Excerpted in Piero Weiss and Richard Taruskin, *Music in the Western World* (New York: Schirmer Books, 1984), p. 314.
8. Ibid., p. 315.
9. Quoted in Donald Jay Grout, *A History of Western Music* (New York: W. W. Norton & Company, 1960), p. 453.
10. Excerpted in Weiss and Taruskin, *Music in the Western World*, p. 315.
11. Excerpted in H. C. Robbins Landon, ed., *The Collected Correspondence and London Notebooks of Joseph Haydn* (London: Barrie and Rockliff, 1959), p. 124.
12. Quoted in Alexander Wheelock Thayer, *Thayer's Life of Beethoven*, ed. Elliot Forbes (Princeton, N.J.: Princeton University Press, 1967), p. 87.
13. Ibid., pp. 304–305.
14. Ibid., p. 376.
15. Ibid., p. 534.
16. Louis Untermeyer, trans., *RCA Records*, 1952.
17. Excerpted in Weiss and Taruskin, *Music in the Western World*, p. 333.
18. *Thayer's Life of Beethoven*, p. 1057.

CHAPTER 20

Age of Romanticism: A New Cultural Orientation

Eugene Delacroix, *Scenes from the Massacres at Chios,* (1822–1824), oil on canvas, 13'10" x 11'7" (4.22 x 3.53 m), Musée du Louvre, Paris.

This painting is based upon the actual massacre of 20,000 Greeks on the island of Chios during the Greek War of Independence. Delacroix's focuses his attention on the victims in the foreground and on those in the background who are waiting to be slaughtered.

(Louvre/Réunion des Musées Nationaux/Art Resource, NY)

A FTER THE DEFEAT OF NAPOLEON, the traditional rulers of Europe, some of them just restored to power, were determined to protect themselves and society from future revolutions. As defenders of the status quo, they attacked the reformist spirit of the philosophes, which had produced the French Revolution. In *conservatism,* which championed tradition over reason, hierarchy over equality, and the community over the individual, they found a philosophy to justify their assault on the Enlightenment and the Revolution.

But the forces unleashed by the Revolution had penetrated European consciousness too deeply to be eradicated. One of them was *liberalism,* which aimed to secure the liberty and equality proclaimed by the Revolution. Another was *nationalism,* which sought to free subject peoples and unify fragmented nations.

The postrevolutionary period also witnessed the flowering of a new cultural orientation. *Romanticism,* with its plea for the liberation of human emotions and the free expression of personality, challenged the Enlightenment stress on rationalism. Although it was primarily a literary and artistic movement, Romanticism also permeated philosophy and political thought, particularly conservatism and nationalism.

The period opened with the Congress of Vienna, which drew up a peace settlement after the defeat of Napoleon, and closed with the revolutions that swept across most of Europe in 1848.

THE RISE OF IDEOLOGIES

Conservatism: The Value of Tradition

To the traditional rulers of Europe—kings, aristocrats, and clergy—the French Revolution was a great evil that had inflicted a near-fatal wound on civilization. Disgusted and frightened by the revolutionary violence, terror, and warfare, the traditional rulers sought to refute the philosophes' worldview, which had spawned the Revolution. In conservatism, they found a political philosophy to counter the Enlightenment ideology.

Edmund Burke's *Reflections on the Revolution in France* (1790) was instrumental in shaping conservative thought. Burke (1729–1797), an Anglo-Irish statesman and political theorist, wanted to warn his countrymen of the dangers inherent in the ideology of the revolutionaries. Although writing in 1790, he astutely predicted that the Revolution would lead to terror and military dictatorship. To Burke, fanatics armed with pernicious principles—abstract ideas divorced from historical experience—had dragged France through the mire of revolution. Burke developed a coherent political philosophy that served as a counterweight to the ideology of the Enlightenment and the Revolution.

Entranced by the great discoveries in science, the philosophes and French reformers had believed that the human mind could also transform social institutions and ancient traditions according to rational models. Progress through reason became their faith. Dedicated to creating a new future, the revolutionaries abruptly dispensed with old habits, traditional authority, and familiar ways of thought.

To conservatives, who venerated the past, this was supreme arrogance and wickedness. They regarded the revolutionaries as presumptuous men who had recklessly severed society's links with ancient institutions and traditions and condemned venerable religious and moral beliefs as ignorance. By attacking time-honored ways, the revolutionaries had deprived French society of moral leadership and had opened the door to anarchy and terror. By despising and discarding their nation's inheritance, said Burke, the revolutionaries made a fateful mistake. Once ancient beliefs and rules of life are taken away, a country has no compass to guide it, no safe port to which to steer.

The philosophes and French reformers had expressed unlimited confidence in the power of human reason to understand and to change society. While appreciating human rational capacities, conservatives also recognized the limitations of reason. They saw the Revolution as a natural outgrowth of an arrogant Enlightenment philosophy that overvalued reason and sought to reshape society according to abstract principles.

Conservatives did not view human beings as good by nature. Human wickedness was not caused by a faulty environment, as the philosophes had proclaimed, but lay at the core of human nature, as Christianity taught. Evil was held in check not by reason, but by tried and tested institutions, traditions, and beliefs. Without these habits inherited from ancestors, said conservatives, sinful human nature threatened the social order.

Because monarchy, aristocracy, and the church had endured for centuries, argued the conservatives, they had worth. By despising and uprooting these ancient institutions, revolutionaries had caused people to commit terrible outrages on one another and on society.

Conservatives viewed equality as another pernicious abstraction that contradicted all historical experience. For conservatives, society was naturally hierarchical, and they believed that some men, by virtue of their intelligence, education, wealth, and birth, were best qualified to rule and instruct those less able.

Liberalism: The Value of the Individual

The decades after 1815 saw a spectacular rise of the bourgeoisie. Talented and ambitious bankers, merchants, manufacturers, professionals, and officeholders wanted to break the stranglehold of the landed nobility—the traditional elite—on political power and social prestige. They also wanted to eliminate restrictions on the free pursuit of profits. The political philosophy of the bourgeoisie was most commonly liberalism. While conservatives sought to strengthen the foundations of traditional society, which had been severely shaken in the period of the French Revolution and Napoleon, liberals strove to alter the status quo and to realize the promise of the Enlightenment and the French Revolution.

THE SOURCES OF LIBERALISM   In the long view of Western civilization, liberalism is an extension and development of the democratic practices and rational outlook that originated in ancient Greece. Also flowing into the liberal tradition is Judeo-Christian respect for the worth and dignity of the individual endowed by God with freedom to make moral choices. But nineteenth-century liberalism had its immediate historical roots in seventeenth-century England. At that time, the struggle for religious toleration by English Protestant Dissenters established the principle of freedom of conscience, which is easily translated into freedom of opinion and expression in all matters. The Glorious Revolution of 1688 set limits on the power of the English monarchy. At the same time, John Locke's natural rights philosophy declared that the individual was by nature entitled to freedom, and it justified revolutions against rulers who deprived citizens of their lives, liberty, or property.

The French philosophes helped to shape liberalism. From Montesquieu, liberals derived the theory of the separation of powers and of checks and balances—principles intended to guard against despotic government. The philosophes supported religious toleration and freedom of thought, expressed confidence in the capacity of the human mind to reform society, maintained that human beings are essentially good, and believed in the future progress of humanity—all fundamental principles of liberalism.

The American and French Revolutions were crucial phases in the history of liberalism. The Declaration of Independence gave expression to Locke's theory of natural rights, the Constitution of the United States incorporated Montesquieu's principles and demonstrated that people could create an effective government, and the Bill of Rights protected the person and rights of the individual. In destroying the special privileges of the aristocracy and opening careers to talent, the French National Assembly of 1789 had implemented the liberal ideal of equality under the law. It also drew up the Declaration of the Rights of Man and of the Citizen, which affirmed the dignity and rights of the individual, and a constitution that limited the king's power. Both revolutions explicitly called for the protection of property rights, another basic premise of liberalism.

The liberals' primary concern was the enhancement of individual liberty. If uncoerced by government and churches and properly educated, a person can develop into a good, productive, and self-directed human being. To guard against the absolute and arbitrary authority of kings, liberals demanded written constitutions that granted freedom of speech, the press, and religion; freedom from arbitrary arrest; and the protection of property rights. To prevent the abuse of political authority, they called for a freely elected parliament and the distribution of power among the various branches of government. Liberals held that a government that derived its authority from the consent of the governed, as given in free elections, was least likely to violate individual freedom.

Many bourgeois liberals viewed with horror the democratic creed that all people should share in political power. To them, participation of commoners in politics meant a vulgar form of despotism and the end of individual liberty. They saw the masses—uneducated, unpropertied, inexperienced, and impatient—as lacking both the ability and the temperament to maintain liberty and protect property.

Because bourgeois liberals feared that democracy could crush personal freedom as ruthlessly as any absolute monarch, they called for property requirements for voting and officeholding. They wanted political power to be concentrated in the hands of a safe and reliable—that is, a propertied and educated—middle class. Such a government would prevent revolution from below, a prospect that caused anxiety among bourgeois liberals.

Although liberalism was the political philosophy of a middle class that was generally hostile to democracy, the essential ideals of democracy flowed logically from liberalism. Eventually, democracy became a later stage in the evolution of liberalism because the masses, their political power enhanced by the Industrial Revolution, pressed for greater social, political, and economic equality. Thus, by the early twentieth century, many European states had introduced universal suffrage, abandoned property requirements for officeholding, and improved conditions for workers.

Nationalism

Nationalism is a conscious bond shared by a group of people who feel strongly attached to a particular land and who possess a common language, culture, and history, marked by shared glories and sufferings. Nationalists contend that one's highest loyalty and devotion should be given to the nation. They exhibit great pride in their people's history and traditions and often feel that their nation has been specially chosen by God or history. They assert that the nation—its culture and history—gives meaning to an individual's life and actions. Like a religion, nationalism provides the individual with a sense of community and with a cause worthy of self-sacrifice. Identifying with the nation's collective achievements enhances feelings of self-worth.

In an age when Christianity was in retreat, nationalism became the dominant spiritual force in nineteenth-century European life. Nationalism provided new beliefs, martyrs, and "holy" days that stimulated reverence; it offered membership in a community, which satisfied the overwhelming psychological need of human beings for fellowship and identity. And nationalism gave a mission—the advancement of the nation—to which people could dedicate themselves.

The Romantic Movement awakened nationalist feelings. By examining the language, literature, and folkways of their people, Romantic thinkers instilled a sense of national pride in their compatriots. Johann Gottfried Herder (1744–1803), a prominent German writer, conceived the idea of the *Volksgeist*—the soul of the people. For Herder, each group of people was unique and creative; each expressed its genius in language, literature, monuments, and folk traditions. Herder did not make the theoretical jump from a spiritual or cultural nationalism to political nationalism; he did not call for the formation of states based on nationality. But his emphasis on the unique culture of a people stimulated a national consciousness among Germans and the various Slavic peoples who lived under foreign rule. Fascination with the Volksgeist prompted intellectuals to investigate the past of their own people, to rediscover their ancient traditions, and to extol their historic language and culture. From this cultural nationalism, it was only a short step to a political nationalism that called for national liberation, unification, and statehood.

The Romantics were the earliest apostles of German nationalism. Resisting the French philosophes, who sought to impose universal norms on all peoples, German Romantics stressed the uniqueness of the German nation and its history. They restored to consciousness memories of the German past, and they emphasized the peculiar qualities of the German folk and the special destiny of the German nation. The Romantics glorified medieval Germany, they saw the existence of each individual as inextricably bound up with folk and fatherland, and they found the self-realization for which they yearned in the uniting of their own egos with the national soul. To these Romantics, the national community was the source of artistic and spiritual creativity and the vital force, giving the individual both an identity and a purpose in life. The nation stood above the individual; the national spirit linked isolated souls into a community of brethren.

In the early 1800s, liberals were the principal leaders and supporters of nationalist movements. They viewed the struggle for national rights—the freedom of a people from foreign rule—as an extension of the struggle for the rights of the individual. There could be no liberty, said liberal nationalists, if people were not free to rule themselves in their own land.

Liberals called for the unification of Germany and Italy, the rebirth of Poland, which was ruled by Russia, the liberation of Greece from Turkish rule, and the granting of autonomy to the Hungarians of the Austrian Empire. Liberal nationalists envisioned a Europe of independent states based on nationality and popular sovereignty. Free of foreign domination and tyrannical princes, these newly risen states would protect the rights of the individual and strive to create a brotherhood of nationalities in Europe.

But in the last part of the century, nationalism grew increasingly more extreme, and in the twentieth century, it was a principal cause of the two world wars and the rise of Nazism.

Revolution and Reaction

In 1815, the Great Powers of Europe met at Vienna, drew up a peace settlement awarding territory to the states that had fought Napoleon, and restored to power some rulers dethroned by the French emperor. The Congress of Vienna also organized the Concert of Europe to preserve the Vienna settlement and to guard against the resurgence of the revolutionary spirit that had kept Europe in turmoil for some twenty-five years.

However, their efforts to turn the clock back to the Old Regime could not contain the forces unleashed by the French Revolution. Between 1820 and 1848, a series of revolts rocked Europe. In 1830, a revolution in France led to the overthrow of the reactionary Charles X and his replacement with a more moderate ruler, Louis Philippe. Catholic Belgians successfully revolted against the rule of Protestant Holland. The Russians savagely crushed a revolt by Polish patriots fighting to restore Poland's independence, and the Austrians suppressed an uprising by Italian nationalists.

The year 1848 was decisive in the struggle for liberty and nationhood. In February 1848 French democrats overthrew Louis Philippe and established the Second French Republic in which all male citizens were eligible to vote. However, the new government did little to relieve the misery of the urban poor, who also rose in revolt in June 1848. The revolt was crushed after bitter street fighting in Paris. The great majority of Frenchmen opposed the demands of the urban poor for government programs to assist them and elected as president Louis Bonaparte (1808–1873), nephew of the great Napoleon, whom they expected to prevent future working-class disorders. In 1852, he took the title of emperor and ruled in an authoritarian manner.

In 1848 Italian liberal revolutionaries failed to drive out the Austrian Hapsburgs and unite the country. The attempt by German liberals and nationalists to unite the thirty-nine German states, each ruled by a prince, into one country also failed. As we shall see, both countries would soon attain unity, but not through revolution.

THE ROMANTIC REVOLT AGAINST THE ENLIGHTENMENT

The Romantic Movement, which began in the closing decades of the eighteenth century, dominated European cultural life in the first half of the nineteenth. Most of Europe's leading cultural figures came under its influence.

Exalting Imagination and Feelings

Perhaps the central message of the Romantics was that the individual's imagination should determine the form and content of an artistic creation. This outlook ran counter to the rationalism of the Enlightenment, which had been a reaction against the otherworldly Christian orientation of the Middle Ages. Whereas the philosophes had attacked faith because it thwarted and distorted reason, Romantic poets, philosophers, and artists now denounced the rationalism of the philosophes because it crushed the emotions and impeded creativity.

The philosophes, said the Romantics, had turned flesh-and-blood human beings into soulless thinking machines. For human beings to be restored to their true nature, to become whole again, they needed to be emancipated from the tyranny of excessive intellectualizing and their feelings nurtured and expressed. Championing Rousseau's idea of the "noble savage," Romantics yearned to rediscover in the human soul the pristine freedom and creativity that had been squashed by "the chains" of civil society—habits, values, rules, and standards imposed by civilization. The philosophes had concentrated on people in general, focusing on the elements of human nature shared by all people. Romantics, on the other hand, emphasized human diversity and uniqueness—those traits that set one human being apart from others. Discover and express your true self, the Romantics urged: Play your own music; write your own poetry; paint your own vision of nature; live, love, and suffer in your own way.

Whereas the philosophes had asserted the mind's autonomy—its capacity to think for itself and not depend on authority—Romantics gave primary importance to the autonomy of the personality—the individual's need and right to find and fulfill an inner self. To the philosophes feelings were an obstacle to clear thinking, but to the Romantics they were the essence of being human. People could not live by reason alone, said the Romantics. They agreed with Rousseau, who wrote: "For us, to exist is to feel and our sensibility is incontestably prior to our reason."[1] For the Romantics, reason was cold and dreary, and its understanding of people and life was meager and inadequate. Reason could not grasp or express the complexities of human nature or the richness of human experience. By always dissecting and analyzing, by imposing deadening structure and form, and by demanding adherence to strict rules, reason crushed inspiration and creativity and barred true understanding. "The Reasoning Power in Man," wrote William Blake, the British poet, artist, and mystic, is "an Incrustation over my Immortal/Spirit."[2]

The Romantics saw spontaneous, unbounded feelings, rather than the constricted intellect, as the avenue to truth. By cultivating emotions, intuition, and the imagination, individuals could experience reality and discover their authentic selves. The Romantics wanted people to feel and to experience—"To bathe in the Waters of Life," said

Blake.[3] Consequently, they insisted that imaginative poets had a greater insight into life than analytical philosophers. "I am certain of nothing but of the holiness of the Heart's affections and the truth of Imagination," wrote John Keats. "O for a Life of Sensations rather than of Thoughts."[4]

The Enlightenment mind had been clear, critical, and controlled. It had adhered to standards of aesthetics, thought to be universal, that had dominated European cultural life since the Renaissance. Romantic poets, artists, and musicians broke with these traditional styles and uniform rules and created new cultural forms and techniques. "We do not want either Greek or Roman Models," Blake declared, "but [should be] just & true to our own Imaginations."[5] Victor Hugo, the dominant figure among French Romantics, urged in the Preface to his play *Cromwell:* "Freedom in art! . . . Let us take the hammer to the theories, the poetics [the analysis of poetry] and the systems."[6] The Romantics felt deeply that one did not learn how to write poetry or paint pictures by following textbook rules, nor could one grasp the poet's or artist's intent by judging works according to fixed standards. The Romantics also explored the inner life of the mind, which Freud would later call *the unconscious.* It was this layer of the mind—the wellspring of creativity, mysterious, primitive, more elemental and more powerful than reason—that the Romantics yearned to revitalize and release.

Nature, God, History

The philosophes had viewed nature as a lifeless machine: a giant clock, all of whose parts worked together with precision and in perfect harmony. Nature's laws, operating with mathematical certainty, were uncovered by the methodology of science. To the Romantics, nature was alive and suffused with God's presence. Nature stimulated the creative energies of the imagination; it taught human beings a higher form of knowledge. As William Wordsworth wrote in his poem "The Tables Turned,"

> One impulse from a vernal [spring] wood
> May teach you more of man,
> Of moral evil and of good,
> Than all the sages can.[7]

Regarding God as a great watchmaker—a detached observer of a self-operating mechanical universe—the philosophes tried to reduce religion to a series of scientific propositions. Many Romantics, on the contrary, viewed God as an inspiring spiritual force and condemned the philosophes for weakening Christianity by submitting its dogmas to the test of reason. For the

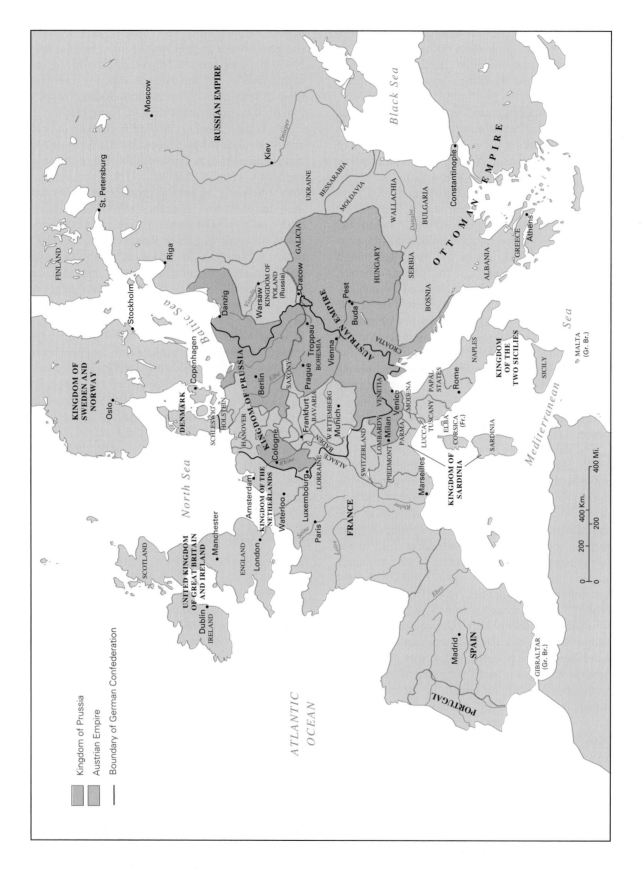

Romantics, religion was not science and syllogism, but a passionate and authentic expression of human nature. They called for acknowledgment of the individual as a spiritual being and for cultivation of the religious side of human nature. This appeal accorded with their goal of restoring the whole personality, which, they were convinced, had been fragmented and distorted by the philosophes' excessive emphasis on the intellect.

The philosophes and the Romantics viewed the Middle Ages very differently as well. To the former, that period was a time of darkness, superstition, and fanaticism; the surviving medieval institutions and traditions only barred progress. The Romantics, on the other hand, revered the Middle Ages. To the Romantic imagination, the Middle Ages abounded with Christian mysteries, heroic deeds, and social harmony—clergy, lords, and peasants, each group performed a role that served the overall good of society.

The Romantics also disagreed with the philosophes on their conception of history. For the philosophes, history served a didactic purpose by providing examples of human folly. Such knowledge helped people prepare for a better future, and for that reason alone history was worth studying. To the Romantics, a historical period, like an individual, was a unique entity with its own soul. They wanted the historian to portray and analyze the variety of nations, traditions, and institutions that constituted the historical experience, always recognizing what is particular and unique to a given time and place. The Romantics' insistence on comprehending the specific details of history and culture within the context of the times is the foundation of modern historical scholarship.

Searching for universal principles, the philosophes had dismissed folk traditions as peasant superstitions and impediments to progress. The Romantics, on the other hand, rebelled against the standardization of culture, and saw native languages, songs, and legends as the unique creations of a people and the deepest expression of national feeling. The Romantics regarded the legends, myths, and folk traditions of a people as the fount of poetry and art and the spiritual source of a people's cultural vitality, creativity, and identity. Consequently, they examined these earliest cultural expressions with awe and reverence. In this way, Romanticism played a part in shaping modern nationalism.

Map 20.1   Europe in 1815   Intent on regaining the security and stability of prerevolutionary years, the Great Powers redraw the map of Europe at the Congress of Vienna (1814–1815).

GOETHE AND GERMAN ROMANTICISM

German Romanticism began in the early 1770s with the literary movement known as *Sturm und Drang* (Storm and Stress), which decried both social convention and the inordinate emphasis placed on rational thought by Enlightenment thinkers. Instead, the Romantics emphasized imagination, spontaneity, feeling, and passion, and they appreciated the consummate power of nature. In addition, they disdained any constraints that might be placed on the passionate, creative genius and applauded originality, eccentricity, and the exotic.

Sturm und Drang was closely associated with the writings of the young Johann Wolfgang von Goethe (1749–1832). In the tradition of Richardson's *Pamela* (1740) and Rousseau's *Julie* (1761), Goethe in 1774 published his epistolary novel, *The Sorrows of Young Werther*. In his early twenties, Werther falls in love with the nineteen-year-old Lotte, who is engaged to the thirty-year-old Albert. Although Lotte feels some affection for Werther, she cannot return his unconditional love. Werther senses the hopelessness of his quest, but after she and Albert are married, his love for Lotte only intensifies. On one occasion, while Albert is out of town on business, Werther succumbs to his passion, kisses Lotte, and proclaims his undying love. Lotte, although moved by his love, flees Werther and locks herself in her room. On the very next day, the disconsolate Werther takes Albert's pistols and commits suicide. For Goethe the story of Werther was largely autobiographical, because for two years before writing the novel, Goethe was in love with Charlotte Buff. She, like Lotte, could not return his love, for she was engaged to an older man. But rather than commit suicide like Werther, Goethe simply left town.

The highly successful novel had an immense impact throughout Europe. Young men of the period copied Werther's clothing by wearing a blue coat and a yellow leather waistcoat, along with brown boots and a felt hat, and reportedly there was a sudden increase in suicides.

Goethe's best-known work is *Faust: A Tragedy*, which had an enormous impact on his age and beyond. By Goethe's day, the legend of Faust and the Faustian theme of selling one's soul to the devil was already centuries old. Goethe's *Faust* describes the emptiness of a man whose pursuit of science and philosophy has separated him from a deeper wisdom that is the source and sustainer of life. The learned Faust, restless and striving, yearns to plumb the depths of his senses. His revolt against quietude and his yearning for joy and excitement exemplifies the Romantics' intense passion for feeling. Reminiscent of the bargain made between

God and Satan in the biblical Book of Job, Goethe's Prologue occurs in heaven, where God and Mephistopheles, as a manifestation of the Devil, enter into a wager. God allows Mephistopheles to try to lure Faust away from the course of good. But if he fails, Mephistopheles must acknowledge that humanity is not as corrupt as he believed.

In the opening scene, Faust acknowledges that the knowledge he has acquired is nothing more than a set of facts and that his life is devoid of understanding and inner joy. Hoping to find some sort of inner meaning, Faust turns to magic, gets results, but ultimately recognizes its lack of value and considers suicide. Faust thus laments the emptiness of his life:

> I have pursued, alas, philosophy,
> Jurisprudence, and medicine,
> And, help me God, theology,
> With fervent zeal through thick and thin.
> And here, poor fool, I stand once more,
> No wiser than I was before.
> They call me Magister, Doctor, no less,
> And for some ten years, I would guess,
> Through ups and downs and tos and fros
> I have led my pupils by the nose—
> And see there is nothing we can know!
> It fair sears my heart to find it so.[8]

Mephistopheles later appears at Faust's study door. They make a pact, sealed in blood, in which Mephistopheles promises to fulfill Faust's every desire in this life. In return, however, Faust must, on his death, become Mephistopheles' servant in hell.

Mephistopheles makes it possible for Faust to seduce an innocent young girl named Margaret. Desirous of making love with Faust in the very bedroom she shares with her mother, Margaret gives her mother a sleeping potion, which accidentally kills her. Margaret's brother, who learns of his sister's affair, confronts Faust and challenges him to a duel, but Faust, assisted by Mephistopheles, kills him. The guilt-ridden Margaret then kills the infant fathered by Faust, a crime for which she is put on trial and condemned to death. While in prison, Margaret goes insane, but is ultimately redeemed and ascends to heaven. In the conclusion of Part Two, Goethe also permits Faust to be saved.

Goethe wrote additional novels and dramas, but his enduring legacy was *Faust*. Perhaps the most important of its many rich themes, the one that appealed most to the Romantic temperament was that of the seeker. Such people strive mightily to transcend all intolerable limits and restrictions and to break through all confining restraints that prevent them from experiencing everything life has to offer. Of course, such a cosmic ambition, such a craving for the impossible, does not come without a price, for it ultimately leads to tragic suffering.

Goethe's play has also given rise to two widely used terms: *Faustian man* and *Faustian bargain*. Faustian man has been used to describe modern Westerners who, breaking with traditions that defined a person's place in society, strove relentlessly to alter the conditions of their life, explore both earth and the heavens, and master nature. When someone says "I will sell my soul for that," and then actually does—that is, behaves ruthlessly and immorally in order to achieve the end for which he or she desperately yearns—that person has entered into a Faustian bargain.

ENGLISH ROMANTIC POETRY

The French Revolution deeply influenced English literary figures, demonstrating that the same revolutionary zeal that had swept aside the traditional political and social order was capable of inspiring fresh literary ventures. In direct contrast to the Neoclassical tradition of Dryden, Pope, and Johnson (see Chapter 18), who viewed poetry as an art form created according to formal rules of rhyme and meter and filled it with classical allusions and scholarly artifices, a new breed of English poets asserted that artists must not be bound by the textbook rules and ancient models but should trust their own sensibilities and inventiveness.

Wordsworth and Coleridge

The theory and practice of writing poetry were revolutionized when William Wordsworth (1770–1850) and Samuel Taylor Coleridge (1772–1834) published their *Lyrical Ballads, With a Few Other Poems* in 1798. In his "Preface" to the second edition of *Lyrical Ballads* (1800), Wordsworth delineated the difference between poetry that is "formally conceived" and poetry that is the result of "the spontaneous overflow of powerful feelings."[9] For Wordsworth and his like-minded contemporaries, a poem was not a lifeless literary form, but rather, an imaginative activity. Wordsworth commented on the purpose and style of the poems contained in the *Lyrical Ballads*: "I have said that each of these poems has a purpose: . . . namely to illustrate the manner in which our feelings and ideas are associated in a state of excitement."[10]

The appreciation of nature and the expression of powerful emotions link the *Lyrical Ballads* to the Age of Romanticism. Together, Wordsworth and Coleridge began the poem "The Rime of the Ancient Mariner," for the *Lyrical Ballads*, but Wordsworth retired from the undertaking early on, leaving Coleridge to complete it. Fashioned in seven distinct parts, the poem is an allegorical voyage through sin, repentance, and atonement. Coleridge only wrote one other poem for the *Lyrical Ballads*—"The Nightingale: A Conversational Poem." Finding the bird's warblings so beautiful, he wants every child to "grow up familiar with these songs."

> 'Tis the merry Nightingale
> That crowds, and hurries, and precipitates
> With fast thick warble his delicious notes,
> As he were fearful, that an April night
> Would be too short for him to utter forth
> His love-chant, and disburthen [unburden] his
>   full soul
> Of all its music! . . .
> So many Nightingales: and far and near
> In wood and thicket over the wide grove
> They answer and provoke each other's
>   songs — . . .
> Stirring the air with such an harmony,
> That should you close your eyes, you might
>   almost
> Forget it was not day![11]

Such an appreciation of the awesome beauty and power of Nature was a hallmark of both English poets and English landscape painters (see later discussion) during the Age of Romanticism.

From 1791 until 1792, Wordsworth traveled throughout France, savoring the sights and sounds of freedom. However, when the French radicals seized control of the government and began their Reign of Terror (see Chapter 19), Wordsworth felt betrayed and became despondent. With Wordsworth on the verge of a total mental collapse, Wordsworth's sister, Dorothy, and Coleridge suggested he return to the Wye River Valley, where England meets Wales, to recapture his poetic muse by communing with Nature. There he wrote "Lines Written a Few Miles above Tintern Abbey," which shows the power of nature to uplift the soul.

> Five years have passed; five summers, with the
>   length
> Of five long winters! And again I hear
> These waters, rolling from their mountain-
>   springs
> With a sweet inland murmur. . . .
>   Though absent long,
> These forms of beauty have not been to me,
> As is a landscape to a blind man's eye:
> But oft, in lonely rooms, and mid the din
> Of towns and cities, I have owed to them,
> In hours of weariness, sensations sweet . . .
>   And this prayer I make,
> Knowing that Nature never did betray

> The heart that loved her; 'tis her privilege,
> Through all the years of this our life, to lead
> From joy to joy: for she can so inform
> The mind that is within us, so impress
> With quietness and beauty, and so free
> With lofty thoughts, that neither evil tongues,
> Rash judgments nor the sneers of selfish men,
> Nor greetings where no kindness is, nor all
> The dreary intercourse of daily life,
> Shall e'er prevail against us, or disturb
> Our cheerful faith that all which we behold
> Is full of blessings.[12]

Lord Byron

Throughout the nineteenth century, Europeans viewed George Gordon (1788–1824), better known as Lord Byron, as the one person who embodied the fundamental attributes of Romanticism and sought to emulate him. Byron led an unconventional life, loved adventure, disdained convention, and epitomized the creative genius in rebellion against society. From the beginning of his life, Byron knew ridicule, and later in life, he learned to mock those members of "polite society" who had given him such great grief by satirically criticizing the social conventions that allowed them to think that they were better than he was.

Byron was a descendant of two aristocratic families—his great-uncle was the fifth Baron Byron of Rochdale (know as the "Wicked Lord") and his mother, Catherine Gordon, was the last of a prominent Scottish family. During the first ten years of his life, Byron lived in Aberdeen, Scotland, where his mother raised him as a strict Calvinist. Byron, however, soon rebelled against his dogmatic upbringing. Disabled by congenital lameness, he spent much of his early life trying to overcome it by swimming, boxing, fencing, and becoming an expert horseman. At Trinity College in Cambridge, he became self-indulgent and sexually promiscuous. (Recounting Byron's numerous love affairs, in which he engaged throughout his lifetime, would necessitate a chapter in itself.) In 1809, after attaining his Master of Arts degree, Byron and a close friend journeyed to Turkey, Albania, Greece, Malta, Spain, and Portugal. These travels served as the basis for Byron's first and last masterpieces: *Childe Harold's Pilgrimage* and *Don Juan.*

In 1812, Byron published the first two books of *Childe Harold's Pilgrimage,* detailing his recent travels, and he became an overnight sensation. He added Book III to the poem in 1816, after visiting Waterloo, where Napoleon, who fascinated Byron, suffered his great defeat, and journeying up the Rhine River into Switzerland. During his stay at Lake Geneva, Byron and Shelley (see the later

room. The Yorkshire setting ("wuthering" itself means "stormy") continuously parallels the tempestuous relationship between Heathcliff and Catherine.

In 1816, Mary Wollstonecraft Godwin Shelley (1797–1851), encouraged by her neighbor and friend, Byron, put her pen to paper to write the Gothic classic *Frankenstein, or, the Modern Prometheus*. Her mother, Mary Wollstonecraft, a path breaker in the struggle for female equality, died giving birth to Mary; her father, William Godwin, was a prominent political theorist. As a teenager, Mary met Percy Bysshe Shelley, and in 1814, they blissfully abandoned her family and his wife to travel. Following the suicide of his wife in 1816, Percy and Mary were married. Percy also edited Mary's manuscript for *Frankenstein* and wrote the preface for it, using her name. Upon its publication on January 1, 1818, *Frankenstein*, which excels in horror, the dominant device of the Gothic Romance novel, became an immediate success. Moreover, the plot enabled Mary Shelley to deal with such typically Romantic themes as creating something or someone as an extension of a side of oneself and the role science should, or should not, play in human affairs.

The form of the novel is a series of letters written by Robert Walton, the captain of a ship bound for the North Pole, to his sister in England recalling the plight of Victor Frankenstein, a scientist who created a human being through artificial means. Walton first meets Victor when his ship becomes trapped in the ice. The exhausted Victor Frankenstein, who has been traveling north by dogsled into the Arctic, boards Walton's ship and relates the horrific tale of his monster. He recalls his days of studying chemistry and natural philosophy and his obsession with discovering the secret of human life. Following the escape of his creation, Victor learns of the death of his youngest brother, suspects the monster, and discovers that an unsuspecting, innocent young girl has been tried, condemned, and sentenced to death for committing the murder. Realizing that he alone is responsible for the deaths of two innocent young people, Victor becomes despondent.

To assuage his grief, Victor vacations in the mountains, only to encounter the monster on a glacier. When the monster, feeling friendless and dejected, admits to Victor that he murdered his brother to reap revenge on Victor for creating him in the first place, Victor accedes to his wishes and agrees to create a female companion for him. But plagued by self-doubt and questioning the ethics of his action, Victor ultimately destroys his new creation—an act that further enrages the monster, who vows to seek vengeance on him on his wedding night. Although Victor sends his fiancée

away, the monster finds her and murders her. Then it is Victor who vows revenge and pursues his monster northward over the ice.

The narrative then returns to the present, as Captain Walton rescues Victor, who describes the anguish his quest to create life has caused:

> I felt as if I were destined for some great enterprise. . . .This sentiment of the worth of my nature supported me, when others would have been oppressed; for I deemed it criminal to throw away in useless grief those talents that might be useful to my fellow-creatures. When I reflected on the work I had completed, no less a one than the creation of a sensitive and rational animal, I could not rank myself with the herd of common [schemers]. But this feeling, which supported me in the commencement of my career, now serves only to plunge me lower in the dust. All my speculations and hopes are as nothing; and like the archangel who aspired to omnipotence, I am chained in an eternal hell. . . . I trod heaven in my thoughts, now exulting in my powers, now burning with the idea of their effects. From my infancy I was imbued with high hopes and a lofty ambition; but how am I sunk! Oh! my friend, if you had known me as I once was, you would not recognize me in this state of degradation. Despondency rarely visited my heart; a high destiny seemed to bear me on, until I fell, never, never again to rise.[19]

Walton relates the remainder of the story, recounting how Victor becomes ill and dies and how he comes to find the monster in Victor's room, crying over his creator. The monster then tells Walton about his enormous grief, suffering, solitude, regret, and hatred.

> You, who call Frankenstein your friend, seem to have a knowledge of my crimes and his misfortunes. But, . . . he could not sum up the hours and months of misery which I endured, wasting in impotent passions. For whilst I destroyed his hopes, I did not satisfy my own desires. They were for ever ardent and craving; still I desired love and fellowship, and I was still spurned. Was there no injustice in this? Am I to be thought the only criminal, when all human kind sinned against me? . . . I, the miserable and the abandoned, am an abortion, to be spurned at, and kicked, and trampled on. Even now my blood boils at the recollection of this injustice.[20]

Cognizant of the fact that, like his creator, he too must now die, the monster departs for the northernmost regions of ice.

Frankenstein lends itself to various interpretations. On one level it is a modern example of what the ancient Greek called hubris—overweening pride that invites suffering and disaster. In seeking to create life in order to demonstrate his superior talents, Victor overstepped the bounds of moderation; he forgot that he was only a mortal man, not a god. Such hubris demands punishment. The novel is also a work of social commentary. The monster does not become violent and dangerous until he has suffered rejection by society. "I am malicious because I am miserable," he laments. Mary shared the views of both her husband and her father, who argued that antisocial behavior is the product of an unjust society, a particularly poignant maxim in an age of social upheaval caused by rapid industrialization.

French Literature: The Gothic Novel and Social Reform

The poet, novelist, and dramatist, Victor Hugo (1802–1885), is viewed as one of France's great national treasures and his tomb is in the Panthéon. In addition to his monumental literary output, Hugo encouraged artists to be aware of their awesome responsibility to further the progress of humanity. Hugo himself became an advocate of the poor and dispossessed and a supporter of republicanism.

In 1830, Hugo's best-known play, *Hernani,* made him the unchallenged leader of the Romantic movement in France. The play encapsulates the last great battle between the Romantics and the Classicists for European dominance. At its premiere on February 25, 1830, many of those in attendance hissed and hooted, because Hugo's plot audaciously violated the rules of classicism. The mixing together of social classes, the colloquial language, and the deaths shown on the stage were all considered inappropriate for classical tragedy.

Soon after the July Revolution of 1830, Hugo published *Notre-Dame de Paris: 1482* (better known as *The Hunchback of Notre Dame),* which combines historical fiction with melodrama and Gothic horror. It features the deaf hunchback, Quasimodo; a priest, Frollo, who is haunted by his vow of celibacy; and a young orphan girl, La Esmeralda, who represents the Parisian underclass. Nevertheless, in a very real sense, the Gothic cathedral itself is the main character, for within the novel, Hugo appeals for conservation of the structure. Thus, the novel influenced the creation of an official organization committed to the preservation of French historical monuments, and it secured Hugo's lasting fame.

Nearly thirty years later, Hugo published his greatest novel—*Les Misérables (The Underclass)*—set in the Parisian underworld with an ex-convict, Jean Valjean, as the protagonist. The novel reflects both Hugo's passion for social justice and his abiding concern for the suffering poor—the *Misérables.* During the twentieth century, the novel inspired the long-running Broadway musical of the same name, as well as a number of motion pictures. When Hugo turned seventy, his birthday was declared a national holiday, and when he died, his body lay in state in the Arc de Triomphe, where two million people came to venerate him.

CREATING A TRULY AMERICAN LITERATURE

During the early years of the nineteenth century, the United States defended itself against the British in the War of 1812, even while American statesmen such as Thomas Jefferson, James Madison, Benjamin Franklin, and James Monroe were gaining prominence in Europe. By the middle of the century, pioneers had pushed the American frontier across the Mississippi River, across the Rocky Mountains, onto the shores of the Pacific Ocean, and even into the northwestern territory of Alaska. These achievements stirred the Romantic imagination and fostered nationalism. Concurrent with the material successes of the United States was the expansion of culture, including an enhanced appreciation of literature that was indigenous in both tradition and character.

Even though American literature of the age was characterized as Romantic, it was not intended as a reflection of European culture. Instead, American authors such as Washington Irving, James Fenimore Cooper, Nathaniel Hawthorne, Edgar Allan Poe, Ralph Waldo Emerson, Henry David Thoreau, and Herman Melville sought to portray the virtue of the American way of life. Moreover, they sought to express the wonder of the new territories and to articulate the hope that the ideals of the Enlightenment, particularly the inevitable progress toward human perfection, could be brought to fruition in the United States.

Irving and Cooper

American authors deeply appreciated the various forms that Gothic Romantic literature took, including historical tales, historical novels, and the Gothic Romance. Washington Irving (1783–1859) wrote under the pseudonyms Dietrich Knickerbocker, Jonathan Oldstyle, and Geoffrey Crayon when he wrote his tales and histories of New York. In 1809, Irving, as Dietrich Knickerbocker, published his comic *History of New York,* detailing the early Dutch administration of the region. Irving also led a group of the first truly American school of authors—the *Knickerbocker Group.*

Irving built on his successes when he compiled *The Sketchbook of Geoffrey Crayon,* a series of short stories, including his two most famous ones— "The Legend of Sleepy Hollow," with the unforgettable characters of Ichabod Crane and the Headless Horseman, and "Rip Van Winkle," the tale of a farmer who wanders into the Catskill Mountains only to fall into a deep sleep that lasts for twenty years. These tales established the short story as a new literary genre in America and gave children their first literature. Moreover, Irving's histories and biographies, most especially his *Life of George Washington* (1855–1859), were written in a style that made them popular entertainment, instead of dry, scholarly tomes.

Irving's contemporary, James Fenimore Cooper (1789–1851), introduced the first truly American frontier hero, Natty Bumppo, in five novels—*The Pioneers* (1823), *The Last of the Mohicans* (1826), *The Prairie* (1827), *The Pathfinder* (1840), and *The Deerslayer* (1841)—which are collectively referred to as his *Leatherstocking Tales.* Bumppo not only appears as Leatherstocking but also as Pathfinder, Hawkeye, and Deerslayer. In them, Cooper combined elements of Rousseau's "noble savage" with the medieval idea of the gallant knight of the courtly romance, thereby creating a composite character whose adventures take place on American soil. For example, *The Prairie* (1827) describes the death of the venerable Leatherstocking—as the American version of the Byronic hero—assisting the Pawnee tribe and some white pioneers against the Sioux tribe in the western plains.

Poe's Tales of Terror

When someone mentions Gothic horror in American fiction, the name that generally comes to mind is Edgar Allan Poe (1809–1849), one of America's most popular and enduring authors. Although Irving established the American short story as a genre, it was Poe who transformed it into an art form of the first magnitude. In addition, Poe was an accomplished poet and essayist, and he gave America its first detective stories, even while perfecting the tale of psychological terror.

His father, David Poe, Jr., and his mother, Elizabeth Arnold Hopkins, were both touring actors who died before Poe was three years old. He was then taken in by John Allan, an affluent businessman from Richmond, Virginia. When Poe accumulated huge gambling debts, John Allan cut him off financially, and Poe enlisted in the army. Upon his temporary reconciliation with John Allan, Poe received an appointment to West Point. After only six months, he was dismissed from the academy, but his fellow cadets raised enough money to have

a second edition of his poems published—the first having been *Tamerlane and Other Poems,* written in the style of Byron and published in 1827.

Poe then moved to Baltimore where, in 1832, the *Philadelphia Saturday Courier* published five of his short stories, including the horrific "Berenice," and he won a $50 prize from the *Baltimore Saturday Visitor* for his short story "Ms. [Manuscript] Found in a Bottle." In 1835, Poe moved to Richmond, became editor of the *Southern Literary Messenger,* and married Maria Clemm, the fourteen-year-old daughter of his widowed aunt Virginia. In the *Messenger,* Poe published a number of his short stories and critical reviews. Although his literary efforts increased the circulation of the periodical, Poe's alcoholism and the subject matter of his poems and short stories— including a mother who comes back to life by living through her daughter, premature burial, and a shadow that is neither man nor God—offended his employer, who dismissed him in 1837.

In 1845, Poe wrote an essay, *The Philosophy of Composition,* which included a specific discussion of his most famous poem, "The Raven." In deciding to write a poem with a melancholy tone, Poe asked himself two questions: "Of all melancholy topics, what . . . is the *most* melancholy?" "And when is this most melancholy of topics most poetical?" He decided that the death of a beautiful women "is, unquestionably, the most poetical topic in the world."[21] Therefore, the poem is about a lover lamenting his deceased mistress, Lenore. Poe, however, was faced with the problem of how to bring together the lover and the Raven, whose incessant reply is "Nevermore." "I determined, then, to place the lover in his chamber . . . and . . . to introduce the bird . . . [on] a night tempestuous, first to account for the Raven's seeking admission, and secondly, for the effect of contrast with the (physical) serenity of the chamber."[22] Once the lover admits the Raven into his chamber, the suspense and dread are escalated by his questioning of the bird. When the lover asks "if he shall meet his mistress in another world,"[23] he is greatly distressed with the Raven's response, because it offers him no hope.

> "Prophet!" said I, "thing of evil!—prophet still,
>   if bird or devil!
> By that Heaven that bends above us—by the God
>   we both adore—
> Tell this soul with sorrow laden if, within the
>   distant Aidenn [Eden, Paradise],
> It shall clasp a sainted maiden whom the angels
>   name Lenore—
> Clasp a rare and radiant maiden whom the
>   angels name Lenore."
>   Quoth the Raven, "Nevermore."

"Be that word our sign of parting, bird or fiend!"
I shrieked, upstarting—
"Get thee back into the tempest and the Night's
Plutonian shore!
Leave no black plume as a token of that lie thy
soul hath spoken!
Take that beak from out my heart, and take thy
form from off my door!"
Quoth the Raven, "Nevermore."[24]

Poe concludes his essay by explaining how the Raven is "emblematical of *mournful and Never-ending Remembrance,*" and how this is not evident to the reader "until the very last line of the very last stanza":

And the Raven, never flitting still is sitting, still is
sitting,
On the pallid bust of Pallas [Athena] just above
my chamber door;
And his eyes have all the seeming of a demon's
that is dreaming,
And the lamplight o'er him streaming throws his
shadow on the floor;
And my soul *from out that shadow* that lies
floating on the floor
Shall be lifted—nevermore.[25]

Poe considered his masterpiece to be the short story "Fall of the House of Usher." The darkly Gothic tale, first published in 1839 in *Burton's Gentleman's Magazine,* relates the macabre relationship of Roderick and Madeline Usher to their home. In the opening pages, the narrator portends the effect for the entire story, which is melancholic, dark, dreary, cold, and cheerless.

During the whole of a dull, dark, and soundless day in the autumn of the year, when the clouds hung oppressively low in the heavens, I . . . at length found myself . . . within view of the melancholy House of Usher. I know not how it was— but, with the first glimpse of the building, a sense of unsufferable gloom pervaded my spirit. . . . There was an iciness, a sinking, a sickening of the heart—an unredeemed dreariness of thought which no goading of the imagination could torture into aught of the sublime. What was it—I paused to think—what was it that so unnerved me in the contemplation of the House of Usher? It was a mystery all insoluble.[26]

The ending of Poe's life is similar to the mystery of the House of Usher, for on the evening of October 3, 1849, Poe was found on a Baltimore street in a demented state of mind. Four days later, he died, but his legacy of forty-eight poems, his philosophy of composition, his Gothic short stories, and his detective stories gave rise to a new type of fiction emphasizing psychological introspection and symbolism that would be evident in the works of other American authors, notably Nathaniel Hawthorne and Herman Melville.

Images of Light and Dark: Hawthorne, Melville, and the Transcendentalists

In recounting the history of Gothic Romantic literature, Nathaniel Hawthorne (1804–1864) occupies a significant place, because he developed a unique type of Romance novel. At the beginning of his most famous Romance, *The Scarlet Letter* (1848), Hawthorne wrote a long, introductory sketch, called "The Custom-House," wherein he described a romance as "somewhere between the real world and fairy-land where the Actual and the Imaginary may meet, and each imbue itself with the nature of the other."[27] The novelist, said Hawthorne, must be concerned with atmosphere—"moonlight and sunshine, and the flow of firelight, were just alike in my regard"—and must explore the inner conflict of his characters so as "to spiritualize the burden; . . . to seek, resolutely, the true and indestructible value that lay hidden in the petty and wearisome incidents, and ordinary characters"[28]

From English Romance novels and the works of Shakespeare, Hawthorne appropriated three traits: the use of elaborately detailed scenes, conceived on a large scale, to intensify dramatic effects; the inclusion of minor characters, to add "comic relief"; and the introduction of a mysterious stranger, to further entangle the plot. From *The Pilgrim's Progress* Hawthorne appropriated Bunyan's style of allegory and his concern with sin and redemption (see Chapter 16). But in one of the *Twice-Told Tales,* "The Celestial Railroad," Hawthorne gives an ironic twist to Bunyan's allegory, for although the train is scheduled to arrive in the Celestial City, in reality, its final destination is Hell itself. Because Hawthorne disguises the road to Hell as the way to Heaven, the reader expectantly endures an onslaught of conventional values being turned upside down.

Hawthorne was also particularly fascinated by what he consistently called "secret sin." Nowhere is this more evident than in *The Scarlet Letter,* where the Reverend Dimmesdale is tortured by the secret he bears: he is the father of Hester Pyrnne's daughter, Pearl, and he is the reason Hester must wear the stigma of the scarlet letter "A" of adultery emblazoned on her clothing. In each of his other three Romance novels—*The House of the Seven Gables* (1851), *The Blithedale Romance* (1852), and *The Marble Faun* (1860)— Hawthorne sought what he called "the thoughtful moral" behind the foibles and follies of human existence.

Seeking to implement *utopian socialist* and transcendentalist hopes for perfection, Hawthorne, at the encouragement of his future wife, Sophia Peabody, invested in the Brook Farm community in 1841. But less than a year later, he left the community totally disenchanted with this early socialist experiment. Hawthorne also drew on this experience as subject matter for *The Blithedale Romance*, a book that enabled him to work through issues pertaining to human nature, including power, passion, and egoism, which he believed led to the demise of Brook Farm so soon after its establishment.

The *Transcendentalists* were one of the most important intellectual forces in New England from 1836 until 1844. The group of writers comprising the Transcendental Club met at the Concord home of Ralph Waldo Emerson (1803–1882) and included such important figures as the progressive educator Bronson Alcott (father of Louisa May Alcott, best known for her novel *Little Women*); pioneers in public education Elizabeth, Mary, and Sophia Peabody; the early feminist writer and editor Margaret Fuller (1810–1850); the author of *Walden*, Henry David Thoreau (1817–1862), and for a time, Hawthorne.

In the tradition of Plato, Transcendentalists held that truth can be arrived at independently of the senses; the soul has the capacity to transcend the world of experience and grasp ultimate truth. They asserted that intuition was a superior avenue to truth over either logical reasoning or empiricism—knowledge derived from sense experience. They also stressed the spiritual unity of the world, identifying God, whom they called the Over Soul, with Nature and maintained that a higher truth can be attained through Nature's spiritual power as described by Emerson in his essay, *Nature* (1836).

> Standing on the bare ground,—my head bathed by the blithe air and uplifted into infinite space—all mean egotism vanishes. I become a transparent eyeball; I am nothing; I see all; the currents of the Universal Being circulate through me; I am part or parcel of God. . . . The greatest delight which the fields and woods minister is the suggestion of an occult relation between man and the vegetable. I am not alone and unacknowledged. They nod to me, and I to them.[29]

Like the Romantic poets, Transcendentalists valued nature as a source of inspiration and saw poetry as an avenue to truth. "The true philosopher and the true poet are one," declared Emerson, "and a beauty, which is truth, and a truth, which is beauty, is the aim of both."[30]

The Transcendentalists' concern with the inner life led them to stress self-reliance, moral responsibility, optimism concerning an individual's capacity for self-improvement, and tolerance and to support reform movements, including mandatory universal education, elimination of child labor, and the abolition of slavery. They also expressed disdain for the pursuit of wealth and possessions; such materialism, they feared, corrupted the soul. In *Walden; or, Life in the Woods* (1854), Thoreau, reflecting on the years 1845–1847 when he lived alone in a small shack on the edge of Walden Pond (occupying 64 acres in Concord), expressed his concern that the values associated with an emerging industrial age would direct people away from what was truly important: moral self-improvement.

> Men think that it is essential that the *Nation* have commerce, and export ice, and talk through a telegraph, and ride thirty miles an hour. . . . If we do not . . . forge rails, and devote days and nights to the work, but go to tinkering upon our *lives* to improve *them*, who will build railroads? And if railroads are not built, how shall we get to heaven in season? But if we stay at home and mind our business, who will want railroads? We do not ride on the railroad; it rides upon us.[31]

The Transcendentalists also had their detractors, one of whom was Herman Melville (1819–1891), who rejected the entire notion of the Over Soul and the truths Transcendentalists reputedly derived from it. As an empirical naturalist, Melville was concerned with physical reality and abjured the Transcendentalists' belief in God as the Over Soul. For Melville, no such God as the Over Soul existed. Melville was born in New York City and, until his father died in 1832, led a comfortable life. His mother then became a domineering force in his life as did the dogmatic form of Calvinism she practiced, which Melville was compelled to endure. Throughout his life, as is evident in his letters, his short stories, and his novels, Melville was skeptical about organized religion, but uncomfortable with the prospect of atheism.

In 1839, he enlisted as a deckhand on a merchant ship, and for the next five years, Melville traversed the world; later, he signed on as a seaman on the warship *United States*. These adventures gave rise to a number of novels, including *Typee* (1846), *Omoo* (1847), *Redburn* (1849), *Mardi* (1849), *White-Jacket* (1850), and Melville's most famous book—*Moby Dick; or, The Whale*—which many critics regard as the best American novel of the era.

As Melville worked and reworked his story of a whaling adventure, he credited Hawthorne for its actual transformation into a compelling masterpiece and dedicated it to him when it appeared in 1851. Melville's rebellion against what he perceives to be a false idea of God is symbolized by Captain Ahab and his quest for "The White

Whale." Ahab believes that if he can only "pierce the mask"—penetrate the physical reality of the whale and thus get beyond the superficial—he can know the truth about the whale, which will lead him to the truth about God. In his "Cetology [the study of whales] Chapters," Melville meticulously details the attack, death, and processing of each whale, piece by piece, in hope of discovering some ultimate meaning and truth. The novel is laden with mystical images of both the demonic and the heavenly. For example, the three chief shipmates represent various opinions about religion and the capacity of human beings. The first mate, Starbuck, is a Christian idealist who "bucks" the course that Ahab has laid out for his ship, the *Pequod*. In contrast, Stubb is a self-professed fatalist, who accepts life without critically questioning it. He is cheerful and optimistic, but he fails to grasp the seriousness of Ahab's quest for the White Whale, and it is Stubb who dispassionately abandons the cabin boy, Pip, at sea when he is washed overboard. Finally, Flask represents the materialist dolt who never thinks critically about anything, except the task immediately in front of him. When Ahab nails a gold doubloon to the main mast as a reward for whomever sites the White Whale, Flask can only contemplate buying cigars if he wins it.

The images of evil, however, are less clear-cut. Consider, for example, three of the crew: Queequeg, the Manxman, and Fedallah. Queequeg, a Muslim, is covered in mystical tattoos, and he fashions his own coffin, which ultimately serves as the life raft for the ship's only survivor, Ishmael. The Manxman, from the Isle of Man, hence his name, serves as a prophet figure, much like the biblical Elijah. He interprets omens, which Ahab consistently ignores, foretelling doom for the *Pequod*. Fedallah, a *Zoroastrian,* is a quiet, obscure figure that some critics interpret to be the Devil Incarnate, whereas others view him as a disembodied soul. Finally, there is the complex relationship of Ahab and the White Whale. In a very real sense for Ahab, Moby Dick represents evil, for it is he who is responsible for Ahab's physical deformity—the loss of a leg. But Melville consistently represents Moby Dick as "the White Whale," with the whiteness representing The Good, The True, The Beautiful. If such is the case, then it is Ahab who is the personification of evil, and Moby Dick becomes God's agent of divine retribution on a sinful humanity.

Melville, who died in total obscurity as the "Dark Man of American Letters," was soon, like his sole survivor Ishmael, to rise again in the twentieth century—as a restless, questioning reading public started to seek answers to questions of human existence and the meaning of human life.

ROMANTIC ART

Valuing spontaneous creativity, Romantic artists departed from the accepted norms and conventions that underlay Neoclassicism. Rather than conform to artistic models regarded as universal, they aspired to listen to their own inner voice, to trust their own aesthetic judgment. Instead of embracing harmony, balance, symmetry, simplicity, and restraint, Romantic artists sought to create individually unique (sometimes eccentric) art forms and were fascinated with the "exotic" artistic forms of the Far East. Rather than looking back to the decorum of Raphael (see Chapter 13) and Poussin (see Chapter16), Romantic artists were more interested in the drama and passion of Michelangelo (see Chapter 13) and Rubens (see Chapter 16).

Painting

English landscape painters, the first of the Romantic artists, left the studio to study nature itself so as to portray the natural world in all its splendor. Like the Romantic poets, English painters viewed nature as a particularly appropriate outlet for their feelings. They used new theories of light and color to express their personal feelings about nature.

CONSTABLE   One of the early great landscape painters, John Constable (1776–1837), was greatly influenced by the landscapes of Gainsborough (see Chapter 18) and by the color and brushwork of Rubens (see Chapter 16). Nonetheless, it was his own study of the light of the sky that made it possible for Constable to portray his mystical view of nature in landscapes such as *The Hay Wain* (Figure 20.1). When *The Hay Wain* was on exhibition at the Royal Academy in 1821, he wrote: "[A] landscape painter who does not make his skies a very material part of his composition, neglects to avail himself of one of his greatest aids. . . . The sky is the source of light in nature, and governs everything."[32] All of the colors and every part of *The Hay Wain* are affected by the light of the sky: the clouds bounce off the water, the trees themselves are reflected in the stream, and bits of light reflect from the leaves. Constable's great love of the countryside, a key element of the Romantic attitude, is palpable in such a scene, with the human figure at one with nature.

TURNER   The best of the Romantic landscape painters, often called England's finest painter, was Constable's contemporary, Joseph Mallord William Turner (1775–1851). The son of a barber, his artistic ability was evident at an early age; he exhibited a watercolor at the Royal Academy

Figure 20.1   John Constable, *The Hay Wain*, 1821, 51 1/4" x 73" (1.3 x 1.85 m), oil on canvas, National Gallery, London.   Constable's great love of the countryside, a key element of the Romantic attitude, is palpable in such a scene, with the human figure at one with Nature. All of the colors and every part of *The Hay Wain* are affected by the light of the sky. *(National Gallery, London/The Bridgeman Art Library International)*

when he was fifteen years old. His visionary landscapes, which feature shadow and sunlight, mountains and the sea, epitomize the Romantics' veneration of nature's beauty and awesome power. Translating what he saw into scenes that expressed his own romantic feelings, Turner is known for his dramatic treatment of natural light and atmospheric effects in his landscapes. He once stated that wherever there is light, there is color, because "Light is . . . color." Another time, he declared: "Color, the use of which aids, exalts, and in true union with Light and Shadow, makes a whole."[33] Turner applied these sentiments in many of his paintings, but never more spectacularly than in *The Burning of the Houses of Lords and Commons, 16th October, 1834* (Figure 20.2). The light of the fire illuminates the boats in the Thames River, where many, including Turner, are witnessing the spectacular destruction of the British Houses of Parliament, engulfed in flames that shoot into the night sky. On the right, the light of the fire spreads over the bridge and the smoke obliterates all but a small patch of blue sky. Throngs of people, visible in the foreground and on the bridge, watch the nocturnal conflagration.

Constable's *Hay Wain* is a glorification of preindustrial England, but Turner's *The Fighting "Téméraire," Tugged to Her Last Berth to Be Broken Up* (Figure 20.3) announces the new industrial

age. Turner observed the actual towing of the *Téméraire* and then created a celebration of light and color that expressed his powerful feelings. The *Téméraire*, having participated in the Battle of Trafalgar in 1805 when the British navy crushed Napoleon's combined French and Spanish fleet, had a grand and glorious past. But now, in 1838, it is being towed away to its destruction by a modern, steam-powered tugboat, shooting smoke and fire into the air. The spectacular sunset immerses the entire scene with light, transforming the water into a lake of fire on which the image of the two ships is reflected. Turner's unfettered and elevated use of light and color anticipated and influenced the style of Monet and the Impressionists (see Chapter 22).

GÉRICAULT   Like the English, French painters were inspired by the spirit of Romanticism, but their art also reflected the political fervor of nineteenth-century France. Napoleon's official painter during the campaign in northern Italy in 1793, Antoine-Jean Gros (1771–1835), is known as the father of Romantic painting in France. But Théodore Géricault (1791–1824) was the first French painter to make a decisive break with Neoclassicism. His early work was influenced by Gros, but from 1816 to 1817, Géricault studied in Florence and Rome, where he discovered the work of Michelangelo.

Figure 20.2   Joseph Mallord William Turner, *The Burning of the Houses of Lords and Commons, 16th October, 1834*, 1835, 36 1/4″ x 48 1/2″ (92 x 123 cm), oil on canvas, Philadelphia Museum of Art. The light of the fire illuminates the boats in the Thames River where Turner actually witnessed the spectacular destruction of the British Houses of Parliament, engulfed by flames that shoot into the night sky. *(The Philadelphia Museum of Art/The Bridgeman Art Library International)*

Following his return to Paris, Géricault completed his most famous painting in 1819—the *Raft of the Medusa* (Figure 20.4)—exemplifying the Romantic theme of humanity pushed beyond limits. Three years earlier, in 1816, the *Medusa*, a French government ship full of Algerian immigrants, capsized. One hundred forty-nine of the immigrants escaped on a raft fabricated from the wood of the sinking ship. Thirteen days later, fifteen people who had survived on wine and human flesh were rescued.

In preparation for the painting, Géricault interviewed survivors, made sketches of them, and built a replica of the raft. Amid a scene filled with death, he captures the moment when the jubilant survivors first spot their rescue ship. The painting employs two cross axes. The one axis encompasses the Michelangelesque forms of the fifteen survivors (and several corpses), who are arranged in a pyramid that extends from the lower left to the upper right. The cross axis descends from the sail and storm clouds in the upper left to the corpse half submerged in the water in the lower right.

The tragedy came to symbolize the corruption in the government of Louis XVIII. Because the painting was officially condemned, it was simply listed as "A Shipwreck" during its exhibition in Paris. Disheartened by the lack of appreciation for his arduous portrayal of the conflict between human beings and nature, Géricault took the

Figure 20.3   Joseph Mallord William Turner, *The Fighting "Téméraire," Tugged to Her Last Berth to Be Broken Up*, 1838, 35 1/4″ x 48″ (89.5 x 121.9 cm), oil on canvas, National Gallery, London. Having once participated in the Battle of Trafalgar, crushing Napoleon's combined French and Spanish fleet, the ship is now being towed away to its destruction by a modern, steam-powered tugboat. *(National Gallery, London/The Bridgeman Art Library International)*

Figure 20.4 Théodore Géricault, *Raft of the Medusa,* 1818–1819, 16′ 1″ x 23′ 6″ (4.9 x 7.16 m), oil on canvas, Musée du Louvre, Paris. In 1816, the *Medusa,* a French government ship full of Algerian immigrants, capsized. One hundred forty-nine of them escaped on a raft fabricated from the wood of the sinking ship. But thirteen days later, only fifteen jubilant survivors were still alive to spot their rescue ship. *(Louvre/Réunion des Musées Nationaux/Art Resource, NY)*

16- × 23-foot painting to England, where he displayed it commercially.

Upon his return to France, Géricault executed an innovative series of ten paintings depicting the psychological conflict of insane people for Dr. Georget, an early pioneer in the field of psychiatry. Each canvas features a different psychotic condition, including delusions of grandeur and klepto-

mania. Géricault's work was unparalleled, for he portrayed the insane, not as the object of laughter and ridicule but, rather, as helpless victims of a debilitating mental illness.

Although it appeared that Géricault would indeed become the visionary leader of high Romanticism in France, in 1824 he was thrown from a horse and died as a result of his injuries. Thus, it

Figure 20.5 Eugene Delacroix, *Death of Sardanapalus,* 1827, 12′ 1 1/2″ x 16′ 2 7/8″ (3.7 x 4.95 m), oil on canvas, Musée du Louvre, Paris. Because he is about to be captured, Sardanapalus orders the destruction of his concubines and slaves. He watches the slaughter of his people and animals from the couch, which will soon serve as his own funeral pyre. *(Louvre/Réunion des Musées Nationaux/Art Resource, NY)*

was Delacroix, Géricault's younger friend, who became the leading French Romantic painter.

DELACROIX The Romantic sentiments of Eugene Delacroix (1798–1863) flowed from his love of literature, especially Shakespeare and Dante, and the works of his contemporaries, Goethe, Byron, and Hugo. In addition, Delacroix was inspired by the old masters—Raphael, the Venetian painters of the Renaissance, and especially Rubens—and by contemporary English artists. In 1824, Delacroix saw Constable's *Hay Wain* win a gold medal at the exhibition at Paris, and the following year he spent three months in England studying the works of English painters.

Between 1822 and 1828, Delacroix executed three important paintings—*Virgil and Dante Crossing the Styx,* illustrating a passage from Dante's *Divine Comedy; Scenes from the Massacres at Chios,* inspired by a contemporary event; and *Death of Sardanapalus,* drawn from the poetic drama *Sardanapalus: A Tragedy,* by Byron —which made him the acknowledged leader of the Romantic painters in France. *Scenes from the Massacres at Chios* (see chapter opening), like Géricault's *Raft of the Medusa,* was based on an actual event. In 1822, during the Greek War of Independence, Turks massacred 20,000 Greeks on the island of Chios. Delacroix's portrayal focuses attention on both the victims in the foreground (some already dead and others dejectedly awaiting their fate) and those in the background, also waiting to be slaughtered. The vibrant, rich, contrasting colors and the luminescent sky, which became

a staple of his work, show the influence of Constable. Critics who were enamored with Neoclassicism condemned the painting's composition, proportion, drawing, and color. One even remarked that it was not the massacres of Chios, but rather "the massacre of painting."

The exotic scene in *Death of Sardanapalus* (Figure 20.5) depicts the ancient king about to be captured by his enemies. Consequently, Sardanapalus orders the destruction of his concubines and slaves, as well as himself. He watches the slaughter of his people and animals from the couch, which soon will serve as his funeral pyre. When it was exhibited, critics and the public alike attacked the painting, claiming that the disorderly scene was too colorful, violent, and sensual.

Delacroix's *Liberty Leading the People* (Figure 20.6), his most famous work, has been called the first political painting in modern art. In the wake of the Revolution of 1830, Delacroix wrote to his brother, "[I]f I have not fought for the country, at least I will paint for her."[34] As an allegory, the painting idealizes and glorifies the idea of liberty. Lady Liberty, the seminude woman, holds a musket in one hand and waves the tricolor flag of the French Revolution in the other, leading the people in their armed revolt. But it is also a history painting that celebrates the uprising of the various classes of the French people on July 28, which forced Charles X to abdicate his throne. Especially chilling was the menacing figure with the sword on the left, who represents the underclass, and the street urchin brandishing pistols to the right of Liberty. Conservatives feared that this work would

Figure 20.6 Eugene Delacroix, *Liberty Leading the People*, 1830, 8′ 6″ x 10′ 8″ (260 x 325 cm), oil on canvas, Musée du Louvre, Paris. This painting, in which Lady Liberty holds a musket in one hand and waves the tricolor flag of the French Revolution in the other, celebrates the uprising of the various classes of the French people. Of special note is the menacing figure with the sword, on the left, who represents the underclass, and the street urchin brandishing pistols. *(Louvre/Erich Lessing/Art Resource, NY)*

Figure 20.7 François Rude, *Departure of the Volunteers of 1792*, 1833–1836, approx. 42′ x 26′ (12.8 x 7.93 m), Arc de Triomphe, Place de l'Étoile, Paris. The volunteers who joined with the regular troops to halt the Prussian invasion, at Valmy, in 1792 are led by the winged figure of Victory. *(Giraudon/Art Resource, NY)*

inspire further unrest, and the new king, Louis Philippe, purchased it and hid it from public view. But following the Revolution of 1848, the painting was again exhibited publicly. It continues to be an enduring symbol of French liberty—adorning the hundred-franc note in 1979 and a postage stamp in 1982.

In 1832, Delacroix journeyed to Morocco as part of a French diplomatic mission. This experience inspired him to introduce exotic themes into his paintings, such as clashes between African animals and Arabs in their colorful dress, whom Delacroix called "nature's noblemen,"[35] uncorrupted by European excess. As a result, he is credited with introducing Orientalism into French art. By the 1840s, Delacroix's style was overshadowed by the new Realism of painters such as Gustave Courbet (see Chapter 21), but he continued to be a prolific painter until his death in 1863.

Sculpture: Rude

Generally speaking, Romantic sculpture was conceived for public buildings and monuments, as is evidenced by the most impressive of these works, *Departure of the Volunteers of 1792* (Figure 20.7) by François Rude (1784–1855). Executed between 1833 and 1836 for the Arc de Triomphe on the Champs Elysées, it depicts the volunteers who joined the regular troops of the army to halt the Prussian invasion at Valmy in 1792, a critical event in the French Revolution. The volunteers are driven onward by the winged figure of Victory above them.

Figure 20.8 Charles Barry and A. W. N. Pugin, *Houses of Parliament*, 1836–1860, London. Although the basic plan was Barry's, Pugin was responsible for the Gothic decoration, and taken together, their work is regarded as the culmination of the Gothic Revival in England. *(National Monuments Record © English Heritage)*

Figure 20.9 Richard Upjohn, *Trinity Church*, 1839–1846, New York City, New York. Upjohn was a devoted member of the Protestant Episcopal Church, the American cousin of the Church of England, which had embraced the Gothic revival. The success of the Gothic design for Trinity Church occasioned many additional commissions for churches, mostly Episcopal.

Although the figure of Victory and the poses and armor of the volunteers are reminiscent of Classicism, the ebullient mood of patriotism is purely Romantic. Soon, Rude's work came to be known as *The Marseillaise*, so-named after the French national anthem, written soon after the battle.

The Gothic Revival in Architecture

Along with the rise of the Gothic novel in England came the Gothic Revival in architecture. This was due not only to the Romantic enchantment with things medieval, but because the English also believed that the Gothic style best reflected their past; they dated the origins of their democracy to the signing of the Magna Carta in 1215 during the Middle Ages. Consequently, when the old Houses of Parliament burned in 1834, a competition was held to select an architect for a new structure. One of the chief requirements was that all entries had to be in English Gothic style to match Westminster Abbey, which had escaped the fire. The winners of the competition were Charles Barry (1795–1860)

and A. W. N. Pugin (1812–1852), who between 1836 and 1860, built the *Houses of Parliament* (Figure 20.8). The basic plan was Barry's, whereas Pugin, the foremost proponent of the Gothic style in England, was responsible for the decoration. Taken together, their work is viewed as the culmination of the Gothic Revival in England.

Subsequently, the Neo-Gothic style was introduced in the United States by Richard Upjohn (1802–1878), who emigrated from his native England to the United States in 1829. Upjohn was a devoted member of the Protestant Episcopal Church, the American cousin of the Church of England, which had embraced the Gothic Revival. In 1839, Upjohn designed *Trinity Church* (Figure 20.9) in New York City in the British Gothic style of the early fourteenth century. The success of the Gothic design for Trinity Church occasioned many additional commissions for churches, mostly Episcopal. For those parishes that could not afford to build in stone, in 1852 Upjohn published *Rural Architecture*, a design for wooden rural churches in the Gothic style.

ROMANTIC MUSIC

Romantic composers placed an unparalleled emphasis on individualism and the composer's creative genius. Nearly all composers of the nineteenth century viewed Beethoven as their spiritual and musical mentor, and they consistently chose Beethoven's *Ninth Symphony* (see Chapter 19) as the line of demarcation between Classical and Romantic music. Nonetheless, Romantic composers continued to employ many of the musical forms of their Classical predecessors, but they imbued them with an emotional intensity previously unheard. Music was no longer simply composed to entertain guests on a special occasion or to provide "background" to a state function. Like Romantic painters, composers employed a palette of tone color to capture the unspeakable sadness of unrequited love or to arouse nationalistic zeal. Ultimately, Romantic composers developed new musical forms, most notably program music, to tell a story with a moral or a meaning that was truly "extramusical"—thereby transcending the Classical conventions of pitch, dynamics, rhythm, and harmony.

During the age of Romanticism, the status of musicians changed. Instead of relying on the patronage of the aristocracy and the church, they now drew their support from a wider public, middle-class people of wealth who commissioned performances. Furthermore, musicians believed that they had been "called" to fulfill some sort of special mission. Robert Schumann (see following discussion) succinctly summarized this calling when he declared: "To cast light into the depths of the human heart—the artist's mission!"[36] The training of this new generation of composers and performers was also transformed at musical conservatories, specialized educational institutions that replaced the apprenticeship of musicians to princely courts or to the service of the church.

Like their literary and artistic contemporaries, Romantic composers were drawn to "supernatural" texts, including Goethe's *Faust,* and viewed nature as a fountain of hidden powers. Composers of program music thus discovered innovative ways to make their musical ideas symbolize philosophical ideas, emotional states of mind, dramatic affairs, or individual people and things. Moreover, as the Napoleonic wars aroused a sense of national identity among conquered peoples, Romantic composers began to use music as an instrument to accentuate national pride. Many of their compositions were inspired by folk dances and tunes, as well as a variety of ethnic stories and historical legends, which were often laden with patriotic tones. Such nationalistic sentiments were particularly decisive in the battle between Italian and German composers over who was the true heir of opera (see Chapter 22).

Because the character of Romantic music was both international and indigenous, it is virtually impossible to define "the Romantic style" of music. Nonetheless, definite ingredients can be identified. To achieve the most expressive and heartfelt sounds, composers aspired to find fresh ways of combining tone colors. They employed a wider range of sound by varying the dynamics (loudness and softness), and they created new sounds by improving the quality of instruments (particularly woodwind instruments, such as the flute) and by adding new instruments to the orchestra. For example, the harp became part of the strings section; cymbals and the triangle were added to the percussion section; tubas and trombones became mainstays of the brass section; and the character of the woodwinds section was virtually transformed with the addition of the English horn, bass clarinet, contrabassoon, and piccolo. Thus, the Romantic orchestra, with approximately 100 members, was significantly larger than the orchestra of the Classical era, which numbered between twenty and sixty players.

Throughout the Age of Romanticism, the piano (vastly improved during the 1820s and 1830s) became the preferred instrument of musicians. The instrument was made stronger by adding a cast iron frame to hold the strings in great tension.

Moreover, the hammers (which struck the strings) were covered with felt to tone down the strident sound of the wooden hammer hitting the exposed string. Finally, a damper (loud) pedal was affixed to permit a more resonant blending of tones to enhance the entire spectrum of sound the piano could produce. Therefore, one could truthfully say that the piano did indeed "sing."

Beyond their exploitation of new and exciting tone colors, Romantic composers achieved greater emotional intensity by emphasizing fuller, often more discordant, harmonies. In some cases they abandoned the traditional major and minor scales of seven different tones in favor of the chromatic scale consisting of twelve tones. By delaying the resolution of the dramatic intensity of dissonant chords, melodies became longer. Moods of mystery, anxiety, or desire could also be heightened by means of tempo—which became more extreme—ranging from *larghissimo* (very broad) to *prestissimo* (very, very fast). Furthermore, a new innovation, called **tempo rubato,** meant that the performer and/or conductor was freed from adhering to a strict tempo. This permitted the creative genius of the musician to "speak" through the music.

One of the most distinctive forms of music during the Age of Romanticism was the **art song**—a composition for piano and solo voice. In such a composition, poetry and music are inextricably fused, and the piano and the soloist virtually "sing" a duet. Both the piano and the soloist share the interpretive task of characterizing the beauty of nature, creating a mood, relating a story, inspiring joy, lamenting love unfulfilled, or plumbing the depths of the human soul. For example, vocal melodies can stress certain tones or change dynamic levels to suit the demands of the text. Similarly, the piano accompaniment can make use of chords in the lower registers of sound to create dark, sinister moods or employ the higher registers to depict pleasure and delight. The mood is generally announced by a brief piano introduction and summarized by a piano section at the end—termed a *postlude.* Romantic art songs can also be assembled in a *song cycle,* in which the various songs are linked to one another with a plot line that appears in each of the poems or by a musical motif that connects each of the songs. The three acknowledged masters of this musical genre were Franz Peter Schubert, Robert Schumann, and Johannes Brahms.

Schubert

Romantic traits began to appear in the German *lied* (song, plural *lieder*) by the end of the eighteenth century, but the earliest master of the lied was Franz Peter Schubert (1797–1828). Like many of his contemporaries, Schubert believed he was called to music ("I have come into the world for no other purpose than to compose"[37]), and he died tragically at the early age of thirty-one.

Schubert composed 600 songs during his lifetime, including his *Erlkönig (Elf King)*, arranged when he was just eighteen years old. As related in Goethe's narrative ballad, on which Schubert based his musical setting, the Elf King symbolizes death. The song relates the tale of a desperate father, riding his horse through a tumultuous thunderstorm while holding his sick son in his arms. In the lower registers of the piano, Schubert creates the sound of the galloping horse. In a higher register, he depicts the son crying out: "Father, don't you see the Elf King?" With a gleeful tune, played and sung very quietly, Schubert has the Elf King ask: "My handsome boy, will you come with me?" The son's stunned response is related loudly, in a higher register, as he, once again, tries to convince his father that he sees and hears the Elf King. A narrator then sings about how the father rides on, holding the groaning child in his arms, and how "he finally reaches the courtyard weary and anxious." The piano accompaniment then abruptly ceases and a plaintive recitative relates that "in his arms the child was dead."[38] Schubert eventually drew on Goethe's poems for an additional fifty-eight songs.

By 1822, Schubert began to feel the exhausting effects of venereal disease. Nevertheless, he composed some of his finest works in his last years, including two great symphonies: *Symphony in B minor* (dubbed the "Unfinished Symphony") and the *Symphony in C Major* (which Schumann anointed "The Great," a name that has remained to the present day). Today, Schubert is best remembered not only for these two symphonies, but also for his *Mass in G Major* (in the style of Haydn), which continues to be the most often performed mass from the nineteenth century. But Schubert's most enduring legacy is a lied that came to be called "Ave Maria" ("Hail Mary").

Eight days before Beethoven's death in 1827, Schubert visited him. He did so knowing that he had achieved his lifelong ambition—to have his work recognized by "the Master." Beethoven's first biographer recounted how much Beethoven respected Schubert's talent when he exclaimed: "That man has a divine spark!"[39] When Schubert served as a torchbearer at Beethoven's funeral on April 3, few could have guessed that in a little over a year Schubert would die from the effects of venereal disease, probably syphilis. On November 29, 1828, Schubert was buried in Währing Cemetery, thus fulfilling his last wish—to be buried near his beloved Beethoven.

The Schumanns

Schubert's successor in the composition of lieder, and another one of Beethoven's great admirers, was Robert Schumann (1810–1856). Beginning in 1830, Schumann composed his first pieces for the piano, but when he began to experience serious problems with the fourth finger on his right hand, he was compelled to turn his attention from performing to writing musical criticism. In 1834, Schumann founded the musical journal *The New Journal of Music*. During the ten years he was editor, the journal became one of the most influential musical periodicals of the nineteenth century. In his journal articles, Schumann revealed himself to be a true Romantic—idealistic, intuitive, and self-absorbed; he was rarely wrong when it came to assessing the abilities of emerging artists. Schumann is credited with "discovering" a number of successful Romantic composers, including Felix Mendelssohn, Frédéric Chopin, and Johannes Brahms (see following discussion).

Schumann suffered from severe mental illness, which drove him to attempt suicide by throwing himself into the Rhine River. Two years later, his wife, Clara Wieck (1819–1896), herself a gifted pianist, was forced to institutionalize him in an asylum, where he died shortly after. Despite his tragic life, Schumann made great contributions to Western music. Many of his compositions became popular because Clara returned to the concert stage to perform them. Both his lieder and his piano music reveal Schumann's deep love of a lyrical line and his passion for good literature—ranging from the Greek classics to those of Byron and Sir Walter Scott, the prominent English historical novelist. Although his orchestral works remain truer to the Classical tradition of Haydn, Mozart, and the early Beethoven, they do evidence a number of Romantic tendencies, including poetic lyricism, experimentation with form (aside from the structure of sonata form) and the mixing of literary and musical ideas, for Schumann considered music in autobiographical, literary, and emotive ways.

In 1857, Clara moved to Berlin to teach, to perform, and to edit her husband's works. Her piano playing was characterized as technically masterful, yet poetically sensitive. Moreover, in more than thirty-eight concert tours outside Germany, she was heralded for her thoughtful interpretation of all composers' works. In an age when women found opportunities to express themselves as performers, they were hindered by innumerable social and cultural obstacles when it came to composing. Clara was a shining exception, for she wrote twenty works for solo piano, twenty-nine lieder, and four compositions for piano and orchestra and arranged *cadenzas* (elaborate flourishes near the end of a piece of music) for three Beethoven and Mozart piano concertos. Many of her musical works were drawn from the writings of her contemporaries, including Goethe and the Scottish poet Robert Burns.

Mendelssohn

The most Classical musician of the nineteenth century was Felix Mendelssohn Bartholdy (1809–1847), who was born into a distinguished Jewish family—his father was a banker and his grandfather, Moses Mendelssohn, a prominent philosopher. In 1816, the family converted to Christianity, taking the additional surname—Bartholdy. A child prodigy, Mendelssohn composed his first music at age eleven, his first symphonies by the time he was thirteen, and his *Overture to a Midsummer Night's Dream,* which he based on Shakespeare's play, at the age of seventeen. Mendelssohn gained an international reputation at the age of twenty, when he conducted a performance of Bach's *Saint Matthew Passion* in Berlin. This event marked the beginning of the "Bach Revival" of the nineteenth century. Over the next several years, Mendelssohn traveled extensively in Italy, England, and Scotland, resulting in works such as his "Italian Symphony" (1833) and his "Scottish Symphony" (1842). A much sought after conductor, some of his command performances were for dignitaries such as England's Queen Victoria (1837–1901).

In 1843, Mendelssohn composed a type of program music—called *incidental music*—for the staging of Shakespeare's play, *A Midsummer Night's Dream.* (It included the music that, ever since, has been called "The Wedding March.") Incidental music is not actually a part of the drama itself, but rather it is played in the background to set a scene or mood. The modern-day equivalent to this type of music is the musical score of a motion picture.

Mendelssohn composed in every genre except opera. His most Romantic pieces are his lieder and some of his shorter piano works, in which he demonstrates his ability to draw extramusical associations from his great love of literature. Most of Mendelssohn's works, however, exude a sense of grace and proportion reminiscent of Haydn and Mozart, and one of his greatest works—the oratorio *Elijah*—demonstrates the influence of the choral works of Bach and Handel. In 1846 Mendelssohn premiered the work in Birmingham, England, to a stupendous reception. Following the path of Schubert and Schumann, he died at the age of thirty-eight from a series of strokes.

Berlioz

One of the first great composers of program music was the Frenchman Hector Berlioz (1803–1869), who was profoundly influenced by both the poetry of Shakespeare and the music of Beethoven. Writing in his *Memoirs,* Berlioz recalls:

> Thunderclaps occasionally follow one another in the life of an artist as rapidly as during certain storms in which the clouds, replete with electric fluid, seem to toss the lightning back and forth and to breathe the hurricane. . . . I saw the immense Beethoven rise up. The impact on me was nearly comparable to that which I had felt with Shakespeare. He opened up for me a new world in music, just as the poet had revealed to me a new universe in poetry.[40]

In 1830, Berlioz composed his most famous piece—*Symphonie fantastique* (Fantastic Symphony)—which deals, in part, with his obsessive love for Harriet Smithson, an Irish Shakespearean actress who had rebuffed him. Prior to the concert in Paris, Berlioz requested that a program be distributed to prepare the audience better for what they were about to hear. In his notes on the symphony, Berlioz wrote:

> I take as my subject an artist blest with sensibility and a lively imagination . . . who meets a woman who awakens in him for the first time his heart's desire. He falls desperately in love with her. Curiously, the image of his beloved is linked inseparably with a musical idea representing her graceful and noble character. This *idée fixe* [fixed idea], haunts him throughout the symphony,[41] [and] the image of the beloved never presents itself to the artist's imagination except tied to a musical idea— *idée fixe* (fixed idea).[42]

In the first part, "Daydreams—Passions," the artist sees his beloved for the first time. She is introduced by the *idée fixe*—a forty-measure musical theme that represents his love—which recurs throughout all five movements of the symphony. In the second part, "A Ball," the artist continues to contemplate his beloved, but her image brings trouble to his spirit, which is further enhanced in the third part, "Country Scene," when the artist's visions of happiness degenerate into dark forebodings. In the fourth part, "March to the Scaffold":

> Having become convinced that his love is not returned, the artist poisons himself with opium. The dose of narcotic, too weak to kill him, plunges him into a sleep beset with the most horrible visions. He dreams he has murdered the one he loved; he has been sentenced, is being led to the

scaffold, is *witnessing his own execution*. . . . At the end of the march, the first four measures of the *idée fixe* reappear like a last thought of love interrupted by the fatal blow [of the guillotine].[43]

And in the final part, "Dream of a Sabbath Night," the artist sees his funeral as a type of witches' sabbath peopled "by a hideous crowd of spirits, sorcerers, monsters of every kind," even his beloved takes part.[44] Many people were shocked by the program's references to the macabre and the demonic, nor did they appreciate Berlioz's dramatic and innovative orchestration, including his use of cymbals, English horn, tuba, harp, cornet, and chimes, to depict the satanic and the phantasmagorical.

Today, Berlioz's work is recognized for its success in transforming the *abstract* musical form of the symphony into a completely *dramatic* one. Throughout the five movements of the symphony, Berlioz demonstrated an amazing ability to express a variety of complex moods. By coming and going throughout the piece, the *idée fixe* serves to develop the actual excitement of the piece as the young artist repeatedly encounters his beloved and then loses her. One of the most impressive examples of orchestration comes from the third movement, where Berlioz wrote a solo passage for the English horn and four tympani (kettledrums), suggesting the "distant sound of thunder."

As a result of winning the *Prix de Rome*, Berlioz spent two years studying in Rome. Following his return to Paris, he was introduced to Harriet Smithson, who had attended a performance of the *Symphonie fantastique* and realized that the symphony was, in a sense, portraying her. They were married on October 3, 1833, but the marriage ended in 1841.

Great literature also inspired Berlioz to compose a number of innovative symphonies, including *King Lear* (1831) and *Romeo and Juliet* (1839), based on Shakespeare's tragedies, and *Harold in Italy* (1834), inspired by Byron's poem *Childe Harold's Pilgrimage*. Berlioz also created dramatic choral works such as his cantata *The Damnation of Faust*, based on Goethe's work, and his *Requiem*, which justifiably stands alongside those of Mozart, Beethoven, Brahms, and Verdi. Moreover, Berlioz's program music served to inspire both Franz Liszt and Richard Wagner (see Chapter 22).

Due to his immense interest in the seemingly boundless possibilities for orchestration and the various combinations of instrumental sounds, in 1844 Berlioz wrote *Treatise on Orchestration*. To this day, Berlioz's treatise is regarded as one of the best sources concerning instrumentation in the field, and his efforts in this area advanced the expansion and development of the modern symphony orchestra.

Chopin

Before concertizing in Warsaw and Vienna, Frédéric Chopin (1810–1849) was trained at the newly established Warsaw Conservatory of Music. When he was twenty years old, Chopin traveled to Paris, where he was soon appreciated by Berlioz, Delacroix, Hugo, and the distinguished female novelist who took the name George Sand (see Chapter 21). Most of Chopin's performances were for small audiences of less than 200 people, not unlike the performances that once entertained French aristocrats in the salons during the eighteenth century.

From 1831 until 1847, George Sand was the dominating presence in Chopin's life. Writing about Chopin's innate genius, as well as his tortured path to get his ideas down on paper, Sand remarked:

His creation was spontaneous and miraculous. He found it without seeking it, without foreseeing it. It came on his piano suddenly, complete, sublime, or it sang in his head during a walk, and he was impatient to play it to himself. But then began the most heart-rending labor I ever saw. . . . He shut himself up for whole days, weeping, walking, breaking his pens, repeating and altering a bar [measure] a hundred times, writing and erasing it as many times, and recommencing the next day with a minute and desperate perseverance.[45]

Sand cared for Chopin even while his health continued to deteriorate after their love affair ended in 1847; he died less than two years later from tuberculosis.

Chopin's genius as a pianist–composer was evident in the innovative sounds he evoked from the instrument. Drawing on the entire spectrum of color the piano could produce, the always introspective Chopin found an outlet for his private thoughts. Regarded as one of Poland's first nationalist composers, most of his melodies, harmonies, and rhythms were drawn from native Polish themes. Typical Polish dance tunes are evident in Chopin's mazurkas, polonaises, and waltzes. Similarly, his **nocturnes** (French for "night piece") and preludes reflect a melancholic (yet nationalistic) longing for his homeland. Commenting on such pieces for the London *Daily News*, a reviewer wrote:

In these various pieces he showed very strikingly his original genius as a composer and his transcendental powers as a performer. His music is as strongly marked with individual character as that of any master who has ever lived. It is highly finished, new in its harmonies, full of contrapuntal skill and ingenious contrivance. . . . The performer seems to abandon himself to the impulses of his fancy and feeling to indulge in a reverie and to pour out unconsciously, as it were, the thoughts and emotions that pass through his mind.[46]

Chopin performed his own works and those of other composers with equal mastery, and he was a consummate virtuoso at improvisation.

—————

The Impact of the Romantic Movement

The Romantic revolt against the Enlightenment had an important and enduring impact on European history. By focusing on the creative capacities inherent in the emotions—intuition, instinct, passion, spontaneity, empathy, and compassion—the Romantics shed light on a side of human nature that the philosophes had often overlooked or undervalued. By encouraging freedom of expression and diversity in art, music, and literature, they greatly enriched European cultural life. Future artists, writers, and musicians would proceed along the path opened by the Romantics. Modern art, for example, owes much to the Romantic Movement's emphasis on the legitimacy of human feeling and its exploration of the hidden world of dreams and fantasies. The Romantics' emphasis on feeling sometimes found expression in humanitarian movements that fought slavery, child labor, and poverty. Romantics were among the first to attack the emerging industrial capitalism for subordinating individuals to the requirements of the industrial process and treating them as mere things. By recognizing the distinctive qualities of historical periods, peoples, and cultures, the Romantics helped to create the modern historical outlook. By valuing the nation's past, Romanticism contributed to modern conservatism and nationalism.

However, the Romantic Movement had a potentially dangerous side: it served as background to the extreme nationalism of the twentieth century. By waging their attack on reason with excessive zeal, the Romantics undermined respect for the rational tradition of the Enlightenment and thus set up a precondition for the rise and triumph of fascist movements. Although their intention was cultural and not political, by idealizing the past and glorifying ancient folkways, legends, native soil, and native language, the Romantics introduced a highly charged nonrational component into political life, particularly in Germany. When transferred to the realm of politics, the Romantics' idealization of the past and fascination with inher-

ited national myths as the source of wisdom reawakened a way of thinking about the world that rested more on feeling than on reason. In the process, people became committed to nationalist and political ideas that were fraught with danger. The glorification of myth and the folk community constitutes a link, however unintended, between Romanticism and extreme nationalism, which culminated in the world wars of the twentieth century.

Key Terms

Conservatism	utopian socialists
liberalism	Transcendentalists
nationalism	Zoroastrian
Romanticism	*tempo rubato*
Volksgeist	art song
Sturm und Drang	cadenza
"Byronic hero"	incidental music
Gothic Romance	nocturnes

Notes

1. Quoted in H. G. Schenk, *The Mind of the European Romantics* (Garden City, N.Y.: Doubleday, 1969), p. 4.
2. William Blake, *Milton*, in *The Poetry and Prose of William Blake*, ed. David V. Erdman (Garden City, N.Y.: Doubleday, 1965), plate 40, lines 34–36.
3. Ibid., plate 41, line 1.
4. Letter of John Keats, November 22, 1817, in *The Letters of John Keats*, ed. Hyder E. Rollins (Cambridge, Mass.: Harvard University Press, 1958), 1: 184–185.
5. Blake, *Milton*, Preface.
6. Quoted in Robert T. Donomm, *Nineteenth-Century French Romantic Poets* (Carbondale: Southern Illinois University Press, 1969), p. 28.
7. From William Wordsworth "The Tables Turned," in *The Complete Poetical Works of Wordsworth*, ed. Andrew J. George (Boston: Houghton Mifflin, 1904, rev. ed., 1982), p. 83.
8. Johann Wolfgang von Goethe, *Faust: A Tragedy*, trans. Walter Arndt, ed. Cyrus Hamlin, 2nd ed. (New York and London: W. W. Norton, 2002), p. 12.
9. William Wordsworth and Samuel Coleridge, *Lyrical Ballads*, ed. R. L. Brett and A. R. Jones (London: Methuen & Co. Ltd., 1971), p. 246.
10. Ibid., pp. 247, 250–251.
11. Ibid., pp. 44, 42.
12. Wordsworth and Coleridge, *Lyrical Ballads*, "Lines written Above Tintern Abbey" (lines 1–4, 23–28, and 122–135), pp. 113, 114, and 117.

13. Lord Byron, "Don Juan," *The Norton Anthology of English Literature*, ed. M. H. Abrams (New York: W. W. Norton, 1968), pp. 331–332.

14. Bennett A. Cerf and Donald S. Klopper, eds., *John Keats and Percy Bysshe Shelley: Complete Poetical Works with the Explanatory notes of Shelley's poem by Mrs. Shelley* (New York: The Modern Library, n.d.), p. 835.

15. Ibid., p. 228.

16. Ibid., p. 618.

17. Ibid., p. 185.

18. Emily Brontë, *Wuthering Heights* (New York: Scholastic Book Services, 1961), pp. 191, 192, 194, 195.

19. Mary Shelley, *Frankenstein: Complete, Authoritative Text with Biographical, Historical and Cultural Contexts, Critical History, and Essay from Contemporary Critical Perspectives*, ed. Johanna M. Smith (Boston and New York: Bedford/St. Martin's, 2000), p. 180.

20. Ibid., p. 188.

21. W. H. Auden, ed., *Edgar Allan Poe: Selected Prose, Poetry, and Eureka* (New York: Holt, Rinehart and Winston, Inc., 1950), p. 427.

22. Ibid., p. 428.

23. Ibid., p. 430.

24. Ibid., p. 471.

25. Ibid., p. 431.

26. Ibid., pp. 1–2.

27. Nathaniel Hawthorne, *The Portable Hawthorne*, ed. Malcolm Cowley (New York: Penguin Books, 1979), p. 327.

28. Ibid., pp. 328 and 329.

29. Ralph Waldo Emerson, *Nature Address and Lectures* (Boston and New York: Houghton Mifflin, 1903, reprinted AMS Press, 1968), p. 10.

30. Ibid., p. 55.

31. *The Annotated Walden: Or, Life in the Woods, Together with "Civil Disobedience," a Detailed Chronology and Various Pieces About Its Author the Writing and Publishing of the Book*, ed. Philip van Doren Stern (New York: Bramhall House, 1970), p. 223.

32. Quoted in David M. Robb, *The Harper History of Painting: The Occidental Tradition* (New York: Harper & Brothers, 1951), p. 721.

33. Quoted in Gerald Finley, *Angel in the Sun: Turner's Vision of History* (Montreal and Kingston: McGill-Queen's University Press, 1999), p. 188.

34. Quoted in Barthélémy Jobert, *Delacroix* (Princeton, N.J.: Princeton University Press, 1997), p. 130.

35. Helen Gardner, *Gardner's Art Through the Ages*, ed. Horst de la Croix and Richard G. Tansey, 6th ed. (New York: Harcourt Brace Jovanovich, Inc., 1975), p. 676.

36. Excerpted in Piero Weiss and Richard Taruskin, *Music in the Western World: A History in Documents* (New York: Schirmer Books, 1984), p. 361.

37. Quoted in Roger Kamien, *Music: An Appreciation* (Boston: McGraw-Hill, 1998), p. 218.

38. Ibid., pp. 221–222.

39. Quoted in Alexander Wheelock Thayer, *Thayer's Life of Beethoven*, ed. Elliot Forbes (Princeton, N.J.: Princeton University Press, 1967), p. 1044.

40. Excerpted in Weiss and Taruskin, *Music in the Western World*, p. 352.

41. Jason C. Lee, *Hector Berlioz: Symphonie Fantastique* [online] Available http://www.ugcs.caltech.edu/~jclee/music/fantastique.html June 11, 2001

42. Excerpted in Weiss and Taruskin, *Music in the Western World*, p. 355.

43. Ibid., p. 356.

44. Ibid., p. 357.

45. Ibid., p. 370.

46. Ibid., pp. 370–371.

21

Thought and Literature in an Age of Science and Industrialism: Realism, Secularism, and Reform

William Powell Frith, Charles Dickens, c. 1850s, oil on canvas

In his early novels, Dickens attempted to show that society must be fundamentally changed or it will implode, but in his later ones, he blamed social institutions for the misery of the downtrodden.

(Corbis)

T HE SECOND HALF OF THE NINETEENTH CENTURY was marked by great progress in science, a surge in industrialism, and a continuing secularization of life and thought. The main intellectual and literary currents of the century's middle decades reflected these trends. Realism, Darwinism, Marxism, and liberalism all reacted against romantic, religious, and metaphysical interpretations of nature and society, focusing instead on the empirical world. In one way or another, each movement derived from and expanded the Enlightenment tradition. Adherents of these movements relied on careful observation and strove for scientific accuracy. This emphasis on objective reality helped to stimulate a growing criticism of social ills, for despite unprecedented material progress, reality was often sordid, somber, and dehumanizing.

In the last part of the nineteenth century, European life was profoundly affected by accelerating industrialization and nationalism that was growing more extreme and dangerous.

THE HISTORICAL SETTING

Accelerating Industrialization

In the last part of the eighteenth century, as a revolution for liberty and equality swept across France and sent shock waves through Europe, a different kind of revolution, a revolution in industry, was transforming life in Great Britain. In the nineteenth century, the Industrial Revolution spread to the United States and to the European continent. Today, it encompasses virtually the entire world; everywhere the drive to substitute machines for human labor continues at a rapid pace.

After 1760, dramatic changes occurred in Britain in the way goods were produced and labor organized. New forms of power, particularly steam, replaced animal strength and human muscle. Better ways of obtaining and using raw materials were discovered, and a new way of organizing production and workers—the factory—came into common use. In the nineteenth century, technology moved from triumph to triumph with a momentum unprecedented in human history. The resulting explosion in economic production and productivity transformed society with breathtaking speed.

Rapid industrialization caused hardships for the new class of industrial workers, many of them recent arrivals from the countryside. Arduous and monotonous, factory labor was geared to the strict discipline of the clock, the machine, and the production schedule. Employment was never secure. Sick workers received no pay and were often fired; aged workers suffered pay cuts

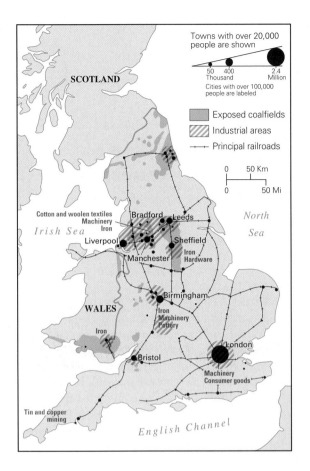

Towns with over 20,000 people are shown

50 400 2.4
Thousand Million

Cities with over 100,000 people are labeled

Exposed coalfields

Industrial areas

Principal railroads

0   50 Km

0   50 Mi

or lost their jobs. During business slumps, employers lowered wages with impunity, and laid-off workers had nowhere to turn for assistance. Because factory owners did not consider safety an important concern, accidents were frequent. Yet the Industrial Revolution was also a great force for human betterment. Ultimately, it raised the standard of living, even for the lowest classes, lengthened life expectancy, and provided more leisure time and more possibilities for people to fulfill their potential.

The Industrial Revolution dramatically altered political and social life at all levels, but especially for the middle class, whose engagement in capitalist ventures brought greater political power and social recognition. During the course of the nine-

Map 21.1 The Industrial Transformation in England, ca. 1850 Industry developed in the areas rich in coal and iron fields. Important cities sprang up nearby and were soon linked by a growing railway network.

Map 21.2 Major Uprisings and Reforms, 1848–1849 In no other year had as many revolts broken out simultaneously; in many cases the revolutions led to reforms and new constitutions.

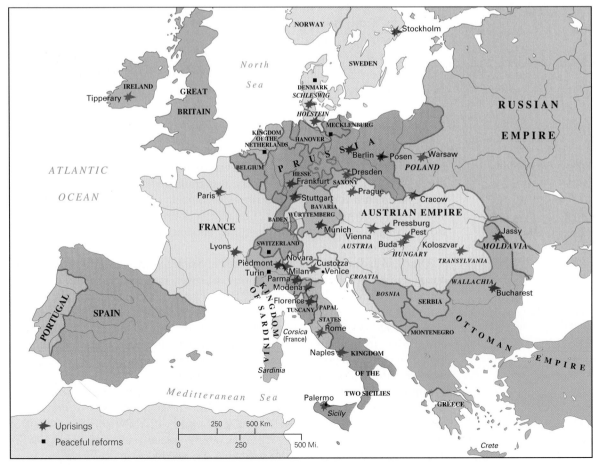

★ Uprisings

■ Peaceful reforms

0   250   500 Km.

0   250   500 Mi.

Figure 21.1   Gustave Dore.   This painting by the French artist depicts the overcrowded and unsanitary conditions in industrial London. Because municipal authorities were unable to cope with the rapid pace of urbanization, the working class was forced to live in dwellings such as these row houses that did not have adequate sanitation or recreational facilities. *(Prints Division, New York Public Library, Astor, Lenox, and Tilden Foundations)*

teenth century, the bourgeoisie came to hold many of the highest offices in western European states, completing a trend that had begun with the French Revolution.

Cities grew in size, number, and importance. Municipal authorities were unable to cope with the rapid pace of urbanization, and without adequate housing, sanitation, or recreational facilities, the exploding urban centers became another source of working-class misery (Figure 21.1). In preindustrial Britain, most people had lived in small villages. They knew where their roots were; relatives, friends, and village church gave them a sense of belonging. The industrial centers separated people from nature and from their places of origin, shattering traditional ways of life that had given men and women a sense of security.

The plight of the working class created a demand for reform, but the British government, committed to laissez-faire economic principles that militated against state involvement, was slow to act. In the last part of the nineteenth century, however, the development of labor unions, the rising political voice of the working class, and the growing recognition that the problems created by industrialization required state action led the government to speed up the pace of reform. Rejecting the road of reform, Karl Marx called for a working-class revolution that would destroy the capitalist system.

The Rise of Extreme Nationalism

The revolutions of 1848 ended in failure, but nationalist energies were too powerful to contain. In 1867, Hungary gained the autonomy it had sought in 1848, and by 1870 the unification of Italy and Germany was complete.

The leading architects of Italian and German unification, Count Camillo Benso di Cavour (1810–1861) and Otto von Bismarck (1815–1898), were not liberal idealists or romantic dreamers of the type who had fought in the revolutions of 1848; they were tough-minded practitioners of ***Realpolitik,*** "the politics of reality." Shrewd and calculating statesmen, they respected power and knew how to wield it; focusing on the actual world, they dismissed ideals as illusory, noble sentiments that impeded effective action. Realpolitik was the political counterpart of Realism in the arts. Both outlooks shared the desire to view things coldly and objectively as they are, rather than as idealists would like them to be.

Map 21.3 The Unification of Italy, 1859–1870   While liberals failed to unite the Italian nation in 1848, Cavour, who was a tough-minded practitioner of Realpolitik, succeeded in doing so.

Nationalism, gaining in intensity in the last part of the nineteenth century, was to become the dominant spiritual force in European life. Once German unification was completed as a result of the Franco-Prussian War (1870–1871), German nationalists sought to incorporate Germans living outside the Reich into the new Germany and to build a vast overseas empire. Russian Pan-Slavs dreamed of bringing the Slavs of Eastern Europe under the control of "Mother Russia." Growing increasingly resentful of Magyar and German domination, the Slavic minorities of the Hapsburg

Empire agitated for recognition of their national rights. In the late 1800s, nationalism became increasingly belligerent, intolerant, and irrational, threatening both the peace of Europe and the liberal-humanist tradition of the Enlightenment.

The extreme nationalism of the late nineteenth and early twentieth centuries contributed to World War I and to the rise of fascism after the war; it was the seedbed of totalitarian nationalism. Concerned exclusively with the greatness of the nation, extreme nationalists or **chauvinists** rejected the liberal emphasis on political liberty. Liberals regarded the state as a community of individuals voluntarily bonded by law and citizenship and entitled to the same rights. To extreme nationalists, however, the state was the highest development of a folkish-racial spirit inherited from their ancestors. In their eyes, profound and irreconcilable differences separated "their people" from those who did not share this ancestry. Even if they had dwelled in the land for centuries, such people, particularly Jews, were seen as dangerous aliens. Increasingly, nationalists attacked parliamentary government as an obstacle to national power and greatness and maintained that authoritarian leadership was needed to meet national emergencies. The needs of the nation, they said, transcended the rights of the individual.

Extreme nationalists also rejected the liberal ideal of equality. Placing the nation above everything, chauvinists accused national minorities of corrupting the nation's spirit, and they glorified war as a symbol of the nation's resolve and will. In the name of national power and unity, they persecuted minorities at home and stirred up hatred against other nations. Increasingly, they embraced militaristic, imperialistic, and racist doctrines. At the founding of the Nationalist Association in

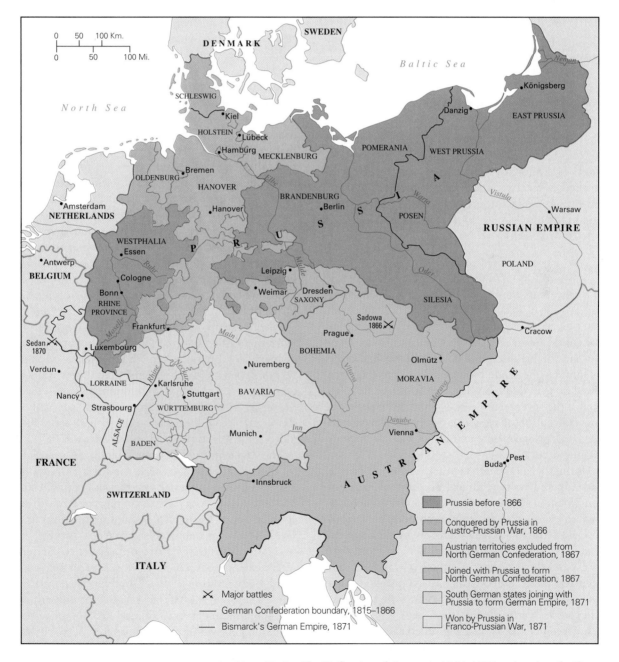

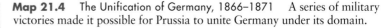

Map 21.4   The Unification of Germany, 1866–1871   A series of military victories made it possible for Prussia to unite Germany under its domain.

Italy in 1910, one leader declared: "Just as socialism teaches the proletariat the value of class struggle, so we must teach Italy the value of international struggle. But international struggle is war? Well, then, let there be war! And nationalism will arouse the will for a victorious war . . . the only way to national redemption."[1]

Interpreting politics with the logic of emotions, extreme nationalists insisted that they had a sacred mission to regain lands once held in the Middle Ages, to unite with their kinfolk in other lands, or to rule over peoples considered inferior. Loyalty to the nation-state was elevated above all other allegiances. The ethnic state became an object of religious reverence; the spiritual energies that formerly had been dedicated to Christianity were now channeled into the worship of the nation-state.

CURRENTS OF THOUGHT

The belief that the problems of society, including those caused by the Industrial Revolution, could be rationally understood and resolved, a growing respect for the scientific method, and an increasing secularization of life all found expression in the intellectual currents of the mid and late nineteenth century.

Darwinism

In a century distinguished by scientific discoveries, perhaps the most important scientific advance was the theory of evolution formulated by Charles Darwin (1809–1882), an English naturalist. Darwin did for his discipline what Newton had done for physics: he made biology an objective science based on general principles. The Scientific Revolution of the seventeenth century had given people a new conception of space. Darwin radically altered our conception of time and biological life, including human origins.

During the eighteenth century, almost all people had adhered to the biblical account of creation contained in Genesis: God had instantaneously created every river and mountain and the various species of animal and plant life, giving each species a finished and permanent form distinct from that of every other species. All this, it was believed, occurred some 6,000 years ago. Gradually, this view was questioned, but Darwin was the most effective in overturning it.

In December 1831, Darwin sailed as a naturalist on the *H.M.S. Beagle*, which surveyed the shores of South America and some Pacific islands. During the five-year expedition, Darwin collected and examined specimens of plant and animal life; he concluded that many animal species had perished, that new species had emerged, and that there were links between extinct and living species. In the *Origin of Species* (1859) and the *Descent of Man* (1871), Darwin used empirical evidence to show that the wide variety of animal species was due to a process of development over many millennia, and he supplied a convincing theory that explained how evolution operates.

Darwin adopted the theory of the British political economist, Thomas R. Malthus (1766–1834) that the population reproduces faster than the food supply, causing a *struggle for existence*. Not all infant organisms grow to adulthood; not all adult organisms live to old age. The principle of *natural selection* determines which members of the species have a better chance of survival. The organism favored by nature is more likely to reach maturity, to mate, and to pass on its superior qualities to its offspring, some of which will acquire the advantageous trait to an even greater degree than the parent. Over many generations, the favorable characteristic becomes more pronounced and more widespread within the species. Over millennia, natural selection causes the death of old, less adaptable species and the creation of new ones. Very few of the species that dwelt on earth ten million years ago still survive, and many new ones, including human beings, have emerged. People themselves are products of natural selection, evolving from earlier, lower, nonhuman forms of life.

Like Newton's law of universal gravitation, Darwin's theory of evolution had revolutionary consequences in areas other than science. *Social Darwinists*—those who transferred Darwin's scientific theories to social and economic issues—used the terms "struggle for existence" and "survival of the fittest" to buttress an often brutal economic individualism and political conservatism.

The application of Darwin's biological concepts to the social world, where they did not apply, also buttressed imperialism, racism, nationalism, and militarism—doctrines that preached relentless conflict. Social Darwinists insisted that nations and races were engaged in a struggle for survival in which only the fittest survive and deserve to survive.

The theory of evolution was a great achievement of the rational mind, but in the hands of the Social Darwinists, it served to undermine the Enlightenment tradition, which emphasized human equality and peaceful progress. Darwinism also contributed to the waning of religious belief (see below) and to a growing secular attitude.

Religion in a Secular Age

Several developments in the middle of the nineteenth century served to undermine traditional Christian belief. A growing secular attitude pushed religion to the periphery of human concerns for many people. New trends in biblical scholarship questioned the established opinion about the authenticity of the text of the Bible. Darwin's theory of evolution challenged traditional Christian beliefs and, to some, undermined the infallibility of Scripture and the conviction that the Bible was indeed the Word of God.

Darwin's theory touched off a great religious controversy between Christians who defended a literal interpretation of Genesis and those who advocated the new biology (Figure 21.2). In time, however, most religious thinkers tried to reconcile evolution with the Christian view that there was a Creation and that it had a purpose. These Christian thinkers held that modifications within a species were made by an intelligent creator—that God created and then directed the evolutionary process, that he steered evolution so that it would culminate in the human being. The Bible, they contended, was a work of spiritual truth and was never intended to serve as a textbook in science. Many sections of the Bible had an allegorical meaning and should not be taken literally. For many, however, the conclusion seemed inescapable: Nature contained no divine design or purpose, and the human species itself was a chance product of impersonal forces. The core idea of Christianity—that people were children of God participating in a drama of salvation—rested more than ever on faith rather than reason. Some even talked openly about the death of God.

Confronted by this assault on orthodox belief, some Christians continued to believe that the Bible was true in all its parts; it was the divinely inspired storehouse of knowledge about God and the world. These defenders of traditional Christianity rejected evolution and any other scientific discovery that appeared to be in conflict with their reading of Scripture.

New trends in biblical scholarship also challenged traditional Christian beliefs. Fortified by the discoveries of anthropologists and psychologists, "higher critics" examined the Old and New Testaments and the rise of Christianity in a historical and critical way. Generally, Protestant scholars, particularly Germans or those trained in Germany, took the lead in the new biblical scholarship.

In his *Life of Jesus* (1835), David Friedrich Strauss (1808–1874), a German theologian, examined the Gospels in a critical spirit, attempting to discern what was historically valid. He maintained

Figure 21.2 Darwin's theory of evolution touched off a great religious controversy between Christians who defended a literal interpretation of Genesis, and those who advocated the new biology. In this caricature, mocking his theory, an apelike Darwin, holding a mirror, is explaining his theory to a fellow ape. *(Bettmann Corbis)*

that the New Testament was replete with myths, unconscious inventions by the Gospel writers, who embellished Jesus' life and words with their own messianic longings and with inherited legends. The Gospels contain much mythical–religious content, Strauss said, but little history. Prior to the publication of Strauss' work, most students of religion had viewed the Gospels as a reliable historical source. But Strauss argued that the Jesus of faith is not the same as the Jesus of history. The belief that history, as presented in the Gospels, provided a firm basis for belief in Christian teachings had been permanently undermined.

In his *Essence of Christianity* (1841), Ludwig Feuerbach (1804–1872), a German philosopher, argued: "Religion is the dream of the human mind,"[2] and God is a human creation, a product of human feelings and wishes. Human beings believe in the divine because they seek assistance from it in life and fear death. He called theology a "web of contradictions and illusions."[3] Religion, said Feuerbach, is a form of self-alienation, for human beings diminish their humanity when they invest their finest qualities in a nonexistent God and reserve their worst qualities for themselves. God represents the externalization of an idealized human being. When individuals measure themselves against this God–ideal, they see only miserable, contemptible, and worthless creatures. "To enrich God, man must become poor; that God may be all, man must become nothing. . . . [M]an is wicked, corrupt, incapable of good; but, on the other hand, God is only good—the Good Being."[4]

For Søren Kierkegaard (1813–1855), a Danish theologian, truth is subjective and personal, reached through passion and commitment. To find a truth that has an all-consuming meaning, to find an idea for which one can live and die—this should be the individual's highest aim. According to Kierkegaard, all philosophical systems fail because they are concerned with objective certainty and humanity in general and not with what truly matters—the individual standing alone and making choices based on passionately held beliefs. It is this experience that brings the individual face-to-face with God.

Because Christian truths surpass reason, Kierkegaard said that true Christians must commit themselves to beliefs that are seemingly unintelligible and plunge, with confidence, into the absurd. But it is this "leap of faith" that enables Christians to conquer the agonizing feeling that life, in its deepest sense, means nothing and to give meaning to their own existence. Such a faith, based on total commitment, is thus the true avenue of self-discovery.

A movement of Catholic intellectuals called modernism sought to liberalize the church, to make it more accepting of modern liberal political ideals and modern science, and to reexamine the Gospels and Catholic teaching in the light of modern biblical scholarship. In many of these instances, modernists took positions that directly challenged core Catholic principles. Thus, Alfred Firmin Loiry (1857–1940), a scholarly priest, questioned the historicity of the Virgin Birth and the bodily Resurrection of Jesus, rejected the infallibility of papal and council pronouncements, and contended that Jesus did not impart God's permanent truths, that both he and the Gospels had to be interpreted within the context of their historical times. Pius X (1903–1914) strongly condemned modernism for undermining revelation and fostering agnosticism. The church also suppressed modernist journals, placed a number of modernist works on the Index of Forbidden Books, dismissed some modernist instructors, and excommunicated a number of the movement's staunchest supporters.

Marxism

Karl Marx (1818–1883) (Figure 21.3) was born of German–Jewish parents (both descendants of prominent rabbis). To save his job as a lawyer, Marx's father converted to Protestantism. Enrolled at a university to study law, Marx switched to philosophy. In 1842, he was editing a newspaper, which was soon suppressed by the Prussian authorities for its outspoken ideas. Leaving his native Rhineland, Marx went to Paris, where he met another German, Friedrich Engels (1820–1895), who was the son of a prosperous textile manufacturer. Marx and Engels entered into a lifelong collaboration and became members of socialist groups. In February 1848, they published the *Communist Manifesto*, which called for a working-class revolution to overthrow the capitalist system. Forced to leave France in 1849 because of his political views, Marx moved to

Figure 21.3 Interpreting history in economic terms, Karl Marx predicted that socialism would replace capitalism. He called for the proletariat to overthrow capitalism and to establish a classless society. *(Corbis)*

London, where he remained to the end of his life. There he spent years writing *Das Kapital (Capital)*—a study and critique of the modern capitalistic economic system, which, he predicted, would be destroyed by a socialist revolution.

Like other thinkers influenced by the Enlightenment, Marx believed that human history, which paralleled the operations of nature, was governed by scientific law. As a strict materialist, Marx rejected all religious and metaphysical interpretations of both nature and history. Consequently, he sought to fashion an empirical science of society.

Marx believed that the world could be rationally understood and changed. For Marx, the historical process was governed by objective and rational principles. Marx also held that history advanced dialectically—that the clash of opposing forces propelled history into higher stages. The clash of classes, which represented conflicting economic interests, accounted for historical change and progress. This conflict is called *dialectical materialism.* According to Marx, the driving forces in history are the ways in which goods are produced and wealth distributed. They account for historical change and are the basis of all culture—politics, law, religion, morals, and philosophy.

Throughout history, said Marx, there has been a class struggle between those who own the means of production and those whose labor has been exploited to provide wealth for this upper class. The opposing tension between classes has pushed history forward into higher stages. During the Middle Ages, when land was still the predominant mode of production, the struggle was between lord and serf. In the modern industrial world, the capitalists who owned the factories, mines, banks, and transportation systems were confronted by the exploited wage earners (the *proletariat*).

According to Marx, the class with economic power also controls the state and uses its political power to protect and increase its property and to hold down the laboring class. Furthermore, Marx asserted that the class that controls material production also determines the ideas that become the dominant ideas of society, which are regarded as the truth by oppressor and oppressed alike. In reality, however, these ideas merely reflect the special economic interests of the ruling class. Thus, said Marx, liberal bourgeois ideologists insist that natural rights and laissez-faire economics are laws of nature and have universal validity. But, they are unaware of the real forces motivating their thinking.

Capitalism, as Marx saw it, alienated people from their work, themselves, and one another. He believed that capitalist control of the economy and

the government would not endure forever; capitalist society produced its own grave diggers—the working class. The capitalist system would perish, just as the feudal society of the Middle Ages and the slave society of the ancient world had perished. From the ruins of a dead capitalist society, a new socioeconomic system—socialism—would emerge.

Marx also predicted how capitalism would be destroyed. First, periodic unemployment would increase the misery of the workers and intensify their hatred of capitalists. Then, owners of small businesses and shopkeepers, unable to compete with the great capitalists, would sink into the ranks of the working class, greatly expanding its numbers. Finally, society would become polarized into a small group of immensely wealthy capitalists and a vast proletariat of poor, embittered, and desperate people.

Growing increasingly conscious of their misery, the workers—aroused, educated, and organized by Communist intellectuals—would revolt. The working-class revolutionaries would smash the government, confiscate the property of the capitalists, abolish private property, place the means of production in the workers' hands, and organize a new society. Thus the *Communist Manifesto* ends with a strident call for revolution: "The Communists . . . openly declare that their ends can be attained only by the forcible overthrow of all existing social conditions. Let the ruling classes tremble at a Communist revolution. The proletarians have nothing to lose but their chains. They have a world to win. Workingmen of all countries, unite!"[5]

With the destruction of capitalism, the distinction between capitalist and worker would cease and with it the class conflict. Because this classless society would contain no exploiters, there would be no need for a state. The state would thus wither away. The production and distribution of goods would be carried out through community planning and communal sharing, which would replace the capitalist system of competition.

Marxism had immense appeal both for the downtrodden and for intellectuals. It promised to end the injustices of industrial society; it claimed the certainty of science; and it assured adherents that the triumph of their cause was guaranteed by history. In many ways, Marxism was a secular religion: The proletariat became a chosen class, endowed with a mission to achieve worldly salvation for humanity.

Marx's influence grew during the second wave of industrialization, in the closing decades of the nineteenth century, when class bitterness between the proletariat and the bourgeoisie seemed to worsen. Many workers thought that liberals and

simple work—*A Christmas Carol* (1843). Although Dickens often criticized institutionalized religion, he enjoyed celebrating Christmas, and the writing of his "little book" (as Dickens called it) touched him deeply. Ebeneezer Scrooge sacrifices love, joy, and happiness for a life of avarice and exploitation of his employees, especially Bob Cratchit, father of a lame son, Tiny Tim. As Marley's Ghost (Scrooge's former partner) and the ghosts of Christmases Past, Present, and Yet to Come confront Scrooge with his misdeeds on Christmas Eve, he is ultimately redeemed. Tiny Tim's exclamation at the conclusion of the story—"God Bless Us, Every One!"—once again, encapsulates Dickens' message of how society, like Scrooge, can be redeemed through love, compassion, and generosity.

ELIOT   The foremost female English author of the Victorian Age was George Eliot (born Mary Ann Evans, 1819–1880), who, like Dickens, filled her novels with autobiographical detail, focused on the trials and tribulations of everyday people, and rejected escapist Romantic literature; but unlike Dickens, Eliot's novels shun violence and melodrama. Her abiding concern was to explore human nature and human existence without resorting to literary artifice or exaggeration. In 1856, Eliot wrote an article, "Silly Novels by Lady Novelists," which condemned the pervasiveness of melodrama in Victorian fiction. In each of her seven novels, Eliot allows her characters to evolve gradually, portraying them with psychological depth. This allows the reader to understand both the behavior of her characters as well as the moral choices that they make.

Eliot's abilities as a Realist author are abundantly evident in her detailing of the mill, the Floss River, the trees, and the countryside in *The Mill and the Floss* (1860). Her descriptions are reminiscent of the English landscapes of Constable and Turner (see Chapter 20), whom Eliot greatly admired:

A wide plain, where the broadening Floss hurries on between its green banks to the sea, and the loving tide, rushing to meet it, checks its passage with an impetuous embrace. . . . Far away on each hand stretch the rich pastures, and the patches of dark earth, made ready for the seed of broad-leaved green crops, or touched already with the tint of the tender-bladed autumn-sown corn. . . . How lovely the little river is, with its dark, changing wavelets! It seems to me like a living companion while I wander along the bank and listen to its low placid voice. . . . And this is Dorlcote Mill. I must stand a minute or two here on the bridge and look at it, though the clouds are threatening. . . . Even in this leafless time of February it is pleasant to look at—perhaps the chill damp season adds a charm to the trimly-kept, comfortable dwelling-house, as old as the elms and chestnuts that shelter it from the northern blast.[31]

Silas Marner: The Weaver of Raveloe (1861) is Eliot's best-known novel. The short length and simple form of *Silas Marner,* the story of a miserly recluse whose lost gold is replaced by the love of an orphaned girl named Eppie, has made the novel standard fare in children's literature.

The intricate plot of *Middlemarch* (1872), Eliot's masterpiece, involves people from all walks of life—landed aristocracy, country gentry, merchants, professionals, intellectuals, politicians, and industrialists. Throughout the novel, Eliot deals with the realities of various kinds of marriage. She deprecates the idealistic notion that love conquers all in her treatment of the ill-fated marriage of the extravagant Rosamond Vincy and the idealistic doctor, Tertius Lydgate. Eliot also assails the idea that the purpose of marriage is for a man to take care of a woman by recounting the relationship of the headstrong Dorothea Brooke and the much older aristocratic clergyman, Edward Casaubon, who expects her to worship and adore him. Eliot is the least critical of the marriage of compatibility. Such marriages tend to work out better, because the woman generally has a greater say about what is important in the marriage. Evidence of this is Eliot's treatment of the marriage of Fred Vincy and Mary Garth. Mary tells Fred that she will forgo her dream of being a social reformer and marry him, but only if he agrees not to become a clergyman. In the end, her condition saves Fred from a miserable entrapment in an occupation he never liked anyway.

When *Middlemarch* appeared, critics assailed Eliot for not writing the type of fiction that a woman ought to write. Instead of a conventional romance that concluded with a happy ending, they claimed that Eliot's novel was too intellectual and too depressing. Today, the novel, in both structure and content, is viewed as being on the cutting edge of where the future of the modern novel rested—layers of meanings, multiple relationships and story lines, and the reader's changing sympathies for characters.

Russian Realism: Turgenev, Tolstoy, Chekov, and Dostoevsky

TURGENEV   Russian writers were among the leading Realists. In *A Sportsman's Sketches* (1852), the novelist, dramatist, and short-story writer Ivan Turgenev (1818–1883) provided a true-to-life picture of Russian rural conditions, particularly the brutal life of serfs. In an unpolemical style, Turgenev showed that serfdom not only debased the serfs but also their masters, the rural nobility, who did not recognize serfs as human beings. Inheriting from his mother an estate of 15,000 acres and some 2,000 male serfs, Turgenev freed some, providing them with fields, and gave others an opportunity to acquire their own land. In 1862 Turgenev published his masterpiece, *Fathers and Sons,* which deals, in part, with the theme of nihilism—the rejection of all values. To Bazarov, a young physician, the values of an idealistic, older generation—faith, romantic love, and personal honor—are merely superstitions born of ignorance. The novel was not well-received, and Turgenev determined to live outside Russia, primarily in France. Personally and artistically, Turgenev was a liberal who stood between the spirit of revolutionary zeal that was overtaking many of his contemporaries and the reactionary government of the tsar.

TOLSTOY Another aristocrat, Leo Tolstoy (1828–1910), was a soldier during the Crimean War (1853–1856) and following it, he traveled widely throughout Europe. In 1862, he married Sophie Andreyevna Behrs, and they produced fifteen children. Tolstoy not only managed his family and his estate, but he worked actively to set up schools for peasants patterned after those he had encountered during his travels. During this happy time in his life, Tolstoy wrote his two best-known novels: *War and Peace* (1863–1869) and *Anna Karenina* (1874–1876).

In *War and Peace,* Tolstoy describes the tragedies that attended Napoleon's invasion of Russia and the outlook and manners of the Russian nobility. More than 500 people appear in his epic, yet each one has a recognizable personality—a tribute to the author's talent for characterization. Seeking to provide a historically accurate description of the war, Tolstoy examined letters and diaries of participants and spoke with veterans. Although the work contains several denunciations of war, it also has positive things to say about military life, notably the camaraderie soldiers shared, the self-sacrifice they demonstrated, and the patriotism showed by the Russian people in resisting Napoleon. Tolstoy's masterful descriptions of magnificent balls, hunting parties, and battles exemplify Realism.

In *Anna Karenina,* Tolstoy probes the complexities of marital relationships, including a wife's adultery, the lure of illicit passion, and a woman's place in society. The Russian aristocracy may have had a casual attitude toward marital fidelity, but

for Tolstoy, a violation of the sacred bond of marriage was a crime that incurred severe punishment. Anna's deceitful relationship with Count Vronsky, who is engaged to Kitty, her sister-in-law's sister, ends in the loss of everything Anna cherishes. This causes Anna to commit suicide. In contrast, the marriage of Kitty and Konstantin Levin provides the spouse with a richer existence. Contributing to Levin's more meaningful life is his discovery that "one should live for the soul." Unlike Anna, who seeks life's purpose totally through romantic love, Levin's concern for spiritual development provides him with a vehicle for meaning and happiness and enhances his marital relationship.

In addition, Tolstoy dealt with social issues, including the decline of the landed nobility and the emergence of a new class of bourgeois capitalists. Tolstoy had no love for industrialization and capitalism, hallmarks of the modern age. On almost every page, he provides the reader with illuminating descriptions of the upper classes of Russian society.

Throughout much of his life, Tolstoy suffered from an inner conflict, for he was torn between his natural instincts and his zest for life and his moral responsibility to make life better for those who had less than he did. By 1877, his inner torment was resolved when he experienced a religious conversion. The centerpiece of Tolstoy's faith was not dogma but morality. For him, Jesus was not divine but a genuine ethical person and teacher who set a noble example of loving humanity and repudiating violence and hate; following Jesus' path was the avenue to personal happiness. Tolstoy put forward his ideas in two books, *What I Believe* (1883) and *What Then Must I Do?* (1886), and his home became a pilgrimage site for disciples from all over the world.

CHEKOV One of Tolstoy's friend's, Anton Chekov (1860–1904), was a physician who turned to literature. Chekov wrote hundreds of short stories and several plays, including his last play, *The Cherry Orchard* (1904), detailing the lives of people who struggle against forces beyond their control. In his dramas, Chekhov sought to elucidate the characters' inner thoughts and deepest feelings, which he analyzed impartially and objectively. Both his short stories and plays are distinguished by simple dialogue devoid of excessive verbiage. Using ordinary language, Chekov succeeded in conveying human fears and weaknesses in the face of personal tragedy. His major dramas concentrate on the realities, often ugly, of provincial life among dissolute landowning nobles, who squander their money, drink excessively, and do nothing productive to better society. In essence, Chekov was describing a decadent social order in its last throes.

DOSTOEVSKY In 1844, a number of people who discussed socialist and revolutionary ideas, including the novelist Fyodor Dostoevsky (1821–1881), were sentenced to death by the tsar. As they were bound and placed before a firing squad, the tsar's messenger arrived, informing them that the sentence had been commuted to penal servitude. (Actually, the "execution" was merely a charade intended to frighten the group and set an example for those who might hold similar ideas.) Dostoevsky's near-death experience and the five years he spent as a convict in remote Siberia, where he studied the New Testament, deeply affected him. Dostoevsky ultimately abandoned political radicalism, and he placed his faith, instead, in the teachings of the Russian Orthodox Church.

Dostoevsky's fame derives from four major novels: *Crime and Punishment* (1866), *The Idiot* (1868), *The Possessed* (1871), and *The Brothers Karamazov* (1880). In these and other works, he revealed his belief in the need to regenerate Russian spirituality; for him, the truth of Jesus demonstrated by simple Russian peasants was superior to the truth of science heralded by Westerners. He also showed a superb ability to create memorable characters, to probe minds, and to describe vividly and perceptively.

Dostoevsky's genius was richly demonstrated in *Crime and Punishment,* a gripping psychological thriller that takes place during a stifling summer in St. Petersburg swarming with people. With realistic detail, Dostoevsky captures the individuality of his characters and the heartbeat of the city. Raskolnikov, an impoverished student, and, at times, even generous and compassionate, commits murder. Why? He believes that "extraordinary" people have a right to shed blood if the realization of their ideas, which is to the advantage of humanity, requires it.

> It may even be remarked that nearly all these benefactors and teachers of humanity [Solon, Lycurgus, Mohammed, Napoleon, etc.] have been terribly bloodthirsty. Consequently, not only all great men, but all those who by hook or by crook, have raised themselves above the common herd, men who are capable of evolving something new, must, in virtue of their innate power, be undoubtedly criminal, more or less. Otherwise they would not free themselves from trammels; and, as for being bound by them, that they cannot be—their very mission forbidding it.[32]

Does he think committing a murder would prove that he is indeed an extraordinary person, a self-willed Napoleon? ". . . I longed to know if I was vermin, like the majority—or a Man."[33] Does he hope to demonstrate to himself that he has courage?

The man who dares much is the right man in his fellow's opinion. The one who defies and scorns them acquires their respect! . . . [P]ower is only given to the man who dares stoop to pick it up. Nothing more is needed, except courage. From the moment this truth had dawned upon me—a truth as clear as the light of the sun—I longed to dare, and I committed murder.[34]

After the murder, the student's conscience pains him, and encouraged by a religious young prostitute, a tormented Raskolnikov eventually confesses. The work's greatness lies in Dostoevsky's ingenious treatment of Raskolnikov's motives for the crime, how he is psychologically affected by the act, and how his agonizing, subconscious struggles compel him to confess.

Because he perceived human beings as inherently depraved, irrational, and rebellious and probed the unconscious mind, Dostoevsky was also a forerunner of the Modernist movement in thought and culture (see Chapter 23). The work that best links Dostoevsky to the modernist movement is *Notes from Underground* (1864). In this work, the narrator (the Underground Man) rebels against the efforts of rationalists, humanists, liberals, and socialists to define human nature according to universal principles and to reform society so as to promote greater happiness. He rebels against science and reason, against the entire liberal and socialist vision. He does so in the name of human subjectivity: the uncontainable, irrepressible, whimsical, and foolish human will. Human nature, says the Underground Man, is too volatile, too diversified to be schematized by the theoretical mind.

For the Underground Man, there are no absolute and timeless truths that precede the individual and to which the individual should conform. There is only a terrifying world of naked wills vying with one another. In such a world, people do not necessarily seek happiness, prosperity, and peace—all that is good for them, according to "enlightened" thinkers. To the rationalist who aims to eliminate suffering and deprivation, Dostoevsky replies that some people freely choose suffering and depravity because it gratifies them—for some, "even in a toothache there is enjoyment"—and they are repelled by wealth, peace, security, and happiness. If Dostoevsky is right, if individuals do not act out of enlightened self-interest, if they are driven by instinctual cravings that resist reason's appeals, then what hope is there for a social planner wishing to create the "good" society?

In rejecting external security and liberal and socialist concepts of progress—in aspiring to assert his own individuality even if this means acting against his own best interests—the Underground Man demonstrates that a powerful element of irrationality underlies human nature, an element that reason can neither understand nor justify. In succeeding decades, philosophers, social theorists, and literary figures would become preoccupied with this theme.

Realism in Drama: Ibsen

Realism was not restricted to the novel alone. The leading Realist playwright, Henrik Ibsen (1828–1906), a Norwegian, examined with clinical precision the commercial and professional classes, their personal ambitions, business practices, and family relationships. In a period of less than ten years, Ibsen wrote four Realist "problem plays"—*Pillars of Society* (1877), *A Doll's House* (1879), *Ghosts* (1881), and *Enemy of the People* (1882)—that drew attention to bourgeois pretensions, hypocrisy, and social conventions that thwart individual growth. Thus, Ibsen's characters are typically torn between their sense of duty to others and their own selfish wants. Although Ibsen wrote about profound social issues, he viewed himself as a dramatist relating a piece of reality and not a social reformer agitating for reform.

In *Pillars of Society,* Ibsen portrayed entrepreneurs who, aspiring for wealth and status, not only betray loved ones but also engage in unscrupulous business practices at the expense of their fellow citizens. Thus, the title itself is ironic, for the "pillars of society" are actually corrupt hypocrites.

In *A Doll's House,* Ibsen took up a theme that shocked late-nineteenth-century bourgeois audiences: a woman leaving her husband and children in search of self-realization. Nora Helmer resents being a submissive and dutiful wife to a husband who does not take her seriously, who treats her like a child, a doll. Before walking out on Torvald, Nora tells him:

> In all these eight years—longer than that—from the very beginning of our acquaintance, we have never exchanged a word on any serious subject. . . . When I was at home with papa, he told me his opinion about everything, and so I had the same opinions; and if I differed from him I concealed the fact, because he would not have liked it. He called me his doll-child, and he played with me just as I used to play with my dolls. And when I came to live with you . . . I was simply transferred from papa's hands into yours. You arranged everything according to your own taste, and so I got the same tastes as you—or else I pretended to, I am really not sure which—I think sometimes the one and sometimes the other. . . . I have existed merely to perform tricks for you, Torvald. But you

would have it so. You and papa have committed a great sin against me. It is your fault that I have made nothing of my life.[35]

By recognizing the truth about her life up to that point in time and then by resolving "to educate myself . . . to understand myself and everything about me," Nora now has the possibility of achieving individual freedom—of becoming a person in her own right.

Ibsen's next play, *Ghosts,* continued with this theme of a loveless marriage in a bourgeois home. Helene Alving, like Nora, dwells in an oppressive environment; also like Nora, she hides her true feelings and lives an unauthentic existence. Angered by Ibsen's depiction of marital unhappiness, critics accused him of undermining the sanctity of marriage and family life, which they saw as the very foundation of bourgeois society. Adding to their ire and Ibsen's image as a moral subversive was his treatment of the unmentionable, scandalous topic of venereal disease.

Although a comedy, *An Enemy of the People* deals with themes that are crucial to modern democratic society: the failure of the majority to break with inherited ideas and beliefs that do a disservice to society and the ease with which people, driven by self-interest, will close their minds to truth and morality. Dr. Stockmann discovers that the spring water given to guests at a Norwegian spa has been polluted by sewage. Was the infected spring a symbol for a diseased bourgeois society? When Stockmann announces his discovery, town officials and businessmen who profit from the spa conspire to silence him. When he refuses to stay quiet, townspeople attack his house, smash his windows, get him fired, and shun him. However, Stockmann gains inner strength when he stands alone against a hostile society.

Ibsen's plays were often penetrating psychological explorations into the forces, hidden below the surface, that mold a person's character. If he had a message to relate, it was that people should overcome self-deception and be morally honest with themselves.

AMERICAN LITERATURE

Realism and the American Novel: Stowe, Twain, Howells, and Crane

Like their European counterparts, American authors also rejected romantic sentimentality in literature. They set their novels, short stories, and poems in recognizable American locales, even capturing the essence of "local color" in both dialect and dialogue. Like Dickens, American Realists often portrayed the bleak realities of mundane life in the city and illustrated the breakdown of traditional systems of morality. The general public was enticed by the Realist authors, because they could see themselves as characters in the books: Were they not also engaged in real-life struggles with themselves, with society, with the environment, and with governmental institutions?

STOWE   One of the most effective early Realist writers in America was Harriet Beecher Stowe (1811–1896). On June 5, 1851, she began to publish her antislavery novel, *Uncle Tom's Cabin,* in the abolitionist periodical the *National Era.* Although it was only the first of ten novels that Stowe wrote, it overshadows all the others. During the first week of publication, 10,000 copies were sold, and 300,000 copies sold by the end of 1852. It made Stowe an immediate celebrity, and she conducted antislavery speaking tours in both America and Europe. Compelled to refute her critics who claimed that the brutalities she depicted were not authentic, in 1853, Stowe published *A Key to Uncle Tom's Cabin* in which she painstakingly documented, page by page and chapter by chapter, the realities on which her novel was based. In 1862, ten years after the controversial novel's publication, Stowe visited President Lincoln in the White House, where he reputedly greeted her by saying: "So you are the little lady who made this great war." Although Lincoln had always insisted that his goal during the Civil War was to preserve the Union, not to abolish slavery, the efforts of Stowe and other abolitionists made slavery a matter of central concern and caused him to issue the *Emancipation Proclamation,* freeing the slaves, in 1862.

The novel is based on Stowe's personal experiences with Christian morality, slavery, and the **underground railroad.** In 1832, Stowe's father, a powerful evangelical preacher, decided to assume the presidency of Lane Theological Seminary and moved his family from Connecticut to Cincinnati, Ohio. Across the Ohio River from Cincinnati was the slave state of Kentucky, and Ohio had a number of key stations on the underground railroad. (The underground railroad was neither "underground" nor a "railroad," but rather a network of people who helped fugitive slaves escape to freedom in Canada.) The novel thus has two plots—one concerned with bondage, the other with freedom.

The freedom narrative relates the story of Eliza, George Harris, and Harry. Eliza is a "quadroon" (three-quarters white) personal maid to Emily Shelby, the mistress of a Kentucky plantation worked by slaves. When Emily's husband, Arthur,

incurs huge gambling debts, he decides to sell off some of his slaves, including Eliza's son Harry. Frantic about the possibility of losing her son, Eliza flees with him and, with the help of the underground railroad, reaches Canada, where they are eventually joined by her husband, George Harris, a slave on a neighboring plantation. Following their reunion in Canada, they travel to France so that George can acquire an education. The Harris family then returns to the United States for a time, before founding a freedom colony for ex-slaves in Africa.

The bondage narrative deals with another slave that Arthur Shelby sold, "Uncle Tom," an old Christian who has improved his life by learning to write and to read the Bible. Instead of escaping, Uncle Tom remains loyal to his new master, Mr. Haley, to whom Harry had also been sold. Haley pursues Eliza and Harry with dogs across the Ohio River, before shipping Tom to New Orleans, where he is to be sold again. On the trip south, Tom becomes friends with the virtuous child, "Little Eva" St. Clare, whom he saves from drowning. Eva convinces her father to buy Tom, and before her untimely death, she persuades her father to free him. However, before Mr. St. Clare can take the appropriate legal action, he dies, and Mrs. St. Clare sells Tom to the despicable Simon Legree to pay off their debts. Legree is an alcoholic, Yankee slave owner in the South who compels his slaves to live in deplorable conditions and has his overseers, Quimbo and Sambo, beat them viciously on a regular basis. Throughout his ordeal, Tom seeks solace in his faith, which makes Legree despise him even more.

> At first, Tom used to read a verse or two of his Bible, by the flicker of the fire, after he had returned from his daily toil; but, after the cruel treatment he received, he used to come home so exhausted, that his head swam and his eyes failed when he tried to read; and he was fain to stretch himself down, with the others, in utter exhaustion. . . .
>
> One evening, . . . a coarse laugh roused him; he looked up,—Legree was standing opposite to him.
>
> "Well, old boy," he said, "you find your religion don't work, it seems!"
>
> . . . The cruel taunt was more than hunger and cold and nakedness. Tom was silent.
>
> "You were a fool," said Legree; "for I meant to do well by you, when I bought you. You might have been better off than Sambo, or Quimbo either, and had easy times; and, instead of getting cut up and thrashed, every day or two, ye might have had liberty to lord it round, and cut up the other niggers; and ye might have had, now and

then, a good warming of whiskey punch. Come, Tom, . . . join my church!"

"The Lord forbid!" said Tom, fervently.

"You see the Lord an't going to help you; if he had been, he wouldn't have let me get you! This yer religion is all a mess of lying trumpery, Tom. I know all about it. Ye'd better hold to me; I'm somebody, and can do something!"

"No, Mas'r," said Tom; "I'll hold on. The Lord may help me, or not help; but I'll hold to him, and believe him to the last!"

"The more fool you!" said Legree, spitting scornfully at him, and spurning him with his foot. "Never mind; I'll chase you down, yet, and bring you under,—you'll see!" and Legree turned away.[36]

Even as Quimbo and Sambo are beating Tom to death, he remains steadfast in his Christian faith and forgives his tormentors; deeply moved by the Christ-like Tom, Quimbo and Sambo subsequently embrace Christianity. For years the term "Uncle Tom" referred to a man who never loses his faith and dignity in the face of adversity; today, however, it is often used in a derogatory manner to refer to any black man who is perceived to be submissive.

TWAIN Portraying true-to-life characters, situations, and dialogue, the journalist, philosopher, humorist, and novelist Samuel Langhorne Clemens (1835–1910), better known as Mark Twain (a term used by riverboat pilots meaning "two fathoms"), exemplified American Realism. Twain's boyhood in Hannibal, Missouri, on the Mississippi River, is evident in his novels *Tom Sawyer* (1876) and *The Adventures of Huckleberry Finn* (1884). Twain had little formal education, but learned a great deal about people and life working as a riverboat pilot, prospector, and journalist.

Following the Civil War, Southerners introduced **"Jim Crow" laws** that curtailed the freedom of former slaves and legalized new forms of oppression. Twain chose to write an antislavery novel twenty years after the Civil War had ended, because in his eyes, Jim Crow was as insidious as slavery. Racism and slavery are the dominant themes of *Huck Finn*, and the themes are centered on the relationship between Huck Finn and the runaway slave, Jim. Their adventures together also allow Twain to explore the issue of child abuse, to question the merit of "sivilizing" Huck, and to analyze the social and moral development of Huck Finn and Tom Sawyer, the young boy who was the principal character in Twain's previous book.

Huck Finn, the sequel to *Tom Sawyer*, begins by acquainting the reader with the events contained in the earlier work, including the discovery of a cache of robber's gold. Huck, the protagonist and narrator of the novel, is the thirteen-year-old son of Pap, the town drunk, who beats him regularly. Huck, therefore, is compelled to survive by his own initiative. When Huck goes to live with the Widow Douglas and her sister, Miss Watson, they effectively "sivilize" him by teaching him manners and cleanliness and by sending him to church and to school. Pap, however, comes after the gold, kidnaps Huck, and imprisons him in a cabin on the Mississippi River. To free himself from Pap, Huck escapes and fakes his own death. But while he is hiding out waiting for the commotion over his death to subside, he meets Jim, one of Miss Watson's slaves, who is fleeing the plantation, because he has overheard her say that she intends to sell him. Huck and Jim live contentedly on an island in the river, until Huck learns that people on shore believe that Jim is holed up on the island, and they issue a reward for his capture. Jim and Huck then decide to flee up the Ohio River and into the "free states" of the North, where slavery is illegal. Throughout their adventures together, Huck is continually faced with the moral choice of whether or not to hand over Jim, because he is someone else's "property."

> Once I said to myself it would be a thousand times better for Jim to be a slave at home where his family was, as long as he's *got* to be a slave, and so I'd better write a letter to Tom Sawyer and tell him to tell Miss Watson where he was. But I soon give up that notion for two things: she'd be mad and disgusted at his rascality and ungratefulness for leaving her, and so she'd sell him straight down the river again; and if she didn't, everybody naturally despises an ungrateful nigger, and they'd make Jim feel it all the time, and so he'd feel ornery and disgraced. And then think of *me!* It would get all around that Huck Finn helped a nigger to get his freedom; and if I was ever to see anybody from that town again I'd be ready to get down and lick his boots for shame. That's just the way: a person does a low-down thing, and then he don't want to take no consequences of it. . . . The more I studied about this the more my conscience went to grinding me, and the more wicked and low-down and ornery I got to feeling.[37]

Jim and Huck subsequently team up with a pair of con artists, the Duke and the Dauphin, pretenders to the French throne, who sell Jim to a local farmer. Huck then makes the conscientious choice to free his friend with the help of Tom. In executing Tom's elaborate scheme to free Jim, Tom is shot in the leg, and Jim sacrifices his own freedom to help Tom. The novel ends with the

Realism, Impressionism, and Later Romanticism in Art and Music

Richard Wagner with Franz Liszt and Liszt's daughter Cosima, anonymous, 19th century oil on canvas, Wagner Museum, Bayreuth, Germany.

While Wagner (center) was completing his tale of forbidden love, *Tristan und Isolde,* he was engaged in an illicit love affair with Cosima (left), the daughter of Franz Liszt (right), who was still married to Hans von Bülow, the conductor of *Tristan und Isolde.* Their love affair produced two children, and when Wagner's wife died, he finally married Cosima.

(The Bridgeman Art Library International)

LIKE SCIENTISTS AND WRITERS, REALIST ARTISTS carefully investigated the empirical world. In a matter-of-fact style and without any attempt at glorification, Realist artists painted commonplace scenes: laborers breaking stones, peasants tilling the soil, a country burial, bathers, floor scrapers, rag pickers, prostitutes, and beggars. Impressionists continued in the tradition of Realists, but their experiments with color, light, and space also represented a change of direction that makes them forerunners of modern art. At the same time that Realist writers and artists were breaking with Romantic models, mid- and late-nineteenth-century composers carried forward the Romantic musical style initiated by their predecessors earlier in the century by taking the opera, symphony, lieder, and ballet to the next level. However, they also engaged in a great debate about where the future of music lay, which resulted in new musical forms, most notably the music drama and the tone poem.

Nationalism, which was gaining in intensity in the last part of the nineteenth century, had a profound influence on late Romantic music. Some nationalist composers simply tried to break the hold that the Germans had on music. Others saw music as a way to protest political domination of their country by a foreign power and to arouse patriotic fervor among their people. All of them sought to express their national identity by rendering themes drawn from their nation's folklore, legends, heroes, heroines, and histories. Composers were inspired by the melodies of their national folk tunes and the rhythms of their folk dances, which frequently served as the foundation for their symphonic compositions and were often played on musical instruments associated with their native culture.

REALISM IN ART

The accurate representation of the natural world, the aim of Western art since the Renaissance, was the central concern of Realist artists in the middle decades of the nineteenth century. Realist painting was fostered by the widespread faith in science, which relied on careful observation of the physical world, and by photography, which could precisely replicate real life.

Photography

Painters had used the camera obscura technique—a lens in a box that projects an image onto a wall or screen (see Chapter 16)—for at least two centuries, but no one had been able to create permanent images, until the late 1830s, when the Frenchman Louis-Jacques-Mandé Daguerre (1789–1851) produced his first photograph. It was called a *daguerreotype*—a positive print made on light-sensitive copper. In 1851, Frederick Scott Archer (1813–1857) invented the first practical photographic process involving the use of glass negatives. Although the process was painstaking and required a great amount of equipment, it produced precise and clear prints.

Photography and Realism in art emerged simultaneously. Gaspard-Félix Tournachon (1820–1910), using the pseudonym Nadar, adopted Archer's process and elevated the art of portraiture. Like Realist painters, Nadar aspired to obtain an exact representation of his subjects and to capture their distinctive character in his portraits. Similarly, Nadar shared the Realists' concern with light, an issue that he addressed in 1857: "Everywhere you can see working at photography an artist who has never painted. . . . The theory of photography can be learnt in an hour; the first ideas of how to go about it in a day. . . . What can't be learnt . . . is the feeling for light."[1] Although some painters feared that photographs would eliminate the need for paintings, others used photographs of their subjects as the basis for their portraits. During the mid-nineteenth century, Nadar's studio became a meeting place for Parisian writers and artists, whose visages Nadar captured in portraits.

Soon after the development of photography, Matthew Brady (1823–1896) and his group of assistant photographers used the camera to capture the realities of the American Civil War. Their 7,000 photographs document nearly every facet of the war, except the actual fighting, which could not be caught by the slow-speed cameras of the day. Some of the most haunting pictures are photographs of the dead, taken after the battle before they could be buried. *Soldiers on the Battlefield at Antietam* (Figure 22.1) shows some of the bodies of the Confederate soldiers who died in that battle in 1862. When Brady exhibited his Antietam photographs at his New York City studio, a mass audience was exposed to the horror and brutality of war for the first time ever.

Painting

Unlike Romantic artists, who painted their own subjective world—the world of their imagination—Realists strove for an objective depiction, warts and all, of the world of common people and everyday life. France was the center of Realism, but the French Academy, the conservative keepers of artistic style, often found such works ugly. Under state control, the French Academy was the official body charged with organizing an annual exhibition called the *Salon*. The name derived from the *Salon d' Apollon* (Apollo Room) in the Palace of the Louvre—the place where the exhibition was held. Concerned about class divisions and hoping to improve the lives of the common people, most Realists were republicans, and some were socialists. Consequently, they occasionally came into conflict with the government of King Louis Philippe and later Emperor Napoleon III, as well as with the official

Figure 22.1 Matthew Brady, *Soldiers on the Battlefield at Antietam*, Albumen silver print by Alexander Gardner (1862), National Archives, Washington, D.C. Brady's haunting photographs document nearly every facet of the Civil War, including this one, which shows some of the bodies of the Confederate soldiers who died at the Battle of Antietam in 1862. *(The Granger Collection, New York)*

Figure 22.2   Gustave Courbet, *The Stone-Breakers*, 1849, 5′3″ x 8′6″ (1.5 x 2.59 m), oil on canvas, formerly Gemäldegalerie, Dresden (destroyed 1945).   The Revolution of 1848 inspired Courbet to create a new style to match his republican and socialist political beliefs. *The Stone-Breakers* depicts a scene Courbet actually witnessed: two peasants are engaged in the backbreaking activity of crushing stones into gravel to patch a highway. The social message of the painting was subsequently praised by the leading French socialist, Pierre-Joseph Proudhon. *(Gemaldegalerie, Dresden/The Bridgeman Art Library International)*

art community. Initially, the works of the Realists were rejected by the jury that selected paintings to be exhibited in the Salon. In 1863, the jury for the Salon refused so many paintings that Napoleon III ordered the creation of the *Salon de Refusés* (Salon of the Rejected) to exhibit the spurned paintings, many of which turned out to be among the best works of the period.

The greatest of the French Realist painters was Gustave Courbet (1819–1877). Born into a prosperous farming family in Ornans, his father sent him to Paris to study law in 1840. Instead, Courbet involved himself in the art world, spent his time painting, and achieved some early successes. The Revolution of 1848 inspired Courbet to create a new style to match his republican and socialist political beliefs. In 1849, while on a visit with his family in Ornans, he painted *The Stone-Breakers* (Figure 22.2). Depicting a scene Courbet had actually witnessed, the painting shows two peasants engaged in the backbreaking activity of crushing stones into gravel to patch a highway. The lifesize figures in the huge painting (5′3″ x 8′6″) are solid and palpable, partially because of

Courbet's method of first applying paint thickly with a palette knife. Only after this paint was dry did he use a brush to fill in color and to affect light.

The painting's social message was subsequently praised by the leading French socialist, Pierre-Joseph Proudhon (1809–1865):

That old man, kneeling, bent over his hard task, who breaks the stone by the side of the road with a long-handled hammer, certainly invites your compassion. . . . This man, however, has seen better days; . . . if, for him, the present is without illusion, without hope, he has at least his memories, his regrets, to sustain him, . . . while that deplorable boy who carries the stones will never be acquainted with any of the joys of life; chained before his time to day labor, he is already falling apart. . . . Ground down in his adolescence, he will not live. . . . The condition of the stone-breakers is that of more than six million souls in France. . . .

Some peasants . . . wanted to have it . . . put . . . on the high altar of their church. The Stone-Breakers is worth a parable from the Bible; it is morality in action.[2]

Figure 22.3 Gustave Courbet, *Burial at Ornans,* 1849, 10'3 1/2" x 21'9" (3.1 x 6.6 m), oil on canvas, Musée du Louvre, Paris. All of the individuals in the painting were either part of Courbet's family or other local folk, including two veterans of the French Revolution. In contrast to the glamorous settings and brilliant colors of the Romantic painters, Courbet portrayed peasants in realistic settings with subdued colors. *(Musée d'Orsay, Paris/Réunion des Musées Nationaux/Art Resource, NY)*

Still at home, Courbet painted the huge *Burial at Ornans* (Figure 22.3), which may portray the funeral of his own grandfather, a veteran of the French Revolution, who died in 1848. All of the individuals in the painting were either part of Courbet's family or other local folk, including (in the center foreground) two veterans of the French Revolution. While he was working on the painting, Courbet wrote to a friend: "Here models are to be had for the asking; everyone wants to appear in the *Burial*; I'll never be able to satisfy them all; I'll make plenty of enemies."[3] Each of the nearly fifty people is treated with an intense objectivity, and no one person appears to be more important than the others.

In both *The Stone-Breakers* and the *Burial,* Courbet portrayed peasants in realistic settings with subdued colors, in contrast to the glamorous settings and brilliant colors of the Romantic painters. Although well received in Ornans, the paintings were vilified by critics when they were exhibited in Paris at the Salon of 1850. One critic's comments epitomize the typical reaction to the *Burial*:

One has never seen, and never could see, anything so frightful and so eccentric. . . . It is in fact abominably ugly. . . . [A]ll the persons, ranged in a line in the foreground, are on the same plane; . . . there is no perspective, no arrangement, no composition; all the rules of art are overthrown and despised; we see black [darkly clothed] men laid on black women, and behind, . . . four black bearers favoured with a democ[ratic]-soc[ialist] beard. . . . There! Good God, how ugly it is.[4]

Another critic compared it to a defective photograph: "In that scene, which one might mistake for a faulty daguerreotype, there is the natural coarseness which one always gets in taking nature as it is, and in reproducing it just as it is seen."[5]

In 1855, Courbet executed *The Studio: A Real Allegory Concerning Seven Years of My Artistic Life* (Figure 22.4). It is in the genre of Velázquez's *Las Meninas* (see Chapter 16) and Goya's *Family of Charles IV* (see Chapter 19), but the artist has been moved from the left background into the center of the painting. The nude model with him was painted from a photograph, which Courbet had requested from a friend, to whom he explained, "She will stand behind my chair in the middle of the picture."[6] Perhaps she represents the Truth, which Courbet wished to proclaim in his paintings. The figures on the right are people whom Courbet knew in Paris. Those on the left, Courbet explained, depict "society at its best, its worst, and its average; in short it's my way of seeing society in its interests and passions; it's the people who come to my studio to be painted."[7]

Courbet submitted *The Studio* and *The Burial* to the jury for the Universal Exposition of 1855, but the works were refused. Consequently, Courbet built his own gallery, which opened with forty of his paintings and four drawings. In the catalogue for the showing, Courbet stated that it was his goal "to create living art."[8] After attending Courbet's exhibition, Delacroix (see Chapter 20) wrote in his Journal: "I stayed there for nearly an hour and discovered a masterpiece in the picture [*The Studio*] which they rejected. . . . They have rejected one of the most remarkable works of our time, but Courbet is not the man to be discouraged by a little thing like that."[9]

Courbet continued to paint portraits, sensuous female nudes, animals, and landscapes in his controversial Realist style. In 1871, Courbet was arrested for democratic political activities, briefly imprisoned, and given a huge fine, which ruined him financially. In 1874, he went into exile in Switzerland, where he died on New Year's Eve 1877.

Courbet's contemporary and fellow republican, Honoré Daumier (1808–1879), was originally a caricaturist, who satirized the government, politicians, lawyers, and the bourgeoisie. In 1832, he even was imprisoned because of a caricature of King Louis Philippe. In the mid-1840s, he began to paint, and his most famous work, *Third Class Carriage* (Figure 22.5), was executed between 1863 and 1865. The viewer is an anonymous fellow passenger in a crowded public transit carriage reserved for the poor. The figures in the foreground are a mother and her child and a grandmother, with a basket on her lap and her grandson sleeping at her side. The barely completed figures in the background are crowded together, as they share the burden of their common poverty. The subdued, almost monochromatic colors add to the poignancy of the scene. Rather than existing as portraits of individual people, these people represent the poor in spirit as well as the poor in possessions.

Figure 22.4   Gustave Courbet, *The Studio: A Real Allegory Concerning Seven Years of My Artistic Life*, 1854–1855, 11'10" x 19'7 3/4" (3.61 x 5.99 m), oil on canvas, Musée d'Orsay, Paris.   Courbet is in the center of the painting, whereas his nude model stands behind his chair, perhaps as a representation of Truth, which Courbet hoped to proclaim in his paintings. The figures on the right are people whom Courbet knew in Paris. *(Musée d'Orsay/Giraudon /The Bridgeman Art Library International)*

Figure 22.5 Honoré Daumier, *Third Class Carriage*, 1863–1865, 25 3/4″ x 35 1/2″ (65.4 x 90.2 cm), oil on canvas, The Metropolitan Museum of Art, New York. The viewer is an anonymous fellow passenger in a crowded public transit carriage reserved for the poor. Rather than existing as portraits of individual people, these people represent the poor in spirit as well as the poor in possessions. *(The Metropolitan Musem of Art, H.O. Havemeyer Collection, Bequest of Mrs. H.O. Havemeyer, 1929 [29.100.129] Photograph © 1985 The Metropolitan Museum of Art)*

IMPRESSIONISM

The generation of French painters who followed the Realists is termed Impressionists. ***Impressionism*** was the logical extension of the Realists' preoccupation with light and color. Impressionists generally concluded that what they saw was not the object itself, but rather light reflecting from objects, forms, and surfaces. Intrigued by the impact that light has on objects, Impressionists left their studios for the countryside, where they painted landscapes or scenes of contemporary life under an open sky. The Impressionists began a major breach with the Renaissance tradition because their real subject was light rather than the scenes themselves. They attempted to understand the permutations of light and color, "to get an impression of," or to capture the moment when the eye perceives light on various surfaces during different times of the day. The Impressionists also violated the Renaissance traditions of perspective and three-dimensional space by acknowledging the two-dimensional surface of the painting. A contemporary observer explained the Impressionists' interest with painting scenes naturally:

[T]he Impressionist is . . . a modernist painter endowed with an uncommon sensibility of the eye. He is one who, forgetting the pictures amassed through the centuries in museums, forgetting his optical art school training—line, perspective, color—by dint of living and seeing frankly and primitively in the bright open air, that is, outside his poorly lighted studio, whether the city street, the country, or the interiors of houses, has succeeded in remaking for himself a natural eye, and in seeing naturally and painting as simply as he sees.[10]

Like the Realists, the Impressionists depicted ordinary experiences and everyday life. But in contrast to the Realists, whose subjects were drawn from rural toil and lower-class life, Impressionists painted the middle class at leisure.

The movement began in 1874 when several artists whose works were not in harmony with the ideals of the official Salon organized an independent exhibition of their work. One of the paintings exhibited was Claude Monet's *Impression—Sunrise*, from which the term "Impressionism" is derived. Between 1874 and 1886, the Impressionists held eight more of these independent exhibitions.

Manet

The artist who is the bridge between the Realists and the Impressionists was Édouard Manet (1832–1883). He was born into a moderately well-to-do upper-middle-class family in Paris, and in 1850, after twice failing the examinations to attend the naval college, his father allowed Manet to enter the studio of Thomas Couture (1815–1879). Although he often clashed with Couture, Manet remained in his studio for six years. His first independent painting was rejected for the Salon of 1859, and the two paintings that were accepted in 1861 received harsh treatment from critics.

In 1863, the Salon rejected Manet's *Le Déjeuner sur l'Herbe* (*Luncheon on the Grass;* Figure 22.6), but he was able to exhibit it at the first *Salon de Refusés*. The painting shows two clothed men and two women, one partially clothed and the other completely nude, sharing a meal somewhere in the Parisian countryside. The inclusion of the nude woman created an enormous scandal among the Parisians, for she exists neither as a goddess nor as part of an allegory, as was the customary way to depict female nudes. Instead, she was Manet's favorite model, a contemporary Parisian, who seems boldly to ogle the crowds who come to view the painting. Criticism was also leveled against the style and form of the painting—there is no chiaroscuro and the forms are flat. But this was precisely Manet's aim—to make the human figures stand out from the natural surroundings by using a frontal light (instead of lighting from one side) to flatten the forms and to reduce the shadows. The frontal light also makes the luminous flesh of the nude woman the focus of the painting. One dismayed critic reflected the typical reaction:

> A commonplace woman . . . as naked as can be, shamelessly lolls between two dandies dressed to the teeth. These latter look like schoolboys on a holiday, . . . and I search in vain for the meaning of this. . . . This is a young man's practical joke. . . . The landscape is well handled, . . . but the figures are slipshod.[11]

Some of Manet's paintings continued to be rejected by the Salon during the 1870s, but in 1881, the Salon chose to award Manet a medal for his work. The following year, Manet exhibited his final masterpiece at the Salon, *Bar at the Folies-*

Figure 22.6 Édouard Manet, *Le Déjeuner sur l'Herbe*, 1863, 7' x 8'10" (2.13 x 2.64 m), oil on canvas, Musée d'Orsay, Paris. This painting shows two clothed men and two women, one partially clothed and the other completely nude, sharing a meal somewhere in the Parisian countryside. By painting the nude woman as neither a goddess nor as part of an allegory, as was customary, Manet created an enormous scandal among Parisian audiences. *(Musée d'Orsay, Paris/Giraudon/The Bridgeman Art Library International)*

Figure 22.9 Claude Monet, *Rouen Cathedral in Full Sunlight,* 1892–1893, 39 1/2" x 25 3/4" (100.3 x 65.4 cm), oil on canvas, Museum of Fine Arts, Boston. This painting is from Monet's most famous series, depicting the high Gothic façade of the Rouen Cathedral catching the play of light at different times of the day and in diverse weather conditions. Like the other paintings in the series, the Cathedral occupies the entire canvas with hardly any foreground or background showing. *(Juliana Cheney Edwards Collection, 39.671. Courtesy, Museum of Fine Arts, Boston. Reproduced with permission. © 2002 Museum of Fine Arts, Boston. All Rights Reserved)*

the series, the Cathedral occupies the entire canvas with hardly any foreground or background.

For 43 years, Monet lived at Giverny, which is located on the right bank of the Seine River, 45 miles northwest of Paris in Normandy. There he concentrated on the water garden he so lovingly designed and built. Monet painted water lily scenes of his gardens on both large canvases and panels until his death. Today, his *Water Lily* paintings decorate two immense, oval rooms at the Orangerie in Paris.

Morisot, Renoir, Degas, and Cassatt

One of the original members of the Impressionist group, Berthe Morisot (1841–1895), was greatly influenced by Manet with whom she had a friendship beginning in 1868 and whose brother, Eugène, she married in 1874. In that same year, she exhibited several works in the First Impressionist Exhibition. Many of Morisot's paintings deal with home life, women, and domestic scenes, as can be seen with *In the Dining Room* (Figure 22.10), which she executed in 1886. As the viewer looks into a cluttered dining room, a servant girl pauses from her work, while a small dog begs for attention. The only other objects depicted are a landscape, visible through the window, and a soiled tablecloth, which hangs over the cabinet door. The liberated brushwork and expressive use of light and shade are typical of Morisot's style.

One of the most famous Impressionist scenes of middle-class leisure was painted by Pierre August Renoir (1841–1919). On a Sunday afternoon, in a happy moment of carefree intimacy, young couples gather at tables or dance under the trees at *Le Moulin de la Galette* (Figure 22.11), an outdoor café in the Montmartre region of Paris. The broken brushwork creates the dabs of sunlight filtering through the trees and the shadows. The light, color, and open air epitomize the spirit of Impressionism, and the painting was included in the Third Impressionist Exhibition of 1877. Less than four years later, Renoir had come to an impasse as an Impressionist painter and began to feel that the Impressionist abolition of form and line was too great a loss. On a trip to Italy, he studied the works of the past, especially Raphael, and upon his return to Paris, he began to focus on the female nude. His new direction was signaled by *The Bathers* (Figure 22.12), which Renoir exhibited in 1887. Only the landscape might be labeled Impressionist. The substantive figures, positioned in a traditional pyramidal grouping, are well-modeled forms, and this was a renunciation of Impressionism, which Renoir now believed was a passing fad.

Although he did exhibit with the Impressionists, Edgar Degas (1834–1917) always insisted that he was a Realist; consequently, his work is more difficult to classify. Degas' use of color and his interest in the fleeting moment make him comparable to the Impressionists, but his interest in rendering a well-modeled human form and his many renderings of figures painted indoors, rather than outdoors in their natural setting, separated him from the Impressionists. Like Monet's series paintings, Degas executed a number of paintings on a single motif. His most famous series is his representation of ballet dancers, in which he attempted to capture their movements in brief snapshots. In 1876, he painted a very different type of scene in *Glass of Absinthe* (Figure 22.13), which focuses on human character rather than movement. Like an off-center, candid photograph (Degas was an amateur photographer), the painting captures a lonely, saturnine couple as they sit in a Parisian café (one that Degas and Manet often frequented). Actually, the pair is inebriated, for they have been drinking absinthe—an addictive green liqueur that brings about trancelike intoxication. Through the positioning of objects in both the foreground and the background, Degas added spatial depth and perspective to the brooding scene.

Also connected to the Impressionist group was an American artist, Mary Cassatt (1844–1926), who settled in Paris in 1874. Cassatt's paintings depict ordinary, domestic scenes focusing on

Figure 22.10   Berthe Morisot, *In the Dining Room*, 1886, 24 1/8″ x 19 3/4″ (61.3 x 50.2 cm), oil on canvas, National Gallery of Art, Washington, D.C. Morisot was one of the original members of the Impressionist group. Many of her paintings, such as this one, deal with home life, women, and domestic scenes. The liberated brushwork and expressive use of light and shade are hallmarks of her style. *(National Gallery of Art, Washington, Chester Dale Collection, Photograph © Board of Trustees)*

**Figure 22.11   Pierre August Renoir, *Le Moulin de la Galette*, 1876, 4'3 1/2" x 5'9"
(1.31 x 1.75 m), oil on canvas, Musée d'Orsay, Paris.**
On a Sunday afternoon, in a happy moment of carefree intimacy, young couples gather at
tables or dance under the trees at an outdoor café in the Montmartre region of Paris. The
light, color, and open air epitomize the spirit of Impressionism. Dabs of color create the
effect of sunlight filtering through the trees, as well as shadows. *(Musée d'Orsay,
Paris/Giraudon/ The Bridgeman Art Library International)*

**Figure 22.12   Pierre August Renoir, *The Bathers*, 1887, 3'10 3/8" x 5'7 1/4" (1.18
x 1.71 m), oil on canvas, Philadelphia Museum of Art.**   Renoir abandoned the
Impressionist styling following a trip to Italy. These substantive, well-modeled figures,
positioned in a traditional pyramidal grouping, were viewed as a renunciation of
Impressionism. *(Renoir, Pierre Auguste, The Bathers, 1887, oil on canvas, 46-3/8 " x 67-1/4 "
Philadelphia Museum of Art: Mr. And Mrs. Carroll S. Tyson Collection)*

Figure 22.13   Edgar Degas, *Glass of Absinthe*, 1876, 36" x 27" (91.3 x 68.7 cm), oil on canvas, Musée d'Orsay, Paris.
Like an off-center, candid photograph, this painting captures a lonely, saturnine couple as they sit in a Parisian café. However, the man and the woman are actually inebriated, for they have been drinking an addictive green liqueur called absinthe. *(Musée d'Orsay, Paris/Giraudon/The Bridgeman Art Library International)*

women and children. She exhibited her first important painting of a child, *Girl in the Blue Armchair*, in the Salon of 1875. Three years after the final Impressionist Exhibition of 1886, she painted *Mother and Child* (Figure 22.14); in this work, she differentiated the background, with its free, light-filled strokes, from the clearly delineated, interwoven human forms in the foreground. The poignancy of the moment is heightened by the positioning of the heads of the mother and her child, as the child tenderly reaches up to touch the mother's face. When the painting was exhibited in France, it was simply titled *Maternité*, to suggest that Cassatt had captured the very essence of motherhood.

Sculpture: Rodin

The man who transformed sculpture during the same years as the Impressionists' breakthrough in painting was Auguste Rodin (1840–1917), the

greatest sculptor since Houdon (see Chapter 19) and arguably the best since Bernini (see Chapter 16). Rodin's early works were rejected by the Salon, because they did not conform to the contemporary idealized, Neoclassical sculptural style. In 1875, Rodin traveled to Italy, where the works of Michelangelo and Donatello (see Chapter 13) had a decisive influence on him. In executing his marble sculptures, Rodin did not actually cut the marble; instead, he made clay models, and stonecutters did the actual cutting of the stone from plaster casts of the original models. Rodin's most famous work in marble is *The Kiss,* executed between 1888 and 1898. The entwined couple represent Paolo Malatesta and Francesca da Rimini, the tragic lovers of Dante's *Inferno,* the first part of *The Divine Comedy.* Rodin did a number of smaller models of *The Kiss,* which proved to be immensely popular. Consequently, the French

Figure 22.14   Mary Cassatt, *Mother and Child,* 1889, 35 1/2" x 25 3/8" (89.8 x 64.4 cm), oil on canvas, Wichita Art Museum.
The poignancy of the moment is heightened by the positioning of the heads of the mother and her child, as the child tenderly reaches up to touch the mother's face. In France, the painting was titled *Maternité,* suggesting that Cassatt captured the very essence of motherhood. *(M109.53, Mary Cassatt, Mother and Child, ca. 1890, oil on canvas, 35-1/2 x 25-3/8" The Roland P. Murdock Collection, Wichita Art Museum, Wichita, Kansas)*

Figure 22.15 Auguste Rodin, *The Kiss*, 1888–1898, marble, over lifesize, Musée Rodin, Paris. The entwined couple represent Paolo Malatesta and Francesca da Rimini, the tragic lovers of Dante's *Inferno*. This larger-than-life version was commissioned by the French government for the 1889 World's Fair in Paris. *(Musée Rodin, Paris/The Bridgeman Art Library International)*

government commissioned him to render this larger-than-life version (Figure 22.15), which premiered at the 1889 World's Fair in Paris, even before Rodin was completely finished with it. Rodin finished the marble himself, in a soft blurry surface to heighten the eroticism of the sculpture. By the 1880s, Rodin was the leading sculptor in France, and his impact on the future of sculpture was enormous. Although most sculptors rejected his naturalism and turned to less natural modeling, no one surpassed him as the heir to Renaissance classical modeling, individualism, and realism.

ARCHITECTURE

During the nineteenth century, new forms of architecture were made possible by the advent of a new building material—metal. Although iron had been used since the end of the eighteenth century to construct bridges and aqueducts, its use in large-scale buildings did not commence until the middle of the nineteenth century. Iron was often used to construct arches to span the central halls of

railway stations. The *Central Railway Station, Newcastle-upon-Tyne* (Figure 22.16), which was officially opened by Queen Victoria in 1850, employed iron vaulting to support the metal and glass roof.

Metal architecture was assured of an even brighter future when a new method of converting pig iron into steel was introduced. In 1856, the British engineer Henry Bessemer (1813–1898) invented a special furnace, called a **convertor**, to mass-produce large quantities of steel. The converter worked by blowing air into the bottom of the furnace so that it then bubbled up through the molten pig iron, thus removing the carbon and further refining the steel. In 1860, John Brown of Sheffield, England, bought the first license to produce Bessemer steel, and Sheffield went on to dominate the steel-making industry, supplying steel for railway parts, armor plates, and construction. In all types of large structures, steel soon replaced iron, because of its strength, and because it was not susceptible to fire.

Joseph Paxton

In 1850, Queen Victoria and her husband, Prince Albert, announced a design competition for a huge temporary structure to accommodate the London Great Exhibition of 1851. Joseph Paxton (1803–1865), a builder of greenhouses, submitted the winning proposal and, in less than nine months, he built *The Crystal Palace* (Figure 22.17) in Hyde Park. It covered more than eighteen acres and provided nearly one million square feet of exhibition space, making *The Crystal Palace* the

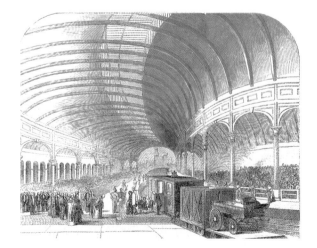

Figure 22.16 John Dobson, *Central Railway Station, Newcastle-upon-Tyne*, 1846–1850. Iron was often used to construct arches to span the central halls of railway stations, as is evident in this structure, which employed iron vaulting to support the metal and glass roof. *(Illustrated London News, 1850/Mary Evans Picture Library)*

Figure 22.17   Joseph Paxton, *The Crystal Palace*, 1851.   Covering more than eighteen acres and nearly one million square feet of exhibition space, *The Crystal Palace* was the largest enclosed space up to that time. Notice how the iron skeleton shows through the glass, making the hall like a gigantic greenhouse. *(The Fotomas Index, U.K.)*

largest enclosed space up to that time. Essentially, it was a huge greenhouse, for the central, vaulted transept and the walls—with the iron skeleton showing through glass covering—furnished natural light for the interior. Following the Great Exhibition, *The Crystal Palace* was dismantled and moved to a location south of London, where it was reconstructed, before burning to the ground in 1936.

Charles Garnier

During the Second Empire, under Napoleon III, Paris experienced a vast transformation of its landscape, including parks and a network of wide boulevards. The centerpiece of the newly constructed district was *The Paris Opéra* (Figure 22.18), built by Charles Garnier (1825–1898). The original Paris Opéra—the Royal Academy of

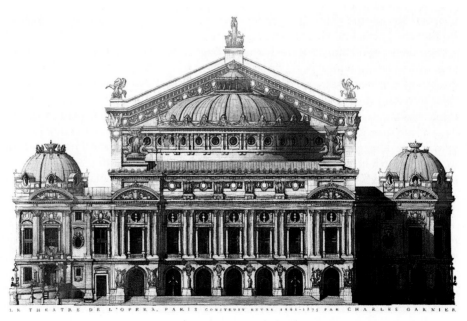

Figure 22.18   Charles Garnier, *The Paris Opéra*, 1861–1875.   Echoing the designs of the great architects of the Renaissance and the Baroque eras, the Opéra employs steel supports, which are completely concealed by marble and plaster. *(Aquatint etching by Andrew Ingamells, Smith Village Gallery, London/Private Collection/The Bridgeman Art Library International Ltd)*

Music and Dance—was destroyed by fire in 1781. And due to political upheaval, reconstruction did not begin again until 1857, when Napoleon III announced a competition for the creation of a vast new opera house. Although the twenty-five-year-old Garnier was trained in Classical architecture, he won the competition by submitting plans that echoed the designs of the great architects of the Renaissance and the Baroque eras. The Empress Eugénie objected to the design, however, because she claimed that it was too ostentatious and eclectic and did not favor any particular style.

In spite of the Empress' objections, the Paris Opéra was begun in 1861 and completed in 1875, four years after the collapse of the Second Empire. For its construction, Garnier used the new structural device of steel supports, but unlike the exposed skeleton of the Crystal Palace, he completely concealed the structural metal with marble and plaster. The interior of the palatial Opéra is the epitome of opulence, where the old nobility, the new aristocracy, and the wealthy industrialists could parade themselves in their sumptuous finery. Thus, the Paris Opéra came to represent all that was right with *eclecticism* in architecture.

LATER ROMANTICISM IN MUSIC

In the middle decades of the nineteenth century, a great debate arose between the advocates of Classical music, for which Haydn and Mozart had set the standard, and *program music,* which aspired to continue in the Romantic genre forged by Beethoven. The acknowledged leaders of the new school of program music were Richard Wagner and Franz Liszt, the most highly regarded concert pianist of the age. They abandoned the formal rules in sonata form (see Chapter 19) of Classical music and favored a type of music that relied heavily on the poetic inspiration of the composer, who chose a variety of specific musical motifs to express changing human emotions. Liszt explained the difference between the two styles:

> In so-called Classical music, the recurrence and thematic development of themes are determined by formal rules that are looked upon as irrevocable. . . . In program music, on the other hand, the recurrence, alternation, transformation, and modulation of motifs are determined by their relationship to poetic conception. Here one theme does not elicit another in accordance with formal requirements, here the motifs are not a result of stereotyped juxtapositions or contrast of timbres [tones or pitches], and the coloring as such does not determine the grouping of ideas. . . . The artist

who favors . . . [program music] enjoys the advantage of being able to link all the affections (which the orchestra can express so powerfully) to a poetic model.[15]

Franz Liszt

Of Hungarian-German ancestry, Franz Liszt (1811–1886), who began concertizing at age eleven, did miraculous things with the piano. A contemporary described one of Liszt's performances.

> After the concert, Liszt stands there like a conqueror on the field of battle, . . . vanquished pianos lie about him, broken strings flutter as trophies and flags of truce, frightened instruments flee in their terror into distant corners, the hearers look at each other in mute astonishment as after a storm from a clear sky; . . . and he . . . now treats his beloved, the piano, tenderly, then tyrannically; caresses, pouts, scolds, strikes, drags by the hair, and then all the more fervently, with all the fire and glow of love, throws his arms around her with a shout, and away with her through all space; he stands there bowing his head, leaning languidly on a chair, with a strange smile, like an exclamation mark after the outburst of universal admiration: this is Franz Liszt![16]

Liszt, the greatest pianist of his generation, retired from the concert stage in 1848 to concentrate on composing and conducting. Between 1848 and 1861, he served as the Director of Court Music in Weimar, where he premiered many important Romantic works, including a number by Schumann, Berlioz, Verdi, and Wagner. In 1861, Liszt traveled to Rome, where he began religious studies, eventually taking minor orders and becoming Abbé Liszt. While in Rome, he composed liturgical music, primarily masses and oratorios.

In 1868, Liszt emerged from religious seclusion to teach, to compose, and to perform in Weimar, Rome, and Budapest. Liszt is credited with inventing the modern piano recital, and his compositions for the piano are some of the most difficult ever written. At his piano recitals, Liszt often played *transcriptions*—modified versions of monumental operatic and orchestral scores that could be played on the piano. Liszt did the transcriptions for works by well-known composers, including Mozart, Beethoven, Schubert, Mendelssohn, Verdi, and Wagner. Using the piano, he sought to replicate the sounds of the orchestra, thus making symphonic music accessible to ordinary middle-class citizens. Small cities and towns could not afford symphony orchestras, but now people could listen to piano arrangements of great operas and symphonies performed by distinguished pianists on a concert tour.

Liszt is also credited with inventing the symphonic poem or *tone poem,* a musical composition that creatively integrates music and poetry, some of them famous literary masterpieces. Tone poems are most often based on a literary idea that is presented in a single, long movement without being tied to exposition, development, and recapitulation, the traditional format of the sonata (see Chapter 19).

Liszt's best-known original work is, perhaps, his *Faust Symphonie* (1854), which relies heavily on the musical artifice known as **thematic transformation** to portray the story of Goethe's play. Rather than simply varying the original theme through tempo, dynamics, or key changes, as was customary, Liszt transformed or altered specific musical ideas to unite the entire work. Sometimes he changed only one note at a time, but he kept on changing the original theme until it was totally transformed into a new theme—hence the term "thematic transformation."

All of Liszt's works composed during his final years, but particularly his piano pieces, evidence experiment in form that anticipated many of the features of twentieth-century composers, including the works of Gustav Mahler, Richard Strauss, Claude Debussy (see the following discussion), and Arnold Schönberg (see Chapter 23).

Italian Opera: Giuseppe Verdi

Throughout the nineteenth century, the battle over "true" opera was waged primarily between the Italians and the Germans. Because the Germans did not possess the long tradition of opera experienced by the Italians, German composers were freer to experiment with form and style. Most of the themes for German operas are drawn from German mythology, legend, or history and involve both supernatural events and superhuman beings. Because the German operatic tradition favors the mysterious and untamed character of nature, as well as the pastoral and sublime, it stands in contrast to Italian opera, which pays scant attention to nature. The treatment of worldly events is also an area of stark contrasts. Whereas Italian opera tends to deal with the reality of the human condition, German opera soars into the realm of the spirit and the ideal, and at times conveys a nationalist message: the German cultural spirit, exemplified by the will and idealism of the German nation, represents a superior cultural tradition.

The music itself is also treated differently. In Italian opera, the melodic line is the central focus, but in German opera, the emphasis is on the inner harmonic voices of the orchestra, which reinforce the link to the ideal, the spiritual. Finally, German composers emphasize recurring musical themes instead of underscoring the total independence of themes in the various movements of a symphony or an opera as did their Italian contemporaries.

The leading Italian composer of the nineteenth century was Giuseppe Verdi (1813–1901), whose operas (and even his last name) became a rallying cry for the unification of Italy. For nearly fifty years, the history of Italian music focused almost exclusively on Verdi. He became the music director for the town of Busseto, in the province of Parma, and married his patron's daughter, with whom he had two children. But in less than two years, unspeakable tragedy struck Verdi's life; both his two children and his wife died.

Stirred by the *Risorgimento*—the nationalist movement advocating Italian liberation from Austrian domination and the creation of a unified Italy—Verdi, in 1842, composed the opera *Nabucco (Nebuchadnezzar),* the most successful of his early operas. In *Nabucco,* Verdi likened the situation of the Jews in exile in Babylon in the sixth century B.C. to the situation of the Italians under Austrian rule. In the third part of *Nabucco,* a chorus of slaves sings: "Go, my thoughts, on golden wings." This chorus came to symbolize the Italian struggle for independence. Even today, when the first chords are sounded, audiences often rise to their feet singing Verdi's chorus.

Between 1857 and 1867, Verdi continued to experiment with grand opera, the most successful of which was *Don Carlo* (1867). After *Don Carlo,* Verdi did not compose another opera for nearly twenty years. When *Otello* finally premiered at La Scala on February 5, 1887, it was hailed as the climax of Italian tragic opera, and Verdi's final opera, *Falstaff,* is considered to be the pinnacle of *opera buffa* (see Chapter 19).

Following in the footsteps of Mozart, Beethoven, and Berlioz, Verdi also composed a *Requiem Mass* (1874), which many music critics consider to be the finest example of the genre ever written. Although Verdi only lived one year into the twentieth century, his operas (and his *Requiem*) continue to be standard fare of musical repertoires around the world.

German Opera: Richard Wagner

Without question, the most significant (and polarizing) composer of German opera during the nineteenth century was Richard Wagner (1813–1883). Like Verdi, Wagner's most outstanding compositions are those he composed for the stage. But unlike Verdi, Wagner abandoned the Classical tonality of Western music as well as the Classical conventions of opera. Wagner viewed himself as a poet, dramatist, and composer who was about to create a *Gesamtkunstwerk*, total work of art (see Chapter 16), by uniting music with all other art forms, including poetry, drama, painting, and dance, even as the setting and the plot of the story were being played out on stage. Although his vehicle was opera, Wagner succeeded in transforming opera into *music drama*—larger-than-life epics of sung poetry supported by complex, colorful orchestration to create moods using continuous melody and *leitmotifs*—short musical labels associated with a person, an idea, or an object. In his music dramas, Wagner used the orchestra to describe a character, a thought, a feeling, or an object. For example, the brass section expressed a king's majesty, clarinets and flutes a lovely maiden, and bassoons and oboes a cruel witch. A harp's melody represented glittering light as the gods crossed over a rainbow bridge and the violin's shimmering high notes stood for the Holy Grail. In a Wagnerian opera, there are times when characters stand motionless and speechless, their deepest thoughts conveyed by the music.

In 1852, in complex and grandiloquent language, Wagner wrote about his decisive break with the Classical operatic tradition, which led to the *Neudeutsche Schule* (New German School) of music:

> With *Rienzi*, my intention was still only to write an "opera." . . . With *The Flying Dutchman* I entered upon a new path, in that I myself grew to be the artificer of a material that lay before me only in its simple, unelaborated outline as a folk saga. From then on I was, in relation to all my dramatic works, first a *poet*; and only as I fully worked out the poem did I again become a musician. . . . But that which is expressed in the language of music consists solely of *emotions* and *sensations*. . . . That which, accordingly, remains inexpressible to absolute [Classical] music is the precise identification of the emotion's or sensation's cause. . . . [T]he musical language's range of expression consists, then, in acquiring also the capacity to indicate with recognizable precision the individual, the particular; and this it acquires only by being wedded to the word-language. . . . [T]he content of that which must be expressed by the word and tone poet becomes self-evident: it is *the purely human, released from all conventions*. . . . I could not, in shaping it [poetic material] proceed otherwise than by gradually and totally abolishing, of necessity, the *operatic form* I had inherited. . . . As I drafted my scenes, I was not in the least constrained, by the nature of the material thus conceived, to have a care for any particular musical form in advance, for the scenes themselves dictated the musical working out as intrinsic and necessary to them.[17]

When the Revolution of 1848 broke out, Wagner fled to Zurich, Switzerland, where he continued to develop his theories of art and music—the most famous of which is his two-volume work, *Opera and Drama* (1851), and the most infamous, his vitriolic, anti-Semitic polemic, *Judaism in Music* (1850) (see chapter end-piece). Although he composed no operas while in Switzerland, Wagner did complete the librettos for his renowned music dramas—a cycle of four, based on the Norse legends regarding *Der Ring des Nibelungen* (The Ring of the Nibelung).* For the next twenty-five years, this cycle of music dramas occupied most of Wagner's attention. In 1862, he interrupted his work on them to assume a position of patronage under Ludwig II (1845–1886), the eighteen-year-old king of Bavaria. As Wagner's fanatical supporter, Ludwig placed all of the resources of the Munich Opera Company at his disposal.

During this period, Wagner completed his tale of forbidden love, *Tristan und* (and) *Isolde* (1865), which was ironically apropos. At the time, Wagner was engaged in an illicit love affair with Liszt's daughter, Cosima, who was still married to Hans von Bülow, the conductor of *Tristan and Isolde*. Their affair produced two children, and when Wagner's wife died, he married Cosima (see chapter opening). In 1868, he returned to Switzerland and completed the most lighthearted of his music dramas, *Die Meistersinger von Nürnberg (The Master-Singer of Nuremberg)*.

Wagner's conception of the music drama is epitomized by the entirety of the *Ring* cycle—*Das Rheingold (The Rhine Gold,* 1857), *Die Walküre (The Valkyrie,* 1857), *Siegfried* (after 1857), and *Götterdämmerung (The Twilight of the Gods,* 1874). As Wagner completed each opera, he became more impatient to find a theater worthy of such a monumental undertaking, including staging, sound, choreography, and lighting. Again, King Ludwig assisted him by constructing the Bayreuth Opera House, where the first complete performance of the *Ring* cycle was held in 1876. However, the *Ring* cycle proved to be a theatrical and financial disaster. The audience was unimpressed with the sets, the sound, the staging, and the choreography. The only thing they did like was Wagner's music.

Wagner developed and maintained the action of the *Ring* cycle through the innovative use of leitmotifs. He sought to weave a seamless web of more than thirty leitmotifs into the story line of the

---

*The opera cycle is based on Norse mythology concerning the treasure of the Nibelungs, dwarfs who lived under the earth. Whoever possesses the gold, and forges a ring out of it will rule the world. Because of its power, the ring is often stolen and used for evil purposes. Wagner's opera cycle recounts the various struggles to recover the ring.

A FOLK TALE FROM WEST AFRICA

Rooted in an oral culture, African storytelling is a communal activity that involves interaction between the storyteller and the audience. These tales (which have only been collected and written down since the middle of the nineteenth century) entertain, instruct, inform, and pass folk wisdom from generation to generation. The following tale, *The Beaten Path,* is one of many stories about Spider, a trickster who can be wise, foolish, amusing, or selfish, but who always teaches a lesson. This tale is from Ghana, and its typical opening consists of a call by the storyteller, "Hear my tale!" and a response from the audience, "Tell us!"

At first there was only one path in the whole world, and the reason why there are more now is as follows:

Grandfather Sky God had a daughter. He said he would give her to whichever man could tell her name. Of course, all the young men were eager to find out her name, and they asked all the elders of the town, but no one knew the name. One day when Spider was walking alone along the path, he said to himself, "I wonder what I could do to find out this girl's name so that I could marry her." The path replied, "I can easily tell you that, but then you will go and tell people who it was who told you, and they will come and beat me for telling you and not them." Spider said, "Oh, I would never do that. I swear." At this point Path told Spider what he would pay for the information. Path demanded a hare, a dwarf, and a python.

Spider said, "That is no problem," and went off and returned shortly after with all that Path had asked for. Path now revealed the name of Grandfather Sky God's daughter, "Mpensaaduasa." Spider said, "Oh, Oh! Thank you for that. Today I will be getting married."

Spider went off and told Grandfather Sky God that he would name his daughter publicly before all the elders, if Grandfather Sky God would convene a celebration for him on the next day. The Sky God, who had named his child secretly on the path before he brought her home, and did not know that the path had told Spider her name, thought Spider was bluffing. "Yoo!" said Spider. On the day of the celebration all the men present were invited to come out and speak the girl's name. No one could. Spider was called last, and he came forward and said straightaway that she was called Mpensaaduasa. Grandfather Sky God was very surprised but agreed that Spider had said the correct name. Everybody acclaimed Spider, calling out "Yee yee! Spider O! Spider O!"

Then God said, "I will give you my daughter in marriage, Spider, but you must tell me who told you her name, or else I will have to deal with you." Spider wasn't happy about this, but at last he said, "It was the path, the path, the path." God then ordered all the people to go and beat the path.

Spider went ahead to show them Path's house, singing: "Path, oh! God's Path oh! I thank you I've got Mpensaaduasa. I thank you, Path O, I thank you." They beat the path until it was broken up into many more paths. That is why we now have many paths.

Source: West African Folktales, *trans. Jack Berry, ed. Richard Spears (Evanston, Ill.: Northwestern University Press, 1991), pp. 121–122.*

drama, but only a determined listener is able to discover each of them. Wagner also heightened dramatic intensity through a creative use of both chromaticism and dissonance. Even after his death in 1884, Wagner's rejection of the Classical notion of tonality continued to inspire new systems of harmony (including the twelve-tone system discussed in Chapter 23), which characterizes so much of the music of the twentieth century and beyond.

Romantic Classicism: Johannes Brahms

In 1859, the music of the New German School, as represented by Liszt and Wagner, was publicly condemned in an article written by Johannes Brahms (1833–1897) for Schumann's *The New Journal of Music*. In the article, Brahms "deplored" and "condemned" the music of the New German School for not following basic rules, which made it "contrary to the most fundamental essence of music."[18] Within a year, Brahms found himself (albeit reluctantly) the leader of the "Romantic Classicists," who viewed themselves as the musical heirs of Bach, Haydn, and Mozart and the opponents of the Romantic Radicalism of the New German School.

As a teenager, Brahms arranged music for his father's orchestra and made money by playing the piano in local dance halls and taverns. In 1853, while Brahms was on tour in Hungary, he was introduced to Schumann, who praised his playing:

> [I]t has seemed to me that . . . there would and must suddenly appear some day one man who would be singled out to make articulate in an ideal way the highest expression of our time. . . . And he is come, a young creature over whose cradle graces and heroes stood guard. His name is *Johannes Brahms,* and he comes from Hamburg where he has been working in silent obscurity. . . . Seated at the piano, he at once discovered [for] us wondrous regions. We were drawn into a circle whose magic grew on us more and more. To this was added an altogether inspired style of playing which made of the piano an orchestra of lamenting and exultant voices. . . . [E]very work [was] so distinct from any other that each seemed to flow from a different source. And then it seemed as though . . . he united them all as in a waterfall.[19]

In spite of Schumann's review, Brahms spent years trying to gain recognition as a composer and conductor. Brahms' musical reputation was finally established in 1869 with the premier of his great vocal work, the *German Requiem*. Drawing freely on passages from the Bible, without adhering to any particular denominational tradition, Brahms created a work of both national and personal importance. His

Variations on a theme by Haydn in B Major, for two pianos, brought him further critical acclaim when it premiered on February 19, 1874.

Brahms was also the acknowledged successor to Schubert and Schumann in the composition of lieder. Some of his more than 200 lieder were inspired by poetry (including Goethe's), some by gypsy songs, others by nature, and still others by the subject of love. One simple lied—*Wiegenlied* (Cradle Song)—has served as Brahms legacy. "Brahms' Lullaby," as the lied is known today, is a tune (and text) that probably every child knows.

Although it took Brahms nearly fifteen years to write his first symphony, today he is regarded as one of the greatest symphonic composers. Such a delay was not due to a lack of talent on his part, but rather, Brahms' reluctance to compose a musical form for which Beethoven was the acknowledged master. Friends often quoted Brahms as remarking: "You don't know what it means to the likes of us when we hear his [Beethoven's] footsteps behind us."[20] When Brahms was forty-three years old, his *Symphony No. 1 in C minor* premiered in Vienna, and Eduard Hanslick, the famed Viennese music critic, exclaimed: "The new symphony of Brahms is a possession of which the nation may be proud, an inexhaustible fountain of sincere pleasure and fruitful study."[21]

Over the course of the next eight years, Brahms composed three more symphonies before abandoning this musical form forever. On December 30, 1877, in Vienna, Brahms triumphantly introduced his *Symphony No. 2 in D minor,* with the great maestro Hans Richter conducting. His *Symphony No. 3 in F Major* premiered in December 1883, with Hans Richter again conducting the Vienna Philharmonic. Hanslick immediately hailed it a masterpiece. In less than a year, Brahms completed his *Symphony No. 4 in E minor* and conducted the symphony's premiere in October 1885 in Meiningen, the home of one of Germany's preeminent orchestras. Although the work was well received in Meiningen, the Viennese critics responded coolly to it.

When Brahms turned sixty-four in 1897, he attended a concert in Vienna, where his *Fourth Symphony* was performed. Following the concert, he was given an extraordinary ovation, and although he was terminally ill with liver cancer, Brahms managed to leave his theater box to acknowledge the ovation. His own symphony was the last he heard, for in less than a month, he was dead.

In assessing Brahms' greatness, the famed conductor and pianist Hans von Bülow (1830–1894) referred to "the Three Bs"—Bach, Beethoven, and Brahms—and he dubbed Brahms' *First Symphony* "Beethoven's Tenth." Echoing the same sentiments, Hans Richter equated Brahms' *Second Symphony* with Beethoven's *Pastorale* (No. 6) and his *Third Symphony* with Beethoven's *Eroica* (No. 3).

The Post-Wagnerians: Mahler and Strauss

The premier conductor of the late nineteenth century was the Bohemian-born composer Gustave Mahler (1860–1911), who was the son of an Austrian-Jewish innkeeper. During his youth, Mahler was exceedingly conflicted, for he was a German-speaking Jew living in a predominately Catholic Czech region. At the age of fifteen, Mahler went to live and to study in Vienna, where he spent most of the rest of his life. In 1897, Mahler agreed to convert to Catholicism so that he might accede to the post of director for the Vienna Opera. During his tenure, he enhanced the opera's stature and brought it international renown. But in 1907, partly because of pervasive anti-Semitism, Mahler resigned his post in Vienna and accepted the position of director for the Metropolitan Opera in New York City; the next year, he became the director of the New York Philharmonic. Less than two years later, however, Mahler was compelled, for health reasons, to return to Vienna, where he died on May 18, 1911.

By pairing lofty, sophisticated themes with lyrical, native folk tunes, dance rhythms, and marches, Mahler's symphonies are both complicated and simple. Nowhere is this more evident than in his *Symphony No. 2 in C minor* (1895), in which Mahler deals with a strictly Christian theme, the Resurrection, asking the questions: "Why have you lived? Why have you suffered? Is all this merely a great horrible jest?"[22] The climax of this symphony, hereafter known as Mahler's "Resurrection Symphony," employs vocal parts, making it like Beethoven's *Ninth Symphony* (see Chapter 19). The massive orchestra plays a passage to depict the dawning of the Day of Resurrection just before the soloists and chorus sing a setting of an eighteenth-century German Resurrection ode.

Mahler surpassed the monumentality of his *Resurrection Symphony* with his *Symphony No. 8 in E flat,* nicknamed "the symphony of a thousand," because it required an even larger array of singers and orchestra members for its two movements than had the *Resurrection Symphony.* His innovative orchestration is reminiscent of Berlioz, but his inspiration was drawn from the medieval church and Goethe. Whereas the first movement is a rendering of the Latin hymn *Veni Creator Spiritus (Come, Creator Spirit),* the second movement considers the entirety of the damnation and redemption of Faust, making it nearly an oratorio unto itself.

Although Mahler composed music throughout his lifetime, his work generally received little critical acclaim. He did, nonetheless, continue to assert that the time would come when his work would be appreciated, and he was indeed proven correct. Today his nine symphonies are not only regarded as the summation of the late Romantic tradition, but his experimentation with their form is viewed as foreshadowing the work of the groundbreaking Viennese composer Arnold Schönberg, discussed in the next chapter.

Another acclaimed conductor of the age was the German-born composer Richard Strauss (1864–1949). At the age of seventeen, Strauss premiered his first symphony, and three years later the second one. But in 1886, Strauss went to Italy in search of his own musical style. A year later, he premiered his symphonic fantasy, *Aus Italien (From Italy),* which demonstrated his conversion to the thinking of Wagner and Liszt and the New German School. Strauss then began to compose powerful, dramatic tone poems, which firmly established his reputation as a composer: *Don Juan* (1889), based on the story of the legendary lover (see Chapters 19 and 20); *Tod und Verklärung (Death and Transfiguration,* 1889), a philosophic work detailing the progress of the human soul from suffering to self-realization; *Till Eulenspiegels lustige Streiche (Till Eulenspiegel's Merry Pranks,* 1894), a lighthearted, melodic adventure piece; *Also sprach Zarathustra (Thus Spake Zarathustra,* 1896), a philosophical composition inspired by Friedrich Nietzsche's concept of a new type of Western hero (discussed in the next chapter); and *Don Quixote* (1894), based on Cervantes' epic (see Chapter 15). His autobiographical tone poem *Ein Heldenleben (A Hero's Life,* 1898) was hailed as the wave of the future because of his use of dissonance.

Strauss next set his sights on opera, where he was determined to make an impact. Although his first two operas (produced in 1894 and 1901) were failures, the operatic success of *Salomé* (1905) not only created a scandal but also caused Strauss to be viewed as the prophet of modern decadence. Based on a French play by the Irish writer Oscar Wilde (1854–1900), the subject matter alone still raises eyebrows today. The legend of Salomé is linked to the beheading of John the Baptist as the wish fulfillment of Herod the Great's decadent stepdaughter, who is never mentioned by name (Matthew 14:1–12 and Mark 6:16–29). The Wilde/Strauss version, however, focuses on the psyche of Salomé. She demands John the

Baptist's head on a silver platter—not only as a test of her stepfather's depraved desire for her, but also as an act of simple revenge against John the Baptist, who has spurned her sexual advances.

The entire opera takes place in only one act. As Narraboth, the young captain of the guards, sings about his love for Salomé, she revels inside Herod's banquet hall with the other guests. But from the depths of a cistern, the voice of Jokanaan (John the Baptist) prophesies the coming of the Messiah. Fascinated by Jokanaan's voice, Salomé, using her feminine wiles, convinces Narraboth to bring him to her. Jokanaan's condemnation of her family only serves to incite Salomé's passion, and she attempts to seduce him. Overwhelmed by Salomé's outrageous behavior and his own rejection by her, Narraboth commits suicide. Herod subsequently slips and slides through Narraboth's blood and makes an incestuous suggestion to Salomé, which enrages his wife. She and five Jews then demand to know why Herod has not turned Jokanaan over to the Jews. Seeking to avoid controversy, Herod asks Salomé to dance for him. She agrees, on the condition that when she is finished Herod will grant her any wish. Salomé then performs the "Dance of the Seven Veils" and demands the head of John the Baptist on a silver platter. Upon receiving the prize of Jokanaan's severed head, Salomé sings deliriously about how she finally possesses him, and she kisses him on his dead lips. Repulsed by the sight, Herod orders his soldiers to crush Salomé with their shields.

In his later years, Strauss recounted the reactions of the audience at the premier, including their response to the innovative orchestration, founded in dissonance and chromaticism, which even drew objections from the woman cast in the role of Salomé:

> At the staging rehearsals, the highly dramatic Frau Wittich, who . . . had been entrusted with the part of the 16-year-old princess with the Isolde-voice— "You can't write music like that, Mr. Strauss: make up your mind!"—went on strike periodically with the indignant objection . . . "That I refuse to do; I'm a decent woman!"

Moreover, Strauss recalled that when he "strummed parts" of the music "at the piano" for his father, also a prominent musician, how he groaned miserably, "Dear Lord, all this nervous music! It's like having your trousers full of crawling June bugs."[23] Finally, Strauss mentioned "the puritans of New York" who, in 1907, succeeded in suspending the opera's performance after only one semipublic rehearsal at the Metropolitan Opera in New York City.

Strauss' next opera, *Elektra*, based on the Orestian trilogy of Aeschylus, the ancient Greek dramatist, was equally provocative and scandalous. Many critics decried the libretto as signaling the end of opera and the disappearance of the human voice as an instrument of art.

Strauss' decade-long descent into the decadent and the avant-garde ended as abruptly as it began. For beginning with his immensely popular *Der Rosenkavalier* (*The Rose Cavalier*, 1911), a comedic opera set in Vienna during the eighteenth century, Strauss performed the musical equivalent of an about face. The Classical opera, in the style of Mozart (see Chapter 19), placed emphasis on the human voice as an artistic instrument. It is also laden with rich, Romantic harmonies, German folk dances, and folk songs.

Throughout the 1920s, as Strauss traveled widely in Europe and North and South America, he continued to compose operas in this more Classical style. During the 1930s, he accepted the post of Director of Chamber Music under the Nazi regime. Following the defeat of the Nazis, Strauss composed his impassioned lament, *Metamorphoses* (1945). Four years later, Strauss died quietly at his home; his last work, bearing the ironic title *Last Four Songs* (1948), was composed in the graceful style of his beloved Mozart.

Dvořák and Sibelius: Nationalist Expressions

When Bohemia (today part of the Czech Republic) became part of the Austro-Hungarian empire during the sixteenth century, the German language was imposed on the people. This resulted in a diminution of Czech culture. But during the nineteenth century, a renaissance in Czech culture took place. The leading musical proponent of this renaissance was Antonín Dvořák (1841–1904), who began his musical career as an organist. As a nationalist composer, Dvořák incorporated Bohemian legends, dance tunes, folk songs, and rhythms into nearly everything he composed. His first composition was *Slavonic Dances* (1878), which brought him international renown. Dvořák was particularly appreciated in England, where he composed the choral works, *The Spectre's Bride* (1884) and *Requiem Mass* (1890), as well as his *Symphony No. 7 in D minor* (1885).

In 1892, Dvořák traveled to the United States to become the director of the National Conservatory of Music in New York City—a post he held for three years. There, he composed his best-known composition, *Symphony No. 9 in E minor (From the New World)*, which is simply known today as "The New World Symphony." Dvořák based some of the symphony on a Czech translation of Longfellow's poem, "Hiawatha"; he also utilized what he called "Negro melodies":

I am now satisfied that the future music of this country must be founded upon what are called Negro melodies. This must be the real foundation of any serious and original school of composition to be developed in the United States.[24]

Dvořák's words proved to be prophetic indeed, for jazz (see Chapters 24 and 25) is a uniquely American art form whose influence is now worldwide.

In 1896, after returning to Prague, Dvořák published four of his most famous tone poems: *The Water Goblin, The Noon Witch, The Golden Spinning Wheel,* and *The Wild Dove.* Having established an international reputation, Dvořák received an honorary doctorate from Cambridge University in England, and the Austrian government made him a senator. But the people of Bohemia considered Dvořák to be their statesman of culture. Unfortunately, because he sold his compositions for such little money, Dvořák died a very poor man in 1904.

Like the Bohemians under the Hapsburgs, the Finnish longed for independence from the Russian Empire, which had ruled them since 1809. During the ensuing years, the ideas of Herder (see Chapter 20) found fertile ground in Finland. The Finnish were attracted to his argument that the nation exists only if it possesses a distinctive cultural identity based on the language and oral traditions of its people. Until the second half of the nineteenth century, however, Swedish was the language of both education and government in Finland. But in 1849, Elias Lönnrot published the Finnish national epic *Kalevala* in the Finnish language. Although few people could read it in their native tongue, they were attracted to the powerful myths contained in the epic—stories about ancient times when all aspects of life were governed by a myriad of invisible gods and spirits. Moreover, there were myths about the origin of the world, the growth cycle of the primeval world, and people who could magically summon the powers of the "Otherworld."

In 1899 a national pageant was organized that sought to make Finland culturally more Russian. Jean Sibelius (1865–1957) responded differently. Inspired by the *Kalevala* and the northern countryside of Finland, which abounded in lakes and forests, he submitted his tone poem *Finlandia.* Almost immediately, Sibelius was hailed as Finland's national composer, an achievement that was particularly remarkable, especially because no indigenous musical tradition existed in Finland. In 1917, *Finlandia* was banned, because it had come to embody Finnish nationalistic aspirations, which were finally achieved in 1920. Most of Sibelius' significant compositions were composed before 1925, including seven symphonies and a number of tone poems.

Sibelius' birthday eventually became a national holiday, and on his seventieth birthday, he was honored at a banquet that was attended by all of the past presidents of Finland as well as the prime ministers of the other Scandinavian countries: Denmark, Norway, and Sweden.

"The Mighty Handful" in Russia

In 1882, the librarian Vladimir Vasilievich Stasov (1824–1906) published his encyclopedic survey of Russian literature, architecture, painting, and music, *Twenty-five Years of Russian Art,* in which he identified five Russian nationalist composers, whom he dubbed "the mighty handful." The inclusion of uniquely Russian material and the breaking away from traditional musical forms were hallmarks of the musical compositions of the Russian nationalists. The self-appointed leader of the group was Mily Balakirev (1837–1910), the only member of the group who was a trained, professional musician. In 1861, Balakirev went to St. Petersburg where he became familiar with Mikhail Glinka's (1804–1857) patriotic opera, *A Life of the Tsar* (1836), which is credited with inaugurating Russian music. Russian folk tales and Russian folk tunes are the foundation of Balakirev's compositions, as is evident in his tone poem *Russia* (1887).

César Cui (1835–1918), the least known of The Mighty Handful, composed hundreds of songs in French, Polish, and German, as well as in Russian, and fourteen operas, including several children's operas that were actually performed by children. Even though he is best remembered for his acerbic musical criticism, which supersedes his somewhat mundane musical compositions, he is regarded as a Russian nationalist because of the Russian songs that he composed.

Like Cui, Alexander Borodin (1833–1887), a professor of chemistry, was originally an adherent of Romantic music, particularly Mendelssohn (see Chapter 20); but under Balakirev's influence, he became a fervent nationalist. Although his lyrical, descriptive style is reminiscent of Mendelssohn, Borodin's first symphony, which appeared in 1876, and a symphonic sketch, *In the Steppes of Central Asia* (1880), demonstrate his determination to compete with Western European Classical music. His four-act opera, *Prince Igor,* remained unfinished when Borodin died, but the work was completed by another member of The Mighty Handful—Nicolas Rimsky-Korsakov (1844–1908).

The musical output of Rimsky-Korsakov is the link between the early Russian nationalists and the more avant-garde Russian composers of the twenti-eth century, including Igor Stravinsky, who was Rimsky-Korsakov's pupil (see Chapter 23). In 1873, Rimsky-Korsakov abandoned his naval career to study with Balakirev, but during the 1880s, he moved away from Balakirev's extreme nationalism to create a more eclectic type of music, but which still included themes based on Russian folk tunes and dances. Rimsky-Korsakov's flights of fancy are evident in his symphonic suite *Scheherazade* (1888), based on the tale from *The Thousand and One Arabian Nights*, and in his best-known piece, *Flight of the Bumblebee*, from the orchestral work *Tsar Saltan* (1903). Rimsky-Kor-sakov's music is commonly viewed as being in dia-metric contrast to that of Modest Mussorgsky (1839–1881), whose works he often edited.

Mussorgsky is generally considered to be a Realist and the most important of The Mighty Handful. His first important orchestral work—the symphonic fantasy *Night on Bald Mountain*—was published in 1867, and seven years later, his opera *Boris Godunov* was successfully staged. Mussorgsky's most famous work, *Pictures at an Exhibition*, also appeared in 1874. The "pictures" are actually a series of ten piano pieces (not counting the *Promenade*, which opens the composition and recurs throughout the work) that were inspired by a memorial exhibition of sketches by Mussorgsky's close friend, Victor Hartmann, an architect, designer, and artist who died at the age of thirty-nine. In his musical treat-ment of sketch after sketch, Mussorgsky, true to his Realist tendencies, moves the listener from one psychological state of mind to another. Moreover, he uses the sketches to give fuller expression to his sense of Russian pride and patriotism, as he gave musical illustration to Hartmann's scenes of Russ-ian life at all levels of culture.

Although only six of Hartmann's sketches are known with certainty, Mussorgsky's intentions are well known. He creates an otherworldly atmo-sphere to paint *Gnomus*, a gnome-shaped nut-cracker. In *The Old Castle*, Mussorgsky portrays a troubadour singing outside a medieval castle, which is followed by the shortest piece, *Tuileries*, depicting visitors to the famous Parisian garden. Peasant laborers are the subject of *Bydlo*, literally "ox cart," which precedes the *Ballet of Chicks in their Shells*, the first movement for which Hart-mann's sketch is known with certainty. (Because Hartmann was working on a ballet, he designed costumes that were shaped like eggs, and the chick breaking through the shell served as a type of hel-met for the dancers.) Two Jewish men, one rich, one poor, are the subjects of *Samuel Goldenberg and Schmuyle*, which leads deftly into the sights

and sounds of the *Limoges Market*. Mussorgsky's lament for his friend is evident in the *Catacombs*, including the Latin dirge *cum mortuis in lingua mortua* (with the dead in a dead language), which is a musical transformation of the opening *Prome-nade* theme. The somber mood of the previous piece stands in stark contrast to the freneticism that characterizes *The Hut on Fowl's Legs*. It por-trays Baba Yaga, the witch of Russian fairy tales, who lures lost children into her hut (actually a clock that sits on chicken legs) only to crush them to death.

The final piece, *The Great Gate of Kiev*, is Mus-sorgsky's nationalistic declaration of affection for his homeland. Hartmann originally presented a design to be considered by the committee charged with building a grand new entrance to Kiev as a way to commemorate the unsuccessful assassi-nation attempt on the life of Tsar Alexander II (1818–1881). However, no winner was ever announced, and no gate was ever built. Yet, Hart-mann's sketch and Mussorgsky's piano piece became an immense source of Russian pride and heritage, particularly after the French Impression-ist composer Maurice Ravel (1873–1937) arranged the piano pieces for full orchestra—the way they are best known today.

Tchaikovsky and the Russian Ballet

The Mighty Handful were harsh critics of Russia's most important composer for the **ballet,** Pyotr Ilyich Tchaikovsky (1840–1893), but he was greatly appreciated by the Russian public. Tchaikovsky studied music at Russia's first conser-vatory of music in St. Petersburg, where he learned to respect the mainstream European musical tradi-tion scorned by his nationalist contemporaries. Following his graduation, Tchaikovsky became a professor of harmony at the Moscow Conserva-tory of Music and began to compose feverishly. His early works included an opera, *The Voyevoda* (1869), a couple of symphonies, his tone poem *Romeo and Juliet* (1869), and his enormously popular *Piano Concerto No. 1 in B flat minor* (1875). Although Tchaikovsky was comfortable with composing beautiful Romantic melodies that were supported by colorful orchestrations, he was ill at ease with the traditional musical conventions. As a consequence, his works were criticized by both his instructors and his peers.

Much of Tchaikovsky's music is semiautobio-graphical, often portraying inner torment. His tur-moil centered on his homosexuality, with which he was never content. Seeking to fit into mainstream society, Tchaikovsky entered into a disastrous marriage in 1877. After only two weeks, he abandoned his wife, attempted suicide, and suffered a mental breakdown. That same year, Tchaikovsky acquired the patronage of the wealthy widow Nadezhda von Meck, with whom he corresponded for fourteen years, even though they never met. He also scored his first ballet, *Swan Lake* (1877), which premiered at the Bolshoi Theater in Moscow.

Three years later, Tchaikovsky began work on a commission to commemorate the seventieth anniversary of Napoleon's retreat from Russia. The work, *"1812" Overture in E-flat major*, premiered on August 20, 1882, and was immediately hailed as a triumph. In 1974, the legendary conductor of the Boston Pops orchestra, Arthur Fiedler, included the piece as part of the fireworks finale for the Fourth of July festival. Ever since, Tchaikovsky's *"1812" Overture*, replete with cannon fire, church bells, and chimes, has become standard fare for Fourth of July celebrations throughout the United States.

During the 1890s, the "Big Three" of Russian ballet—*The Sleeping Beauty* (1890), *The Nutcracker* (1892), and the reworked *Swan Lake* (1895)—were staged. The hallmarks of his ballet music are the tunefulness of the melodies, the well-conceived orchestrations to evoke human emotion and to further the story line, and his sensitivity to theatrical staging.

Debussy: French Impressionism

Impressionism in music was inspired by the French Impressionist painters and was founded by Claude-Achille Debussy (1862–1918), who considered himself a "post-Wagnerian" reacting to the dramatic emotionalism of Wagner and the New German School. Like an Impressionist painting, Debussy's music has no distinct shape (clear-cut form) nor hard line (melody), but rather picturesque splashes of orchestral color and exotic rhythms. He wanted his music to sound as if it had just come into his mind and had never been written down, only improvised. Debussy's first major orchestral work—the tone poem *Prélude à l'après-midi d'un faune (Prelude to the Afternoon of a Faun*, 1894)—was inspired by the poet Stéphane Mallarmé's (1842–1898) poem with a similar title. The piece established Impressionism as a style of music and inaugurated Debussy's most productive period, lasting almost twenty years.

Debussy's two books of piano *Preludes* (1910–1913)—with titles such as the "Sounds and Scents Revolve in the Evening Air" and "What the West Wind Saw"— are still considered the most significant piano pieces since Chopin's. But Debussy's most famous composition for the piano is undoubtedly *Clair de lune (Moonlight)* from his *Suite bergamasque* (1893). He also composed the orchestral suites *Nocturnes* (1899), *La Mer* (The Sea, 1905), *Images* (1905 and 1907), and in 1908, he dedicated his *Children's Corner Suite* to his daughter, Claude-Emma.

Debussy's musical style is considered to be the link between Later Romantic composers and Modern composers. His handling of harmony was revolutionary, for he used chords more for the tone color (the difference between pitches) they produced than for resolving dissonant harmonies; Debussy often left his own musical dissonances totally unresolved. Moreover, he abandoned standard major and minor scales, preferring instead the medieval church modes, the Javanese pentatonic (five-tone) scale, and the whole-tone scale. In the whole-tone scale, no single note stands out, for the scale is composed of six different notes, each note being a whole step away from the previous one. There is no "leading" tone; each note stands on its own, rather than being linked to the one that comes either before it or after it. These innovations enabled Debussy to produce different, even strange, unearthly melodies and harmonies. But they were also intriguing and appealing. In a conversation with his former teacher, Ernest Guiraud (1837–1918), Debussy summed up his views concerning conventions in music:

> [I have] no faith in the supremacy of the C Major scale. The tonal scale must be enriched by other scales. . . . Rhythms are stifling. Rhythms cannot be contained within bars [measure markings]. It is nonsense to speak of "simple" and "compound" time. There should be an interminable flow of both. Relative keys are nonsense, too. Music is neither major nor minor. . . . The mode is that which one happens to choose at the moment. It is inconstant. There must be a balance between musical demands and thematic evocation. Themes suggest their orchestral coloring.[25]

Nationalism and the Arts

By glorifying the nation's past, bemoaning its current humiliations, or assigning it a special mission, some literary figures, artists, and musicians contributed to the shaping of nationalist feelings. Often they expressed only a healthy pride in their nation and its accomplishments as is evident in the poetry of Walt Whitman, which celebrated

American democracy and the spirit of its people. Sometimes they voiced a longing to correct a historic injustice. Thus, Polish poet Adam Mickiewicz (1798–1855), while living abroad, wrote passionately about Poland's suffering and the need to liberate it from Russian rule:

Lord! we are very sad and lonely now;
We, once so free and happy, mourn in bonds;
Our burden heavier than we can bear;
Still heavier—compared with freedom gone.[26]

British writers such as Rudyard Kipling (1865–1936) spoke glowingly about Britain's overseas empire as the fulfillment of the nation's destiny. In his short stories, novels, and poetry, Kipling promoted the belief that the British were a superior race with a noble mission to spread the blessing of civilization—"the White Man's Burden," he called it—to lesser peoples, "Half-devil and half-child." At the end of the nineteenth century, when Britain ruled a vast empire, Kipling mirrored the outlook of many, few of whom questioned the racist assumptions that underlay imperial expansion.

Some writers propagated ideas, often irrational, that made nationalism more extreme and dangerous. This can be seen in the writings of Fyodor Dostoevsky. Rejecting the liberal-rationalist tradition of modern Western Europe, Dostoevsky glorified the Russian peasant who was mystically attached to the soil and devoted to the Orthodox Church, the one true faith. He urged Russian intellectuals to draw inspiration from their native soil and people and to reject alien Western ways. To this extent he conflicted with Russian intellectuals, who wanted Russia to overcome its backwardness by emulating the progressive and liberal changes taking place in the West. He also sided with Pan-Slavs who believed that Russia, with its superior spiritual qualities, had a messianic mission to lead the Slavic peoples against the rotting West, a view he graphically expressed in *The Possessed* (1872).

Nationalist feelings also found expression in the music of Chopin, Verdi, Dvořák, Sibelius, Mussorgsky, and others. Richard Wagner was a key figure in giving German nationalism an irrational component that contributed to its dangerousness. His immensely popular operas glorified ancient, pre-Christian Germanic myths and warriors and heroines. To many Germans, Wagner's operas, particularly the *Ring* cycle, represented true German idealism, a heroic spirit now corrupted by materialism and greed. This hoary Teutonic past bound Germans together and set them apart from other Europeans; the Enlightenment and parliamentary democracy, associated with France and Britain, were foreign ideas that corrupted the true

German spirit. Wagner also promulgated Jew-hatred, a central doctrine of militant German nationalists, who regarded Jews as an alien and dangerous element in their midst.

In his *Judaism in Music*, first published in 1850 under a pseudonym and republished in 1869 under his own name, Wagner, who resented the fame of the Jewish composers Felix Mendelssohn (who had converted to Lutheranism) and Giacomo Meyerbeer, asserted that Jews debased German music. They could not possess nor express the feelings that animated the German soul; they had their own folk soul, which had been shaped by a degenerate culture. Devoid of a creative imagination and concerned only with self-centered materialist pursuits, said Wagner, Jews were incapable of making a creative contribution to European culture. Because Jews were the opposite of German artists, who set aside personal gain to pursue the ideal, Wagner insisted that Jews could only have a detrimental influence on German cultural life. He expressed the view many of the German elite had toward acceptance of Jews who had been recently emancipated, that is, allowed to leave the ghettos to which they had been confined and to participate in professional and public life that had been previously denied them: "For with all our speaking and writing in favor of Jewish emancipation, we always felt instinctively repelled by any real, active contact with Jews. . . . [The German people have] the most profound repugnance for the Jewish nature." And in the concluding passage of the essay, Wagner wrote: "There is only one possible way of redeeming the Jews from the terrible curse that hangs over them—annihilation."[27] (No doubt he meant the disappearance of the Jewish religion and the Jews as a people and not their physical annihilation, which the Nazis attempted.)

In later essays published in the Wagnerian journal, the *Bayreuther Blätter,* and in private correspondence and conversations, Wagner's anti-Semitism grew even more vitriolic and racist. "I hold the Jewish race to be the born enemy of pure humanity and everything noble in it. It is certain that it is running us Germans to the ground."[28] Wagner and his immediate circle, including his wife Cosima, reviled Judaism as a curse, considered Jews inferior, and maintained that they were taking over Germany. They frequently referred to Jews as vermin, bacilli, and lice, the very language that Nazi mass murderers would employ. Holding that artistic creativity was a function of ethnicity, Wagner saw Jews as the deadly opponent of the German spirit, the contaminators of the arts in Germany, and rejected their participation in the regeneration of the nation's culture, which he hoped to inspire. He also doubted that Jesus was Jewish and called for severing Christianity's relationship from its Jewish roots, believing that such a connection ruined it.

German anti-Semites regarded Wagner as their apostle: they sent him their anti-Semitic publications for approval and viewed the master's home as a shrine. A young Adolf Hitler was obsessed with Wagner's music, which he felt embodied the Germanic soul; it may have inspired him to believe that he was the man of destiny needed to regenerate Germany and save it from the Jews, whom Wagner accused of dominating the country. When he was struggling for power, Hitler attended the Bayreuth Festival that celebrated Wagner's music, a sign that he had adopted Wagner's popular nationalist and anti-Semitic ideas. And Wagner's family and disciples viewed Hitler as the savior of the German soul. Once in power, the Nazis utilized, for propaganda purposes, the music and words of Wagner, whom they unreservedly revered.

At the time that Wagner, and many other German intellectuals, were spreading their venomous anti-Semitic myths, Jews, who constituted less than one percent of Germany's population, considered themselves loyal Germans, were devoted to German culture, and were making immense contributions to medicine, science, the arts, and commerce. But a long tradition of anti-Semitism had poisoned the minds of Germans (and other peoples) against the Jews, leading them to accept irrational anti-Jewish myths as truth.

Key Terms

daguerreotype	transcriptions
The Salon	thematic transformation
Salon de Refusés	tone poem
Impressionism	music drama
convertor	*leitmotif*
eclecticism	ballet
program music	

Notes

1. Quoted in Aaron Scharf, *Pioneers of Photography* (New York: Harry N. Abrams, Inc, 1976), p. 106.
2. Excerpted in Linda Nochlin, *Realism and Tradition in Art, 1848–1900: Sources and Documents* (Englewood Cliffs, N.J.: Prentice Hall, 1966), pp. 52–53.
3. Quoted in Jack Lindsay, *Gustave Courbet: His Life and Art* (Bath, Somerset: Adams & Dart, 1973), p. 61.
4. Ibid., p. 76.
5. Quoted in Aaron Scharf, *Art and Photography* (Baltimore: Penguin Books, 1974), p. 128.
6. Quoted in Van Deren Coke, *The Painter and the Photograph from Delacroix to Warhol* (Albuquerque: University of New Mexico Press, 1964), pp. 12–13.
7. Ibid., p. 127.
8. Nochlin, *Realism and Tradition in Art*, p. 34.
9. *The Journal of Eugene Delacroix*, ed. Hubert Wellington, trans. Lucy Norton (London: Phaidon Press, 1995), pp. 308–309.
10. Excerpted in Linda Nochlin, *Impressionism and Post-Impressionism, 1874–1904: Sources and Documents* (Englewood Cliffs, N.J.: Prentice Hall, 1966), p. 15.
11. Quoted in George Heard Hamilton, *Manet and His Critics* (New York: W. W. Norton & Co., 1969), p. 45.
12. Ibid., p. 251.
13. Quoted in Charles F. Stuckey, *Monet: A Retrospective* (New York: Hugh Lauter Levin Associates, 1985), p. 196.
14. Nochlin, *Impressionism and Post-Impressionism*, p. 35.
15. Excerpted in Piero Weiss and Richard Taruskin, *Music in the Western World: A History in Documents* (New York: Schirmer Books, 1984), p. 383.
16. Ibid., p. 365.
17. Ibid., pp. 374–375.
18. Ibid., p. 385.
19. Ibid., p. 362.
20. Matt Boynick, ed., *Classical Music Pages Homepage*, trans. Elizabeth Schwarm Glesner, [online] Available http://igor.rz-berlin.mpg.de/cmp/brahms_sym1.html, March 22, 2001.
21. Ibid.
22. Excerpted in Piero Weiss and Richard Taruskin, *Music in the Western World*, p. 414.
23. Ibid., p. 415–416.
24. David Isadore Lieberman, *Notes on Symphony No. 9 in E minor, "From the New World" (1893)*, [online] Available http://www.loudounsymphony.org/notes/dvorak-9.html, July 6, 2001.
25. Excerpted in Piero Weiss and Richard Taruskin, *Music in the Western World*, pp. 417–418.
26. Excerpted in Louis L. Snyder, ed., *The Dynamics of Nationalism* (Princeton, N.J.: D. Van Nostrand, 1964), p. 230.
27. Quoted in Jacob Katz, *The Darker Side of Genius: Richard Wagner's Anti-Semitism* (Hanover, N.H.: Brandeis University Press and University Press of New England, 1986), pp. 35–36.
28. Ibid., p. 115.

23

Modern Consciousness: New Views of Nature and Human Nature

T HE MODERN MENTALITY MAY BE SAID TO HAVE PASSED through two broad phases: early modernity and late modernity. Formulated during the era of the Scientific Revolution and the Enlightenment, early modernity stressed confidence in reason, science, human goodness, and humanity's capacity to improve society. Then, in the late nineteenth and early twentieth centuries, a new outlook took shape. Late modern thinkers and scientists achieved revolutionary insights into human nature, the social world, and the physical universe; and writers and artists opened up hitherto unimagined possibilities for artistic expression.

These developments produced a shift in European consciousness. The mechanical model of the universe, which had dominated the Western outlook since Newton, was fundamentally altered. The Enlightenment view of human rationality and goodness was questioned, and the belief in natural rights and objective standards governing morality came under attack. Rules of aesthetics that had governed the arts since the Renaissance were discarded. Shattering old beliefs, late modernity left Europeans without landmarks—without generally accepted cultural standards or agreed-upon conceptions about human nature and the meaning of life.

The late modern period was marked by extraordinary creativity in thought and the arts. Yet imaginative and fruitful as these changes were for Western intellectual and cultural life, they also helped to create the disoriented, fragmented, and troubled era that marked the twentieth century. These intellectual and cultural currents occurred at a time when Western Europe was experiencing rapid industrial growth and extending its power throughout the globe.

POLITICS AND SOCIETY

Europe at the Turn of the Century

The pace of technological innovation and industrialization accelerated to such a degree in the closing decades of the nineteenth century that historians refer to this period as the Second Industrial Revolution. A few industrialized European states dominated the world market for manufactured goods. The people of Europe, more numerous than ever, were concentrated in ever-growing cities, several of them now with populations exceeding one million.

Gaining in wealth and power, the middle class lived comfortably; taxes were low, inflation was not a problem, and cheap domestic help was plentiful. They also viewed condescendingly the urban poor, whose housing, work, dress, habits, and education separated them from the genteel lifestyle of the bourgeoisie.

Edvard Munch,
The Scream,
1893, 36" x 29"
(91.3 x 73.7 cm),
tempera and pastel
on cardboard
Nasjonalgalleriet,
Oslo.

Munch attempted to express his inner self and the pathos of human relations in his paintings, as is evident in this painting, which expresses an overwhelming sense of dread and anguish.

(Nasjonalgalleriet, Oslo/Erich Lessing/Art Resource, NY © 2002 The Munch Museum/The Munch-Ellingsen Group/Artists Rights Society (ARS), NY)

Aided by the skill of its scientists and inventors, Germany became a leader in the chemical and electrical industries. It possessed the most extensive sector of large-scale, concentrated industrial and corporate capitalism of any Great Power. Within a short period, Germany had become a strong, industrialized state, ready and eager to play an important role in world affairs. But its growing industrial and military might, linked with an aggressive nationalism, alarmed other countries. This combination of German vitality, aggressiveness, and the fears of its rivals helped lead to World War I.

RUSSIA: TSARIST AUTOCRACY   In the middle of the nineteenth century, Russia differed fundamentally from Western Europe. The great movements that had shaped the outlook of the modern West—Renaissance, Reformation, Scientific Revolution, Enlightenment, and Industrial Revolution—had barely penetrated Russia. Autocracy, buttressed by the Orthodox Church, reigned supreme; the small and insignificant middle class did not possess the dynamic, critical, and individualistic spirit that characterized the Western bourgeoisie, and the vast majority of the people were illiterate serfs.

Alexander II (1855–1881) was determined to preserve autocratic rule. However, he wanted Russia to achieve what had made Western Europe strong: the energetic support and free enterprise of its citizens. Toward this end, he emancipated the serfs in 1861 and permitted closer ties with Europe. Increasingly a rising class of businesspeople and professionals looked to the West and adopted Western middle-class standards. By the end of the nineteenth century, Russia was experiencing a rapid industrialization that created a new class of discontented workers and a new breed of revolutionaries, Marxists, who believed that under the right historical conditions, revolution would succeed in Russia, which could then be transformed into a socialist society. Both Marxists and liberals, who advocated peaceful and gradual change, were thwarted by the instruments of tsarist autocracy—censorship, secret police, and banishment to Siberia.

CURRENTS OF THOUGHT

Irrationalism

Although many intellectuals continued to adhere to the outlook identified with the Enlightenment, some thinkers in the late nineteenth century challenged the basic premises of the philosophes and their nineteenth-century heirs. In particular, they repudiated the Enlightenment conception of human rationality, stressing instead the irrational side of human nature. Regarding reason as sovereign, the philosophes had defined human beings by their capacity to think critically; now thinkers saw blind strivings and animal instincts as the primary fact of human existence. It seemed that reason exercised a very limited influence over human conduct and that impulses, drives, and instincts—all forces below the surface—determined behavior much more than did logical consciousness.

The problem of *irrationalism* is manifold. Some thinkers, although they recognized the weakness of reason, continued to value it and sought to preserve it as an essential ingredient of civilized life. Some studied manifestations of the irrational in myth, religion, the arts, and politics in a logical and systematic way in order to gain a more complete understanding of human nature and human behavior. Others, concentrating on the creative potential of the irrational, urged nourishing the feelings, which they considered vital to artistic creativity and a richer existence. Still others celebrated violence as a healthy expression of the irrational.

The new insights into the irrational side of human nature and the growing assault on reason had immense implications for political life. In succeeding decades, these currents of irrationalism would become ideologized and politicized by unscrupulous demagogues, who sought to mobilize and manipulate the masses. The popularity of fascist movements, which openly denigrated reason and exalted race, blood, action, and will, demonstrated the naiveté of nineteenth-century liberals, who believed that reason had triumphed in human affairs.

NIETZSCHE   The principal figure in the "dethronement of reason" and the glorification of the irrational was the German philosopher Friedrich Nietzsche (1844–1900). Nietzsche's writings are not systematic treatises but collections of aphorisms, often containing internal contradictions. Consequently, his philosophy lends itself to misinterpretation and misapplication, as manifested by Nazi theorists, who distorted Nietzsche to justify their theory of the German master race.

Modern bourgeois society, said Nietzsche, was decadent and enfeebled—a victim of the excessive development of the rational faculties at the expense of will and instinct. Against the liberal–rationalist stress on the intellect, Nietzsche urged recognition of the dark, mysterious world of instinctual desires—the true forces of life.

Christianity, with all its prohibitions, restrictions, and demands to conform, also stifles the human impulse for life, said Nietzsche. Therefore, Christian morality must be obliterated, for it is fit only for the weak, the slave. It is life-denying—it gives man a sick soul. It makes humility, weakness, and self-abnegation virtues and pride a vice. In short, Christianity extinguishes the spark of life.

"God is dead," proclaimed Nietzsche. God is man's own creation. There are no higher worlds, no transcendental or metaphysical truths, no morality derived from God or nature, and no natural rights, scientific socialism, or inevitable progress. Individuals must recognize that old values and truths have lost their intelligibility. However, Nietzsche insisted, man can create new values and achieve self-mastery. Europe can only be saved by the emergence of the *Übermensch*—a higher type of man, who will not be held back by the egalitarian rubbish preached by Christians, democrats, and socialists. To end the dominion of "inferior man," said Nietzsche, "higher man" must declare war on the masses.

Nietzsche conceived of the higher man as a new kind of man who breaks with accepted morality and sets his own standards. He does not repress his instincts but asserts them. He destroys old values and asserts his prerogative as master. Free of Christian guilt, he proudly affirms his own being; dispensing with Christian "thou shalt not," he instinctively says, "I will." He dares to be himself. Because he is not like other people, traditional definitions of good and evil have no meaning for him. He does not allow his individuality to be stifled. He makes his own values, those that flow from his very being. He knows that life is meaningless but lives it laughingly, instinctively, fully. This "will to power" is not a product of rational reflection but flows from the very essence of human existence. As the motivating force in human behavior, it governs everyday life and is the determining factor in political life. The masses, cowardly and envious, will condemn the higher man as evil; this has always been their way. Thus, Nietzsche castigates democracy because it "represents the disbelief in great human beings and an elite society."[3]

Nietzsche foresaw the future as violent, sordid, and nihilistic—an age without meaning or values. In a world where nothing is true, all is permitted. Nietzsche urged individuals to face themselves and live a life free of illusions, pretense, and hypocrisy. However, no social policy could be derived from Nietzsche's heroic individualism. Nietzsche thought only of great individuals, humanity's noblest specimens, who overcome mediocrity and the artificiality of all inherited values; the social community and social injustice did not concern him.

Likewise, Nietzsche had no constructive proposals for dealing with the disintegration of rational and Christian certainties. Instead, his vitriolic attack on European institutions and values helped erode the rational foundations of Western civilization. This assault appealed immensely to intellectuals in central Europe, who saw Nietzsche's philosophy as liberating an inner energy. Thus, many young people, attracted to Nietzsche, welcomed World War I; they viewed it as an aesthetic experience and thought that it would clear a path to a new heroic age.

Nazi theorists, recasting Nietzsche in their own image, viewed themselves as Nietzsche's *supermen*, members of a master race who, by force of will, would conquer all obstacles and reshape the world according to their self-created values. Nietzsche himself, however, detested German nationalism and militarism, scoffed at the notion of German racial superiority, disdained (despite some unfortunate remarks) anti-Semitism, and denounced state worship.

Nonetheless, Nietzsche's extreme and violent denunciation of Western democratic principles, including equality; his praise of power; his call for the liberation of the instincts; his elitism, which denigrates and devalues all human life that is not strong and noble; and his spurning of humane values provided a breeding ground for violent, antirational, antiliberal, and inhumane movements. His philosophy, which included loose talk about the virtues of pitiless warriors, the breeding of a master race, and the annihilation of the weak and the ill, is conducive to a politics of extremes that knows no moral limits.

FREUD: A NEW VIEW OF HUMAN NATURE

In many ways, Sigmund Freud (1856–1939), an Austrian–Jewish physician who spent most of his adult life in Vienna, was a child of the Enlightenment. Like the philosophes, Freud identified civilization with reason and regarded science as the avenue to knowledge. But in contrast to the philosophes, Freud focused on the massive power and influence of nonrational drives. Whereas Nietzsche glorified the irrational and approached it with a poet's intuition, Freud sought to comprehend it scientifically and recognized its potential danger. Unlike Nietzsche, Freud did not belittle the rational but always strove to salvage respect for it.

Freud held that people are not fundamentally rational; human behavior is governed primarily by powerful inner forces, which are hidden from consciousness. These instinctual strivings, rather than rational faculties, constitute the greater part of the mind. Freud's greatest achievement was his exploration of the world of the unconscious with the tools and temperament of a scientist. He showed that the irrational contained a structure that could be empirically explained and rationally explored.

After graduating from medical school, Freud specialized in the treatment of nervous disorders. His investigations led him to conclude that childhood fears and experiences, often sexual in nature, accounted for neuroses—disorders in thinking, feeling, and behavior that interfere with everyday acts of personal and social life. So painful and threatening were these childhood emotions and experiences that his patients banished them from conscious memory to the realm of the unconscious. This was Freud's concept of *repression.*

In 1900, Freud published his *Interpretation of Dreams,* in which he asserted that he had found the key to the unconscious. An individual's dreams, said Freud, reveal his or her secret wishes—often socially unacceptable desires and frightening memories. The *id,* the subconscious seat of the instincts, said Freud, is a "cauldron full of seething excitations," which constantly demand gratification. The id is primitive and irrational. It knows no values and has no awareness of good and evil. Unable to endure tension, it demands sexual release, the termination of pain, and the cessation of hunger. Gratifying the id is our highest pleasure. But the full gratification of instinctual demands is detrimental to civilized life. That is why the *ego,* which stands for reason, seeks to hold the id in check, to bring it in line with reality.

Freud postulated a harrowing conflict between the relentless strivings of our instinctual nature and the requirements of civilization. Civilization, for Freud, required the renunciation of instinctual gratification and the mastery of animal instincts, a thesis he developed in *Civilization and Its Discontents* (1930). Although Freud's thoughts in this work were, no doubt, influenced by the great tragedy of World War I, the main theme could be traced back to his earlier writings. Society's demand for repression of instincts in the interest of civilization causes terrible frustration. Equally distressing, the violation of society's rules under the pressure of instinctual needs evokes terrible feelings of guilt. Either way, people suffer; civilized life simply entails too much pain for people. It seems that the price we pay for civilization is neurosis. Most people cannot endure the amount of instinctual renunciation that civilization requires. "Civilization imposes great sacrifices not only on man's sexuality but also on his aggressivity,"[4] said Freud. People are not good by nature, as the philosophes had taught; on the contrary, they are "creatures among whose instinctual endowments is to be reckoned a powerful share of aggressiveness." Their first inclination is not to love their neighbor, but to "satisfy their aggressiveness on him, to exploit his capacity for work without compensation, to use him sexually without his consent, to seize his possessions, to humiliate him, to cause him pain, to torture and to kill him."[5]

Freud's awareness of the irrational and his general pessimism regarding people's ability to regulate it in the interests of civilization did not lead him to break faith with the Enlightenment tradition, for Freud did not celebrate the irrational. He was too cognizant of its self-destructive nature for that. Civilization is indeed a burden, but people must bear it because the alternative is far worse.

Although Freud was undoubtedly a child of the Enlightenment, in crucial ways he differed from the philosophes. Regarding the Christian doctrine of original sin as myth, the philosophes had believed that people's nature was essentially good. If people took reason as their guide, evil could be eliminated. Freud held to a more pessimistic view. He saw evil as rooted in human nature rather than as a product of a faulty environment. Education and better living conditions would not eliminate evil, as the philosophes had expected, nor would abolition of private property, as Marx had declared. The philosophes venerated reason; it had enabled Newton to unravel nature's mysteries and would permit people to achieve virtue and reform society. Freud, who wanted reason to prevail, understood that its soft voice had to compete with the thunderous roars of the id. Freud broke with the optimism of the philosophes. His awareness of the immense pressures that civilization places on our fragile egos led him to be generally pessimistic about the future.

Unlike Marx, Freud had no vision of utopia. He saw the crude, destructive tendencies of human nature as an ever-present obstacle to harmonious social relations. The fact that Freud was hounded out of Vienna by the Nazis and his four sisters were murdered by them simply for being Jewish is a telling footnote to his view of human nature, the power of the irrational, and the fragility of civilization.

Modern Physics

Until the closing years of the nineteenth century, the view of the universe held by the Western mind rested largely on the classical physics of Newton. It included the following principles: (1) time, space, and matter were objective realities that existed independently of the observer; (2) the universe was a giant machine, whose parts obeyed strict laws of cause and effect; (3) heated bodies emitted radiation in continuous waves; and (4) complete knowledge of the physical universe was possible.

In 1900, Max Planck (1858–1947), a German physicist, proposed the *quantum theory,* which holds that a heated body radiates energy not in a continuous unbroken stream, as had been believed, but in intermittent spurts, or jumps, called quanta. Planck's theory of discontinuity in energy radiation challenged a cardinal principle of classical physics: that action in nature was strictly continuous. In 1913, Niels Bohr, a Danish scientist, applied Planck's theory of energy quanta to the interior of the atom and discovered that the Newtonian laws of motion could not fully explain what happened to electrons orbiting an atomic nucleus. As physicists explored the behavior of the atom further, it became apparent that its nature was fundamentally elusive and unpredictable.

Newtonian physics says that, given certain conditions, we can predict what will follow. For example, if an airplane is flying north at four hundred miles per hour, we can predict its exact position two hours from now, assuming that the plane does not alter its course or speed. Quantum mechanics teaches that in the subatomic realm we cannot predict with certainty what will take place; we can only say that, given certain conditions, it is *probable* that a certain event will follow. This principle of uncertainty was developed in 1927 by the German scientist Werner Heisenberg, who showed that it is impossible to determine at one and the same time both an electron's precise speed and its position. In the small-scale world of the electron, we enter a universe of uncertainty, probability, and statistical relationships. No improvement in measurement techniques will dispel this element of chance and provide us with complete knowledge of the universe.

The *theory of relativity,* developed by Albert Einstein (1879–1955), a German–Swiss physicist of Jewish lineage, was instrumental in shaping modern physics. Newtonian physics had viewed space as a distinct physical reality, a stationary medium through which light traveled and matter moved. Time was deemed a fixed and rigid framework that was the same for all observers and existed independently of human experience. For Einstein, however, neither space nor time had an independent existence; neither could be divorced from human experience. Once asked to explain briefly the essentials of relativity, Einstein replied: "It was formerly believed that if all material things disappeared out of the universe, time and space would be left. According to the relativity theory, however, time and space disappear together with the things."[6]

Einstein's work also encompassed motion, matter, and energy. We can only describe the motion of one body in relative terms, that is, by comparing it with another moving body. This means that there is no motionless, absolute, fixed frame of reference anywhere in the universe. In his famous equation, $E = mc^2$, Einstein showed that matter and energy are not separate categories, but rather two different expressions of the same physical entity. The source of energy is matter, and the source of matter is energy. Tiny quantities of matter can be converted into staggering amounts of energy. The atomic age was dawning.

The discoveries of modern physics transformed the world of classical physics. Whereas nature had been regarded as something outside the individual—an objective reality existing independently of ourselves—modern physics teaches that our position in space and time determines what we mean by reality and that our very presence affects reality itself. Nature is not fully knowable, as the classical physics of Newton had presumed; uncertainty, probability, and even mystery are inherent in the universe.

Like Darwin's theory of human origins and Freud's theory of human nature, the modifications of the Newtonian picture by modern physicists have enlarged our understanding. At the same time, they have contributed to the sense of uncertainty and disorientation that characterized the twentieth century.

THE MODERNIST MOVEMENT

At the same time as Freud and Nietzsche were breaking with the Enlightenment view of human nature and society, artists and writers were rebelling against traditional forms of artistic and literary expression that had governed European cultural life since the Renaissance. Rejecting both Classical and Realist models, they subordinated form and objective reality to the inner life—to feelings, imagination, and the creative process. These avant-garde writers and artists found new and creative ways to express those explosive forces within the human psyche that increasingly had become the subject of contemporary thinkers. Their experimentations produced a great cultural revolution called *Modernism,* which still profoundly influences the arts. In some ways, Modernism was a continuation of the Romantic Movement, which had dominated European culture in the early nineteenth century. Both movements subjected to searching criticism cultural styles that had been formulated during the Renaissance and had roots in ancient Greece.

Even more than Romanticism, Modernism aspired to an intense introspection—a heightened awareness of self—and saw the intellect as a barrier to the free expression of elemental human emotions. Modernist artists and writers abandoned conventional literary and artistic models and experimented with new modes of expression. They liberated the imagination from the restrictions of conventional forms and enabled their audience, readers and viewers alike, to share in the process of creation, often unconscious, and to discover fresh insights into objects, sounds, people, and social conditions. They believed that there were further discoveries to be made in the arts, further possibilities of expression, that past masters had not realized.

Like Freud, Modernist artists and writers probed beyond surface appearances for a more profound reality hidden in the human psyche. Writers such as Marcel Proust, James Joyce, August Strindberg, D. H. Lawrence, and Franz Kafka explored the inner life of the individual and the psychopathology of human relations in order to lay bare the self. They dealt with the predicament of men and women who rejected the values and customs of their day, and they depicted the anguish of people burdened by guilt, torn by internal conflicts, and driven by an inner self-destructiveness. Besides showing the overwhelming might of the irrational and the seductive power of the primitive, they also broke the silence about sex that had prevailed in Victorian literature.

From the Renaissance through the Enlightenment and into the nineteenth century, Western aesthetic standards had been shaped by the conviction that the universe embodied an inherent mathematical order. A corollary of this conception of the outer world as orderly and intelligible was the view that art should imitate reality, that it should mirror nature. Since the Renaissance, artists had deliberately made use of laws of perspective and proportion; musicians had used harmonic chords, which brought rhythm and melody into a unified whole; writers had produced works according to a definite pattern, which included a beginning, middle, and end.

Modernist culture, however, acknowledged no objective reality of space, motion, and time that has the same meaning to all observers. Rather, reality can be grasped in many ways; a multiplicity of frames of reference apply to nature and human experience. Consequently, reality is what the viewer perceives it to be through the prism of the imagination. "There is no outer reality," said the modernist German poet Gottfried Benn, "there is only human consciousness, constantly building, modifying, rebuilding new worlds out of its own creativity."[7] Modernism is concerned less with the object itself than with how the artist experiences it—with the sensations that an object evokes in the artist's very being and with the meaning the artist's imagination imposes on reality. Dispensing with conventional forms of aesthetics, which stressed structure and coherence, Modernism propelled the arts onto uncharted seas.

MODERNIST LITERATURE

Modernist writers abandoned the efforts of the Realists and the Naturalists to produce a clinical and objective description of the external world; instead, they probed subjective views and visions and the inner world of the unconscious. Recoiling from a middle-class, industrial civilization, which prized rationalism, organization, clarity, stability, and definite norms and values, Modernist writers were fascinated by the bizarre, the mysterious, the unpredictable, the primitive, the irrational, and the formless. They attempted to represent ideas, emotions, and sensations in a uniquely personal way, free of rules and customary conventions. Writers, for example, experimented with new techniques to convey the intense struggle between the conscious and the unconscious and to explore the aberrations and complexities of human personality and the irrationality of human behavior. In particular, they devised a new way, the *stream of consciousness,* to exhibit the mind's every level—both conscious reflection and unconscious strivings—and to capture how thought is punctuated by spontaneous outbursts, disconnected assertions, random memories, hidden desires, and persistent fantasies.

Instead of presenting the plot, characters, and descriptive narration in the conventional linear way, stream-of-consciousness technique relates the action through images and symbols that are conjured up in the mind of one or more of the characters. What matters most is not the articulation of ordered, verbalized thoughts, but rather the psychological state of each character. Often a third-person omniscient narrator describes everything about each of the characters, how they think, what they feel, and why they do what they do. Omniscient narrators often express themselves in the form of soliloquies whereby, talking only to themselves, they reveal to the reader not only the character's but also their own innermost thoughts. The introspective turn in the novel is also expressed through *interior monologue,* in which a character's meandering and disconnected comments progressively penetrate deeper into the unconscious, disclosing buried fears and torments.

Modernist writers also made use of symbols, attributing a larger meaning to particular phenom-

TWENTIETH-CENTURY JAPANESE POETRY

UNTIL JAPAN WAS OPENED UP TO THE WEST during the second half of the nineteenth century, Japanese poetry was confined to its traditional forms of *tanka* and *haiku*. But influenced by the style of European poets, particularly the British, modern Japanese poetry exhibits a freedom of form not seen previously. The following poets characterize the range of modern Japanese poetry in the first half of the twentieth century. Among the best of modern Japanese lyric poets is Nakahara Chuya (1907–1937), who died in obscurity at the age of thirty. His poem, "Cold Night," is typical of his verses that express the loneliness of the soul.

On a winter night
My heart is sad
Sad for no reason
My heart is rusty, purple.

Beyond the heavy door
Past days are vague
On top of the hill
Cotton seeds burst open.

Here firewood smoulders
Smoke climbs from it
As if it even knows itself.

Without being invited
Or even wishing
My heart smoulders.

Takahashi Shinkichi (b. 1901), a modernist poet who was greatly influenced by Dada as a youth, turned to Zen Buddhism in his thirties. The following stanzas, selected from his poem, "Beach Rainbow," typify his free verse poetry.

Heedless of the spray from the steaming waves,
The shell sleeps.
Buried in sand, rolled by the sand shifting as the tide shifts,
Not hearing the noise of the thundering waves,
The shell lies down lightly.

The shell does not worry about the far future,
Does not covet the form of the clouds drifting in the sky,
Does not pine after its lost body parted by death.

In a typhoon, bending its ear to the din:
Baked on the sand in the burning sun:
Picked up by a man in a daydream:
Turned into a button, even. Unconcerned.

Sea shell,
Beach rainbow,
Keep your eyes on your beautiful dream.

Source: The Penguin Book of Japanese Verse, *trans. Geoffrey Bownas and Anthony Thwaite (Harmondsworth, Middlesex, England: Penguin Books, 1964), pp. 205–206, 213.*

ena and events. All the elements of the novel—the actions of characters and the ways in which they are presented—have symbolic meanings. These particularities convey larger implications about the human condition. A bird in a cage can represent entrapment and a bird spreading its wings symbolizes self-actualization. A fog can stand for confusion, a jungle for primal instincts, and taking off one's clothes can symbolize the shunning of societal norms that stifle self-expression. The moon can represent not only the mythic power of the universe but also romantic and sexual notions of love. Bodies of water, particularly the ocean, represent escape and freedom, as does sleep, which often precedes moments of self-realization.

Literary Introspection: Proust, Joyce, and Woolf

Aspiring to transcend Realism, which emphasized an accurate description of physical reality, Modernist authors sought to explore a deeper reality that lay beneath the surface. It was this inner reality, the interior of the mind, rather than the objective world, that concerned them. To penetrate this hidden existence (and to give meaning to their own deeply personal feelings), Modernists devised new literary techniques, particularly stream of consciousness and interior monologue. The writings of Marcel Proust, James Joyce, and Virginia Woolf exemplify this concern with literary introspection.

Marcel Proust's (1871–1922) father was a physician, and his Jewish mother was a successful stockbroker. Proust enjoyed a privileged existence but chronic asthma kept him constantly sick. Beginning when he was eighteen, he led a self-indulgent life of ease, rubbing shoulders with intellectuals, artists, musicians, and writers. But in 1896, the Dreyfus Affair engendered a disenchantment with the military and social elites he had come to admire. At the age of twenty-two, Proust took his first homosexual lover. In 1903, his father died, and two years later, so too did his mother, to whom Proust was deeply devoted. Perhaps as a consequence of these life-altering experiences, Proust, in 1909, had a life-altering vision—causing him to lock himself up in his apartment for the rest of his life to devote himself to writing.

In his masterpiece, a semiautobiographical cycle of novels, *Remembrance of Things Past* (1913–1927), Proust cursorily deals with his hero's development from childhood to the time when he decides to devote himself completely to a literary career. But each book of the novel cycle is more acutely concerned with portraying the psychological, sociological, and philosophical underpinnings of French society during "the Banquet Years"—the period covering the concluding years of the Second Empire to the onset of World War I—as seen through the eyes of his omniscient, introspective narrator.

Beneath Proust's episodic, cyclical scheme, a number of interconnected themes emerge: personal growth and transformation, the finality of death, the obsessiveness of jealous love, and the relentless onslaught of time, which ultimately leaves an individual only in possession of her or his memories. These themes are enlivened through Proust's use of metaphorical language—such as "seascape, with frieze of girls," to describe the narrator's encounter with a group of young girls—and sense imagery, as is evident in the following passage drawn from a thirty-page description of the narrator's thoughts as he tosses and turns in bed, suffering from insomnia:

> I would fall asleep, and often I would be awake again for short snatches only, just long enough to hear the regular creaking of the wainscot [wall moldings], or to open my eyes to settle the shifting kaleidoscope of the darkness, to savour, in an instantaneous flash of perception, the sleep which lay heavy upon the furniture, the room, the whole surroundings of which I formed but an insignificant part and whose unconsciousness I should very soon return to share. Or, perhaps, while I was asleep I had returned without the least effort to an earlier stage in my life, now forever outgrown; and had come under the thrall of one of my childish terrors, such as that old terror of my great-uncle's pulling my curls, which was effectually dispelled on the day—the day of a new era to me—on which they were finally cropped from my head. I had forgotten that event during my sleep; I remembered it again immediately I had succeeded in making myself wake up to escape my great-uncle's fingers; still, as a measure of precaution, I would bury the whole of my head in the pillow before returning to the world of dreams.[8]

Passages such as these reveal the ability of the mind to personify physical reality so that a person actually becomes one with it and to shift spontaneously and randomly between the present and the past.

Ultimately, Proust's narrator discovers that with time, human memory fades, thus making it an unreliable source for remembering things past. He also concludes that many memories, particularly those related to homosexual and heterosexual love, are inordinately painful and cause immense emotional suffering. Proust's ability to interpret such deeply personal experiences had a profound effect on the generations of novelists and thinkers who have followed him, and his work is viewed as a key component in the development of Modernism.

The man whom many regard as *the* most influential Modernist writer was James Augustine Aloysius Joyce (1882–1941). He was born into an Irish Catholic merchant family in a suburb of Dublin, Ireland. Although Joyce left his homeland early in life, it remained the inspiration for his major works, including the *Dubliners* (1914), his autobiographical *Portrait of the Artist as a Young Man* (1916), and *Ulysses* (1922), in which Joyce took stream of consciousness to a deeper level by exploring "dream consciousness." Through *Ulysses,* Joyce critiques the social institutions of bourgeois Ireland during the early 1900s, particularly those foisted on Irish Catholics by the Anglo-Irish Protestant aristocracy, including a ban on the use of the Irish language. Joyce himself acknowledged his ultimate purpose: "I want to give a picture of Dublin so complete that if the city one day suddenly disappeared from the earth it could be reconstructed out of my book."[9]

Joyce chose Homer's epic hero Ulysses for his novel, because he regarded the introspective Ulysses (Odysseus, in the Greek) to be the "complete all-round character" and superior to Shakespeare's brooding Hamlet (see Chapter 15):

> Hamlet is a human being, but he is a son only. Ulysses is son to Laertes, but he is father to Telemachus, husband to Penelope, lover of Calypso, companion in arms of the Greek warriors around Troy and King of Ithaca. He was subjected to many trials, but with wisdom and courage came through them all. Don't forget that he was a war dodger who tried to evade military service by simulating madness. . . . But once at the war the conscientious objector becomes a *jusqu'auboutist* [right-to-the-ender]. When the others want to abandon the siege he insisted on staying till Troy should fall.[10]

Consequently, each episode in Joyce's novel corresponds to an incident in Homer's epic, even though Joyce does not give the reader any clues to this fact in the chapter headings; only through his private correspondence and conversations does he make his intentions clear. For example, in one episode, Joyce uses the image of Proteus—the sea god of Book IV of Homer's *Odyssey* who can alter his form—to explore the conscious and unconscious mind of Stephen Dedalus, the hero of *Portrait of the Artist as a Young Man,* as he muses about life and speculates about the future.

The whole of Joyce's epic (it numbers around 700 pages) involves only one day in the lives of the citizens of Dublin. The novel begins on June 16, 1904, at 8:00 A.M. and ends at approximately 3:00 A.M. on June 17. The central characters are the haughty, unyielding artist Stephen Dedalus and the Jewish-Dubliner businessman Leopold Bloom. Joyce chooses Bloom to be his hero and elucidates his conflicted status as both a citizen of Dublin and an exiled Jew, and as both a "father" to "son" Dedalus, and as a victim of his wife's sexual infidelity. To reproduce with words the ramblings of the human mind, Joyce dispenses with conventional sentences and creates his own private language. Thus, in the final chapter, which is a long, interior monologue by Bloom's wife, Molly, Joyce uses virtually no punctuation marks (the first sentence alone contains 2500 words, and only eight periods appear in the entire chapter), little capitalization, and no paragraph indentations. In the passage, Molly muses about sexual reproduction as the basis of human existence and how the female exclaiming "yes" to sex, figuratively keeps the universe in motion:

> [T]he day I got him to propose to me yes first I gave him the bit of seedcake out of my mouth and it was leapyear like now yes 16 years ago my God after that long kiss I near lost my breath yes he said I was a flower of the mountain yes so we are flowers all a womans body yes that was one true thing he said in his life and the sun shines for you today yes that was why I like him because I saw he understood or felt what a woman is and I knew I could always get round him and I gave him all the pleasure I could leading him on till he asked me to say yes and I wouldnt answer first only looked out over the sea and the sky I was thinking of so many things he didn't know . . . . I asked him with my eyes to ask again yes and then he asked me would I yes to say yes my mountain flower and first I put my arms around him yes and drew him down to me so he could feel my breasts all perfume yes and his heart was going like mad and yes I said yes I will Yes.[11]

Through this episode, beginning and ending with the female saying "yes," Joyce intended to demonstrate how the female is the sole focus of sexual reproduction, which "turns like the huge earth ball slowly surely and evenly round and round spinning."[12]

Ulysses served to inspire the Modernist writing of Virginia Woolf (1882–1941), one of Joyce's most fervent admirers who, in her novel *Mrs. Dalloway* (1925), copied Joyce's technique of interior monologue. Like Proust and Joyce, Woolf drew heavily on personal experience in writing her novels, particularly the emotional travail that led to at least three mental breakdowns. For her first great novel, *Mrs. Dalloway,* Woolf called on her own life experiences to give definition to the character of her protagonist—Clarissa Dalloway, the middle-aged, upper-crust wife of Richard Dalloway, a member of

Parliament, who is frustrated by his inability to accede to a Cabinet post. Like Joyce's *Ulysses,* the events of Woolf's *Mrs. Dalloway* take up only one day, in the middle of June, during the 1920s. The action centers on an evening dinner party to be hosted by Mrs. Dalloway who, as she prepares for her party, reminisces about her past, including a lover whom she had rejected.

Parallel to Mrs. Dalloway's interior monologue are the thoughts of Septimus Warren Smith, a World War I veteran suffering from shell shock, whose suicide has a profound effect on Mrs. Dalloway when she learns of it at her dinner party. Before the war, Septimus loved Shakespeare and wanted to be a poet; now, however, he fears that life has no meaning, and he hears voices and "talks" to his dead friend, Evans, a casualty of the war. On one occasion, as he and his wife Lucrezia stroll in a park, Septimus discusses the merits of suicide as a way to bring an end to suffering. When Lucrezia can no longer deal with her husband's mental affliction, she arranges for him to visit the eminent doctor, Sir William Bradshaw, who specializes in "nerve cases." But Dr. Bradshaw treats Septimus callously, even suggesting that his affliction is nothing more than a reflection of his inability to place things in their proper perspective. He advises Septimus to go to a sanatorium in the country to rest, but while the couple awaits the arrival of the attendants who will take him there, Septimus commits suicide by jumping out a window.

In contrast to Septimus' suicidal reflections, Clarissa Dalloway reminisces about her former lover, Peter Walsh, whose affections she rebuffed even though he made her feel alive and appreciated. She rejected Peter, a commoner, so that she could marry Richard Dalloway, a member of the upper echelons of society. Spurned by Clarissa, Peter travels to India, returns unexpectedly, and drops by Clarissa's house. When their uneasy conversation is interrupted by Clarissa's daughter, Peter goes to a nearby park to reflect on their past. There, he sees Lucrezia and Septimus, whom he believes are engaged in a lover's quarrel. Upon returning to his apartment, Peter hears the sound of the ambulance carrying Septimus' broken body. Later that evening, he attends Clarissa's party, and although everyone is having a good time, Clarissa worries that they are not. Adding to her concern is the late arrival of Sir William Bradshaw, who announces that one of his patients, a young veteran, has committed suicide.

In one of the most compelling passages in the novel, Clarissa reflects on Septimus' suicide, which she attributes to a society peopled with insensitive curs, like Bradshaw.

What business had the Bradshaws to talk of death at her party? A young man had killed himself. And they talked of it at her party—the Bradshaws talked of death. He had killed himself—but how? Always her body went through it, when she was told, first, suddenly, of an accident; her dress flamed, her body burnt. He had thrown himself from a window. Up had flashed the ground; through him, blundering, bruising, went the rusty spikes. There he lay with a thud, thud, thud in his brain, and then a suffocation of blackness. So she saw it. But why had he done it? And the Bradshaws talked of it at her party![13]

Regretting that she had allowed herself to give up the possibility of a loving marriage with Peter, only to become the snobbish "Mrs. Richard Dalloway" and to lose her unique identity as Clarissa, she ponders her own suicide.

Then (she had felt it only this morning) there was the terror; the overwhelming incapacity, one's parents giving it into one's hands, this life, to be lived to the end, to be walked with serenely; there was in the depths of her heart an awful fear. . . . She had escaped. But that young man had killed himself.

Somehow it was her disaster—her disgrace. It was her punishment to see sink and disappear here a man, there a woman, in this profound darkness, and she forced to stand here in her evening dress.[14]

Despite Woolf's additional successful novels, including *To the Lighthouse* (1927), *A Room of One's Own* (1929), and *The Waves* (1931), she continued to be plagued by mental illness. Finally, on March 18, 1941, fearing that she was undergoing a mental breakdown from which she would never recover, Virginia Woolf left notes for her husband and sister, loaded her pockets with stones, and drowned herself in the Ouse River.

The Dark Side of Human Nature: Conrad

Behavior driven by the unconscious and the human being's capacity to act irrationally and cruelly—the dark side of human nature, which was the subject of Freud's investigations—intrigued many Modernist writers, including British novelist Joseph Conrad (1857–1924), born Jozel Tendor Konrad Korzeniowski. In 1862, when Conrad was not yet five years old, his father, who had participated in an insurrection to liberate Poland from Russian rule, was exiled to northern Russia. In this harsh environment, his mother died of tuberculosis in 1865. His father, who translated the works of French and English authors into Polish, which the precocious young Conrad read voraciously, made the difficult decision to place his only child in the care of Joseph's maternal uncle in Poland, where he attended school. Joseph lost his father when he was twelve, and five years later, he left school to become an apprentice seaman on a French merchant ship. In 1878, speaking only a few words of English, he joined the British merchant navy.

During his twenty years at sea, Conrad visited exotic lands and experienced danger. These adventures found literary expression in Conrad's novels and short stories, including *An Outcast of the Islands* (1896), *Lord Jim* (1900), *Heart of Darkness* (1902), *Nostromo* (1904), and *The Secret Agent* (1907). But Conrad was far more than a masterful renderer of adventure stories. His reputation as one of England's finest novelists derives from both his compelling prose and his creative exploration of human depravity, a phenomenon to which he seemed irresistibly drawn. In 1891, after a four-month stay in the Congo Free State, a land notoriously exploited and brutalized by agents of the Belgian King Leopold, Conrad suffered psychological trauma. His experiences in the heart of Africa led him to write his most compelling work, *Heart of Darkness*

The two principal characters in the work are Kurtz, a company agent who runs a very successful ivory trading post deep in the Congo, and Marlow, a riverboat pilot, who is repelled by the cruelty inflicted on Africans by the company's agents. Marlow, who narrates his experiences, pilots a steamer upriver to Kurtz's station. Slowly he learns about Kurtz from the other agents of the company, including those accompanying him, and from a young Russian devoted to Kurtz, whom Marlow spots on the shore near Kurtz's post. Marlow finds out that not only is Kurtz a poet, musician, and painter with politically progressive views, but that when he first came to Africa, Kurtz was imbued with humanitarian sentiments. One company employee describes him as "an emissary of pity and science and progress"[15] who intended to bring enlightenment to "savage" Africans. But in the primeval African jungle, his other self, long repressed by European values, comes to the fore. Kurtz becomes a depraved tyrant, who decorates the fence poles around his house with human heads. The charismatic Kurtz has made disciples of the villagers, who view him as a godlike figure; they heed his every word and, at his command, launch murderous raids against nearby villages for more ivory. Kurtz engages in mysterious ceremonies—Conrad leaves the nature of these ceremonies to the reader's imagination, but it is likely that they are human sacrifices—that contribute to his uncanny power over the Africans.

Although shriveled by disease, Kurtz is reluctant to return with Marlow, but eventually relents. As the ship travels down the river, Marlow engages Kurtz in long conversations. During one of these talks, Kurtz senses that death is imminent, and suddenly gripped by "craven terror," he blurts out: "The horror! The horror!"[16] He dies later that evening. Here too, as in the case of the ceremonies, Conrad relies on the reader to determine the meaning of Kurtz's agonizing cry.

There now exists a rich body of commentary analyzing the layers of meaning in Conrad's work. One obvious interpretation is that Conrad intended to write an indictment of imperialism, for *Heart of Darkness* expressed his revulsion of avaricious European imperialists who, in their quest for riches, plundered and destroyed African villages and impressed the natives into forced labor. Their greed, callousness, and brutality belied the altruism that they claimed was their motivation for coming to Africa.

Most commentators also regard *Heart of Darkness* as a tale of moral deterioration: The forbidding jungle environment, far from the restraints of European civilization, and the repulsive scramble for riches disfigure Kurtz, who is transformed into a sadist driven by dark urges no longer buried within his unconscious. The wilderness "whispered to him things about himself which he did not know, things of which he had no conception till he took counsel with this great solitude—and the whisper had proved irresistibly fascinating."[17] When the dying Kurtz cries out: "The horror! The horror!" in "that supreme moment of complete knowledge,"[18] was he referring to his own moral collapse? Thus "darkness" refers not only to the jungle interior, but also to the destructive tendencies that are at the core of human nature. Marlow's travels into the dark interior of Africa in search of Kurtz can be seen as a descent into the dark interior of the unconscious. Civilization, as Freud maintained, is very fragile; only a thin barrier separates it from barbarism. Given the right circumstances, all human beings are capable of the moral disfigurement experienced by Kurtz.

In 1979, director Francis Ford Coppola adapted Conrad's *Heart of Darkness* for his Academy Award–winning motion picture, *Apocalypse Now*. The movie's journey into the heart of darkness begins in Saigon, South Vietnam, where the CIA operative and assassin U.S. Army Captain Willard (the parallel to Conrad's Marlow) receives orders to infiltrate the renegade special forces camp of Colonel Kurtz and terminate his command. Kurtz reputedly has gone insane, commanding a private army in the jungles of Cambodia, where he is worshiped as a god by the tribal Cambodians. When

Willard finally arrives at Kurtz's jungle camp, he sees countless bodies hanging in the trees and an immense collection of heads. The climactic end of the movie involves Willard killing Kurtz, whose final words are: "The horror! The horror!" *Apocalypse Now* was thus seen as an indictment of the United States' imperialistic involvement in Southeast Asia, just as *Heart of Darkness* was viewed as an indictment of European imperialism in Africa. And Colonel Kurtz's descent into moral depravity parallels the moral deterioration of Conrad's Kurtz.

Irrationality: Kafka

The Modernist concern with human irrationality was captured brilliantly by Franz Kafka (1883–1924), whose major novels, *The Trial* and *The Castle*, were published after his death and did not receive recognition until after World War II. Yet perhaps better than any other novelist of his generation, Kafka grasped the dilemma of the modern age. There is no apparent order or stability in Kafka's world. Human beings strive to make sense out of life, but everywhere ordinary occurrences thwart them. They are caught in a bureaucratic web that they cannot control; they live in a nightmare society dominated by oppressive, cruel, and corrupt officials and amoral torturers. In Kafka's world, cruelty and injustice are accepted facts of existence, power is exercised without limits, and victims cooperate in their own destruction. Traditional values and ordinary logic do not operate. Our world, thought to be secure, stale, and purposeful, easily falls apart.

Like Kierkegaard, Kafka understood the intense anxiety that torments modern people. In *The Trial* (1925), for example, an ordinary man who has no consciousness of wrongdoing is arrested. "K. lived in a country with a legal constitution, there was universal peace, all the laws were in force; who dared seize him in his own dwelling?"[19] Josef K. is never told the reason for his arrest, and he is eventually executed, a victim of institutional evil that breaks and destroys him "like a dog." In these observations, Kafka anticipated the emerging totalitarian state. (Kafka's three sisters perished in the Holocaust.)

A German-speaking Jew in the alien Slav environment of Czechoslovakia, Kafka died of tuberculosis at an early age. In voicing his own deep anxieties, Kafka expressed the feelings of alienation and isolation that characterize the modern individual. He explored life's dreads and absurdities, offering no solutions or consolation. In Kafka's works, people are defeated and unable to comprehend the irrational forces that contribute to their destruction. Although the mind yearns for coherence, Kafka tells us that uncertainty, if not

chaos, governs human relationships. We can be sure neither of our own identities nor of the world we encounter, for human beings are the playthings of unfathomable forces, too irrational to master.

A brooding pessimism about the human condition pervades Kafka's work. One reason for the intensified interest in Kafka after World War II, observes Angel Flores, "is that the European world of the late 30s and 40s with its betrayals and concentration camps, its resulting cruelties and indignities, bore a remarkable resemblance to the world depicted by Kafka in the opening decades of the century. History seems to have imitated the nightmarish background evoked by the dreamer of Prague."[20]

Sex Outside the Victorian Closet: Chopin and Lawrence

The Victorian Age is generally regarded as prudish and sexually repressive; well-bred Victorians were expected to resist sexual temptation. Victorians assumed that "decent" women had no sexual appetites and that men represented a sinful, lustful, and fallen humanity who preyed on women. Women came to be portrayed in one of two ways— either as insatiable sexual harlots or as chaste and frigid innocents. But an American female writer, Kate Chopin, and a British male writer, D. H. Lawrence, put an end to such stereotypical characterizations. In their novels, they created portraits of women who fight to end their subjugation to men and are vibrant and sexually responsive.

After her husband's death in 1882, Kate Chopin (1850–1904), with her six children, moved back to St. Louis, the city of her birth, and began a career as a celebrated "local color" writer. In 1889, Chopin published her first novel, *The Fault*, which contrasts two different types of love—one heartfelt, the other restrictive. Although the novel was a failure, it did establish the theme for which Chopin is best known—a submissive woman struggling to end her subjugation to a man.

In 1899, Chopin dealt with the theme of female oppression and a woman's need to feel emotionally and sexually fulfilled in her scandalous novel *The Awakening*. The St. Louis *Republic* labeled the novel "poison," and the St. Louis *Dispatch* considered it "disturbing—even indelicate."[21] The novel opens with the image of a caged parrot endlessly repeating *"Allez vous-en! Allez vous-en! That's all right!"*[22] to symbolize the entrapment of the novel's protagonist, Mrs. Edna Pontellier. Edna feels confined by her role as mother and wife to Léonce, who is twelve years her senior and views her as "a valuable piece of personal property." While vacationing with Léonce at Grand Isle, Edna makes the acquaintance of Madame

Lebrun's son, Robert (two years her junior), with whom she enters into an adulterous relationship. Using symbols of the sea, Chopin documents the emerging passion of Edna for Robert as she awakens to herself as a sexual being. On one occasion, when Robert invites her to go swimming, Edna resists, for she is a weak swimmer, but she is lured by the sea's "sonorous murmur" and Robert's insistence, with its sexual overtones, "You mustn't miss your bath. Come on. The water must be delicious; it will not hurt you. Come."[23]

By the end of the novel, however, Robert has left, and Edna's awakening to her sexual self has cut against the grain of her identity as Mrs. Pontellier and mother to her children. A despondent Edna makes the decision to drown herself. As she walks on the beach, she hears the sea beckoning her, "seductive, never ceasing, whispering, clamoring, murmuring, inviting the soul to wander in abysses of solitude." She also finds a bird with a broken wing, symbolizing her own shattered existence. However, she sheds all of her clothing— symbolic of her freeing herself from the confinement of societal norms—and steps into the open air: "How strange and awful it seemed to stand naked under the sky! how delicious! She felt like some new-born creature, opening its eyes in a familiar world that it had never known."[24] Finally, she enters the sea, embracing it as she would a lover, and drowns herself in its passion.

> She walked out. The water was chill, but she walked on. The water was deep, but she lifted her white body and reached out with a long, sweeping stroke. The touch of the sea is sensuous, enfolding the body in its soft, close embrace.
>
> She went on and on. . . . She did not look back now, but went on and on. . . . She thought of Léonce and the children. They were a part of her life. But they need not have thought that they could possess her, body and soul.
>
> Exhaustion was pressing upon and overpowering her.
>
> "Good-bye—because, I love you."[25]

In spite of those who found the ending of the novel offensive, because a woman commits suicide to escape the self-limiting roles of wife and mother, the late-nineteenth-century historian Larzer Ziff esteemed *The Awakening* as "the most important piece of fiction about the sexual life of a woman" and the renowned literary critic Edmund Wilson hailed it as "anticipating D. H. Lawrence in its treatment of infidelity."[26]

David Herbert Lawrence (1885–1930), the son of an illiterate British coal miner whose bawdy drunkenness conflicted severely with his wife's gentility, was one of the most important, yet controversial, novelists of the twentieth century.

Lawrence was saddened and angered by the consequences of industrial society: the deterioration of nature; tedious, regimented work divorced from personal satisfaction; and a life-denying quest for wealth and possessions at the expense of humanitarian concerns. Thus, in *Women in Love* (1921), the new owner of the family coal mine, determined to utilize modern management techniques in order to extract greater wealth from the business, dismisses the human needs of the workers:

> Suddenly he had conceived the pure instrumentality of mankind. There had been so much humanitarianism, so much talk of sufferings and feelings. It was ridiculous. The sufferings and feelings of individuals did not matter in the least. . . . What mattered was the pure instrumentality of the individual. As a man as of a knife: does it cut well? Nothing else mattered.
>
> Everything in the world has its function and is good or not good in so far as it fulfills this function. . . . Was a miner a good miner? Then he was complete.[27]

Lawrence looked back longingly on preindustrial England and wanted people to reorient their thinking away from moneymaking and suppression of the instincts.

Lawrence's affirmation of sexual passion as both necessary and beneficial for a fulfilling life led him to rail against cultural norms, including puritanical attitudes that stifled human sexuality and disfigured it with shame and guilt. His feelings about sex were poignantly expressed in his highly erotic novel, *Lady Chatterley's Lover* (1928). Because of its use of four-letter words and intimate descriptions of sexual activity, Lawrence was forced to publish it in Italy. An unexpurgated version was not released in Britain until 1960, after a celebrated trial.

Lady Chatterley, married to Sir Clifford, who considers sex distasteful, has an affair with the gamekeeper, Mellors, a commoner who exudes sexuality and whose passionate lovemaking is deeply tender. Sir Clifford, still unaware of the affair, asks his wife if she likes her body. She replies:

> "I love it!" And through her mind went [Mellor's] words: "It's the nicest, nicest woman's arse as is!"
>
> "But that is really rather extraordinary, because there's no denying it's an encumbrance. But then I suppose a woman doesn't take a supreme pleasure in the life of the mind."
>
> "Supreme pleasure?" she said, looking up at him. "Is that sort of idiocy the supreme pleasure of the life of the mind? No thank you! Give me the body. I believe the life of the body is a greater reality than the life of the mind: when the body is really wak-

ened to life. But so many people . . . have only got minds tacked on to their physical corpses."

He looked at her in wonder.

"The life of the body," he said, "is just the life of the animals."

"And that's better than the life of professional corpses. But it's not true! The human body is only just coming to real life. With the Greeks it gave a lovely flicker, then Plato and Aristotle killed it and Jesus finished it off. But now the body is coming really to life, it is really rising from the tomb. And it will be a lovely, lovely life in the lovely universe, the life of the human body."[28]

And after a night of lovemaking with Mellors, she reflects on sexual passion:

> In the short summer night she learnt so much. She would have thought a woman would have died of shame. Instead of which, the shame died. She felt, now, she had come to the real bed-rock of her nature, and was essentially shameless. She was her sensual self, naked and unashamed. She felt a triumph, almost a vainglory. So! That was how it was! That was life! That was how oneself really was! There was nothing left to disguise or be ashamed of. She shared her ultimate nakedness with a man, another being. . . .
>
> What liars poets and everybody were! They made one think one wanted sentiment. When what one supremely wanted was this piercing, consuming, rather awful sensuality. To find a man who dared do it, without shame or sin or final misgiving! If he had been ashamed afterwards, and made one feel ashamed, how awful![29]

Like nineteenth-century Romantics, Lawrence found a higher truth in intuition and deep-seated passion than in reason. Like Nietzsche, he believed that excessive intellectualizing destroyed the life-affirming, instinctual part of human nature. In 1913, he wrote:

> My great religion is a belief in the blood, the flesh, as being wiser than the intellect. We can go wrong in our minds. But what our blood feels and believes and says is always true. The intellect is only a bit and a bridle. What do I care about knowledge. All I want is to answer to my blood without fribbling intervention of mind, or moral, or what not. . . . We have got so ridiculously mindful, that we never know that we ourselves are anything.[30]

Naturalism and Beyond: Strindberg

Although essentially a Realist-Naturalist playwright, Ibsen (see Chapter 21), by grappling with contemporary social problems and by probing deeply into a character's psychological state, also was a precursor of Modernist drama. August Strindberg (1849–1912), another Scandinavian dramatist, articulated these concerns with great dramatic power; in the process, he experimented with techniques that are crucial to the shaping of the Modernist play.

A strange, tormented soul, Strindberg's life is itself a fitting subject for Modernist theater. He was a prolific dramatist and novelist—some of his novels are autobiographical sketches in which he bared his demons. He was also an accomplished painter, composed music, experimented with chemistry, and was a proficient linguist—in addition to knowing several European languages, he also taught himself enough Chinese to catalog Chinese manuscripts while employed by the Royal Library in Stockholm. But Strindberg was a creative genius who lived on the edge of madness. He was drawn to the occult, mysticism, alchemy (he was certain that he had discovered the formula to transform base metals into gold), and black magic (he was equally certain that he had the ability to cause harm to his enemies merely by wishing it). For a period of time he did go over the edge. He thought that he was being attacked by demons, that a neighbor was trying to kill him with electronic currents, and that a physician friend, who was treating him, wanted to steal his secret formula for making gold.

In contrast to Ibsen and George Bernard Shaw (see following discussion), Strindberg was a misogynist who maintained that women were physically, intellectually, and morally inferior to men and that motherhood and homemaker were their proper roles. At times, he warned men that feminists were conspiring to enslave them. His three marriages, two to actresses and one to a writer, were filled with discord and ended in divorce. Women were often treated unmercifully in his plays.

The same personality traits that accounted for Strindberg's haunted existence may also explain his intense curiosity about human behavior, the keenness with which he observed it, and the brilliance with which he deciphered it. In dealing with conflicts between men and women, parents and children, siblings, love rivals, and upper and middle classes, Strindberg demonstrated an intuitive ability to enter into the mind's subterranean crevices.

In his early plays, *The Father* (1887), *Miss Julie* (1889), and *Creditors* (1889), Strindberg employed the conventional Naturalist style favored by Zola and Ibsen. *Miss Julie* treats tensions between the sexes and social classes. Miss Julie, the daughter of a count, is physically attracted to Jean, her father's valet. Disregarding her station, she dances with Jean on a Midsummer Eve, a time of pagan revelry, and acts the coquette. Because of her unhappy relationship with her parents, Julie may have had an unconscious desire to lower herself by sleeping with the valet.

After first resisting her advances, Jean relishes the opportunity to make love to this upper-class lady. Jean, intelligent but callous, wants desperately to ascend the social ladder. He has a recurring dream that he is climbing a tall tree at the top of which is a bird's nest with golden eggs. Seeing himself engaged in a Darwinian struggle for survival, he will use Julie any way he can to get ahead. He fantasizes that his sexual encounter with Julie will provide him with money and eventually a title.

In the end, both Julie and Jean act in accordance with their social status and upbringing. After they have been intimate, Julie becomes despondent for allowing herself to be shamed by a servant, and Jean is fearful that the count, on his return, will order his arrest for dishonoring his daughter. When the count returns, he rings the bell for his valet to bring his boots and coffee. Jean, revealing his true servant status, cringes uncontrollably. Julie, eyeing Jean's razor, thinks of slitting her throat, which Jean cleverly urges her to do. By choosing honorable suicide, Julie remains true to her class; Jean, the servant, is incapable of such a noble gesture. In the gender battle, the strong, masculine Jean defeats the weaker female, but in the conflict of social classes, he is only a sniveling, petrified servant, while Julie is a noble lady.

Strindberg intended to write a Naturalistic drama. The characters, he tells us in the foreword, are products of their heredity and environment, which is the basic premise of a Naturalistic literary work, and the dialogue is not a "symmetrical, mathematical construction,"[31] but wanders as it does in real life, for people's thoughts are often disconnected. Nor are the characters one-dimensional types, but as in real life, they display conflicting feelings. However, *Miss Julie* also contains elements that anticipate Strindberg's departure from Naturalism in his later plays. For example, Julie's father, the count, never appears, but his presence dwells ominously in Jean's mind. At the mere sight of his master's gloves lying on the chair, or his boots standing on the floor, or the bell with which the count summons him, Jean is gripped by an unnatural panic. Such symbolism and deep psychological probing of the unconscious, together with Strindberg's use of dreams, mark a break with Naturalism; they would become more pronounced in his later plays, which are replete with sexual symbolism and explorations of the subconscious, including analyses of dreams, in order to clarify a distorted and tormented reality. The new direction that Strindberg traveled is seen in his explanatory note to *A Dream Play* (1907):

In this dream play as in his earlier dream play *To Damascus*, the author has tried to imitate the disconnected but apparently logical form of a dream. Everything can happen; everything is possible and likely. Time and space do not exist; on an insignificant basis of reality the imagination spins and weaves new patterns: a blending of memories, experiences, free inventions, absurdities, and improvisations. . . . [A]nd as the dream is usually painful, less frequently cheerful, a note of sadness and sympathy for every living creature runs through the swaying story. Sleep, the liberator, appears often as painful, but, when the torture is at its very peak, waking comes reconciling suffering with reality, which however painful it may be is still at this moment is a delight compared with the tormenting dream.[32]

The Problem Play: Shaw

Henrik Ibsen had introduced the problem play that dealt with contemporary social problems, including marital discord, capitalist greed and corruption, and the clash of generations. He also introduced poignant discussions in which the principal characters aired their views. Modernist playwrights, including the prolific Irish dramatist George Bernard Shaw (1856–1950), continued in the directions pioneered by Ibsen. Shaw's plays are distinguished by brilliant intellectual discussions around themes that reveal the dramatist's own political and ideological convictions and his moral passion to remedy injustice. (At the time, critics protested that didactic discussions have little dramatic appeal; they cannot hold an audience's interest, but for the most part, Shaw made them work.)

Shaw was a democratic socialist committed to the cause of social justice for the poor. He also denounced munitions manufacturers, imperialism, and the pursuit of military glory and was concerned with the preservation of personal integrity in a society that demanded conformity to tradition and acquiescence to authority. Shaw used drama as a vehicle for his ideas; he believed that drama was a way of compelling the public to rethink its morals, of influencing and converting minds. His plays, even the comedies, are replete with challenging, often significant, philosophical ideas, penetrating dialectical exchanges between articulate individuals who hold conflicting views, and critical analyses of current issues. For example, in an early play, *Widower's Houses* (1892), he posed the question: Should a bridegroom accept a dowry from his fiancé's father, a slumlord, who had obtained his wealth and middle-class respectability by shamelessly exploiting the poor?

In several plays, his principal characters are strong-willed women striving to overcome enormous obstacles. In *Mrs. Warren's Profession* (originally, 1893, but censored until 1924), a poor woman decides to sell her body, over which she has control, because it is preferable to toiling long hours for starvation wages in a factory. For Shaw, prostitution "is not caused by female depravity . . . but simply by underpaying, undervaluing, and overworking women so shamefully that the poorest of them are forced to resort to prostitution to keep body and soul together."[33] In time, Mrs. Warren is managing several successful brothels and is able to provide her daughter with a good education and a comfortable bourgeois existence. The high point of the play comes when the daughter discovers her mother's unseemly profession.

Pygmalion (1912), a comedy about English class foibles, prejudices, and pains, also focuses on the character development of a spirited woman. Because of Frederick Loewe's and Alan Jay Lerner's adaptation of Shaw's play for their Broadway musical, *My Fair Lady* which premiered on March 15, 1956, and enjoyed a run of 2,717 performances, lasting more than nine years, and won an Academy Award for "Best Picture" in 1965, the public is well aware of the story of Henry Higgins and Eliza Doolittle. Higgins, a prominent authority on phonetics, observes Eliza hawking her flowers on the street and is appalled at her mutilation of the English language and her lower-class mannerisms. Higgins enters into a wager with Colonel Pickering that in six months he can transform this "so deliciously low—so horribly dirty"[34] flower girl, Eliza, into a lady. "I shall make a duchess of this draggletailed guttersnipe."[35] In the process of preparing Eliza for high society, the insensitive Higgins routinely bullies and insults her. Pickering asks Higgins: "Does it occur to you Higgins, that the girl has some feelings?" Higgins, looking at her, critically replies; "Oh no. I don't think so. Not any feelings that we need bother about."[36]

The experiment succeeds brilliantly. However, Eliza's triumph at the ambassador's ball, where she intrigues the elegant dignitaries with her charm, grace, and meticulous diction, is not the end of the play—as one might expect—for now she lets the arrogant and overbearing Higgins know that she resents being treated as a laboratory animal so that he can demonstrate his genius. "I want a little kindness," she tells Higgins,[37] who maintains that he "created this thing out of . . . squashed cabbage leaves."[38] In the final scene, Eliza demonstrates that she has become a self-confident and independent woman capable of turning the tables on her mentor. She tells Higgins that she has offered herself as an assistant to a teacher of phonetics, whom Higgins detests, so that she can earn enough money to open her own flower shop, for she is determined not to go back to the street. The

thought of Eliza teaching "that toadying ignoramus . . . my methods,"[39] infuriates Higgins, who raises his hand to strike her, but Eliza, showing spirit, refuses to back down. By forcing Higgins to lose his carefully guarded self-control, Eliza achieves a victory. Getting over his loss of temper, Higgins gains new respect for Eliza:

> Higgins: By George, Eliza, I said I'd make a woman of you; and I have. I like you like this.
>
> Liza: Yes, you can turn 'round and make up to me now that I am not afraid of you, and can do without you.
>
> Higgins: Of course I do, you little fool. Five minutes ago you were like a millstone around my neck. Now you're a tower of strength: a consort battleship.[40]

The canonization of Joan of Arc, the young peasant girl who led the French army to victory over England in the early fifteenth century, was the inspiration for Shaw's *Saint Joan*, his most famous play. Joan believed that heavenly voices had called on her to save France, which she did. Captured by the English, she was tried by an English-dominated church court and executed in 1453 as a heretic and a witch.

In Shaw's version, Joan is a saint, who received revelation, and a genius, who saw further and probed deeper than others. She was altogether an "uncommonly woman" who had a zest for soldiering. A natural leader of men and a superb tactician, Joan knew how to instill courage in her troops and plan military campaigns. Shaw also viewed Joan as a forerunner of the Protestant Reformation, because in obeying her voices, she was interpreting God's will on her own without relying on the church. The medieval church, which considered itself the intermediary between God and human beings, condemned as heretics those who maintained that they were in direct communication with God, who set their "private judgment above the instructions of your spiritual directors."[41] The clash between the strong-willed Joan, determined to do what God had commanded through her voices, and the church, which considered such behavior a presumptuous denial of its God-given authority to lead, has all the elements of high drama.

Born a Protestant, but essentially a freethinker, Shaw, in *Saint Joan*, was affirming the cause of individual liberty and religious toleration. Nevertheless, in defiance of nineteenth-century Protestant opinion, he did not treat the church's inquisitors as villains. Rather, he saw them as well-meaning judges who, acting according to the beliefs and laws of their day, made a regrettable mistake. Moreover, they gave Joan every chance to save herself, but she continued to insist—she could do nothing less—that her actions were commanded by God. The dialectical tension between the clergy and Joan, elevated by Shaw's masterful dialogue, makes for a dramatic *tour de force*.

THE INQUISITOR. If the Church Militant tells you that your revelations and visions are sent by the devil to tempt you to your damnation, will you not believe that the church is wiser than you?

JOAN. I believe that God is wiser than I; and it is His commands that I will do. All the things that you call my crimes have come to me by the command of God. I say that I have done them by the order of God: it is impossible for me to say anything else. If any Churchman says the contrary I shall not mind him: I shall mind God alone, whose command I always follow.

LADVENU [pleading with her urgently]. You do not know what you are saying, child. Do you want to kill yourself? Listen. Do you not believe that you are subject to the Church of God on earth?

JOAN. Yes. When have I ever denied it?

LADVENU. Good. That means, does it not, that you are subject to our Lord the Pope, to the cardinals, the archbishops, and the bishops for whom his lordship stands here today?

JOAN. God must be served first.

D'ESTIVET. Then your voices command you not to submit yourself to the Church Militant?

JOAN. My voices do not tell me to disobey the Church; but God must be served first.

CAUCHON. And you, and not the Church, are to be the judge?

JOAN. What other judgment can I judge by but my own?

THE ASSESSORS [scandalized]. Oh! [They cannot find words.]

CAUCHON. Out of your own mouth you have condemned yourself. We have striven for your salvation to the verge of sinning ourselves: we have opened the door to you again and again; and you have shut it in our faces and in the face of God. Dare you pretend, after what you have said, that you are in a state of grace?[42]

MODERN ART

Probably the clearest expression of the Modernist viewpoint is found in art. During the late nineteenth century, artists began to turn away from the standards that had characterized art since the Renaissance. No longer committed to depicting how an object appeared to the eye or to organizing space mathematically, they searched for new forms of representation. Increasingly artists moved further away from reproducing an exact likeness of a physical object or human being, and artists sought to penetrate the deepest recesses of the unconscious, which they saw as the wellspring of creativity and the dwelling place of a higher truth. Paul Klee (1879–1940), a prominent Swiss painter, described modern art in these words: "Each [artist] should follow where the pulse of his own heart leads. . . . Our pounding heart drives us down, deep down to the source of all. What springs from this source, whether it may be called dream, idea or phantasy—must be taken seriously."[43]

Throughout the period from the late 1880s to 1914, artists were de-emphasizing the objective world and stressing the expressive power of such formal qualities as line, color, and space. This trend culminated in abstract art, a nonobjective art totally devoid of reference to the visible world. In breaking with the Renaissance view of the world as inherently orderly and rational and stressing the power of the imagination, Modern artists opened up new possibilities for artistic expression. They also exemplified the growing appeal and force of the nonrational in European life.

Post-Impressionism: Cézanne, Seurat, Gauguin, and van Gogh

During the 1880s, a new group of younger artists replaced the Impressionists in the vanguard of painting. Because all of them had either shown their work in the Impressionist exhibitions or had been influenced by one of the Impressionists, they came to be known as the **Post-Impressionists.** Further revolutionizing the artist's sense of space and color, they tried, even more than the Impressionists, to make art a vivid emotional experience and to produce a personal impression of reality, rather than a photographic copy of objects.

The artist who has been called the father of modern art, Paul Cézanne (1839–1906), was born in Aix-en-Provence, in southern France, to a struggling shopkeeper, Louis-Auguste Cézanne, who later became an affluent banker. He wanted his son to study law, but finally allowed him to join his childhood friend, Émile Zola, in Paris in 1861 to become a serious painter. Cézanne, the closest of all the Post-Impressionists to the Impressionists, embraced the Impressionists' fascination with light and color and displayed his work at the Impressionist exhibitions of 1874 and 1877, but he did not share their vision of capturing a moment of light. Cézanne stated that his intention was "to make of Impressionism something solid and durable, like the art of the museums,"[44] by developing a pictorial style that was more structured, orderly, and monumental. But also, seeking to portray his own visual perception of an object,

Cézanne deliberately distorted perspective, subordinating the objective appearance of the individual object to the requirements of the total design, as he perceived it. For Cézanne, the design, or total effect, was more important than reproducing an exact copy of an object. Thus, in his *Still Life with Basket of Apples* (Figure 23.1), the fruit, the basket, the plate, and the bottle do represent real objects, but their significance within the painting resides more in their relationship to each other than in their unique individual reality. The wine bottle, tipping precariously, is set off by the apples in the foreground, which appear to be resisting gravity. Only the biscuits on the imperfectly rounded plate seem to be stable.

Although Cézanne visited Paris often and lived there for brief periods, for most of his life he lived and painted in his native Aix. Similar to Monet's obsession with the Rouen Cathedral, Cézanne was captivated by *Mont Sainte-Victoire,* a mountain near his home, which he painted more than sixty times. Although his paintings of the mountain are somewhat similar, they do differ depending on the atmospheric conditions and the time of day. In one of his final depictions of *Mont Sainte-Victoire* (Figure 23.2), just prior to his death, the colors are darker than many of the series, and although the objects—the houses and the vegetation—are ascertainable, they are not distinct. Rather than reproducing the object itself, Cézanne sought to represent it, to create his own visual perception of it, as he did here with strong, rectangular brush strokes. Rather than a *reproduction* of nature, Cézanne's landscape is a personal *representation* of nature. Cézanne's interest in irregular form and flattened space later

instructed Pablo Picasso and Georges Braque, the founders of Cubism (see later discussion).

Cézanne's work was not well received until he was fifty years old. The critics felt that his representation of reality was quite faulty, that he did not have the skill to depict mountains, houses, and apples in a naturalistic manner. Cézanne himself was uneasy and uncertain about his own skills as a painter, which became clear in 1886 when his friend Zola sent him a copy of his new novel—the story of an inept painter who commits suicide. Seeing a caricature of himself, he terminated his lifelong friendship with Zola.

As a consequence of his study of contemporary theories of color and light, Cézanne's younger contemporary, Georges Seurat (1859–1891), developed a new approach that came to be called ***pointillism*** or *divisionism.* Seurat's huge masterpiece was his *Sunday Afternoon on the Island of La Grande Jatte* (Figure 23.3), which he entered in the final Impressionist Exhibition of 1886. To construct this typical Impressionist scene of outdoor leisure, Seurat made numerous preliminary color studies outdoors and then painted the picture in his studio, working day and night. Rather than the short brush strokes of the Impressionists, he employed tiny round points of color, nearly identical in size, which, rather than being blended on the artist's palette, are intended to merge in the eyes of the observer. The formal composition and the somewhat flat forms of the stiff figures are in contrast to the Impressionist celebration of light and nature. Nonetheless, because Seurat's subject matter was similar to that of the Impressionists—leisurely weekend

Figure 23.1   Paul Cézanne, *Still Life with Basket of Apples,* 1890–1894, 24 3/8" x 31" (62.5 x 79.5 cm), oil on canvas The Art Institute of Chicago.
The fruit, the basket, the plate, and the bottle represent real objects, but their significance within the painting resides more in their relationship to each other than in their unique, individual reality. The tipping wine bottle is set off by the apples in the foreground, which appear to be resisting gravity. Only the biscuits on the imperfectly rounded plate seem to be stable. *(Helen Birch Bartlett Memorial Collection, 1926.252 © The Art Institute of Chicago. All Rights Reserved)*

Figure 23.2 Paul Cézanne,
Mont Sainte-Victoire,
1902–1906, 25 1/2" x 32"
(65 x 81 cm), oil on canvas
Philadelphia Museum
of Art (V.799; R.911), Gift of
Mrs. Louis C. Madeira.
Cézanne was captivated by this
mountain near his home, which
he painted more that sixty
times. But rather than
reproducing the object itself,
Cézanne sought to represent it,
to create his own visual
perception of it. *(Philadelphia
Museum of Art, The George W.
Elkins Collection. Photo by
Graydon Wood, 1994)*

diversions—he and his associates came to be known as Neo-Impressionists.

A more radical break with the past was made by Paul Gauguin (1848–1903), who renounced not only the Impressionists' vision of capturing an instant of light but also the entire Western notion that the painter should reproduce the physical world as it actually appears. Gauguin was a successful Parisian stockbroker until 1883, when he abandoned the marketplace for the life of a professional painter. Two years later, Gauguin left his wife and five children, and the next year he moved to Brittany, in western France, to live a simpler life.

Gauguin wrote of the Impressionists: "They sought for things at the visible level and not at the mysterious center of thought, and for this reason they fell into scientific reasoning."[45] It was this "mysterious center of thought," the deeper reality, that Gauguin tried to convey with his art. In 1888, Gauguin painted *Vision after the Sermon* (Figure 23.4)—the work that marks his break from Impressionism and Naturalism. On the far right is the priest who has preached the sermon, while the group of women experience a vision concerning the biblical story of Jacob wrestling with an angel (Genesis 32: 24–26). The flat modeling and perspective, influenced by medieval stained glass windows, accentuates the mood of spiritual ecstasy among the women. Gauguin himself explained why neither the color nor the proportion is true to nature:

Figure 23.3 Georges Seurat,
Sunday Afternoon on the Island
of La Grande Jatte, **1884–1886,**
6'9 1/2"x 10'1 1/4" (2.07 x
3.08 m), oil on canvas, The Art
Institute of Chicago. Seurat
entered this masterpiece in the final
Impressionist Exhibition of 1886.
But rather than using the short
brush strokes of the Impressionists,
he employed tiny round points of
color, nearly identical in size, which
are intended to mix in the eyes of
the observer, instead of being
blended on the artist's palette.
*(Helen Birch Bartlett Memorial
Collection, 1926.224 © The Art
Institute of Chicago. All Rights
Reserved)*

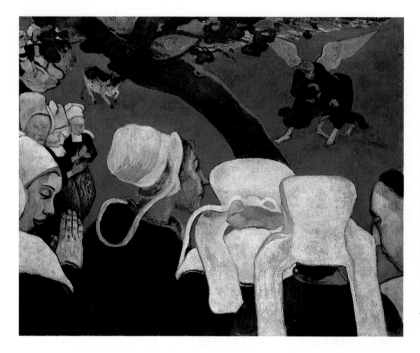

Figure 23.4   Paul Gauguin, *Vision after the Sermon*, 1888, 28 3/4" x 36 1/2" (73 x 92.7 cm), oil on canvas, The National Galleries of Scotland, Edinburgh.   This painting marks Gauguin's break from Impressionism and Naturalism. On the far right is the priest who has preached the sermon, while the group of women experience a vision concerning the biblical story of Jacob wrestling with an angel. *(The National Galleries of Scotland)*

For me in this painting the landscape and the fight exist only in the imagination of the people praying after the sermon, which is why there is a contrast between the people, who are natural, and the struggle going on in a landscape which is non-natural and out of proportion.[46]

In 1891, Gauguin, attempting to escape what he viewed as a corrupt European civilization, abandoned France for the island of Tahiti in the South Pacific. During his first two years in Tahiti, Gauguin painted sixty-six canvases, one of which was *Manao Tupapao (The Spirit Watches Over Her)* (Figure 23.5), depicting his mistress, Tehura, whom he found one night terrified by "the Tupapaü"—the spirits of the dead. Writing in his journal, Gauguin recalled, "The intensity of fright which had dominated her as the result of the physical and moral power of her superstitions had transformed her into a strange being,"[47] and he made the incident the subject of his painting.

> I have to explain this fright . . . and this is what I am doing. General harmony: dark, sad, frightening, resounding in the eye like a funeral knell. The violet, the dark blue, and the yellow-orange. I am making the linen greenish-yellow. . . . This yellow links the orange-yellow and the blue and so completes the musical harmony. There are a few flowers in the background, but they must not be real since they are imagined; I make them look like sparks. For the Kanaka, the night phosphorescences are connected with the spirit of the dead; they believe this and are frightened by it.[48]

The figure of the Tupapao, which she had invoked, stands at the foot of the bed in the guise of an old woman.

Among Gauguin's artistic friends, before he fled to Tahiti, was the tragic figure Vincent van Gogh (1853-1890). The son of a Dutch Protestant minister, van Gogh was initially drawn to a career in the church. After a brief period at a missionary school near Brussels, he became a missionary to the coal miners in a village in southern Belgium in 1878. Because of his zeal—he lived like a pauper with the miners, slept on the floor, and gave away all his possessions—he was dismissed by the church, but he never lost his mystical faith and love of humanity. In 1880, he turned to art and lived in poverty for the next five years, while developing his skills as a painter. Van Gogh arrived in Paris in 1886, where he lived for two years with his brother, Theo, who owned an art gallery. There, he met the Impressionists, whose influence transformed his style. In February of 1888, due to emotional instability and depression, van Gogh moved to Arles, in southern France, where he hoped to find some peace of mind. At Arles, his painting went through a profound change that is characterized by thick paint, strong brush strokes, and glowing color. In a letter to Theo, he explained that he was using color to express his feelings because it has a language all its own:

> [W]hat I learned in Paris is leaving me. . . . And I should not be surprised if the impressionists soon will find fault with my way of working. . . . Because, instead of trying to reproduce exactly what I have before my eyes, I use color more arbitrarily, in order to express myself forcibly.[49]

Van Gogh's new expressive use of color is apparent in his painting, *Vincent's Bedroom in Arles* (Figure 23.6), which may also give the

member of the group was Henri Matisse (1869–1954), whose *Bonheur de Vivre (The Joy of Life)* (Figure 23.8) embodies the spirit of *Fauvism.* This Saturnalia obviously occurs in a meadow in a forest, but Matisse intended to simplify the entire scene, both the human forms and nature. Concerning the human form, Matisse explained:

> I have to paint the body of a woman: first of all I give it grace and charm, but something more is necessary. I will condense the meaning of this body by seeking out its essential lines. The charm will be less apparent at first glance, but it should eventually arise from the new image I have obtained, which will have a broader meaning, *one more fully human.*[53]

Matisse further asserted: "An artist must recognize . . . that his picture is an artifice; but when he paints, he should feel that he has copied nature. And even when he consciously departs from nature, it must be with the conviction that it is only to render it more completely."[54] By rendering nature "more completely," Matisse meant reducing the scene to its barest essentials, an activity that somewhat distorted reality. Thus, in *The Joy of Life* he simplified the human bodies, flattened the perspective, and used flat tints, with soft brush strokes, rather than the colors of nature.

Matisse's *Red Studio* (Figure 23.9), which depicts his own studio with several of his paintings decorating the wall, is another example of simplification. At first glance, the monochromatic red makes it appear to be a flat surface, but on closer inspection one discovers different planes in the painting. The outline of the table top, the chairs, and the chest, along with the paintings and the small sculptures, give the scene a feeling of three-dimensionality. In addition, the paintings on the floor and the lines connecting them suggest a corner in the room, even though there is no vertical line to form one. By delineating the horizontal and the vertical planes with so few lines, Matisse rendered the scene as simply as possible, nearly deserting Renaissance perspective.

Expressionism: Munch, Der Blaue Reiter, and Kandinsky

At the turn of the century, there were several groups of avant-garde painters in Germany, which were later grouped together under the term *Expressionism.* Rather than seeking to portray objective reality, Expressionist painters created innovative forms to *express* the intensity of their feelings. Influenced by Gauguin, van Gogh, and the Fauves, Expressionists created an art characterized by harsh colors and distorted shapes to express their emotions.

The Norwegian painter Edvard Munch (1863–1944) was a forerunner of the German Expressionists. He designed stage sets for his friend, Ibsen, but went far beyond him in expressing his profound feelings of isolation in scenes that portray fear and death. Munch was no stranger to death and mental suffering—both his mother and a sister died of tuberculosis, another sister became chronically insane, and Munch himself suffered a severe nervous breakdown. Consequently, like his fellow countryman, Strindberg, Munch attempted to express his inner self and the pathos of human relations in his paintings. One such work, *The Scream* (see chapter opening), expresses an overwhelming dread and anguish. As Munch later explained:

Figure 23.8   Henri Matisse, *The Joy of Life*, 1905–1906, 5′8 1/2″ x 7′9 3/4″ (1.74 x 2.38 m), oil on canvas, The Barnes Foundation, Merion, Penn. Matisse was the leader of a group of avant-garde artists that critics dubbed "Fauves" (wild beasts), because they distorted form and used color with great freedom to express intense feelings in their paintings. His simplified rendering of nature and the human forms in this Saturnalia are typical of his style. *(The Barnes Foundation, Merion, Pa/The Bridgeman Art Library International © 2002 Succession H. Matisse, Paris/Artists Rights Society (ARS), New York)*

Figure 23.9 Henri Matisse (1869–1954), *The Red Studio*, Issy-les-Moulineaux, 1911. Oil on canvas, 71 1/4 x 72 1/4". This painting is another example of simplification by Matisse. Although the monochromatic red makes it appear to be a flat surface, upon closer inspection, one discovers different planes within the painting. *(Mrs. Simon Guggenheim Fund © Museum of Modern Art, New York/Scala/Art Resource, NY. © 2002 Succession H. Matisse, Paris/Artists Rights Society (ARS), New York)*

One evening I was walking along a path—on one side lay the city and below me the fjord. I was tired and ill—I stopped and looked out across the fjord—the sun was setting—the clouds were dyed red like blood. I felt a scream pass through nature; it seemed to me that I could hear the scream. I painted this picture—painted the clouds as red as real blood.—The colors were screaming.[55]

The bright colors, along with the curved brush strokes, appear to make the scream reverberate throughout the landscape and the sky.

German Expressionism originated in Dresden when a group of artists began to live and work together as a brotherhood in 1905. They called themselves *Die Brücke* (The Bridge) and saw themselves as a bridge to a better future. Soon thereafter, a second source of German Expressionism came into existence with *Der Blaue Reiter* (The Blue Rider), a loosely organized group of avant-garde painters in Munich, whose stated goal was "to push back the existing limits of artistic expression."[56] One of the leaders of the group was Vassily Kandinsky (1866–1944), a Russian who arrived in Munich in 1896 at the age of thirty. Between 1910 and 1914, Kandinsky painted a series of *Improvisations* and *Compositions* in which he gradually abandoned representational subject matter, thus becoming the first abstract painter. Kandinsky gradually removed all traces of the physical world from his painting, creating a

Figure 23.10 Vassily Kandinsky, *Composition no. 7*, 1913, oil on canvas, 6'6 3/4" x 9'11 1/8" (200 x 300 cm), Tretyakov Gallery, Moscow. Kandinsky was a leader of a group of avant-garde painters in Munich, called *Der Blaue Reiter* (The Blue Rider), whose goal was to challenge the limits of artistic expression. In this painting, he has removed virtually all traces of the physical world, thereby creating a nonobjective artwork that bears little, or no, resemblance to the natural world. *(Tretyakov Gallery, Moscow/The Bridgeman Art Library International)*

nonobjective art that bears no resemblance to the natural world. In declaring that he "painted . . . subconsciously in a state of strong inner tension,"[57] Kandinsky explicitly expressed a distinguishing quality of modern Western art: the artist's private inner experience of the world.

Just prior to World War I, apocalyptic themes were common in Kandinsky's paintings. Although Kandinsky's *Composition no. 7* (Figure 23.10) might seem at first glance a simple array of brushed shapes and colors, its themes—its inner content—are documented in the more than thirty preliminary studies for the final version. In the final version, there is a boat with three oars, outlined in black, in the lower left corner (the theme of the Deluge); long blue shapes in the upper right suggest trumpets (the theme of the Last Judgment and the Resurrection); and in the middle right there are two purple oval shapes, situated diagonally, to represent a couple (the theme of the Garden of Eden). Kandinsky painted the final version in a little over three days, in late November of 1913.

Although *Der Blaue Reiter* came to an end with World War I, Kandinsky's paintings signaled the advent of abstract art, which continues to exert a powerful influence on art today.

Cubism: Picasso and Braque

During the first decade of the twentieth century, a revolutionary new style, called *Cubism*, pushed Modern art into new directions. Exploring the interplay between the flat world of the canvas and the three-dimensional world of visual perception, these painters sought to depict a reality deeper than what the eye sees at first glance. One art historian describes Cubism as follows: "The cubist is not interested in usual representational standards. It is as if he were walking around the object he is analyzing, as one is free to walk around a piece of sculpture for successive views. But he must represent all these views at once."[58] The Cubists' effort to depict something from multiple perspectives rather than from a single point in space and their need to deliberately deform objects in order to achieve this effect mark a radical break with artistic conventions. The two men responsible for the development of Cubism were Pablo Picasso (1881–1973) and Georges Braque (1882–1963).

Picasso, born the son of an art professor in Málaga, Spain, studied art in Barcelona before arriving in Paris in 1900. During the next six years, the gifted Picasso went through his successful "Blue" and "Rose" periods, but it was his monumental *Les Demoiselles d'Avignon (The Young Ladies of Avignon)* (Figure 23.11) of 1907 that

began a period of creativity seldom matched in the history of art. What motivated Picasso to create such a scene? He was probably influenced by the 1906 exhibition of ancient Spanish sculptures, which he saw at the Louvre, and African masks, which he discovered at another exhibit in Paris. The faces of the three women on the left resemble the primitive faces of the sculptures, and the faces of the two women on the right look like the African masks. Finally, Picasso may have intended *Les Demoiselles* to be the antithesis of Matisse's *Joy of Life* (which was first exhibited in 1906). Picasso's "young ladies" are not Matisse's joyfully cavorting young people in a meadow; instead, these flattened figures are prostitutes, grouped in a parlor in a brothel on Carrer d'Avinyo, a street in the red light district of Barcelona. An earlier version of the painting included two clothed male customers, but in the final version, only the five prostitutes stare out at the viewer, who now plays the role of the customer. Matisse proclaimed this painting to be a betrayal of modern art, and even Picasso's friends were perplexed. It was not formally exhibited until Picasso sold it in 1920; since

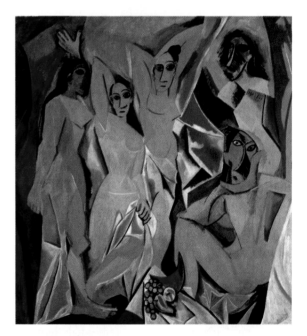

Figure 23.11 Pablo Picasso, (1881–1973), *Les Demoiselles d'Avignon,* **June–July 1907. Oil on canvas 8′ x 7′8″.** While the faces of the three women on the left resemble the primitive faces of ancient Spanish sculptures, the faces of the two women on the right look like African masks. Picasso's "young ladies" are prostitutes, grouped in a parlor at a brothel on Carrer d'Avinyo, a street in the red light district of Barcelona. *(Acquired through the Lille P. Bliss Bequest (333.1939). © Museum of Modern Art, New York, NY/Scala/Art Resource, NY. © 2002 Estate of Pablo Picasso/Artists Rights Society (ARS), New York)*

A.D. 1850   **A.D. 1900**

Politics/Society

World War I (1914–1918) ●
Bolsheviks take power in Russia (1917) ●
Germany signs Treaty of Versailles (1919) ●
The Harlem Renaissance (1920s) ●
Mussolini seizes power in Italy (1922) ●
Death of Lenin; Stalin succeeds to power (1924) ●
Start of the Great Depression (1929) ●
Hitler becomes chancellor of Germany (1933) ●
Stalin orders mass purges in the Soviet Union (1936–1938) ●

Art/Architecture

Lumiere brothers create the first film (1895) ●
Matisse and other artists named the *Fauves* by critics (1905) ●
Picasso's *Les Demoiselles d'Avignon* first Cubist painting (1907) ●
Beginning of Futurist art movement in Italy (1909) ●
Picasso and Braque turn to Synthetic Cubism (1912) ●
Duchamp submits *Fountain* to art exhibition; first Dada work of art (1917) ●
Gropius founds the Bauhaus school (1919) ●
Dada art movement ends; beginning of Surrealism (1924) ●
Brancusi's sculpture *Bird in Space* completed (1928) ●

Literature/Music

● Ragtime music (c. 1890–1920)
Shaw, *Pygmalion* (1912) ●
Schönberg's *Five Pieces for Orchestra* performed; first atonal piece (1912) ●
Popularity of new music genres such as jazz and blues (1920s) ●
Eliot, *The Waste Land* (1922) ●
Woolf, *Mrs. Dalloway* (1925) ●
Kafka, *The Trial* (1925) ●
Fitzgerald, *The Great Gatsby* (1925) ●
Hemingway, *The Sun Also Rises* (1926) ●
Lawrence, *Lady Chatterley's Lover* (1928) ●
Brecht, *The Three Penny Opera* (1928) ●
Remarque, *All Quiet on the Western Front* (1929) ●

Philosophy/Science/Religion

● Nietzsche, *The Anti-Christ* (1888)
Freud, *The Interpretation of Dreams* (1900) ●
Planck develops quantum theory (1900) ●
Einstein develops theory of relativity (1905) ●
Freud, *Civilization and Its Discontents* (1930) ●

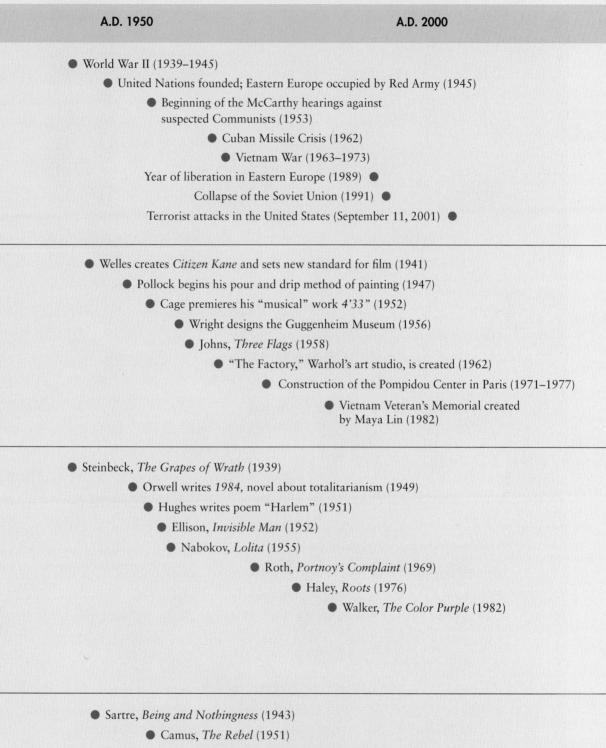

● World War II (1939–1945)

    ● United Nations founded; Eastern Europe occupied by Red Army (1945)

      ● Beginning of the McCarthy hearings against
        suspected Communists (1953)

          ● Cuban Missile Crisis (1962)

          ● Vietnam War (1963–1973)

Year of liberation in Eastern Europe (1989) ●

       Collapse of the Soviet Union (1991) ●

Terrorist attacks in the United States (September 11, 2001) ●

● Welles creates *Citizen Kane* and sets new standard for film (1941)

    ● Pollock begins his pour and drip method of painting (1947)

      ● Cage premieres his "musical" work *4'33"* (1952)

        ● Wright designs the Guggenheim Museum (1956)

        ● Johns, *Three Flags* (1958)

          ● "The Factory," Warhol's art studio, is created (1962)

            ● Construction of the Pompidou Center in Paris (1971–1977)

             ● Vietnam Veteran's Memorial created
              by Maya Lin (1982)

● Steinbeck, *The Grapes of Wrath* (1939)

    ● Orwell writes *1984,* novel about totalitarianism (1949)

      ● Hughes writes poem "Harlem" (1951)

      ● Ellison, *Invisible Man* (1952)

      ● Nabokov, *Lolita* (1955)

        ● Roth, *Portnoy's Complaint* (1969)

        ● Haley, *Roots* (1976)

          ● Walker, *The Color Purple* (1982)

● Sartre, *Being and Nothingness* (1943)

    ● Camus, *The Rebel* (1951)

          ● Creation of the Internet (1983)

317

24

World War I and Its Aftermath: The Lost Generation and the Jazz Age

Constantin Brancusi, *Bird in Space*, 1928, Bronze, 54" x 8 1/2" x 6 1/2" (137.2 x 21.6 x 16.5 cm), Collection, The Museum of Modern Art, New York.

With its exceedingly simplified form—a tall, slender, elliptical shape ending in a point—this sculpture expresses the essence of a bird in flight.

(Given anonymously. © Museum of Modern Art, NY/Scala/Art Resource, NY. © 2002 Artists Rights Society (ARS), New York/ADAGP, Paris)

TO MANY EUROPEANS, THE OPENING YEARS of the twentieth century seemed full of promise. Advances in science and technology, the rising standard of living, the expansion of education, and the absence of wars between the Great Powers since the Franco-Prussian War (1870–1871) all contributed to a general feeling of optimism. Yet these accomplishments hid disruptive forces, particularly an overheated nationalism, that were propelling Europe toward a cataclysm—World War I. "There will be wars as never before on earth," predicted Nietzsche. World War I bore him out. Modern technology enabled the combatants to kill with unprecedented efficiency.

After World War I, Europeans looked at themselves and their civilization differently. It seemed that in science and technology they had unleashed powers that they could not control, and belief in the stability and security of European civilization appeared to be an illusion. Also illusory was the expectation that reason would banish the vestiges of darkness, ignorance, and injustice and usher in an age of continual progress. European intellectuals felt that they were living in a "broken world." In a time of heightened brutality and mobilized irrationality, the values of old Europe seemed beyond recovery. "All the great words," wrote D. H. Lawrence, "were canceled out for that generation."[1] The fissures discernible in European civilization before 1914 had grown wider and deeper.

The sense of disillusionment and disenchantment found expression in cultural life; many intellectuals, feeling that they were part of a "lost generation," questioned traditional values, and their works often demonstrated a pessimistic outlook about the human condition. At the same time, Modernist experimentation continued to produce innovations in the arts. An entire generation of American authors left the United States to take up residence in Europe, particularly Paris. Their bohemian lifestyle of pleasure seeking and capriciousness opened the door for later generations of writers and artists who established themselves as a counterculture. Those American writers who remained at home attempted to come to grips with the glitz, glamour, and free-spending habits of the postwar generation, but at the same time, they tried to give meaning to the anxiety, hypocrisy, exploitation, and corruption that they believed characterized their age.

WORLD WAR I AND THE RUSSIAN REVOLUTION

On June 28, 1914, Archduke Frances Ferdinand, heir to the throne of Austria-Hungary, was assassinated by Gavrilo Princip, a young Serbian nationalist (and Austrian subject), at Sarajevo in the Austrian province of Bosnia, inhabited largely by South Slavs. The assassination triggered those explosive forces that lay beneath the surface of European life, and six weeks later, Europe was engulfed in a general war that altered the course of Western civilization.

Belligerent, irrational, and extreme nationalism was a principal cause of World War I. Placing their country above everything, nationalists in various countries fomented hatred of other nationalities and called for the expansion of their nation's borders—attitudes that fostered belligerence in foreign relations. Wedded to nationalism was a militaristic view that regarded war as heroic and as the highest expression of individual and national life.

Yet Europe might have avoided the world war had the nations not been divided into hostile alliance systems. By 1907, the Triple Alliance of Germany, Austria-Hungary, and Italy confronted the loosely organized Triple Entente of France, Russia, and Great Britain.

A danger inherent in an alliance system is that a country, knowing that it has the support of allies, may pursue an aggressive foreign policy and may be less likely to compromise during a crisis; also, a war between two states may well draw in the other allied powers. These dangers materialized in 1914.

In the diplomatic furor of July and early August 1914, following the assassination of Francis Ferdinand, several patterns emerged. Austria-Hungary, a multinational empire dominated by Germans and Hungarians, feared the nationalist aspirations of its Slavic minorities. The nationalist yearnings of neighboring Serbia aggravated Austria-Hungary's problems, for the Serbs, a South Slav people, wanted to create a Greater Serbia by uniting with South Slavs of Austria-Hungary. If Slavic nationalism gained in intensity, the Austro-Hungarian (or Hapsburg) Empire would be broken into states based on nationality. To prevent this, Austria-Hungary decided to use the assassination as justification for crushing Serbia.

The system of alliances escalated the tensions between Austria-Hungary and Serbia into a general European war. Germany saw itself threatened by the Triple Entente (a conviction based more on paranoia than on objective fact) and regarded Austria-Hungary as its only reliable ally. Holding that at all costs its ally must be kept strong, German officials supported Austria-Hungary's decision to crush Serbia. Fearing that Germany and Austria-Hungary aimed to extend their power into southeastern Europe, Russia would not permit the destruction of Serbia. With the support of France, Russia began to mobilize, and when it moved to full mobilization, Germany declared war. Because German battle plans, drawn up years before, called for a war with both France and Russia, France was drawn into the conflict; Germany's invasion of neutral Belgium, which Britain was pledged to defend, brought the British Empire into the war.

Most European statesmen and military men believed the war would be over in a few months. Virtually no one anticipated that it would last more than four years and that the casualties would number in the millions.

The most terrible war the world had experienced ended in November 1918; in January 1919, representatives of the victorious powers assembled in Paris to draw up a peace settlement. The *Versailles Treaty* required Germany to cede territory to France and the newly created Poland, to surrender her colonies, to disarm, and to pay reparations, the exact amount left for future determination. The Germans denounced the treaty, which they regarded as an Anglo-French plot to keep Germany economically and militarily weak. The treaty's defenders argued that if Germany had won the war, it would have forced far more ruthless terms on France and other losing countries.

What is most significant about the Treaty of Versailles is that it did not solve the German problem. Germany was left weak but unbroken—its industrial and military power only temporarily contained, and its nationalist fervor undiminished. The real danger in Europe was German unwillingness to accept defeat or surrender the dream of expansion.

One consequence of the war that influenced the course of European and world history in momentous ways was the Russian Revolution of 1917 and the resultant triumph of the Bolsheviks (soon to be called Communists). The people of Russia had initially responded to the war with a show of patriotic fervor. By January 1917, however, virtually all Russians—and, most of all, the soldiers—had lost trust in their autocratic government. The ill-equipped and poorly led Russian armies suffered huge losses, and by 1916 the home front began to fall apart. Shops were empty, money had no value, and hunger and cold stalked the working quarters of cities and towns. But Tsar Nicholas II, determined to preserve autocracy, resisted any suggestion that he liberalize the regime for the sake of the war effort.

Autocracy was ready to collapse at the slightest blow. In early March, a strike, riots in the food lines, and street demonstrations in Petrograd (formerly Saint Petersburg) flared into sudden, unpremeditated revolution. The soldiers, who during the unrest of 1905 had stood by the tsar, now rushed to support the striking workers. The Romanov dynasty, after three hundred years of rule (1613–1917), came to an end.

The Provisional Government, after July 1917 guided by Aleksandr Kerensky (1881–1970), sought to transform Russia into a Western-style liberal state, but the government failed to comprehend the urgency with which the Russian peasants wanted the landlords' land and soldiers and the masses wanted peace. Resentment spiraled. Kerensky's increasing unpopularity and the magnitude of the popular unrest seemed to Vladimir Lenin (1870–1924), head of the Bolsheviks, a revolutionary Marxist party, an invitation to seize power. In November 1918, the Bolsheviks, supported by the workers and soldiers in Petrograd, overthrew the Kerensky government.

A brutal civil war followed. Opponents of the Bolsheviks (Reds) were led by elements of the tsarist aristocracy (Whites). The Bolsheviks proved to be the only force capable of holding together a country faced with defeat, revolution, civil war, foreign intervention, and economic ruin. The government became a socialist dictatorship with Lenin at its head. Soviet Russia was guided by Marxist ideology adapted by Lenin to Russian conditions, and it was run by the professional revolutionaries of the Communist party. Lenin believed that among the raw and violence-prone peoples of Russia, discipline had to be enforced by compulsion and even terror, if their country was to survive. The civil war—a counterrevolution that threatened the very existence of the Communist regime—was for Lenin a pressing reason for employing terror.

LITERATURE

The Experience of War

At the outbreak of World War I, several poets, notably Englishman Rupert Brooke (1887–1915), greeted the conflict as a glorious adventure, a God-given opportunity to experience life fully.

> Oh! We, who have known shame, we have found release there,
> Where there's no ill, no grief, but sleep has mending,
> Naught broken save this body, lost but breath;
> Nothing to shake the laughing heart's long peace there
> But only agony, and that has ending;
> And the worst friend and enemy is but Death.[2]

Volunteering for service, Brooke received a commission in the Royal Naval Division. His brief experience with combat, before becoming seriously ill and dying on a hospital ship, further convinced him of the justice of the British cause and the virtue of self-sacrifice, ideals that he expressed in his war poetry.

Several British poets who fought in the trenches, including Siegfried Sassoon (1886–1967), Wilfred Owen (1893–1918), Robert Graves (1895–1985), Charles Hamilton Sorley (1895–1915), Edmund Charles Blunden (1896–1974), and Isaac Rosenberg (1890–1918), bitterly rejected Brooke's effort to transform the indiscriminate slaughter of Europe's youth into an idealistic venture. In angry, unsentimental tones and graphic imagery, they depicted the brutality of trench warfare.

Wilfred Owen, who volunteered for duty in 1915, sustained shellshock at the battle of the Somme and was sent to a hospital in Britain. In 1918, he returned to the front and was awarded the Military Cross for bravery; he died one week before the Armistice. In "Anthem for a Doomed Youth," he writes that there are no solemn church funerals "for those who die as cattle."

> What passing-bells for these who die as cattle?
> —Only the monstrous anger of the guns.
>
> Only the stuttering rifles' rapid rattle
> Can patter out their hasty orisons [prayers].
> No mockeries now for them; no prayers nor bells;
> Nor any voice of mourning save the choirs,—
> The shrill, demented choirs of wailing shells;
> And bugles calling for them from sad shires.[3]

In "Disabled," Owen portrays the enduring misery of those whose wounds leave them invalids for life.

> He sat in a wheeled chair, waiting for dark,
> And shivered in his ghastly suit of gray,
> Legless, sewn short at elbow. Through the park
> Voices of boys rang saddening like a hymn,
> Voices of play and pleasure after day,
> Till gathering sleep mothered them from him.
>
> About this time Town used to swing so gay
> When glow-lamps budded in the light blue trees,
> And girls glanced lovelier as the air grew dim,—
> In the old time, before he threw away his
>   knees. . . .
> He asked to join, He didn't have to beg;
> Smiling they wrote his lie: aged nineteen years.
> Germans he scarcely thought of; all their guilt,
> And Austria's, did not move him. And no fears
> Of Fear came yet. He thought of jeweled hilts
> For daggers in plaid socks; of smart salutes;
> And care of arms; and leave; and pay arrears;
> *Esprit de corps;* and hints for young recruits.
> And soon, he was drafted out with drums and
>   cheers. . . .
>
> Now, he will spend a few sick years in Institutes,
> And do what things the rules consider wise,
> And take whatever pity they may dole.

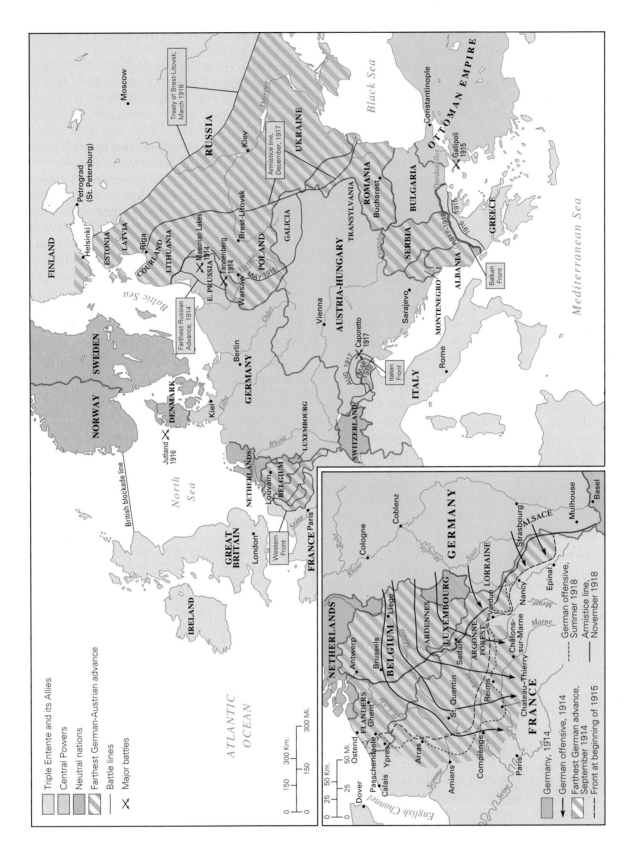

Tonight he noticed how the women's eyes
Passed from him to the strong men that were
  whole.
How cold and late it is! Why don't they come
And put him into bed? Why don't they come?[4]

Like many other educated and well-to-do Englishmen, Siegfried Sassoon enlisted in the early days of the war, but quickly lost his initial enthusiasm and published antiwar poems, even while earning a Military Cross for bravery. Frontline soldiers often looked with contempt on generals who, from a safe distance, ordered massive assaults against well-defended enemy lines that could cost the lives of tens of thousands of soldiers in just a few days. In "Base Details," Sassoon showed his disdain for these callous commanders. The poem draws a sharp distinction between the "glum heroes" at the front and their "bald," "short of breath," "puffy" generals.

If I were fierce, and bald, and short of breath,
I'd live with scarlet Majors at the Base,
And speed glum heroes up the line to death.
You'd see me with my puffy petulant face,
Guzzling and gulping in the best hotel,
Reading the Roll of Honor. "Poor young chap,"
I'd say—"I used to know his father well;
Yes, we've lost heavily in this last scrap."
And when the war is done and youth stone dead,
I'd toddle safely home and die—in bed.[5]

In addition to poetry, the experience of war gave rise to numerous novels, many of them written by combatants. Henri Barbusse's *Le feu* (*Under Fire*), written in 1916, while the war still raged, was the most significant French war novel. Barbusse, a veteran of the front driven by a compulsion to bear witness, denounced the war and indicted the society that spawned it. He focused on average conscripts struggling to survive, not on members of the elite, testing their valor in chivalric combat, the theme of traditional war literature. He realistically described life in the trenches—coping with lice, rats, and excrement, enduring relentless artillery bombardments, and watching one's comrades killed or dismembered. Occasionally Barbusse shows respect for the courage and devotion to a cause evidenced by soldiers. Nevertheless, *Under Fire* is essentially a protest against war; debunking the pursuit of glory, it finds no virtue in the profession of arms. In a world where artillery shells and machine gun fire kill indiscriminately, the hero's quest for honor and glory seems ludicrously out of place. Modern technological warfare is simply brutality and butchery devoid of glamour.

The most famous literary work to emerge from the war was *All Quiet on the Western Front* (1929), written by Erich Maria Remarque (1898–1970), a German novelist and himself a veteran of the trenches. In addition to his memorable descriptions of mind-numbing artillery bombardments and hand-to-hand combat in the trenches, Remarque captured the disillusionment that would affect the postwar generation. A young German soldier in the novel ponders the war's effect on his generation:

I am twenty years old; yet I know nothing of life but despair, death, fear, and fatuous superficiality cast over an abyss of sorrow. I see how peoples are set against one another, and in silence, unknowingly, foolishly, obediently, innocently slay one another. I see that the keenest brains of the world invent weapons and words to make it yet more refined and enduring. . . . [A]ll my generation is experiencing these things with me. . . . What do they expect of us if a time ever comes when the war is over? Through the years our business has been killing. . . . Our knowledge of life is limited to death. What will happen afterwards?[6]

The best American novel to come out of the Great War was *A Farewell to Arms* (1929) by Ernest Hemingway, whom many regard as the greatest American novelist of the twentieth century (see later discussion). It is a memorable love story, intense and tragic, involving Lieutenant Frederick Henry, an American ambulance driver serving in the Italian army, and Catherine Barkley, a beautiful English volunteer nurse. It also provides a gripping description of the disastrous rout of the Italians by the Austrians and Germans at the battle of Caporetto. Although Hemingway did not experience the battle, he had served as a volunteer ambulance driver and was himself wounded. With the sensibilities of a great novelist, he depicted the confusion of an army in retreat and the mood of weary and demoralized soldiers. The roads are littered with abandoned trucks, carts, and supplies; soldiers throw away their rifles and shout, "We're going home." Special units, the "battle police," hunt for officers separated from their men and accuse them of treachery. In questioning the officers, they employ inane nationalistic rhetoric that has no meaning for these battle-weary soldiers.

"It is you and such as you that have let the
  barbarians onto the sacred soil of the
  fatherland."
"I beg your pardon," said the lieutenant-colonel.

Map 24.1   The First World War in Europe   The trench war on the western front was concentrated in Belgium and northern France, while the war in the east encompassed an enormous territory.

"It is because of treachery such as yours that we have lost the fruits of victory."

"Have you ever been in a retreat?" the lieutenant-colonel asked.

"Italy should never retreat."[7]

Hemingway brilliantly captures the mentality of these young true believers who became executioners in the conviction that they were saving their country.

We stood in the rain and were taken out one at a time to be questioned and shot. So far they had shot every one they had questioned. The questioners had that beautiful detachment and devotion to stern justice of men dealing in death without being in any danger of it.[8]

Before the Great War, German writer Thomas Mann (1875–1955) had earned a reputation for his short stories and novels, particularly *Buddenbrooks* (1901), which portrays the decline of a prosperous bourgeois family. At the outbreak of the war, Mann was a staunch conservative who disliked democracy. After the war, he drew closer to liberalism, supporting the Weimar republic and attacking the Nazi cult of irrationalism.

In *The Magic Mountain*, begun in 1912 and completed in 1924, Mann reflected on the decomposition of bourgeois European civilization. The novel is set in a Swiss sanitorium, just prior to World War I. The patients, drawn from several European lands, suffer from tuberculosis and are diseased in spirit as well as body. The sanitorium symbolizes Europe. It is the European psyche that is sick and rushing headlong into a catastrophe.

One patient, the Italian Ludovico Settembrini, stands for the humanist ideals of the Enlightenment: reason, individual liberty, and progress. Although Mann is sympathetic to these ideals, he also indicts Settembrini for his naive faith in progress, his shallow view of human nature, which gives little significance to the will, and his lofty rhetoric. He belongs to the League for the Organization of Progress, which combats

human suffering by the available sound methods, to the end of finally eliminating it altogether; mindful also of the fact that this lofty task can only be accomplished by the aid of sociology the end and aim of which is the perfect state. . . . [The League has drawn up a] comprehensive and scientifically executed programme, . . . embracing all projects for human improvement conceivable at the moment. . . . The League envisions . . . the resolution of the class conflict by means of all the social amelioration which recommend themselves for that purpose, and finally the doing away with national conflicts, the abolition of war through the development of international law.[9]

Overestimating the power of the rational, Settembrini foolishly believes that people will mend their ways once they are enlightened by reason. Thus, he even claims that he cured a sick person merely by looking at him "rationally." Settembrini represents a decaying liberalism.

Pitted against Settembrini is Leo Naphta, a Spanish-trained Jesuit of Jewish-Polish descent, who represents the revolt against reason in Mann's generation. Naphta completely rejects the Italian's liberal-humanist values. Combining Catholic hostility to the modern liberal age with Marxist zeal to redeem society, Naphta, complex and sinister, is worthy of Dostoevsky. An authoritarian, he insists that people do not need freedom, but only authority and discipline imposed by state or church. He is a fanatic, supporting discipline and terror as ways to impose authority. Convinced that the dictatorship of the proletariat is the means of salvation demanded by the age, Naphta embraces Marxism. Borrowing from medieval mysticism, Nietzschean irrationalism, and Marxist militancy, he attacks every facet of the existing liberal order. For him, "the principle of freedom has outlived its usefulness." A person's deepest pleasure, he says, comes not from freedom, but from obedience.

Another character, a wealthy Dutch planter from Java, named Mynheer Peeperkorn, is nonintellectual, illogical, and inarticulate, but he radiates pure vitality and emotional intensity. This charismatic personality dwarfs the humanist Settembrini and the authoritarian Naphta and dominates the patients, who find him irresistible.

The Magic Mountain, which ends with the advent of World War I, raised, but did not resolve, crucial questions. Was the epoch of rational humanist culture drawing to a close? Did bourgeois Europe welcome its spiritual illness in the same way that some of the patients in the sanitorium had a will to illness? How could Europe rescue itself from decadence?

The Lost Generation: Gertrude Stein

The focus of much of the cultural life of the 1920s was the Parisian salon, on the Left Bank (Rive Gauche) of the Seine River, of the American author Gertrude Stein (1874–1946). She initially studied psychology at Johns Hopkins medical school with the philosopher William James, but beginning in 1912, she took up residence with her lifelong companion, Alice B. Toklas (1877–1967). Stein's 1933 autobiography was titled *The Autobiography of Alice B. Toklas,* which made it appear that it was the autobiography of her friend, Alice, instead of being about Stein herself. The enormously popular book describes the types of discussions, advice, and creative inspiration that radiated from their apartment at 27 Rue de Fleurs. The apartment itself became the literary and artistic landmark for avant-garde painters, including Matisse, Cézanne, Braque, and Picasso, who painted Stein's portrait in 1906, and expatriate American authors such as Sherwood Anderson (1876–1941), who wrote *Winesburg, Ohio* (1919), a collection of tales that demonstrated his appreciation of ordinary Americans, F. Scott Fitzgerald (see the following discussion), and Hemingway.

In the early 1920s, Anderson gave Hemingway a letter of introduction to Stein's salon, and during one of his visits with her, Stein described the generation of expatriates in Paris as "***the lost generation.***" For three major reasons, the writers of the lost generation are significant: they capably described the spiritual isolation and alienation of the American expatriates, their criticism of the traditional values of their age gave rise to new literary expression, and their lifestyle of pleasure seeking and impetuousness paved the way for later generations of writers and artists who established themselves as a counterculture entity.

Influenced by Stein's remark, "You are all a lost generation," Hemingway published, *The Sun Also Rises* (1926), the title of which is derived from a passage in the biblical book of Ecclesiastes (1:5), and for the frontispiece, he appropriated Stein's epithet. All of the characters in the novel are based on people that Hemingway knew, and even though he changed their names and created composites of some characters, a number of people did recognize themselves and were irritated with Hemingway for the manner in which he portrayed them. Robert Cohn, a shy Jewish man, takes up boxing and marries the first woman he meets. When she leaves him, he travels to California, meets another woman, and they then embark for Europe, where Robert writes a novel. He also has occasion to meet the journalist Jake Barnes, a veteran of World War I whose unnamed injury has left him impotent. Both men fall in love with Lady Brett Ashley, who is already engaged to Mike Campbell, who busies himself with bouts of drunkenness while he awaits his inheritance to pay off his debts. Although Brett does love Jake, her insatiable desire for sex leads to affairs with Cohn and the bullfighter, Pedro Romero. As the expatriates living in Europe seek to provide meaning in their lives, scenes of excessive drinking, brawling, meaningless sex, and partying abound, but the characters ultimately discover that they are indeed "lost." Thus, Jake's friend tells him:

> "You're an expatriate. One of the worst type. Haven't you heard that? Nobody that ever left their country ever wrote anything worth printing. Not even in the newspaper. . . . You're an expatriate. You've lost touch with the soil. You get precious. Fake European standards have ruined you. You drink yourself to death. You become obsessed by sex. You spend all your time talking, not working. You are an expatriate, see? You hang around cafés."[10]

Like a journalist reporting a story, Hemingway relates what he has to say as simply as possible. His writing is free of stylistic devices—metaphors, similes, image-signs—and he rarely uses adjectives and adverbs to modify his carefully chosen nouns and verbs. Hemingway's direct, clipped, bare, and hard prose style continues to exert an incalculable influence on modern writers. "Hemingway as much as any other man has put the raw language of the street, the poolroom, the barracks and the brothel into modern literature."[11]

The Sun Also Rises brought Hemingway an international reputation as a writer, which was enhanced by some of his later works, particularly *A Farewell to Arms* (see p. 323), *For Whom the Bell Tolls* (1940), and *The Old Man and the Sea* (1952), for which he received the prestigious Pulitzer Prize. In 1954, Hemingway was awarded the Nobel Prize for literature. But in the last years of his life, he produced no major work; these years were marked by physical and mental deterioration and in 1961, he took his own life with a shotgun.

The "Roaring Twenties" in America

By 1914, the United States had become a major industrial power. It entered World War I in 1917 and it played a decisive role in Germany's defeat. Like their European counterparts, Americans were profoundly disillusioned by the brutality of the Great War, a carnage that caused them to view the Victorian social morality of the late nineteenth and early twentieth centuries as pretentious hypocrisy. A wave of materialism, fueled by people consuming and spending at an alarming rate, was initiated by the unprecedented rise in the stock market. Gains in the stock market meant that potentially people from any social class could become rich. However, the "old rich" in America often spurned the "new rich." Enormous sums of money could also be made in bootleg liquor when the Eighteenth Amendment (1919) banned the sale and consumption of alcohol. The law resulted in an underground culture of partying at "speakeasies"—clandestine clubs that sold liquor and avoided the police.

American novelists also tried to put their finger on the pulse of America during this era. They not only sought to understand the glitz, glamour, free spending, and the "new woman" (with her "bobbed" hair and short skirts), but also to give meaning to the wickedness, deceit, and corruption that characterized the age. Through it all, each author recognized that the accepted norms—that had governed everything from the manners and customs of ordinary human interaction to establishing standards for literature, art, and music—were now fading away, and many wondered aloud where America was headed.

WHARTON The novels of Edith Wharton (1862–1937) detail the complicated life of upper-class society, a world that she knew well, because she was born into a prestigious, wealthy family who educated her by European governesses. Through her writing, Wharton exposed the social hypocrisy that had helped to shape the powerful, upper echelons of American society. Many of her characters, such as Lily Bart in *House of Mirth* (1905), *Ethan Frome* (1911), and Undine Spragg of *The Custom of the Country* (1913), are tragic victims of callous social conventions engendered by the conflict between the social-climbing *nouveau riche* (new rich), who had made their fortune in manufacturing and industry, and the "old" elite families, who traced their lineage back to the landed aristocracy of Europe or settlers who acquired huge estates in early America.

In 1921, Wharton was awarded the Pulitzer Prize for *The Age of Innocence* (1920), a historical novel tracing the rapidly changing world of post–Civil War New York society during the 1870s, which Wharton knew as a child, to a time thirty years later.

Wharton's careful descriptions of "old" New York are balanced by her ability to portray conflicted characters who must choose between lust and reason, dreams and duty, and freedom and responsibility. At the same time, she depicts the desire of the "new" generation to simultaneously honor the traditions of their ancestors even while they seek to forge a path of their own in life. Most of all, Wharton allows her readers to choose who is right and wrong in their choices.

LEWIS Although Edith Wharton won the Pulitzer Prize for *The Age of Innocence*, the jury actually voted for Sinclair Lewis' (1885–1951) novel *Main Street*—an exposé about small-town life in Gopher Prairie, Minnesota. According to Wharton's recollection, the Columbia University trustees overturned the decision because they found that his novel had "offended a number of prominent persons in the Middle West,"[12] especially because the Pulitzer was intended to be awarded to the American novel that "best present[s] the wholesome atmosphere of American life and the highest standard of American manners and manhood."[13] But Sinclair Lewis' novel sold 500,000 copies, making him an instant celebrity.

When Sinclair Lewis was eighteen, his father sent him to Yale University, where he met Upton Sinclair (1878–1968) whose novel, *The Jungle* (1906), about the abuses of the Chicago meat-packing industry, caused such a public outcry that the government launched an investigation and Congress passed laws to regulate food processing. During the war years, Lewis wrote five novels, all of them failures. He then decided to attack the myth of the American town of little white cottages with a picket fence surrounding each with his novel *Main Street* (1920); two years later, he dedicated his novel *Babbitt* to Edith Wharton.

George F. Babbitt is a successful businessman who lives in the fictional town of Zenith (patterned after Minneapolis). But at the age of forty-six, Babbitt, a prosperous real estate agent who is dissatisfied with his life, engages in fantasies about a fairy girl who makes him feel like a gallant young man. Moreover, his friend Paul Riesling is equally dissatisfied with his marriage and dreams about becoming a concert violinist. Seeking freedom from their monotonous lives, the two decide to take a getaway vacation to Maine, but subsequently return to their stultifying lives, that is, until Riesling decides to have an affair. Although Babbitt preaches to Riesling about the importance of appearances in society, Riesling, who regards life as miserable, feels no guilt about his affair. When Riesling argues with his wife again, he shoots her, and he is sent to the state penitentiary for three years.

Devastated by the loss of his friend, Babbitt longs for a tangible manifestation of his fairy girl and finds her in the person of the widow, Tanis Judique, with whom he has an illicit affair. As a result, Babbitt's opinions about social conventions change, even to the point of supporting the claims of workers in Zenith who plan a general strike. Although Babbitt's friends and his wife, Myra, try to get him to see the error of his ways, he refuses to conform, and his business begins to go downhill. But when Myra becomes gravely ill, Babbitt once again becomes a devoted husband, thus regaining his friends and his social standing. Finally, acknowledging that he can never break the vicious cycle of his monotonous life, Babbitt encourages his son, Ted, not to conform and to do whatever he wants in life.

In 1927 Lewis wrote *Elmer Gantry*—an exposé of a charlatan preacher in which he attacked hypocritical religious revivalism. A clergyman in New

England urged Lewis be put in prison for defaming the ministry. However, H. L. Mencken (1880–1956), the feisty man of letters, countered such arguments:

> I am no prophet, but it seems to be quite possible that this simple (but far from idle!) tale may accomplish at one stroke what ten billion kilowatt hours of argument and invective have failed to accomplish. It may awaken the Americano to the dangers of the Methodist tyranny, as *Babbitt* awakened him to the imbecility of the Rotary-Kiwanis blather. In six months every Wesleyan spouter in the land may be jeered at as a Gantry, as every gabby tradesman is now sneered at as a Babbitt. The book may turn out a bugle-blast to topple over the evangelical wall, now so high and frowning. It may be the bomb foreordained to blow up the citadel.[14]

In actuality, *Elmer Gantry* was an unparalleled success for Lewis and a bitter pill for his detractors to swallow.

Today, the titles of Lewis' novels—*Main Street, Babbitt,* and *Elmer Gantry*—have become euphemistic expressions as part of ordinary American speech. Main Street stands for stereotypical "middle America," Babbitt represents a figure from middle-class life in rebellion against its values, and Elmer Gantry has come to mean any charlatan who is engaged in bilking honest people out of their hard-earned money.

FITZGERALD The decade of the 1920s is defined as *The Jazz Age,* because of the term coined by the American author Francis Scott Key Fitzgerald (1896–1940), who was named for his ancestor, Francis Scott Key, the composer of "The Star-Spangled Banner." In his most famous novel, *The Great Gatsby* (1925), Fitzgerald worked through a number of issues and themes that paralleled his own life as well as events that elucidated the American scene during the 1920s. The story of Jay Gatsby, the protagonist of the novel, is told exclusively through the eyes of the novel's narrator, Nick Carraway.

Through Gatsby and Nick, Fitzgerald explores his contradictory feelings about the opulence, excess, glitz, and glamour of the Jazz Age, as well as its cynicism and sense of alienation. Both Nick and Fitzgerald come from Minnesota and attend Ivy League colleges, Nick, Yale, and Fitzgerald, Princeton. Both Nick and Fitzgerald relish the power that money brings but both are also aware of the deceitful, moral vacuum in which people, driven by greed and extravagance, exist. Both Gatsby and Fitzgerald have an obsessive love for a woman, whom they believe personifies idealized perfection, and both pay a price for this obsession. Fitzgerald pursues Zelda, a Southern belle, who finally agrees to marry him after he becomes a successful author. She relentlessly pursues an extravagant lifestyle and becomes mentally unbalanced. Gatsby falls in love with the beautiful and beguiling Daisy, who promises him her love, but when Gatsby leaves for World War I, she abandons him for the arrogant socialite, Tom Buchanan. Gatsby subsequently enters into a series of questionable deals (most notably bootlegging and trading in stolen securities) and throws lavish parties with the hope of impressing Daisy and winning her back. Both Gatsby and Fitzgerald suffer tragedies. Gatsby is murdered for something he didn't do; Fitzgerald's mentally ill wife is confined to a sanatorium, where she dies. Fitzgerald himself becomes an alcoholic and suffers a fatal heart attack at age forty-four.

The themes of *The Great Gatsby* are inextricably linked to the symbols in the novel. The theme concerning the conflict between the "old money" and "new money" is symbolized by the geography of Long Island: East Egg symbolizes the deep-rooted old moneyed families and West Egg the ambitious newly rich. The individual's pursuit of the American Dream is symbolized by Gatsby's pursuit of Daisy and by the green light at the end of Daisy's dock.

The emotional and physical wasteland following World War I is exemplified by the Valley of Ashes—a large area between West Egg and New York City that has been set aside for the dumping of industrial ashes. It is managed by George Wilson, who himself was victimized by the moral laxity of his superiors. In the Valley of Ashes there is also a fading billboard featuring the glasses on the face of Dr. T. J. Eckleburg. Although Fitzgerald never makes it explicit, Dr. Eckleburg may symbolize God as judge of America as he looks down from above.

On the beach of Long Island, Nick's melancholic reflections on Gatsby's life summarize the themes of the novel, most particularly Gatsby's pursuit of the American Dream as symbolized by his pursuit of Daisy. Nick likens Gatsby's starstruck wonder in his early years—when he first met Daisy and began to pursue both her and the American Dream—to what the Dutch explorers must have experienced when they first landed in the new world.

> And as I sat there brooding on the old, unknown world, I thought of Gatsby's wonder when he first picked out the green light at the end of Daisy's dock. He had come a long way to this blue lawn, and his dream must have seemed so close that he could hardly fail to grasp it. . . .

Gatsby believed in the green light, the orgiastic future that year by year recedes before us. It eluded us then, but that's no matter—tomorrow we will run faster, stretch out our arms farther. . . . And one fine morning—

So we beat on, boats against the current, borne back ceaselessly into the past.[15]

Continued Modernist Experiments

Poets, novelists, and playwrights continued to experiment with ways to express the intense struggle between the conscious and the unconscious and to explore the aberrations and complexities of human personality and the irrationality of human behavior. Expressionist writers concerned themselves with the inner reality of the mind, with the hidden self that was often revealed in fantasies, dreams, and hallucinations. They portrayed frenzied and irrational behavior that gave expression to intense, subjective feelings. To dramatize this behavior, dramatists and novelists punctuated dialogue with nervous and explosive outbursts. Deliberately reacting against Realism and Naturalism, which aspired to an accurate and objective depiction of external reality and human behavior, Expressionist writers deliberately distorted shapes and movements.

During the early decades of the twentieth century, writers continued to use symbolism drawn from personal experience, history, and classical antiquity; stream-of-consciousness style was also still popular, as is evident in William Faulkner's novel, *The Sound and the Fury* (1929), which relates the struggle of the "Old" South against the emerging "New" South. T. S. Eliot, along with Ezra Pound (1885–1972), is credited with starting a "poetic revolution" that transformed the rhyme, diction, and verse of traditional poetic norms. William Butler Yeats, along with Eliot, struggled to find appropriate metaphors for the fear, anxiety, disillusionment, despair, and spiritual desolation of "the lost generation."

ELIOT   The American-English playwright, literary critic, and acknowledged leader of Modernist poetry was T. S. (Thomas Stearns) Eliot (1888–1965). The poetic revolution began in 1917 when Eliot published his *The Love Song of J. Alfred Prufrock,* which recounts the ruminations of Prufrock, who, like Sinclair Lewis' Babbitt, is a middle-aged man who believes that both youth and happiness have passed him by.

But though I have wept and fasted, wept and prayed,
Though I have seen my head (grown slightly bald) brought in upon a platter,

I am no prophet—and here's no great matter;
I have seen the moment of my greatness flicker,
And I have seen the eternal Footman hold my coat, and snicker,
And in short, I was afraid.[16]

Moreover, in expressing the bleakness of Prufrock's life, Eliot made use of symbols drawn from ordinary life, such as, "I have measured out my life with coffee spoons."[17]

In expressing the alienation they experienced as a result of the Great War, industrialization, and urban society, Eliot and Pound often chose metaphors and symbols that were deeply rooted in the history and literature of the Western tradition, from antiquity through the Middle Ages and the Renaissance. A critical feature of their work, however, is that they consistently make reference to obscure figures and passages with which few people are familiar. This is particularly evident in Eliot's most famous poem, *The Waste Land* (1922), which is often unintelligible even to the most sophisticated reader. The five parts of the 433-line poem, which is dedicated to Pound, who edited it, are essentially poetic vignettes. Eliot acknowledged that much of the symbolism of the poem was suggested by the medieval quest for the Holy Grail (the cup Jesus reputedly used during his Last Supper with his disciples). Many literary critics regard the poem as the poetic equivalent to James Joyce's *Ulysses* (see Chapter 23) in defining Modernism. Similarly, they are equally divided about what the poem really means. Some view it as a poem about the death of Europe. Others consider it to be a manifesto of "imagism"—lacking in order and rationality, pointing to evidence of Eliot's emotional distress and unhappy marriage. Still others view Eliot as the new Homer, who takes his readers into the depths of Hades. Whatever Eliot's meaning, *The Waste Land* captured the imagination of his generation, for he gave voice to the suffering of many lost souls.

Expressing the anxiety, despair, and disillusionment of the generation following World War I, Eliot depicts a barren world of conspicuous lust and neurotic fears as humanity waits for some kind of "second coming" (as Yeats described it) to redeem it. He also gave expression to a feeling of foreboding. In his image of a collapsing European civilization, Eliot creates a macabre scenario. Hooded hordes, modern-day barbarians, swarm over plains and lay waste to cities. Jerusalem, Athens, Alexandria, Vienna, and London—each once a great spiritual or cultural center—are now collapsing. In the secular city of spiritual desolation, people search for a moral absolute to fill their empty lives.

MOHANDAS K. GANDHI AND PASSIVE RESISTANCE

MOHANDAS GANDHI (1869–1948) WAS THE KEY FIGURE in the drive to secure the independence of India from Great Britain. Determined to practice passive resistance in the struggle for liberation from British rule, he rose to be an outstanding political leader, widely worshiped as *Mahatma,* a model of high-mindedness and spiritual power. Several times, when the British jailed him, Gandhi fasted until he was almost dead. After his death, his message of passive resistance remained a hopeful vision and later inspired the American civil rights leader Martin Luther King Jr.'s nonviolent protests in the United States. In the following selection below, Gandhi describes the essence of passive resistance.

Passive resistance is a method of securing rights by personal suffering; it is the reverse of resistance by arms. When I refuse to do a thing that is repugnant to my conscience, I use soul-force. For instance, the Government of the day has passed a law which is applicable to me. I do not like it. If by using violence I force the Government to repeal the law, I am employing what may be termed body-force. If I do not obey the law and accept the penalty for its breach, I use soul-force. It involves sacrifice of self. . . .

No man can claim that he is absolutely in the right or that a particular thing is wrong because he thinks so, but it is wrong for him so long as that is his deliberate judgement. It is therefore meet that he should not do that which he knows to be wrong, and suffer the consequence whatever it may be. This is the key to the use of soul-force. . . .

To use brute-force . . . is contrary to passive resistance, for it means that we want our opponent to do by force that which we desire but he does not. And if such a use of force is justifiable, surely he is entitled to do likewise by us. . . . Those who believe that they are not bound to obey laws which are repugnant to their conscience have only the remedy of passive resistance open to them. Any other must lead to disaster. . . .

What do you think? Wherein is courage required—in blowing others to pieces from behind a cannon, or with a smiling face to approach a cannon and be blown to pieces? . . . Believe me that a man devoid of courage and manhood can never be a passive resister.

This however, I will admit: that even a man weak in body is capable of suffering this resistance. One man can offer it just as well as millions. Both men and women can indulge in it. It does not require that training of an army; it needs no jiu-jitsu. Control over the mind is alone necessary, and when that is attained, man is free like the king of the forest and his very glance withers the enemy.

Source: Mohandas K. Gandhi, "Passive Resistance," from Hind Swaraj, or Indian Home Rule *(Ahmedabad: Navajivan Pub. House, 1939), pp. 79–82.*

What are the roots that clutch, what branches
  grow
Out of this stony rubbish? Son of man,
You cannot say, or guess, for you know only
A heap of broken images, where the sun beats,

And the dead tree gives no shelter, the cricket no
  relief,
And the dry stone no sound of water.[18]

YEATS One of the most important poets of the twentieth century was the Anglo-Irish dramatist and writer of prose, William Butler Yeats (1865–1939). After World War I he captured the essence of a world falling apart, without a "center" to hold its values in place, in his poem *The Second Coming* (1921):

Turning and turning in the widening gyre [cycle]
The falcon cannot hear the falconer;
Things fall apart; the centre cannot hold
Mere anarchy is loosed upon the world,
The blood-dimmed tide is loosed, and
  everywhere
The ceremony of innocence is drowned;
The best lack all conviction, while the worst
Are full of passionate intensity.[19]

Yeats was known to have described the poem as a subconscious prophecy regarding the rise of fascism (see Chapter 25) to fill the moral vacuum of the postwar generation.

FAULKNER One of the greatest American novelists and short story writers was William Faulkner (1897–1962), whose novel cycle about the fictional Yoknapatawpha County, in Mississippi, earned him the Nobel Prize for literature in 1949. Faulkner was born in New Albany, Mississippi, and was raised in Oxford, Mississippi, by a black woman named Caroline Barr, for whom he had a great deal of respect and admiration. In a letter, written in 1940 to the Methodist Bishop Robert Jones, Faulkner recalled that Aunt Callie (as he called her) encouraged him to tell the truth, to avoid wastefulness, and to be considerate of others, especially the weak and the elderly. He immortalized Aunt Callie as Dilsey Gibson in *The Sound and the Fury* and as Mollie Beauchamp in *Go Down, Moses*. Faulkner thus became a beleaguered spokesperson for the white liberal position with regard to the issue of race in the South.

In slightly over one decade (from 1929 to 1942), Faulkner achieved greatness as an author, in spite of never having graduated from either high school or college and growing up in one of the poorest states in the nation during the Great Depression. Following his first novels, *Soldier's Pay* (1926) and *Mosquitoes* (1927), Faulkner experienced an epiphany that transformed his writing.

> With *Soldier's Pay* and *Mosquitoes* I wrote for the sake of writing because it was fun. Beginning with *Sartoris* I discovered that my own little postage stamp of native soil was worth writing about and that I would never live long enough to exhaust it, and by sublimating the actual into apocryphal I would have complete liberty to use whatever talent I might have to its absolute top. . . . I like to think of the world I created as being a kind of keystone in the Universe; that, as small as that keystone is, if it were ever taken away, the universe itself would collapse.[20]

In *Sartoris,* for the first time, Faulkner introduces the reader to the fictional town of Jefferson and to the Snopes and Sartoris families, who figure so prominently in his Yoknapatawpha cycle of novels.

One of the most antagonistic families in all of Faulkner's fiction is the Snopes family, led by its patriarch Ab Snopes, a former horse thief and barn-burning sharecropper. The family represents an affront to the ideals and values embraced by members of the aristocracy of the "Old South," including the Sartorises. In the years following the Civil War, as plantation owners' wealth and prestige declined, that of the socially mobile Snopeses ascended. This upward social mobility is best exemplified by Ab's son, Flem Snopes, whose progress from sharecropper, to townsman, to mansion owner is captured in Faulkner's "Snopes trilogy" novels—*The Hamlet* (1931), *The Town* (1957), and *The Mansion* (1959)—which also include the Sartoris family.

Faulkner considered *The Sound and the Fury* to be the best novel he ever wrote, and many critics continue to agree. By focusing on the promiscuous behavior of Candace "Caddy" Compson, the novel traces the demise of the Compson family, once the most prominent family in Jackson, Mississippi. Faulkner, using stream-of-consciousness technique, tells Caddy's story through the eyes of her three brothers: Benjamin, Quentin, and Jason. To help the reader follow the shifting time sequences, Faulkner once considered having the publisher use different colors of ink to indicate a change in time, but he abandoned the idea, because it was too expensive. Instead, to indicate a shift in time, he put much of Benjy's section of the narrative in italics. But Benjy's narrative is still, by far, the most challenging, because Benjy is mentally retarded and unable to care for himself properly. As his thought processes skip backward and forward in time, Benjy relives events of the past, even while living in the present. Therefore, Faulkner is actually conducting an experiment in stream-of-consciousness technique. He also makes considerable use of symbolism. For example, Quentin regards Caddy's sexual behavior as a symbol of the dissolution of the "Old South" with its emphasis on honor, duty, and loyalty, a realization that causes him to commit suicide.

The character of Benjy also gave rise to the title of the novel, which Faulkner borrowed from Shakespeare's tragedy, *Macbeth,* to describe the meaninglessness of human existence:

> To-morrow, and to-morrow, and to-morrow
> Creeps in this petty pace from day to day
> To the last syllable of recorded time;
> And all our yesterdays have lighted fools
> The way to dusty Death. Out, out, brief candle!
> Life's but a walking shadow, a poor player
> That struts and frets his hour upon the stage
> And then is heard no more. It is a tale
> Told by an idiot, full of sound and fury,
> Signifying nothing.[21]
> (*Macbeth* Act V, Scene v, lines 19–28)

O'NEILL   Although Expressionism as a movement died out by the mid-1920s, its techniques, assimilated by playwrights, became a permanent part of drama. Social questions were another concern of dramatists in the period between the two world wars. Liberal and Marxist playwrights focused on the plight of the poor and the misbehavior of capitalists. Among the leading playwrights of this generation was Eugene O'Neill.

Eugene Gladstone O'Neill (1888–1953), considered by many to be America's finest dramatist, grew up in a troubled household; the love-hate that consumed relationships among his father, a prominent actor, his morphine-addicted mother, his alcoholic brother, and himself were dramatized in his plays, particularly in the autobiographical *Long Day's Journey into Night,* published posthumously in 1956.

After being expelled for misbehavior from Princeton at the end of his freshman year, O'Neill worked at various jobs, including a gold prospector in Honduras, a seaman, and a reporter before he decided to become a playwright. O'Neill established himself in the 1920s as a major dramatist with more than a dozen plays, including *The Emperor Jones* (1920), *The Hairy Ape* (1922), and *Strange Interlude* (1928).

The Emperor Jones, which depicts a man coming apart emotionally, is an experiment in depth psychology. It shows how easily our rational faculties break down, and at such times, the unconscious, a storehouse of primitive feelings shared collectively by all human beings, takes control of us. Influenced by Expressionism, O'Neill sought to penetrate the mind's deepest recesses.

Brutus Jones, an American black man and former Pullman porter, has in two years climbed from stowaway to emperor of an island in the West Indies. Self-confident and intelligent, he is able to dominate the islanders: "I cracks de whip and dey jumps through."[22] He tells his credulous subjects that because of his strength only a silver bullet could kill him. He had a silver bullet molded, he tells them, "I'm de on'y man in de world big enuff to git me. No use'n deir tryin'. And dey falls down and bumps deir heads. [He laughs] I does dat so's I kin take a walk in peace widout no jealous nigger gunnin' at me from behind de trees."[23] But he has stored stolen money in foreign banks just in case. "I ain't no fool. I know dis Emperor's time is sho't . . . [W]hen I see dese niggers gittin' up deir nerve to tu'n me out, and I'se got all de money in sight, I resign on de spot and beats it quick."[24] Thus, when his guards and servants desert him, he flees into the forest filled with confidence. He asks contemptuously: "Think dese ign'rent bush niggers dat ain't got brains enuff to know deir own names even can catch Brutus Jones?"[25]

In the dark woods, however, Jones loses his way and is unable to locate the supplies he had hidden in preparation for flight. Soon he is gripped by terror, which is intensified by the rhythmic thumping of tom-toms beaten by his pursuers; hunted down by assassins in this eerie setting, the once-powerful emperor loses his mind. He hallucinates successively about shapeless creatures with "glittering little eyes"; a Pullman porter he had once murdered over a dice game; a prison guard whom he had killed while toiling on a chain gang in the South; a slave market where the auctioneer sells him to a planter. A disoriented Jones takes a shot. Now only his silver bullet remains, and the constantly pulsating tom-tom beats grow louder and quicker.

Resting in a clearing, the exhausted and terrified Jones continues to hallucinate. Descending further back into his unconscious, he now sees himself aboard a slave transport huddled with other shackled blacks wearing only loincloths and wailing in despair to the rhythm of the tom-toms in the distance. In his final hallucination, Jones evokes a distant primitive past. He is at the edge of a river, by the foot of a gigantic tree next to which is an altar make of boulders. Jones seems to remember this place from his African past. A witch doctor, painted red, springs from behind the tree. His dancing and incantations before Jones, who is "paralyzed with awed fascination by this new apparition,"[26] tell a story with a message: the forces of evil demand a human sacrifice. Stretching out his arms by the river, the witch doctor calls to a god in the waters, and a huge crocodile starts to move toward Jones, the sacrificial victim, who begs God to save him. As if his prayer has been answered, Jones remembers the remaining silver bullet and shoots the crocodile.

At dawn the trackers find Jones and kill him with recently molded silver bullets forged from coins, for as their leader says: "My mens dey got um silver bullets. . . . Lead bullet no kill him. He got um strong charm."[27]

The Hairy Ape deals with alienation, a crucial concern in modern urban and industrial society. Yank, the principal character, toils as a stoker fueling the furnaces in the bowels of a transatlantic liner. The stokers are all hard-drinking, hairy-chested, long-armed, powerful men. All of them fear and respect Yank for his superior strength. A passenger on the ship, Mildred, a wealthy and attractive young woman of twenty, who had done social work in the slums of the East Side of New York, visits the stokerhole "anxious . . . [to] investigate how the other half lives and works on ships."[28] Accompanied by two engineers, Mildred, wearing a white dress, enters the blazing hot stokerhole, where the men, stripped to the waist, rhythmically shovel coal into the fiery furnace. She hears an annoyed Yank loudly cursing someone blowing a shrill whistle. When Yank turns and glares into her eyes, she is paralyzed by his *"abysmal brutality, naked and shameless,"* and covers her eyes *"to shut out the sight of his face."* "Take me away! Oh, the filthy beast,"[29] she whimpers and then faints. The engineers carry her out. When the iron door clangs shut, an enraged Yank hurls his shovel at it. He cannot stop thinking about it. "Hairy ape. . . . Dat's de way she looked at me. . . . Hairy ape! So dat's me, huh?"[30]

Three weeks later Yank, still seething from the insult, is walking on swanky Fifth Avenue in Manhattan. Seeing well-dressed parishioners exiting from church, he makes crude passes at a lady, who stalks by without looking at him. He insults others who also choose not to acknowledge him. "Look at me, why don't you dare?" he cries. He directs his rage at the men, bumping them viciously, but in a distortion of objective reality, it is he, not those whom he had so strongly jarred, who recoils from the collisions. (This departure from reality is another example of Expressionism in O'Neill's early dramas.) All of them ignore Yank's appeal to fight; without seeming to notice him, they all answer with affected politeness: "I beg your pardon."

The upper classes view Yank as a primitive man-beast and totally ignore him. Even a labor union, which fights for workers like Yank, rejects him. When Yank wants to blow up the steel works owned by Mildred's father, the union official regards him as a "dirty spy, a rotten agent provo-cator" and tells him to "go back and tell whatever skunk is paying you blood-money for betraying your brothers that he's wasting his coin. And tell him that all he'll ever get on us, or ever has got, is just his own sneaking plots that he's framed up to put us in jail." Several husky men kick and throw Yank sprawling into the middle of the cobbled street. Sitting like Rodin's sculpture "The Thinker," a brooding Yank mutters bitterly: "so dem boids don't tink I belong, neider."[31]

The next day Yank visits the zoo and sees a gorilla squatting on his haunches in much the same position as the "The Thinker." Identifying with the gorilla, Yank takes a jimmy from under his coat, forces the lock, and addresses the beast: "Step out and shake hands! I'll take yuh for a walk doen Fif' Avenoo. We'll knock'em offen de oith and croak wit de band playing. Come on brother."[32] The gorilla crushes Yank in a death hug. "He got me, aw right. I'm trou. Even him didn't think I belonged. *[Then with sudden passionate despair]* Christ, where do I get off at? Where do I fit in?"[33]

In *The Emperor Jones, The Hairy Ape,* and other early plays, O'Neill employed Expressionist techniques, which were very much in vogue. In *Strange Interlude,* a nine-act play that takes almost six hours to perform, O'Neill, like Joyce, experimented with internal monologues, in which Nora, the leading character, in addition to her conventional speeches, reflects introspectively. At times revealing her deepest unconscious thoughts, Nora's asides are heard by the audience, but not the other characters who share the stage with her.

The Harlem Renaissance

During and immediately after World War I, in the so-called **Great Migration,** some 450,000 blacks moved from the rural South to northern cities to work in factories. Many of these blacks were share-croppers eager to escape the vicious cycle of poverty, landlessness, and debt to unscrupulous landowners; or they were fleeing southern racism, which subjected them to humiliation and violence. But the North was no "Promised Land," as some northern black newspapers touted it, for blacks were segregated into ghettos and were victims of white bigotry. In 1919, race riots broke out in 36 cities, the worst being Chicago, where a riot lasted for three weeks and 38 people died. Nevertheless, the Great Migration was a benefit to blacks. A new urbanized middle class emerged, and blacks became more organized in their struggle to end racial injustice and more determined to take their rightful place as Americans of African descent.

Migration to northern urban centers also stimulated intellectual and artistic pursuit among blacks. Nowhere was this more evident than in the Harlem district of New York City, which witnessed a cultural explosion.

Popular histories of the **Harlem Renaissance** conveniently tend to choose the year 1920 to mark the beginning of the period. Others point to March 1924, when a formal dinner was held at New York's Civic Club to celebrate the publication of Jessie Fauset's *There Is Confusion*, the first novel published by the movement. Whenever it may have begun, the Harlem Renaissance is generally recognized for the prose and poetry of African American writers, but it also included a number of artists and jazz musicians. For example, *the Cotton Club* in Harlem, which opened in the fall of 1923, brought international attention to America's jazz music, and it became the home to accomplished musicians, including Duke Ellington (see later discussion). Moreover, African American art was finally being taken seriously, and for the first time ever, the artists themselves were speaking out loud about what it was like to be an African American living in the United States. But with the advent of the **Great Depression,** in the early 1930s, the Harlem Renaissance virtually ended.

Many of the African American writers of the Harlem Renaissance acknowledged their indebtedness to (William Edward Burghardt) W. E. B. DuBois (1868–1963), who wrote *The Souls of Black Folk* (1903), which enabled Negroes, as he called them, to see that America belonged as much to them as it did to white people. In the opening essay of the volume, DuBois spoke of the "twoness" of the American Negro:

> After the Egyptian and Indian, the Greek and Roman, the Teuton and Mongolian, the Negro is a sort of seventh son, born with a veil, and gifted with second-sight in this American world,—a world which yields him no true self-consciousness, but only lets him see himself through the revelation of the other world. It is a peculiar sensation, this double-consciousness, this sense of always looking at one's self through the eye of others, of measuring one's soul by the tape of a world that looks on in amused contempt and pity. One ever feels his twoness,—an American, a Negro; two souls, two thoughts, two unreconciled strivings; two warring ideals in one dark body, whose dogged strength alone keeps it from being torn asunder.[34]

The book thrust DuBois into a position of leadership that often found him engaged in a lonely quest. Disenchanted with race relations in America, DuBois spent his final years in self-imposed exile in Ghana, where he died at the age of ninety-five.

One of the most original talents of the Harlem Renaissance was Jean Toomer (1894–1967), whose book *Cane* (1923)—an anthology of sketches, short stories, and poetry—was highly acclaimed by his contemporaries but found little acceptance by publishers or the reading public. Some of his most innovative and poignant pieces deal with his experiences in Georgia while he was the principal of a school. In one of them, Toomer speaks of the intensely beautiful young girl, Karintha, who becomes a prostitute, gets pregnant, and is forced, too soon, into becoming a woman who must support her young child: "Karintha is a woman. Men do not know that the soul of her was a growing thing ripened too soon. They will bring their money; they will die not having found it out . . . Karintha at twenty, carrying beauty, perfect as dusk when the sun goes down. Karintha."[35]

One of the major forces in the development of African American culture and literature was the scholar, critic, author, and philosopher Alain Locke (1886–1954), whose publication *The New Negro* (1925) signaled the end of the "Old Negro," whom he characterized as "more a myth than a man."

> His has been a stock figure perpetuated as an historical fiction partly in innocent sentimentalism, partly in deliberate reactionism. . . . So for generations in the mind of America, the Negro has been more of a formula than a human being—a something to be argued about, condemned or defended, to be "kept down," or "in his place," or "helped up," to be worried with or worried over, harassed or patronized, a social bogey or a social burden.[36]

Locke describes the "New Negro" as full of "self-respect and self-dependence," and he points to the significance of Harlem as helping him achieve both.

> Here in Manhattan is not merely the largest Negro community in the world, but the first concentration in history of so many diverse elements of Negro life. It has attracted the African, the West Indian, the Negro American; has brought together the Negro of the North and the Negro of the South; the man from the city and the man from the town and village; the peasant, the student, the business man, the professional man, artist, poet, musician, adventurer and worker, preacher and criminal, exploiter and social outcast. Each group has come with its own separate motives and for its own special ends, but their greatest experience has been the finding of one another. . . . So what began in terms of segregation becomes more and more, as the elements mix and react, the laboratory of a

great race-welding. . . . In Harlem, Negro life is seizing upon its first chances for group expression and self-determination.[37]

The poets of the Harlem Renaissance, including James Weldon Johnson, Claude McKay, Arna Bontemps, Countee Cullen, and Langston Hughes, were masters at melding the African American experience with poetic language to foster a greater understanding of what it meant to be black in white America. James Weldon Johnson (1871–1938) was an essayist, songwriter, and pioneer in the fledgling civil rights movement as well as being a poet. In 1927, he published a volume of poetry called *God's Trombones,* which contained a vivid poetical account of the Genesis story of creation from an African American perspective, entitled "The Creation: A Negro Sermon":

And God stepped out on space,
And He looked around and said,
"I'm lonely—
I'll make me a world."
And far as the eye of God could see
Darkness covered everything,
Blacker than a hundred midnights
Down in a cypress swamp.

Then God smiled,
And the light broke,
And the darkness rolled up on one side,
And the light stood shining on the other,
And God said, *"That's good!"*[38]

And after God made "the sun a-blazing in the heavens," the moon and the stars, the valleys and mountains, "the seven seas," the "fishes and fowls" and "beast and birds," he walked around and declared: "I'm lonely still." Johnson then recounts how God decided to make man.[39]

Up from the bed of the river
God scooped the clay;
And by the bank of the river
He kneeled Him down;
And there the great God Almighty,
Who lit the sun and fixed it in the sky,
Who flung the stars to the most far corner of the
    night,
Who rounded the earth in the middle of His
    hand—
This Great God,
Like a mammy bending over her baby,
Kneeled down in the dust
Toiling over a lump of clay
Till He shaped it in His own image

Then into it He blew the breath of life,
And man became a living soul.
Amen. Amen.[40]

One of the more radical writers of the Harlem Renaissance was the Jamaican-born poet-novelist Claude McKay (1891–1948), who came to America in 1912 and whose volume of poetry, *Harlem Shadows* (1922), is often viewed as the beginning of the Harlem Renaissance. In 1953, *Selected Poems of Claude McKay* was published posthumously, and it contained the poem "America," about his bittersweet love for his adopted nation.

Although she feeds me bread of bitterness
And sinks into my throat her tiger's tooth,
Stealing my breath of life, I will confess
I love this cultured hell that tests my youth!
Her vigor flows like tides into my blood,
Giving me strength erect against her hate.
Her bigness sweeps my being like a flood.
Yet as a rebel fronts a king in state,
I stand within her walls with not a shred
Of terror, malice, not a word of jeer.
Darkly I gaze into the days ahead,
And see her might and granite wonders there,
Beneath the touch of Time's unerring hand,
Like priceless treasures sinking in the sand.[41]

One of the key figures in the dissemination of African American literature, particularly to children, was Arna Bontemps (1902–1973). In an early poem from the 1920s, "A Black Man Talks of Reaping," he reflected a vexation akin to that of McKay.

I have sown beside all waters in my day.
I planted deep, within my heart the fear
    that wind or fowl would take the grain away.
I planted safe against this stark, lean year.

I scattered seed enough to plant the land in rows
    from Canada to Mexico
    but for my reaping only what the hand
    can hold at once is all that I can show.

Yet what I sowed and what the orchard yields
    my brother's sons are gathering stalk and root;
    small wonder then my children glean in fields
    they have not sown, and feed on bitter fruit.[42]

Perhaps the most classical poet of the Harlem Renaissance was Countee Cullen (1903–1946), who acknowledged that he patterned much of his poetic style after that of John Keats (see Chapter 20). A Phi Beta Kappa as an undergraduate at New York University, Cullen went on to receive his master's degree from Harvard University. Following graduation from Harvard, he became an editor for *Opportunity,* which championed the works of African American writers. Between 1934 and 1945, Cullen taught in Harlem, where he collaborated on a play, *St. Louis Woman,* with his friend Arna Bontemps, whose novel, *God Sends Sunday,* inspired their play. In his poem, "Yet Do I Marvel," written early in Bontemps' career but not published until 1947 in a volume of poetry entitled *On These I Stand,* he references classical mythology to talk about the tortuous life of an African American poet.

> I doubt not God is good, well-meaning, kind.
> And did He stoop to quibble could tell why
> The little buried mole continues blind,
> Why flesh that mirrors Him must some day die,
> Make plain the reason tortured Tantalus
> Is baited by the fickle fruit, declare
> If merely brute caprice doom Sisyphus
> To struggle up a never-ending stair.
> Inscrutable His ways are, and immune to
>   catechism by a mind too strewn
> With petty cares to slightly understand
> What awful brain compels His awful hand.
> Yet do I marvel at this curious thing:
> To make a poet black, and bid him sing![43]

Langston Hughes (1902–1967) incorporated blues forms, the language of the street, and jazz rhythms into his poetry. In the poem "Harlem," included in *Montage of a Dream Deferred* (1951), he gave the American public a lasting and prophetic image of the mood of blacks.

> What happens to a dream deferred?
>
> Does it dry up
> like a raisin in the sun?
>
> Or fester like a sore—
> And then run?
> Does it stink like rotten meat?
> Or crust and sugar over—
> Like syrupy sweet?
>
> Maybe it just sags
> like a heavy load.
>
> *Or does it explode?*[44]

In these few lines, Hughes captured the underlying resentment, fear, alienation, and even hatred that eventually spilled over into violence, as the American Civil Rights Movement took hold during the 1960s.

In 1958, the poem appeared as the introduction to the award-winning play *A Raisin in the Sun,* by Lorraine Hansberry (1930–1965), the first African American woman to have a play produced on Broadway. The drama traces the trials and tribulations of an African American family, but it found a universal appeal because of Hansberry's ability to penetrate the psyche of all human beings who laugh, cry, and feel compassion for one another.

ART

The new directions taken in art before World War I—Abstractionism and Expressionism—continued in the postwar decades, and during this time, artists such as Picasso, Kandinsky, Matisse, and Braque continued to refine their styles. But new art trends also emerged that mirrored the trauma of a generation who, because of "The Great War," had lost their faith in Europe's moral and intellectual values. Many artists, like literary figures, regarded the Enlightenment belief in human goodness, reason, and the progress of humanity as expressions of naive optimism.

Postwar Disillusionment

Because of their dehumanizing experiences during the Great War, many German artists expressed the disillusionment of their generation with modern civilization. Otto Dix (1891–1969), who was wounded several times during the war, fought in the German army on the Western Front and witnessed the barbarity of trench warfare. In addition to his many paintings, Dix produced a book of etchings of maimed, dying, and dead soldiers, *The War* (1924), which was a powerful, visual indictment of World War I's cruelty and suffering. Another veteran of World War I was Max Beckmann (1884–1950), whose service as a medical corpsman in the German army made him acutely aware of violence and brutality. Before the war, Beckmann was greatly influenced by Impressionism, but his exposure to dead and maimed soldiers occasioned a totally different artistic style after the war. *The Night* (Figure 24.1) is an alarming scene, which, with its distressing colors and long brush strokes, depicts human beings engaging in mindless depravity and cruelty. Through his paintings, Beckmann gave expression to the disillusionment and spiritual unease that afflicted postwar Germany.

Other German artists who expressed their revulsion against violence and war and the civilization that spawned it were George Grosz (1893–1959) and Käthe Kollwitz (1867–1945). And in 1915, even before the end of the war, artists and writers in Zurich founded a movement called Dada, which expressed revulsion against the war and the European civilization that produced it.

Dada: Duchamp

Spreading from neutral Switzerland to Germany, Paris, and New York, Dada shared in the postwar mood of disorientation and despair. *Dadaists* viewed artistic and literary standards with contempt and rejected both God and reason. They

Figure 24.1   Max Beckmann, *The Night,* **1918–1919, 52 3/8" x 60 1/4" (1.33 x 1.53 m), oil on canvas, Kunstsammlung Nordrhein-Westfalen, Düsseldorf.** This alarming scene, with its distressing colors and long brush strokes, depicts human beings engaging in mindless depravity and cruelty. Through his paintings, Beckmann gave expression to the disillusionment and spiritual unease that afflicted postwar Germany. *(Kunstsammlung Nordrhein-Westfalen, Düsseldorf; Walter Klein, Düsseldorf, photographer © 2002 Artists Rights Society (ARS), New York-VG Bild-Kunst, Bonn)*

celebrated nihilism for its own sake. "Through reason man becomes a tragic and ugly figure," said one Dadaist; "beauty is dead," said another. Dadaists regarded life as essentially absurd (Dada is a nonsense term) and cultivated indifference. "The acts of life have no beginning or end. Everything happens in a completely idiotic way," declared the poet Tristan Tzara, one of Dada's founders and its chief spokesman. Tzara elevated spontaneity above reason:

> What good did the theories of the philosophers do us? Did they help us to take a single step forward or backward? . . . We have had enough of the intelligent movements that have stretched beyond measure our credulity in the benefits of science. What we want now is spontaneity because everything that issues freely from ourselves, without the intervention of speculative ideas . . . represents us.[45]

For Dadaists, the world was nonsensical, and reality disordered; hence, they offered no solutions to anything. "Like everything in life, Dada is useless," said Tzara.[46]

Dadaists showed their contempt for art (one art historian calls Dada "the first anti-art movement on record"[47]) by deliberately producing works that seemed devoid of artistic value. In New York, Marcel Duchamp (1887–1968) invented the readymade—an ordinary mass-produced object, removed from its original function and given artistic significance by the artist, such as *Fountain*

(Figure 24.2), a urinal turned on its back. It was considered a work of art simply because, in 1917, Duchamp chose to submit it to the unjuried exhibition of the American Society of Independent Artists in New York, signed with the pseudonym "R. Mutt." Despite the fact that the exhibition was held to allow all artists who paid an entry fee of six dollars to display their work, the members of the society rejected Duchamp's *Fountain*. That same year, Duchamp "improved" a reproduction of Leonardo da Vinci's *Mona Lisa* (see Chapter 13) by providing her with a moustache and a goatee. Despite the Dadaists' nihilistic aims and "calculated irrationality," says art historian H. W. Janson, "there was also liberation, a voyage into unknown provinces of the creative mind."[48]

Surrealism: Ernst, Miró, and Dali

As a formal movement, Dada ended in 1924 and was succeeded by *Surrealism.* From Dada, Surrealists inherited a contempt for reason, but they also stressed fantasy and made use of Freudian insights and symbols in their art as they sought to reproduce the raw state of the unconscious and to arrive at truths beyond reason's grasp. To penetrate the interior of the mind, said André Breton, a French Surrealist poet, the writer should "write quickly without any previously chosen subject, quickly enough not to dwell on and not to be tempted to read over what you have written."[49] Writing should not be dictated by the intellect but should flow automatically from the unconscious. Surrealists tried to portray the world of fantasy and hallucination, the marvelous and the spontaneous. Breton urged artists to live their dreams, even if it meant seeing "a horse galloping on a tomato." In the effort to break through the constraints of rationality so that they might reach a higher reality, that is, a "surreality," leading Surrealists produced works of undeniable artistic merit.

Max Ernst (1891–1976), who was deeply influenced by Freudian psychology, studied philosophy, psychiatry, and art history at the University of Bonn from 1909 to 1914. Although he served in the German army during World War I, Ernst was able to participate in the first Dada event in Zurich in 1915. After the war, he helped found Dadaism in Cologne, and in 1922 Ernst moved to Paris and joined Breton's Surrealist group. There he developed a procedure that he called *frottage* (from *frotter*, to rub) in which he laid a sheet of paper over a textured surface, such as wood or stone, and then rubbed the paper with a soft pencil, creating images that he could then alter in a painting. Ernst later devised a method whereby he spread paint on two canvases and then, before the paint was dry, pressed the two canvases together. When the canvases were separated, the random images (like the frottage images) became the raw material for some of his most terrifying paintings. Perhaps the most forceful example is *Europe after the Rain* (Figure 24.3), executed between 1940 and 1942, which Ernst began while he was hiding from the Germans during the occupation of Paris. It depicts a silent, desolated landscape with two lonely figures surveying the devastation of Europe.

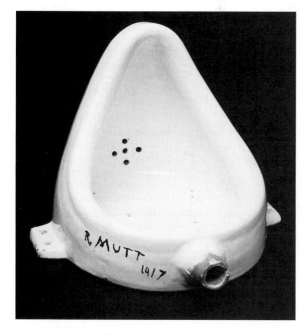

Figure 24.2 Marcel Duchamp (American, b. France, 1887–1968), *Fountain* **(Second Version), 1950. Readymade: glazed sanitary china with black paint, h: 12″; w: 15″; d: 18″ (acc. #1998-74-1).** This is an example of a Duchamp readymade, created by taking an ordinary mass-produced object—such as this urinal turned on its back—removing it from its original function, and giving it artistic significance by exhibiting it in an art gallery. *(Philadelphia Museum of Art: Gift (by exchange) of Mrs. Herbert Cameron Morris. Photo: Graydon Wood, 1998. © 2002 Artists Rights Society (ARS), New York/ADAGP, Paris/Estate of Marcel Duchamp)*

Figure 24.3 Max Ernst, *Europe after the Rain,* **1940–1942, 21 5/8″ x 51 1/4″ (54.9 x 148 cm), oil on canvas, Wadsworth Atheneum, Hartford, Connecticut, The Ellen Gallup Sumner and Mary Catlin Sumner Collection.** This painting portrays a silent, desolated landscape with two lonely figures surveying the devastation of Europe during World War II. *(Wadsworth Atheneum, Hartford, Connecticut, The Ellen Gallup Sumner and Mary Catlin Sumner Collection)*

Figure 24.4 Joan Miró, *Harlequin's Carnival*, 1924–1925, 26" x 36 5/8" (66 x 93 cm), oil on canvas, Albright-Knox Art Gallery, Buffalo, New York, Room of Contemporary Art Fund. This dreamlike, whimsical painting—with its distorted animal figures, twisted shapes, cubes, and geometrical forms—is characteristic of the many Surrealist scenes that Miró painted. *(Albright Knox Art Gallery, Buffalo, New York, Room of Contemporary Art Fund, 1940 © 2002 Successio Miro/Artists Rights Society (ARS), New York/ADAGP, Paris)*

Another important Surrealist was Joan Miró (1893–1983) who, after studying art in his native Barcelona, arrived in Paris in 1919, where Picasso introduced him to Cubism and Fauvism. Miró's first Surrealist work, *Harlequin's Carnival* (Figure 24.4), was completed in 1925, soon after he joined the Surrealists. It is a colorful picture of fantastic creatures dancing and reveling in a one-window room, furnished with a table. This dreamlike, whimsical painting—with its distorted animal figures, twisted shapes, cubes, and geometrical forms—is characteristic of the many Surrealist scenes that Miró painted during his long life, as he endeavored to release the creative forces of the unconscious.

Miró's fellow Spaniard, Salvador Dali (1904–1989), joined the Surrealists in 1929, and two years later, he executed *The Persistence of Memory* (Figure 24.5)—arguably the most famous Surrealist painting. Greatly influenced by Freud, Dali developed a paranoia-critical method in which the sane person, deliberately abandoning reason, nurtures a very real form of paranoia; in actuality, delirium becomes reality. Dali stated that *The Persistence of Memory* was a result of the paranoia-critical method. He believed that he had extracted from his irrational unconscious a higher truth than mathematics and science could offer.

Figure 24.5 Salvador Dali (1904–1989), *The Persistence of Memory*, 1931. Oil on canvas, 9 1/2" x 13". Dali acknowledged that this painting was a result of his paranoia-critical method. Influenced by Freud, Dali developed a paranoia-critical method in which the sane person, abandoning reason, begins to nurture a form of paranoia that results in delirium becoming reality. *(© Museum of Modern Art, New York/Scala/Art Resource, NY © 2002 Salvador Dali, Gala-Salvador Dali Foundation/Artists Rights Society (ARS), New York/ ADAGP, Paris)*

Figure 24.6 Piet Mondrian, *Composition with Red, Blue, and Yellow,* 1920, 20 1/2″ x 20 5/8″ (52 x 60 cm), oil on canvas, Stedelijk Museum, Amsterdam. Mondrian developed a purely non-naturalistic, abstract style of painting, which he called Neo-Plasticism. Working in only primary colors, he painted only a flat surface with horizontal and vertical black lines outlining the blocks of color. *(Stedelijk Museum, Amsterdam)*

My limp watches are not just a fanciful and poetic image of the real; this vision of runny cheese is in fact the most perfect definition that the highest of mathematical speculations can give of space-time. The image was born spontaneously in me and on the basis of this paranoia-inspired picture one can consider that I have wrested from the irrational one of the most colossal archetypes of its arsenal of secrets. For, better than any mathematical equation, the limp watches give a definition of life: space-time condensed to the highest potential, to create the Camembert whose putrefaction brings forth the mushrooms of the mind, sparks that are capable of igniting the great cosmic motor.[50]

Although he does not explicitly make the connection, the limp watches may also be symbolic of Dali's sexual impotence, about which he had much to say. No matter the interpretation, the tiny (9 1/2″ x 13″) painting is visually distressing; Dali's use of a realistic style makes his irrational world even more disturbing.

Surrealism was an important art style, and with its emphasis on free form, it furnished a major artistic alternative to contemporary Cubism. Moreover, the Surrealists' emphasis on the significance of the unconscious for creativity greatly influenced the artists who introduced Abstract Expressionism in the United States after World War II (see Chapter 26).

De Stijl: Mondrian

In 1917, a small group of Dutch artists launched a periodical entitled *De Stijl (The Style),* which was devoted to attaining a clear vision of the universal reality that underlies all appearances. The most important of these artists was Piet Mondrian (1872–1944), who took abstract art to a new level. Mondrian was initially influenced by Cubism, but he subsequently abandoned it. He declared that his aim for doing so was to express "universal reality," without natural forms:

> Gradually I became aware that Cubism did not accept the logical consequences of its own discoveries; it was not developing abstraction toward its ultimate goal, the expression of pure reality. . . . Cubism intended to express volume [forms]. Intrinsically it remained naturalistic. Abstract Art attempts to destroy the corporeal expression of volume: to be a reflection of the universal aspect of reality.[51]

Mondrian developed a purely nonnaturalistic, abstract style of painting, which he called Neo-Plasticism. He explained why he rejected natural forms: "The appearance of natural forms changes but reality remains constant. To create pure reality plastically, it is necessary to reduce natural forms to the constant elements of form and natural color to *primary color.*"[52] An early example of this new style is his *Composition with Red, Blue, and Yellow* (Figure 24.6), which he designed and painted in 1920. As in all of his later Neo-Plastic works, Mondrian totally eliminated three-dimensional forms, curved lines, and representation of natural forms. He painted only a flat surface, with horizontal and vertical black lines outlining blocks of the primary colors—red, blue, and yellow—against a white, and occasionally gray, background.

Sculpture: Brancusi, Giacometti, and Moore

In the early years of the twentieth century, during the development of Fauvism and Expressionism in painting, there was no similar avant-garde movement in sculpture. Rodin (see Chapter 22) was the leading Western sculptor, and from 1900 until his death in 1917, young artists from all over Europe came to Paris to work with him or to visit with him. One of those young artists was Constantin Brancusi (1876–1957), the son of a free peasant in

Figure 24.7   Alberto Giacometti, *Hands Holding the Void (Invisible Object)*, 1934, cast 1935, Bronze, 60 1/4" x 13 1/4" x 9 1/4" (153 x 33.7 x 23.5 cm), The Saint Louis Art Museum, Friends Fund.
As the woman's body tilts forward, it appears as if it might move, but the arms are joined with the frame to constrain any possible motion. Her hands grasp an invisible object, or perhaps they hold nothing because the object is the void. *(The Saint Louis Art Museum, Friends Fund)*

Romania. Brancusi graduated from the academy of art in Bucharest in 1902, and two years later, he went to Paris to further his studies. During this time, Brancusi began to detach himself from both Rodin's method and his style. Rather than modeling with clay and then allowing a stonecutter to do the actual cutting, Brancusi did his own cutting and finished his own stone and wood sculptures. Also, much in the spirit of Mondrian, Brancusi took a bold step in the direction of Abstractionism in sculpture, which he connected with the "essence" of things: "[W]hat is real is not the external form but the essence of things. Starting from this truth it is impossible for anyone to express anything essentially real by imitating its exterior surface."[53] This sentiment is convincingly illustrated by a series of twenty-seven bird sculptures, rendered over a period of more than thirty years. Brancusi's first was his *Maiastra* (1912), a highly stylized but recognizable rendition of a legendary bird in Romanian folklore. After several more versions, Brancusi began to streamline his birds, as in the highly polished *Bird in Space* (see chapter opening), completed in 1928. Its exceedingly simplified form—its tall, slender, elliptical shape, which ends in a point—expresses the essence of "bird" in flight. One of Brancusi's birds occasioned one of the more dramatic incidents in the history of modern art. When he arrived in New York for his first extensive exhibition in 1926, the United States Customs Office levied a forty percent tax on *Bird in Space,* insisting that it was a manufactured object, not a work of art. Brancusi paid the tax, then sued the Customs Office, thus pitting traditionalist sculptors against those who defended the principles of modern art. When the verdict of 1928 went in Brancusi's favor, it marked the beginning of the acceptance of Abstractionism in America.

Another important sculptor of the early twentieth century was Alberto Giacometti (1901–1966), the son and nephew of Swiss Post-Impressionist painters. In 1923, he moved to Paris, where he initially created Cubist-styled sculptures. In 1930, André Breton bought one of his sculptures and invited him to join the Surrealist group, and Giacometti soon became the leading Surrealist sculptor, as he created numerous pieces during the next four years. In 1934, he executed his Surrealist masterpiece, *Hands Holding the Void (Invisible Object)* (Figure 24.7). As the woman's body tilts forward, it appears as if it might move, but the arms are joined with the frame to constrain any possible motion. Her hands grasp an invisible object, or perhaps they hold nothing, as the object is the void. Part of the

Figure 24.8 **Henry Moore,** *Reclining Figure,* **1929, Brown Hornton Stone, 22 1/2″ x 33″ x 15″ (57 x 83.8 x 38 cm), Leeds City Gallery, England.** Evoking the archetypal earth mother, this powerful, yet erotic, stone sculpture is indicative of Moore's favorite theme: the reclining nude female figure, leaning on one elbow with her knees raised. *(Leeds Museums and Galleries, City Art Gallery, UK/The Bridgeman Art Library International)*

French title, *maintenant le vide,* suggests a philosophical interpretation—"now the void," "the emptiness," or "the nothingness." Giacometti originally intended it to have a naturalistic head, but dissatisfied with his efforts, he replaced it with a metal mask that he had found. His desire to sculpt a naturalistic head may have signaled the abrupt turn that Giacometti was about to take, as in the fall of 1934, he rejected Surrealist Abstractionism and devoted himself to reproducing what he saw. He later recalled that the Surrealists considered this to be "a reactionary and treacherous activity. . . . [T]here was not public excommunication. But I lost all my friends. . . . From that day I . . . decided anew to reproduce the human form as truly as possible."[54] Giacometti finally succeeded in his quest for a unique sculptural style in 1945, when his human figures began to take on the slender, elongated form that characterized his subsequent work and assured his fame.

A third great sculptor of the first half of the twentieth century was Henry Moore (1898–1986), the youngest son of an English coal miner. After attending the Leeds School of Art for two years, Moore moved to London in 1921 to study at the Royal College of Art. Influenced by sculptors like Brancusi, he preferred carving to model-

ing, in order to allow the stone or the wood to dictate the position of a body, or parts of a body. In speaking about his method of sculpting, Moore said, "It's as though you have something which is trying to make itself come to a shape from inside itself. . . . [Y]ou begin with the block and have to find the sculpture that's inside it."[55] Moore's distinctive style was affected by his appreciation of the primitive and non-Western art in the British Museum. It is evident in the treatment of his favorite theme—the reclining nude female figure, leaning on one elbow with her knees raised. The first one of these was *Reclining Figure* (Figure 24.8) of 1929. Evoking the archetypal earth mother, this powerful, yet erotic, stone sculpture sat in Moore's studio until 1941, when he sold it to the Leeds Art Gallery.

Moore's work was not readily accepted, as is evidenced by the words of one art critic: "The cult of ugliness triumphs at the hands of Mr. Moore. He shows an utter contempt for the natural beauty of women and children, and in doing so, deprives even stone of its value as a means of aesthetic and emotional expression."[56] During the 1930s, Moore's sculptures became even more abstract, and he became involved with Surrealism, exhibiting his work at the International Exhibition of

Surrealism of London in 1936. By the 1940s, criticism of Moore's work was more muted, and he came to be acknowledged as one of the premier sculptors in the West, and by the end of his life, his international reputation was assured.

MUSIC

Ragtime: Scott Joplin

In the bars, bordellos, and dance halls of the Midwest and South, a type of piano music, called *ragtime,* was popularized by primarily African American pianists. Ragtime lasted from approximately 1890 until 1920. The major characteristic of ragtime is its syncopated rhythm—a metric pattern that emphasizes the weak beats of a measure instead of the strong ones. For example, in 4/4 time, the first and third beats traditionally are emphasized, but in ragtime, the second and fourth beats are accented. Similarly, in the waltz rhythm of 3/4, in which the first beat is accented, the second and third beats receive emphasis in ragtime.

CD 24.1 The most famous composer of ragtime music was Scott Joplin (1868–1917), who is best remembered for his *Maple Leaf Rag* and the music for the movie *The Sting* (starring Robert Redford and Paul Newman), which used as its theme Joplin's rag, *The Entertainer.* Joplin's father was a slave who became a free man with the Emancipation Proclamation in 1863. He encouraged his children's love of music, and by the time the family moved to St. Louis, Scott, largely self-taught, was an accomplished pianist. Because Joplin excelled in the popular ragtime music of the day, his music had great appeal. However, his efforts at a ragtime ballet, *The Ragtime Dance,* and a ragtime opera, *The Guest Of Honor,* were commercial failures, even if the tunes included in them remained popular. Personal tragedies—a failed marriage, the death of a child, and declining health—prevented Joplin from ever achieving success as a classical composer, a recognition he desperately craved. In spite of his problems, Joplin did finish his ragtime opera, *Treemonisha,* but he was not able to find financial backing to stage it. Consequently, Joplin himself paid for a run-through performance in 1915, but it also failed. Two years later, Joplin, in the final stages of venereal disease, was hospitalized and died.

During the 1970s, ragtime burst on the musical scene again. In large part this was due to Gunter Schuller's New England Conservatory Jazz Repertory Orchestra and his Ragtime Ensemble. Once again, Joplin's rags such as *Chrysanthemum, Elite Syncopations, Solace I,* and *Solace II* became enormously popular. In 1975, Joplin's opera *Treemonisha* was performed by the Houston Grand Opera with Schuller directing. Unfortunately, most of Joplin's other extended compositions have been lost. In 1997, Joplin's music was combined with that of Irving Berlin (1888–1989) in *The Tin Pan Alley Rag*—based on a chance encounter between Joplin and Berlin on the famed street in New York City. Tin Pan Alley was the nickname given to West 28th Street, between Broadway and Sixth Avenue in Manhattan, the location of many popular music publishers. Eventually, Tin Pan Alley became the generic term used to describe collectively all of the publishers of popular American sheet music, no matter where they were located.

Blues: Bessie Smith

As a musical genre, *blues* originated in the Mississippi Delta region and Texas, but it soon spread into the northern states, especially New York City, where blues singers, most of whom were women, could get better jobs and make more money by recording their music. Generally speaking, blues is a vocal narrative style derived from earlier field hollers, which features a solo voice accompanied by instruments. By the 1920s, blues style had developed characteristic texts, harmonies, and melodies. The harmony is based on the repetition of three major chords, and the melody is characterized by so-called "blues notes," which embody the bittersweet, emotional lyrics. While the blues vocalist sings, the instrumentalists often improvise solos over the blues chords. For example, to simulate vocal moans and slides, the "bottleneck slide" style of guitar playing came into being, consisting of scraping a glass bottleneck or a knife up the fingerboard of the guitar. Blues has had a significant impact on the development of jazz, country and western music, and rock and roll.

The finest singer of the blues in the United States was undoubtedly Bessie Smith (1894–1937), who was born in Chattanooga, Tennessee, and sang on street corners before becoming a dancer in a black minstrel show. The show also included "Ma" Rainey, whose protégé Smith became, and by 1920, Smith surpassed Rainey to become the headliner in the touring show. Even though musical tastes were different everywhere the show performed, Smith was always a hit, which earned her the title "Empress of the Blues." Despite her successes in northern cities such as Chicago and New York, Smith's real "home" was always in the South. Even though other blues singers made records, only Smith's sold in record numbers, rescuing some dying record companies that were on the verge of bankruptcy. Her rendition of "Lost Your Head Blues"—concerning a woman who is about to leave her man because "he done her wrong"—is considered to be one of the finest examples of blues. It opens with the cornet, played by Joe Smith, and the piano, played by Fletcher Henderson. Bessie Smith then sings, in quivering tones and slides, the blues melody in passages such as "I was with you baby," "throw'd your good gal down," and "days are lonesome, nights are long," phrases that are recapitulated by the instrumental ensemble.

Smith's records cover an array of music—from boisterous and bawdy vaudeville tunes to heart-wrenching blues tunes. She was good with the former because it often reflected her own devil-may-care lifestyle, whereas the latter brought a poignancy of heartfelt emotion. But above all, it was Smith's lush contralto voice and her awe-inspiring delivery that won audiences over. Although she was accompanied by some of the greatest jazz musicians of the day, including Louis Armstrong, Smith was the one who always was in total control of the performance. She refused to allow anyone to rush her slow tempos, and her influence on subsequent blues and jazz singers and musicians alike cannot be overstated.

Early Jazz

As a new musical genre, *jazz* developed in the brothels, saloons, dance halls, and streets of southern cities, particularly New Orleans, primarily among African American musicians. But from there it spread to Chicago, Kansas City, and New York and can be heard anywhere in the world today. Although it probably was around as early as the turn of the twentieth century, no one knows for sure when jazz actually began, because it was intended to be performed rather than written down. It incorporated multicultural influences, including West African rhythms, drumming, percussion, and improvisation, and most importantly, a trait identified as "call and response." In West African music, a soloist's words are echoed by a chorus, but in jazz, the vocalist's phrases are answered by another instrument or the entire jazz ensemble. Call and response also characterizes the African American church service in which the pastor issues a "call" to which the parishioners respond. Other sources of jazz include the blues, the syncopated rhythms of ragtime, as well as gospel hymns, dance tunes, spirituals, and work songs. Moreover, the American band tradition helped shape the sound of early jazz music, which used many band instruments, including drums,

clarinet, trumpet, cornet, and trombone. The premier American band composer was John Philip Sousa (1854–1932), who originally conducted the Marine Corps Band, but who went on to be renowned as "The March King," for his marches such as *The Washington Post March* and *Stars and Stripes Forever,* with its famous piccolo obligato.

Dixieland jazz was immortalized by such performers as Ferdinand "Jelly Roll" Morton (1890–1941) and the trumpeter and vocalist Louis "Satchmo" Armstrong (1900–1971), whose jazz ensembles, Hot Five and Hot Seven, made famous such tunes as "Oh, Didn't He Ramble?," "Hotter Than Hot," and "When the Saints Go Marchin' In." Armstrong became the leading trumpeter of the age by demonstrating that the instrument could be played in a range higher than anyone had ever imagined. Moreover, as a singer, he championed a style called "scat," which is characterized by rhythmically vocalizing nonsense syllables like "do, doot, do, doot," "da da dat da," and "dat-a bat-a dip-da."

During the 1920s a unique style of jazz, called *swing,* came into being. Because this music was intended for the big bands, it needed to be arranged rather than improvised on the spot. Entire sections of the band, either in harmony or in unison, would play the melodies, but the main melody was accompanied by short, repetitive phrases called riffs. In swing jazz, the saxophone took on a leading role as a solo instrument, and the percussion section achieved prominence. Conceivably the most important arranger, composer, and conductor of the swing era was Edward Kennedy "Duke" Ellington (1899–1974). His musical output was prodigious, for it is estimated that Ellington composed more than 2,000 songs, and some music historians estimate that it may be as high as 5,000. Among the many tunes that have become popular standards are "Mood Indigo," "Sophisticated Lady," "In a Sentimental Mood," "Don't Get Around Much Anymore," "I'm Beginning to See the Light," "It Don't Mean a Thing (If It Ain't Got That Swing)," "I Got It Bad and That Ain't Good," and "Satin Doll."

By 1927, Ellington's band was established all along the east coast, including in several prestigious New York City nightclubs. By year's end, he had auditioned successfully for a type of "artist-in-residence" position at Harlem's famed Cotton Club. Ellington's regular radio broadcasts from the Cotton Club, which ended in early 1931, guaranteed an extensive audience. Moreover, Ellington's band tours and recording sessions during the period helped to build his band's popularity. In his later years, Ellington composed musical scores for motion pictures, including *The Asphalt Jungle* (1950), *Anatomy of a Murder* (1959), *Paris Blues* (1960), and *Assault on a Queen* (1966).

George Gershwin (1898–1937) decided to take up music when his older brother, Ira (1896–1983), got a huge piano. George was particularly fond of Classical music and the new music of African American musicians. He became a serious musician in 1912 and studied it conscientiously. In the early 1920s, George and Ira collaborated on a number of songs, with George composing the music and Ira the lyrics. Among the more popular ones from this period are: "The Man I Love" and "Somebody Loves Me." In 1924, the bandleader Paul Whiteman (1890–1967) commissioned George to compose an extended piece of music for his band that combined jazz idioms with Classical music. The result was the enormously famous *Rhapsody in Blue*, which was first performed in New York City, at the Aeolian Hall, with George himself at the piano. George and Ira then hit it big on Broadway with shows such as *Lady, Be Good!, Strike Up the Band,* and *Girl Crazy*. In the orchestra pit for *Girl Crazy* were the soon-to-be-famous big band leaders Glenn Miller, Gene Krupa, and Benny Goodman (see Chapter 26).

World War I and European Consciousness

The Great War profoundly altered the course of Western civilization, deepening the spiritual crisis that had produced it. How could one speak of the inviolability of the individual when Europe had become a slaughterhouse, or of the primacy of reason when nations permitted slaughter to go unabated for four years? How could the mind cope with this spectacle of a civilization turning against itself, destroying itself in an orgy of organized violence? A young French soldier, shortly before he was killed at Verdun, expressed the disillusionment that gripped the soldiers in the trenches: "Humanity is mad! It must be mad to do what it is doing. What a massacre! What scenes of horror and carnage, I cannot find words to translate my impressions. Hell cannot be so terrible. Men are mad!"[57] The war, said British poet Robert Graves, provoked an "inward scream" that still reverberates. Now only the naive could believe in continuous progress. Western civilization had entered an age of violence, anxiety, and doubt.

The war left many with the gnawing feeling that Western civilization had lost its vitality and was caught in a rhythm of breakdown and disintegration. It seemed that Western civilization was fragile and perishable, that Western people, despite their extraordinary accomplishments, were never more than a step or two away from barbarism. Surely, any civilization that could allow such senseless slaughter to last for four years had entered its decline and could look forward to only the darkest of futures.

European intellectuals were demoralized and disillusioned. The orderly, peaceful, rational world of their youth had been wrecked. The Enlightenment worldview, weakened in the nineteenth century by the assault of Romantics, Social Darwinists, extreme nationalists, race mystics, and glorifiers of the irrational, was now disintegrating. The enormity of the war had destroyed faith in the capacity of reason to deal with crucial social and political questions. Civilization seemed to be fighting an unending and hopeless battle against the irrational elements in human nature. It appeared that war would be a recurring phenomenon in the twentieth century.

Scientific research had produced more efficient weapons to kill and maim Europe's youth. The achievements of Western science and technology, which had been viewed as a boon for humanity and the clearest testament to the superiority of European civilization, were called into question. Confidence in the future gave way to doubt. The old beliefs in the perfectibility of humanity, the blessings of science, and ongoing progress now seemed an expression of naive optimism. As British historian A. J. P. Taylor concludes,

> The First World War was difficult to fit into the picture of a rational civilization advancing by ordered stages. The civilized men of the twentieth century had outdone in savagery the barbarians of all preceding ages, and their civilized virtues—organization, mechanical skill, self-sacrifice—had made war's savagery all the more terrible. Modern man had developed powers which he was not fit to use. European civilization had been weighed in the balance and found wanting.[58]

Western civilization had lost its spiritual center. The French writer Paul Valéry summed up the mood of a troubled generation, for whom the sun seemed to be setting on the Enlightenment.

> The storm has died away, and still we are restless, uneasy as if the storm were about to break. Almost all the affairs of men remain in a terrible uncertainty. We think of what has disappeared, and we

are almost destroyed by what has been destroyed; we do not know what will be born, and we fear the future, not without reason. We hope vaguely, we dread precisely; our fears are infinitely more precise than our hopes; we confess that the charm of life is behind us. There is no thinking man . . . who can hope to dominate this anxiety, to escape from this impression of darkness. . . . But among all these injured things is the Mind. The Mind has indeed been cruelly wounded; its complaint is heard in the hearts of intellectual men; it passes a mournful judgment on itself. It doubts itself profoundly.[59]

This disillusionment heralded a loss of faith in liberal-democratic values—a loss of faith that contributed to the widespread popularity of fascist ideologies in the postwar world. Having lost confidence in the power of reason to solve the problems of the human community, in liberal doctrines of individual freedom, and in the institutions of parliamentary democracy, many people turned to fascism as a simple saving faith. Far from making the world safe for democracy, as President Wilson and other liberals had hoped, World War I gave rise to totalitarian movements that would nearly destroy democracy.

The war produced a generation of young people who had reached their maturity in combat. Violence had become a way of life for millions of soldiers hardened by battle and for millions of civilians aroused by four years of propaganda. The astronomical casualty figures—some ten million dead and twenty-one million wounded—had a brutalizing effect. Violence, cruelty, suffering, and even wholesale death seemed to be natural and acceptable components of human existence. The sanctity of the individual seemed to be liberal and Christian claptrap.

The fascination with violence and contempt for life persisted in the postwar world. Many returning veterans yearned for the excitement of battle and the fellowship of the trenches—what one French soldier called "the most tender human experience." After the war, a young English officer reminisced: "There was an exaltation, in those days of comradeship and dedication, that would have come in few other ways."[60] A fraternal bond united the men of the trenches. But many veterans also shared a primitive attraction to war's fury. A Belgian veteran expressed it this way:

The plain truth is that if I were to obey my native animal instincts—and there was little hope for anything else while I was in the trenches—I should enlist again in any future war, or take part

in any sort of fighting, merely to experience again that voluptuous thrill of the human brute who realizes his power to take away life from other human beings who try to do the same to him. What was first accepted as a moral duty became a habit . . . had become a need.[61]

The veterans who aspired to recapture the exhilaration experienced in combat made ideal recruits for extremist political movements that glorified action and promised to rescue society from a decadent liberalism. Both Hitler and Mussolini, themselves ex-soldiers imbued with the ferocity of the front, knew how to appeal to veterans. The lovers of violence and the harbingers of hate who became the leaders of fascist parties would come within a hairbreadth of destroying Western civilization. The intensified nationalist hatreds following World War I also helped fuel the fires of World War II. The Germans swore to regain lands lost to the Poles; some Germans dreamed of a war of revenge. Italy, too, felt aggrieved because it had not received more territory from the dismembered Austro-Hungarian Empire.

Yet while some veterans clung to an aggressive militarism, others aspired to build a more humane world. Such veterans embraced democratic and socialist ideals and resolved that the horror should never be repeated. Tortured by the memory of the Great War, European intellectuals wrote pacifist plays and novels and signed pacifist declarations. In the 1930s, an attitude of "peace at any price" discouraged resistance to Nazi Germany in its bid to dominate Europe.

World War I was total war; it encompassed the entire nation and was without limits. States demanded total victory and total commitment from their citizens. They regulated industrial production, developed sophisticated propaganda techniques to strengthen morale, and exercised ever-greater control over the lives of their people, organizing and disciplining them like soldiers. This total mobilization of nations' human and material resources provided a model for future dictators. With ever-greater effectiveness and ruthlessness, dictators would centralize power and manipulate thinking. The ruthless dictatorships that emerged in Russia, Germany, and Italy were products of the war. The war gave communists the opportunity to seize power in Russia, and the mentality of the front helped to mold the fascist movement that emerged in Italy and Germany. The barbarism of the trenches would be eclipsed in the postwar era by the horrors inflicted on people by totalitarian regimes.

Key Terms

Versailles Treaty	Surrealism
"the lost generation"	frottage
The Jazz Age	ragtime
Great Migration	blues
Harlem Renaissance	jazz
Great Depression	swing
Dadaists	

Notes

1. Quoted in Barbara Tuchman, *The Guns of August* (New York: Macmillan, 1962), p. 440.
2. Rupert Brooke, "Peace," in *Collected Poems of Rupert Brooke* (New York: Dodd, Mead, 1941), p. 111.
3. *The Poems of Wilfred Owen,* ed. Edmund Blunden (London: Chatto and Windus, 1967), p. 80.
4. Ibid, pp. 75–76.
5. *The War Poems of Siegfried Sassoon,* ed. Rupert Hart-Davis (London: Faber and Faber, 1983), p. 71.
6. Erich Maria Remarque, *All Quiet on the Western Front,* trans. A. W. Wheen (Boston: Little, Brown, 1929), p. 224.
7. Ernest Hemingway, *A Farewell to Arms* (New York: Collier Books, Macmillan, 1986), p. 223.
8. Ibid., p. 224.
9. Thomas Mann, *The Magic Mountain,* trans. H. T. Lowe-Porter (New York: Vintage Books, 1969), pp. 244, 245.
10. Ernest Hemingway, *The Sun Also Rises* (New York: Charles Scribner's Sons, 1954), p. 115.
11. Michael F. Moloney, "Ernest Hemingway: The Missing Third Dimension," in *Hemingway and His Critics,* ed. Carlos Baer (New York: Hill and Wang, 1961), p. 185.
12. Edith Wharton, *The Age of Innocence; Complete Text with Introduction; Historical Context; Critical Essays* (Boston: Houghton Mifflin Company, 2000), p. 383.
13. Ibid., p. 381.
14. *Introduction to Elmer Gantry* [online] Available http://xroads.virginia.edu/~ UG00/lambert/ introduction.html October 11, 2001, p. 1.
15. F. Scott Fitzgerald, *The Great Gatsby* (New York: Charles Scribner's Sons, 1953) p. 182.
16. T. S. Eliot, *Collected Poems: 1909–1962* (New York: Harcourt, Brace & World, Inc., 1963), p. 6.
17. Ibid., p. 4.
18. Ibid., p. 53.
19. William Butler Yeats, *The Collected Poems of W. B. Yeats* (New York: Macmillan Company, 1951), p. 184.
20. James B. Meriwether and Michael Millgate, eds., *Lion in the Garden: Interviews with William Faulkner, 1926–1962* (Lincoln and London: University of Nebraska Press, 1968), p. 255.
21. *The Complete Plays and Poems of William Shakespeare,* ed. William Allan Neilson and Charles Jarvis Hill (Cambridge, Mass.: The Riverside Press, 1942), p. 1210.
22. Eugene O'Neill, *The Emperor Jones, Anna Christie, The Hairy Ape* (New York: Vintage Books, 1972), p. 13.
23. Ibid., p. 14.
24. Ibid., p. 15.
25. Ibid., p. 19.
26. Ibid., p. 47.
27. Ibid., p. 52.
28. Ibid., p. 184.
29. Ibid., pp. 191–192.
30. Ibid., p. 198.
31. Ibid., p. 225.
32. Ibid., p. 231.
33. Ibid., p. 232.
34. W. E. Burghardt DuBois, *The Souls of Black Folk* (New York: The New American Library, 1969), p. 45.
35. Jean Toomer, "Karintha," in *Black Voices: An Anthology of Afro-American Literature,* ed. Abraham Chapman (New York: The New American Library, 1968), p. 65.
36. Alain Locke, "The New Negro," in *Black Voices,* p. 513.
37. Ibid., pp. 514–516.
38. James Weldon Johnson, "The Creation: A Negro Sermon," in *Black Voices,* p. 364.
39. Ibid., pp. 364–365.
40. Ibid., 366.
41. Claude McKay, "America," in *Black Voices,* p. 374.
42. Arna Bontemps, "A Black Man Talks of Reaping," in *Black Voices,* p. 424.
43. Countee Cullen, "Yet Do I Marvel," in *Black Voices,* p. 383.
44. Langston Hughes, "Harlem," in *Black Voices,* pp. 430–431.
45. Tristan Tzara, "Lecture on Dada (1922)," trans. Ralph Mannheim, in *The Dada Painters and Poets,* ed. Robert Motherwell (New York: Witterborn, Schultz, 1951), pp. 248, 250.
46. Ibid., p. 251.
47. Edward Lucie-Smith, in Donald Carrol and Edward Lucie-Smith, *Movements in Modern Art* (New York: Horizon Press, 1973), p. 49.
48. H. W. Janson, *History of Art,* 5th ed. (New York: Harry N. Abrams, 1995), p. 784.
49. André Breton, *What Is Surrealism?* trans. David Gascoyne (London: Faber & Faber, 1936), p. 62.
50. *The Unspeakable Confessions of Salvador Dali, As Told to André Parinaud,* trans. Harold J. Salemson (New York: William Morrow, 1976) p. 143.
51. Piet Mondrian, *The New Art—The New Life. The Collected Writings of Piet Mondrian,* ed.

and trans. Harry Holtzman and Martin S. James (Boston: G. K. Hall & Co., 1986), pp. 338, 350.

52. Ibid., p. 338.

53. Quoted in George Heard Hamilton, *Painting and Sculpture in Europe, 1880 to 1940* (Baltimore: Penguin Books, 1967), p. 309.

54. Quoted in Reinhold Hohl, ed., *Giacometti: A Biography in Pictures* (Ostfildern, Germany: Verlag Gerd Hatje, 1998), p. 83.

55. Excerpted in Philip James, ed., *Henry Moore on Sculpture: A Collection of the Sculptor's Writings and Spoken Words,* ed. Philip James (New York: The Viking Press, 1971) pp. 62, 137.

56. Quoted in *London Morning Post* (11 April 1931); [online] available (November 2001) http://www.henry-moore-fdn.co.uk/hmf/biography.htm

57. Quoted in Alistair Horne, *The Price of Glory* (New York: Harper, 1967), p. 240.

58. A. J. P. Taylor, *From Sarajevo to Potsdam* (New York: Harcourt, Brace & World, 1966), pp. 55–56.

59. Paul Valéry. *Variety* (New York: Harcourt, Brace, 1927), pp. 27–28.

60. Quoted in Modris Eksteins, *Rites of Spring: The Great War and the Birth of the Modern Age* (New York: Doubleday Anchor Books, 1989), p. 232.

61. Quoted in Eric J. Leed, *No Man's Land: Combat and Identity in World War I* (New York: Cambridge University Press, 1979), p. 201.

fascist parties that glorified combat and organized private armies. A third contributing factor was the inability of democratic parliamentary governments to cope with the problems that burdened postwar Europe. Having lost confidence in the procedures and values of democracy many people joined fascist movements that promised strong leadership, an end to party conflicts, and a unified national will.

Fascism's appeal to nationalist feelings also drew people into the movement. In a sense, fascism expressed the aggressive racial nationalism that had emerged in the late nineteenth century. Fascists saw themselves as dedicated idealists engaged in a heroic struggle to rescue their nations from domestic and foreign enemies; they aspired to regain lands lost by their countries in World War I or to acquire lands denied them by the Paris Peace Conference.

Fascists glorified instinct, will, ties of blood and native soil, and battle as the true forces of life; they openly attacked the ideals of reason, liberty, and equality—the legacies of the Enlightenment and the French Revolution.

Benito Mussolini (1883–1945), founder of the Italian Fascist party, came to power in 1922. Although he established a one-party state, he was less successful than Adolf Hitler (1889–1945), the leader of the German National Socialists, in controlling the state and the minds of the people. Moreover, Mussolini's state hesitated to impose the brutal terror that distinguished Stalin's and Hitler's regimes. For these reasons, fascist Italy is more accurately called authoritarian, rather than totalitarian.

Many extreme racist-nationalist and paramilitary organizations sprang up in postwar Germany. Adolf Hitler, a veteran of World War I, joined one of these organizations, which became known as the National Socialist German Worker's party (commonly called the Nazi party). Hitler had uncanny insight into the state of mind of postwar Germans, and at mass meetings he used his power as an orator to play on their dissatisfactions with the Weimar Republic, the new democratic government established after a revolution brought down the monarchy in the last days of the war.

In November 1923, Hitler attempted to overthrow the state government in Bavaria as the first step in bringing down the Weimar Republic. But the Nazis quickly scattered when the Bavarian police opened fire. Hitler was arrested and sentenced to five years' imprisonment—he served only nine months. While in prison, Hitler wrote *Mein Kampf* (My Struggle), in which he presented his views. The book came to be regarded as an authoritative expression of the Nazi worldview and served as a kind of sacred writing for the Nazi movement.

Hitler's thought comprised a patchwork of nineteenth-century anti-Semitic, Volkish, Social Darwinist, antidemocratic, and anti-Marxist ideas. From these ideas, many of which enjoyed wide popularity, Hitler constructed a worldview rooted in myth and ritual. Nazism rejected both the Judeo-Christian and the Enlightenment traditions and sought to found a new world order based on racial nationalism. For Hitler, race was the key to understanding world history. He believed that a reawakened, racially united Germany, led by men of iron will, would carve out a vast European empire and would deal a decadent liberal civilization its deathblow. It would conquer Russia, eradicate communism, and reduce to serfdom the subhuman Slavs, "a mass of born slaves who feel the need of a master."[3]

In the tradition of crude nineteenth-century German racial nationalists and Social Darwinists, Hitler divided the world into superior and inferior races and pitted them against each other in a struggle for survival. For him, this fight for life was a law of nature and of history.

An obsessive and virulent anti-Semitism dominated Hitler's mental outlook. In waging war against the Jews, Hitler believed that he was defending Germany from its worst enemy, a sinister force that stood in total opposition to the new world he envisioned. In his mythical interpretation of the world, the Aryan was the originator and carrier of civilization. As descendants of the Aryans, the Germans embodied creativity, bravery, and loyalty. As the opposite of the Aryan, the Jew personified the vilest qualities. "Two worlds face one another," said Hitler, "the men of God and the men of Satan! The Jew is the anti-man, the creature of another god. He must have come from another root of the human race. I set the Aryan and the Jew over and against each other."[4] Everything Hitler despised—liberalism, intellectualism, pacifism, parliamentarianism, internationalism, Marxism, modern art, and individualism—he attributed to Jews.

Hitler's anti-Semitism served a functional purpose as well. By concentrating all evil in one enemy, "the conspirator and demonic" Jew, Hitler provided true believers with a simple, all-embracing, and emotionally satisfying explanation for their misery. By defining themselves as the racial and spiritual opposites of Jews, Germans of all classes felt joined together in a Volkish union.

The surrender to myth served to disorient the German intellect and to unify the nation. When the mind accepts an image such as Hitler's image of Jews as vermin, germs, and satanic conspirators, it has lost all sense of balance and objectivity. Such a disoriented mind is ready to believe and to obey, to be manipulated and led, to brutalize and

MODERN CHINESE POETRY

Early in the twentieth century, a new form of poetry came into existence in China, which was inspired by the many intellectuals who began to look to the West in order to modernize their country. The new poetry used the vernacular, rather than the ancient traditional literary language. Hsü Chih-mo (1895–1931), generally regarded as the greatest poet of his generation, was the founder of the *Crescent Monthly,* a magazine devoted to the new poetry. Hsü studied literature at Cambridge University in England, where he became enamored with nineteenth-century Romantic poetry. Western influence, particularly Hsü's romantic appreciation of nature, is reflected in *The Rebirth of Spring* (1929).

Last night
As already the night before
Spring
Took possession of Winter's dead body.

Don't you feel the yielding underfoot?
Don't you feel the mild breath at your temples?
On the branches, a wash of green,
Ripples on the pond, endlessly weaving,
And for both of us, through our limbs,
In our breast, a new kind of beating:

On your cheeks already the peach-blossoms open,
And ever more keenly I gather to me
Your beauty, drink down
The bubbling of your laughter.

Don't you feel these arms of mine
Ever more insistent, demanding to hold you?
My breath homing to strike against your body
As though a myriad of fireflies swarmed to the flame
All these, and so many more beyond the telling
Join with the eager wheeling of the birds
And hand in hand unite to hymn [praise]
The rebirth of Spring.

Source: Twentieth Century Chinese Poetry: An Anthology, *trans. and ed. Kai-yu Hsu (New York: Anchor Books, 1964), pp. 92–93.*

to tolerate brutality. It is ready to be absorbed into the will of the collective community. That many people, including intellectuals and members of the elite, accepted these racial ideas shows the enduring power of mythical thinking and the vulnerability of reason.

Hitler understood that in an age of political parties, universal suffrage, and a popular press—the legacies of the French and Industrial Revolutions—the successful leader must win the support of the masses. This could be achieved best with propaganda. To be effective, said Hitler, propaganda must be aimed principally at the emotions. The masses are not moved by scientific ideas or by objective and abstract knowledge, but by primitive feelings, terror, force, and discipline. Propaganda must reduce everything to simple slogans, incessantly repeated, and must concentrate on one enemy. The masses are aroused by the spoken, not the written, word—by a storm of hot passion erupting from the speaker, "which like hammer blows can open the gates to the heart of the people."[5]

The most effective means of stirring the masses and strengthening them for the struggle ahead, Hitler had written in *Mein Kampf,* is the mass rally. Surrounded by tens of thousands of people, individuals lose their sense of individuality and no longer see themselves as isolated. They become members of a community, bound together by an *esprit de corps* reminiscent of the trenches during the Great War.

Many Germans, viewing Hitler as a nationalist leader who would undo the hated Versailles Treaty and restore Germany's power in world affairs, were attracted to his movement. The middle and upper classes, fearing for their property, saw Hitler as the best defense against the hated Communist and Democratic Socialist parties, which drew their support from the working class. The failure of the Weimar Republic to solve Germany's domestic problems, particularly during the Depression when unemployment soared, turned many Germans against democratic parliamentary government. Moreover, unlike Britain, France, and the United States, Germany lacked a strong liberal-democratic tradition; thus, during the difficult times of the Depression, many Germans were eager to replace what they considered a failed experiment in democracy with authoritarian leadership. And there was always the immense attraction of Hitler. Germans were won over by his fanatical sincerity, his iron will, and his conviction that he was chosen by fate to rescue Germany from defeat and despair.

In the election of July 31, 1932, the Nazis received 37.3 percent of the vote, far more than any other party, but still not a majority. The aging president, Paul von Hindenburg (1847–1934) was persuaded to appoint Hitler chancellor, a decision that had the support of German industrialists and aristocratic landowners, who regarded Hitler as a useful instrument to fight Communism, block social reform, break the backs of organized labor, and rebuild the armament industry, which had been forbidden by the Treaty of Versailles.

After gaining power as chancellor of the German government in 1933, Hitler moved to establish a totalitarian state that controlled all phases of political, social, and cultural life. Utilizing modern methods of administration and communication, the Nazi state manipulated the lives and thoughts of its citizens to a much greater extent than had absolute and tyrannical governments of the past. Rejecting central liberal principles, it outlawed competing political parties, made terror a government policy, and drew no distinction between the individual's private life and the interests of the state. The Nazi regime aspired to shape a "new man," one who possessed a sense of mission and was willing to devote body and soul to the party, its ideology, and its leader, *Der Führer,* who was endowed with attributes of infallibility.

World War II

Hitler sought power to build a great German empire in Europe, a goal that he revealed in *Mein Kampf.* In 1935, Hitler declared that Germany was no longer bound by the Versailles Treaty and would restore military conscription. In 1936, Germany remilitarized the Rhineland and in 1938 incorporated Austria into the Third Reich—both prohibited by the Versailles Treaty. Although these actions violated the Versailles Treaty, Britain and France offered no resistance.

In 1938, Hitler also threatened war if Czechoslovakia did not cede to Germany the Sudetenland, with its large German population—of the 3.5 million people living in the Czech Sudetenland, some 2.8 million were Germans. In September 1938, Hitler met with other European leaders at Munich. Prime Minister Neville Chamberlain (1869–1940) of Great Britain and Prime Minister Édouard Daladier (1884–1970) of France agreed to Hitler's demand, despite France's mutual assistance pact with Czechoslovakia and the Czechs' expressed determination to resist the dismemberment of their country. Both Chamberlain and Daladier were praised by their compatriots for ensuring, as Chamberlain declared, "peace in our time."

Britain and France pursued a policy of *appeasement*—giving in to Germany in the hope that a satisfied Hitler would not drag Europe into another war. Appeasement expressed the widespread British desire to heal the wounds of World War I and to correct what many British officials regarded as the injustices of the Versailles Treaty. Some officials, lauding Hitler's anticommunism, regarded a powerful Germany as a bulwark against the Soviet Union. Britain's lack of military preparedness was another compelling reason for not resisting Hitler.

On September 1, 1939, German troops crossed into Poland, precipitating World War II. Poland fell in four weeks to the Nazi *blitzkrieg,* that is, lightning war marked by fast-moving mechanized columns. In the months that followed, land battles consisted only of a few skirmishes on the Franco-German border. Then in April 1940, Germany attacked Denmark and Norway. The following month Hitler launched his offensive in the west with an invasion of neutral Belgium, Holland, and Luxembourg. Within a few days, German troops penetrated France. The battle for France turned into a rout, and on June 22, France signed an armistice.

Finding Britain unwilling to come to terms, Hitler proceeded in earnest with invasion plans. In early August 1940, the *Luftwaffe* (air force) began massive attacks on British air and naval installations. Virtually every day during the Battle of Britain, weather permitting, hundreds of planes fought in the sky above Britain. The development of radar by British scientists, the skill and courage of British fighter pilots, and the inability of Germany to make up its losses in planes compelled Hitler to call off the invasion.

The obliteration of Bolshevism and the conquest, exploitation, and colonization of Russia by the German master race were cardinal elements of Hitler's ideology. In the early hours of June 22, 1941, the Germans launched their offensive over a wide front, inflicting horrendous losses in men and material on the Russians. By the end of 1941, Germany had conquered vast regions of Russia but had failed to bring the country to its knees.

Over conquered Europe the Nazis imposed a "New Order" marked by exploitation, torture, and mass murder. The Germans took some 5.5 million Russian prisoners of war, of whom more than 3.5 million perished; many of these prisoners were deliberately starved to death. The Germans imprisoned and executed many Polish intellectuals and priests and slaughtered vast numbers of Gypsies. Using the modern state's organizational capacities and the instruments of modern technology, the Nazis murdered six million Jews, including one and a half million children—two-thirds of the Jewish population of Europe. Gripped by the mythical, perverted worldview of Nazism, the SS, Hitler's elite guard, and their collaborators from several lands, carried out these murders with dedication and idealism; they believed that they were exterminating subhumans who threatened the German nation. Jews were herded into crowded ghettos, where they were decimated by malnutrition and disease; killed en masse by gunfire at execution grounds; and transported in sealed cattle cars to infamous death camps—Treblinka, Sobibor, Auschwitz-Burkenau, Belzec, Chelmno, Magdanek—where they perished immediately in gas chambers or later from hunger, disease, and abuse.

While Germany was subduing Europe, its ally, Japan, seeking raw materials and scarce markets for Japanese goods and driven by a xenophobic and racist nationalism, was extending its dominion over Asia. Japan hoped that a quick strike against the American fleet in the Pacific would give it time to enlarge and consolidate its empire. On December 7, 1941, the Japanese struck with carrier-based planes at Pearl Harbor in Hawaii, drawing the United States, with its immense industrial capacity, into the war. By the spring of 1942, the Axis powers held the upper hand. The Japanese empire included the coast of China, Indochina, Thailand, Burma, Malaya, the Dutch East Indies, the Philippines, and other islands in the Pacific. Germany controlled Europe almost to Moscow. When the year ended, however, the Allies seemed assured of victory. Three decisive battles—Midway in the Pacific, Stalingrad in Russia, and El Alamein in North Africa—reversed the tide of war.

After their victory at Stalingrad, the Russians moved relentlessly westward toward Germany. On June 6, 1944, D-Day, the Allies landed on the beaches of Normandy in France. By April 1945, British, American, and Russian troops were penetrating into Germany from east and west. On April 30, 1945, with the Russians only blocks away, Hitler took his own life. On May 7, 1945, a demoralized and devastated Germany surrendered unconditionally.

On August 6, 1945, the United States dropped an atomic bomb on Hiroshima, killing more than 78,000 people. President Harry S Truman said that he ordered the atomic attack to avoid an American invasion of Japan, which would have cost hundreds of thousands of lives. After a second atomic bomb was dropped on Nagasaki on August 9, the Japanese asked for peace.

World War II was the most destructive war in history. Estimates of the number of dead range as high as fifty million, including some twenty-five million Russians, who sacrificed more than the other participants in both population and material resources. Material costs were staggering. Everywhere cities were in rubble; bridges, railway systems, waterways, and harbors destroyed; farmlands laid waste; livestock killed; coal mines wrecked. Homeless and hungry people wandered the streets and roads. Europe faced the gigantic

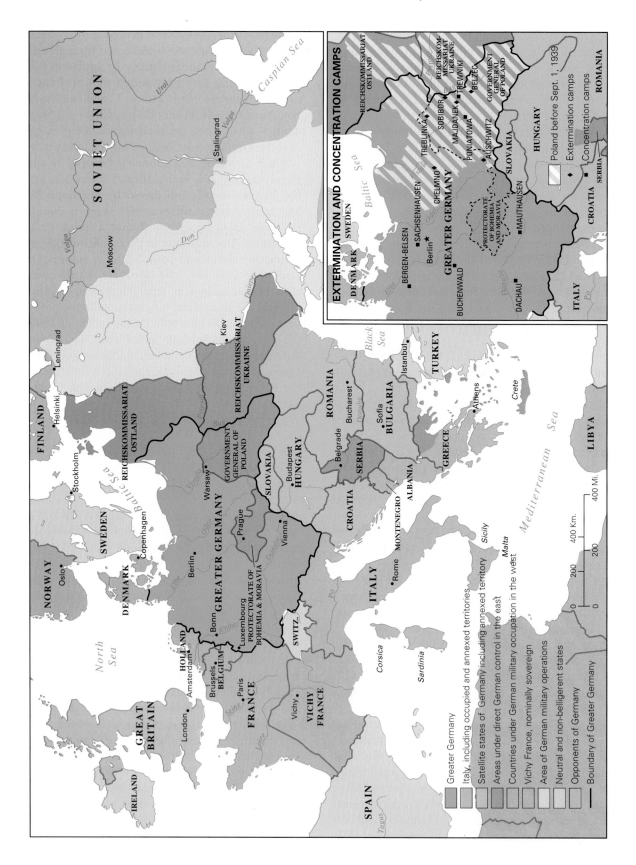

SOVIET UNION

Caspian Sea

Ural

Volga

Stalingrad

Don

Moscow

Leningrad

Kiev

Dnieper

REICHSKOMMISSARIAT
UKRAINE

FINLAND

Helsinki

NORWAY

Oslo

SWEDEN

Stockholm

DENMARK

Copenhagen

Baltic Sea

REICHSKOMMISSARIAT
OSTLAND

Vistula

Bug

Warsaw

GOVERNMENT
GENERAL
OF POLAND

SLOVAKIA

Budapest

HUNGARY

ROMANIA

Bucharest

Danube

Belgrade

SERBIA

BULGARIA

Sofia

CROATIA

ALBANIA

MONTENEGRO

GREECE

Athens

TURKEY

Istanbul

Black Sea

Crete

Mediterranean Sea

LIBYA

GREAT BRITAIN

London

IRELAND

North Sea

HOLLAND

Amsterdam

BELGIUM

Brussels

Paris

Seine

FRANCE

Vichy

VICHY FRANCE

Loire

SPAIN

Tagus

Corsica

Sardinia

ITALY

Rome

Po

Sicily

Malta

GREATER GERMANY

Berlin

Bonn

Luxembourg

Elbe

Oder

Rhine

PROTECTORATE OF
BOHEMIA & MORAVIA

Prague

Vienna

Danube

SWITZ.

EXTERMINATION AND CONCENTRATION CAMPS

REICHSKOMMISSARIAT
OSTLAND

REICHSKOM-
MISSARIAT
UKRAINE

TREBLINKA

SOBIBOR

TREWNIKI

MAJDANEK

PONIATOWA

BELZEC

GOVERNMENT
GENERAL
OF POLAND

AUSCHWITZ

ROMANIA

SLOVAKIA

HUNGARY

CROATIA

SERBIA

ITALY

Po

Danube

MAUTHAUSEN

PROTECTORATE
OF BOHEMIA
AND MORAVIA

DACHAU

BUCHENWALD

Berlin ★

GREATER GERMANY

SACHSENHAUSEN

CHELMNO

BERGEN-BELSEN

DENMARK

SWEDEN

Baltic Sea

Elbe

Oder

Poland before Sept. 1, 1939

◆ Extermination camps

■ Concentration camps

Greater Germany

Italy, including occupied and annexed territories

Satellite states of Germany including annexed territory

Areas under direct German control in the east

Countries under German military occupation in the west

Vichy France, nominally sovereign

Area of German military operations

Neutral and non-belligerent states

Opponents of Germany

Boundary of Greater Germany

400 Mi.

400 Km.

200

200

0

0

task of rebuilding. Yet Europe did recover from this material blight, and with astonishing speed.

The war produced a shift in power arrangements. The United States and the Soviet Union emerged as the two most powerful states in the world. The traditional Great Powers—Britain, France, and Germany—were now dwarfed by these *superpowers.*

After World War I, nationalist passions had intensified. After World War II, Western Europeans progressed toward unity. The Hitler years had convinced many Europeans of the dangers inherent in extreme nationalism, and fear of the Soviet Union prodded them toward greater cooperation.

World War II accelerated the disintegration of Europe's overseas empires. The European states could hardly justify ruling over Africans and Asians after they had fought to liberate European lands from German imperialism. Nor could they ask their people, exhausted by the Hitler years and concentrating all their energies on reconstruction, to fight new wars against Africans and Asians pressing for independence. In the 1950s and 1960s, virtually every colonial territory gained independence. Where a colonial power resisted granting the colony independence, the price was bloodshed.

The consciousness of Europe, already profoundly damaged by World War I, was again grievously wounded. Nazi racial theories showed that even in an age of advanced science, the mind remains attracted to irrational beliefs and mythical imagery; Nazi atrocities proved that people will torture and kill with religious zeal and machine-like indifference. The Nazi assault on reason and freedom demonstrated anew the fragility of Western civilization. This assault would forever cast doubt on the Enlightenment conception of human goodness, secular rationality, and the progress of civilization through advances in science and technology. Both the Christian and the Enlightenment traditions had failed the West.

Some intellectuals, shocked by the irrationality and horrors of the Hitler era, drifted into despair.

Map 25.1   The Nazi New Order in Europe, 1942 At the zenith of its power in 1942, Nazi Germany controlled much of Europe. Concerned most immediately with winning the war, the Nazis sought to coordinate the economies of their satellite states and conquered territories. But they also began establishing what was supposed to be an enduring new order in eastern Europe. The inset shows the location of the major Nazi concentration camps and of the six extermination camps the Nazis constructed in what had been Poland.

To these thinkers, life was absurd, without meaning; human beings could neither comprehend nor control it. In 1945, only the naive could have faith in continuous progress or believe in the essential goodness of the individual. The future envisioned by the philosophes seemed more distant than ever. Nevertheless, this profound disillusionment was tempered by hope. Democracy had, in fact, prevailed over Nazi totalitarianism and terror. Perhaps, then, democratic institutions and values would spread throughout the globe, and the newly established United Nations (1945) would promote world peace.

LITERATURE

Writers in the 1930s were principally concerned with the plight of the downtrodden made manifest by the Great Depression, the socialist experiment in Russia, and the threat to liberty posed by the fascist regimes in Italy and Germany. World War II and the revelation of Nazi atrocities provided writers with new concerns and new themes.

Social Justice: Steinbeck and Brecht

STEINBECK   More than any other novel of the period, John Steinbeck's (1902–1968) *The Grapes of Wrath* (1939) captured the suffering of rural America during the Depression. In several southern and western states, prolonged drought and constant winds had deprived the land of topsoil, causing crops to fail and animals to die. Deprived of their livelihood, hundreds of thousands of families saw their property foreclosed or were forced to sell at a fraction of its value. A work of social protest, *The Grapes of Wrath* movingly describes the ordeal of the Joad family, downtrodden Oklahoma farmers who, driven off their land, head to California to find work as farm laborers. On the long journey west, the Joads suffer hardships: Grampa Joad immediately suffers a fatal stroke; when Granma Joad dies, the family does not have the money for a proper burial.

When the Joads arrive in California, they stay at a squatters' camp, where conditions are deplorable; California is not the "Promised Land" they had expected when they began their arduous journey. The migrants have to cope with filth, chaos, and abuse by brutal police and their deputies. The Joads move to another camp, this one set up by the government. Because of effective management, including the active participation of the migrants themselves on committees, the camp is orderly and clean, a sign that common folk, organized and working together, can improve the conditions under which they live.

Knowing that the migrants are desperate for work, greedy orchard owners cut their pay and use the police to squash strikers, "them goddam reds," as they are referred to. Eight members of the Joad family—four men, two women, and two children—work all day picking peaches. At five cents a box they earn only a dollar and are overcharged for food at the company store. Tom Joad speaks with Jim Casy, who leads a group of pickets outside the orchard. Casy is an ex-preacher whose spiritual nature and humanitarian feelings draw him in fellowship to others. Casy tells Tom how the orchard owners have mistreated the migrants:

> A heavy silence fell in the tent. Casy stared out the entrance, into the dark night. "Lookie, Tom," he said at last. "We come to work there. They says it's gonna be fi' cents. They was a hell of a lot of us. We got there an' they says they're payin' two an' a half cents. A fella can't even eat on that, an' if he got kids—So we says we won't take it. so they druv us off. An' all the cops in the worl' come down on us. Now they're payin' you five. When they bust this here strike—ya think they'll pay five?"
>
> "I dunno," Tom said. "Payin' five now."
>
> "Lookie," said Casy. "We tried to camp together, an' they druv us like pigs. Scattered us. Beat the hell outa fellas. Druv us like pigs. They run you in like pigs, too. We can't las' much longer. Some people ain't et for two days. You goin' back tonight?"
>
> "Aim to," said Tom.
>
> "Well—tell the folks in there how it is, Tom. Tell 'em they're starvin' us an' stabbin' theirself in the back. 'Cause sure as cowflops she'll drop to two an' a half jus' as soon as they clear us out."
>
> "I'll tell 'em," said Tom. "I don' know how. Never seen so many guys with guns. Don' know if they'll even let a fella talk. An' folks don' pass no time of day. They jus' hang down their heads an' won't even give a fella a howdy."
>
> "Try an' tell 'em, Tom. They'll get two an' a half, jus' the minute we're gone. You know what two an' a half is—that's one ton of peaches picked an' carried for a dollar."
>
> He dropped his head. "No—you can't do it. You can't get your food for that. Can't eat for that."[6]

At the book's end, the Joads are living in a makeshift boxcar camp, where in the rain and mud they struggle to build an embankment that would protect them from a perilous flood. The Joads and the other migrants, hungry, some to the point of starvation, penniless, and ill, have hit bottom. Yet the novel ends on a hopeful note. One of the Joads, Rose of Sharon, who has just given birth to a still-born baby, offers her life-sustaining mother's milk to a starving stranger. Written during hard times, *The Grapes of Wrath* was both a cry of pain and an affirmation of life that urges people to be more humane, to be more compassionate, and to recognize their moral obligation to care about others, particularly the downtrodden, with whom they share a common humanity.

Steinbeck's novel, which was the leading best-seller in 1939, came under attack, sometimes viciously, from conservatives and California farm groups. Rumors circulated that Steinbeck was a Jew and a communist—he was neither—out to undermine the American economy. In 1942, a Senate investigation confirmed the "shocking degree of human misery"[7] endured by migrant farm workers.

BRECHT Bertolt Brecht's (1898–1956) experience in the German medical corps during World War I drew him to pacifism; his distress with the chaotic conditions in Germany immediately following the war turned him against capitalism. Contempt for capitalists, whom he saw as exploiters and greedy war profiteers, contributed to his embracing Marxism. When Hitler came to power, Brecht went into exile (the Nazis reacted by burning his books and banning his plays), where he wrote against the Nazi regime. He came to the United States in 1941.

Like the Expressionists, Brecht was critical of contemporary Realist and Naturalist dramas but for different reasons. Like George Bernard Shaw, Brecht regarded the theater as an instrument of social change. A play, he said, should promote critical thinking among the spectators that would foster productive reforms. Because they stir the emotions rather than the intellect, said Brecht, Realist-Naturalist dramas are incapable of such effort. Moreover, because such dramas lead theatergoers to identify with the hero, to interpret the events occurring on the stage from the hero's point of view, they are prevented from reflecting critically on the play's moral and social meaning. He favored what he called *epic theater*—plays dealing with past rather than current events. Properly performed, these historical dramas would stimulate the audience's critical faculties, encouraging them to ponder the lessons that could be learned from these events. What concerns the epic theater is not the characters' inner life, but their behavior, their actions, and their relations with each other; it is these interactions that provoke a thoughtful response by the spectators. Among Brecht's most important plays are *The Three Penny Opera* (1928), *Life of Galileo* (1938–1939; English version, 1947), and *Mother Courage and Her Children* (1939).

The setting for *Mother Courage and Her Children* is the Thirty Years' War (see Chapter 16) that devastated Europe in the seventeenth century. The brutality of war, which Brecht lamented, was also an expression of his pacifism. Mother Courage, a traveling merchant who peddles liquor, clothing, and other commodities to the soldiers, at times driving her cart through bombardments, earns her money from the war. For this unsavory activity, she will pay. The war causes the death of each of her three children one after the other. Her business activities prevent her from saving even one of them. Left alone and reduced to beggary, Mother Courage continues to ply her trade with the soldiers, and the play ends with her dragging her cart hurrying to catch up with the soldiers. Brecht regarded Mother Courage as a war profiteer, whose pursuit of profits contributed to her children's death, and as a foolish woman who, learning no lesson from the death of her children, continues to earn her income from the war. Nevertheless, her suffering and determination never fail to evoke audience sympathy.

Indictment of Totalitarianism: Silone, Koestler, and Orwell

The economic misery of the Depression and the rise of fascist barbarism led many intellectuals to find a new hope, even a secular faith, in communism. They praised the Soviet Union for supplanting capitalist greed with socialist cooperation, for replacing a haphazard economic system marred by repeated depressions with one based on planned production, and for providing employment for everyone when joblessness was endemic in capitalist lands. American literary critic Edmund Wilson said that in the Soviet Union, one felt at the "moral top of the world where the light never really goes out."[8] British political theorists Sidney and Beatrice Webb declared that there was no other country "in which there is actually so much widespread public criticism and such incessant reevaluation of its shortcomings as in the USSR."[9] To these intellectuals, it seemed that in the Soviet Union a vigorous and healthy civilization was emerging and that only communism could stem the tide of fascism. For many, however, the attraction was short-lived. Sickened by Stalin's purges and terror, the denial of individual freedom, and the suppression of truth, they came to view the Soviet Union as another totalitarian state and communism as another "god that failed."

SILONE   Ignazio Silone (1900–1978), an Italian writer and a one-time communist, was expelled from his homeland by the fascists. After viewing the performance of both Russian communists and Italian fascists once they had gained power, Silone grew disillusioned with ideologies: They promised earthly salvation but ended up oppressing people. Motivated by sincere compassion for the poor and oppressed, Silone believed that a combination of socialist idealism and Christian ethics offered the best approach to resolving society's problems. This synthesis figured in his political novels of the 1930s, especially *Bread and Wine* (1937). The protagonist Pietro tells his old schoolmaster, Nunzio, that the fascist dictatorship must be resisted.

"Freedom is not a thing you can receive as a gift," Pietro said. "One can be free even under a dictatorship on one simple condition, that is, if one struggles against it. A man who thinks with his own mind and remains uncorrupted is a free man. A man who struggles for what he believes to be right is a free man. You can live in the most democratic country in the world and if you are lazy, callous, servile, you are not free, in spite of the absence of violence and coercion, you are a slave. Freedom is not a thing that must be begged from others. You must take it for yourself, whatever share you can."

Nunzio was thoughtful and troubled. "You are our revenge."[10]

Wanted by the police for his antigovernment activities, Pietro disguises himself as the priest Don Paolo. To protest the fascist state's suppression of liberty and its invasion of Ethiopia, Don Paolo scrawls antifascist slogans in several public places. As the police search for the dissident, Don Paolo explains the purpose of resistance to a young woman he has befriended.

"The dictatorship is based on unanimity," he said. "It's sufficient for one person to say no and the spell is broken."

"Even if that person is a poor, lonely sick man?" the girl said.

"Certainly." . . .

"Under every dictatorship," he said, "one man, one perfectly ordinary little man who goes on thinking with his own brain is a threat to public order. Tons of printed paper spread the slogans of the regime; thousands of loudspeakers, hundreds of thousands of posters and freely distributed leaflets, whole armies of speakers in all the squares and at all the crossroads, thousands of priests in the pulpit repeat these slogans *ad nauseam,* to the point of collective stupefaction. But it's sufficient for one little man, just one ordinary, little man to say no and the whole of that formidable granite order is imperilled."[11]

Pietro also questions his allegiance to communism. Has not a noble ideal been stifled by a political party that has evolved into a Machiavellian political sect?

As soon as he had finished his coffee he went out into the garden, sat on the bench under the rowan tree, and started writing again, with the notebook resting on his knees: "Is it possible to take part in political life, to put oneself in the service of a party and remain sincere? Has not truth for me become party truth and justice party justice? Have not the interests of the organization ended in my case too by getting the better of all moral values, which are despised as petty bourgeois prejudices, and have those interests not become the supreme value? Have I, then, escaped from the opportunism of a decadent Church only to end up in the Machiavellism of a political sect?"[12]

KOESTLER An intellectual and correspondent for a leading Berlin newspaper chain, Arthur Koestler (1905–1983) joined the Communist party at the very end of 1931, because he "lived in a disintegrating society thirsting for faith," was moved by the suffering caused by the Depression, and saw communism as the "only force capable of resisting the onrush of the primitive [Nazi] horde."[13] Born in Budapest of Jewish ancestry and educated in Vienna, Koestler visited the Soviet Union in 1933, experiencing firsthand both the starvation brought on by forced collectivization and the propaganda that grotesquely misrepresented life in Western lands. Although his faith was shaken, he did not break with the party until 1938, in response to Stalin's liquidations.

In *Darkness at Noon* (1941), Koestler explored the attitudes of the Old Bolsheviks who were imprisoned, tortured, and executed by Stalin. These dedicated communists had served the party faithfully, but Stalin, fearful of opposition, hating intellectuals, and driven by megalomania, denounced them as enemies of the people. The leading character in *Darkness at Noon*, the imprisoned Rubashov, is a composite of the Old Bolsheviks. Although he is innocent, Rubashov, without being physically tortured, publicly confesses to political crimes that he never committed.

Rubashov is aware of the suffering that the party has brought to the Russian people:

[I]n the interests of a just distribution of land we deliberately let die of starvation about five million farmers and their families in one year. . . . [to liberate] human beings from the shackles of industrial exploitation . . . we sent about ten million people to do forced labour in the Arctic regions and the jungles of the East, under conditions similar to those of antique galley slaves. . . . to settle a difference of opinion, we know only one argument: death. . . . Our poets settle discussions on questions of style by denunciations to the secret police. . . . The people's standard of life is lower than it was before the Revolution, the labour con-

ditions are harder, the discipline is more inhuman. . . . Our Press and our schools cultivate Chauvinism, militarism, dogmatism, conformism and ignorance. The arbitrary power of the Government is unlimited, and unexampled in history. Freedom of the Press, of opinion and of movement are as thoroughly exterminated as though the proclamation of the Rights of Man had never been. We have built up the most gigantic police apparatus, with informers made a national institution, and with the most refined scientific system of physical and mental torture. We whip the groaning masses of the country towards a theoretical future happiness, which only we can see.[14]

Pained by his own complicity in the party's crimes, including the betrayal of friends, Rubashov questions the party's philosophy that the individual should be subordinated, and if necessary, sacrificed to the regime. Nevertheless, Rubashov remains the party's faithful servant. True believers do not easily break with their faith. By confessing to treason, Rubashov performs his last service for the Revolution. For the true believer, everything—truth, justice, and the sanctity of the individual—is properly sacrificed to the party.

ORWELL George Orwell (1903–1950), a British novelist and political journalist, wrote two powerful indictments of totalitarianism: *Animal Farm* (1945) and *1984* (1949). In *Animal Farm*, based in part on his experiences with communists during the Spanish Civil War, Orwell satirized the totalitarian regime built by Lenin and Stalin in Russia. In *1984*, Orwell, who was deeply committed to human dignity and freedom, warned that these great principles are now permanently menaced by the concentration and abuse of political power. "If you want a picture of the future, imagine a boot stamping on a human face forever," says a member of the ruling elite as he tortures a victim in the dungeons of the Thought Police.[15]

The society of *1984* is ruled by the Inner Party, which constitutes some 2 percent of the population. Heading the Party is Big Brother—most likely a mythical figure created by the ruling elite to satisfy people's yearning for a leader. The Party indoctrinates people to love Big Brother, whose picture is everywhere. Party members are conditioned to accept unquestioningly the Party's orthodoxy, with all its contradictions, twists, and reversals. Doublethink, the prescribed way of thinking, brainwashes people into holding two contradictory beliefs simultaneously. The Party's philosophy of government is revealed in three slogans: "WAR IS PEACE," "FREEDOM IS SLAVERY," "IGNORANCE IS STRENGTH." The Ministry of Truth resorts to thought control to dominate and manipulate the masses and to keep Party members loyal and subservient. Independent thinking is destroyed. Objective truth no longer exists. Truth is whatever the Party decrees at the moment. If the Party were to proclaim that "2 + 2 = 5," it would have to be believed.

Anyone thinking prohibited thoughts is designated a Thoughtcriminal, a crime punishable by death. The Thought Police's agents are ubiquitous. Using hidden microphones and telescreens, they check on Party members for any signs of deviance from Party rules and ideology. Posters displaying Big Brother's picture carry the words "BIG BROTHER IS WATCHING YOU." Convinced that "who controls the past controls the future," the Ministry of Truth alters old newspapers to make the past accord with the Party's current doctrine. In this totalitarian society of the future, all human rights are abolished, people are arrested merely for their thoughts, and children spy on their parents. The society is brutalized by processions of chained prisoners of war, by public mass executions, and by the Two Minutes Hate ritual, which rouses the participants to a frenzy against Party enemies. A steady supply of cheap gin and pornographic literature keeps the masses, called proles, dull-witted and out of political mischief.

Orwell's anti-utopian novel focuses on Winston Smith, who works for the Ministry of Truth and is arrested by the Thought Police for harboring anti-Party sentiments. Smith rebels against the Party in order to reclaim his individuality—to think and feel in his own way rather than in accordance with the Party's dictates. Tortured brutally, humiliated, and brainwashed, Smith confesses to crimes that both he and the Party know he did not commit.

The Inner Party seeks to capture the inner mind, to transform people into mindless robots. O'Brien of the Thought Police tells Smith: "You will be hollow. We shall squeeze you empty, and then we shall fill you with ourselves." Thus, the Party does not kill Smith but "reshapes" him, by breaking his will and transforming him into a true believer in Big Brother. Smith comes to believe that "the struggle was finished. He had won the victory over himself. He loved Big Brother."[16]

The War Novel: Shaw, Jones, Mailer, Heller, Böll, and Grass

World War II generated a prodigious output of fiction from several countries that dealt imaginatively with the elemental nature of combat and the ordeal of the frontline soldier. Among American novelists who produced memorable works are Norman Mailer, *The Naked and the Dead* (1948), Irwin Shaw, *The Young Lions* (1948), Herman Wouk, *The Caine Mutiny* (1951) and *The Winds of War*

(1971), James Jones, *From Here to Eternity* (1951) and *The Thin Red Line* (1962), and Joseph Heller, *Catch-22* (1961). These novels explored many of the often-conflicting emotions evidenced by men at war—fear, cowardice, brutality, fanaticism, patriotism, loyalty, courage, camaraderie, decency, altruism, longing; they showed men who loved war and the power it gave them, and delved into those elusive qualities of character demonstrated by effective leaders even under the most trying of circumstances. They contained powerful descriptions of the horror and tragedy of conflict that killed and maimed indiscriminately and in staggering numbers and touching scenes of compassion and loyalty. At times they analyzed the ideological and moral issues that were central to the war: the nature and appeal of fascism and its threat to freedom and civilized values. Several of the war novelists, reared on the social issues of the 1930s, were sensitive to bigotry that minorities, particularly Jews and blacks, faced in the service. Examining the prewar life of recruits who made up the heterogeneous American army, these novelists offered penetrating insights into American sexual behavior, social classes, and regional cultures.

SHAW *The Young Lions*, by Irwin Shaw (1913–1984), who was born and educated in New York City, is a novel of ideas, replete with ideological and social concerns. Although treating the prejudices and ignorance of some American soldiers, it also pays homage to their idealism, courage, and commitment. A distinguishing feature of the work is Shaw's treatment of the mind of a German soldier. As the war progresses, Christian Dietsl, who had vaguely believed that Nazism would produce a better world, gradually degenerates into a committed Nazi who discovers his own potential for evil: he arrests Jews in hiding in Paris, participates in a deliberate massacre of English soldiers in North Africa, and demonstrates a zest for killing. He regards as a mentor Lt. Hardenburg, who, now terribly disfigured, speaks to him from a hospital bed:

> For the purpose of our country we need an empty Europe. It is a mathematical problem and the equalizing sign is slaughter. . . . We can be prosperous only if all Europe is a pauper. . . . Do I want the illiterate Pole, drunk on potato alcohol in the winter mud of his village, to be prosperous? Do I want the stinking goaters in the Dolomites [mountains in Italy] to be rich? . . . Why I want servants, not competitors. And failing that, I want corpses. . . . If we announced to the world that for every day of war, we would kill one hundred thousand Europeans and kept our promise, how long do you think the war would last? And not Jews, because everyone is used to seeing Jews killed.[17]

As the war is drawing to a close, Diestl is persuaded by Brandt, an old comrade and friend, to seek refuge with him in the house of his French girlfriend. Diestl goes with him but then has second thoughts; he reports Brandt to the SS, even joining them as they make the arrest. He then tries to find his way back to the German lines eager only to kill for the cause and for the satisfaction it brings him. The war and Nazism have completely annihilated his humanity.

JONES   *The Thin Red Line* by James Jones 1921–1977 captures the emotions and behavior of infantrymen fighting a brutal war in the jungles of the South Pacific.

> Corporal Fife scampered along with Jenks's squad shooting every Japanese he could see, filled with both terror and elation to a point where he could not separate one from the other. Then Jenks went down with a loud squak and a rifle bullet through the throat, and Fife had the squad for himself, and the responsibility, and found he loved it, and all of them. John Bell, his panic of last night gone, ran leading the squad and yelling them on, but mainly watching coolly to keep casualties down. Don Doll ran grinning with his rifle in one hand and his pistol in the other, and when the pistol was empty he . . . began using his rifle. . . . [T]hey found the majority of the Japanese killing themselves with grenades, guns or knives, which was just as well because most of those who did not were shot or bayoneted.
>
> When it was all over, they began shaking hands with the guys from Item Company, grinning at each other out of blackdirty faces. A few men sat down and wept. Charlie Dale garnered many gold teeth. . . . Coming on a Japanese sitting dejectedly on a doorstop with his head in his hands, this beautiful watch sticking out like a big diamond on his wrist, Dale shot him through the head and took the watch.[18]

MAILER   Written by Norman Mailer 1923–, a twenty-five-year-old veteran who had served two years in the Philippines as a rifleman, *The Naked and the Dead*, like *The Thin Red Line*, contains gripping scenes of men in combat on a Pacific island. But it is also an intellectually powerful novel with an undercurrent of pessimism about the future of liberal values in America. The two most commanding, resolute, and effective men, General Cummings and Sgt. Croft, are neofascists, who, Mailer fears, represent America's future. General Cummings engages the liberal Lt. Hearn in political discussions. But Hearn's defense of equality and social justice seems weak and ineffectual when pitted against Cummings's vigorous and self-confident affirmation of elitism, authoritarianism, and man's will to power. Cummings declares "that the only morality of the future is a power morality, and a man who cannot find his adjustment to it is doomed. There's one thing about power. It can flow only from the top down. When there are little surges of resistance at the middle levels, it merely calls for more power to be directed downward, to burn it out."[19]

HELLER   Brooklyn-born Joseph Heller (1923–1999), author of *Catch-22*, enlisted in the United States Air Force in 1942, serving as a B-25 wing bombardier on his tour of duty in Europe. *Catch-22* is like no other war novel. It contains realistic accounts of men under attack on bombing missions, their panic and dying screams as their plane, hit by enemy fire, plummets to earth. But it also transcends the stark, documentary realism of traditional war novels. It is punctuated by outrageous satirical humor, which leads the reader into the bizarre world of the military bureaucracy, with its insane logic, and the Freudian world of mentally disjointed individuals. The comic satire that runs through the book mocks a romantic vision of war; for Heller, combat is not adventure, glory, or honor but madness. Also coming under satirical attack are bureaucratic authority, the profit motive, psychiatry, sexual encounters, religion, and patriotism. The "death" of Doc Daneeka, who keeps complaining that the war has deprived him of his lucrative medical practice, exemplifies the military's macabre bureaucratic machinery. Fearful of flying, Doc Daneeka has the records falsified to show that he is collecting flight time. He is supposedly on a plane that crashes and learns that according to official records he is dead. "You didn't come down in a parachute, so you must have been killed in the crash," he is told.[20] Considered dead and ostracized by his squadron, "he drew no pay or PX rations and depended for life on the charity of Sergeant Tower and Milo, who both knew he was dead. Colonel Cathcart refused to see him, and Colonel Korn sent word through Major Danby that he would have Doc Daneeka cremated on the spot if he ever showed up at Group Headquarters."[21] The War Department officially notifies Doc Daneeka's wife of his demise. Easing her grief is the knowledge that she will receive substantial sums from various life insurance policies and that the U.S. government will provide pension benefits for her and her dependents. And, in a safety deposit box, she discovers $18,000 in cash on which income tax had not been paid and will never have to be paid. Titillated by the flirtatious behavior of her best friends' husbands, the recent "widow" dyes her hair. When she receives a letter from Doc Daneeka urging her to tell the authorities of the mistake, she moves and leaves no forwarding address.

The novel's principal character is Captain Yossarian, a paranoid American bombardier, who believes that people everywhere want to kill him. Knowing that the war is almost over, he no longer cares whether his bombs hit their target. He only wants to stay alive. He seeks to finish the required number of missions needed to be sent home. But as soon as the men of his squadron approach the figure, Colonel Cathcart raises it and keeps raising it; and air force regulations mandate obedience to a commander's orders. This is Catch-22. Using this ploy, the colonel keeps Hungry Joe, who has now completed fifty missions—twice the number originally required—from going home. By now Hungry Joe is crazy; he experiences fearful nightmares and goes about Rome looking for women to photograph naked. Colonel Cathcart believes that setting a record for missions will make him a general and realize his dream of getting his picture in the *Saturday Evening Post*. From his desk, he bravely volunteers his squadron for the most dangerous missions.

Determined to stay alive, Yossarian does everything he can to avoid flying missions, including feigning sickness to gain the security of the hospital and ordering his plane to return to base before the mission is completed. On one mission, Snowden, the radio gunner, is hit and spills his guts all over Yossarian. Traumatized by the ordeal, Yossarian walks around naked, refusing to wear the uniform that had been drenched with Snowden's blood. A frantic Yossarian begs Doc Daneeka to ground him because of insanity. But an army regulation, another Catch-22, states specifically that anyone asking to be grounded could not be insane because he is showing concern for his personal safety, which is a sign of mental health. A truly insane person is someone who cavalierly goes on missions showing no regard for his own life, a description that does not fit Yossarian. Unknown to anyone, Yossarian's roommate, Orr, had been frequently crash-landing his plane as practice runs for an escape to neutral Sweden. When Yossarian learns that Orr had made it, he resolves to follow him to Sweden. In his determination to survive and to break free from an impersonal bureaucracy that is crushing his humanity—to take control over his own life in an increasingly irrational world—Yossarian affirms the enduring value of the individual.

BÖLL AND GRASS Immediately after World War II, few German writers sought to discuss the moral dimensions of the war. Most books dealing with the war were often self-pitying accounts of the horrors suffered by German soldiers fighting in Russia. As economic conditions improved and Germans grew accustomed to their new democratic government, more novelists and playwrights took the Hitler years as their theme. The works of German authors Heinrich Böll (1917–1985) and Gunter Grass (1927–) reveal moral concerns, in particular a determination to compel their countrymen to ponder and learn from the ethical collapse exhibited in their recent past. Both won the Nobel Prize for literature—Böll in 1972 and Grass in 1999—the most prestigious award given writers.

As a young man Böll was never sympathetic to the Nazis, managing to avoid membership in the Hitler Youth. Drafted into the army, he was wounded four times and at the end of the war was taken prisoner by the Americans. Because he chastised his fellow Germans for their selective memory, if not amnesia, about the Nazi years, he was called "the conscience of a nation," a label he rejected. In his numerous essays, short stories, and novels, particularly *Adam Where Are Thou?* (1955), Böll attacked the war's madness, reflected on the Nazis' inhumane mind-set, and indicted Germans for attempting to escape their guilt for the crimes committed by the Nazi regime by blaming everything on Hitler and his party; individuals are responsible for the evil acts they commit, he maintained. Böll also wrote movingly of average Germans—widows, fatherless children, disillusioned veterans—struggling immediately after the war to rebuild their lives in devastated cities and villages where corruption and black markets reigned, and hunger and despair were everyday experiences. Böll's reminder of Germany's dark past was tied to his concern for the injustices of his own day: the plight of the unemployed, intellectuals denied freedom of thought, ethnic bigotry, and asylum seekers fleeing oppressive regimes. He passionately attacked the materialism of the new Germany and injustice and institutional authority that violated the rights of the individual wherever they existed.

Gunter Grass served in the Luftwaffe and ended up as a prisoner of war. Like Böll, he deplored Nazism and the war and pressed his fellow Germans to confront their past, to remember that they had once embraced the lies that they were now eager to bury. Also like Böll, he rejected the idea that Germans were simply victims of history, a specious argument that enables individuals to escape responsibility for their actions. Throughout his long career, Grass remained committed to humane and civilized values, the kind the Nazis sought to destroy. In 1959, Grass achieved instant recognition with *The Tin Drum*, a highly inventive novel that synthesizes stark realism, mocking satire, grotesque fantasy, and outrageous humor. The story takes place where Grass was born, the Baltic city of

Danzig (now Gdansk), populated by both Poles and Germans. Grass shows how many of the German lower bourgeoisie, supposedly good little people, eagerly embrace Nazism, something they were later quick to deny or to forget. The principal character, Oskar, at age three, protesting the cruelties of German history, wills himself not to grow and remains a midget. At the same time he is given a tin drum as a gift, which he constantly beats—even interrupting a Nazi rally with his drumming—for this is how he communicates or drives people away. The tin drum and his glass-shattering voice are devices by which he protects himself from a hostile adult world. *The Tin Drum* was followed by two sequels, *Cat and Mouse* (1961) and *Dog Years* (1963). Collectively known as the Danzig Trilogy, these works provide penetrating insights into the attraction of Nazism for many Germans, Nazi brutality—"mounds of bones," "stench of corpses," and "mass grave"—and the way Germans, after the war, conveniently suppressed or forgot their own complicity and guilt.

The Holocaust: Wiesel and Schwarz-Bart

After liberation, survivors felt a compulsion to bear witness to the willful extermination of a people and a culture. One such survivor, Elie Wiesel (1928–), who received instant acclaim with the French publication of *Night* in 1958, has since become a distinguished man of letters. Among his many honors is the Nobel Peace Prize, awarded in 1986. (Actually, he was born in Romania; his village became part of Hungary during the war and was returned to Romania after the war.) Wiesel was transported from Hungary in 1944 with his family to Auschwitz, the infamous extermination camp. His mother and sister were gassed on arrival; his father, weakened by the death march from Auschwitz to Buchenwald, much of it by foot in freezing weather and with little food, died in early 1945, shortly before the liberation. In this passage from *Night*, which has the quality of sacred poetry, Wiesel describes his entry into another planet—Auschwitz.

> Never shall I forget that night, the first night in camp, which has turned my life into one long night, seven times cursed and seven times sealed. Never shall I forget that smoke. Never shall I forget the little faces of the children, whose bodies I saw turned into wreaths of smoke beneath a silent blue sky.
>
> Never shall I forget those flames which consumed my faith forever.
>
> Never shall I forget that nocturnal silence which deprived me, for all eternity, of the desire to live. Never shall I forget those moments which murdered my God and my soul and turned my dreams to dust. Never shall I forget these things, even if I am condemned to live as long as God Himself. Never.[22]

In addition to the testimony of those who experienced the Holocaust, creative writers, many not themselves survivors, have tried to express through their art happenings that exceed the bounds of historical experience and human imagination. Often for the authors, using the Holocaust to tell a story or to compose verse was a painful but necessary catharsis; they also regarded their words as a memorial to the millions who had suffered. Widely regarded as a memorable literary treatment of the Holocaust is the *Last of the Just* (1959) by André Schwarz-Bart (1928–), a French Jew who fought in the resistance and whose entire family had been murdered in the Nazi death camps. In the book's last scene, the SS club Jewish men, women, children, and patriarchs into the gas chamber. Ernie Levy, whose family God has granted one Just Man for generations, embraces the little children he had been tending since the deportation to lessen their suffering, and he tells them to breathe deeply. The children, "in their last agonies," cry out: "Mama! But I was a good boy! It's dark! It's dark!" The doomed Jews recite a sacred prayer that affirms their commitment to God's oneness and sovereignty:

> When the layers of gas covered everything, there was a silence in the dark sky of the room for perhaps a minute, broken only by the shrill, racking coughs and gasps of those too far gone in their agonies to offer a devotion. At first a stream, and then a cascade, an irresistible majestic torrent, the poem that through the smoke fires and above the funeral pyres of history the Jews . . . unfurled in the gas chamber, enveloped it . . . : "SHEMA YISRAEL ADONOI ELOHENU ADONOI EH'OTH . . . Hear, O Israel, the Lord is our God, the Lord is One. O Lord, by your grace you nourish the living, and by your great pity you resurrect the dead, and you uphold the weak, cure the sick, break the chains of the slave. And faithfully you keep your promises to those who sleep in the dust. Who is like unto you, O merciful Father, and who could be like unto you . . . ?"[23]

The Holocaust has given rise to a vast and growing body of literature. During the war, Jews in the ghettos, concentration camps, or hiding, virtually all of whom eventually perished, wrote poems and kept diaries so that the world, which they felt had forsaken them, would know of their ordeal. These writings were also a means of spiritual sustenance and defiance during the darkest of times. Anne Frank (1929–1945), a young girl who lived in a secret annex in Amsterdam, kept a diary of her experience that survived her capture and death in the notorious Bergen Belsen concentration camp. First published in 1947 and translated into many languages, *The Diary of a Young Girl* has become a modern classic. Made into a play in 1956, it was performed simultaneously in seven German cities before audiences that sat in stunned silence.

Indictment of American Racism: Wright and Ellison

In the 1950s and 1960s, American blacks and their white sympathizers, in what is known as the *Civil Rights Movement,* actively fought to end legal segregation in the South. After the genocidal madness of Nazi racism, it became increasingly more difficult to defend southern racism. Because of their powerful indictment of racial injustice, two novels by black authors, Richard Wright and Ralph Ellison, helped stir public opinion to support the struggle for civil rights.

WRIGHT   The most powerful novel about the racial situation in America, prior to World War II, was *Native Son* (1940) by Richard Wright (1908–1960). Immediately after publication, Wright was in demand as a lecturer, particularly on the subject of "How 'Bigger' Was Born." Bigger Thomas, the protagonist of the novel, "is resentful toward whites, sullen, angry, ignorant, emotionally unstable, depressed and unaccountably elated at times, and unable even, because of his own lack of inner organization which American oppression has fostered in him, to unite with the members of his own race."[24]

Wright centered the narrative entirely on Bigger, dividing it into three long sections—*Fear, Flight,* and *Fate*—detailing how Bigger becomes the chauffeur for the millionaire philanthropist, Mr. Dalton, who owns the apartment building in Chicago in which Bigger's family lives; how he accidentally kills Dalton's daughter, Mary; how Bigger tries to frame Mary's communist boyfriend, Jan, for her death; how he rapes and then bludgeons to death his girlfriend Bessie, because she knows the truth; and how Bigger is ultimately accused of the rape and murder of Mary, is found guilty at trial, and is sentenced to death in the electric chair. In the *Fear* section, Wright recounts Bigger's own fear as he attends to a drunken Mary—how he carries her into her room and lays her on her bed just as her blind mother enters the room:

> He turned and a hysterical terror seized him, as though he were falling from a great height in a dream. A white blur was standing by the door, silent, ghostlike. It filled his eyes and gripped his body. It was Mrs. Dalton. He wanted to knock her out of his way and bolt from the room.
>
> "Mary!" she spoke softly, questioningly.

> He felt Mary trying to rise and quickly he pushed her head back to the pillow. . . . He wanted to move from the bed, but was afraid he would stumble over something and Mrs. Dalton would hear him, would know that someone besides Mary was in the room. Frenzy dominated him. . . . Mary mumbled and tried to rise again. Frantically, he caught a corner of the pillow and brought it to her lips. He had to stop her from mumbling, or he would be caught. . . . Mary's fingernails tore at his hands and he caught the pillow and covered her entire face with it, firmly. Mary's body surged upward and he pushed downward upon the pillow with all of his weight, determined that she must not move or make any sound that would betray him. . . . Then suddenly her fingernails did not bite into his wrists. Mary's fingers loosened. He did not feel her surging and heaving against him. Her body was still.[25]

Wright acknowledged that he patterned the plight of his character Bigger after the dire straits of many other "Biggers" he had met in his own life:

> Bigger No. 1 . . . was a bareheaded, barefoot kid in Jackson, Mississippi, . . . who terrorized me and all of the boys I played with. . . . And never was he happier than when he had someone cornered and at his mercy. . . . I longed secretly to be like him and was afraid. . . . The hardness of . . . Bigger No. 2 was not directed toward me or the other Negroes, but toward the whites who ruled the South. He bought clothes and food on credit and would not pay for them. He lived in the dingy shacks of the white landlords and refused to pay rent. . . . When we asked him why he acted as he did, he would tell us . . . that white folks had everything and he had nothing. . . . We longed to believe and act as he did, but we were afraid. . . . There was Bigger No. 3, whom the white folks called a "bad nigger." . . . [He] was killed during the days of Prohibition: while delivering liquor to a customer he was shot through the back by a white cop. And then there was Bigger No. 4, whose only law was death. The Jim Crow laws of the South were not for him. . . . His rebellious spirit made him violate all the taboos and consequently he always oscillated between moods of intense elation and depression. . . . Then there was Bigger No. 5, who always rode the Jim Crow streetcars without paying . . . and sitting in the white section.[26]

During his trial, Bigger is defended by Boris A. Max, a Jewish Communist, who takes Bigger's case *pro bono* as a favor to Jan. Max attempts to save Bigger from the death penalty by demonstrating that he has been conditioned by his environment to act as he did. As Max pleads Bigger's case before the court, he contends that Bigger's crimes are, at least partially, to be blamed on a white society that is filled with institutionalized bigotry and racism:

> Your Honor, consider the mere physical aspect of our civilization. How alluring, how dazzling it is! How it excites the senses! . . . These bright colors may fill our hearts with elation, but to many they are daily taunts. Imagine a man walking amid such a scene, a part of it, and yet knowing that it is *not* for him!
>
> We planned the murder of Mary Dalton, and today we come to court and say: "We had nothing to do with it!" But every school teacher knows that this is not so, every school teacher knows the restrictions which have been placed upon Negro education. The authorities know that it is not so, for they have made it plain in their every act that they mean to keep Bigger Thomas and his kind within rigid limits. All real estate operators know that it is not so, for they have agreed among themselves to keep Negroes within the ghetto-areas of cities. Your Honor, we who sit here today in this courtroom are witnesses. We know this evidence, for we helped to create it. . . .
>
> This boy's crime was not an act of retaliation by an injured man against a person who he thought had injured him. If it were, then this case would be simple indeed. This is the case of a man's mistaking a whole race of men as a part of the natural structure of the universe and of his acting toward them accordingly. He murdered Mary Dalton accidentally, without thinking, without plan, without conscious motive. But, after he murdered, he accepted the crime. And that's the important thing. It was the first full act of his life; it was the most meaningful, exciting and stirring thing that had ever happened to him. He accepted it because it made him free, gave him the possibility of choice, of action, the opportunity to act and to feel that his actions carried weight.[27]

Through Wright's characterization of his unromantic hero, Bigger Thomas, he not only capably portrayed African American reactions to life in the South, vacillating between rebelliousness and submission, but he also depicted their attraction to communist ideology and the possibility that it held out for social action in behalf of the oppressed. Wright faithfully characterized social conditions, including squalid housing conditions in Chicago and the propensity of "white cops" to arrest "black loners" and charge them with rape with no evidence to support their charges. *Native Son* shocked its readers into an awareness of the magnitude of American racism, a fact that the literary critic and historian of American-Jewish culture, Irving Howe (1920–1993), recognized when he

wrote: "The day *Native Son* appeared, American culture was changed forever."[28]

ELLISON Ralph Waldo Ellison (1914–1994), whose parents were former slaves, was born in Oklahoma City and named for the transcendentalist Ralph Waldo Emerson (see Chapter 20). As a young boy, Ellison loved literature, and as a teenager, he aspired to be a "Renaissance Man." He studied music, became an accomplished jazz trumpeter, played football, and dabbled in electronics. In 1933, Ellison left Oklahoma on a music scholarship to study at the Tuskegee Institute in Alabama, where he became fascinated with sociology and sculpture. There he met Alain Locke, who enabled Ellison to meet Langston Hughes and Richard Wright; at Tuskegee, he also discovered the powerful language and symbols of T. S. Eliot's poem, *The Waste Land,* which later became a hallmark of Ellison's own writing.

During World War II, Ellison joined the merchant marine and began his one and only novel: *Invisible Man* (1952). The story line of the 500-plus-page novel is often convoluted, for it is replete with complex symbols that have multiple layers of meaning, reminiscent of *The Waste Land.* Ellison relates situations that cause people, both black and white, to be blind to people as unique individuals, preferring to see them as cogs in a piece of machinery or as some "thing" to help them further their own social or political agenda. This leads to a loss of personal identity. The unnamed narrator, the book's principal character, becomes increasingly aware that people seek to impose their values and expectations on him. By forcing him to become someone other than himself, by regarding him "simply [as] a material, a natural resource to be used,"[29] they deprive him of his identity, making him even more invisible. This is why he has decided to live underground in a manhole, which is illumined by light bulbs that he has electrified by siphoning off power from New York City.

> I am a man of substance, of flesh and bone, fiber and liquids—and I might even possess a mind. I am invisible, understand, simply because people refuse to see me. . . . When they approach me they see only my surroundings, themselves, or figments of their imagination—indeed, everything and anything except me.[30]

The series of puzzling, disenchanting, and debilitating events that led to the narrator's decision allow Ellison to explore his own feelings about race and to seek to understand the various ways black and white Americans relate to each other. In particular, he depicts the humiliations that black people of his generation had to endure.

When he takes a job at Liberty Paints, where the managers are all white and are paid considerably more than the black employees, the narrator helps to make a product called "Optic White." This is one of Ellison's more complex symbols, but it allows him to make his ideas about color known in a literal way. Billed as the "Right White," Optic White is "so white you can paint a chunka coal and you'd have to crack it open with a sledge hammer to prove it wasn't white clear through!"[31] Ellison is thus making a penetrating comment about how white society completely diminishes black culture, which leads the narrator to muse to himself, "If you're white, you're right." One of the more ironic connotations of the symbol is that Optic White is made by swirling very dark colors into the paint mixture, depriving the colors of their true identity. Black workers perform this crucial task, and they are viewed as an integral part of the machinery, a fact that the narrator's foreman makes clear when he remarks: "They got all this machinery, but that ain't everything; *we are the machines inside the machine*."[32] The final layer of meaning to this symbol becomes evident when an explosion occurs. It knocks the narrator unconscious and covers him with white paint—symbolizing his total subjugation to white society.

Following his recovery, the narrator attracts the attention of the political organization called the Brotherhood, which he believes will aid him in his quest for social justice and racial equality. But again, he is acutely aware of his invisibility, for his supposed "brothers" only want to use him to further their own political goals. When the narrator offends the black nationalist leader, Ras the Exhorter, Ellison begins to explore the conflict within the black community about how best to respond to social injustice and racial prejudice. Whereas the Brotherhood believes in a program of political action, Ras represents the beliefs of the black nationalist leader Marcus Garvey (1887–1940) who flaunted his blackness, and refused to be invisible. The cornerstones of his philosophy were black pride, black identity, and black solidarity, and he advocated racial redemption through black separatism. This meant giving blacks their own homeland in Africa, to parallel the white homeland of Europe. He opposed the integration advocated by men like W. E. B. DuBois because he believed that it led to the diminution of blacks in white society and the loss of black identity.

The narrator comes to another crucial conclusion: his inner being is limited not only by racial prejudice but also by ideologies such as those professed by the accommodationist Dr. Bledsoe at the college he once attended, by the politically active Brotherhood, by the separatist Ras, and by the charlatan preacher Rinehart. Eventually, the narrator comprehends how invisible he has become, and for the first time, he finally understands the type of accommodation that his grandfather had made by always saying "yes" to his white master.

> I didn't know what my grandfather had meant, but I was ready to test his advice. I'd overcome them with yeses, undermine them with grins, I'd agree them to death and destruction. . . . I'd yes them, but wouldn't I yes them! I'd yes them till they puked and rolled in it. All they wanted of me was one belch of affirmation and I'd bellow it out loud. Yes! Yes! YES! That was all anyone wanted of us, that we should be heard and not seen, and then heard only in one big optimistic chorus of yassuh, yassuh, yassuh! . . . They wanted a machine? Very well, I'd become a supersensitive confirmer of their misconceptions, and just to hold their confidence I'd try to be right part of the time. Oh, I'd serve them well and I'd make invisibility felt if not seen, and they'd learn that it could be as polluting as a decaying body, or a piece of bad meat in a stew.[33]

By the end of the novel, the narrator concludes that while going underground, his invisibility has brought him safety, but his isolation will not bring about social equality or put an end to racial prejudice. Consequently, in the Epilogue, he determines to emerge from his underground cave in a manner very much like the individual in Plato's "Allegory of the Cave," who must give up the shadows of the cave for the light of truth. By exerting his power as a "visible" man—free of the stereotypes that others, in their blindness, have thrust on him—the narrator resolves to make a visible difference in society.

> In going underground, I whipped it all except the mind, the *mind*. And the mind that has conceived a plan of living must never lose sight of the chaos against which that pattern was conceived. That goes for societies as well as for individuals. Thus, having tried to give pattern to the chaos which lives within the pattern of your certainties, I must come out, I must emerge.[34]

ART

Painting and Totalitarianism

The goal of totalitarian governments was to dominate totally all aspects of society, including culture. In the early years of the Soviet Union, the Bolsheviks favored the avant-garde artists, who ardently supported the revolution. But when Stalin succeeded Lenin in 1924, a new tone was set, so that

Figure 25.1 Pablo Picasso, *Guernica*, 1937, 11′6″ x 25′8″. Colored only in shades of black, white, and gray, this painting is perhaps the most successful antiwar painting in art history. As a metaphor of extreme violence and intolerable suffering, it memorializes the victims of the saturation bombing of the town by Nazi pilots supporting General Franco. *(Museo del Prado/Giraudon/Art Resource, NY © 2002 Estate of Pablo Picasso/Artists Rights Society (ARS), New York)*

by 1932, there existed an official standard for art called *Socialist Realism.* Artists were required to belong to the "Union of Soviet Artists," under state control, and their paintings had to glorify the collectivist ideals of communism. Soviet Socialist Realist painters produced overly dramatic works that depicted larger than life political leaders, citizens engaged in wholesome activities such as farming, and soldiers valiantly defending the homeland.

In Germany, the avant-garde artists did not support Hitler; they generally were on the left of the political spectrum. Hitler, who himself had been a mediocre painter as a young man, hated avant-garde art, which he referred to as "artistic Bolshevism." Soon after he became chancellor in 1933, he began his campaign to purify Germany of such "degenerate" art. Official Nazi paintings featured scenes that celebrated the athletic prowess, health, strength, and beauty of the Aryan race and glorified family, motherhood, the fatherland, and *Der Führer.*

Although most avant-garde artists were politically on the left, Dali was a conservative. He was expelled from the Surrealist group in Paris, because he supported General Franco (1892–1975), the neo-Fascist leader who led the forces that overthrew the republican government during the Spanish Civil War (1936–1939) and who ruled Spain until 1975.

In contrast, Picasso never evidenced much interest in politics until the Spanish Civil War broke out, when he became an avowed opponent of

Franco. In April 1937, he had a chance to show his support for the republicans when Nazi pilots supporting Franco decimated the town of Guernica, in northern Spain, with saturation bombing, killing hundreds of civilians, including women and children. To memorialize the tragic event, Picasso painted his huge (11′6″ × 25′8″) *Guernica* (Figure 25.1), which evidences the influence of the Surrealists, even though he was never a member of their group. The painting was exhibited during the summer of 1937 in the Spanish Pavilion at the International Exhibition in Paris. Colored only in shades of black, white, and gray, it is perhaps the most successful antiwar painting in art history. It is a metaphor of extreme violence and intolerable suffering. On the right a woman screams, with her arms spread wide, fleeing a burning house, and in the far left a mother, looking upward and wailing, holds her dead child. Above her is a bull, which represents Franco and the fascists, and above a dead warrior is a dying horse, symbolizing the moribund republic and the people of Spain. The electric light bulb in a shade is the all-seeing eye that, with the help of the lantern held by a woman, illuminates the horror of the scene for all to witness.

American Artists: Hopper, O'Keeffe, Lange, and Adams

As modern art was developing in Europe at the turn of the twentieth century, most American artists continued to elaborate on the Realist tradition of nineteenth-century Europe. However, a few artists were introduced to modern art during trips to France and Germany, and when they returned home, mostly to New York, they began to introduce modern art to America. In 1905, Alfred Stieglitz (1864–1946), often referred to as the father of modern photography, opened a gallery in New York, which in 1907 began to exhibit paintings as well as photographs. Six years later, the International Exhibition of Modern Art was held in the Sixty-Ninth Regiment Armory in New York, where the works of Matisse, Kandinsky, Picasso, Braque, and Duchamp (among others) were shown. Although the critics were harsh, galleries devoted to the new idiom soon opened, including the Museum of Modern Art in New York City in 1929.

During the 1930s and the 1940s, America became a refuge for European artists just as Europe had been a haven for avant-garde expatriate authors in the 1920s. Many European artists—including Duchamp, Ernst, Mondrian, and Dali—emigrated to the United States to escape the totalitarian regimes in Europe. But even though European Modernists found asylum in the United States, American Modernism was soon superseded by a new type of Realism.

One of the most successful practitioners of the new Realism was Edward Hopper (1882–1967). At the same time that Matisse, Picasso, and Braque were creating the genre of modern art, Hopper visited Paris three times, between 1906 and 1910. Nonetheless, these experiences seemed to have had no influence on his style. Hopper sold his first painting at the Armory Show in New York in 1913, but it was not until about 1930 that he developed the style that made him the most notable American Realist of the twentieth century. In his most famous painting, *Nighthawks* (Figure 25.2), Hooper depicts loneliness and alienation—one of his favorite themes. The scene occurs in an all-night diner in New York City in 1942, where a couple seem disconnected, as the man converses with the waiter. The fourth figure, with his back to the viewer, is not identified. Exposed and vulnerable in the bright light, these people suffer an existential loneliness, with no door for entry or exit.

One of the pioneers of American Modernism, Georgia O'Keeffe (1887–1986), was trained entirely in the United States. O'Keeffe attended Columbia Teachers College in New York, where she was introduced to Post-Impressionism and to Asian art. The first showing of her work was in 1916, when a series of abstract charcoal drawings

Figure 25.2   Edward Hopper, *Nighthawks,* **1942, 33″ x 60″ (83.8 x 152.4 cm), oil on canvas, The Art Institute of Chicago.**   One of Hopper's favorite themes is loneliness and alienation, which is evident in this, his most famous painting. As the man converses with the waiter in an all-night diner, he and the woman seem disconnected. Exposed and vulnerable in the bright light, these people suffer from a type of existential loneliness, which provides no door for entry or exit. *(Friends of American Art Collection, 1042.51 © The Art Institute of Chicago. All Rights Reserved)*

MUSIC

Developments in Jazz and Blues

Billie Holiday (1915–1959) is regarded as one of the finest blues vocalists. Her teenage mother was Sadie Harris (a.k.a. Fagan), and her father probably was Clarence Holiday, a guitar and banjo player who worked with Fletcher Henderson's band in the early part of the 1930s. By the time she was sixteen, Holiday had learned how to bear up under extreme conditions, including parental neglect, physical abuse (including rape at age eleven), racial prejudice, and abject poverty in the Harlem ghetto. Holiday had little schooling and no formal musical training, but she did have an intuitive feel for jazz and blues.

Holiday's big break came when she was spotted by the well-connected record producer John Hammond, Jr., who had come to the 133rd Street Club to listen to another blues singer but ended up hearing Holiday, who impressed him with her sense of phrasing and uncanny ability to remember all the lyrics to her songs. Hammond brought noted jazz musicians to hear her sing, including Benny Goodman, with whom she recorded three records late in 1933. In spite of the prowess of her instrumentalists, "The Lady" (the nickname she earned in Harlem for her sense of dignity which was later modified to "Lady Day.") managed to imprint her own style on the vocal refrains, for which she earned the respect of prominent jazz musicians.

She went on to sing with the big bands of Count Basie and Artie Shaw: she was one of the first black singers to star with an all-white band. She also did a motion picture (1935) with the legendary jazz musician Duke Ellington. But while performing with Shaw in the South in the spring of 1938, Holiday got into trouble with racists and left the band before the end of the year, vowing never again to be a band member.

In 1939, a racially integrated nightclub in New York's Greenwich Village, Café Society, opened. For nine months, Holiday performed there and premiered her song-poem, "Strange Fruit," about a lynching—written by a white Jewish schoolteacher, Abel Merropol, using the pseudonym Lewis Allan.

Southern trees bear strange fruit,
Blood on the leaves. Blood at the root,
Black bodies swinging in the southern breeze,
Strange fruit hanging from the poplar trees.

Pastoral scene of the gallant south,
The bulging eyes and the twisted mouth,
The scent of magnolia sweet and fresh,
Then the sudden smell of burning flesh!

Here is a fruit for the crows to pluck,
For the rain to gather, for the wind to suck,
For the sun to rot, for the tree to drop,
Here is a strange and bitter crop.

"Strange Fruit" was an immediate success, and Holiday became known as a singer of socially significant ballads. On April 29, 1939, the controversial song was recorded on the Commodore label, because her own recording studio refused to do so. Later, it was considered as one of the songs to champion the Civil Rights Movement of the 1950s and 1960s, even before "We Shall Overcome" became its standard-bearer.

Today, Billie Holiday is regarded as a truly innovative blues artist for her use of vibrato and tonal variation, her ease with vocal phrasing, and her emotional attachment to the lyrics of her songs. Moreover, her uncanny ability to couple blues with clear diction, even while improvising on a theme, which could be flirtatious, joyous, disillusioned, moody, haughty, demanding, or defiant, demonstrates her musical ability as nothing short of genius quality.

During the 1940s, *Bebop jazz* developed for those audiences who were adept at listening to complex harmonies, melodies, and rhythms. Celebrated Bebop performers of the decade were the saxophonist Charlie "Bird" Parker (1922–1955), the trumpeter Dizzy Gillespie (1917–1993), and the pianist Thelonious Monk (1917–1982). John Coltrane (1926–1967) was an important improvisation artist, playing the tenor and soprano saxophones, who helped to make free jazz popular. As its name implies, *free jazz* is not driven by any regular patterns pertaining to chord structure, rhythm, or melody. The bandleader and trumpeter Miles Davis (1926–1991), spanned several styles of jazz, including the relaxed, "cool" tones of cool jazz, which was made possible by incorporating new instruments into the jazz ensemble, among them the cello, the flute, and the French horn. Davis also is connected to the fusion of jazz with rock music during the 1960s, 1970s, and 1980s.

The Big Band

The 1930s and 1940s were the heyday of the *big bands.* Some of America's greatest musicians played in these bands, and the leader was generally a virtuoso performer: clarinetists Benny Goodman (1919–1986), Artie Shaw (1910–), and Woody Herman (1913–1987); drummer Gene Krupa (1919–1973); trombonists Glenn Miller (1905–1944) and Tommy Dorsey (1905–1956); trumpeter Harry James (1916–1983); and pianist Stan

Kenton (1911–1979). Arguably, the best of the big bands, in these years of racial segregation and discrimination, were all-black ensembles led by men of dazzling talent, including Duke Ellington, piano; Count Basie (1904–1984), piano; Louis Armstrong (1901–1971), trumpet; and Chick Webb (1909–1939), drums. Virtually all the bands featured vocalists, several of whom became legendary figures in American popular music, including Frank Sinatra (1915–1998), Mel Torme (1925–1999), Dick Haymes (1916–1980), Joe Williams (1918–1999), Helen O'Connell (1920–1993), Ella Fitzgerald (1917–1996), and Peggy Lee (1920–2002).

Combining pulsating rhythms with creative arrangements of tunes by America's leading songwriters, the big band had Americans listening to live radio broadcasts, buying records in unprecedented numbers and "jumpin' and jivin'" in the many ballrooms that sprang up in cities and towns throughout the country. An engagement in their town by a prominent big band was a gala event for young people, who danced swing (also called "jitterbug" or the "Lindy Hop," after the aviator Charles Lindbergh) with great intensity or swayed to sentimental ballads; often they congregated in front of the stage to cheer a band's unique sound and the soloist's artistry.

One of the most popular bands was led by Benny Goodman (1909–1986). Born into a poor Russian-Jewish immigrant family that settled in Chicago, as a youngster Goodman studied classical clarinet under a demanding German-born instructor, who insisted on technical mastery. Goodman's solos, which demonstrated his matchless control, combined with Fletcher Henderson's (1897–1952) creative arrangements, led him to be crowned "king of swing." Henderson, who had earlier distinguished himself as the leader of a black orchestra, added a Harlem influence to the pop tunes and traditional jazz numbers played by the Goodman band, a formula that appealed to Goodman's white audience. Concerned only with talent, musicians were among the first to bypass color barriers. Goodman, for example, hired Lionel Hampton (1914–), the outstanding vibraphone soloist and drummer, pianist Teddy Wilson (1912–1986), who had exquisite feeling for melody, and Charlie Christian (1916–1942), the innovative guitarist, who tragically died of tuberculosis at the age of twenty-six.

Playing in a big band was demanding; it required constant travel and often temperamental leaders with exacting standards who could make rehearsals an ordeal. Yet for many musicians, it was a priceless experience. Harold Wax, who played accordion for Artie Shaw's Navy band during World War II, one of the finest ever assembled, because it drew on the talent of top musicians now in the service, reflects on the big band experience:

> With complete brass, woodwind, and rhythm sections, the big band could constantly innovate, and soloists, performing jazz improvisations, would be complemented by background riffs that enhanced the music's richness and originality. New and exciting sounds were created as when Glenn Miller had a clarinet play the lead melody backed up by four saxophones. Musicians felt that they were originating a new style of music and relished the opportunity to perform with colleagues, many of them with extraordinary talent, who shared their enthusiasm for the new sound. And they fed off the dancers and listeners, who showed their admiration for the music by spontaneously breaking out in applause and cheers. All of these factors working concurrently created an electricity that made the emotions soar. At times it seemed we were lifted to another dimension; the feeling was almost spiritual.[39]

The Modern Predicament

The process of fragmentation, which had begun in European thought and arts at the end of the nineteenth century, accelerated after World War I. Increasingly, philosophers, writers, and artists expressed disillusionment with the rational-humanist tradition of the Enlightenment. They no longer shared the Enlightenment's confidence in either reason's capabilities or human goodness, and they viewed perpetual progress as an illusion.

For some thinkers, the crucial problem was the great change in the European understanding of truth. Since the rise of philosophy in ancient Greece, Western thinkers had believed in the existence of objective, universal truths: truths that were inherent in nature and applied to all peoples at all times. (Christianity, of course, also taught the reality of truth as revealed by God.)

It was held that such truths—the natural rights of the individual, for example—could be apprehended by the intellect and could serve as a standard for individual aspirations and social life. The recognition of these universal principles, it was believed, compelled people to measure the world of the here and now in the light of rational and universal norms and to institute appropriate reforms. Philosophy had the task of reconciling human existence with the objective order.

During the nineteenth century, the existence of universal truth came into doubt. A growing historical consciousness led some thinkers to maintain that what people considered truth was merely a reflection of their culture at a given stage in history—their perception of things at a specific point in the evolution of human consciousness. These thinkers, called historicists, held that universal truths were not woven into the fabric of nature. There are no natural rights of life, liberty, and property that constitute the individual's birthright; there are no standards of justice or equality inherent in nature and ascertainable by reason. It was the people, said historicists, who elevated the beliefs and values of an age to the status of objective truth. The normative principles—the self-evident truths proclaimed by Jefferson—which for the philosophes of the Enlightenment constituted a standard for political and social reform and a guarantee of human rights, were no longer linked to the natural order, to an objective reality that could be confirmed by reason. As political philosopher Hannah Arendt noted, "We certainly no longer believe, as the men of the French Revolution did, in a universal cosmos of which man was a part and whose natural laws he had to imitate and conform to."[40]

This radical break with the traditional attitude toward truth contributed substantially to the crisis of European consciousness that marked the first half of the twentieth century. Traditional values and beliefs, either those inherited from the Enlightenment or those taught by Christianity, no longer gave Europeans a sense of certainty and security. People were left without a normative order to serve as a guide to living—and without such a guide might be open to nihilism. For if nothing is fundamentally true—if there are no principles of morality and justice that emanate from God or can be derived from reason—then it can be concluded, as Nietzsche understood, that everything is permitted. Some scholars interpreted Nazism as the culminating expression of a nihilistic attitude grown ever more brutal.

By the early twentieth century, the attitude of Westerners toward reason had undergone a radical transformation. Some thinkers, who had placed their hopes in the rational tradition of the Enlightenment, were distressed by reason's inability to resolve the tensions and conflicts of modern industrial society. Moreover, the growing recognition of the nonrational—of human actions determined by hidden impulses—led to doubts that reason plays the dominant role in human behavior. The intellect did not seem autonomous and self-regulating, but instead seemed subject to the rebellious demands of unconscious drives and impulses. Men's and women's propensity for goodness, their capacity to improve society, and their potential for happiness seemed severely limited by an inherent irrationality. Indeed, civilization itself seemed threatened by people's instinctual needs, as Freud had proclaimed.

Other thinkers viewed the problem of reason differently. They attacked reason for fashioning a technological and bureaucratic society that devalued and crushed human passions and stifled individuality; these thinkers insisted that human beings cannot fulfill their potential, cannot live wholly, if their feelings are denied. They agreed with D. H. Lawrence's critique of rationalism: "The attribution of rationality to human nature, instead of enriching it, now seems to me to have impoverished it. It ignored certain powerful and valuable springs of feeling. Some of the spontaneous, irrational outbursts of human nature can have a sort of value from which our schematism was cut off."[41]

These thinkers pointed out that reason was a double-edged sword: it could demean, as well as ennoble, the individual. They attacked all theories that subordinated the individual to a rigid system, including Marxism, for making social class a higher reality than the individual. Rebelling against political collectivization, which regulated individual lives according to the needs of the corporate state, they assailed modern technology and bureaucracy. These creations of the rational mind, they claimed, had fashioned a social order that devalued and depersonalized the individual, denying people an opportunity for independent growth and a richer existence. According to these thinkers, modern industrial society, in its drive for efficiency and uniformity, deprived people of their uniqueness and reduced flesh-and-blood human beings to mere cogs in a mechanical system. Were not the systematic extermination of European Jewry that depended on modern technology (gas chambers and crematoria designed for maximum efficiency) and bureaucracy (administrators who diligently organized deportations to the death camps, gearing them to railroad schedules) both the creations of calculating reason?

Responding to the critics of reason, other philosophers maintained that it was necessary to reaffirm the rational tradition, first proclaimed by the Greeks and given its modern expression by the Enlightenment. Reason, said these thinkers, was indispensable to civilization. What they advocated was broadening the scope of reason to accommodate the insights into human nature advanced by the Romantics, Nietzsche, Freud, Modernist writers and artists, and others who explored the world of feelings, will, and the unconscious. They also stressed the need to humanize reason so that it could never threaten to reduce a human being to a thing.

In the decades shaped by world wars and totalitarianism, intellectuals raised questions that went to the heart of the dilemma of modern life. How can civilized life be safeguarded against human irrationality, particularly when it is channeled into political ideologies that idolize the state, the leader, the party, or the race? How can individual human personality be rescued from a relentless rationalism that reduces human nature and society to mechanical systems and seeks to regulate and organize the individual as it would any material object? Do we, as human beings, have the moral and spiritual resolve to use properly the technological and scientific creations of modern civilization, or will they devour us? Do the values associated with the Enlightenment provide a sound basis on which to integrate society? Can the individual find meaning in what many came to regard as a meaningless universe? World War II and the Holocaust gave these questions a special poignancy.

Key Terms

totalitarianism	International Style
Five Year Plans	*Bauhaus*
fascism	organic architecture
appeasement	Bebop jazz
epic theater	free jazz
Civil Rights Movement	big band
Socialist Realism	

Notes

1. Hannah Arendt, *The Origins of Totalitarianism* (New York: World, Meridian Books, 1958), p. 469.
2. Karl Dietrich Bracher, *The Age of Ideologies,* trans. Erwald Osers (New York: St. Martin's Press, 1984), p. 83.
3. *Hitler's Secret Conversations, 1941–1944,* with an introductory essay by H. R. Trevor Roper (New York: Farrar, Straus & Young, 1953), p. 28.
4. Quoted in Lucy S. Dawidowicz *The War Against the Jews 1933–1945* (New York: Holt, Rinehart & Winston, 1975), p. 21.
5. Adolf Hitler, *Mein Kampf* (Boston: Houghton Mifflin, 1962), p. 107.
6. John Steinbeck, *The Grapes of Wrath* (New York: Penguin Books, 1992), pp. 522–523.
7. Quoted in Jackson J. Benson, *John Steinbeck, Writer* (New York: Penguin Books, 1990), p. 422.
8. Quoted in David Caute, *The Fellow Travellers* (New York: Macmillan, 1973), p. 64.
9. Ibid., p. 92.
10. Ignazio Silone, *Bread and Wine,* trans. Richard Crossman (New York: Signet, 1986), p. 63.
11. Ibid., pp. 209–210.
12. Ibid., p. 88.
13. Richard Crossman, ed., *The God That Failed* (New York: Bantam Books, 1951), pp. 15, 21.
14. Arthur Koestler, *Darkness at Noon* (New York: Macmillan, 1941), pp. 158–159.
15. George Orwell, *1984* (New York: Harcourt Brace, 1949; paperback, *The New American Library,* 1961), p. 220.
16. Ibid., pp. 211, 245.
17. Irwin Shaw, *The Young Lions* (New York: Signet, 1948), pp. 256–257.
18. James Jones, *The Thin Red Line* (New York: Delta, 1998), pp. 463–464.
19. Norman Mailer, *The Naked and the Dead* (New York: Rinehart, 1948), p. 323.
20. Joseph Heller, *Catch-22* (New York: Dell, 1970), p. 351.
21. Ibid., p. 353.
22. Elie Wiesel, *Night* (New York: Avon Books, 1969), p. 44.
23. André Schwarz-Bart, *The Last of the Just* (New York: Bantam, 1961), pp. 420–421.
24. Richard Wright, *Native Son, with an Introduction "How 'Bigger' Was Born"* (New York: Harper & Row, Publishers, 1940), p. xxi.
25. Ibid., pp. 84–85.
26. Ibid., pp. viii, ix, and x.
27. Ibid., pp. 363–364.
28. Quoted in Kenneth Kinnamon, ed., *New Essays on Native Son* (Cambridge: Cambridge University Press, 1990), p. 24.
29. Ralph Ellison, *Invisible Man* (New York: New American Library, 1952), p. 439.
30. Ibid., p. 7.
31. Ibid., p. 190.
32. Ibid.
33. Ibid., pp. 439–440.
34. Ibid., p. 502.
35. Ansel Adams, *An Autobiography,* with Mary Street Alinder (Boston: Little, Brown and Company, 1985), p. 112.
36. *World Unity Magazine* (Sept. 1928) 2: 393–395.
37. Quoted in Robert C. Twombly, *Frank Lloyd Wright: An Interpretive Biography* (New York: Harper and Row, 1973), p. 276.
38. Quoted in Meryle Secrest, *Frank Lloyd Wright* (New York: Alfred A. Knopf, 1993), p. 548.
39. A discussion with Marvin Perry, December 2001.
40. Quoted in Harry S. Kariel, *In Search of Authority* (Glencoe, Ill.: The Free Press, 1964), p. 246.
41. Quoted in Anthony Arblaster, *The Rise and Decline of Western Liberalism* (Oxford: Basil Blackwell, 1984) p. 81.

26

The Contemporary Age

T HE DECADES SINCE WORLD WAR II HAVE WITNESSED momentous changes in both Western and world history: the Cold War between the Soviet Union and the United States, both armed with weapons of mass destruction, ended with the collapse of the Soviet empire in Eastern Europe and the disintegration of the Soviet Union itself; the global map was rapidly altered as the European colonial powers surrendered their overseas empires; non-European countries have been transformed by the spread of Western ideas, institutions, and cultural forms throughout the globe; and in the first decade of the twenty-first century, militant Islamic terrorism, exemplified by the suicide attacks on the World Trade Center and the Pentagon on September 11, 2001, has become an increasingly dangerous force. The United States, which now stands as the only superpower, has also come to play a major role in both Western and world cultural life. American popular music, films, and television programs travel the globe, and American authors, artists, and musicians now occupy a prominent place in the evolution of the Western humanist tradition.

A NEW EUROPE AND A NEW WORLD

At the end of World War II, Winston Churchill, Britain's pugnacious wartime leader, lamented: "What is Europe now? A rubble heap, a charnel house, a breeding ground for pestilence and hate."[1] Everywhere the survivors counted their dead. War casualties were relatively light in Western Europe. Britain and the Commonwealth suffered 460,000 casualties; France, 570,000; and Italy, 450,000. War casualties were heavier further east: 5 million people in Germany, 6 million in Poland (including 3 million Jews), 1 million in Yugoslavia, and more than 25 million in the Soviet Union. The material destruction was unprecedented. Cities and farmland lay in ruins. Industry, transportation, and communication had come to a virtual standstill. Now members of families searched for each other; prisoners of war made their way home; Jews were liberated from concentration camps and came out of hiding places to return to open life; and displaced persons by the millions sought refuge. However, aided by the United States through the Marshall Plan, Western Europe recovered with extraordinary speed, and with the memory of two ruinous world wars still vivid, many Western Europeans were determined to build a new Europe that rejected extreme nationalism and emphasized a common cultural heritage and commitment to democratic values.

As the same time that Western Europe was struggling to rebuild, it faced another crisis: the expansion of Soviet power, for in pursuing Hitler's armies,

David Smith, Cubi XIX, 1964, height 9'5 3/8" (2.88 m), Tate Gallery, London.

Smith produced several series of sculptures, this being but one example, which were inspired by Cubism. All of the monumental cubes, cubic rectangles, and cylinders, are constructed out of polished and brushed stainless steel which Smith himself constructed. The carefully balanced cubis are meant to be displayed outdoors where they capture and reflect every change in the natural light.

(Tate Gallery, London/Art Resource, NY © David Smith/Licensed by VAGA, New York, NY)

Soviet troops had overrun Eastern Europe and penetrated into the heart of Germany. Europe's future now depended on two countries, the United States and the Soviet Union, which soon became embroiled in a bitter struggle. The Soviet Union, exhausted by World War II and anxious about security, imposed its grim tradition of dictatorship in Eastern Europe. The Berlin Blockade and airlift, the Communist coup in Czechoslovakia, and the formal partition of Germany in the late 1940s, followed by the creation of adversarial alliances and the definitive division of Eastern and Western Germany by the Berlin Wall and barbed-wire-fringed free-fire zones, manifested irreconcilable differences and served as powerful symbols of potential conflict between the two camps.

The Cold War took on a global dimension with the establishment of a Communist government in China in 1949; the invasion of the pro-American regime in South Korea by the pro-Soviet Communist regime in North Korea in 1950; the Soviet attempt to install nuclear missiles in Communist Cuba in 1962, which almost led to war between the two superpowers; and the failed attempt of the United States to prevent Communist North Vietnam from taking over South Vietnam in the 1960s and early 1970s.

Soviet rule was never firmly rooted. The Eastern Europeans under Soviet domination traditionally looked westward, benefiting from economic, religious, and cultural ties with Western Europe. They also carried over from their past a strong nationalist ambition for independence. In the Soviet Union, too, opposition mounted; the communist system did not improve the quality of life as promised. As Western Europe recovered from World War II, the discrepancy between the poverty of the countries of the Soviet bloc and the prosperity of their Western neighbors added a further source of anticommunist agitation.

Inevitably, the craving for independence and freedom caused mounting tensions in Soviet-controlled Eastern Europe. By the end of 1989, all communist regimes there, except in Albania, had been overthrown. (Communist rule in Albania ended in 1991.) And in the Soviet Union, the reforms instituted by Mikhail Gorbachev (1931–) in 1986 led to the dissolution of the communist empire at the end of 1991. Within three years, the once-mighty Soviet superpower had disintegrated unexpectedly and in a remarkably peaceful manner. Its ideology discredited, its economy shattered, and its government transformed into a confederation of sovereign states, the Soviet Union had collapsed as a major force in world affairs. Only one superpower remained. The Cold War was over. The sudden and unexpected collapse of Commu-

nism in Eastern Europe in 1989 seemed to discredit Marxism irrevocably. Reformers in Eastern European lands liberated from communist oppression expressed revulsion for the socialist past and a desire to regenerate their countries with an infusion of Western liberal ideals and institutions.

The recovery of Western Europe and the Cold War were two major developments in the decades after World War II. Another was decolonization, the end of European empires in Asia and Africa. Western imperialism had everywhere introduced Western institutions, goods, and ideals, including the right of self-determination. World War II had stirred up the non-Western peoples living under Western colonial rule to liberate themselves. When World War II ended, the militancy of anticolonial movements increased. The political agitation of the war, in which many colonial soldiers had loyally fought for their masters, sparked the desire for political independence. After all, freedom and self-determination had been prominent Allied war slogans. Exhausted by the war and aware that colonial rule conflicted with their own ideals, European powers eventually abolished all overseas empires and propelled their former subjects into independent statehood. Decolonization quickly became a major issue in the Cold War, as the two superpowers competed with each other for influence in the emerging states of Africa and Asia.

Decolonization everywhere sparked protracted and often brutal struggles to build modern states among peoples who had been utterly unprepared for this effort by their colonial rulers and who were also divided by their past animosities, as well as by the competition between the superpowers. Given these countries' lack of preparation, Western practices such as capitalism and democracy proved too complex. The Soviet model seemed more suitable; besides, it offered the new leaders the attraction of absolute power. Yet how long could that model hold its own against the capitalist rival, whose riches exerted an even stronger attraction? Decolonization inevitably expanded the influence of Western ways of life in the newly independent nations, even though one-party governments and dictatorships remain in power in many countries.

In the twenty-first century, globalization continues relentlessly; the world is being knit together by the spread of Western ideas, popular culture (particularly American), free market capitalism, and technology. High government officials and business and professional people all over the world are dressed in Western clothes. Women follow Western fashions in clothes, hairstyles, and makeup. People in both Western and non-Western lands follow Western lifestyles—lining up to eat at McDonald's or to see

Map 26.1   The Dissolution of the Soviet Union   As a crisis gripped the Soviet system by the late 1980s, the republics of the Soviet Union began declaring first their sovereignty, then their independence. Most of the fifteen republics that had made up the Soviet Union became part of a much looser confederation, the Commonwealth of Independent States, in 1991 and 1992.

a movie made in Hollywood; eager to adopt the latest technology; and in general, seeking to share in the benefits of Western modernity.

Advanced technology intensifies the means of communication, not only through television and radio, but also with faxes, e-mail, cellular phones, and the Internet—all means of instantaneous individual communication that have become commonplace in the past decade. These developments promote shared interests among individuals and businesses throughout the globe, reducing the importance of national frontiers.

The ideals of freedom and democracy, historical accomplishments of Western civilization, exert a powerful influence worldwide, but unlike technology, they cannot easily be put into practice outside the lands of their origin. However, they inspire human ambitions everywhere. They have even become part of the rhetoric of dictatorships.

At the same time, traditional ways of life persist, interacting, and often clashing, with the forces of modernity. All these factors combined are reshaping non-Western societies in a relentless process of cultural adjustment. A striking example of the clash of cultures is the hatred radical Muslim fun-

damentalists have for the West, which they view as a threat to traditional Islam. These Muslim militants, organized in an international network, al-Qaeda, with well-financed cells in dozens of countries, including the United States, were behind the bombing of the World Trade Center and the Pentagon on September 11, 2001, the worst terrorist attacks in history; in all, more than 3,000 people died.

The leader of al-Qaeda is Osama bin Laden (c. 1957–), scion of an immensely wealthy Saudi Arabian family. Operating from Afghanistan, with the protection and support of the radical fundamentalist Taliban, who once ruled that country, he and his followers are dedicated to the destruction of Western civilization, which they see as immoral and an affront to God, the restoration of the Islamic empire that had existed in the Middle Ages, and the imposition of strict Islamic law in all Islamic lands. For them Western values—pluralism, secularism, separation of church and state, equal rights for women, and the free exchange of ideas—threaten the true faith. When Taliban leaders refused to turn bin Laden over to the United States, President George W. Bush

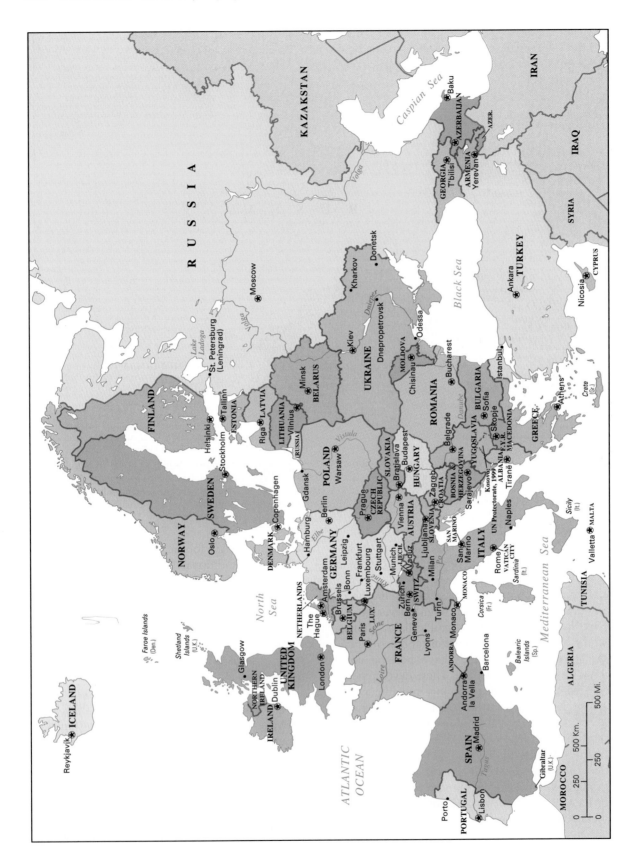

(1946–), supported by a coalition of many states, launched a military campaign, the ultimate goal of which was the destruction of international terrorism. Local Afghan forces opposed to the Taliban, assisted by American air power, which proved decisive, defeated the Taliban in a few weeks. But with al-Qaeda cells located in many countries, the war against international terrorism is far from over.

THOUGHT

Existentialism

The philosophical movement that best exemplified the anxiety and uncertainty of Europe in an era of world wars was *existentialism.* Like writers and artists, existentialist philosophers were responding to a European civilization that seemed to be in the throes of dissolution. Although existentialism was most popular after World War II, expressing the anxiety and despair of many intellectuals who had lost confidence in reason and progress, several of its key works were written prior to or during the war. What route should people take in a world where old values and certainties had dissolved, where universal truth was rejected and God's existence denied? How could people cope in a society where they were menaced by technology, manipulated by impersonal bureaucracies, and overwhelmed by feelings of anxiety? If the universe lacks any overarching meaning, what meaning could one give to one's own life? These questions were at the crux of existentialist philosophy.

Existentialism does not lend itself to a single definition, because its principal theorists did not adhere to a common body of doctrines. For example, some existentialists were atheists, such as Jean Paul Sartre (1905–1980); or omitted God from their thought, such as Martin Heidegger (1889–1976); others, such as Karl Jaspers (1883–1969), believed in God but not in Christian doctrines; still others, such as Nikolai Berdyaev (1874–1948) and Gabriel Marcel (1889–1973), were Christians; and Martin Buber (1878–1965) was a believing Jew. Perhaps the following principles contain the essence of existentialism, although not all existentialists would subscribe to each point or agree with the way it is expressed.

Map 26.2 Europe in the Early Twenty-First Century The reunification of Germany and the breakup of the Soviet Union, Yugoslavia, and Czechoslovakia fundamentally altered the map of Europe during the 1990s.

1. Reality defies ultimate comprehension; there are no timeless truths that exist independently of and prior to the individual human being. Our existence precedes and takes precedence over any presumed absolute values. The moral and spiritual values that society tries to impose cannot define the individual person's existence.

2. Reason alone is an inadequate guide to living, for people are more than thinking subjects who approach the world through critical analysis. They are also feeling and willing beings, who must participate fully in life and experience existence directly, actively, and passionately. Only in this way does one live wholly and authentically.

3. Thought must not be merely abstract speculation but must have a bearing on life; it must be translated into deeds.

4. Human nature is problematic and paradoxical, not fixed or constant; each person is like no other. Self-realization comes when one affirms one's own uniqueness. One becomes less than human when one permits one's life to be determined by a mental outlook—a set of rules and values—imposed by others.

5. We are alone. The universe is indifferent to our expectations and needs, and death is ever stalking us. Awareness of this elementary fact of existence evokes a sense of overwhelming anxiety and depression.

6. Existence is essentially absurd. There is no purpose to our presence in the universe. We simply find ourselves here; we do not know and will never find out why. Compared with the eternity of time that preceded our birth and will follow our death, the short duration of our existence seems trivial and inexplicable. And death, which irrevocably terminates our existence, testifies to the ultimate absurdity of life.

7. We are free. We must face squarely the fact that existence is purposeless and absurd. In doing so, we can give our life meaning. It is in the act of choosing freely from among different possibilities that the individual shapes an authentic existence. There is a dynamic quality to human existence; the individual has the potential to become more than he or she is.

Postmodernism

The term *Postmodernism,* which came into vogue in the 1970s, is used broadly to describe avant-garde developments in the arts, in architecture, and in thought. Postmodernist thinkers mark a fundamental break with the modern humanist tradition that emerged in the Renaissance. This tradition, which achieved full expression in the Enlightenment, gave central place to the autonomous self and to independent reason. Postmodernism is a radical critique of the Enlightenment tradition and an attack on its values—the autonomous self, reason's primacy, objective science, universal norms, and progress through reason. *Deconstruction,* a technique for reading literary and philosophic works developed by Jacques Derrida (1930–), is closely identified with Postmodernism. Derrida held that a rigorous reading of a text shows that its underlying arguments and premises are fundamentally ambiguous, inconsistent, and contradictory. The text tells a story that differs from and may even be opposed to the one the author may have intended. Simply stated, deconstructionists hold that it is impossible for language to say what the author means. Moreover, authors cannot help acting as mouthpieces of the dominant ideology of the day; unwittingly, their words are used to sustain the privileged and to suppress the powerless. In effect, the authors do not control their words but are controlled by them. Deconstruction denies the possibility of determining truth or certainty. Facts are unverifiable; no rational principle exists either in a text or in the universe. For deconstructionists, the canonical books of Western thought are not creative works of art possessing an inherent worth, works of insight, inspiration, and stylistic excellence that the reader should approach with respect. Rather, deconstructionists seek to discredit, expose as fraudulent, or relegate as obsolete ideas and ideals that are at the heart of the Western tradition, particularly in its modern form, and dismiss standards of aesthetics as irrelevant.

Postmodernists reject universal principles and seek the dismantling of all systems and beliefs; for them, there is no possibility of ever finding truth. Recognition that we live in an uncentered universe, they say, fosters a creative cultural diversity and an exciting plasticity in lifestyles. It compels us to acknowledge the legitimacy of a plurality of perspectives and to scrutinize ideas constantly, for at bottom, all interpretations are subjective, and all knowledge is relative and fallible.

Thinkers committed to traditional Western ideals decry the Postmodernist dismantling of values, denial of objectivity, and repudiation of the Enlightenment's goal of the rational improvement of society. They denounce deconstruction as an insidious attack on the great works of Western literature. Are there no standards by which we can judge the aesthetic merit or lack of merit of a poem or a novel? Do authors have so little control over their words that all stated meanings are suspect? Is language so elusive that we must treat all texts as fundamentally unintelligible—as unsolvable puzzles—and must equate reading a text with getting stuck in a revolving door?

Postmodernism's radical critique of self-sufficient reason, say these critics, erodes the foundations of democratic government, which rests on rational discourse. It also promotes a dangerous nihilism, in which all is permissible. Is there no free will that allows us to rise above impulse, no autonomous subject responsible for its behavior? Are there no moral norms by which we can condemn genocide, cannibalism, infanticide, torture, slavery, religious or racial persecution, rape, incest, child abuse, drug abuse, or drunken driving? Are there no criteria by which we can characterize something as an improvement—as progress?

LITERATURE

Literature in the last half of the twentieth century reflected many of the concerns and problems faced by Europeans and Americans. With the United States emerging as a superpower and its popular culture spreading throughout the globe, the works of American writers assumed new importance. In this concluding chapter, we discuss some of the key literary themes and figures since World War II.

Communist Oppression: Solzhenitsyn

The writings of Russian historian and novelist Alexander Solzhenitsyn (1918–) focused international attention on the brutality of the communist regime in his beloved Russia. During World War II, Solzhenitsyn was captain of the artillery, but in 1945, he was arrested for writing a private letter in which he denigrated Joseph Stalin. Consequently, for the next eight years, Solzhenitsyn spent time in prison and in Soviet labor camps, which was followed by four years of compulsory exile before he was permitted to return to central Russia in 1956. He then began writing about his experiences, beginning with his first short novel, *One Day in the Life of Ivan Denisovich* (1962), which brought him immediate recognition. The next year, Solzhenitsyn published a collection of short stories, which the government sought to ban, but which he had published secretly. In the meantime, he garnered an international literary reputation with the novels *The First Circle* (1968), *Cancer Ward* (1968), and *August 1914* (1971). In 1970, Solzhenitsyn was awarded the Nobel Prize, but refused to travel to Stockholm to accept it for fear of not being allowed to return to the Soviet Union. In Paris, in December of 1973, Solzhenitsyn published the first of three volumes of his *Gulag Archipelago* (1973–1975). Two months later, he was arrested, charged with treason, and exiled; he came to the United States and settled in Cavendish, Vermont, where he continued to write.

Subtitled "An Experiment in Literary Investigation," Solzhenitsyn makes use of "gulag" (an acronym for the Soviet agency that administered the labor camps) and "archipelago" (a chain of islands) as a metaphor for the string of prisons and labor camps that were spread all over the Soviet Union, stretching from the Bosporus Straits to the Bering Sea. Interjecting excruciatingly painful details, Solzhenitsyn describes how the Soviets knowingly tortured and killed millions of their own people. He recounts innumerable incidents of prisoners and their families at various stages of arrest, interrogation, conviction, transportation, imprisonment, slave labor, and/or death. Solzhenitsyn interlaces his often-indignant narrative with a personal account of his own years in the gulag, revealing the full horror of a regime that imprisoned and executed millions of innocent people. For Solzhenitsyn, communist ideology spawned the atrocities for which not only the cruel and paranoid Stalin, but also Lenin, was responsible.

In his final years, Solzhenitsyn became a harsh critic of what he perceived to be the extreme individualism and moral laxity of the West, and after the fall of the Soviet Union, he became an even harsher critic of the "new" Russia, which failed to honor its roots in Orthodox Christianity. In 1990, Solzhenitsyn's citizenship was restored, and four years later, he returned to his homeland.

The Dark Side of Human Nature: Golding, Malamud, and Capote

The darker side of human nature, a reality made manifest by the atrocities of World War II, intrigued William Golding (1911–1993), a veteran of the British Royal Navy. The title of his novel, *Lord of the Flies* (1954), comes from the bloody pig's head that is impaled on a post by Jack, one of the main characters, who symbolizes power and brutality. As the novel progresses, it becomes a beastly, satanic symbol—the embodiment of the power of evil. ("Lord of the flies" is actually a translation of the name of the biblical demon Beelzebub.) Due to nuclear war, all the children of Britain are evacuated, but one airplane carrying both adults and children crashes into a deserted island. All of the adults die, leaving the children to create their own society. Ralph, the protagonist of the novel, symbolizes order in society; Roger represents savagery and blood vengeance; Piggy symbolizes the rational, sci-

entific mind of the civilized world; and Simon embodies humanity's inherent goodness. Soon, however, they all lose their innocence, their "civilization" degenerates into barbarism, and before the novel's end, murder is committed. By exploring the loss of innocence, Golding exposes a savage element in human nature, which is capable of great evil, including torture and murder.

The evil acts committed against European Jews over the centuries by people whose attitude toward Jews was shaped by bizarre myths exemplifies the dark side of human nature. Russian-born, American-Jewish writer Bernard Malamud (1914–1986) employs the centuries-old canard, that Jews slaughter Christian children to use their blood for making the Passover matzoh, as a means of demonstrating human wickedness. During the Middle Ages this absurd allegation, a product of hate and delusion, led to the torture and death of numerous Jews. The belief persisted into the modern world, and several Jews accused of ritual murder were placed on trial in various European countries to the horror of enlightened people. The setting for Malamud's Pulitzer Prize–winning novel, *The Fixer* (1966), is tsarist Russia in the early twentieth century, where the protagonist Yakov Bok, a Jewish handyman or "fixer," stands accused of ritual murder of a Christian boy. (In the Russia of that day, a Jew actually did stand trial for this charge and the case drew international attention.) Most of the action takes places in jail. The reader learns that Yakov's acts of kindness and generosity have been rewarded with unbelievable cruelty and denigration. Yakov discovers that he can fix almost anything—except the human heart. Even though he is persecuted by an all-powerful state, Yakov never succumbs to the inhumanity of his persecutors, thus becoming their moral superior in the process. Due to the medium of motion pictures Malamud's everlasting fame, however, rests with his first novel, *The Natural* (1952), the story of a baseball hero (with Robert Redford appearing in the title role) who seems to possess miraculous powers, particularly in his bat.

The murder of Herbert Clutter and his family on November 14, 1959, in Holcomb, Kansas, motivated the writer Truman Capote (1924–1984), to travel there to research an article he wanted to write about the murder for the *New Yorker*. The end result, after more than five years of labor, was Capote's novel *In Cold Blood: A True Account of Multiple Murder and Its Consequences* (1966). He believed that by re-creating the lives of the murderers, Richard Eugene Hickock and Perry Edward Smith, in a journalistic style that probed in microscopic sociological and psychological detail that he had invented a new genre of literature—"the nonfiction novel." Capote relates how each of the four family members died—the two teenage daughters and their parents were shot in the head; Herbert Clutter was also stabbed and had his throat slit. Capote follows the investigation that led to the arrest and confession of Hickock and Smith. Finally, Capote penetrates what was going on in the minds of the petty criminals turned brutal murderers before, during, and after their heinous crime. The reader thus comes to know each of the tragedy's victims and to probe the minds of the aberrant personalities who could so willingly kill "in cold blood"— when Mr. Clutter could not come up with the stash of cash in a safe that Hickock and Smith believed he possessed. Prior to their hanging at the Kansas State Penitentiary on April 14, 1965, Smith spoke from the gallows about the cruelty of capital punishment while Capote watched.

Religious Concerns: O'Connor, Beckett, and Potok

In an increasingly secular age, some authors remained motivated by religious concerns. A human being's alienation from God characterizes much of the work of Flannery O'Connor (1925–1964), a novelist and short story writer, who set most of her works in the rural South. O'Connor was uncharacteristically raised as a Roman Catholic in Georgia, which was viewed as part of the evangelical "Bible Belt." In 1950, she was afflicted with her first attack of lupus—a skin disease that killed her father and from which she eventually died at a comparatively young age. Two years later, O'Connor published her first novel, *Wise Blood,* the story of a young religious zealot who attempts to found a church without Christ. Six years later, she followed up on the theme with her book *The Violent Bear It Away.* In her collection of short stories, *A Good Man Is Hard to Find* (1955), and in the nine stories of *Everything That Rises Must Converge,* which were published posthumously in 1965, O'Connor deals with two principal themes: redemption of misfits and the role of revelation among reluctant prophets. Critics now believe that these two themes were very personal to her and reflective of her own religious understanding.

Many critics and audiences have interpreted the tragicomedy *Waiting for Godot* (1952) by the Irish playwright Samuel Beckett (1906–1989), as Westerners waiting for God to rescue them from the misery of their meaningless lives. Critics view Beckett's play as the first dramatic success for the so-called *Theater of the Absurd.* The two-act play is a series of conversations between the two homeless protagonists: Estragon and Vladimir, who await the coming of a mysterious character named Godot. Estragon is beaten up each night in the ditch where he sleeps, and his memory extends no further than the present moment. Consequently, he relies on Vladimir to remember everything for him, but Vladimir constantly questions whether his mind is playing tricks on him. Vladimir's friendship with Estragon is based on the fact that he actually appreciates being forced to recall past events. And it is Vladimir who continually compels Estragon to wait for Godot, whose arrival, he claims, is imminent, but who never appears. Some critics have compared Estragon to the body, without the mind, which is provided by Vladimir. In essence, the pair has no idea why they are on earth, and consider hanging themselves even while they continue to hope for the arrival of Godot to enlighten them. Such a hope for the future, however, causes them to rise above their mere existence and become noble characters in search of truth.

The confrontation between traditional religious beliefs and modern ways is at the heart of the novels written by Chaim Potok (1929–2002), the son of Polish immigrants to America. Raised as a strict Orthodox Jew, he became an ordained Conservative rabbi in the somewhat less observant form of Judaism. Potok acknowledges that his novels are about the "confrontation of ideas, of cultures in tension." He also explains that the novelist "forces us . . . to look at what it is we are doing and urges us to think about it, to see if something can be learned or understood about ourselves and our species by observing this confrontation."[2] In his novel *The Chosen* (1967), Potok demonstrates the conflict of religious values between the narrator, Reuven Malter, whose liberal father, David, is actively involved in the Zionist movement to create an independent Jewish state, and Danny Saunders, a Hasidic Jew, whose father, Reb (a Yiddish word meaning master, teacher, or rabbi that shows respect), instructs his brilliant son in the often intricate commentaries on Jewish law compiled in the *Talmud.* When David Malter suffers a heart attack, Reuven comes to live in the Saunders household. There, he speaks of his father's ambitions, which infuriates Reb, who believes that a secular Jewish state is a violation of Jewish law. Later, after the boys have enrolled in college, Reb learns about a speech David has given in which he states that the Holocaust will only have value if a Jewish state is made a reality. As a consequence, he forbids Danny from associating with Reuven. But although the relationship between the two friends becomes strained, it does not prevent Reuven from encouraging Danny to pursue his doctorate in psychology. This opens up new possibilities for Danny, whose life had been determined for him by his father's insistence that he become a tzaddik ("righteous one") and succeed him as spiritual leader of the Hasidic community.

Potok describes these "two elements of ongoing tension" (religious and secular) by pointing out that the Saunders' tradition represents those who claim "'I don't need the outside world to solve my problems,'" and the Malters' tradition, which "insists on an openness toward the outside world."[3] For *The Chosen*, Potok gained an international reputation, and the book was applauded for its realistic re-creation of the closed community of Hasidic Jews. In 1969, Potok published a sequel to *The Chosen* entitled *The Promise*, and he returned to the same theme with his novels: *My Name is Asher Lev* (1972) and its sequel *The Gift of Asher Lev* (1990).

Coming of Age: Salinger

Teenagers coming of age, currently a popular motif in motion pictures, was the subject of *Catcher in the Rye* (1951), the only novel ever published by J. D. (Jerome David) Salinger (1919–). The work details just two days in the life of its sixteen-year-old protagonist, Holden Caulfield, who has been dismissed from prep school. Disenchanted and bewildered, Caulfield begins a quest to find truth, even as he berates the deceitfulness of grown-ups. When his search leaves him emotionally exhausted, Caulfield frequents a psychiatrist to assist him with his recovery, subsequently recounting his experiences for the reader. The humor and earthy language of Salinger's novel are reminiscent of Mark Twain's *Huck Finn* (see Chapter 21), for which it engendered an equal amount of controversy, but it too ultimately was acclaimed by both readers and critics for its self-conscious insights into a teenager in search of meaning in his life.

Gender Relationships: Williams, Nabokov, Roth, and Albee

Playwrights and novelists continue to be fascinated by the various types of relationships between men and women, young and old; upper, middle, and lower class; married and unmarried. Often these writers explore sexual relationships.

The playwright Tennessee Williams (1911–1983) detailed the moral and emotional demise of the former Southern belle, Blanche DuBois, in his play *A Streetcar Named Desire*, for which he won the Pulitzer Prize for drama in 1947. Although she still takes on airs as a *femme fatale*, Blanche's delusions are made painfully evident to the audience through the character of her brother-in-law, Stanley Kowalski, who is a new breed of Southern male and in the prime of his life as a lover, a factory worker, and a brawler. He feels intense passion for his wife, Stella and is committed to his friends, but he is ruthlessly abusive to Blanche, as is evident when he rapes her. The audience learns that Blanche has arrived in New Orleans from Laurel, Mississippi, where she had been an English teacher and married to a tortured young man who, on discovering his homosexuality, committed suicide. Blanche, filled with shame and regret, then witnessed the dissolution of her prestigious family as each of her relatives died. The demise of her family paralleled her own emotional collapse as she entered into a series of illicit sexual relationships for which she incurred the wrath of the Laurel community. Now living in New Orleans with her sister Stella and Stanley, she feigns dignity and position, but Stanley, who sees right through her pretensions, ridicules her; Stella does little for Blanche, because she loves Stanley so intensely. For Williams, the brute animal that Stanley is represents the reality of the new South of primal passion in which gentility is dead. Williams later returned to this same theme in *Cat on a Hot Tin Roof* (1955), in which the "cat" is a sexually frustrated woman whose husband is consumed with the suicide of his past roommate, and *Sweet Bird of Youth* (1958), in which Williams recounts the destructive relationship between a fading beauty and a male companion.

The introspective musings of Humbert Humbert—the antihero, narrator, murderer, and widowered pedophile who lusts after the twelve-year-old nymphet Delores Haze, whom he calls his Lolita—created a literary firestorm in 1955, when the Russian-born American novelist and literary critic, Vladimir Nabokov (1899–1977) published his novel *Lolita, Or the Confession of a White Widowed Male*. The unorthodox allegorical novel is about sex and murder, but the language of Nabokov's narrative—laden with allusions, puns, and double entendres—allows the reader to explore the psychology of inner passions, particularly those motivated by Freudian theories pertaining to sexual relations and aggression, the most basic of human instincts. Thus, the language of Humbert's narrative is designed to portray him in the best possible way, for he is accustomed to getting whatever he wants in life, and he gratifies his body with whatever it craves. At the beginning of the novel, because he wants a marriage, he marries Valeria, who leaves him for another man. When he desires to make love to Lolita, he marries her mother, Charlotte, to get nearer to Lolita. When he craves revenge on Clare Quilty, the

Morrison calls into question the validity of the typical American nuclear family, emphasizing individualism, for Milkman's identity surfaces only through the communalism that he believes he has found in his African past.

During the 1980s, Morrison authored *Beloved* (1987), which most critics and audiences agree is her best novel. It is the story of the former slave, Sethe, who early in her life, before emancipation, murders her daughter so that she will not grow up to be a slave. The image of the Beloved of the novel operates on a variety of levels. On one level it is the spirit of Sethe's dead child, on another the spirit of Sethe's African mother, whom she never knew, and on a third, the Beloved symbolizes the horrific yet inescapable history of slavery, which continues to plague the present. On the third level, Beloved's allure becomes progressively diabolical, but it does serve to foster Sethe's emotional development so that she can free herself from the past, which preys on her so heavily. Ultimately, the reader learns that the novel's title is a result of Sethe's simple misunderstanding of what the pastor meant at her daughter's funeral when he said "dearly beloved." Although he was addressing the living, Sethe interpreted it as a greeting to her dead daughter. For Morrison's portrayal of the physical and spiritual desolation caused by slavery and how it shaped the identity of slaves, many of whom continued to feel alienated even after they were granted their freedom, she received the Pulitzer Prize in 1988, and in 1993 she became the first black woman to be awarded the Nobel Prize for literature. Today, Morrison continues to write and is the Robert F. Goheen Professor in the Council of Humanities at Princeton University, making her the first African American woman writer to occupy a named chair at an Ivy League college.

Alice Walker's (1944–) poems, short stories, and novels focus primarily on the battle of black women to find racial and sexual equality. Sexism and racism are the dominant themes of Walker's Pulitzer Prize–winning novel, *The Color Purple* (1982), for which she also received the American Book Award and the National Book Critics Circle Best Fiction Award.

The Color Purple is a complicated novel about racial and sexual identity. Holding that black women in both Africa and America endure the same physical abuse and dominance by black males, Walker asserts that it is futile to attempt to analyze racial identity without first addressing the status of black women, and she is equally incensed by the racist attitudes of American blacks toward Africans. Written in epistolary form, the first half of the novel deals with Celie's letters to God in which she details the repeated rapes by her stepfa-ther, Alphonso, and the physical abuse by her husband, referred to as Mr. ____, who is frustrated about not being able to marry Celie's sister, Nettie. Celie also recognizes that the type of Christianity she practices subjugates women to men, thus compounding the tragedy of her situation. With the help of Shug Avery, the worldly-wise blues singer and a former lover of Mr. ____, Celie begins to discover her own sexuality. Shug also helps put an end to most of Celie's physical abuse and assists her in discovering Nettie's letters, which Mr. ____ had hidden from Celie for so many years. Through Nettie's letters, Celie learns that Nettie had traveled as a missionary in Africa with Samuel and Corrine, a childless black couple who unknowingly took in Celie's two children, born after Celie had been raped by her stepfather. Although Nettie, Samuel, and Corrine expect to be received as brothers and sisters in Africa, they discover that they are viewed as outsiders and a threat to the African way of life. Moreover, just as the African people cannot understand why Nettie, Samuel, and Corrine cannot comprehend the role that blacks played in the European colonization of Africa, neither can Nettie, Samuel, and Corrine come to grips with why African people are not more aware of their own complicity in the North and South American slave trade. In 1985, *The Color Purple* was turned into an award-winning motion picture by the talented director Steven Spielberg (see later discussion).

The Power of Fantasy and Science Fiction: Bradbury, Tolkein, and Vonnegut

Fantasy and science fiction writers deal imaginatively with the impact of scientific and technological change on our world or on a hypothetical world. They explore how these changes affect the past, the present, the future, or some yet unknown planet or civilization.

The self-proclaimed fantasy writer Ray Bradbury (1920–) confronted the pitfalls of unrestrained technology and weighed the pros and cons of different types of colonization in his fictional account of NASA's settlement of Mars, *The Martian Chronicles* (1950).

Bradbury's most popular fictional work, *Fahrenheit 451* (1953), is an allegory about a world in which the state controls all media, with the title referring to the temperature at which paper burns. Set in the twenty-fourth century, the firemen of Bradbury's creation, including Guy Montag, the thirty-year-old protagonist of the novel, burn books and the houses in which such "illegal contraband" is found. But the inquisitiveness and humane nature of Montag's sixteen-year-old neighbor, Clarisse McClellan, causes him to become introspective. Ultimately, Montag risks everything to preserve learning in the world. He connects with a man named Granger, an intellectual and former author, who tells Montag how some people have memorized books, hoping that someday it will be safe to print books again. When war is declared, bombs destroy their city, and Granger and Montag set out to form a new society in which books and freedom of expression are valued and where people are free to learn and to develop to their fullest potential.

Science fiction in the genre of mythic fantasy is at the heart of J. R. R. Tolkein's (1892–1973) trilogy, *The Lord of the Rings* (1954–1956). The book that actually served as a prologue to the series was *The Hobbit* (1937), which depicts a fanciful world of Middle Earth peopled with elves, dwarfs, and hobbits—humanlike creatures who prize peace and a simple home life. The protagonist is Bilbo Baggins who, while on a quest with twelve dwarfs, recovers a magical ring that makes its wearer invisible. In his quest, the homebody Bilbo must become a courageous warrior to fight against evil. *The Lord of the Rings* cycle—*The Fellowship of the Ring, The Two Towers,* and *The Return of the King*—subsequently details various battles between the forces of good and evil for possession of the ring.

The terrors and incongruities of life in the twentieth century are, perhaps, best expressed by the American novelist Kurt Vonnegut (1922–), who uses science fiction fantasy to relate his pessimistic view of life. For example, in his first novel, *Player Piano* (1952), Vonnegut depicts workers in a New York City factory as incapable of fending off the dehumanizing effects of mechanized society.

Slaughterhouse Five; or, The Children's Crusade: A Duty-Dance with Death (1969), Vonnegut's masterpiece, encapsulated the counterculture of the Vietnam War years. His own experiences as a soldier during World War II left an indelible impression on Vonnegut's philosophical outlook and his writing. While he was away fighting the Germans in 1944, his mother (who suffered from mental illness) committed suicide. In December, Vonnegut was taken prisoner by the Germans at the Battle of the Bulge. As a prisoner of war, Vonnegut worked in a militarily insignificant factory in Dresden, which was firebombed by the Allied Forces on February 13, 1945. To protect themselves, Vonnegut and his fellow POWs took cover in the meat locker of a slaughterhouse. Upon their emergence, Vonnegut learned that the death count of innocent civilians numbered more than 130,000 (historians set 35,000 as the most likely number), which he believed was greater than the death toll of

71,000 people who died as a result of the atomic blast on Hiroshima. This horrific event of human tragedy and mass destruction not only helped to shape Vonnegut's pacifist views toward war, but twenty-five years later, during the height of the war in Vietnam, it also inspired him to write *Slaughterhouse-Five*. In the novel, Vonnegut deftly blends his own historical experience in Dresden with a science fiction account of Billy Pilgrim, who lives simultaneously on Earth as a soldier involved in World War II and as a citizen of the faraway planet Tralfamadore. Because the Tralfamadorians know the future, they are philosophically resigned to the impending destruction of the universe. Consequently, during his time on Earth, Billy professes their fatalistic approach to life epitomized by their saying "so it goes." Vonnegut's "antiwar" novel was thus a conscious attempt to write a book that ran counter to war novels that glorified war, making it look like an adventure worth taking.

ART

Abstract Expressionism: Pollock and Rothko

During World War II, many European artists—including Max Ernst, Salvador Dali, and Piet Mondrian—moved to New York City. These European artists greatly influenced the American artists who introduced **Abstract Expressionism,** also known as the New York School, which was the first internationally important American art movement. Although there were sharp differences in the personal styles of these artists, they shared an outlook that championed individuality and espoused the freedom to express themselves purely through the use of color and abstract, nonrepresentational forms. Abstract Expressionism thus marked America's conversion to modern art.

Abstract Expressionism had deep roots in Surrealism. Abstract Expressionists shared in the Surrealists' emphasis on the significance of the Freudian unconscious for creativity. Some American artists found an additional inspiration in the ideas of the Swiss psychiatrist Carl Jung (1875–1961), who, in contrast to Freud's idea of the individual unconscious, developed a concept of the "collective unconscious," common memories shared by all of humanity. Jung claimed that great art is an expression of this creative, semidivine part of the psyche.

The most famous Abstract Expressionist was Jackson Pollock (1912–1956). Pollock was born in Cody, Wyoming, but he grew up in Arizona and California. At the age of eighteen, he moved to New York City to study at the Art Students League, and within three years, he was already

Figure 26.1   Jackson Pollock (American 1912–1956), *Autumn Rhythm (Number 30),* ***1950* oil on canvas, 105 x 207" (57.92).**   In 1947, Pollick began his *pour* and *drip* *method* of painting on huge unstretched canvases which he attached to the floor. His method was soon to be dubbed *action painting.* In its coloring and organization, this painting evokes a sense of nature. *(The Metropolitan Museum, George A. Hearn Fund, 1957 (57.92) Photograph © 1998 The Metropolitan Museum of Art © 2002 The Pollock-Krasner Foundation/Artists Rights Society (ARS), New York)*

painting in a semiabstract manner. Pollock came under the influence of Jung in 1939, when he began four years of psychotherapy, which gave him a new appreciation for the therapeutic role of art. In 1944, when he was asked about the importance of the European Surrealists who then lived in New York, he replied: "I am particularly impressed with their concept of the source of art being the unconscious."[5] And in an interview in 1956, just prior to his death, he said that "all of us [are] influenced by Freud, I guess. I've been a Jungian for a long time."[6]

In 1943, Peggy Guggenheim gave Pollock his first solo show at her gallery in New York. Two years later, Pollock married Lee Krasner, who introduced him to several influential abstract artists. In 1947, he began his *pour and drip method* of painting on huge unstretched canvases, which he attached to the floor. In essence, this involved allowing his unconscious to take over his painting, as he explained later that year:

On the floor I am more at ease. I feel nearer, more a part of the painting, since this way I can walk around it, work from the four sides and literally be in the painting. . . . When I am in the painting, I'm not aware of what I'm doing. . . . [T]he painting has a life of its own. . . . [T]here is pure harmony, an easy give and take, and the painting comes out well.[7]

Pollock's method was soon to be dubbed ***action painting,*** of which *Autumn Rhythm (Number 30)* (Figure 26.1) is one example. Even though it is abstract, it invokes a sense of nature in its coloring and organization. In an interview given soon after completing *Autumn Rhythm,* Pollock further explained how he applied paint to the canvas: "Most of the paint I use is a liquid, flowing kind of paint. The brushes I use are used more as sticks rather than brushes—the brush doesn't touch the surface of the canvas, it's just above."[8] Because Pollock dripped the paint onto the canvas, it is quite thick in spots. Six years after painting *Autumn Rhythm,* Pollock died in an automobile accident.

The youngest child of a Jewish pharmacist in Divnsk, Russia, Mark Rothko (1903–1970) emigrated to Portland, Oregon, with his family when he was ten years old. After spending two years at Yale University, Rothko moved to New York, in 1923, where he took art classes at the Art Students League. His first exhibitions came in 1931, one in Portland and the other in New York. Although Rothko is categorized among the Abstract Expressionists, his mature style of the 1950s, which is called ***color-field painting,*** is rather different from Pollock's style. *Orange and Yellow* (Figure 26.2) comprises two soft-edged rectangles, one yellow and the other orange, on a red background. This typically large canvas (more than seven and one-half feet tall) was painted on an easel, not on the floor. Rothko applied his paints quite thinly, with no visible brush strokes (somewhat similar to watercolor spreading on wet paper), allowing the texture of the canvas to be seen. He intended his paintings to be hung low, in dim light, to immerse the viewer in the color field. Some critics have described Rothko's paintings as meditative, in contrast to Pollock's expressive style.

Pop Art: Johns, Rauschenberg, and Warhol

The phrase *Pop Art* was first used in England in the late 1950s to signify paintings that exalted postwar consumerism and celebrated popular culture. Pop Art was a postmodern reaction against nonrepresentational abstract art, including the painting of its most recent practitioners, the Abstract Expressionists, whom the Pop artists thought were pretentious and overly serious with their concept of the collective unconscious. The Pop artists, who converted common objects into works of art, were influenced by Dada and by Marcel Duchamp's ready-mades (see Chapter 24). Pop artists scoffed at the idea of the unique art object.

Of the early painters in the Pop Art movement in the United States, Jasper Johns (1930–) was the foremost. Born and raised in South Carolina, Johns studied briefly at the University of South Carolina before moving to New York City in the early 1950s. Largely self-taught as an artist, he began to paint common objects such as targets, maps, and especially flags, in 1954. Four years later, he executed one of his most famous paintings, *Three Flags* (Figure 26.3), which is literally three canvases superimposed on each other, creating a reverse perspective, with the smallest flag moving into the space of the viewer. It is simultaneously a painting and a relief sculpture. Johns used thick encaustic paint, pigments mixed in a medium of wax (a method used in antiquity by the Romans), to create his flag paintings. The meaning of these paintings was debated at the time. As one critic wrote in 1957:

> Take Jasper Johns' work, which is easily described as an accurate painted replica of the American flag but which is as hard to explain in its unsettling power as the reasonable illogicalities of a Duchamp ready-made. Is it blasphemous or respectful, simple-minded or recondite? One suspects here a vital neo-Dada spirit.[9]

The work of Robert Rauschenberg (1925–) has also, like Johns', often been described as "Neo-Dada." In 1948, Rauschenberg studied at Black Mountain College in North Carolina, where he met the musician John Cage (see later discussion), with whom he later collaborated. In 1949, he went to New York and studied at the Art Students League. After traveling in Europe, in 1955 he rented a studio in New York in the same building as Johns. At this time, Rauschenberg began to produce works that he called *combines*—somewhat like Picasso's collages and Duchamps' found items or ready-mades. Also called "assemblages," they were neither paintings nor sculptures, but a combination of the two. Rauschenberg's *Canyon* (Figure 26.4)—a mixture of collage work and three-dimensional found items—combines paint, a photograph (of himself as a boy), paper, metal, fabric, and wood on canvas, as well as a stuffed eagle perched on a box and a suspended pillow. The disorder reflects Rauschenberg's own sense of the chaos of modern life, as he himself declared: "I only consider myself successful when I do something that resembles the lack of order I sense."[10]

Figure 26.2   Mark Rothko, *Orange and Yellow* (1956), oil on canvas, 91" x 71" (231 x 180.3 cm), Albright-Knox Art Gallery, Buffalo, New York   This is an example of Rothko's "color-field painting," in which two soft-edged rectangles, one yellow and the other orange, are displayed on a red background. Rothko applied his paints quite thinly, with no visible brushstrokes (somewhat similar to watercolor spreading on wet paper), allowing the texture of the canvas to be seen. *(Albright-Knox Art Gallery, Buffalo, New York, Gift of Seymour H. Knox, Jr., 1956. © 2002 Artists Rights Society (ARS), New York/ADAGP, Paris)*

Figure 26.3 Jaspar Johns, *Three Flags* (1958), encaustic paint on canvas, 30 7/8 x 45 1/2 x 5" (78.4 x 115.6 x 12.7 cm), collection of Whitney Museum of American Art, New York. This painting is literally three canvases superimposed on each other, creating a reverse perspective with the smallest flag moving into the viewer's space. It is simultaneously a painting and a relief sculpture. *(Collection of Whitney Museum of American Art, New York © Jasper Johns/Licensed by VAGA, New York, NY., Photo © 2000)*

The man whom the media called "The Prince of Pop," Andy Warhol (1928–1987), was also influenced by Duchamp. After studying painting and commercial design at the Carnegie Institute of Technology in his native Pittsburgh, Warhol moved to New York in 1948, where he soon became a successful commercial artist. In 1962,

Warhol turned to depicting popular culture in "The Factory," his art studio on East 87th Street, where he mass-produced prints and posters. His favorite printmaking technique was silk-screening photo images on canvas. Photo silk screen printing is accomplished by creating a stencil on a piece of stretched silk gauze and then forcing paint or ink through the stencil onto the printing surface. One screen is used for each color. Warhol used ordinary objects, often in multiple forms, such as Campbell Soup cans and Coca-Cola bottles, as well as images of celebrities, such as Marilyn Monroe. Warhol's *Marilyn Diptych* (Figure 26.5) of 1962 consists of two panels, each with twenty-five images of the masklike face. The left, multicolored panel shows Marilyn the star, the sex symbol; the panel on the right, perhaps, shows her life, and as she fades out in the upper right, represents her

Figure 26.4 Robert Rauschenberg, *Canyon* (1959), collage, 6'1" x 5'6" x 2' 3/4" (1.85 x 1.68 x 0.63 m), Collection Ileana and Michael Sonnabend, New York, on extended loan to The Baltimore Museum of Art. This work, called an assemblage, is neither a painting nor a sculpture, but a combination of the two. It combines paint, a photograph, paper, metal, fabric, and wood on canvas, as well as a stuffed eagle perched on a box and a suspended pillow. *(Courtesy Sonnabend, New York. Photography courtesy The Baltimore Museum of Art © Robert Rauschenberg/Licensed by VAGA, New York, NY)*

death by suicide in the same year. Warhol not only portrayed popular culture; he also celebrated it, as when he wrote: "The Pop artists did images that anybody walking down Broadway could recognize in a split second—comics, picnic table, men's trousers, celebrities, shower curtains, refrigerators, Coke bottles—all the great modern things that the Abstract Expressionists tried so hard not to notice at all."[11]

Sculpture: Smith, Lin, Puryear, and Gormley

The work of sculptors during the second half of the twentieth century evidences both continuity with the Modernist sculpture of the pre-World War II period and radical change. Although the work of sculptors like Giacometti and Moore continued to evolve within the Modernist aesthetic, younger sculptors began to experiment. The major movement, from the 1970s, was *Minimalism*— simple, symmetrical sculpture, made of modern materials that engaged the viewer and, by implication, spurned depicting the human body. Minimalism marked the end of Modernism in sculpture. Although it is impossible to know who will be remembered as the "great" sculptors of the later part of the twentieth century, we have chosen to focus on four representative artists.

One of the most important American sculptors was David Smith (1906–1965), who flourished during the Abstract Expressionist era. Smith, the son and grandson of blacksmiths in Decatur, Indiana, first studied art briefly at Ohio University in Athens, Ohio. After working at an automobile plant in the summer of 1925, where he learned metalworking, he attended the Art Students League in New York in 1926, where he studied painting and became acquainted with Cubism. When Smith was asked in an interview in 1961 what led him to turn from painting to sculpture, he answered:

> I think it was seeing Picasso's iron sculpture in [an art book]. . . about 1928 or 1929. Seeing iron and factory materials used in producing art was quite a revelation, and since I had worked in factories and I have known iron and metal and metalworking since I have been very young, it came to me that it should be.[12]

Smith began to sculpt in metal in 1933. During the 1950s and early 1960s, Smith produced several series of sculptures, including his Cubi series, which was inspired by Cubism. *Cubi XIX* (see chapter opening), of 1964, is representative of the series. All of the cubis are constructed of monumental cubes, cubic rectangles, and cylinders, which Smith himself constructed out of polished and brushed stainless steel. The carefully balanced cubis are meant to be displayed outdoors where they capture and reflect every change in the

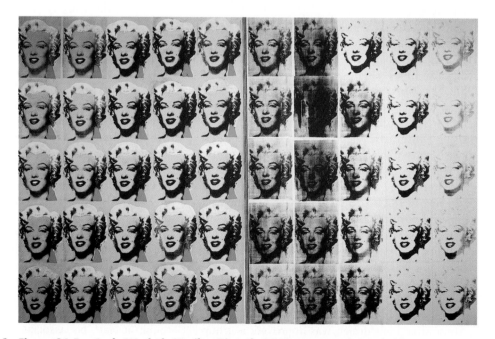

Figure 26.5 Andy Warhol, *Marilyn Diptych*, 1962, two panels, each 82" x 57".
Each of the two panels consists of twenty-five images of Marilyn's mask-like face. The left, multicolored panel shows Marilyn the star, the sex symbol; the panel on the right, perhaps, shows her life, and as she fades out in the upper right, represents her recent death by suicide. *(Tate Gallery, London/Art Resource, NY. © 2002 Andy Warhol Foundation for the Visual Arts/ ARS, New York.)*

Figure 26.6 Maya Ying Lin, *Vietnam Veterans' Memorial* (1982), height 10′ (3.05 m), length 500′ (152 m), Constitution Gardens, Washington, D.C. This memorial is often regarded as the consummate example of Minimalist sculpture. The memorial, two walls of black granite, bears the names of the nearly 58,000 who died in Vietnam between 1959 and 1975. (*© Peter Aaron/Esto. All rights reserved.*)

natural light. With the cubis, Smith was an early participant in Minimalism. The year after sculpting *Cubi XIX,* Smith died in an automobile accident.

The *Vietnam Veterans Memorial* (Figure 26.6) in Washington D.C., designed by Maya Ying Lin (1960–), is perhaps the consummate Minimalist sculpture. Lin, a Chinese-American from Athens, Ohio, was an undergraduate student in architecture at Yale University when her design was chosen over 1,424 others to memorialize the dead and missing during the Vietnam War. The memorial consists of two walls of black granite, each nearly 250 feet long, which meet at a 136-degree angle at the center, where they are ten feet tall. The names of the nearly 58,000 dead are inscribed on the wall beginning with the first in 1959 and ending with the final death in 1975. With one arm pointing toward the Lincoln Memorial and the other toward the Washington Monument, the wall, partially below ground level, almost appears to be growing organically from the ground of Constitutional Gardens on the Mall.

Soon after Lin's design was approved, a group of veterans protested against it, saying it was an insult to those who had died in the war. One of them referred to the wall as "the black gash of shame." In 1984, to calm the criticism, a traditional monument, featuring three soldiers, was erected near the wall. Despite the controversy, the Memorial remains one of the most visited in Washington, D.C., and those who visit invariably encounter the tragedy of the war in their own reflection in the highly polished stone.

Born in Washington, D.C., Martin Puryear (1941–) is the foremost African American sculptor today. After graduating from Catholic University in 1963, Puryear joined the Peace Corps and went to Sierra Leone, where he taught in a remote village and learned traditional methods of woodworking. In 1966, he went to Sweden, where he learned more about working with wood. After returning to the United States, he earned a Master of Fine Arts degree in sculpture at Yale University in 1971. Although Puryear's career began during the height of Minimalism, his own work, mostly in wood, is noted for its independence and meticulous craftsmanship, of which *Lever No. 3* (Figure 26.7) is characteristic. Because of its simplicity and because he created several of these levers, he might be compared with Brancusi. However, unlike Brancusi's birds, it does not represent any specific thing; it can be associated with a variety of things—the prow of a ship, a long-necked animal, or a plant.

After receiving his degree in archaeology and art history at Trinity College, Cambridge, Antony Gormley (1950–) studied at various art schools in

Figure 26.7   Martin Puryear, *Lever No. 3,* **1989, 84 1/2" x 162" x 13" (215 x 412 x 33 cm), National Gallery of Art Washington, D.C.**   Although Puryear's career began during the height of Minimalism, his own work, mostly in wood, is noted for its independence and meticulous craftsmanship, of which this sculpture is characteristic. *(National Gallery of Art, Washington, Gift of the Collectors Committee, Photograph © Board of Trustees)*

his native London and in 1981 had his first one-person exhibition. He has since become a leading Western sculptor, and as such, his work is part of a movement returning to the human image, which had mainly been missing in sculpture since the 1950s. Throughout his career, Gormley has used a cast of his own body to produce sculptures of the human form that delve into what it feels like to be in a body and what the relationship of a body to architecture and to nature is. He first makes a full-body plaster cast of himself in various positions—standing, sitting, lying, crouching—which he then overlays with sheets of lead. One example is *Testing a World View* (Figure 26.8) of 1993, in which Gormley placed five identical figures in different parts of a room. While he was still working on the sculpture, Gormley sought to explain his motivation during an interview:

I'm thinking of calling the work *Testing a World View.* The work is a kind of psychological Cubism. An identical body cast is made from the interior of a body case five times, which I then try to test against architecture. The piece expresses the polymorphousness of the self; that in different places we become different and I think this is physical. If Cubism is about taking one object and making multiple views of it in one place, this is a dispersion of one object into several cases for itself.[13]

Earlier in the same interview, Gormley also stated that he was interested "in the space that the body is[,] . . . [in] finding the other half of life that my upbringing excluded me from—which is an encounter with the earth, the body and the unconscious."[14] This is an allusion to his upbringing as a Catholic and to the period of time he spent in the

Figure 26.8   Antony Gormley, *Testing a World View,* **movable installation, 1993.**   Throughout his career, Gormley has used a cast of his own body to produce sculptures of the human form that delve into what it feels like to be in a body and what the relationship of a body to architecture and to nature is. *(Courtesy the artist and Jay Jopling/White Cube, London)*

Figure 26.9 *Centre National d'Art et de Culture Georges Pompidou* **(1972–1977), Paris, France.** With all of the working parts of the building—its blue air-conditioning ducts, green water pipes, yellow electrical units, red elevators, and the escalator—on the exterior, the Pompidou Center has effectively been turned inside-out. *(Renzo Piano and Richard Rogers, Centre National d'Art et de Culture Georges Pompidou, Paris) (Courtesy Centre National d'Art et de Culture Georges Pompidou, Paris)*

Middle East investigating Buddhist meditation immediately after his undergraduate studies. Therefore, as this work suggests, Gormley's use of the body has spiritual, mystical overtones.

Gormley and Puryear illustrate the pluralism that has defined sculpture since the 1980s. With the decline of Minimalism, no new style has taken hold to replace modern art; instead there are many styles, sometimes grouped under the label *Postmodernism.*

New Forms of Expression in the Visual Arts

Ever since the Armory show of 1913 introduced modern art to America (see Chapter 25), avant-garde artists had been pushing the boundaries in painting and sculpture. Later in the twentieth century, some artists, in true Postmodern fashion, completely rejected traditional norms for painting and sculpture and turned to new forms of expression, such as performance, photography, and video, thereby shocking the sensibilities of many people. These new forms of expression were closely connected with *Conceptualism*—art that attempts to engage the mind, rather than the emotions or the aesthetic values, of the viewer.

One such artist was the Korean American Nam June Paik (1932–), a classical pianist and composer of electronic music, who was influenced by John Cage (see the later discussion). Desiring to give his music a visual dimension, Paik incorporated video imagery into his art. One of his most famous works, *TV Bra for Living Sculpture,* was performed in 1969 in collaboration with the classical cellist, Charlotte Moorman, who wore a bra made of two tiny video monitors that projected video while she played the cello. With this assimi-

lation of music and visual art, Paik wished to eroticize and personalize technology.

Postmodern Conceptualism endured into the 1980s in the work of Laurie Anderson (1947–), who made performance art mainstream. In 1980, she recorded *O Superman,* a satire of America's superpower status, which became the number two hit on England's pop charts. Her 1983 punk opera, *United States,* was a multimedia production that integrated music, photography, film, drawings, and animation; its complex lighting, sound, and text were all perfectly choreographed. Anderson accompanied complicated narratives with her own voice, which could change octaves and shift from male to female simply through the use of a harmonizer. Organized into four sections—Transportation, Politics, Money, and Love—and consisting of 78 segments, *United States* ran for more than six hours at its first performance at the Brooklyn Academy of Music.

Postmodern artists have also used photography as a tool to criticize the media and popular culture, as is evident in the work of Cindy Sherman (1954–). Sherman's images are self-portraits in which she uses costumes to evoke the feeling of an old film still or to become the subject of a famous painting. These emotionally charged, often open-ended images raise questions about female stereotypes as depicted in media and art, as well as other issues dealing with gender, class, and sexuality.

Janine Antoni (1962–) is an artist who has addressed similar issues through personally unique means of performance. In 1993, she performed *Loving Care,* using her own hair as a paintbrush to "mop" a gallery floor with Clairol's Loving Care black hair dye. As Antoni later explained in an interview, the performance referred to male-dominated art movements: "So for me, this piece relates to abstract expressionism, to Jackson Pollock and probably most closely to Yves Klein [1928–1962], with the performances where there were women covered in blue paint and then rolled on the canvas. Klein has a great quote: 'Rather than to paint the model, I wanted to paint with the model.' My response is that this is about the conflict of trying to be the model and the master at the same time."[15]

Architecture: Piano and Rogers, Graves, and Gehry

Postmodernism has become the prevailing aesthetic in late twentieth-century architecture. Its beginnings can be dated from 1966, when the architect Robert Venturi (1925–) retorted to Mies van der Rohe's saying, "Less is more," with his own witticism, "Less is a bore." Historians differ about the meaning of "Postmodernism" and about how the term should be applied to architecture, but it is clear that the era of the simple box-like modern architecture has passed. In its place is an architecture that manifests a whimsical use of both historical and amusing forms.

The *Centre National d'Art et de Culture Georges Pompidou* (Figure 26.9) in Paris, designed by Renzo Piano (b. 1937) and Richard Rogers (b. 1933), is often cited as one of the first Postmodern structures. Constructed from 1971 to 1977, the architects turned the Pompidou Center inside out, with all of the working parts of the building on the exterior—its blue air-conditioning ducts, green water pipes, yellow electrical units, red elevators, and the escalator. All of the interior space is left available for the exhibitions of the National Museum of Modern Art. On sunny days, the plaza next to the building attracts amateur street performers of various types, as well as soap-box orators and drifters, which has led Parisians to disagree about whether the building can be a serious art museum. There are also jokes about the beauty of the design, but the building attracts more than eight million visitors a year.

A leading proponent of architectural Postmodernism is Michael Graves (1934–), who was educated at the University of Cincinnati and at Harvard University. A professor of architecture at Princeton University, Graves has received numerous architectural awards. In a 1982 essay, he contrasted the Postmodern aesthetic to the Modern approach in architecture. He compared Modern architecture with the standard form of language used in literature. The "Modern Movement," Graves asserted, is dominated by "the metaphor of the machine," and its goal is "to build with only utility in mind."[16] Graves compared his own philosophy of architecture with the poetic form of language, defining it as the "figurative" approach to design that allows architecture "to represent the mythic and ritual aspirations of society."[17] Graves has completed a large number of important projects that have advanced this aesthetic both in the United States and Japan, but the work that may best illustrate the difference between his Postmodern designs and the Modern approach is his *1500 Ocean Drive* (Figure 26.10) in Miami Beach,

Figure 26.10 Michael Graves, *1500 Ocean Drive* (1999). As an example of Postmodern architecture, this fifteen-floor high-rise building contains a retail center on the ground level and 113 residential condominiums. Graves carefully designed the structure to reflect the oceanfront location and the surrounding neighborhood. *(Photo Courtesy of Michael Graves & Associates)*

Figure 26.11 Frank O. Gehry, *Peter B. Lewis Building,* **Case Western Reserve University, Cleveland, Ohio.** This five-story building houses the Weatherhead School of Management, with its faculty offices, classrooms, and meeting areas, covering an area of 149,000 square feet. Gehry is best known for his innovative use of materials, and he is famous for the way that he twists, turns, and bends metal into shapes that affect the emotions. *(Peter B. Lewis Building, Weatherhead School of Management, Case Western Reserve University, Cleveland, OH. Photograph by Michael W. Sands © 2002 Weatherhead School of Management, CWRU. All rights reserved.)*

Florida. When one compares Graves' design with Mies van der Rohe's simple and stark steel and glass design in *Lake Shore Drive Apartment Towers* (see Chapter 25), the contrast is evident. Graves has been careful to allow his design and colors to reflect the oceanfront location and the surrounding neighborhood. Completed in 1999, this fifteen-floor high-rise building contains a retail center on the ground level and 113 residential condominiums.

The most famous architect of the early twenty-first century is Frank O. Gehry (1929–), who received his degree in architecture from the University of Southern California in 1954. In succeeding years, he worked for several architectural firms, spent a brief period studying urban planning at the Graduate School of Design at Harvard University, and worked for a year in Paris. In 1962, he returned to California and opened his own firm in Santa Monica. In 1989, Gehry won the Pritzker Architecture Prize, often called "the Nobel of architecture." His work is found not only in the United States but also in Japan and in several European countries. Gehry's aesthetic has evolved from Modernism to a distinctive idiom that evidences his interest in painting and his friendship with contemporary artists. Gehry once expressed his theory of architecture in an interview, "[M]y theory is that our buildings, the ideas that come from buildings are from art. . . . So, paintings and sculptures have been very crucial to my world and my life."[18] Although he has refused to be categorized, his aesthetic is compatible with Postmodernism. Gehry is best known for his innovative use of materials, and he is famous for the way that he twists, turns, and bends metal into shapes that affect the emotions. One of his most recent ven-

tures is the *Peter B. Lewis Building* [Figure 26.11] at Case Western Reserve University, in Cleveland, Ohio, completed in 2002. The five-story building houses the Weatherhead School of Management, with faculty offices, classrooms, and meeting areas, covering an area of 149,000 square feet. Gehry has described its roof—which is built of stainless steel shingles, overlaid, to look like fish scales—as resembling water flowing over rocks. In a 2001 interview about the building, he exclaimed:

> Why these shapes? Why do you twist and turn like that? Why would anybody do that? It has to do with my belief that a building can have feeling. That there can be buildings that are deadly inert and don't give you anything. My favorite buildings, you either hate'em or you love'em. You get emotional. You can go into great buildings and they evoke some kind of an emotion and a lot of modern architecture is deadly and doesn't.[19]

In an earlier interview, in 1993, Gehry explained that his firm starts "with shapes, sculptural forms. Then we work into the technical stuff."[20] This is made possible by computer software that creates and manipulates the sculptural forms that dominate his architecture.

MUSIC

The Future of "Classical" Music: Copland and Cage

Music for popular consumption, instead of salons, churches, and opera houses, continues to be the hallmark of the music produced since 1945. This trend is particularly evident in the body of work of Aaron Copland (1900–1990), the son of Jewish-Lithuanian immigrants, whose musical career spanned seventy years. Copland grew up in New York City, where he was attracted to European Classical music, and at the age of twenty, he went to France on a scholarship to study with the conductor, performer, and composition teacher Nadia Boulanger (1887–1979). He wrote his first symphony, *Symphony for Organ and Orchestra* (1924), and, later, *Symphony for Orchestra,* commissioned by Madame Boulanger for her performances with the New York Philharmonic and the Boston Symphony Orchestra. These early works were inspired by Copland's appreciation of American jazz themes, which motivated him to compose his unique form of symphonic music, which he hoped would eventually become as popular as jazz.

By the 1930s, audiences and critics alike regarded Copland as the leader of classical music in America. Copland composed musical scores for several motion pictures and ballet music, including *Rodeo* (1942) for Agnes DeMille and *Appalachian Spring* (1944) for Martha Graham, which earned him the Pulitzer Prize. In all of these works, Copland's music was characterized by simplicity and tuneful melodies, which he believed were indicative of American folk tunes. During World War II, Copland composed two of his most popular, and patriotic, pieces for the Cincinnati Symphony: *Fanfare for the Common Man* and *A Lincoln Portrait,* incorporating portions of Lincoln's addresses, which have been read by such men as the poet Carl Sandburg and the Academy Award–winning actor Charlton Heston. As a way of honoring America following the tragedy of September 11, 2001, it was performed by the Boston Pops Orchestra at Super Bowl XXXVI, on February 3, 2002, with former presidents Jimmy Carter, Gerald Ford, and George H. Bush reading Lincoln's words, along with Nancy Reagan, the wife of former president Ronald Reagan.

The most avant-garde of the classical composers, John Cage (1912–1992), pioneered experimental music, particularly the so-called music of chance, which recognizes that sounds occurring simply by chance can still be appealing. During the 1930s, he studied the twelve-tone technique with Arnold Schönberg (see Chapter 23), but discovered he had "no feel for harmony." Consequently, Cage soon became a proponent of *musique concrete*—the movement that combined conventional sounds with electronics and ultimately resulted in the synthesizer. This innovation was one of the biggest influences on rock groups during the 1970s and 1980s, including Jerry Garcia and The Grateful Dead. A number of Cage's ideas were directly inspired by Marcel Duchamp's ready-mades, for both believed that music and art are all around us and that they do not necessarily emanate from the inner being of the artist. In his "music," Cage employed such ready-made sounds as radio static, doors slamming, and water pouring. For example, *Imaginary Landscape No. 4* (1951) utilizes twelve radios being played simultaneously; the music performed depends completely on the chance broadcast at that particular time, in that particular place. Cage also invented the "prepared piano technique"—inserting ordinary objects such as screws, boards, or metal plates into the soundboard of the piano, thereby altering its customary sound.

During the 1960s, Cage was deeply influenced by Zen Buddhism and was fascinated by the *I Ching* (Book of Changes), which enabled him to create his own type of experimental music. One of his more innovative pieces of this sort involves cutting apart a prerecorded tape and then reassembling it based on information gleaned from reading the *I Ching.* Nonetheless, Cage's most famous composition is still his *4′33″,* which premiered in 1952 with David Tudor as the pianist. Tudor approached the piano, sat down, used his fingers to show the audience which of the four movements he was playing, and then sat at the piano without touching the keys, and turned each page of the imaginary score at unplanned intervals. The "music" thus produced was the variety of sounds randomly generated by the audience, including whispering, shuffling of feet, coughing, sneezing, unwrapping a breath mint, or restlessly shifting in their seats.

Rock and Roll

The term "rock and roll" was coined by Alan Freed, a disc jockey in Cleveland, Ohio, who worked for WJW radio. In its early years, rock and roll was characterized by a hard-driving beat and made extensive use of the electric guitar and amplification. The earliest form of rock (which gave it its so-called "roll") was the African American rhythm and blues (R&B for short) dance music. But rock and roll was also heavily influenced by blues, jazz, gospel, country western, and folk music. Although rock and roll began as dance music, by the late 1960s, it had lost a great deal of its tunefulness and danceable rhythms—thus "rock" abandoned its "roll" and became known simply as "rock" music. Its lyrics often addressed social concerns: civil rights for blacks, women's rights, hostility to the war in Vietnam, and experimenting with drugs.

Rock and roll entered its so-called "Golden Decade" (1954–1963) when Bill Haley and the Comets introduced their megahit "Rock Around the Clock" (1954). But it was Elvis Presley (1935–1977), now known simply as "The King," who popularized rock and roll as an international genre of musical expression. Like Bill Haley, Elvis was a white man who could capably perform R&B songs, but unlike Haley, Elvis was equally at home with country western, gospel, and bluegrass music. By fusing country western with R&B, Elvis created a new style of music, known as *rockabilly*, which served as the foundation for his early hits for Sun Records, including "Heartbreak Hotel," "All Shook Up," "Jailhouse Rock," and "A Big Hunk O' Love." Elvis's megahit, the double-sided single "Don't Be Cruel"/"Hound Dog," earned him a performance on Ed Sullivan's popular television show "Toast of the Town" on September 9, 1956, which thrust him into the national spotlight. Because Sullivan viewed Elvis's trademark—sensual hip gyrations—as too risque for his show, Elvis was shown only from the waist up. He concluded his performance, which was watched by 85 percent of the people who were tuned in that evening, with the tender ballad "Love Me Tender," which signaled the new direction in which Elvis wanted his music to go.

During the 1960s, rock and roll moved in a new directions with the advent of the *Motown Sound*, so-named for the Detroit (Motor City) office of Motown's founder, Berry Gordy (1929–). Black groups such as The Four Tops ("Sugar Pie, Honey Bunch"), Diana Ross and the Supremes ("You Can't Hurry Love"), Smokey Robinson and the Miracles ("I Second That Emotion"), and The Temptations ("My Girl") sang songs that blended pop melodies, backed by rich harmonies, with R&B. This combination brought black popular music into the mainstream of American society, and throughout the early 1960s, the songwriting team of Eddie Holland, Lamont Dozier, and Brian Holland turned out one number one hit after another.

Rock and roll returned to its more rebellious roots in the working-class pubs and clubs of Liverpool, England, with the music of The Beatles: Paul McCartney (1942–), John Lennon (1940–1980), George Harrison (1943–2001), and Ringo Starr (1940–). This "mop-top" act unleashed a "British Invasion" of rock groups, which included The Yardbirds, The Kinks, The Who, and the "bad boys of rock," The Rolling Stones. The songwriting partnership of Lennon and McCartney was one of the most imaginative and creative in the history of pop music, and The Beatles were simultaneously the most *popular* and the *best* at what they did.

Generally regarded to have brought literacy to rock lyrics, Bob Dylan (1941–) has developed into a commanding figure in popular music. Dylan's music and poetry were influenced by R&B, folk music, and blues. During the early 1960s, Dylan's most popular pieces were his "topical songs," that dealt with the American Civil Rights Movement and the Vietnam War, which he opposed. "Blowin' in the Wind," recorded by Peter, Paul, & Mary in 1963, help to create his persona as an antiestablishment figure.

The watershed of rock music was reached in 1969, on a farm in Bethel, New York, with the rock festival Woodstock. For three days (August 15–17), 500,000 young people (who endured a twenty-mile traffic jam) listened to the likes of Joan Baez, Arlo Guthrie, Ravi Shankar, Sly and the Family Stone, The Who, Country Joe and the Fish, The Grateful Dead, Janis Joplin, The Band, Jimi Hendrix, and Sha-Na-Na. Although there were numerous drug busts and two deaths reported, for the most part a sense of community prevailed among the participants.

During the last three decades of the twentieth century, rock music, like jazz, became fragmented. Now audiences can choose from a variety of rock sounds, including country rock, pop rock, heavy metal, punk rock, alternative, and rap—one of the most popular forms of rock music in the new millennium. During the 1970s, rap was inaugurated by black teenagers on street corners, in school yards, and at block parties in New York City, Washington, D.C., and Philadelphia. Early raps were often boastful putdowns aimed at other rappers, but at other times, rappers cried out about the travail of ghetto life, spoke about drugs, and lauded sexual potency. The first big mainstream recording was "Rapper's Delight" by the Sugar Hill Gang, and the first truly successful rappers were Run-D.M.C., Kurtis Blow, and L. L. Cool J. The popularity of rap grew by leaps and bounds during the 1980s through acts such as N.W.A., Public Enemy, and Ice-T. In its purest form, rap is characterized by a type of spoken-word poetry, disc jockeys scratching records on turntables for sound effects, sampling of other artists, and a steady beat to reinforce the poetic line.

THE MOTION PICTURE INDUSTRY

The beginning of the motion picture industry can be traced back to the laboratory of Thomas A. Edison (1847–1931), where his assistant, William Kennedy Laurie Dickson, developed the kinetograph—a camera that was capable of capturing movement—which Edison patented in 1893. The next year, Edison pioneered the coin-operated kinetoscope, which enabled a single viewer to watch a continuous loop of film in a bulky viewfinder box. In 1895, Edison's technology was soon subverted by the *cinematographe*—the combination of a projector and movie camera, which could project an image to more than one spectator—the brainchild of the French brothers Louis and Auguste Lumiere. Their first film, *Workers Leaving the Lumiere Factory* (1895), showed nothing more than workers leaving the factory for a lunch break or going home for the day. Edison reentered the picture in 1896, when he purchased Vitascope from Thomas Armat and screened a ballet sequence in New York to paying customers; a year later, the first cinema theater was built in Paris.

During these early years, motion pictures were called "silent movies," even though they were accompanied by such things as pianos, organs, orchestras, sound effects, and sometimes even live actors speaking dialogue. The American director D. W. Griffith (1875–1948) introduced close-ups, fade-outs, and flashbacks to the art of filmmaking with his landmark film, *Birth of a Nation* (1915).

The leading male actor in the age of the silent screen was Charlie Chaplin (1889–1977). Insightful, intelligent, musical, and artistic, Chaplin transformed silent film comedy, which was largely slapstick, into an art form. In *The Tramp* (1915), Chaplin played a gentleman tramp, the character with which he would always be identified. The "little tramp" wore baggy pants, a derby, fingerless gloves, and a shabby dress coat, handled a bamboo cane with great dexterity, and shuffled as he walked.

American technology soon revolutionized the motion picture industry when Warner Bros. unveiled Vitaphone—a sound system that synchronized sound, dialogue, and the moving picture. In 1926, Warner Bros. premiered its film *Don Juan*, starring the legendary actor John Barrymore (1882–1942), nicknamed "The Great Profile." Fox Film Corporation subsequently launched their Movietone system, placing the soundtrack directly onto the film, which supplanted Vitaphone. Nonetheless, the advent of the "talkies" is generally regarded as the premier of Warner Bros. film *The Jazz Singer* (1927), starring Al Jolson (1888–1950), which included six songs on a partially synchronized musical soundtrack.

The decade of the 1930s is acknowledged as Hollywood's "Golden Age," for it not only saw the further development of "talking pictures," but also witnessed the appearance of gangster films, musicals, horror films, and westerns.

During World War II, Hollywood directors made training films and war documentaries. But they also responded to the effects of wartime with films that ran the gamut from escapism, to pacifism, to patriotism, to *film noir* (black film), which focused on dark, brooding plots, often involving femme fatales.

In 1940, Alfred Hitchcock (1899–1980), a recent immigrant from England, directed *Foreign Correspondent*, which concluded with an appeal to the United States government to thwart the spread of Nazism in Europe. Over the next fifty years, Hitchcock became the best-known and most influential director in the history of global cinema with films such as *Spellbound* (1945), *Notorious* (1945), *Dial M for Murder* (1954), *Vertigo* (1958), *North by Northwest* (1959), *Psycho* (1960) with its infamous shower scene murder, *The Birds* (1963), and *Frenzy* (1972), films that gave rise to the appellation "Hitchcockian Thriller."

By the age of twenty-four, Orson Welles (1915–1985) had already panicked America with his radio broadcast of a supposed Martian invasion of earth, based on H. G. Wells's book, *The War of the Worlds* (1898), but in 2000, his film, *Citizen Kane* (1941), topped critics' lists of "the best hundred movies of all time." Welles served as cowriter, director, and star of the film, which bore a very strong resemblance to the life of the newspaper magnate William Randolph Hearst (1863–1951), who did everything in his power to prevent the motion picture's dissemination. The plot is advanced through a mosaic of interlocking flashbacks as Charles Foster Kane is described by the different characters who knew him. The film also makes use of innovative techniques, including deep-focus optical effects, unusual camera angles, low-level lighting, close-ups, and unique sound editing.

The motion picture industry was, however, soon threatened by the increasing popularity of television. But movie studios soon learned the value of airing motion pictures on television. What proved to be the most effective rebuttal to television, however, was the motion picture epic, including *The Robe* (1953), *The Ten Commandments* (1956), *Around the World in 80 Days* (1956), and the most celebrated film of its time (winning eleven Oscars out of the twelve for which it was nominated) *Ben-Hur* (1957), which is best remembered for its climactic chariot race. The most commercially successful and renowned filmmaker of the present day is Steven Spielberg (1946–). He gives expression to his childlike sense of wonder in films such as *Close Encounters of the Third Kind* (1977), *E. T. The Extra-Terrestrial* (1982), and *Raiders of the Lost Ark* (1981), but he also demonstrates his social consciousness and sense of history in films such as *The Color Purple* (1985), based on Alice Walker's novel; *Empire of the Sun*

(1987), which depicts Japanese prisoner-of-war camps in Shanghai during World War II, as viewed through the eyes of a young English boy; and *Schindler's List* (1993), in which Liam Neeson portrays the industrialist Oskar Schindler, who managed to save hundreds of Polish Jews from extermination during the Nazi reign of terror.

The Western Tradition in a Global Age

In recent years, modern Western civilization has come under severe attack from some Western thinkers, loosely called Postmodernists, and advocates of Third World peoples. Expressing disdain for Western humanism, which ascribes an inherent dignity to human beings, urges the full development of the individual's potential, and regards the rational, self-determining human being as the center of existence, Postmodernists claim that humanism has failed. The humanist vision of socialist society ended in Stalinism, and liberal humanism proved no more effective a barrier to Nazism than did Christianity. In our own day, they ask, has the rational humanist tradition been able to solve the problems of overpopulation, worldwide pollution, world hunger, poverty, and war that ravage our planet? Closer to home, has reason coped successfully with the blight of homelessness, violence, racial tensions, or drug addiction that burden our society? Moreover, Postmodernists contend that the Western tradition, which has been valued as a great and creative human achievement, is fraught with gender, class, and racial bias.

Western intellectuals who identify with victims of exploitation, discrimination, and persecution throughout the globe also attack the Western tradition. They point to the modern West's historic abuses: slavery, imperialism, racism, ethnocentrism, sexism, class exploitation, and the ravaging of the environment.

Defenders of the Western heritage, on the other hand, argue that this heritage, despite all its flaws, still has a powerful message for us. They caution against devaluing and undermining the modern West's unique achievements: the tradition of *rationality,* which makes possible a scientific understanding of the physical universe and human nature, the utilization of nature for human betterment, and the identification and reformation of irrational and abusive institutions and beliefs; the tradition of *political freedom,* which is the foundation of democratic institutions; the tradition of *inner freedom,* which asserts the individual's capacity for ethical autonomy; the tradition of *humanism,* which regards individuals as active subjects, with both the right and the capacity to realize their full potential; the tradition of *equality,* which demands equal treatment under the law; and the tradition of *human dignity,* which affirms the inviolable integrity and worth of the human personality and is the driving force behind what is now a global quest for social justice and human rights.

The roots of these ideals are ultimately found in the West's Greek and Judeo-Christian heritage, but it was the philosophes of the Enlightenment who clearly articulated them for the modern age. To be sure, these ideals are a goal, not a finished achievement, and nothing should make people more appreciative of the preciousness of these ideals and more alert to their precariousness than examining the ways in which they have been violated and distorted over the course of centuries. It is equally true that every age has to rethink and revitalize this tradition in order to adapt it to the needs of its own time.

Therefore, it is crucial in this age of globalism, with its heightened sense of ethnic and cultural diversity, that Westerners become sensitized to the histories and traditions of all cultures and resolutely root out racist, sexist, and irrational ideas that have gravely poisoned Western perceptions and history. But it is equally crucial in an era of global interdependence and tension that Westerners continuously affirm and reaffirm the core values of their heritage and not permit this priceless legacy to be dismissed or negated. As the history of the twentieth century demonstrates, when we lose confidence in this heritage, we risk losing our humanity, and civilized life is threatened by organized barbarism. And vital components of this heritage are the Humanities—the achievements in thought, literature, and the arts examined in this text. Experiencing these creative works deepens respect for the civilization that produced them. But the Humanities also have a wider significance. They contribute to personal growth by cultivating the mind and enriching the spirit and to moral growth by leading us to empathize with the humanity of others. Unlike the sciences, the Humanities impel us to ponder the human condition, to explore what it means to be human. This new age of globalism is propelling the Humanities in new directions. Western art forms circulate widely throughout the globe. Asian musicians, for example, have distinguished themselves playing European Classical music, and American jazz and rock musicians perform before large audiences on every continent. African and Asian students read the classics of Western literature. But there is a reciprocal relationship between Western culture and the other cultures of the world. Audiences in Europe and the United States attend performances by African singers, instrumentalists, and dancers. African and Asian artists display their works in Western galleries. Asian and African cultural forms influence Western writers, artists, and musicians. Thus Picasso painted the faces of his French ladies of Avignon like African masks; American jazz musicians were inspired by African rhythms, and The Beatles incorporated Hindu rhythms into their songs; writers such as Alex Haley and Toni Morrison made it commendable for blacks to investigate their African heritage. Increasingly, students in American and European universities are studying the history and cultures of the non-Western world. In a world fraught with political dissension and cultural clashes, it is hoped that the study of the Humanities will contribute to greater tolerance and compassion, to those qualities that make us better human beings.

Key Terms

existentialism

Postmodernism

deconstruction

Theatre of the Absurd

Abstract Expressionism

action painting

color-field painting

Pop Art

combines

Minimalism

Conceptualism

musique concrete

cinematographe

Notes

1. Quoted in Walter Laqueur, *Europe Since Hitler* (Baltimore: Penguin Books, 1970), p. 118.

2. Chaim Potok, "On Being Proud of Uniqueness," lecture given to Southern College of Seventh Day Adventists, March 20, 1986, p. 1. Available [online] http://www.lasierr.edu/~bellen/potol/Potok.unique.html. January 25, 2002.

3. Ibid., p. 2.

4. Harper Lee, *To Kill a Mockingbird* (New York: Warner Books, Inc., 1982), p. 94.

5. Pepe Karmel, ed., *Jackson Pollock: Interviews, Articles, and Reviews* (New York: The Museum of Modern Art, 1999) p. 16.

6. Quoted in Michael Leja, *Reframing Abstract Expressionism: Subjectivity and Painting in the 1940s* (New Haven and London: Yale University Press, 1993), p. 122.

7. Karmel, *Jackson Pollock: Interviews, Articles, and Reviews*, pp. 17–18.

8. Ibid., p. 21.

9. Quoted in Fred Orton, *Figuring Jasper Johns* (Cambridge, MA: Harvard University Press, 1994), p. 140.

10. Quoted in Marilyn Stokstad, *Art History* (New York: Harry N. Abrams, Inc., 1999), p. 1126.

11. Ibid., p. 130.

12. Quoted in Jörn Merkert, ed., *David Smith: Sculpture and Drawings* (Munich: Prestel-Verlag, 1986) p. 162.

13. Quoted in John Hutchinson et al., *Antony Gormley* (London: Phaidon, 2000), p. 137.

14. Ibid., p. 135.

15. Interview, 1996, with City Arts producer Gail Levin, at http://www.thirteen.org/cityarts3/show10/uncutp.html, July 3, 2002.

16. Michael Graves, "A Case for Figurative Architecture," in *Michael Graves: Buildings and Projects, 1966–1981*, ed, Karen Vogel Wheeler, Peter Arnel, and Ted Bickford (New York: Rizzoli International Publications, Inc., 1982), p. 11.

17. Ibid., p. 13.

18. Interview, December 1998, *Architectural Record*, at http://www.archrecord.com/intrview/ghery.asp, July 3, 2002.

19. Interview, Spring 2001, Case Western Reserve University, Weatherhead School of Management [online] Available at http://www.cwru.edu/pubaff/univcomm/vnr/spring01/gehry.htm, February 14, 2002.

20. Frank O. Gehry, "On The American Center, Paris, An Interview," in *Theories and Manifestoes of Contemporary Architecture*, ed. Charles Jencks and Karl Kropf (Chichester, England: Academy Editions, 1997), p. 119.

Abstract Expressionism – also known as the New York School, artists in this modern art movement used color and abstract, nonrepresentational forms in their paintings to express their emotions.

action painting – a method of painting, made famous by Jackson Pollock, in which the artist moves around a canvas on the floor, pouring and dripping paint from above.

Anabaptists – a Protestant sect whose members rejected infant baptism and rebaptized each other as adults.

apocalyptic – referring to a prophetic vision of the catastrophes of the last days of the human race.

appeasement – the policy employed by Britain and France of giving in to Germany in the hope that a satisfied Hitler would not drag Europe into another war.

aquatint – a process using acid to create tonal areas on a plate that had already been etched.

ars nova – (new art) designates music of the 14th century in contrast to the *ars antiqua* (old art) of the 12th and 13th centuries. The music is generally characterized by polyphony.

art song – a composition for piano and solo voice in which poetry and music are inextricably fused, and the piano and the soloist virtually "sing" a duet.

atonal – a style of musical composition that purposefully lacks any particular key as its tonal center and has no identifiable melodic line or harmonic formula.

ballet – Originating in the sixteenth century, a ballet is a theatrical performance emphasizing artistic dancing, supported by costumes, scenery, and a full orchestra.

Baroque Age – the period, primarily during the seventeenth century, when rulers used art and architecture to express their wealth and power.

Bastille – a fortress and symbol of the Old Regime that was stormed and captured on July 14 by Parisians during the French Revolution.

Bauhaus – a school, founded by Walter Gropius, that was based on the concept of combining instruction in the fine arts, the crafts, engineering, and architecture.

Bebop jazz – a term coined in the 1940s to characterize jazz which emphasized complex, often dissonant, improvised solo performances.

big band – ensembles popular during the 1930s and 1940s that featured vocalists and instrumentalists who generally played trumpet, piano, drums, clarinet, and trombone.

blank verse – a style of poetry consisting of unrhymed iambic pentameter; Milton's *Paradise Lost* was composed in this fashion.

blues – a musical style, originating in the Mississippi Delta region and Texas, whose harmony is based on the repetition of three major chords, and whose melody is characterized by so-called "blues notes," which embody the bittersweet, emotional lyrics.

British Palladian style – the movement that dominated British architecture during the eighteenth century, based on the design principles of the Italian Renaissance architect Andrea Palladio.

"Byronic hero" – a literary hero who is self-absorbed, brooding, and impassioned; this hero is evident in Byron's *Don Juan*.

cadenza – an elaborate flourish near the end of a piece of music.

camera obscura – a technique, popularized by Italian artists during the sixteenth century, in which a box projects an image onto a wall or screen for an artist to trace.

chansons – songs that make use of short phrases, thereby skirting the problem of reconciling a substantive text with an extended melody.

chauvinists – extreme nationalists.

chorale – a genre of sacred music, also known as a congregational hymn, that was first published in 1524 by Johann Walther.

cinematographe – a combination of a projector and movie camera, which could project an image to more than one spectator—the brainchild of the French brothers Louis and Auguste Lumiere.

circular motion – a design technique, developed by da Vinci, in which figures are placed in a group in such a way that each seems to be leaning toward, looking at, or pointing to another figure.

"classical" French drama – a style of drama that stressed unity of time, place, and action; it was first expressed by Pierre Corneille (1606-1684).

Civil Rights Movement – the movement in the 1950s and 1960s by American blacks and their sympathizers, that ended legal segregation in the South.

Code Napoléon – a unified code of laws including many principles of the Revolution: equality before the law, the right to choose one's profession, freedom of conscience, protection of property rights, the abolition of serfdom, and the secular character of the state.

collage – a process of constructing a picture, invented by Picasso, that involves pasting shapes of paper and other materials on the picture surface.

color-field painting – a style of abstract expressionist painting, made popular by Rothko, in which huge blocks of color are used on a canvas to express emotion.

combines – works of art produced by Rauschenberg that were both paintings and sculptures, made by combining paint, photographs, paper, metal, fabric, and other objects on a canvas.

conceit – a fixed image that evokes a form of dramatic contrast which is comprehended with intense intellectual effort.

Conceptualism – forms of artistic expression, such as performance, photography, and video, that attempt to engage the mind, rather than the emotions or the aesthetic values, of the viewer.

concerto – a composition for a solo instrument and an orchestra.

Concordat of 1801 – an agreement reached between Napoleon and the pope that recognized Catholicism as the religion of the great majority of the French, rather than as the official state religion.

Congregation of the Index – the church's censorship organ, that condemned the teaching of Copernicanism in 1616 and later forced Galileo to abjure the theory.

Conservatism – an ideology that developed in the nineteenth century as a reaction against the Enlightenment and the French Revolution. Conservatives championed tradition over reform, hierarchy over equality, and the community over the individual.

consistory – a morals court in the church of Geneva, made up of lay elders and pastors, that was designed to enforce Christian discipline.

contrapposto – a pose suspended between resting and walking in which one side of the body is relaxed and the other side tense with the weight carried by one leg.

contrapuntal – also known as counterpoint, its name derives from counter and point, because one note is set against another as if it were constituted by one point against another.

Convertor – a special furnace, created by Henry Bessemer in 1856, that could mass-produce large quantities of steel.

Cubism – an artistic movement, developed by Braque and Picasso, that tried to depict an object from multiple perspectives rather than from a single point in space.

Dadaists – an artistic group who believed that the world was nonsensical; they showed their contempt for art by deliberately producing works that seemed devoid of artistic value.

daguerreotype – the name given to the first photograph, a positive print made on light-sensitive copper.

deconstruction – a technique for reading developed by Jacques Derrida (b. 1930), which holds that a text's underlying arguments and premises are fundamentally ambiguous, inconsistent, and contradictory.

deductive approach – a method employed in mathematics and theoretical physics, in which truths are derived in successive steps from first principles, indubitable axioms, it was championed by Descartes.

deists – eighteenth-century thinkers who sought to fashion a natural religion in accordance with reason and science; they believed in God but rejected revelation and miracles.

dialectical materialism – the Marxist belief that history evolves dialectically—that the clash of opposing forces propels history into higher stages. The

clash of classes, which represents conflicting economic interests, accounts for historical change and progress.

Dreyfus affair – the 1894 trial of Captain Alfred Dreyfus, a Jewish artillery officer who was falsely accused by the army of selling secrets to the Germans left the country deeply divided.

eclecticism – a movement in architecture during the eighteenth and nineteenth centuries that incorporated two or more historical styles.

Elizabethan madrigal – a secular song which proclaims the greatness of Elizabeth I (r. 1558-1603), which ends with the line: "Long live fair Oriana [Elizabeth]."

epic theater – a type of theater, favored by Brecht, that dealt with past rather than current events.

epistolary novel – a novel that is composed of a series of letters; Richardson's *Pamela* is the first example of this style.

Estates – during the eighteenth century, French society was legally divided into three orders, or Estates: the clergy constituted the First Estate, the nobility formed the Second Estate, and the bourgeoisie, the peasants, and the urban workers comprised the Third Estate.

everyman – a literary character meant to represent any person.

existentialism – a philosophical movement popular after World War II that maintained that traditional values are not certainties, the universe is indifferent to our needs, and existence is essentially purposeless and absurd. Nevertheless we must strive to give our life meaning.

Expressionism – a German artistic movement employed harsh colors and distorted shapes in their work to express their emotions.

extreme nationalists – rejecting the liberal emphasis on political liberty, they believed the state was the highest development of a folkish-racial spirit inherited from their ancestors.

fascism – an ideology founded on a hatred of liberalism, democracy, and communism; a commitment to aggressive nationalism; and a glorification of the party leader.

Fauvism – an artistic movement whose members were christened the *Fauves*— the wild beasts—by their critics, because of their distortion of form and color to express intense feelings in their paintings.

Federal period – the period from 1783 to 1830 during which American archi-

tecture was dominated by the Neoclassical style.

fideist – one who simply believes in God without objective, rational proof of his existence.

Five Year Plans – developed under Stalin, this program of rapid industrialization (by force) was designed to make Russia competitive.

fixed forms – during the fourteenth century, *virelai*, *rondeau*, and *ballade* became known as the "fixed forms." The *virelai* (from the Old French word *virelai* meaning to twist or to turn) had its origins in the French dance song, but eventually it ceased to be associated with dance, and became the creative force behind numerous secular compositions. In Italy, the form was associated with the *ballata* or *lauda* and adhered to the earlier medieval monophonic tradition. Like the *virelai*, the more complex *rondeau* had its origins in the "round-dance," to which was added a refrain. *Ballades* were exceptionally simple—two segments of music, the first part sung twice, and the second only once.

free jazz – as its name implies, this style of jazz is not driven by any regular patterns pertaining to chord structure, rhythm, or melody.

frottage – a technique, created by Max Ernst, in which a sheet of paper is placed over a textured surface, and then rubbed with a soft pencil, creating images that he could then alter in a painting.

Futurism – a movement launched by the Italian poet Filippo Marinetti, that sought to depict the dynamism of modern urban life and modern industry, which they linked with war and the destruction of core Western values.

Globe Theater – the theater where most of Shakespeare's plays were performed.

Glorious Revolution – also called the Bloodless Revolution of 1688–1689, it ensured that parliamentary government and the rule of law, not the tyrannical power of a monarch, would prevail in England.

Gothic Romance – novels set in faraway times or locales, whose themes often focused on psychological confinement or physical imprisonment. Therefore, the climax of the Gothic Romance was the liberation of self.

grand manner – Poussin's theory of art, which stated that the subject must be conceived without superfluous details, it must be painted naturally and without affectation, and the style of the painting must flow innately from the artist.

Great Depression – the period of economic collapse that occurred around the world in the 1930s.

Great Migration – the period, during and after World War I, when 450,000 blacks moved from the rural South to northern cities to work in factories.

Harlem Renaissance – the period in the 1920s that witnessed a new growth in the creativity of African–American literature, art, and jazz music, in Harlem, New York.

heliocentric theory – the view, established by Nicolaus Copernicus, that the earth is a planet that orbits a centrally located sun together with the other planets.

humanists – participants in the Renaissance movement of Humanism: an educational and cultural program based on the study of ancient Greek and Roman literature; over the centuries humanists have valued human dignity and pursuits that promote a rich and creative life.

iambic pentameter – a measurement used in poetry – an iambic foot is an unstressed syllable followed by a stressed one; pentameter means that there are five iambic feet per line.

Idealism – a school of German philosophy that held that the world is not something objective, but that human consciousness, the knowing subject, builds the world and determines its form.

idée fixe – (fixed idea) a musical theme that recurs throughout all of the movements of a symphony, representing a person, place, or thing.

Imperial Diet at Worms – a meeting of Church officials in April 1521, at which Luther was ordered to recant his beliefs before the Emperor and all the dignitaries of both the empire and the church. He refused, and was condemned as a heretic and declared an outlaw by an imperial edict.

Impressionism – an artistic movement that attempted to understand the permutations of light and color, "to get an impression of," or to capture the moment when the eye perceives light on various surfaces during different times of the day.

incidental music – first composed by Mendelssohn, this music is not actually a part of the drama itself, but rather it is played in the background to set a scene or mood.

Index of Forbidden Books – a list of dangerous works that no Catholic could read under threat of excommunication.

individualism – a hallmark of the Renaissance, it was the view that human beings have a special dignity: they had the intelligence and talent to accomplish wonders on earth and a special duty to fulfill their potential.

inductive approach – Bacon's method for scientific discovery, which consisted of careful observation of nature and the systematic accumulation of data; drawing general laws from the knowledge of particulars; and testing these laws through constant experimentation.

indulgence – a method whereby sinners could draw on the treasury of merit accrued by Christ, the Virgin Mary, and the saints to remit the temporal punishment for sins. Protestant reformers objected to the sale of indulgences by the Church.

interior monologue – a style of writing in which an author expresses a character's innermost thoughts, which often reveals the character's buried fears and/or torments.

Intermezzi – meaning "in the middle," this term describes the musical interludes that appear before a play, between acts, and at the end of a play.

International Style – a style of architecture that looked to the future instead of the past and in which new architecture would fulfill the needs of the masses and further the development of democracy.

irrationalism – a late nineteenth-century outlook that repudiated the Enlightenment conception of human rationality, stressing instead the importance of hidden forces below the level of consciousness.

jazz – a musical genre, developed by African American musicians, that featured a "call and response," in which a vocalist's phrases are answered by another instrument or the entire jazz ensemble.

"Jim Crow" laws – laws, enacted after the Civil War, that curtailed the freedom of former slaves and legalized new forms of oppression.

justification – a theological term that means "to make a person righteous;" for Luther, justification was a *passive righteousness*, attained through God's gift of faith, and not through any human efforts.

laissez-faire – the economic theory, credited to Adam Smith, that the government should not interfere with the country's economy.

leitmotif – a short musical label associated with a person, an idea, or an object.

liberalism – as developed in the nineteenth century, a political theory in which the central concern was safeguarding individual freedom from abusive governmental authority.

linear perspective – a technique, developed during the Renaissance, that makes it possible to represent three-dimensional space on a flat surface. The central feature of single-point perspective is a vanishing point toward which parallel lines converge.

"the lost generation" – the term used by Gertrude Stein to describe the generation of expatriate artists living in Paris after World War I.

Mannerism – the term given to the period of Italian art from the death of Raphael until about 1600. Mannerism placed an emphasis on instability and discord—the proportions of human bodies are distorted; the principles of space and perspective are similarly violated; and the naturalistic colors are replaced by subjective coloring.

Minimalism – this art movement from the 1970s featured simple, symmetrical sculpture, made of modern materials that engaged the viewer and, by implication, spurned depicting the human body.

minuet – a French dance song of the seventeenth century.

Modernism – a cultural movement originating in the late nineteenth century that abandoned conventional literary and artistic models and experimented with new modes of expression. The artists invited the audience to share in the process of creation, often unconscious, and to discover fresh insights into objects, sounds, people, and social conditions.

monody – a solo song, comes from the Greek *monodia*, which is a combination of *monos*, meaning "alone," and *aidein*, which means "to sing."

moral genre – a type of painting that restored a sense of realism and naturalism to art and attempted to instruct and uplift the viewer. The subject matter often focused on the values and moral standards of the middle class, not of the aristocracy.

motet – early form of polyphonic music, generally in three voice parts, with the *cantus firmus* (fixed songs) sung in the tenor part.

motives – short melodic figures that are too short to be called a theme.

music drama – larger-than-life epics of sung poetry supported by complex, colorful orchestration to create moods using leitmotifs and continuous melody.

musique concrete – a musical movement, made popular by John Cage, that combined conventional sounds with electronics, ultimately resulting in the synthesizer.

nationalism – a conscious bond shared by a group of people who feel strongly attached to a particular land and who possess a common language, culture, and history, marked by shared glories and sufferings.

natural rights – the theory stated by Locke, that human beings have an intrinsic right to life, liberty, and property, and that human beings establish the state to protect these rights; the theory of natural rights was crucial to the development of the modern, liberal-democratic state.

natural selection – the Darwinian theory that an organism favored by nature is more likely to reach maturity, to mate, and to pass on its superior qualities to its offspring, some of whom will acquire the advantageous trait to an even greater degree than the parent. Over time this leads to the death of the old species and the emergence of new ones.

Naturalism – evolving from Realism, followers of this literary movement wrote about the atypical and the seamy side of life, including the criminal element. Naturalists tried to demonstrate a cause-and-effect relationship between human character and the social environment.

New Devotion – a religious order, whose followers were called the Brethren of the Common Life, that influenced northern humanism by establishing schools and operating printing presses.

nocturnes – a lyrical, reflective Romantic musical piece. Chopin's nocturnes feature an "agitated" middle section.

odalisque – a female slave or concubine in a sultan's harem.

organic architecture – Frank Lloyd Wright's idea that a house should appear to grow from the site on which it is built and should blend into its natural environment.

picaresque – a type of novel, such as *Don Quixote*, characterized by a narrator, who appears to be relating his autobiography, who meets numerous characters along his journey.

platonic love – an idea popular in later Renaissance literature, it represents the spiritual intimacy and fervent companionship of two people in a mutual love of God. This spiritual love of the lover and the beloved imitates the manner in which God, through Jesus, loves humanity.

pointillism – the artistic technique that employed tiny round points of color, nearly identical in size, which, rather than being blended on the artist's palette, were intended to merge in the eyes of the observer.

polyphonic – two or more parts, each with its own melody, sung or played simultaneously.

polyrhythm – the combination of different rhythms (such as 3/4 time and 6/8 time) that are played simultaneously.

polytonality – the combination of a number of different melodies, each played in a different key.

Pop Art – a style of painting, made popular by Warhol, which exalted post-war consumerism and celebrated popular culture.

Post-Impressionists – a group of younger artists, influenced by Impressionism, who further revolutionized sense of space and color, and attempted to make art a vivid emotional experience.

postmodernism – the term, which came into vogue in the 1970s, is used broadly to describe avant-garde developments in the arts, in architecture, and in thought.

predestination – a belief, central to Calvin's theology, that even before their birth God determined that some human beings would be saved and others condemned.

principle of inertia – Newton's first law that a body at rest remains at rest unless acted on by a force and that a body in rectilinear motion continues to move in a straight line at the same velocity unless a force acts on it.

program music – a style of music that relied heavily on the poetic inspiration of the composer, who chose a variety of specific musical motifs to express changing human emotions. Also, music that serves a narrative or descriptive function; Vivaldi was a pioneer of this style.

proletariat – the Marxist term for the modern wage earner who was exploited by the capitalists in power.

pyramidal design – a design technique, developed by da Vinci, that establishes a three-dimensional effect by positioning one figure as if at the apex of an imaginary pyramid and then allowing the other figures to fix the corners of the pyramid.

quantum theory – Max Planck's 1900 discovery that holds that a heated body radiates energy not in a continuous unbroken stream, but in intermittent spurts, or jumps, called quanta.

ragtime – a type of piano music, popularized by primarily African American pianists, whose major characteristic is its syncopated rhythm—a metric pattern that emphasizes the weak beats of a measure instead of the strong ones.

Realism – the dominant movement in art and literature in the mid-nineteenth century, it concentrated on the actual world and dealt regularly with social abuses, class divisions, and the ignoble aspects of human behavior.

Realpolitik – meaning "politics of reality," it was the political counterpart of realism, which viewed governments' workings coldly and objectively as they are, rather than as idealists would like them to be.

recitative – a vocal solo which emphasizes a spoken style; used in cantatas, oratorios, and operas to narrate something.

Reign of Terror – the period after the French Revolution, during which Robespierre and others attacked those they considered enemies of the republic; perhaps as many as forty thousand people from all segments of society were executed.

Renaissance – meaning "rebirth," this period of cultural transformation in Italy during the late fourteenth and fifteenth centuries was characterized by a fresh respect for the humanistic and worldly culture of ancient Greece and Rome.

repression – Freud's belief that childhood fears and experiences are too difficult to deal with and are thus banished from conscious memory to the realm of the unconscious.

Rococo – a style of art that emphasized whimsical moods, fanciful, often dreamlike, settings and figures, and soft, often pastel, colors.

Romanticism – a primarily literary and artistic movement that challenged the Enlightenment stress on rationalism with its focus on the liberation of human emotions and the free expression of personality.

Roundheads – led by Oliver Cromwell, these Puritan troops fought against Charles I in the English Civil War of 1642.

Saint Bartholomew's Day Massacre – the day (August 24, 1572) during the religious wars when thousands of Huguenots were brutally murdered in Paris, the center of the atrocity, and throughout France.

Salon de Refusés – the room, created by Napoleon III, to hold paintings rejected from the Salon exhibition; the term literally means "Salon of the Rejected."

Singspiel – during the eighteenth century, the *Singspiel* was a type of comic opera in Germany.

Social Darwinists – this group took Darwin's theory of natural selection and applied it to society, insisting that nations and races were engaged in a struggle for survival in which only the fittest survive and deserve to survive.

Socialist Realism – the official standard for art under Stalin; artists were required to belong to the "Union of Soviet Artists," under state control, and their paintings had to glorify the collectivist ideals of communism.

Society of Jesus – a religious order of the Catholic Church, also called the Jesuits, whose members took a special oath of obedience to the pope, espoused a life of active service, and were committed to Christian education and missionary work.

sonata form – a musical form that dictates the structure of a single movement—*exposition, development,* and *recapitulation.* The exposition states the theme(s); the development enlarges the themes; and the recapitulation restates the themes and brings resolution.

spectaculi – a performance, originating during the second half of the sixteenth century in northern Italy, that included staged combats, equestrian competitions, and dancing. From these events, the French appropriated the word *spectacle* to talk about the dance form known as ballet.

stream of consciousness – a Modernist technique that ignores conventional rules of writing and relates the action through images and symbols that are conjured up in the mind of one or more of the characters.

string quartet – a chamber music group consisting of four stringed instruments, generally two violins, a viola, and a cello.

string quintet – a chamber music group consisting of five stringed instruments, generally two violins, two violas, and a cello.

Sturm und Drang – "storm and stress," a German literary movement from the early 1770s that emphasized imagination, spontaneity, feeling, and passion, and appreciated the consummate power of nature.

Surrealism – an artistic group that stressed fantasy and made use of Freudian insights and symbols in their art as they sought to reproduce the raw state of the unconscious and to arrive at truths beyond reason's grasp.

swing – a style of jazz intended for the big bands, and was therefore arranged rather than improvised on the spot. Entire sections of the band, either in harmony or unison, would play the melodies, but the main melody was accompanied by short, repetitive phrases called riffs.

symphony – originating in the eighteenth century, the symphony became the predominate form of orchestral music. In essence, it is a sonata (see sonata form) for an orchestra.

tabula rasa – Locke's belief that the human mind is a "blank slate," upon which are imprinted sensations derived from contact with the world; therefore, knowledge is derived from experience.

tempo rubato – a musical innovation that freed the performer and/or conductor from adhering to a strict tempo and permitted the creative genius of the musician to "speak" through the music.

tenebrism – a style of painting characterized by figures that emerge from the dark into a type of spotlight—the source of which appears to reside outside the painting.

the cult of the individual – a hallmark of the Romantic movement, this was established by Rousseau and others who championed the freedom of individual personality and expression.

the general will – Rousseau's belief that the state should be governed according to an underlying principle that expressed what was best for the community.

The Jazz Age – the term given to the decade of the 1920s by the author F. Scott Fitzergerald.

The Prince – a treatise on politics, written by Machiavelli, that advises rulers how to gain and maintain power.

The Salon – the name given to the annual art exhibition held by the French Academy.

The Victorian Age – the period from 1837 until 1901 when Queen Victoria ruled England; England was at the height of its power and industrialization and colonization had accelerated.

Theatre of the Absurd – dramatic works of the 1950s in both Europe and the U.S. that embraced the existential concept that human existence is essentially absurd and without meaning.

thematic transformation – the process, made popular by Liszt, of transforming or altering specific musical ideas to unite the entire work.

theory of relativity – developed by Einstein, it holds that neither space nor time is a distinct entity that exists independently of human experience.

Thirty Years' War – the war (1618-1648) resulting from the Emperor Ferdinand's attempt to impose Catholicism on Bohemia in 1618. The Protestant nobles revolted against him and put a Calvinist king on their throne; Spain and Austria responded by sending troops into Bohemia.

tone clusters – a massive dissonance of sound that is created by playing a number of notes that are located very close together.

tone poem – also known as a symphonic poem, this musical style, invented by Liszt, is most often based on a literary or pictorial idea that is presented in a single, long movement free of the traditional conventions of the sonata form.

totalitarianism – a form of government emerging in the twentieth century that abolishes all competing political parties, suppresses individual liberty, eliminates or regulates private institutions, and utilizes the modern state's bureaucracy and technology to impose its ideology and enforce its commands.

Transcendentalists – an intellectual group from nineteenth-century New England who held that truth can be arrived at independently of the senses and who stressed the spiritual unity of the world, identifying God with Nature.

transcriptions – modified versions of monumental operatic and orchestral scores that could be played on the piano.

triptych – an alterpiece consisting of a central panel and two hinged doors.

twelve-tone technique – a musical system, developed by Schönberg, that is based on the twelve tones of the chromatic scale, which included specific rules.

underground railroad – a network of people who helped fugitive slaves escape to freedom in Canada from the United States.

Utopian socialists – early nineteenth-century theorists who drew up plans for ideal cooperative societies. The communities established by their followers generally ended in failure.

Versailles Treaty – the January 1919 Peace Settlement drawn up by the victors of World War I.

Volksgeist – meaning the "soul of the people," the German writer Herder (1744-1803) saw each group of people as unique and creative; each expressed its genius in language, literature, monuments, and folk traditions.

Zoroastrian – a follower of Zoroastrianism, the ancient monotheistic religion that originated in Persia around 600 B.C.

Chapter 13

Baron, Hans, *The Crisis of the Early Italian Renaissance* (1966). An influential interpretation of the origins of civic humanism.

Bouwsma, William J., *Venice and the Defense of Republican Liberty* (1968). The Venetian origins of Western republicanism.

Brucker, Gene A., *Renaissance Florence*, rev. ed. (1983). An excellent analysis of the city's physical character, its economic and social structure, its political and religious life, and its cultural achievements.

Burckhardt, Jacob, *The Civilization of the Renaissance in Italy* (1860), 2 vols. (1958). The first major interpretive synthesis of the Renaissance; still a useful resource.

Burke, Peter, *Popular Culture in Early Modern Europe (1978)*. A fascinating account of the social underside from the Renaissance to the French Revolution.

Eisenstein, Elizabeth, *The Printing Press as an Agent of Change*, 2 vols. (1978). The definitive treatment—informative, argumentative, and suggestive.

Freedberg, Sydney J., *Painting in Italy: 1500-1600*, 2nd ed. (1983). A comprehensive survey of painting in Italy during the sixteenth century.

Hale, John, *The Civilization of Europe in the Renaissance* (1993). An expressive and rich portrait of Europe during the Renaissance.

Hartt, F., *Italian Renaissance Art*, 4th ed. (1993). A standard resource.

Hibbert, Christopher, *The House of Medici: Its Rise and Fall* (1980). An informative and entertaining account of the Medici family.

Holmes, George, *The Florentine Enlightenment, 1400-50* (1969). An impressive study of the early Renaissance in Florence, covering humanism, philosophy, religion, and art.

Kelley, Donald R., *Renaissance Humanism* (1991). A recent synthesis.

King, Margaret L., *Women of the Renaissance* (1991). A useful survey of a burgeoning field of scholarship.

Skinner, Quentin, *The Foundations of Modern Political Thought*, 2 vols. (1978). The first volume covers the Renaissance; informative.

Spitz, Lewis W., *The Renaissance and Reformation Movements. Volume I: The Renaissance*, rev. ed. (1987). A nuanced survey of the entire range of life and thought in the Italian and Northern Renaissance.

Chapter 14

Bainton, Roland H., *Erasmus of Christendom* (1969). A readable, sympathetic biography.

———, *Here I Stand* (1950). An old biography, but still one of the best.

———, *The Travail of Religious Liberty* (1951). A still useful study of the issue of toleration in the sixteenth and seventeenth centuries.

———, *Women of the Reformation in Germany and Italy* (1971). A pioneering study of sixteenth-century women.

Dickens, A. G., *The English Reformation,* 2nd edition (1991). A solid introduction to the Reformation in England.

Goertz, Hans-Jürgen, ed., *Profiles of Radical Reformers: Biographical Sketches from Thomas Müntzer to Paracelsus* (1982). Twenty-one biographical sketches of radical reformers.

Koenigsberger, H. G., *Early Modern Europe, 1500-1789* (1987). An excellent survey by a master historian.

Lindberg, Carter, The *European Reformations (1996)*. The most complete and the most recent coverage of the religious ideas of the sixteenth century and their impact on society.

McGrath, Alister E., *A Life of John Calvin* (1990). Balanced coverage of the life and thought of Calvin.

———, *Reformation Thought: An Introduction,* 2nd edition (1993). A good introduction to Reformation theology.

Oberman, Heiko A., *Luther: Man between God and the Devil* (1989). Luther, the man, in his sixteenth-century context.

———, *The Roots of Anti-Semitism in the Age of the Renaissance and Reformation* (1984). A study of anti-Semitism in the thought of humanists, like Erasmus, and reformers, like Luther.

Olin, John C., *Catholic Reform: From Cardinal Ximenes to the Council of Trent, 1495-1563* (1990). An excellent, balanced treatment of the Catholic Reformation.

Prestwich, Menna, ed., *International Calvinism, 1541-1715* (1985). Studies on the spread and impact of Calvinism during the sixteenth and seventeenth centuries.

Rice, Jr., Eugene F., *The Foundations of Early Modern Europe, 1460-1559* (1970). A compact study that covers all the major aspects of society during the Renaissance and Reformation.

Samuelsson, Kurt, *Religion and Economic Action: A Critique of Max Weber* (1961). A devastating critique of Weber's theory.

Smith, Lacey Baldwin, *This Realm of England, 1399-1688*, rev. ed. (1983). A good, readable survey.

Spitz, Lewis W., *The Protestant Reformation, 1517-1559* (1985). A sympathetic, but fair treatment of the Protestant Reformation in Europe and England, that, despite its title, has an excellent chapter on Catholic reform.

_____, *The Religious Renaissance of the German Humanists* (1963). A fine study of early German humanism up to and including Luther.

Stephens, W. P., *Zwingli: An Introduction to His Thought* (1992). Excellent introduction to the theology of Zwingli.

Chapter 15

Benesch, Otto, *The Art of the Renaissance in Northern Europe*, 2nd ed. (1965). A standard account of Renaissance art in the north.

Brooke, Tucker, *The Tudor Drama* (1911). An old, but still useful history of English drama up to and including Shakespeare.

Christensen, Carl, *Art and the Reformation in Germany* (1979). The impact of the Reformation on the world of art in sixteenth-century Germany.

Frame, Donald M., *Montaigne: A Biography* (1984). A reprint of the 1964 edition of the standard biography of Montaigne.

Grout, Donald Jay, *A Short History of Opera*, 2nd ed. (1965). Begins with Monteverdi.

Inglis, Fred, *The Elizabethan Poets: The Making of English Poetry from Wyatt to Ben Jonson* (1969). A brief study of English poetry in the sixteenth and early seventeenth centuries.

Lewis, C. S., *English Literature in the Sixteenth Century, Excluding Drama* (1954). A survey from the late Middle Ages to Shakespeare; part of the *Oxford History of English Literature.*

Peterson, Douglas L., *The English Lyric from Wyatt to Donne* (1967). The development of English verse from the late Middle Ages to John Donne.

Pattison, Bruce, *Music and Poetry of the English Renaissance* (1970). A standard text on the topic.

Reese, Gustave, *Music in the Renaissance* (1959). Comprehensive account of all types of musical activities from 1400 to 1600.

Snyder, J. *Northern Renaissance Art: Painting, Sculpture, the Graphic Arts, from 1350-1575* (1985). An excellent resource.

Simone, Franco, *The French Renaissance: Medieval Tradition and Italian Influence in Shaping the Renaissance in France* (1969). A study of the Renaissance in France from the mid–fourteenth century, when Petrarch lived in Avignon, until the Reformation.

Tilley, Arthur, *Studies in the French Renaissance* (1968). Reprint of the 1922 edition, covering Rabelais and Montaigne; still a useful study.

Wilson, F. P. *The English Drama, 1485-1585* (1969). Useful survey; part of the *Oxford History of English Literature.*

Chapter 16

Blunt, Sir Anthony, *Art and Architecture in France, 1500-1700*, 5th ed. (1999). An excellent, thorough survey; part of the *Pelican History of Art.*

Brereton, Geoffrey, *French Tragic Drama in the Sixteenth and Seventeenth Centuries* (1973). A survey of the topic from the Renaissance to Racine.

Brown, Jonathon, *The Golden Age of Painting in Spain* (1991). An outstanding survey covering the entire seventeenth century.

Bukofzer, Manfred F., *Music in the Baroque Era, from Monteverdi to Bach* (1947). Thorough treatment of the history of Western music from the 1590s to the mid–eighteenth century.

Bush, Douglas, *English Literature in the Earlier Seventeenth Century, 1600-1660*, rev. ed. (1962). A classic; part of the *Oxford History of English Literature.*

_____, *Mythology and the Renaissance Tradition in English Poetry*, rev. ed. (1963). A classical work on sixteenth- and seventeenth-century poetry.

Emerson, Everett, ed., *Major Writers of Early American Literature* (1972). Essays on Bradstreet and Taylor among others.

Geiringer, Karl, *The Bach Family; Seven Generations of Creative Genius* (1954). A history of the entire Bach clan from the first hint of musical talent in the sixteenth century to the end of its creative genius in the middle of the nineteenth century.

Gerson, H., and E. H. ter Kuile, *Art and Architecture in Belgium, 1600 to 1800* (1960). A thorough study; part of the *Pelican History of Art.*

Greaves, Richard, *John Bunyan and English Nonconformity* (1992). The best recent biography by a master historian.

Haak, Bob, *The Golden Age: Dutch Painters of the Seventeenth Century* (1984). Thorough coverage.

López-Rey, José, *Velazquez' Work and World* (1968). Velazquez' painting in its historical setting.

Nurse, Peter H., *Classical Voices: Studies of Corneille, Racine, Moliere, Mme. de Lafayette* (1971). Challenging, but worthwhile.

Sutherland, James, *English Literature of the Late Seventeenth Century* (1969). Useful survey; part of the *Oxford History of English Literature.*

Swiss, Margo, and David A. Kent, eds, *Heirs of Fame : Milton and Writers of the English Renaissance* (1995). Most essays are on Milton, except for the two essays that connect Milton with Bunyan and Dryden.

Wittkower, Rudolf, *Art and Architecture in Italy, 1600-1750*, 6th ed. (1999). The authoritative source.

Wolff, Christoph, ed., *The New Bach Reader: A Life of Johann Sebastian Bach in Letters and Documents* (1998). Documents that illustrate how Bach viewed himself, how contemporaries saw him, and how he was depicted by historians in the eighteenth and nineteenth centuries; a revised and enlarged edition of *The Bach Reader* of 1966 that was edited by Hans T. David and Arthur Mendel. The definitive work.

Yarrow, Philip J., *The Seventeenth Century, 1600-1715* (1967). Covers the French dramatists and much more; part of the *Literary History of France* series.

Chapter 17

Anchor, Robert, *The Enlightenment Tradition* (1967). A useful survey.

Andrade, E. N. da C., *Sir Isaac Newton* (1954). Brief and clear.

Armitage, Angus, *The World of Copernicus* (1951). Good discussion of the old astronomy and the birth of the new.

Brumfit, J. H., *The French Enlightenment* (1972). A useful survey.

Cohen, I. B., *The Birth of a New Physics* (1960). A classic study.

Cranston, Maurice, *Philosophers and Pamphleteers. Political Theorists of the Enlightenment* (1986). A clear, readable account of the major French thinkers.

Darnton, Robert, *The Literary Underground of the Old Regime* (1982). A collection of essays by a master storyteller.

Drake, Stillman, *Galileo* (1980). By a leading authority.

Gay, Peter, *The Enlightenment: An Interpretation, 2 vols.* (1966). An exhaustive study of the period.

Hampson, Norman, *The Enlightenment* (1968). A useful survey.

Hazard, Paul, *European Thought in the Eighteenth Century* (1954). An old, but still useful survey.

Jacob, James R., *The Scientific Revolution* (1998). The best, most readable account of events from Copernicus to Newton.

McMullen, Ernan, ed., *Galileo Man of Science* (1967). Contains many thoughtful essays on Galileo's life and achievement.

Moss, Jean Dietz, *Novelties in the Heavens. Rhetoric and Science in the Copernican Controversy* (1993). The way scientists from Copernicus to Galileo described their discoveries helps to inform us about their beliefs and values.

Outram, Dorinda, *The Enlightenment* (1995). An accessible recent synthesis.

Rosen, Edward, *Copernicus and the Scientific Revolution* (1984). By a recognized authority.

Strobinski, Jean, *Jean-Jacques Rouseau. Transparency and Obstruction* (1971). One of the greatest biographies ever written of the most important philosophe.

Yolton, John W., ed., *The Blackwell Companion to the Enlightenment* (1991). An excellent reference work for all aspects of the Enlightenment.

Chapter 18

Allen, Walter, *The English Novel: A Short Critical History* (1954). General survey that begins with the eighteenth century.

Butt, John, *The Augustan Age* (1976). Reprint of 1950 edition. Brief, readable treatment, covering Addison, Swift, Pope, and Johnson, among others.

———, *The Age of Johnson, 1740-1789* (1990). Covers poets, dramatists, novelists, and other writers.

———, *The Mid-Eighteenth Century* (1979). Good introduction to major writers of the period; part of the *Oxford History of English Literature.*

Burney, Charles, *A General History of Music from the Earliest Ages to the Present Period (1789)* (1957). Still available in several modern editions.

Dobrée, Bonamy, *English Literature in the Early Eighteenth Century, 1700-1740* (1959). Thorough coverage of the topic; part of the *Oxford History of English Literature.*

Gaunt, William, *The Great Century of British Painting: Hogarth to Turner,* 2nd ed. (1978). An excellent survey by an eminent scholar.

Hitchcock, Henry Russell, *Rococo Architecture in Southern Germany* (1968). A thorough, nicely illustrated, treatment, by a noted architectural scholar, that includes the work of Neumann.

Kalnein, Wend Graf, and Michael Levey, *Art and Architecture of the Eighteenth Century in France* (1972). Painting, sculpture, and architecture during the Enlightenment.

McKillop, Alan D., *The Early Masters of English Fiction* (1979). A brief survey focusing on Defoe, Richardson, and Fielding; a reprint of the 1956 edition.

Niklaus, Robert, *The Eighteenth Century, 1715-1789* (1970). Excellent survey, covering the philosophes and much more; part of the *Literary History of France* series.

Watt, Ian P., *The Rise of the Novel; Studies in Defoe, Richardson, and Fielding* (1957). How the social climate and the change in the reading public affected the development of the new form of the novel.

Chapter 19

Blom, Eric, *Mozart* (1967). An older but venerable biography; reprint of 1937 edition.

Boime, Albert, *Art in an Age of Revolution, 1750-1800* (1987). A synthesis of the art, the ideas, and the politics of the time; volume 1 of *A Social History of Modern Art.*

———, *Art in an Age of Bonapartism, 1800-1815* (1990). An extensive survey of art and society; volume 2 of *A Social History of Modern Art.*

Burk, John N., *The Life and Works of Beethoven* (1943). A concise and accurate account.

Campbell, Peter Robert, *The Ancien Régime in France* (1988). An incisive essay on French society prior to the Revolution.

Carr, John L., *Robespierre* (1972). A biography of the revolutionary leader.

Cronin, Vincent, *Napoleon Bonaparte* (1972). A highly acclaimed biography.

Doyle, William, *The Oxford History of the French Revolution* (1990). A narrative history that incorporates new thinking on the causes and nature of the Revolution.

Geiringer, Karl, *Haydn: A Creative Life in Music,* rev. ed. (1968). A brief, readable biography, followed by a more technical musical section.

Groat, Donald Jay, *A Short History of Opera,* 2nd ed. (1965). Excellent coverage of eighteenth-century opera, including Mozart, in Part 3.

Janson, H. W., *19th-Century Sculpture* (1985). The standard treatment.

Jones, David Wyn, *The Life of Beethoven* (1998). A recent biography that places Beethoven's work within the musical life of the period; part of the *Musical Lives* series.

Markham, Felix, *Napoleon and the Awakening of Europe* (1965). An exploration of Napoleon's influence on other lands.

Middleton, Robin, and David Watkin, *Neoclassical and 19th Century Architecture. Volume 1: The Enlightenment in France and England* (1980). Good coverage of Neoclassical architecture in the eighteenth century; profusely illustrated.

Palmer, R. R., *The Age of the Democratic Revolution, 2 vols.* (1959, 1964). The French Revolution as part of a revolutionary movement that spread on both sides of the Atlantic.

Rosselli, John, *The Life of Mozart* (1998). A readable biography that sets Mozart's life within the history of his time; part of the *Musical Lives* series.

Rudé, George, *Robespierre: Portrait of a Revolutionary Democrat* (1976). A biography of the revolutionary leader.

Thayer, Alexander Wheelock, *Life of Beethoven*, revised and edited by Elliot Forbes (1967). Originally published in German in the middle of the nineteenth century, this is still the standard biography of Beethoven.

Tomlinson, Janis A., *Goya in the Twilight of Enlightenment* (1992). Goya firmly set within his time and place; includes many illustrations.

Chapter 20

Allen, Walter, *The English Novel: A Short Critical History* (1954). Covers the Brontë sisters and the Gothic novel.

Arblaster, Anthony, *The Rise and Decline of Western Liberalism* (1984). A critical analysis of liberalism, its evolution and characteristics.

Clark, Kenneth, *The Romantic Rebellion, Romantic Versus Classic Art* (1973). Excellent coverage of the rebellion of the Romantic painters against Classicism; profusely illustrated.

Daverio, John, *Robert Schumann: Herald of a "New Poetic Age"* (1997). A thorough biography.

Denommé, Robert T., *Nineteenth-Century French Romantic Poets* (1969). The genesis of Romanticism in France; an analysis of several French romantic poets.

Einstein, Alfred, *Music in the Romantic Era* (1947). A useful general survey.

Elliot, J. H., *Berlioz*, rev. ed. (1967). A brief, readable biography.

Elwin, Verrier, *The First Romantics* (1948). The early years of English Romanticism, focusing on Wordsworth and Coleridge.

Hamilton, David, ed., *Metropolitan Opera Encyclopedia: A Comprehensive Guide to the World of Opera* (1991). An excellent, comprehensive guide to opera.

Hayes, Carlton J. H., *Historical Evolution of Modern Nationalism* (1931). A pioneering work in the study of nationalism.

Himmelfarb, Gertrude, *The Idea of Poverty: England in the Early Industrial Age* (1983). A brilliant history of English social thought, focused on the condition of the poor.

Honour, Hugh, *Romanticism* (1979). A study of the influence of Romanticism on the visual arts.

Jack, Ian Robert James, *English Literature, 1815-1832* (1963). An extensive treatment; part of the *Oxford History of English Literature*.

Jacob, Heinrich Eduard, *Felix Mendelssohn and His Times* (1963). An outstanding biography of the Jewish composer.

Klaus, Kenneth B., *The Romantic Period in Music* (1970). An extensive study of music during the period.

Langer, William L., *Political and Social Upheaval: 1832-1852* (1969). An excellent source, with good references and bibliography.

Loesser, Arthur, *Men, Women and Pianos: A Social History* (1954). The piano as the "center" of the social history of the West from the mid–seventeenth century to the mid–twentieth century.

Pascal, Roy, *The German Sturm und Drang* (1967). A wide-ranging study of the movement.

Reed, John, *Schubert* (1997). A brief, readable biography.

Renwick, W. L., *English Literature, 1789-1815* (1963). Covers the early Romantics; part of the *Oxford History of English Literature*.

Schenk, H. G., *The Mind of the European Romantics* (1966). A comprehensive analysis of the Romantic Movement.

Thorslev, Peter, *The Byronic Hero: Types and Prototypes* (1962). Byron and other writers who were alienated heroes.

Weinstock, Herbert, *Chopin: The Man and His Music* (1969). Reprint of 1949 edition; a brief biography, followed by a more technical musical section.

Winnifrith, Tom, *The Brontës and Their Background* (1973). Excellent, readable study of the Brontë sisters within their milieu.

Chapter 21

Allen, Walter, *The English Novel : A Short Critical History* (1954). Covers Realism.

Becker, George J., *Master European Realists of the Nineteenth Century* (1982). Discussions of Flaubert, Zola, Chekhov, and other Realists.

Bullock, Alan, and Maurice Shock, eds., *The Liberal Tradition* (1956). Well-chosen selections from the writings of British liberals; the introduction is an excellent survey of liberal thought.

Charvet, P. E., *The Nineteenth Century, 1789-1870* (1967). A survey of all types of literature from the Revolution to 1870; part of the *Literary History of France* series.

Downs, Brian W., *Modern Norwegian Literature, 1860-1918* (1966). Ibsen within his time and place.

Farrington, Benjamin, *What Darwin Really Said* (1966). A very good short survey.

Kohn, Hans, *Nationalism: Its Meaning and History* (1955). A concise history of modern nationalism by a leading student on the subject.

Latourette, Kenneth Scott, *Christianity in a Revolutionary Age; A History of Christianity in the Nineteenth and Twentieth Centuries*, 5 vols. (1958-1962). An outstanding, exhaustive treatment.

McClellan, David, *Karl Marx: His Life and Thought* (1977). A highly regarded biography.

McElderry, Jr., Bruce R., *The Realistic Movement in American Writing* (1965). Essays on American Realism.

Pollard, Arthur, ed., *The Victorians* (1970). Essays on Victorian thought and literature.

Simmons, Ernest J., *Introduction to Russian Realism* (1965). Brief, readable account.

Tucker, Robert, *The Marxian Revolutionary Idea* (1969). Presents Marxism as a radical social philosophy.

Turner, Paul, *English Literature, 1832-1890: Excluding the Novel* (1989). Thorough treatment of all sorts of literature, except the novel; part of the *Oxford History of English Literature*.

Vogüé, Eugène-Melchior, *The Russian Novel* (1914). Covers the Russian novel through Tolstoy.

Chapter 22

Abraham, Gerald, *A Hundred Years of Music* (1964). A survey of Romantic music, focusing on Wagner, from the 1830s to the 1930s.

Boime, Albert, *The Academy and French Painting in the Nineteenth Century* (1971). A study of the role of the French Academy of Beaux-Arts in the development of French art during the nineteenth century.

Butler, Ruth, *Rodin: The Shape of Genius* (1993). An accomplished biography.

Cardus, Neville, *Composers Eleven* (1958). Good, nontechnical essays on most of the composers covered in this chapter.

Coke, Van Deren, *The Painter and the Photograph: From Delacroix to Warhol*, rev. ed. (1972). A history of the ways that artists have used photographs directly or indirectly in their work since the invention of photography.

Daverio, John, *Nineteenth-Century Music and the German Romantic Ideology* (1993). Covers Shumann, Brahms, Wagner, and Strauss.

Fried, Michael, *Manet's Modernism, Or, the Face of Painting in the 1860s* (1996). An extensive and important study of Manet and his time.

Groat, Donald Jay, *A Short History of Opera*, 2nd ed. (1965). Excellent coverage of nineteenth-century opera in Part 4.

Herbert, James D., *Fauve Painting: The Making of Cultural Politics* (1992). A social, political, and cultural history of Fauve painters and paintings.

Herbert, Robert L., *Impressionism: Art, Leisure, and Parisian Society* (1988). The history of Impressionism within its social, cultural, and political context.

Mead, Christopher Curtis, *Charles Garnier's Paris Opéra: Architectural Empathy and the Renaissance of French Classicism* (1991). A fascinating study, based on the original sources in Paris, that argues that Garnier inspired a renaissance of French classicism with his design of the Opéra.

Newman, Ernest, *The Life of Richard Wagner*, 4 vols. (1933-1946). Comprehensive coverage; the standard biography.

Nochlin, Linda, *Realism* (1971). Realism in art.

Rewald, John, *The History of Impressionism*, 4th rev. ed. (1973). A study of the origins, development, and decline of Impressionism by a master historian of the art of the period.

Scharf, Aaron, *Art and Photography*, rev. ed. (1974). Treats the invention of photography and its impact on art, mostly in England and France.

Toye, Francis, *Giuseppe Verdi : His Life and Works* (1946). The standard biography; an excellent introduction.

Weisberg, Gabriel P., *The Realist Tradition : French Painting and Drawing, 1830-1900* (1980). This work is based on a Realist Exhibition organized by the Cleveland Museum of Art, where the author was Curator of Art History and Education; it includes 237 paintings, with a description of each, and biographical sketches of the more than 70 painters.

Chapter 23

Allen, Walter, *The English Novel: A Short Critical History* (1954). General survey that includes authors covered in this chapter.

Baumer, Franklin, *Modern European Thought* (1977). A well-informed study of modern thought.

Bradbury, Malcolm, and James McFarlane, eds., *Modernism, 1890-1930* (1974). Essays on various phases of modernism; valuable bibliography.

Collaer, Paul, *A History of Modern Music* (1961). An excellent survey of composers from 1887 to 1957.

Everdell, William R. *The First Moderns: Profiles in the Origins of Twentieth-Century Thought* (1997). A very readable introduction to many of the important figures at the turn of the twentieth century.

Ewen, David, *David Ewen Introduces Modern Music: A History and Appreciation—from Wagner to the Avant-Garde* (1969). A readable, entertaining survey of modern music up to the 1960s.

Gay, Peter, *Freud: A Life for Our Times* (1988). A highly recommended study.

Gordon, Donald E., *Expressionism: Art and Idea* (1987). An excellent study of Fauvism and Expressionism.

Hamilton, G. H., *Painting and Sculpture in Europe, 1880-1940* (1967). An authoritative work.

Kaufmann, Walter, *Nietzsche* (1956). An excellent analysis of Nietzsche's thought.

Lucas, Frank L., *The Drama of Ibsen and Strindberg* (1962). Short biographical sketches, followed by analyses of their plays.

Miller, Arthur I., *Einstein, Picasso: Space, Time, and the Beauty That Causes Havoc* (2001). A fascinating study of the parallels in the lives and work of Einstein and Picasso.

Nelson, Benjamin, ed., *Freud and the Twentieth Century* (1957). A valuable collection of essays.

Rewald, John, *Post-Impressionism: From van Gogh to Gauguin*, 3rd rev. ed. (1978). The standard treatment.

Rosenblum, Robert, *Cubism and Twentieth-Century Art* (1960). The origins and development of Cubism and its impact on twentieth-century art.

Stewart, J. I. M., *Eight Modern Writers* (1963). An extensive study that includes some of the authors discussed in this chapter; part of the *Oxford History of English Literature*.

Stromberg, Roland N., *An Intellectual History of Modern Europe* (1975). A fine text.

Chapter 24

Carr, Roy, *A Century of Jazz* (1997). From blues to bop, to swing, to hip-hop.

Curtis, Penelope, *Sculpture, 1900-1945: After Rodin* (1999). An excellent introduction, organized around themes rather than individual sculptors.

Falls, Cyril, *The Great War* (1961). A good narrative of the war.

Gelb, Arthur, and Barbara Gelb, *O'Neill* (1962). An older, but excellent, biography.

Gray, Ronald, *The German Tradition in Literature, 1871-1945* (1965).

Thomas Mann in his historical and political context.

Hale, Oron J., *The Great Illusion, 1900-1914* (1971). European thought, society, and politics just prior to World War I; a volume in the distinguished *Rise of Modern Europe* series.

Huggins, Nathan Irvin, *Harlem Renaissance* (1971). A study of the Harlem Renaissance as an expression of American cultural values.

Jaffe, Hans L., *De Stijl, 1917-1931: The Dutch Contribution to Modern Art* (1986). The origins, development, and importance of De Stijl.

Pizer, Donald, *American Expatriate Writing and the Paris Moment: Modernism and Place* (1996). The impact of Paris on the writing of American authors, including Stein, Hemingway, and Fitzgerald.

Remarque, Erich Maria, *All Quiet on the Western Front* (1969). First published in 1929, this novel has become a classic.

Read, H., *Modern Sculpture: A Concise History* (1987). A history of modern sculpture from Rodin up to the early 1960s.

Rubin, William S., *Dada and Surrealist Art* (1968). Richly illustrated, thorough treatment of Dada and Surrealism.

Schorer, Mark, *Sinclair Lewis: A Collection of Critical Essays* (1962). A collection of critical essays on Lewis.

Service, Robert, *The Russian Revolution, 1900-1927* (1990). A brief overvierw.

Chapter 25

Burleigh, Michael, and Wolfgang Wippermann, *The Racial State: Germany 1933-1945* (1991). Persecution of Jews, gypsies, mentally handicapped, and homosexuals; analysis of racially motivated social policies of the Nazi regime.

Calcocoressi, Peter, and Guy Wint, *Total War* (1972). A good account of World War II.

Cruickshank, John, ed., *Aspects of the Modern European Mind* (1969). A useful collection of sources in modern intellectual history.

Goldhagen, Daniel Jonah, *Hitler's Willing Executioners: Ordinary Germans and the Holocaust* (1996). This controversial book argues that because of profound and pervasive anti-Semitism in Germany, ordinary Germans from all walks of life willingly participated in the extermination of the Jews.

Hilberg, Raul, *The Destruction of the European Jews* (1967). A monumental study of the Holocaust.

Homer, William Innes, *Alfred Stieglitz and the American Avant-Garde* (1977). The life of Stieglitz and his importance as a champion of modern art in America.

Kirkpatrick, Ivone, *Mussolini: A Study in Power* (1964). A solid biography.

Kultermann, Udo, *Architecture in the 20th Century* (1993). Comprehensive coverage.

Marrus, Michael R., *The Holocaust in History* (1987). An excellent summary of key issues and problems.

Mayer, Milton, *They Thought They Were Free* (1955). The lives of ordinary citizens who became Nazis.

Spielvogel, Jackson J., *Hitler and Nazi Germany* (1988). Clearly written, up-to-date survey.

Wiesel, Elie, *Night* (1960). A moving personal record of the Holocaust.

Chapter 26

Barrett, William, *Irrational Man* (1958). Especially good on the intellectual and cultural roots of existentialism.

Coke, Van Deren, *The Painter and the Photograph: From Delacroix to Warhol*, rev. ed. (1972). A history of the ways that artists have used

photographs directly or indirectly in their work since the invention of photography; includes Warhol's *Marilyn Monroe*.

Giannetti, Louis, *Flashback: A Brief History of Film* (2001). An excellent overview of film from its early beginnings with appropriate examples drawn not only from Hollywood but also from world cinema.

Griffiths, Paul, *Modern Music and After* (1995). An excellent introduction to "serious" music in the second half of the twentieth century.

Hitchcock, Henry-Russell, and Philip Johnson, *The International Style*, 2nd ed. (1966). Written by a noted architectural historian and a practitioner of the International style.

Jencks, Charles, *Postmodernism: The New Classicism in Art and Architecture* (1987). An account by the acknowledged expert.

Lewis, Bernard, *What Went Wrong? Western Impact and Middle Eastern Response* (2002). An analysis of the Western eclipse of the Middle East in the past three centuries, and how we feel the aftermath of that today, by an eminent authority on Middle Eastern history.

McEvilley, Thomas, *Sculpture in the Age of Doubt* (1999). An introduction to postmodern sculpture and thought.

Macquarrie, John, *Existentialism* (1972). A lucid discussion of existentialism.

Newhouse, John, *Europe Adrift* (1997). A readable survey of European issues in the late twentieth century.

Polcari, Stephen, *Abstract Expressionism and the Modern Experience* (1991). Treats the roots of Abstract Expressionism and then discusses specific artists.

Rich, Alan, *American Pioneers: Ives to Cage and Beyond* (1995). A readable history of American "classical" music in the twentieth century.

CHAPTER 13

Page 9 From *The Portable Renaissance Reader* edited by Ross and McLaughin. NY: Penguin Putnam Inc. **Pages 11–12** From *History of Italy and History of Florence* by Agnolo Guicciardini, edited by John R. Hale, translated by Cecil Grayson. NY: Simon & Schuster. **Page 15** From *Book of the Courtier* by Baldesar Castiglione, Illustrations editor Edgar Mayhew, translated by Charles S. Singleton. Copyright © 1959 by Charles S. Singleton and Edgar N. Mayhew. Used by permission of Doubleday, a division of Random House, Inc. **Page. 17** From *Lives of the Painters* by Giorgio Vasari, translated by A.B. Hinds, Volumes 1, 2, 3 and 4. NY: Penguin Putnam Inc. **Page 32** Sonnet, "A man with a woman, nay, a god..." by Robert J. Clements from *The Poetry of Michelangelo*, p. 198. Reprinted by permission of NYU Press. **Page 33** Sonnet, "The sculptor's hammer..." quoted in Roland H. Bainton from *Women of the Reformation in Germany and Italy*, Minneapolis: Augsburg Fortress Press, p. 216.

CHAPTER 14

Page 47 From *The Broken Spears: The Aztec Account of the Conquest of Mexico* by Miguel Leon-Portilla. Copyright © 1962, 1990 by Miguel Leon-Portilla. Expanded and Updated Edition © 1992 by Miguel Leon-Portilla. Reprinted by permission of Beacon Press, Boston. **Page 53** From *Luther's Works*: Volume 34, Career of the Reformer IV edited by Lewis W. Spitz, pp. 336–337. Minneapolis: Augsburg Fotress Press, 1960. **Page 54** From *Luther's Works*: Volume 32, Career of the Reformer II edited by George W. Forell, pp. 112–113. Minneapolis: Augsburg Fortress Press, 1958. **Page 59** From *Luther's Works*: Volume 45, The Christian in Society II edited by Walther I. Brandt, p. 229. Minneapolis: Augsburg Fortress Press, 1962. **Page 60** From *Luther's Works*: Volume 47, The Christian in Society IV edited by Franklin Sherman, pp. 268–272. Minneapolis: Augsburg Fortress Press, 1971.

CHAPTER 15

Page 66 From *The Histories of Gargantua and Pantagruel* by Francois Rabelais, translated by J.M. Cohen (Penguin Classics, 1955). Copyright © J.M. Cohen, 1955. Reproduced by permission of Penguin Books Ltd. **Page 71** From "Henry VIII" from *The Complete Plays and Poems of William Shakespeare*, edited by Neilson & Hill, p. 929. Reprinted by permission of Houghton Mifflin Company. **Page 71** From "A Midsummer Night's Dream" from *The Complete Plays and Poems of William Shakespeare* edited by Neilson & Hill, p. 92. Reprinted by permission of Houghton Mifflin Company. **Page 72** From *The Complete Plays and Poems of William Shakespeare* edited by Neilson & Hill, p. 1062. Reprinted by permission of Houghton Mifflin Company. **Page 72** From *The Complete Plays and Poems of William Shakespeare* edited by Neilson & Hill, p. 1066. Reprinted by permission of Houghton Mifflin Company.

CHAPTER 16

Page 97 *Tartuffe by Moliere*, English translation copyright © 1963, 1962, 1961 and renewed 1991, 1990 and 1989 by Richard Wilbur, reprinted by permission of Harcourt, Inc. CAUTION: Professionals and amateurs are hereby warned that this translation, being fully protected under the copyright laws of the United States of America, the British Empire, including the Dominion of Canada, and all other countries which are signatories to the Universal Copyright Convention and the International Copyright Union, are subject to royalty. All rights, including professional, amateur, motion picture, recitation, lecturing, public reading, radio broadcasting, and television, are strictly reserved. Particular emphasis is laid on the question of readings, permission for which must be secured from the author's agent in writing. Inquiries on professional rights (except for amateur rights) should be addressed to Mr. Gilbert Parker, William Morris Agency, 1325 Avenue of the Americas, New York, NY 10019; inquiries on translation rights should be addressed to Harcourt, Inc., Permissions Department, Orlando, FL 32887. The stock and amateur acting rights of *Tartuffe* are controlled exclusively by Dramatists Play Service, Inc., 400 Park Avenue South, New York, NY. No amateur performance of the play may be given without obtaining in advance the written permission of the Dramatists Play Service, Inc., and paying the requisite fee. **Page 99** Andrew Marvell, "On Paradise Lost." Luxon, Thomas H., ed. The John Milton Reading Room, www.dartmouth.edu/~milton/reading_room/pl/note/index.html. April, 2002. Reprinted by permission. **Page 103** Donald Keene, trans., *Major Plays of Chikamatsu* (New York: Columbia University Press, 1990), pp. 55–56.

CHAPTER 17

Page 129 From *Luther's Works*: Volume 54, Table Talk edited by Theodore G. Tappert, pp. 192-193. Minneapolis: Augsburg Fortress Press, 1967. **Page 131** Reprinted by permission of Waveland Press from *Africa Remembered: Narratives by West African from the Era of the Slave Trade* by Philip D. Curtin, pp. 92–93, 95, 97–98. Prospect Heights, IL: Waveland Press, Inc., 1997. All rights reserved.

CHAPTER 18

Page 153 Backhouse, E. and J.O.P. Bland. *Annals and Memoirs of the Court of Peking* (Boston: Houghton Mifflin Company, 1914), pp. 322–326, 330.

CHAPTER 19

Pages 187, 190 From *Thayer's Life of Beethoven*, Part I edited by Alexander Wheelock Thayer and Elliot Forbes. Copyright © 1992 by Princeton University Press. Reprinted by permission of Princeton University Press. **Page 190** Lyrics to Beethoven symphony "Joy is drunk by all God's creatures..." translated by Louis Untermeyer, RCA Records, 1952.

CHAPTER 20

Page 200 From *Faust: A Tragedy, 2/e* translated by Walter Arndt and edited by Cyrus Hamlin, p. 12. Copyright © 2002. NY: W.W. Norton & Co. **Page 205** Harold A. Bierck, Jr., ed., *Selected Writings of Bolivar, Volume One 1810–1822*. Second Edition (New York: The Colonial Press, 1951), pp. 31–32.

CHAPTER 21

Page 236 From *Pere Goriot and Eugenie Grandet* by Honore de Balzac, copyright 1946, 1950 by Random House, Inc. Used by permission of Modern Library, a division of Random

House, Inc. **Page 249** "My life closed twice before its close" by Emily Dickinson. Reprinted by permission of the publishers and the Trustees of Amherst College from *The Poems of Emily Dickinson*, Thomas H. Johnson, ed., Cambridge, Mass.: The Belknap Press of Harvard University Press, Copyright © 1951, 1955, 1979 by the President and Fellows of Harvard College.

CHAPTER 22

Page 268 From *Music in the Western World: A History in Documents*, 1st edition by Piero Weiss and Richard Taruskin. Copyright © 1984. Reprinted with permission of Wadsworth, an imprint of the Wadsworth Group, a division of Thomson Learning. Fax 800 730-2215.

CHAPTER 23

Page 289 'Cold Night' by Nakahara Chuya and 'Beach Rainbow' by Takahashi Shinkichi from *The Penguin Book of Japanese Verse* translated by Geoffrey Bownas and Anthony Thwaite (Penguin Books 1964, Revised edition 1998). Translation copyright © Geoffrey Bownas and Anthony Thwaite, 1964, 1998. Reproduced by permission of Penguin Books Ltd. **Page 290** From *Remembrance of Things Past, Vol. 2* by Marcel Proust, translated by CK Scott Moncrieff & Terence Kilmartin, copyright © 1981 by Random House, Inc. and Chatto & Windus. Used by permission of Random House, Inc. **Page 291** From *Ulysses* by James Joyce. NY: Penguin Putnam Inc. **Page 292** Excerpts from *Mrs. Dalloway* by Virginia Woolf, copyright 1925 by Harcourt, Inc. and renewed

1953 by Leonard Woolf, reprinted by permission of the publisher. **Page 296** From *Lady Chatterley's Lover* by D.H. Lawrence. NY: Penguin Putnam Inc. **Page 298** From *Pygmalion: A Romance in Five Acts* by George Bernard Shaw. NY: Penguin Putnam Inc. **Page 298** From *Saint Joan* by George Bernard Shaw. NY: Penguin Putnam Inc.

CHAPTER 24

Page 324 From *A Farewell to Arms* by Ernest Hemingway. NY: Simon & Schuster. **Page 325** From "Ernest Hemingway: The Missing Third Dimension" in *Hemingway and His Critics* edited by Carlos Baer. New York: Farrar, Straus & Giroux. **Page 329** From *'Hind Swaraj' and Other Writings* by Mohandas Gandhi, edited and translated by Anthony J. Parel. Copyright 1997. Reprinted by permission of Cambridge University Press. **Page 330** "The Second Coming" reprinted with the permission of Scribner, an imprint of Simon & Schuster Adult Publishing Group, from *The Collected Works of W.B. Yeats, Volume 1: The Poems, Revised*, edited by Richard J. Finneran. Copyright 1924 by The Macmillan Company; copyright renewed 1952 by Bertha Georgie Yeats. **Page 334** "The Creation: A Negro Sermon" and "I'm lonely still" from *God's Trombones* by James Weldon Johnson. NY: Penguin Putnam Inc. **Page 334** "America" by Claude McKay from *Selected Poems of Claude McKay*. **Page 334** "A Black Man Talks of Reaping" by Arna Bontemps. Reprinted by permission of Harold Ober Associates Incorporated. Copyright © 1963 by Arna Bontemps. **Page 335** "Harlem" from *The Collected Poems of Langston Hughes* by Langston Hughes,

copyright © 1994 by The Estate of Langston Hughes. Used by permission of Alfred A. Knopf, a division of Random House, Inc. **Page 335** "Yet Do I Marvel" by Countee Cullen. Reprinted by permission of GRM Associates, Inc., Agents for the Estate of Ida M. Cullen. From the book *Color* by Countee Cullen. Copyright © 1925 by Harper & Brothers; copyright renewed 1953 by Ida M. Cullen.

CHAPTER 25

Page 353 From *Twentieth Century Chinese Poetry* by Kai Yu Hsu, translated by Kai-yu Hsu, copyright © 1963 by Kai-yu Hsu. Used by permission of Doubleday, a division of Random House, Inc. **Page 358** From *The Grapes of Wrath* by John Steinbeck. NY: Penguin Putnam Inc. **Page 359** Pietro quote from *Bread and Wine* by Ignazio Silone, translated by Eric Mosbacher. Copyright © 1986 by Eric Mosbacher. Used by permission of the New American Library, a division of Penguin Putnam, Inc. **Page 360** Reprinted with the permission of Scribner, an imprint of Simon & Schuster Adult Publishing Group, from *Darkness at Noon* by Arthur Koestler. Copyright 1941 by Macmillan Publishing Company, renewed © 1969 by Mrs. F.H.H. Henrica. **Page 365** From *Native Son* by Richard Wright. NY: HarperCollins Publishers. **Page 366** From *Invisible Man* by Ralph Ellison, copyright 1947, 1948, 1952 by Ralph Ellison. Copyright renewed 1975, 1976, 19890 by Ralph Ellison. Used by permission of Modern Library, a division of Random House, Inc. **Page 374** "Strange Fruit" by Allan Lewis. NY: Music Sales.